Guide and Index to Texas Confederate Pension Application and Payment Records

1899–1979

Volume 1: A–D

By Anthony Black, Robert de Berardinis and the TSLAC Staff

Edited by Robert de Berardinis

HERITAGE BOOKS
2009

HERITAGE BOOKS
AN IMPRINT OF HERITAGE BOOKS, INC.

Books, CDs, and more—Worldwide

For our listing of thousands of titles see our website
at
www.HeritageBooks.com

Published 2009 by
HERITAGE BOOKS, INC.
Publishing Division
100 Railroad Ave. #104
Westminster, Maryland 21157

Copyright © 2009 Robert de Berardinis

Other Heritage Books by Robert de Berardinis:

Guide and Index to Texas Confederate Pension Application and Payment Records, 1899–1979; Volume 1: A–D
Anthony Black, Robert de Berardinis and the TSLAC Staff, Edited by Robert de Berardinis

Guide and Index to Texas Confederate Pension Application and Payment Records, 1899–1979; Volume 2: E–M
Anthony Black, Robert de Berardinis and the TSLAC Staff, Edited by Robert de Berardinis

Guide and Index to Texas Confederate Pension Application and Payment Records, 1899–1979; Volume 3: N–Z
Anthony Black, Robert de Berardinis and the TSLAC Staff, Edited by Robert de Berardinis

Guide and Index to the Republic of Texas Donation Voucher Files, 1879–1887, and Confederate Script Voucher Files, 1881–1883, in the Texas General Land Office
Texas General Land Office, Edited by Robert de Berardinis

Guide and Index to the Texas Adjutant General Service Records, 1836–1935; Volume 1: Cumulative Index
Anthony Black and the Texas State Archives, Edited by Robert de Berardinis

Guide and Index to the Texas Adjutant General Service Records, 1836–1935; Volume 2: Separate Indexes
Anthony Black and the Texas State Archives, Edited by Robert de Berardinis

Guide and Index to the Texas Confederate Audited Civil and Military Claims, 1861–1865
Texas State Archives, Edited by Robert de Berardinis

Guide and Indexes to the Conserved and Microfilmed Harris County, Texas Records of Oaths and Allegiance, Declarations of Intent, and Final Naturalizations, 1886–1906
Robert de Berardinis

The illustration on the cover is the reverse of the Great Seal of Texas.
It was designed by and donated to the state of Texas
by the Daughters of the Republic of Texas.

All rights reserved. No part of this book may be reproduced or transmitted in any form or by any means, electronic or mechanical, including photocopying, recording or by any information storage and retrieval system without written permission from the author, except for the inclusion of brief quotations in a review.

International Standard Book Numbers
Paperbound: 978-0-7884-4767-9
Clothbound: 978-0-7884-8172-7

Table of Contents

Contents to Volume 1: A–D iii
Contents to Volume 2: E–M iii
Contents to Volume 3: N–Z iv
Preface v
Primer on Texas Confederate Research vi
Confederate Pension Payments Volumes, 1899–1905, 1909–1910,
    1915–1966 1
    Confederate Pension Warrant Registers and Stubs, 1900–1903, 1909–1910,
        1950–1955 4
    Confederate Mortuary Warrant Registers, 1917–66 6
Confederate Pension Application Records, 1899–1979 8
    Confederate Pension Applications, 1899–1979 10
    Miscellaneous Material Relating to Confederate Pension
        Applications, 1903–1934 13
    Confederate Pension Indexes, 1899–1967 19
    Confederate Pension Registers, 1899–1909, 1915–1917 21
    Affidavits of Confederate Military Service, 1909–1917 21
Index to Miscellaneous Material Relating to Confederate Pension
    Applications, 1903–1934 22
Index to Confederate Home Applications 25
Index to Missing Pension Applications 27
Index to Rejected Pension Applications 35
Index to Confederate Pension Applications 134
    A 134
    B 163
    C 253
    D 328

Contents to Volume 2, E–M

Contents to Volume 1: A–D iii
Contents to Volume 2: E–M iii

Contents to Volume 2, E–M, *Continued*

Contents to Volume 3: N–Z iv
Preface v
Primer on Texas Confederate Research vi
Guide to Confederate Pension Payments and Applications 1
Index to Confederate Pension Applications 22
    E 22
    F 39
    G 68
    H 112
    I 194
    J 197
    K 225
    L 247
    M 284

Contents to Volume 3, N–Z

Contents to Volume 1: A–D iii
Contents to Volume 2: E–M iv
Preface v
Primer on Texas Confederate Research vi
Guide to Confederate Pension Payments and Applications 1
Index to Confederate Pension Applications 22
    N 22
    O 37
    P 46
    Q 94
    R 95
    S 144
    T 230
    U 266
    V 268
    W 274
    X 348
    Y 348
    Z 354

Preface

These volumes are "in addition to" rather than "in place of" the online index to the Confederate pension applications and TARO finding aids of the Texas State Library and Archives Commission. True, there are corrections to the online index, but these volumes allow for browsing through a spelling range as well as have separate indexes for the Confederate home, missing, rejected and miscellaneous pension applications. Thus, researchers are given extra tools. Prior to 2006, only the pension applications were widely available through Family History Library (Genealogical Society of Utah) microfilm. Now, the index volumes, the miscellaneous applications, the mortuary warrants, the later payment warrants and stubs, and affidavits of service are now available through microfilming. The film titles are:

1. *Confederate Pension Warrant Registers and Stubs, 1950–1955,*
2. *Texas Confederate Mortuary Warrant Registers, 1917–1966,* and
3. *Confederate Pension Application Records, 1899–1979.*

The microfilmed indexes found under the last title constitute the most important tool. They are the official recordings of who actually received a pension and who did not. Hopefully, some future researcher will check these indexes against the names in the indexes in these volumes to make a final list. The indexes themselves are divided into five types:

1. Pensioners,
2. Widows receiving pensions,
3. Totally Disabled pensioners,
4. Confederate Home pensioners, and
5. Rejected applications.

The Miscellaneous Applications constitute materials sent to the Comptroller's office which do not or cannot pertain to a single pension file. These 281 files contain a variety of varying information such as applications for mortuary warrants (paying for funeral expenses), service records or affidavits pertaining thereto, physician's statements regarding disability, and related other correspondence. For the first time, they are now accessible with individual targets for each folder to make it easier for researchers to find the folders of interest.

Also found in the Pension Application Records is the extremely valuable volume of affidavits of Confederate service. This single volume contains copies of military service sworn to between 1909 and 1917. There is an index at the front of the volume.

Returning to the first two film titles, Confederate Pension Warrant Registers and Stubs, 1950–1955, and Texas Confederate Mortuary Warrant Registers, 1917–1966, they come from the Comptroller's record set, Confederate Pension Payments Volumes, 1899–1905, 1909–1910, 1915–1966. Although part of one record set, they were divided at the time of microfilming for reasons of economy. The three volumes microfilmed from the sub set, Confederate Pension Warrant Registers and Stubs, 1900–1903, 1909–1910, 1950–1955, were done on 16 mm microfilm because the volumes were the old accounting twin post and screw bindings. The four volumes of the mortuary warrants are valuable for an additional reason—they give the cemetery of the deceased.

The Editor

Houston, Texas
The birthday of my mother, Patricia,
Une vraie belle Nouvelle Orléanaise comme sa mère
April 12

Primer on Texas Confederate Research

This primer is designed as a "step by step" beginner's guide using primarily the document collections found in the Texas State Archives and Texas General Land Office rather than solely those of the U.S. National Archives. This is not an exhaustive or definitive treatise. It also addresses as a convenience to researchers, other major microfilm and document collections as well as bibliographies on Confederate research.

The researcher must first acquire all the information from the abstract card for a given officer or enlisted man. These are found in the eight roll microfilm collection, *Texas Confederate Military Service Records*.[1] It is important to note the company commander, the unit designation and name, and the county, if given. In other words, collect all information on the veteran from the card files. With this information, the researcher should then acquire the military roll numbers from the *Index to the Civil War Military Rolls Alphabetical List and by County*.[2] The researcher should also note any information concerning the unit of the soldier in the county section of this index. The county section is alphabetically arranged and begins after "Z" of the main index. The thorough researcher will also consult the *Index to the Civil War Military Rolls by Organizational Units* for any additional information. In all cases, the researcher will be collecting roll numbers.

Armed with these roll numbers, the researcher will then use the *Civil War Military Rolls, 1855–1865*, which are arranged by roll number in ascending order. There are gaps in the numbering but this should not concern the researcher. It is important to note that a roll number may contain more than one document or roll. The rolls themselves may be something other than muster rolls, i.e., election of officers' returns, pay rolls, enlistment rolls, etc. About one-fifth to one-fourth of the documents in the *Civil War Military Rolls, 1855–1865*, are so fragile that they have not been seen by the public in the past twenty years. All of them are designated as "map case" files. Additionally, the finding aid of the *Civil War Military Rolls, 1855–1865*, does identify the forty-three military rolls which were not abstracted onto the cards. They are:

# 73	# 705	# 801	# 844	# 987
# 95	# 734	# 802	# 846	# 989
# 134	# 778	# 803	# 848	# 1173
# 165	# 781	# 804	# 849	# 1354
# 298	# 786	# 833	# 850	# 1383
# 458	# 787	# 834	# 855	# 1562
# 605	# 788	# 836	# 866	# 1577
# 608	# 789	# 837	# 868	
# 614	# 792	# 838	# 912	

---

[1] [Texas State Archives], *Texas Confederate Military Service Records*, 8 rolls (microfilm edition; Austin: Texas State Archives, 1976). This is available for purchase or interlibrary Loan.
[2] Index to the Civil War Military Rolls Alphabetical List and by County (microfilm edition; Austin: CLF, 2004).

There are further avenues for Confederate research with the materials in the Texas State Archives. There are eighteen other sets of source material to be explored.[3] They are:
1. *5th Military District/District of Texas Records, 1865–1870* (Adj. Gen. Dept.),[4]
2. *Adjutant General Service Records*, with Indexes (Adj. Gen. Dept.),[5]
3. *Civil War Records, 1855, 1860–66,* (Adj. Gen. Dept.),
4. *Confederate Pension Application Records, 1899–1979*, with Indexes (Comptroller's Office),[6]
5. *Confederate Pension Payments Volumes, 1899–1905, 1909–1910, 1915–1966*, with Indexes (Comptroller's Office),[7]
6. *Confederate Audited Civil Claims*, with Indexes (Comptroller's Office),
7. *Confederate Audited Military Claims*, with Indexes (Comptroller's Office),[8]
8. *Departmental Correspondence, 1846–1943* (Adj. Gen. Dept.),[9]

---

[3] The compiled finding aid for these items on this list as well as the *Civil War Military Rolls, 1855–65*, may be found online at TARO, Texas Archival Resources Online, at: < www.lib.utexas.edu/taro/index.html>. Always use the archival title, not the microfilm title, for searches. All titles, except the *Confederate Scrip Vouchers*, are at the Texas State Library and Archives Commission.

[4] These were microfilmed as *Military Records of Texas Reconstruction, 1865–70* (microfilm edition; Austin: CLF, 2006).

[5] These records with a new online index are found online at the Texas State Archives website. A print version of all the service record indexes is available as Anthony Black [& TSLAC Staff], *Guide and Index to the Texas Adjutant General Service Records, 1836–1935*, Robert de Berardinis, ed., (Westminster, Md.: Heritage Books, 2008). The relevant portion of microfilm is titled *Confederate & Texas State Troops Service Records, 1861–1865* (Houston: CLF, 2006).

[6] These are currently being digitized for online publication at the website of the Texas State Archives.

[7] These and the previous records have been microfilmed with a new index. The Confederate Pension Applications were microfilmed by the Genealogical Society of Utah. This set is obsolete. Currently, information from the mortuary warrants and pay stubs is being included in the funded pension application folders and being digitized by the Texas State Archives. The payment series, except for the early payment stubs, was microfilmed as *Confederate Pension Warrant Registers and Stubs, 1950–55* (microfilm edition; Houston: CLF, 2005), and *Texas Confederate Mortuary Warrant Registers, 1917–66*, (microfilm edition; Houston: CLF, 2005). There is a comprehensive guide to all of the pension records with a corrected index to the online index as Black, Anthony and Texas State Library and Archives Commission, *Guide & Index to Texas Confederate Pension Application and Payment Records, 1899–1979*, Robert de Berardinis, ed., 2 vols., (Westminster, Md.: Heritage Books, 2008).

[8] An index and guide is available in print as Texas State Library and Archives Commission, *Guide and Index to the Texas Confederate Audited Civil and Military Claims, 1861–1865*, Robert de Berardinis, ed., (Westminster, Md.: Heritage Books, 2008).

[9] The correspondence from 1846 through 1860 was microfilmed as *Ante-Bellum Correspondence of the Texas Adjutant General, 1846–61* (microfilm edition; Austin: CLF, 2006). The Correspondence and Letter Books from 1861 through 1865 was microfilmed as *Civil War Correspondence of the Texas Adjutant General, 1861–65* (microfilm edition; Austin: CLF, 2006). The correspondence from 1865 through 1877 was microfilmed as *Reconstruction Correspondence of the Texas Adjutant General, 1865–77* (microfilm edition; Austin: CLF, 2006). The Indexes to Letters Received and Registers of Letters Received, but not the Letterpress Books from 1870 through 1883 were microfilmed as *Indexes to the Registers of Letters Received by the Texas Adjutant General, 1870–83* (microfilm edition; Houston: CLF, 2005) and *Registers of Letters Received by the Texas Adjutant General, 1870–83* (microfilm edition;

Additional Source Material at the Texas State Archives, *Continued*

9. *Applications for Special Pardons for Former Texas Confederates, 1865–1867* (Secretary of State),
10. *Indigent Confederate Families, 1863–1865*, with Index (Comptroller's Office),[10]
11. *Records of Sam Houston, 1824–1862* (Governor's Office),[11]
12. *Records of Edward Clark, 1861* (Governor's Office),[12]
13. *Records of Francis R. Lubbock, 1861–1881* (Governor's Office),[13]
14. *Records of Pendleton Murrah, 1863–1865* (Governor's Office),[14]
15. *Register of Military Vouchers and Warrants (and Civil Warrants Drawn on Military Appropriations), 1862–1865* (Treasurer's Office),[15]
16. *Special Appropriations Ledgers: Other, 1860–1865, 1879, 1881–1885, 1897–1909* (Comptroller's Office),[16]
17. *Strays Collection, State Military Board Strays, 1860–1864* (Military Board) and
18. *Texas State Military Board Records, 1861–1865, 1955* (Military Board).[17]

At the time of this writing, the Texas State Archives is digitizing the *Adjutant General Service Records* for placement on their web site. Already on the Texas State Archives' web site[18] is a searchable index to those records as well as to the series, *Indigent Confederate Families*, and *Confederate Pension Applications*. There are also printed copies of the *Index to Indigent Confederate Families, 1863–65*, by both surname and county.[19] Photocopies from the *Confederate Pension Applications* may be ordered from the Texas State Archives.[20] There is no index to the *Civil War Records* or the *Departmental Correspondence*. Indeed, the finding aids are very brief as to contents, in many cases giving only beginning and ending dates for files.

There is another avenue for Confederate research, a series of records from the Texas General Land Office, *Confederate Scrip Voucher Files, 1881–1883*. Now available on

---

Houston: CLF, 2005), respectively. This is followed by the series *Early Modern Correspondence of the Texas Adjutant General, 1877–83* (microfilm edition; Austin: CLF, 2006).

[10] These were microfilmed as *Indigent Confederate Families, 1863–65* (microfilm edition; Austin: CLF, 2006). An index is available online and by Robert de Berardinis.

[11] Only the *Executive Record Books of Appointments*, etc. made by President and Governor Houston have been microfilmed already by the Texas State Archives. This is just a small part of this collection.

[12] Only the *Executive Record Books of Appointments*, etc. made by Governor Clark have been microfilmed already by the Texas State Archives. This is just a small part of this collection.

[13] Only the *Executive Record Books of Appointments*, etc. made by Governor Lubbock have been microfilmed already by the Texas State Archives. This is just a small part of this collection.

[14] Only the *Executive Record Books of Appointments*, etc. made by Governor Murrah have been microfilmed already by the Texas State Archives. This is just a small part of this collection.

[15] This was microfilmed as *Civil War Register of Military Vouchers and Warrants, 1862–65* (Houston: CLF, 2005). There is no finding aid or index to this unprocessed volume.

[16] This was microfilmed as *Special Appropriation Ledgers for the Frontier Defense of Texas, 1861–65, 1879* (microfilm edition; Houston: CLF, 2005).

[17] These last two collections are unprocessed, not microfilmed, and without finding aids.

[18] <http://www.tsl.state.tx.us/arc/>, scroll down the page to the database links for each.

[19] See by this author.

[20] Also, at the time of this writing, the David Lowe Chapter of the United Daughters of the Confederacy will be microfilming (with finding aids) the *Civil War Records, 1855–1865*.

microfilm,[21] these are the files documenting claims for land scrip in units of 1,280 acres issued to widows of Confederate soldiers or disabled Confederate soldiers as authorized by legislative act of April 5, 1881. The files include eligibility statements. These files are arranged by file number. To access these numbered files, the researcher should consult the online name index at the Texas General Land Office web site,[22] or the printed version of the index, edited by the author.[23]

Of course, researchers should avail themselves of personal paper collections and source material found at other repositories in Texas and in other states, in particular, the Confederate Memorial Hall collection found at Tulane University Howard-Tilton Libraries Special Collections in New Orleans. Also to be noted is the newly available[24] (on the Internet) text in the otherwise impossibly large, *War of the Rebellion*.[25]

No research on Texas Confederates can be considered thorough without consulting the material found in the U.S. National Archives[26] and their numerous Civil War microfilm publications.[27] At the time of filming, the following list was compiled of available microfilm publications from the National Archives Trust Board (the vendor of the microfilm):

Confederate Service Records and Their Indexes

M227, *Index to Compiled Service Records of Confederate Soldiers Who Served in Organizations from the State of Texas.*
M253, *Consolidated Index to Compiled Service Records of Confederate Soldiers.*
M258, *Compiled Service Records of Confederate Soldiers Who Served in Organizations Raised Directly by the Confederate Government.*
M260, *Records Relating to Confederate Naval and Marine Personnel.*
M323, *Compiled Service Records of Confederate Soldiers Who Served in Organizations From the State of Texas.*
M331, *Compiled Service Records of Confederate Generals and Staff Officers, and Nonregimental Enlisted Men.*
M347, *Unfiled Papers and Slips Belonging in Confederate Compiled Service Records.*
M818, *Index to Compiled Service Records of Confederate Soldiers Who Served in Organizations Raised Directly by the Confederate Government and of Confederate Generals and Staff Officers and Nonregimental Enlisted Men.*
M861, *Compiled Records Showing Service of Military Units in Confederate Organizations.*

---

[21] *Confederate Scrip Voucher Files, 1881–1883* (microfilm edition; Austin: CLF, 2004).
[22] <http:www.glo.tx.us>
[23] Texas General Land Office, *Index and Guide to the Republic of Texas Donation Vouchers, 1879–1887, and Confederate Scrip Voucher Files, 1881–1883, in the Texas General Land Office*, Robert de Berardinis, ed., (Westminster, Md.: Heritage Books, 2008).
[24] At <http://moa.cit.cornell.edu/moa/browse.monographs/waro.html>
[25] Robert N. Scott, comp., *The War of the Rebellion: A Compilation of the Official Records of the Union and Confederate Armies*, 128 vols. (1880–1900 reprint; Gettysburg: National Historical Society, 1971–1972).
[26] Kenneth W. Munden, and Beers, Henry Putney, *Guide to Federal Archives Relating to the Civil War* (Washington: National Archives, 1962). Equally important is Henry Putney Beers, *Guide to the Archives of the Government of the Confederate States of America* (Washington: National Archives, 1968).
[27] For a near complete listing, see [National Archives Trust Board], *Military Service Records: A Select Catalog of National Archives Microfilm Publications* (Washington, D.C.: National Archives Trust Fund Board, 1985) and [National Archives Trust Board], *Microfilm Resources for Research, A Comprehensive Catalog* (Washington, D.C.: National Archives Trust Fund Board, 2000). Of course, to get a current listing, check the U.S. National Archives web site at: <http://www.nara.gov>.

T456, *Reference File Relating to Confederate Medical Officers.*

Confederate Records Relating to Texas

M119, *Letters Sent by Lt. Col. G.H. Hill, Commander of the Confederate Ordnance Works at Tyler, Texas, 1864–1865.*
P2227, *Austin Confederate Court Dockets. 1862–1864.*
P2228, *Galveston Confederate Court Dockets, 1861–1865.*

General Confederate Records

M410, *Index to the Letters Received by the Confederate Adjutant and Inspector General and by the Confederate Quartermaster General, 1861–1865.*
M437, *Letters Received by the Confederate Secretary of War, 1861–1865.*
M469, *Letters Received by the Confederate Quartermaster General, 1861–1865.*
M474, *Letters Received by the Confederate Adjutant and Inspector General, 1861–1865.*
M499, *Letters Received by the Confederate Secretary of the Treasury, 1861–1865.*
M500, *Letters Sent by the Confederate Secretary of the Treasury, 1861, 1864–1865, 1861–1865.*
M522, *Letters Sent by the Confederate Secretary of War, 1861–1865.*
M523, *Letters Sent by the Confederate Secretary of War to the President, 1861–1865.*
M524, *Telegrams Sent by the Confederate Secretary of War, 1861–1865.*
M618, *Telegrams Received by the Confederate Secretary of War, 1861–1865.*
M627, *Letters and Telegrams Sent by the Confederate Adjutant and Inspector General, 1861–1865.*
M628, *Letters and Telegrams Sent by the Engineer Bureau of the Confederate War Department, 1861–1864.*
M836, *Confederate States Army Casualties: Lists and Narrative Reports, 1861–1865.*
M900, *Letters and Telegrams Sent by the Confederate Quartermaster General, 1861–1865.*
M901, *General Orders and Circulars of the Confederate War Department, 1861–1865.*
M909, *Papers Pertaining to Vessels of or Involved With the Confederate States of America: 'Vessel Papers.'*
M935, *Inspection Reports and Related Records Received by the Inspection Branch in the Confederate Adjutant and Inspector General's Office.*
M1091, *Subject File of the Confederate States Navy, 1861–1865.*
T1025, *Correspondence and Reports of the Confederate Treasury Department, 1861–1865.*
T1129, *Records of the Cotton Bureau of the Trans–Mississippi Department of the Confederate War Department, 1862–1865.*

Union Records Pertaining to Confederates

M345, *Union Provost Marshal's File of Papers Relating to Individual Civilians.*
M416, *Union Provost Marshal's File of Papers Relating to Two or More Civilians.*
M598, *Selected Records of the War Department Relating to Confederate Prisoners of War, 1861–1865.*
M621, *Reports and Decisions of the Provost Marshal General, 1863–1866.*
M918, *Register of Confederate Soldiers, Sailors, and Citizens Who Died in Federal Prisons and Military Hospitals in the North, 1861–1865.*
M1163, *Historical Reports of the State Acting Assistant Provost Marshal General and District Provost Marshals, 1865.*

General Civil War Records

M262, *Official Records of the Union and Confederate Armies, 1861–1865.*

M1036, *Military Operations of the Civil War: A Guide Index to the Official Records of the Union and Confederate Armies, Volume 1, 1861–1865.*

M1546, *Petitions Submitted to the U.S. Senate for the Removal of Political Disabilities of Former Confederate Officeholders, 1869–1877.*

M1815, *Military Operations of the Civil War: A Guide Index to the Official Records of the Union and Confederate Armies, Volumes 2–5, 1860–1865.*

P2282, *Correspondence of Military Commands Utilized in The War of the Rebellion: A Compilation of the Official Records of the Union and Confederate Armies, 1861–1865, 1862–1866.*

Robert de Berardinis

Houston, Texas
Sharon Clemon's birthday, my sister in law,
who can brighten the darkest room
August 2

This book is dedicated to
Mary Smith Fay, CG, FASG,

Teacher, friend, and yenta

Confederate Pension Payments Volumes, 1899–1905, 1909–1910, 1915–1966

Beginning in 1899, the Texas Legislature authorized pensions for eligible, indigent Confederate veterans residing in Texas, and their widows. This series consists of twenty-three volumes maintained by the Texas Comptroller's office, which document payments of Confederate pensions. Volumes include five quarterly Confederate pension records, five affidavit registers, nine pension warrant registers or volumes of stubs, and four mortuary warrant registers, with overall dates of 1899–1905, 1909–1910, and 1915–1966.

Historical Sketch

On May 12, 1899, the 26th Texas Legislature, Regular Session, passed the Confederate Pension Law, carrying into effect a Constitutional amendment to grant aid to disabled and dependent Confederate soldiers, sailors and their widows. To qualify for a pension, an applicant had to meet the following requirements, which were modified over the years:

Residency: The applicant must have lived in Texas since 1880 if they (or their husband, if a widow) had enlisted in the Confederate military from a state other than Texas, or since 1899 if they had originally enlisted in Texas. Subsequent legislation gradually lowered the required length of continuous residence for all pensioners (regardless of where they enlisted): thus applicants must have moved to Texas prior to 1900 (1913), prior to 1910 (1925), prior to 1920 (1929), ten years prior to approval (1930), and prior to 1928 (1931). The applicant must have been a resident of the county where he or she made application, for at least six months. Leaving the state for more than six months would disqualify a pensioner.

Age: Male applicants had to be at least 60 years old, unless totally disabled as a direct result of an injury sustained in actual service. (Between 1899 and 1909, soldiers' applications included affidavits of physicians; by 1909, soldiers applying would presumably have met the age requirement.) As of 1913, a widow must have been born prior to 1861 (i.e., she had to be at least 52 years old). As of 1929, she must have been born prior to 1873.

Military Service: The soldier must have served at least three months in the Confederate States Army or Navy, and never deserted. In 1913, legislation extended eligibility to those who served at least six months of the Civil War in the Texas militia (Texas State Troops or Home Guard) or in an organization for the protection of the frontier. Proof of service involved the testimonies of two witnesses, and/or a copy of the soldier's service record on file in the War Department in Washington, D.C., and/or other documentation, such as discharge papers.

Indigence: Applicants had to prove that they were unable to support themselves, "in actual want and destitute of property and means of subsistence." In 1909, indigence was more precisely defined, as follows. Applicants' annual income could not exceed $150 (raised to $300 in 1913). They must not have received any pension or land grant from the federal government (until this provision was dropped in 1927), or from

Confederate Pension Payments

any state government. They could own no real or personal property exceeding $1,000; after 1923, real or personal property could not be worth more than $1,000 exclusive of the homestead, and the assessed value exclusive of household goods could not exceed $2,000. Between 1909 and 1930, tax assessors' certificates were required for proof. At first, they could not be a resident of the Confederate Home or any other state-supported institution. Beginning in 1921, residents of either Confederate Home would receive one-half the normal pension.

Widow's Marital Status: Widows originally had to have been married to an eligible Confederate soldier at least by 1866. In subsequent years this requirement was gradually relaxed, from 1866 to 1880 (in 1909), to 1900 (in 1913), to 1910 (in 1925), to 1912 (in 1929), and to 1921 (in 1931, if they had been married at least ten years before his death). She could not have been separated, divorced, or remarried; in 1925, however, remarried widows were made eligible.

The procedure for applying for a Confederate pension in Texas involved appearing before the county judge, who with the commissioners' court made an initial ruling and forwarded applications deemed acceptable to the Comptroller's office. This is where the Pension Clerk or (after 1909) the Commissioner of Pensions made a final ruling. If accepted, the application would be assigned a unique and consecutive number. Rejected pension applications were retained in the Comptroller's (or the Pension Commissioner's) Office, and many who were rejected later reapplied and were accepted if their circumstances or the law had changed.

Pensioners were initially entitled to a maximum of $24 each quarter, with totally disabled pensioners being paid first, and the rest paid a portion of the appropriated total (not to exceed the allotted maximum, always less in reality). After 1917, every pensioner was given an equal portion of the appropriated money, with those on the Totally Disabled roll classed with other pensioners. Due to the large number of pensioners at first, the initial quarterly payment in 1899 was only $6.81; not until 1920 did the actual payment reach the maximum. During the 1920s, the quarterly payment steadily increased. In 1929, pensions began to be paid monthly, amounting to $25 per month for unmarried soldiers and widows, and $50 per month for married soldiers.

Effective April 1, 1917, mortuary warrants began to be issued, originally not to exceed $30, to help cover burial expenses of deceased pensioners. In 1923 this allotment was raised to $65, in 1929 to $100, and in 1947 to $200. Applications for mortuary warrants had to be received within 40 days of the pensioner's death, and the pension warrant for the quarter in which the death occurred had to be returned unpaid.

Organization

These records have been organized by State Archives staff into four sub series:
Quarterly Confederate Pension Records, 1899–1905, 1915–1916,
Confederate Pension Affidavit Registers, 1900–1901, 1917–1920,
Confederate Pension Warrant Registers and Stubs, 1900–1903, 1909–1910, 1950–1955, and
Confederate Mortuary Warrant Registers, 1917–1966.

Accession Information

These records were transferred to the Texas State Archives by the Texas Comptroller's office on July 19, 1963; September 5, 1968; and unknown other transfers. Two "indexes to mortuary warrants" (1917–1936) were transferred to the Texas State Archives by the Texas Comptroller's office on September 5, 1968. An unknown quantity of Confederate pension

Confederate Pension Payments

warrants was transferred to the Texas State Archives by the Texas Comptroller's office on July 19, 1963. Dates of the other accessions are uncertain.

Quarterly Confederate Pension Records, 1899–1905, 1915–1916

Beginning in 1899, the Texas Legislature authorized pensions for eligible, indigent Confederate veterans residing in Texas, and their widows. This sub series consists of six registers created by the Texas Comptroller's office: five labeled "Quarterly Confederate pension records," 1899–1905, plus one labeled "Record of pension warrants," 1915–16, the bulk of the entries dating 1899–1905.

For each county, the first five registers give name of pensioner, number of application, amounts and numbers of warrants issued for each quarter, and memoranda, e.g., "Dead, mail no. 325, Feb. 18, 1902;" or "At Confederate Home, March 1902;" or "Cancelled, remarried in 1867––see mail no. 1631, Aug. 17, 1903." The first register, which covers October 1, 1899–September 30, 1901 also gives husband's name for widows, plus post office address, i.e. town or city. Since mortuary warrants were not issued until 1917, probably the most valuable use of these registers is to determine when pensions stopped for pensioners who died, moved from the state, or otherwise became ineligible between October 1, 1899 and September 30, 1905.

The register which covers December 1, 1915–February 29, 1916 gives pensioner's name, original county, file number, warrant number, post office, and amount. This is the latest record of payment of Confederate pensions before the issuance of the first Mortuary warrants in 1917.

Arrangement

These volumes have been arranged by State Archives staff roughly chronologically. Therein, the records are arranged by the creator mostly alphabetically by county, then numerically (i.e. chronologically) within each county. The exception is the 1915–16 register, which is arranged by the creator roughly alphabetically by name of pensioner (first by surname, then by given name), then alphabetically by county, then numerically by pension number.

Quarterly Confederate Pension Records, 1899–1905

The following six volumes were not microfilmed.

Volume	
304-2611	Anderson–Zavala County, 1899–1901
304-2612	Anderson–Knox County, 1901–1903
304-2613	Lamar–Zavala County, 1901–1903
304-2614	Anderson–Hopkins County, 1903–1905
304-2615	Houston–Zavala County, 1903–1905

Record of (Confederate) Pension Warrants, 1915-1916

Volume	
304-2929	December 1, 1915–February 29, 1916

Confederate Pension Payments

Confederate Pension Affidavit Registers, 1900–1901, 1917–1920

Beginning in 1899, the Texas Legislature authorized pensions for eligible, indigent Confederate veterans residing in Texas, and their widows. Each pensioner was required to file a quarterly affidavit that conditions affecting his eligibility had not changed since the last payment. This sub series consists of five volumes documenting the filing of Texas Confederate pension affidavits, 1900–1901 and 1917–1920. The two volumes covering July 2, 1900–July 3, 1901 are registers. These give:

>Name of pensioner,
>Number (of affidavit, *NOT* the number of the Confederate Pension Application),
>When received,
>When issued, and
>Warrant number.

The last two items of information are omitted after March 29, 1901. Occasional notations include "held up," or "rejected," or "returned." The three volumes covering June 1, 1917–March 1, 1920 give the following information:

>Name of pensioner,
>Number of application, and
>Check marks under columns representing each of the eleven quarters covered.

When appropriate, quarterly columns are stamped "Dead."

Historical Sketch

Section 7 of the original Pension Law of 1899 required each pensioner to file quarterly with the Comptroller an affidavit "…that he is the identical person to whom a pension has been granted…and that the conditions…on which a pension was originally granted still exist."

Arrangement

These volumes have been arranged by State Archives staff chronologically. Then, the two earlier volumes are arranged by the creator numerically by affidavit number, which is also chronologically. The three later volumes are arranged by the creator alphabetically by county, and therein numerically by Confederate pension application number.

Confederate Pension Affidavit Registers, 1900–1901

The following five wolumes were not microfilmed.

Volume	
304-2616	July 1900–April 1901
304-2617	April–July 1901

Quarterly Affidavits of Confederate Pensioners, 1917–1920

Volume	
304-2927	Anderson–Hutchinson Counties, 1917–1920
304-2926	Irion–Pecos Counties, 1917–1920
304-2925	Rains–Zavala Counties, 1917–1920

Confederate Pension Payments

Confederate Pension Warrant Registers and Stubs, 1900–03, 1909–10, 1950–55

Beginning in 1899, the Texas Legislature authorized pensions for eligible, indigent Confederate veterans residing in Texas, and their widows. This sub series consists of eight volumes which document the issuance of Confederate pension warrants by the State of Texas.

Three of the volumes contain the stubs of Confederate pension warrants for scattered quarters between July 1900 and April 1903. Each stub gives:
    Warrant number,
    Amount,
    Appropriation number,
    Name of pensioner,
    Quarter,
    Application number,
    County, and
    Date.
The third volume includes blank stubs with blank warrants attached.

Five volumes are registers of Confederate pension warrants issued, December 1909–June 1910, December 1910, and September 1950–August 1955. Those for 1909–1910 give date of issue, warrant number, name to whom issued, and amount. Those for 1950–1955 also include pension number and address, while including mortuary warrants and pension warrants.

Arrangement

These volumes have been arranged by State Archives staff chronologically. Arrangement by the creator within each of the stubs volumes is numerical. Arrangement by the creator within each of the registers is chronological, i.e. numerical by warrant number.

Confederate Pension Warrant Stubs, 1900–1903

The following three registers were not microfilmed.

Volume
304-2622   July 1900

Volume
304-2623   February 1901

Volume
304-2621   November 1901–May 1903 (includes blank warrants)

Registers of Confederate Pension Warrants, 1909–1910

The following two registers were not microfilmed.

Volume
304-2618   Number 1, December 1, 1909–June 1, 1910

Volume
304-2619   Number 2, December 1, 1910

Confederate Pension Fund: Registers of Warrants Issued, 1950–1955

The three volumes were filmed as Confederate Pension Warrant Registers and Stubs, 1950–1955

Volume
304-2624   1950–1951

Volume

Confederate Pension Payments

304-2625	1951–1953
Volume	
304-2626	1953–1955

Confederate Mortuary Warrant Registers, 1917–1966

Beginning in 1899, the Texas Legislature authorized pensions for eligible, indigent Confederate veterans residing in Texas, and their widows. Beginning in 1917, mortuary warrants began to be authorized to help cover burial expenses. This sub series consists of four volumes which document the issuance of Confederate mortuary warrants by the State of Texas between 1917 and 1966. Two of them (1917–1966) give the following information:

- Date,
- Mortuary warrant number,
- Claimant,
- Name of pensioner,
- Pension application number, and
- Amount.

The other two volumes (1917–1943) are registers. The register covering May 1917–March 1931 gives:

- Number,
- Payee,
- Amount, and
- Date paid.

The register covering June 1933–August 1943 gives:

- Date of issue,
- Unit amount ($100),
- Month,
- To whom issued, and
- Warrant number.

Mortuary warrants issued beginning September 1943 were included in the registers of monthly pension warrants. Those for 1950–1955 are listed separately, in the sub series Confederate Pension Affidavit Registers.

Historical Sketch

Effective April 1, 1917, mortuary warrants began to be issued, originally not to exceed $30, to help cover burial expenses of deceased Confederate pensioners. In 1923 this allotment was raised to $65, in 1929 to $100, and in 1947 to $200. Applications for mortuary warrants had to be received within 40 days of the pensioner's death, and the pension warrant for the quarter in which the death occurred had to be returned unpaid.

Arrangement

These volumes have been arranged by State Archives staff roughly chronologically. Two of the volumes are arranged by the creator alphabetically by county, and therein numerically (i.e. chronologically) within each county. The two registers are arranged by the creator numerically (and therefore roughly chronologically).

Accession Information

Two "indexes to mortuary warrants" (1917–36) were transferred to the Texas State Archives by the Texas Comptroller's office on September 5, 1968.

Confederate Pension Payments

Record of Confederate Mortuary Warrants (by County), 1917–1966

These four volumes were filmed as Texas Confederate Mortuary Warrant Registers, 1917–1966

Volume
304-2628   1917–1936

Volume
304-2629   1936–1966

Registers of Confederate Mortuary Warrants Issued (Numerical), 1917–1931, 1933–1943

Volume
304-2620   1917–1931

Volume
304-2627   1933–1943

Description by Laura K. Saegert for the Texas State Archives, September 1983, and Tony Black for the Texas State Archives, March 1994 and October 1994, from TARO (Texas Archival Resources Online).

Confederate Pension Application Records, 1899–1979

Beginning in 1899, the Texas Legislature authorized pensions for eligible, indigent Confederate veterans residing in Texas, and their widows. The Confederate pension applications records provide detailed documentation of these persons, as well as the process. This series consists of the following records maintained by the Texas Comptroller's office: Confederate pension applications, 1899–1979; miscellaneous material relating to Confederate pensions, 1904–34; plus sixteen volumes that document applications for Confederate pensions. These volumes include twelve indexes, three registers, and a volume of affidavits of Confederate military service.

An alphabetical union name index is available at Clayton Library or in the Texas State Archives search room, containing the following elements:
- Pension number, if accepted,
- "Rej" if rejected, "Lost" if rejected, but the application file is now missing, "Home" if a Confederate Home resident pension application, or "[Number]" if granted,
- Name of the pensioner,
- County of residence at the time of the application,
- Name of husband if a widow, and
- Husband's pension number if applicable.

Researchers should request each pension application by number or for rejected and Home pension applications by name of applicant. Archives staff routinely checks listings in the index for mail or phone requests, and will copy the records in the files. The Confederate pension application index is also available online at:
<http://www.tsl.state.tx.us/arc/pensions/index.html>.

Historical Sketch

On May 12, 1899, the 26th Texas Legislature, Regular Session, passed the Confederate Pension Law, carrying into effect a Constitutional amendment to grant aid to disabled and dependent Confederate soldiers, sailors and their widows. To qualify for a pension, an applicant had to meet the following requirements, which were modified over the years:

Residency: The applicant must have lived in Texas since 1880 if they (or their husband, if a widow) had enlisted in the Confederate military from a state other than Texas, or since 1899 if they had originally enlisted in Texas. Subsequent legislation gradually lowered the required length of continuous residence for all pensioners (regardless of where they enlisted): thus applicants must have moved to Texas prior to 1900 (1913), prior to 1910 (1925), prior to 1920 (1929), ten years prior to approval (1930), and prior to 1928 (1931). The applicant must have been a resident of the county where he or she made application, for at least six months. Leaving the state for more than six months would disqualify a pensioner.

Age: Male applicants had to be at least 60 years old, unless totally disabled as a direct result of an injury sustained in actual service. (Between 1899 and 1909, soldiers' applications included affidavits of physicians; by 1909, soldiers applying would presumably have met the age requirement.) As of 1913, a widow must have been born prior to 1861

Confederate Pension Application Records

(i.e., she had to be at least 52 years old). As of 1929, she must have been born prior to 1873.

Military Service: The soldier must have served at least three months in the Confederate States Army or Navy, and never deserted. In 1913, legislation extended eligibility to those who served at least six months of the Civil War in the Texas militia (Texas State Troops or Home Guard) or in an organization for the protection of the frontier. Proof of service involved the testimonies of two witnesses, and/or a copy of the soldier's service record on file in the War Department in Washington, D.C., and/or other documentation, such as discharge papers.

Indigence: Applicants had to prove that they were unable to support themselves, "in actual want and destitute of property and means of subsistence." In 1909, indigence was more precisely defined, as follows. Applicants' annual income could not exceed $150 (raised to $300 in 1913). They must not have received any pension or land grant from the federal government (until this provision was dropped in 1927), or from any state government. They could own no real or personal property exceeding $1,000; after 1923, real or personal property could not be worth more than $1000 exclusive of the homestead, and the assessed value exclusive of household goods, which were not to exceed $2000 (Between 1909 and 1930, tax assessors' certificates were required for proof). At first, they could not be a resident of the Confederate Home or any other state–supported institution (Beginning in 1921, residents of either of the Confederate Homes would receive one–half the normal pension.).

Widow's Marital Status: Widows originally had to have been married to an eligible Confederate soldier at least by 1866. In subsequent years this requirement was gradually relaxed, from 1866 to 1880 (in 1909), to 1900 (in 1913), to 1910 (in 1925), to 1912 (in 1929), and to 1921 (in 1931, if they had been married at least ten years before his death). She could not have been separated, divorced, or remarried; in 1925, however, remarried widows were made eligible.

The procedure for applying for a Confederate pension in Texas involved appearing before the county judge, who (with the commissioners' court) made an initial ruling and forwarded applications deemed acceptable to the Comptroller's office, where the Pension Clerk or (after 1909) the Commissioner of Pensions made a final ruling. If accepted, the application would be assigned a unique (and consecutive) number. Rejected pension applications were retained in the Comptroller's (or the Pension Commissioner's) Office, and many who were rejected later reapplied and were accepted if their circumstances (or the law) had changed.

Pensioners were initially entitled to a maximum of $24 each quarter, with totally disabled pensioners being paid first, and the rest paid a portion of the appropriated total (not to exceed the allotted maximum, always less in reality). After 1917, every pensioner was given an equal portion of the appropriated money, with those on the Totally Disabled roll classed with other pensioners. Due to the large number of pensioners at first, the initial quarterly payment in 1899 was only $6.81; not until 1920 did the actual payment reach the maximum. During the 1920s, the quarterly payment steadily increased. In 1929, pensions began to be paid monthly, amounting to $25 per month for unmarried soldiers and widows, and $50 per month for married soldiers.

Confederate Pension Application Records

Effective April 1, 1917, mortuary warrants began to be issued, originally not to exceed $30, to help cover burial expenses of deceased pensioners. In 1923 this allotment was raised to $65, in 1929 to $100, and in 1947 to $200. Applications for mortuary warrants had to be received within 40 days of the pensioner's death, and the pension warrant for the quarter in which the death occurred had to be returned unpaid.

Organization

These records have been organized by State Archives staff into five sub series:
1. Confederate Pension Applications, 1899–1979
2. Miscellaneous Material Relating to Confederate Pension Applications, 1903–1934
3. Confederate Pension Indexes, 1899–1967
4. Confederate Pension Registers, 1899–1909, 1915–1917
5. Affidavits of Confederate Military Service, 1909–1917

Accession Information

Confederate pension applications were transferred to the Texas State Archives by the Texas Comptroller's office in numerous accessions: on February 21 and 24, 1934; during the September 1, 1960–August 31, 1962 biennium (from the Confederate Pension Division); on October 31, 1961 (Confederate Pension Division); November 29, 1965; December 7, 1967; September 5, 1968; November 13, 1969 (via the Records Division of the Texas State Library); February 9, 1977; August 18, 1980; and January 17, 1990.

The Texas Comptroller's office transferred the following to the Texas State Archives: the index to pensioners who were inmates of Confederate Homes, and a list of living Confederate widows drawing pensions, on October 18, 1963; and the index of totally disabled pensioners on October 21, 1964.

25 boxes of Confederate pension affidavits (1919–1931) were apparently transferred to the Texas State Archives by the Texas Comptroller's office (via the Records Management Division of the Texas State Library) on September 6, 1962.

Dates of the other accessions are uncertain.

Confederate Pension Applications, 1899–1979

Beginning in 1899, the Texas Legislature authorized pensions for eligible, indigent Confederate veterans residing in Texas, and their widows. The Confederate pension applications files provide detailed documentation of these persons, as well as the process. This sub series consists of more than 54,600 Confederate pension applications files created by the Texas Comptroller's office, dating 1899–1979. Each file contains an application to the State of Texas for a Confederate pension, plus supporting documents. Accepted applications comprise roughly 89 percent of the total; rejected applications comprise roughly 11 percent of the total; and there are sixty-two Confederate Home applications.

The contents of each veteran's file varies over time, but nearly always includes a four page application containing the basic information:

    Name of veteran,
    Age,
    Where born,
    Length of residency in Texas,
    County where residing and length of residence there,
    Post office address,
    Whether previously rejected for a pension (when and where),
    Occupation,

Confederate Pension Application Records

    Physical condition,
    Disability,
    State in which enlisted,
    Length of service,
    Date and place of discharge,
    Military unit designation (letter of company and number of regiment, battalion, or battery),
    Name of command and length of service if transferred,
    Branch in which enlisted (infantry, cavalry, artillery, or navy),
    Whether recipient of another pension,
    Whether recipient of another veteran's land certificate,
    Real and personal property and its value,
    Property sold within the previous two years and its value, income, and
    Estate of wife and its value.

They also usually contain:
    Affidavits of witnesses to the military service,
    An affidavit of a physician as to disabilities if applicable (especially prior to 1909),
    Certificates of the county judge and county commissioners who approved the application at its initial level, and
    (Between 1909–30) a certificate of the state and county assessor as to the value of any property.

Also usually included in the file is a request from the Comptroller or Commissioner of Pensions to the U.S. War Department (Adjutant General's office) for proof and details of military service, almost always accompanied by the official reply. Beginning in 1917, most files also contain a mortuary warrant application and a copy of the warrant for payment. Other materials may include:
    Additional affidavits and interrogatories relating to any of the requirements for eligibility,
    Correspondence between the Comptroller or Commissioner of Pensions and the applicant, relatives, or friends,
    Original discharges,
    Death certificates, and
    Printed material, including newspaper clippings; etc.

The widow's pension applications provide the following:
    Name of widow,
    Widow's age,
    Birthplace,
    Length of residence in Texas,
    County of residence,
    Length of residency in the county,
    Post office address,
    Occupation,
    Physical condition,
    Name of her husband (veteran),
    Date and place of marriage,
    Date of husband's death,
    County and state where he died,
    Whether divorced or remarried (and if so, whether widowed again),

Confederate Pension Application Records

State in which the husband (veteran) enlisted,
Length of his service (enlistment and discharge dates when known),
Name of unit in which the husband served,
Name of command and date if transferred,
Branch of service,
Whether previously rejected for a pension (when and where),
Whether recipient of another pension,
Whether recipient of another veteran's land certificate,
Real and personal property and its value,
Property sold within the previous two years,
Income,
Property outside of the county, and
Number of husband's pension, if applicable.

The Confederate mortuary warrant applications (beginning in 1917) provide the following information on the veteran or the widow:

Date of death,
City or county of death,
Where death occurred (in home, hospital, etc.),
Relation of person (s) in whose home the pensioner died,
Relationship of the petitioner to the pensioner,
Petitioner's post office address,
Physician's certification (including ailments of pensioner), and
Undertaker's certification.

A number of application files are known to be missing (based on information from the Confederate pension indexes and registers); these are marked with an asterisk in the pension index in the State Archives search room.

An alphabetical union name index is available in the Texas State Archives search room and at Clayton Library, containing the following elements:

Pension number if accepted,
"Rej" if rejected, or "Home" if a Confederate Home pension application;
Name of the pensioner;
County of residence at the time of the application;
Name of husband if a widow, and
Husband's pension number, if applicable.

Researchers should request each pension application by number or for rejected and Home pension applications by name of applicant. Archives staff routinely checks listings in the index for mail or phone requests, and will copy the records in the files. The Confederate pension application index is also available online at:
<http://www.tsl.state.tx.us/arc/pensions/index.html>.

Arrangement

These records have been arranged by State Archives staff numerically by pension number (which is also chronologically) for accepted pension applications, and alphabetically by name of applicant for rejected pension applications, as well as for Confederate Home pension applications. This arrangement was probably the same used by the creator of the records.

Accession Information

Confederate pension applications were transferred to the Texas State Archives by the Texas Comptroller's office in numerous accessions: on February 21 and 24, 1934; during the September 1, 1960–August 31, 1962 biennium (from the Confederate Pension Division); on

Confederate Pension Application Records

October 31, 1961 (Confederate Pension Division); November 29, 1965; December 7, 1967; September 5, 1968; November 13, 1969 (via the Records Division of the Texas State Library); February 9, 1977; and August 18, 1980.

Confederate Pension Applications, 1899–1979

Approved Confederate Pension Applications
#00001 through #52094, #99999

Confederate Home Pension Applications
Aiken, W.C. through Wright, R.S.

Rejected Confederate Pension Applications
Abernathy, T.C. through Zuniga, Felipa Flores de

Miscellaneous Material Relating to Confederate Pension Applications, 1903–1934

Beginning in 1899, the Texas Legislature authorized pensions for eligible, indigent Confederate veterans residing in Texas, and their widows. This sub series consists of records maintained by the Texas Comptroller's Office which pertain to Texas Confederate pension applications, but which for various reasons cannot be assigned to a particular Confederate pension application file. Types of records include:
   Military service records,
   Physician's statements,
   Witness affidavits,
   Mortuary warrant applications, and
   Related correspondence, dating 1903–34.

Arrangement

These records have been arranged by State Archives staff alphabetically by name of applicant.

Miscellaneous Material Relating to Confederate Pension Applications, 1903–1934

Box	
304-3	Adams, Edgar Sheppard (Nacogdoches County)
	Adams, Robert S.
	Adams, S. S. (Limestone County)
	Adamson, J. Q.
	Adamson, J. Q.
	Aiken, J. D.
	Ainsworth, Spencer Montague
	Alexander, H. T.
	Allen, G. W.
	Altum, Newton R. (Bell County)
	Alvis, G. W.
	Anderson, Archibald T.
	Anderson, Marcella J. (Potter County)
	Arnett, N. C.
	Arnold, William B.
	Autrey, A. B.
	Bagby, Arthur P.

Confederate Pension Application Records

Box, Cont.
304-3

Bailey, J. W. (Hill County)
Bailey, W. H.
Ballard, Milton Neal (Shelby County)
Barrett, J. D. (Tarrant County)
Barrett, W. B.
Bass, T. (Smith County)
Bateman, N. M.
Battles, Anderson
Beasley, J. R.
Bell, John L.
Blackstone, James H. (Upshur County)
Blake, John A.
Bourer, S. (Caldwell County)
Bowers, Joe
Bramlett, H. M.
Bridges, William
Brooks, John R. (Tarrant County)
Brown, H. W. (Mrs.) (Harris County)
Brown, J. A.
Brown, J. A.
Brown, John
Brown, W. M.
Bryan, Sydney B.
Burchard, J. Everett
Butler, Benjamin F.
Cage, R. W. (Milam County)
Capman, A. J.
Carlisle, T. R.
Carter, Jake
Catteron, J. B.
Chapmore, G. W. (Hood County)
Clardy, M. J.
Clark, C. C.
Clark, W. J.
Clements, T. W. (Erath County)
Cleveland, J. W. (Shelby County)
Clifton,? (Wood County)
Conaway, John
Cooley, S. A. (Limestone County)
Corker, M. H. (San Saba County)
Crabtree, Isic Newton
Craddock, Erasmus D. (Burnet County)
Crawford, William A.
Cronk, Joseph L.
Crow, Rufus J.

Box
304-4

Davis, F. M.
Davis, Henry H.

Confederate Pension Application Records

Box, Cont.
304-4
    Davis, Susan (Tarrant County)
    Davis, W. G.
    Dean, E. A.
    Dearen, Hampton
    Depew, J. N.
    Draper, G. W. (Travis County)
    Duncan, J. P.
    Edwards, T. J. (Comanche County)
    Eubank, Carter H.
    Evans, Samuel
    Everitt, Joseph R.
    Ewing, E. M.
    Ferguson, Plea F.
    Fleming, J. S.
    Forrest, Calvin J.
    Foster, John C. (Parker County)
    Fox, W. H.
    Freeman, Jesse M.
    Gantier, G. R.
    Gentry, George W.
    Gentry, George W.
    Gilbert, J. F. (Mrs.) (Limestone County)
    Gillion, E. M.
    Glenn, Thomas B.
    Grace, James
    Graham, W. B.
    Graves, Robert Lewis
    Green, John F.
    Gresham, Henry M.
    Guinn, Andy
    Guitry, Virginia (Travis County)
    Gullin, H. H. (Cooke County)
    Hail, Lewis (Hunt County)
    Hale, J. W.
    Hammack, James J.
    Hammonds, J. W.
    Hampton, W. H.
    Hand, W. S.
    Hanes, F. M. (Fannin County)
    Hanscomb, W. H.
    Hansen, J. C.
    Hardin, A. R. (Uvalde County)
    Hardin, G. E.
    Hargrove, J. E.
    Hawkins, E. H. (Erath County)
    Heath, Levi
    Henderson, C. M.
    Hendrick, S. J.

Confederate Pension Application Records

Box, Cont.
304-4

Hendrick, Thomas H.
Henry, Thomas
Hickman, John M.
Hill, James W.
Hill, John
Hill, Richard D.
Hinard, Elija
Hodge, G. A.
Hodges, R. C.
Holder, Henry
Holmes, Seymour W.
Howard, John R.
Hubbard, C. G. (Waller County)
Hughes, R. H. L.
Hunter, Edward F.

Box
304-5

Ireson, A. B. (Nacogdoches County)
Jahn, Frank C. (Waller County)
Jeffries, R. D. (Mrs.)
Johnson, Asa
Johnson, R. J. (Eastland County)
Johnson, T.
Jones, Andrew T. (Lampasas County)
Jones, D. C. W.
Jones, J. C.
Jones, William
Joyner, Lawrence R.
Karnes, Gordon M. (Johnson County)
Killion, G. M.
Lambert, William E.
Landers, James W.
Latham, William (Houston County)
Lawrence, W. D.
Lealling, W. J. (Hunt County)
Lee, Isaac J.
Lee, T. T.
Lewis, Daniel
Lindsey, W. H. (Hunt County)
Locke, Mary F.
Lockhart, C. H.
Loving, J. P. (Fannin County)
Lowrimore or Larrimore, M.
McBride, Wade A.
McCall, Thomas P.
McCarr, H. M.
McDade, R. R. (Waller County)
McDonald, Thomas Benton
McDuffie, Martin A.

Confederate Pension Application Records

Box, Cont.
304-5

McFarland, J. S.
McKinney, William
McLeroy, Olive J. (Hopkins County)
McMahon, Sanders
Madden, James M.
Magee, Abe G. (Harris County)
Mahaffey, W. A. (Tyler County)
Majors, W. J. (Bonham, Fannin County)
Manning, F. M.
Marshall, R. F.
Martin, William J.
Marriott, John W.
Mayfield, George W.
Miller, David A.
Milner, T. F.
Mitchell, Jabez
Mitchell, William C.
Montgomery, J. M.
Moore, J. B.
Moore, J. F.
Moran, John H.
Morgan, William
Morris, A. J.
Munsch, Andrew J.

Box
304-6

Neel, J. C. (Anderson County)
Nichols, J. W.
Norris, A. N.
O'Banion, Peter
Odom, J. S.
O'Neal, Francis
Owens, J. W. (see S. A. Owens, #34077)
Owings, William A.
Parker, Tom
Parks, Leroy (black)
Paschall, Ben F. (Denton County)
Patillo, John Z.
Patrick, John T.
Payne, M. P.
Perkins, Jeremiah W.
Peterson, John Q.
Phillips, Richard (Walker County)
Pier, Sam B. (Waller County)
Porter, J. C.
Post, Wiley G.
Pressler, C. W.
Previt, T. F.
Purviance, John S.

Confederate Pension Application Records

Box, Cont.
304-6
          Raines, C. W.
          Rains, W. A. (Walker County)
          Reich, E. B.
          Richardson, D. K.
          Richey, A. F.
          Riddle, N. B.
          Roberts, William
          Robinson, I. G. (Red River County)
          Rogers, J. S.
          Rogers, William T.
          Roguemore, J. R.
          Ross, Benjamin
          Rutlege, J. A.
          Sampson, Henry
          Sanford, G. A.
          Schmidt, Ed. W.
          Scott, Robert
          Sears, J. R.
          Shappard, A. M.
          Shay, Thomas
          Shepherd, Samuel
          Shugart, L. C.
          Simmons, B. P. (Bastrop County)
          Simmons, R. A.
          Simmons, S. W.
          Smith, J. A.
          Smith, J. W.
          Smith, John Henry
          Smith, Lycurgus (Denton County)
          Smith, Nicholas
          Smith, W. C.
          Smith, William H.
          Smith, William R. (Bexar County)
          Spring, Henry F.
          Spruill, M. J. (Mrs.) (Travis County)
          Stephens, G. W.
          Stewart, D. A. (Navarro County)
          Stoutz, August
          Stovall, William J. (Denton County)
          Strange, William C.
          Strother, W. W. (Mrs.) (Sabine County)
          Sutter, H. Marion

Box
304-7
          Talley, P. T.
          Temple, R. H.
          Temple, T. F.
          Thaveness, Joseph
          Thomas, W. J.

Confederate Pension Application Records

Box, Cont.
304-7
Thompson, Thomas Franklin (Waller County)
Thompson, Warren T.
Tillman, Leroy
Toull, G. W.
Traweek, A. B.
Victor, W. O.
Walden, David M. (Concho County)
Walker, Mary A. (Harris County)
Walsh, J. G. (Fannin County)
Walton, George
Ward, Preston B.
Weaver, L. C.
Wells, Billie (Hopkins County)
Wells, John (Houston County)
West, Thomas Lee
White, E. J.
Williams, Mary (Ellis County)
Wills, W. J.
Willson, J. J.
Wilson, A. J. (Tarrant County)
Wilson, John R.
Wilson, T. A.
Wingose, Fannie (Harris County)
Wood, Thomas
Wooley, R. C.
Wright, J. W. (Somervell County)
Wyatt, John C. (Callahan County)
Young, Emanuel M.

Confederate Pension Indexes, 1899–1967

Beginning in 1899, the Texas Legislature authorized pensions for eligible, indigent Confederate veterans residing in Texas, and their widows. This sub series consists of twelve indexes to Texas Confederate pension applications, covering the period 1899–1967.

Seven of the indexes are to Confederate pensioners, whose applications were accepted between 1899 and 1959. Information given in each index includes surname, Christian name, file number, county, and remarks. Remarks were most commonly, "Dead," often followed by a date from approximately 1921 onward). At least in volumes 1 and 2, rejected ("returned") applications are listed in the back, with the town or city substituted for the file number, and the remarks column indicating the date the application was returned. Indexes Numbers 4 and 6 contain only men, and Numbers 5 and 7 contain only widows; for the latter, the husband's name and number (if he drew a pension) were often added. Please note that the dates provided for each volume in the inventory below correspond to the dates of the applications; later notations, especially concerning deaths, would extend the date span for each volume, up to 1967, the date of the last death recorded.

Separate indexes cover totally disabled pensioners (through 1917), inmates of the Confederate Homes, and rejected applications (1899–1958). This latter index includes:
Surname,

Confederate Pension Application Records

    Christian name,
    Date,
    County, and
    Remarks.

The remarks usually gives the reason for rejection: e.g., "no proof," or "too much property," or "not married 10 years," or "age," or "came to Texas in 1946," or "substitute," or "deserter," or "oath of allegiance," or "Georgia reserves," or "drawing (pension) in Arkansas."

Arrangement

These records have been arranged by State Archives staff chronologically by groups of years during which applications were filed: 1899–1907, 1907–1913, 1913–1915, 1915–1928, and 1928–1948/1959. Within each volume, arrangement by the creator is alphabetical by surname, and within a given surname, numerical (i.e., chronological).

Accession Information

The Texas Comptroller's office transferred the following to the Texas State Archives: the index to pensioners who were inmates of Confederate Homes, and a list of living Confederate widows drawing pensions, on October 18, 1963; and the index of totally disabled pensioners on October 21, 1964. Dates of the other accessions are uncertain.

Confederate Pension Indexes, 1899–1967

Volume	
304-2596	Index 1, Confederate Pensioners, 1899–1907
304-2597	Index 2, Confederate Pensioners, 1907–1913
304-2598	Index 3, Confederate Pensioners, 1913–1915
304-2599	Index 4, Confederate Pensioners, 1915–1928
304-2600	Index 5, Confederate Widows, 1915–1928
304-2601	Index 6, Confederate Pensioners, 1928–1948
304-2602	Index 7, Confederate Widows, 1928–1959
304-2603	Index, Inmates of Confederate Homes
304-2604	Index, Totally Disabled Pensioners, ca. 1899–1917
304-2605	Index, Totally Disabled Pensioners, ca. 1899–1915
304-2606	Index, Rejected Applications, 1899–1958
304-2607	Old Rejected Pension Record, 1902–ca. 1917 (pp. 1–146)

Confederate Pension Application Records

Confederate Pension Registers, 1899–1909, 1915–1917

Beginning in 1899, the Texas Legislature authorized pensions for eligible, indigent Confederate veterans residing in Texas, and their widows. This sub series consists of three registers of Texas Confederate pension applications, covering October 1, 1899–March 31, 1909, and March 1, 1915–December 4, 1917. Information provided includes:

    Name of applicant,
    Post office (town or city),
    County,
    Number of application,
    Date filed (until #8203, September 18, 1901),
    Widow of,
    Service or command (beginning with #8204 or 1901), and
    Disposition (and date, e.g. "approved," or "rejected," or "dead," or "later approved #___.").

The number of the warrant is provided until November 14, 1899.

Arrangement

These records have been arranged by State Archives staff chronologically. Two volumes are arranged by the creator numerically by application number, which is also chronologically. The third volume, covering May 1902–April 1903, is arranged by the creator alphabetically by county; but this volume is incomplete, not covering all the counties for the entire time span.

Confederate Pension Registers

Volume
304-2608   1899–1909

Volume
304-2609   1902–1903 (incomplete)

Volume
304-2607   1915–1917 (pp. 198–298)

Affidavits of Confederate Military Service, 1909–1917

Beginning in 1899, the Texas Legislature authorized pensions for eligible, indigent Confederate veterans residing in Texas, and their widows. One of the key requirements was proof of service in a military unit of the Confederate States of America. This sub series consists of one volume created by the Texas Comptroller's office, containing longhand and typescript transcripts of affidavits of Confederate military service, sworn to between 1909 and 1917. An index is at the front of the volume.

Arrangement

These records have been arranged by State Archives staff chronologically.

Affidavits of Confederate Military Service, 1909–1917

Volume
304-2610   Affidavits of Confederate Military Service, 1909–1917

Description by Laura K. Saegert for the Texas State Archives, September 1983, and Tony Black for the Texas State Archives, March 1994 and October 1994, from TARO (Texas Archival Resources Online).

Index to Miscellaneous Material Relating to Confederate Pension Applications, 1903–1934

Roll number refers to the microfilm, *Confederate Pension Application Records, 1899–1979*. (microfilm edition; Austin: Clayton Library Friends, 2005).

Name	Box	Roll
Adams, Edg. Sheppard (Nacogdoches Co.)	304-3	1
Adams, Robert S.	304-3	1
Adams, S. S. (Limestone Co.)	304-3	1
Adamson, J. Q.	304-3	1
Adamson, J. Q.	304-3	1
Aiken, J. D.	304-3	1
Ainsworth, Spencer Montague	304-3	1
Alexander, H. T.	304-3	1
Allen, G. W.	304-3	1
Altum, Newton R. (Bell Co.)	304-3	1
Alvis, G. W.	304-3	1
Anderson, Archibald T.	304-3	1
Anderson, Marcella J. (Potter Co.)	304-3	1
Arnett, N. C.	304-3	1
Arnold, William B.	304-3	1
Autrey, A. B.	304-3	1
Bagby, Arthur P.	304-3	1
Bailey, J. W. (Hill Co.)	304-3	1
Bailey, W. H.	304-3	1
Ballard, Milton Neal (Shelby Co.)	304-3	1
Barrett, J. D. (Tarrant Co.)	304-3	1
Barrett, W. B.	304-3	1
Bass, T. (Smith Co.)	304-3	1
Bateman, N. M.	304-3	1
Battles, Anderson	304-3	1
Beasley, J. R.	304-3	1
Bell, John L.	304-3	1
Blackstone, James H. (Upshur Co.)	304-3	1
Blake, John A.	304-3	1
Bourer, S. (Caldwell Co.)	304-3	1
Bowers, Joe	304-3	1
Bramlett, H. M.	304-3	1
Bridges, William	304-3	1
Brooks, John R. (Tarrant Co.)	304-3	1
Brown, H. W. Mrs. (Harris Co.)	304-3	1
Brown, J. A.	304-3	1
Brown, J. A.	304-3	1
Brown, John	304-3	1
Brown, W. M.	304-3	1
Bryan, Sydney B.	304-3	1
Burchard, J. Everett	304-3	1
Butler, Benjamin F.	304-3	1
Cage, R. W. (Milam Co.)	304-3	1
Capman, A. J.	304-3	1
Carlisle, T. R.	304-3	1
Carter, Jake	304-3	1
Catteron, J. B.	304-3	1
Chapmore, G. W. (Hood Co.)	304-3	1
Clardy, M. J.	304-3	1
Clark, C. C.	304-3	1
Clark, W. J.	304-3	1
Clements, T. W. (Erath Co.)	304-3	1
Cleveland, J. W. (Shelby Co.)	304-3	1
Clifton, [?] (Wood Co.)	304-3	1
Conaway, John	304-3	1
Cooley, S. A. (Limestone Co.)	304-3	1
Corker, M. H. (San Saba Co.)	304-3	1
Crabtree, Isic Newton	304-3	1
Craddock, Erasmus D. (Burnet Co.)	304-3	1
Crawford, William A.	304-3	1
Cronk, Joseph L.	304-3	1
Crow, Rufus J.	304-3	1
Davis, F. M.	304-4	2
Davis, Henry H.	304-4	2
Davis, Susan (Tarrant Co.)	304-4	2
Davis, W. G.	304-4	2
Dean, E. A.	304-4	2
Dearen, Hampton	304-4	2
Depew, J. N.	304-4	2
Draper, G. W. (Travis Co.)	304-4	2
Duncan, J. P.	304-4	2
Edwards, T. J. (Comanche Co.)	304-4	2
Eubank, Carter H.	304-4	2
Evans, Samuel	304-4	2
Everitt, Joseph R.	304-4	2
Ewing, E. M.	304-4	2
Ferguson, Plea F.	304-4	2
Fleming, J. S.	304-4	2
Forrest, Calvin J.	304-4	2
Foster, John C. (Parker Co.)	304-4	2
Fox, W. H.	304-4	2
Freeman, Jesse M.	304-4	2
Gantier, G. R.	304-4	2
Gentry, George W.	304-4	2
Gentry, George W.	304-4	2
Gilbert, J. F. Mrs. (Limestone Co.)	304-4	2
Gillion, E. M.	304-4	2
Glenn, Thomas B.	304-4	2
Grace, James	304-4	2
Graham, W. B.	304-4	2
Graves, Robert Lewis	304-4	2
Green, John F.	304-4	2
Gresham, Henry M.	304-4	2
Guinn, Andy	304-4	2
Guitry, Virginia (Travis Co.)	304-4	2
Gullin, H. H. (Cooke Co.)	304-4	2
Hail, Lewis (Hunt Co.)	304-4	2
Hale, J. W.	304-4	2

Miscellaneous Material Relating to Confederate Pension Applications

Name	Box	Roll	Name	Box	Roll
Hammack, James J.	304-4	2	McDade, R. R. (Waller Co.)	305-5	3
Hammonds, J. W.	304-4	2	McDonald, Thomas Benton	305-5	3
Hampton, W. H.	304-4	2	McDuffie, Martin A.	305-5	3
Hand, W. S.	304-4	2	McFarland, J. S.	305-5	3
Hanes, F. M. (Fannin Co.)	304-4	2	McKinney, William	305-5	3
Hanscomb, W. H.	304-4	2	McLeroy, Olive J. (Hopkins Co.)	305-5	3
Hansen, J. C.	304-4	2	McMahon, Sanders	305-5	3
Hardin, A. R. (Uvalde Co.)	304-4	2	Madden, James M.	305-5	3
Hardin, G. E.	304-4	2	Magee, Abe G. (Harris Co.)	305-5	3
Hargrove, J. E.	304-4	2	Mahaffey, W. A. (Tyler Co.)	305-5	3
Hawkins, E. H. (Erath Co.)	304-4	2	Majors, W. J. (Bonham, Fannin Co.)	305-5	3
Heath, Levi	304-4	2	Manning, F. M.	305-5	3
Henderson, C. M.	304-4	2	Marshall, R. F.	305-5	3
Hendrick, S. J.	304-4	2	Martin, William J.	305-5	3
Hendrick, Thomas H.	304-4	2	Marriott, John W.	305-5	3
Henry, Thomas	304-4	2	Mayfield, George W.	305-5	3
Hickman, John M.	304-4	2	Miller, David A.	305-5	3
Hill, James W.	304-4	2	Milner, T. F.	305-5	3
Hill, John	304-4	2	Mitchell, Jabez	305-5	3
Hill, Richard D.	304-4	2	Mitchell, William C.	305-5	3
Hinard, Elija	304-4	2	Montgomery, J. M.	305-5	3
Hodge, G. A.	304-4	2	Moore, J. B.	305-5	3
Hodges, R. C.	304-4	2	Moore, J. F.	305-5	3
Holder, Henry	304-4	2	Moran, John H.	305-5	3
Holmes, Seymour W.	304-4	2	Morgan, William	305-5	3
Howard, John R.	304-4	2	Morris, A. J.	305-5	3
Hubbard, C. G. (Waller Co.)	304-4	2	Munsch, Andrew J.	305-5	3
Hughes, R. H. L.	304-4	2	Neel, J. C. (Anderson Co.)	305-6	4
Hunter, Edward F.	304-4	2	Nichols, J. W.	305-6	4
Ireson, A. B. (Nacogdoches Co.)	305-5	3	Norris, A. N.	305-6	4
Jahn, Frank C. (Waller Co.)	305-5	3	O'Banion, Peter	305-6	4
Jeffries, R. D. Mrs.	305-5	3	Odom, J. S.	305-6	4
Johnson, Asa	305-5	3	O'Neal, Francis	305-6	4
Johnson, R. J. (Eastland Co.)	305-5	3	Owens, J. W. (see S. A. Owens, #34077)	305-6	4
Johnson, T.	305-5	3	Owings, William A.	305-6	4
Jones, Andrew T. (Lampasas Co.)	305-5	3	Parker, Tom	305-6	4
Jones, D. C. W.	305-5	3	Parks, Leroy (Black)	305-6	4
Jones, J. C.	305-5	3	Paschall, Ben F. (Denton Co.)	305-6	4
Jones, William	305-5	3	Patillo, John Z.	305-6	4
Joyner, Lawrence R.	305-5	3	Patrick, John T.	305-6	4
Karnes, Gordon M. (Johnson Co.)	305-5	3	Payne, M. P.	305-6	4
Killion, G. M.	305-5	3	Perkins, Jeremiah W.	305-6	4
Lambert, William E.	305-5	3	Peterson, John Q.	305-6	4
Landers, James W.	305-5	3	Phillips, Richard (Walker Co.)	305-6	4
Latham, William (Houston Co.)	305-5	3	Pier, Sam B. (Waller Co.)	305-6	4
Lawrence, W. D.	305-5	3	Porter, J. C.	305-6	4
Lealling, W. J. (Hunt Co.)	305-5	3	Post, Wiley G.	305-6	4
Lee, Isaac J.	305-5	3	Pressler, C. W.	305-6	4
Lee, T. T.	305-5	3	Previt, T. F.	305-6	4
Lewis, Daniel	305-5	3	Purviance, John S.	305-6	4
Lindsey, W. H. (Hunt Co.)	305-5	3	Raines, C. W.	305-6	4
Locke, Mary F.	305-5	3	Rains, W. A. (Walker Co.)	305-6	4
Lockhart, C. H.	305-5	3	Reich, E. B.	305-6	4
Loving, J. P. (Fannin Co.)	305-5	3	Richardson, D. K.	305-6	4
Lowrimore or Larrimore, M.	305-5	3	Richey, A. F.	305-6	4
McBride, Wade A.	305-5	3	Riddle, N. B.	305-6	4
McCall, Thomas P.	305-5	3	Roberts, William	305-6	4
McCarr, H. M.	305-5	3	Robinson, I. G. (Red River Co.)	305-6	4

Miscellaneous Material Relating to Confederate Pension Applications

Name	Box	Roll
Rogers, J. S.	305-6	4
Rogers, William T.	305-6	4
Roguemore, J. R.	305-6	4
Ross, Benjamin	305-6	4
Rutlege, J. A.	305-6	4
Sampson, Henry	305-6	4
Sanford, G. A.	305-6	4
Schmidt, Ed. W.	305-6	4
Scott, Robert	305-6	4
Sears, J. R.	305-6	4
Shappard, A. M.	305-6	4
Shay, Thomas	305-6	4
Shepherd, Samuel	305-6	4
Shugart, L. C.	305-6	4
Simmons, B. P. (Bastrop Co.)	305-6	4
Simmons, R. A.	305-6	4
Simmons, S. W.	305-6	4
Smith, J. A.	305-6	4
Smith, J. W.	305-6	4
Smith, John Henry	305-6	4
Smith, Lycurgus (Denton Co.)	305-6	4
Smith, Nicholas	305-6	4
Smith, W. C.	305-6	4
Smith, William H.	305-6	4
Smith, William R. (Bexar Co.)	305-6	4
Spring, Henry F.	305-6	4
Spruill, M. J. Mrs. (Travis Co.)	305-6	4
Stephens, G. W.	305-6	4
Stewart, D. A. (Navarro Co.)	305-6	4
Stoutz, August	305-6	4
Stovall, William J. (Denton Co.)	305-6	4
Strange, William C.	305-6	4
Strother, W. W. Mrs. (Sabine Co.)	305-6	4
Sutter, H. Marion	305-6	4
Talley, P. T.	305-7	4
Temple, R. H.	305-7	4
Temple, T. F.	305-7	4
Thaveness, Joseph	305-7	4
Thomas, W. J.	305-7	4
Thompson, Thomas Franklin (Waller Co.)	305-7	4
Thompson, Warren T.	305-7	4
Tillman, Leroy	305-7	4
Toull, G. W.	305-7	4
Traweek, A. B.	305-7	4
Victor, W. O.	305-7	4
Walden, David M. (Concho Co.)	305-7	4
Walker, Mary A. (Harris Co.)	305-7	4
Walsh, J. G. (Fannin Co.)	305-7	4
Walton, George	305-7	4
Ward, Preston B.	305-7	4
Weaver, L. C.	305-7	4
Wells, Billie (Hopkins Co.)	305-7	4
Wells, John (Houston Co.)	305-7	4
West, Thomas Lee	305-7	4
White, E. J.	305-7	4
Williams, Mary (Ellis Co.)	305-7	4
Wills, W. J.	305-7	4
Willson, J. J.	305-7	4
Wilson, A. J. (Tarrant Co.)	305-7	4
Wilson, John R.	305-7	4
Wilson, T. A.	305-7	4
Wingose, Fannie (Harris Co.)	305-7	4
Wood, Thomas	305-7	4
Wooley, R. C.	305-7	4
Wright, J. W. (Somervell Co.)	305-7	4
Wyatt, John C. (Callahan Co.)	305-7	4
Young, Emanuel M.	305-7	4

Index of Confederate Home Applications

Name		County	Name of Veteran, if applicable	His No.
Akin, W. C.	Home	Bowie	—	—
Bedell, H. D.	Home	Travis	—	—
Bell, M. E. Mrs.	Home	Travis	Bell, Joseph Athel	10584
Bowles, Green Berry	Home	Travis	—	—
Bozeman, J. R.	Home	Travis	—	—
Bradfield, J. O.	Home	Travis	—	—
Brock, F. M.	Home	Travis	—	—
Burgess, John J.	Home	Travis	—	—
Collins, Eliza Blackshear	Home	Travis	Collins, Charles C.	07629
Davis, S. A. Mrs.	Home	Travis	Davis, Green Hunter	—
Dill, A. J.	Home	Travis	—	—
Doe, E. S.	Home	Travis	—	—
Erwin, Sarah Craig Cattiton	Home	Travis	Cattiton, James Boyd	—
Farmer, Isaac N.	Home	Travis	—	—
Ficklin, J. E.	Home	Travis	—	—
Fitzgerald, David	Home	Travis	—	—
Freeman, Terah Major	Home	Travis	—	—
Garrett, T. J.	Home	Travis	—	—
Gilbreath, Robert	Home	Travis	—	—
Gilliam, John W.	Home	Travis	—	—
Glance, Jacob M.	Home	Travis	—	—
Hardwick, Francis	Home	Travis	Hardwick, William Green Berry	—
Hewett, Josephus	Home	Bexar	—	—
Inge, Amanda Coulson	Home	Travis	Inge, William Marshall	—
Johnston, C. M.	Home	Travis	—	—
Jones, Martha"	Home	Travis	Jones, James M.	07609
Kennedy, Lou	Home	Travis	Kennedy, Wade Holland	10385
Kilpatrick, George W.	Home	Tom Green	—	—
Lynn, Lucy J.	Home	Travis	Lynn, John Henry	11442
Mayo, H. F.	Home	Travis	—	—
McArthur, A. D.	Home	Travis	—	—
McCormick, J. O.	Home	Travis	—	—
Meriwether, D. R. A.	Home	Travis	—	—
Moody, W. L.	Home	Travis	—	—
Moore, Sarah Angeline	Home	Travis	Moore, James William	—
Morris, William C.	Home	Travis	—	—
Norman, Argyle	Home	Travis	—	—
Odom, Mary Hunt	Home	Travis	Odom, Thomas Lawson	—
Parker, Annie R.	Home	Travis	Parker, William James	09861
Parker, Irbin H.	Home	Brown	—	—
Patterson, Elizabeth J.	Home	Travis	Patterson, John Wesley	22987
Pearce, J. T.	Home	Travis	—	—
Quinn, Andrew	Home	Travis	—	—
Remmington, Benjamin Franklin	Home	Travis	—	—
Robertson, B. F.	Home	Travis	—	—
Shackelford, S. H.	Home	Travis	—	—
Shown, Lucille Word	Home	Travis	Word, Preston B.	—
Smith, Thomas	Home	Travis	—	—
South, John P.	Home	Travis	—	—
Spears, James D.	Home	Travis	—	—
Stephens, G. W.	Home	Travis	—	—
Stogner, W. F.	Home	Travis	—	—
Strickland, Hellen	Home	Travis	Strickland, James Jessie	—
Stuart, James W.	Home	Travis	—	—

Confederate Home Pension Applications

Taliaferro, J. N.	Home	Travis	—	—
Vaughn, Mary L.	Home	Travis	Vaughn, Thomas Pinkney	13933
Wallace, Lucia S.	Home	Travis	Wallace, Albert David	20579
Ware, William Henry	Home	Travis	—	—
Wells, Mary E.	Home	Travis	Wells, James Elisha	07998
Wilkins, William B.	Home	Travis	—	—
Williams, George W.	Home	Travis	—	—
Williams, Hugh L.	Home	Travis	—	—
Wilson, J. M.	Home	Travis	—	—
Wright, R. S.	Home	Travis	—	—

Index to Missing Pension Applications

Adair, M. E. Mrs.	08368M	Hunt	
Adams, Fannie Tiberius	RejM	Brown	Adams, Zachariah Burges
Adams, Susan N.	08344M	Henderson	
Ainsworth, Leo	RejM	Callahan	
Alexander, Jason B.	08438M	Panola	
Alexander, L. A. Mrs.	20022M	Titus	
Allen, J. A.	02430M	Lamar	
Allen, M. J. Mrs.	RejM	Houston	
Allen, M. M.	RejM	Williamson	
Arms, Martha	06113AM	Blanco	
Ashley, J. F.	RejM	Rusk	
Ashley, T. G.	RejM	Hill	
Ashmore, A. C.	RejM	Navarro	
Ashworth, Cevena	RejM	Trinity	
Atwood, William M.	08356M	Hood	
Bancone, Michael Mrs.	RejM	Caldwell	Bancone, Michael
Barbee, Sallie	26472M	Hays	
Barnes, A. M.	05509M	Hopkins	
Baron, Thomas	08455M	Robertson	
Bauer, H.	08508M	Victoria	
Beackham, L. L.	RejM	Coryell	
Beasley, E. S.	RejM	San Jacinto	
Beaty, Henry M.	19465M	Collin	
Beau, Robert	RejM	Dallas	
Beau, W. H.	RejM	Denton	
Bedell, H. Mrs.	RejM	Galveston	
Bell, C. C.	08421M	Navarro	
Bell, Hezekiah	RejM	Freestone	
Benson, Sarah J.	08486M	Titus	
Bentoro, H. D.	RejM	Johnson	
Berry, Lou	RejM	Bastrop	
Biggs, C. B. Mrs.	RejM	Llano	
Bigham, W. E.	RejM	Henderson	
Blackburn, E. J. Mrs.	RejM	Bowie	
Blaunt, Thomas W.	RejM	San Augustine	
Blewett, Theresa	RejM	Harris	
Blocker, W. R.	RejM	Collin	
Blount, J. M.	RejM	Hill	
Blue, R. W.	RejM	Van Zandt	
Bogg, J. V.	RejM	Wise	
Bonds, Mittie	RejM	Bexar	
Boroughs, Tom	RejM	Shelby	
Boughman, F. M.	RejM	Archer	
Bounds, Easter	RejM	Madison	
Bra, C. P.	RejM	Leon	
Brachear, W. C.	RejM	Harris	
Brack, H. F.	08432M	Newton	
Braddock, A. M. Mrs.	RejM	Travis	
Bralley, Catherine B.	RejM	Fannin	
Brannon, M. A. Mrs.	RejM	Hill	
Brashear, B. A.	RejM	Lever	
Brewer, S.	08354M	Hood	
Bridges, Eliza	08471M	Smith	
Brooks, W. W.	08518M	Williamson	
Brown, Mary	RejM	Travis	

Missing Confederate Pension Applications

Name	App #	County
Bryant, J. M.	08422M	Navarro
Buchanan, G. W.	08443M	Parker
Bullard, M.	RejM	Smith
Burge, K. F.	08451M	Red River
Burger, Mary R.	RejM	Cherokee
Burke, David	RejM	Harris
Burke, G. F.	RejM	Polk
Burnett, N. P. Mrs.	08360M	Hopkins
Burns, B. F.	RejM	Bexar
Burns, D. S.	RejM	Grayson
Burns, Louisa	RejM	Collin
Burt, R. E.	18884M	Collin
Bynum, Daniel B. A.	08461M	Scurry
Byrun, T. C.	RejM	Titus
Cabitt, John W.	RejM	Upshur
Cain, A. P.	08427M	Newton
Campbell, F. J. Mrs.	08577AM	Wise
Canble, Nannie Mae	RejM	Hill
Caraway, C. M.	RejM	Comanche
Carlton, Margaret	08495M	Trinity
Carothers, Robert Simian	02926M	
Carroll, E. M.	RejM	Jackson
Caruthers, Permelia	RejM	Kaufman
Casber, Millie E.	RejM	Shelby
Casey, James Wilkins	08529M	Caldwell
Catvery, W. J.	RejM	Hill
Caudle, J. H.	08358M	Hopkins
Clarie, E. F. Mrs.	RejM	Harris
Clark, J. K.	RejM	Williamson
Clark, William Wallace	08425M	Navarro
Clary, E. J. Mrs.	08548M	Erath
Clausel, T. N.	08361M	Hopkins
Cloud, Mary	RejM	Van Zandt
Cobb, Calvin L.	RejM	Fannin
Cochran, M. A.	08137M	Newton
Collier, John J.	RejM	Cherokee
Commander, E. L. Mrs.	08497M	Tyler
Conklin, T. B.	08479M	Tarrant
Connon, James William	RejM	Hunt
Corner, James A.	RejM	Dimmit
Cowan, Mary	RejM	Collin
Cox, L. H. Mrs.	RejM	Hunt
Crager, Martin	00059M	Angelina
Cranford, Thomas	08369M	Hunt
Crawson, Jennie	RejM	Fannin
Crews, James	08528M	Brazos
Curry, Amy	08453M	Robertson
Curry, William	RejM	Unknown
Dallar, J. W.	RejM	Collingsworth
Daniel, E.	RejM	Liberty
Darracott, John F.	07464M	Concho
Daugherty, R. F.	08478M	Tarrant
Davis, J. C.	RejM	Freestone
Davis, J. P.	RejM	Robertson
Davis, J. S.	RejM	Leon
Davis, J. W.	RejM	Navarro
Davlin, A. J.	08377M	Kaufman
Dawson, David Duncan	01880M	Brazos
Dean, Mary J.	08535M	Ellis

Missing Confederate Pension Applications

Name	App #	County	Related	Ref #
Dean, N.	RejM	Limestone	—	—
Dean, T. Z.	RejM	Grimes	—	—
Dearcy, L. A. Mrs.	RejM	Brazoria	—	—
Deaver, T. M. Mrs.	RejM	Houston	—	—
Delgao, Servera	08533M	Victoria	—	—
Delhis, M. Z. Mrs.	RejM	Kaufman	—	—
Dennis, Mary A.	08433M	Nolan	—	—
Denton, J. W.	RejM	Newton	—	—
Dick, C. H.	RejM	Austin	—	—
Dickey, W. H.	08537M	Houston	—	—
Dickinson, F. N.	08530M	Callahan	—	—
Dillann, E. Mrs.	RejM	Bowie	—	—
Dillard, R. R.	08392M	Lee	—	—
Dillman, F.	RejM	Marion	—	—
Dillman, John	RejM	Calhoun	—	—
Docus, Maud	RejM	Montgomery	—	—
Donald, R. Q.	RejM	Wise	—	—
Donelson, Charles	RejM	Galveston	—	—
Dooley, George Travis	08509M	Victoria	—	—
Doyle, A. E. Mrs.	RejM	Lee	—	—
Dunn, G. W. Mrs.	RejM	Unknown	—	—
Dupree, J. E.	RejM	Fannin	—	—
Eaves, Dovie	52036M	Robertson	Eaves, James Wade	16322
Edmond, John T.	RejM	Hunt	—	—
Elliott, L. Mrs.	RejM	Cass	—	—
Ellis, John	08411M	Menard	—	—
Ellison, Emily	08437M	Palo Pinto	—	—
Essary, Ceborn Howell	08410M	Medina	—	—
Estoll, Hardie Perry	08380M	Kaufman	—	—
Evans, Elvira C.	08476M	Stephens	—	—
Evans, Lorena	RejM	Brazos	—	—
Fincher, M. C. Mrs.	08415M	Montague	—	—
Finley, Harriett R.	RejM	Dallas	—	—
Fleming, E. B.	08357M	Hopkins	—	—
Florence, E.	RejM	Upshur	—	—
Fowler, George T.	06783M	Van Zandt	—	—
Franklin, Daniel E.	08460M	San Saba	—	—
Franklin, N. H. Mrs.	08547M	Erath	—	—
Fraweek, D. B.	RejM	Goliad	—	—
Fulton, John	08347M	Henderson	—	—
Gage, James M.	11178M	Young	—	—
Gallagher, Peter	00681M	Bexar	—	—
Gann, William	01870M	Angelina	—	—
George, E. B. Mrs.	RejM	Erath	—	—
Gibson, H. A.	RejM	Parker	—	—
Gibson, Thomas J.	08342M	Henderson	—	—
Gilbert, L. A. Mrs.	08473M	Smith	—	—
Gillespie, William Steel	08423M	Navarro	—	—
Glass, M. A. Mrs.	RejM	Cass	—	—
Gleaser, E.	RejM	Bexar	—	—
Goodwin, J. G.	RejM	Rusk	—	—
Gordan, Isaac G.	08893AM	Cooke	—	—
Gorden, W. J., Sr.	08419M	Navarro	—	—
Green, John A.	08400M	Madison	—	—
Grounds, George	08538M	Houston	—	—
Hale, L. T.	11973M	Hunt	—	—
Hall, Charles	RejM	Grayson	—	—
Hall, Dameson E.	43806M	Tarrant	—	—
Hambrick, Thomas J.	08384M	Lampasas	—	—

Missing Confederate Pension Applications

Hammers, S. M.	RejM	Travis	—
Hammers, S. N.	RejM	Travis	—
Hanns, J. W.	RejM	Shackelford	—
Hargrove, J. M.	RejM	Shelby	—
Harrell, E. H. Mrs.	08545M	Erath	—
Harrington, John A.	RejM	Cass	—
Harris, Samuel Washington	13227M	Bexar	—
Hays, George Madison	02924M	—	—
Heathcock, Asa	07388M	Wilson	—
Hewitt, William M.	08348M	Hill	—
Hickman, R. D.	RejM	Rains	—
Hicks, James	08543M	Angelina	—
Hightower, S. A. Mrs.	08424M	Navarro	—
Hill, Elijah J.	04591M	Hays	—
Hobbs, Jobe	08522M	Wilson	—
Holbert, Phebe	RejM	Sabine	—
Holcount, J. H.	RejM	Houston	—
Holcount, W. T.	RejM	Hill	—
Holder, Rachel	RejM	Orange	—
Hollaway, Sarah E.	RejM	Navarro	—
Holly, Polk	RejM	Van Zandt	—
Hookett	RejM	Parker	—
Hopper, E. M.	RejM	Lee	—
Horton, Samuel Houston	01883M	Dallas	—
House, Jane	RejM	Taylor	—
Howell, A. C.	RejM	Tarrant	—
Howell, Sarah	RejM	Upshur	—
Hulzler, Martin	RejM	Medina	—
Hunt, A. D.	05596M	Hunt	—
Hunter, Eveline	08402M	Montague	—
Hunter, Mary L.	RejM	Dallas	—
Hutchings, Stockely	RejM	Unknown	—
Jackson, W. M.	08430M	Newton	—
Jasper, William	RejM	Wilbarger	—
Jernigan, Francis Marion	08500M	Tyler	—
Johnson, E. C. Mrs.	08428M	Newton	—
Johnson, J. F.	RejM	Eastland	—
Johnson, Mary M.	RejM	Johnson	—
Johnson, Thomas	08527M	Brazos	—
Johnston, John Monroe	02090M	Houston	—
Jones, A. L.	08496M	Tyler	—
Jones, Silas	08492M	Travis	—
Keating, Mary	07066M	Galveston	—
Kelley, E. J. Mrs.	08449M	Red River	—
Kerr, Julia Isabella	03760M	Panola	—
Keuhn, J. W.	RejM	Travis	—
Kidd, William	08397M	Leon	—
Kilpatrick, W. T.	08418M	Navarro	—
Kim, Michael	08444M	Parker	—
Kinard, M. N.	01877M	Polk	—
King, A. D. Mrs.	RejM	Nacogdoches	—
King, Peter Beckwith	08487M	Titus	—
King, Selma E.	RejM	Nacogdoches	—
Kireshing, Karoline	RejM	Harris	—
Knuple, Sam	RejM	Gray	—
Koonce, Elizabeth A.	08417M	Nacogdoches	—
Krider, Lucretia	08457M	Rockwall	—
Lamance	RejM	Henderson	—
Langhlin, J. M.	RejM	Dallas	—

Missing Confederate Pension Applications

Name	App No.	County	Veteran
Metts, James Riley	08403M	Marion	
Meyers, Anna Maria	08513M	Webb	
Meyers, F. C.	RejM	Orange	
Miller, Auguste Mrs.	RejM	Washington	
Miller, Hannah	RejM	Williamson	
Miller, Wilburn	RejM	Henderson	
Millhollen, Sarah J.	RejM	Brown	
Mills, T. J.	RejM	Henderson	
Mitchell, Margaret	08394M	Limestone	
Mongham, S. P.	RejM	Upshur	
Moore, A. A. Mrs.	08343M	Henderson	
Moore, H. C.	RejM	Dallas	
Moore, James	08493M	Travis	
Moore, P. C. Mrs.	08385M	Lamar	
Moore, S. A. Mrs.	09548M	Houston	Moore, William H.
Moore, S. T. Mrs.	RejM	Johnson	
Moore, Susan A.	RejM	Bowie	
Moorman, William Henry	01015M		
Moresnau, C. R.	RejM	Deaf Smith	
Morgan, Permelia	RejM	Fannin	
Mulhousen, Frank	RejM	Harrison	
Mullins, Frank M.	RejM	Medina	
Murphy, G. W.	RejM	Hunt	
Murtschin, Auges	RejM	Lee	
Myers, George	RejM	Coryell	
Myers, T. C.	RejM	Orange	
Nance, T. A.	RejM	Tarrant	
Neil, Margaret	RejM	Tarrant	
Neily, M. E. Mrs.	RejM	Rockwall	
Nelson, A. J.	08395M	Limestone	
Nicholson, Jane C.	13271M	Coleman	
Nihols, James C. (Nichols)	08544M	Erath	
Noble, J. R.	RejM	Henderson	
Norris, Matilda	02655M	Knox	
Norton, George Allen	08539M	Houston	
Osburn, M. J. Mrs.	08532M	Milam	
Oteman, John	RejM	Harris	
Owens, Nelson	08466M	Smith	
Palmer, Francis E.	37961M	Walker	
Pangle, J. F.	04658M	Burnet	
Parker, Lucy B.	00250M	Bell	Parker, Needham
Parker, R. B.	08160M	Williamson	
Payne, Annie	08439M	Panola	
Pearce, L. J.	RejM	Coryell	
Pearson, L. J.	RejM	Coryell	
Peck, Joseph	RejM	Red River	
Pfeiffer, John	00905M	Comal	
Pierce, D. V. Mrs.	08541M	Travis	
Pipes, G. W.	27544M	Van Zandt	
Prewitt, Dudley M.	08484M	Tarrant	
Price, G. W.	08374M	Johnson	
Price, Isaac	08462M	Scurry	
Price, Margaret	RejM	Burnet	
Ragan, R. A. Mrs.	RejM	Houston	
Redus, M. S.	RejM	San Patricio	
Reed, Emma	RejM	Houston	
Reeve, Richard	07644M	Navarro	
Renau, James Thomas	08524M	Wood	
Reynolds, J. L. B.	08391M	Lee	

Missing Confederate Pension Applications

Name	Number	County	Alt Name
Rice, A. W.	08467M	Smith	
Richards, E. E. Mrs.	RejM	Dallas	
Richardson, John	RejM	Hall	
Richardson, S. T.	08359M	Hopkins	
Robbs, Barbara	08514M	Webb	
Robinett, W. H.	08420M	Navarro	
Roe, Frances	08445M	Polk	
Rogers, John N.	RejM	Gonzales	
Roscoe, A. L.	RejM	Panola	
Roscoe, Solom	RejM	Limestone	
Russell, Jesse D.	08505M	Van Zandt	
Rutcliff, J. H.	RejM	Houston	
Salmon, E. I. Mrs.	08536M	Harrison	
Sanford, M. J. Mrs.	RejM	Bell	
Schleicher, Franz	09871M	Comal	
Schmidt, Conrad	08481M	Tarrant	
Schulwick, John	RejM	Leon	
Scott, Alexander E.	08351M	Hill	
Scott, J. E. Mrs.	RejM	Bexar	
Scovey, Burchett D.	08549M	Grayson	
Seaman, Patience	08375M	Johnson	
Seay, M. Mrs.	08531M	Llano	
Shadle, M. J.	RejM	Parker	
Shipman, John Landers	08353M	Hood	
Shirey, S. H.	RejM	Unknown	
Sims, A. A.	28837M	Houston	
Sims, Eliza Kirkland	08355M	Hood	
Sims, John L.	RejM	Grayson	
Sinclair, J. S.	37393M	Erath	
Sinclair, R. J. Mrs.	08393M	Leon	
Sisson, E. J.	RejM	Van Zandt	
Smead, S. E. Mrs.	08504M	Van Zandt	
Smith, C. W.	08506M	Van Zandt	
Smith, Henry L. Mrs.	RejM	Runnels	Smith, Henry L.
Smith, John	00095M	Aransas	
Smith, M. A.	RejM	Wise	
Smith, Miles Henry	08371M	Jasper	
Smith, Nathanial	RejM	Upshur	
Smith, R. E. J.	RejM	Karnes	
Smith, Sarah	RejM	Houston	
Smith, W. A. Mrs.	RejM	Henderson	
Smith, W. M.	RejM	Robertson	
Snigleton, J. C.	RejM	Travis	
Sparks, J. J.	08416M	Montague	
Spears, David J.	08440M	Panola	
Spence, L. C. Mrs.	08367M	Hunt	
Stapp, D. A. Mrs.	30605M	Dallas	Stapp, D. A.
Starling, W. T.	08468M	Smith	
Statcup, Margaret	RejM	Collin	
Stembridge, James	08474M	Smith	
Stephens, Alexander B.	08502M	Upshur	
Stevens, M. E. Mrs.	RejM	Eastland	
Stewart, Eliza A.	08498M	Tyler	
Stewart, Jemima	RejM	Cass	
Strong, T.	08450M	Red River	
Suiden, W. H.	08120M	Johnson	
Swan, W. M.	RejM	Rusk	
Tatum, H. S.	RejM	Parmer	
Teal, T. A.	RejM	Brown	

Missing Confederate Pension Applications

Name	Application	County	Veteran
Tharp, J. A.	RejM	Marion	—
Thomahley, S. L. Mrs.	RejM	Van Zandt	—
Thomas, Samuel M.	40019M	—	—
Thomas, Sarah Ann Appling	RejM	San Saba	Appling, John Loyal
Thomas, W. A.	08387M	La Salle	—
Thompson, Ellen C.	RejM	Bell	—
Thompson, Mary J.	08470M	Smith	—
Tindall, Thomas R.	22733M	Erath	—
Tiner, J. M.	RejM	Brazoria	—
Tolson, Julia A.	RejM	Madison	—
Trimble, L. W.	RejM	Travis	—
Trimble, Sarah E.	08448M	Rains	—
Tucker, Amos	09409M	Travis	—
Tucker, Hillarion	08389M	Lavaca	—
Tucker, James Milton	RejM	Gonzales	—
Turlington, Harriet N.	08523M	Wood	—
Turner, James M.	08540M	Montague	—
Underwood, Andrew Jackson	08503M	Upshur	—
Vaden, L.	RejM	Trinity	—
Walker, Jane C.	08454M	Robertson	—
Walters, M.	RejM	Nacogdoches	—
Warner, S. A. Mrs.	08414M	Mills	—
Warren, Jacob R.	RejM	Grayson	—
Warsham, S. A. Mrs.	08346M	Henderson	—
Wasburn, J. A.	RejM	Coryell	—
Watson, Tom	03148AM	Galveston	—
Watson, W. P. Mrs.	RejM	Van Zandt	—
Weaver, John	RejM	Kendall	—
Webb, W. A.	RejM	Bastrop	—
Wells, Richard	07938M	Parker	—
Wheat, Lucius Quntus Cincuna	08365M	Hunt	—
Whillock, J. H.	RejM	Robertson	—
White, J. N.	01612M	Grayson	—
White, W. L.	RejM	Tarrant	—
Wilburn, Amanda	08464M	Shelby	—
Wilkening, Henry L.	RejM	Lampasas	—
Williams, C. J. Mrs.	RejM	Ellis	Williams, John B.
Williams, H. W.	RejM	Harrison	—
Williams, J. E. Mrs.	RejM	Franklin	—
Williams, J. H.	08521M	Wilson	—
Willis, G. W.	RejM	Wise	—
Wilson, Edward Henderson Mrs.	RejM	Chambers	Wilson, Edward Henderson
Wilson, Henry Pendleton Taylor	08515M	Wharton	—
Wilson, Sarah Ann	08501M	Tyler	—
Wilson, William	RejM	Milam	—
Windett, T. J.	RejM	Bell	—
Winfield, Mary	08390M	Lavaca	—
Witt, Eli	RejM	Collingsworth	—
Wolfenberger, H. M.	RejM	Parker	—
Wolston, J. H. A.	RejM	Milam	—
Womack, Nannie	RejM	Unknown	—
Womack, William David	08408M	McLennan	—
Wook, I. T.	RejM	Coleman	—
Wren, Parthenia	08378M	Kaufman	—
Wyatt, J. J.	RejM	Eastland	—
Wyatt, J. T.	RejM	Bowie	—
York, Robert J.	RejM	Comanche	—
Young, E. A. Mrs.	08350M	Hill	—
Zivley, J. H.	08364M	Howard	—

Index to Rejected Pension Applications

Name	Status	County	Veteran	No.
Abernathy, T. C.	Rej	Harris		
Acosta, Bill	Rej	Bexar		
Acree, Alfred W.	Rej	Waller		
Acuff, J. M. W.	Rej	Gregg		
Adams, Collin	Rej	Tarrant		
Adams, Elizabeth	Rej	Red River	Adams, William	
Adams, F. F. Mrs.	Rej	Rusk	Adams, Samuel	
Adams, Fannie Tiberius	RejM	Brown	Adams, Zachariah Burges	
Adams, G. W.	Rej	Nolan		
Adams, J. R.	Rej	Montague		
Adams, James Allen	Rej	Kaufman		
Adams, John Daniel	Rej	Edwards		
Adams, M. E. Mrs.	Rej	Freestone	Adams, John Lumpkin Lamberth	
Adams, M. V. Mrs.	Rej	Hopkins	Adams, J. M. D.	
Adams, N. R. Mrs.	Rej	Llano	Adams, Alexander	34478
Adams, Naoma V.	Rej	Panola	Adams, Lorenzo Harris	
Adams, Renie	Rej	Leon	Adams, Joe	
Adams, S. A. Mrs.	Rej	Robertson	Adams, Robert Hamlin	
Adams, S. H.	Rej	Lubbock		
Adams, W. F.	Rej	San Augustine		
Adams, William M.	Rej	Brazoria		
Adcock, Samuel	Rej	Cherokee		
Addison, A. J.	Rej	Milam		
Aikin, J. F.	Rej	Marion		
Aikin, M. E. Mrs.	Rej	Red River	Aikin, Jacob Willis	
Ainsworth, J. G.	Rej	Limestone		
Ainsworth, Leo	RejM	Callahan		
Aker, J. M.	Rej	Johnson		
Akers, J. H.	Rej	Parker		
Akins, Ophelia E.	Rej	Dallas	Akins, John J.	
Albert, Laura A.	Rej	Harris	Albert, Jules	
Albritton, Asa T.	Rej	Wise		
Aldredge, D. F.	Rej	Camp		
Alexander, Aurelia Alpha	Rej	Taylor	Alexander, Henry Bennett	
Alexander, Carolota D. De	Rej	Webb	Alexander, William J.	
Alexander, Elizabeth J.	Rej	Van Zandt	Alexander, John Marion	
Alexander, G. M.	Rej	Dewitt		
Alexander, Jake	Rej	Webb		
Alexander, R. M.	Rej	Dallas		
Alexander, Rena Cimeon	Rej	Kerr		
Alexander, Sophie	Rej	Potter	Alexander, James E.	
Alexander, W. W.	Rej	Leon		
Alexander, W. W.	Rej	Freestone		
Alford, E. L.	Rej	Harrison		
Alford, J. P.	Rej	Harris		
Alford, James F.	Rej	Fisher		
Alford, Julius Caeser	Rej	Liberty		
Alison, Robert D.	Rej	Collin		
Allard, Sallie	Rej	Clay	Allard, George Washington	47915
Allcorn, Sallie H.	Rej	Washington	Allcorn, John H.	
Allee, M. J. Mrs.	Rej	Houston	Allee, William Mylus	05196
Allen, A. A.	Rej	Collin		
Allen, Fannie Thomason	Rej	McLennan	Thomason, Robert Henry	
Allen, G. H.	Rej	Hopkins		
Allen, H.	Rej	Bosque		

Index to Rejected Confederate Pension Applications

Name	Status	County	Veteran	Number
Allen, H. H.	Rej	Van Zandt	—	
Allen, J. L.	Rej	Mason	—	
Allen, J. R.	Rej	Fayette	—	
Allen, John R.	Rej	Lampasas	—	
Allen, John T.	Rej	Cherokee	—	
Allen, John W. Mrs.	Rej	Falls	Allen, John W.	
Allen, M. J. Mrs.	RejM	Houston	—	
Allen, M. M.	RejM	Williamson	—	
Allen, Mary E.	Rej	Tarrant	Allen, Joseph B.	
Allen, Mat.	Rej	Burnet	—	
Allen, Moses M.	Rej	Sterling	—	
Allen, Nellie	Rej	Wichita	Allen, Virgil Stanley	
Allen, Phillip Tropwell Mrs.	Rej	Johnson	Allen, Phillip Tropwell	
Allen, Rosa	Rej	Tarrant	Allen, Moses A.	
Allen, Sallie C.	Rej	Wise	Allen, J. T.	
Allen, Sarah E.	Rej	Donley	Allen, Abraham B.	
Allen, Sarah Jane	Rej	McLennan	Allen, John Woodson	
Allen, T. J.	Rej	Bell	—	
Allen, T. S.	Rej	Cass	—	
Allen, W. J.	Rej	Hill	—	
Allen, W. W.	Rej	Williamson	—	
Allen, William J.	Rej	Tarrant	—	
Allison, Elizabeth	Rej	Wise	Allison, James William	
Allison, G. A.	Rej	Bowie	—	
Alonzo, Peter	Rej	Milam	—	
Alsabrooks, G. M.	Rej	Cass	—	
Alsobrooks, Mary A.	Rej	Cass	Alsobrooks, George	
Alston, Thomas J.	Rej	Smith	—	
Alston, W. P.	Rej	Bandera	—	
Alsup, Sarah E.	Rej	Milam	Alsup, William E.	
Altwein, Gustave	Rej	Guadalupe	—	
Alwood, Richard Henry	Rej	Cooke	—	
Alwood, Richard Henry Mrs.	Rej	Cooke	Alwood, Richard Henry	
Amidon, Almedia	Rej	Williamson	Amidon, Dwight Calvert	38436
Anders, Henry L.	Rej	Delta	—	
Anders, L. J. Mrs.	Rej	Van Zandt	Anders, L. J.	45127
Anderson, A. J.	Rej	Montgomery	—	
Anderson, B. M.	Rej	Lavaca	—	
Anderson, Ben	Rej	San Augustine	—	
Anderson, Eliza	Rej	Harris	Anderson, Matterson	
Anderson, Frank M.	Rej	Limestone	—	
Anderson, Hugh Stewart Mrs.	Rej	Motley	Anderson, Hugh Stewart	03093
Anderson, I. B.	Rej	Throckmorton	—	
Anderson, I. E.	Rej	Harrison	—	
Anderson, J. I.	Rej	Leon	—	
Anderson, John E.	Rej	Falls	—	
Anderson, John L.	Rej	Harris	—	
Anderson, L. A. Mrs.	Rej	Van Zandt	Anderson, Elijah B.	
Anderson, Lee	Rej	Motley	—	
Anderson, M. C. Mrs.	Rej	Montague	Anderson, Isaac Franklin	
Anderson, Mollie	Rej	Martin	Anderson, Bailey J.	19966
Anderson, Nathan	Rej	Grayson	—	
Anderson, S. J.	Rej	Hunt	—	
Anderson, Susan J. Windham	Rej	Kaufman	Windham, Benjamin B.	
Anderson, Thomas Jefferson	Rej	Taylor	—	
Anderson, W. J.	Rej	Hunt	—	
Anderson, W. P.	Rej	Shelby	—	
Anderson, William Wallace	Rej	Randall	—	
Andrew, Sarah Jane	Rej	Palo Pinto	Andrew, William	

Index to Rejected Confederate Pension Applications

Andrews, Della	Rej	Johnson	Andrews, John Calvin	
Andrews, W. W.	Rej	Hill		
Andrews, William	Rej	Kaufman		
Annan, William R.	Rej	Wilson		
Anthony, Annie E.	Rej	Moore	Anthony, Samuel Wesley	
Anthony, Stephen	Rej	Atascosa		
Anthony, William E. R.	Rej	Hall		
Appel, August Mrs.	Rej	Bexar	Appel, August	
Apperson, Joseph	Rej	Cherokee		
Appleton, Samansie C.	Rej	Tarrant	Appleton, James	09104
Archer, John M.	Rej	Hutchinson		
Archer, Nancy J.	Rej	Limestone	Archer, William J.	32997
Archinard, Samuel	Rej	Harris		
Ard, John	Rej	Hopkins		
Armes, F. H.	Rej	Van Zandt		
Armitage, S. B. Mrs.	Rej	Trinity	Armitage, Wilbur Fisk	
Armitage, Wilber Fisk	Rej	Madison		
Armstrong, Leonora	Rej	Tarrant	Armstrong, Ramsey Clarke	50711
Armstrong, William J.	Rej	Live Oak		
Arnold, Hattie	Rej	Tarrant	Arnold, John Wesley	41417
Arnold, James Mitchum	Rej	Briscoe		
Arnold, Sallie Ann	Rej	Lynn	Arnold, Edward Dorell	
Arnold, William Butler	Rej	Harris		
Arnold, William Thomas Mrs.	Rej	Harrison	Arnold, William Thomas	
Arons, Henry Clay Mrs.	Rej	Limestone	Arons, Henry Clay	
Arrington, Sallie A.	Rej	Brazos	Arrington, Pinkney Henderson	
Arrington, T. W.	Rej	Denton		
Arthur, James	Rej	Anderson		
Ascue, R. B.	Rej	Brown		
Ash, J. F.	Rej	Rusk		
Ashford, Eva	Rej	Foard	Ashford, James	20678
Ashford, Montgomery Paton	Rej	Tarrant		
Ashford, Montgomery Paton Mrs.	Rej	Motley	Ashford, Montgomery Paton	Rej
Ashley, J. F.	RejM	Rusk		
Ashley, Jessie Garrett	Rej	Hill		
Ashley, M. E. Mrs.	Rej	Hunt	Ashley, Moses Samuel McDuffey	
Ashley, Malinda	Rej	Cooke	Ashley, Thomas S.	
Ashley, Robert	Rej	Denton		
Ashley, T. G.	RejM	Hill		
Ashmore, A. C.	RejM	Navarro		
Ashmore, Nancy B.	Rej	Travis	Ashmore, John Bloomer	
Ashworth, Cevena	RejM	Trinity		
Askew, Sarah H.	Rej	Llano	Askew, George Christian	
Aston, W. E. Mrs.	Rej	Scurry	Aston, John Monroe	
Ater, Frances Isabel	Rej	Burnet	Ater, Albert Melvin	
Athey, W. W.	Rej	Van Zandt		
Atkins, G. H. McMillan Mrs.	Rej	Dallas	McMillan, John Thomas	
Atkins, Tom M.	Rej	Hood		
Atkinson, Carrie L.	Rej	Nueces	Atkinson, Edward	33339
Autrey, James	Rej	Tarrant		
Autrey, James L.	Rej	Bexar		
Autry, G. M.	Rej	Karnes		
Autry, Winnie M.	Rej	Jack	Autry, J. A.	
Avance, Sam M.	Rej	Delta		
Aven, A. J.	Rej	Hale		
Aynew, Jane P.	Rej	Eastland	Aynew, A. J.	
Babb, Buna	Rej	Bowie	Babb, Daniel Harrison	
Babb, D. H.	Rej	Bowie		
Bacon, John	Rej	Denton		

Index to Rejected Confederate Pension Applications

Badgett, R. S.	Rej	Wharton	—	—
Baggett, W. J.	Rej	Runnels	—	—
Baggett, W. J.	Rej	Milam	—	—
Bailey, A. L.	Rej	Harris	—	—
Bailey, Ada	Rej	Nacogdoches	Bailey, John	—
Bailey, John G.	Rej	Van Zandt	—	—
Bailey, John T.	Rej	Bexar	—	—
Bailey, Josephus	Rej	Wise	—	—
Bailey, L. C. Mrs.	Rej	Denton	Bailey, James Marshall	—
Bailey, Peter James Mrs.	Rej	Freestone	Bailey, Peter James	17483
Bailey, Sarah M.	Rej	McLennan	Bailey, William Bennett	—
Bailey, Tabitha	Rej	Stephens	—	—
Bailiff, A. J.	Rej	Van Zandt	—	—
Baits, Martha Jane	Rej	Wise	Baits, George Edward	—
Baker, Amanda	Rej	Caldwell	Baker, John White	18859
Baker, Catherine (Katie)	Rej	Liberty	Baker, John	—
Baker, J. A.	Rej	Lamar	—	—
Baker, John F.	Rej	Bexar	—	—
Baker, John W.	Rej	Delta	—	—
Baker, Lizzie	Rej	Cooke	Baker, George W.	—
Baker, Louisa Phenolia	Rej	Brown	Baker, Henry	—
Baker, Martha Ann Johnson	Rej	Cherokee	Johnson, J. N., Sr.	23680
Baker, Mary	Rej	Caldwell	Baker, Green	—
Baker, Mary J.	Rej	Bowie	Baker, A. J.	—
Baker, William	Rej	Houston	—	—
Baldwin, A. M. Mrs.	Rej	Harrison	Baldwin, Benjamin Harris	42429
Baldwin, Fannie C.	Rej	Red River	Baldwin, George Scott	—
Ball, Henderson A.	Rej	Tarrant	—	—
Ball, William Lee	Rej	Bowie	—	—
Ballard, A. E. Mrs.	Rej	Kaufman	Ballard, John Wesley	—
Ballard, James M.	Rej	Red River	—	—
Ballard, Martha A.	Rej	Bexar	Ballard, Christopher A.	—
Ballard, Nannie Carolina	Rej	Bell	Ballard, Leonard	—
Ballou, William Harry Mrs.	Rej	Taylor	Ballou, William Harry	—
Balthrop, Wilie R.	Rej	Hunt	—	—
Bancone, Michael Mrs.	RejM	Caldwell	Bancone, Michael	—
Bandy, John Jefferson	Rej	Bandera	—	—
Bandy, Sarah E. Jones	Rej	Brewster	Jones, Bewford Whittington	—
Banks, Josiphine	Rej	Titus	Banks, John	—
Banks, R. P.	Rej	Titus	—	—
Banks, W. W.	Rej	Cherokee	—	—
Banner, Thomas Jefferson	Rej	Terrell	—	—
Banta, D. B.	Rej	Kerr	—	—
Barclay, J. H.	Rej	Hopkins	—	—
Barclay, J. K. P.	Rej	Milam	—	—
Barefield, John C.	Rej	McLennan	—	—
Barfield, B. T.	Rej	Dallas	—	—
Barker, Ann	Rej	Parker	Barker, J. J.	—
Barker, I. M.	Rej	Llano	—	—
Barker, Joseph G.	Rej	Hill	—	—
Barker, Lou E.	Rej	Eastland	Barker, Thomas Hensie	—
Barker, R. B.	Rej	Williamson	—	—
Barker, Thomas	Rej	Limestone	—	—
Barkwell, Marcellus E.	Rej	Limestone	—	—
Barlow, Alice Ray	Rej	El Paso	Barlow, John E.	—
Barnes, Albert L.	Rej	San Augustine	—	—
Barnes, F. F. Mrs.	Rej	Erath	Barnes, John Burgess	—
Barnes, J. E.	Rej	Fannin	—	—
Barnes, Kathrine	Rej	Wharton	Barnes, Fredrick C.	—

Index to Rejected Confederate Pension Applications

Barnes, M. J.	Rej	Archer	—	
Barnes, Manerva	Rej	Montague	Barnes, J. G.	
Barnes, William A., Sr	Rej	Kaufman	—	
Barnett, A. E. Mrs.	Rej	Wharton	Barnett, Wood Fork	
Barnett, A. L. Mrs.	Rej	Wise	Barnett, John Abb	
Barnett, Lucy Ann	Rej	Williamson	Barnett, John Perry	
Barnett, M. D.	Rej	Kent	—	
Barnett, M. J. Mrs.	Rej	Coleman	Barnett, Rine	
Barnett, N. P.	Rej	Jasper	—	
Barnett, Pearl	Rej	Rusk	Barnett, (henry) Thomas	41004
Barnhill, F. F.	Rej	Montague	—	
Barrett, John	Rej	Hood	—	
Barrett, M. J. Mrs.	Rej	Franklin	Barrett, William Satterwhite	
Barrett, S. E.	Rej	Rains	—	
Barrier, Rebecca C.	Rej	Titus	Barrier, Mike T.	
Barron, Mary F.	Rej	Dallas	Barron, James Powell	
Barron, Robert	Rej	Rockwall	—	
Barrow, L. J.	Rej	Hardin	—	
Barrow, Richard Vincent	Rej	Galveston	—	
Barry, William T.	Rej	Williamson	—	
Bartee, F. E. Mrs.	Rej	San Jacinto	Bartee, John Overton	
Bartlett, Nancy Helen Cruce	Rej	Jones	Cruce, John William Richard	
Bartlett, S. A. Mrs.	Rej	Travis	Bartlett, Otho Francis	
Barton, Hiram	Rej	Upshur	—	
Barton, J. L.	Rej	Wood	—	
Barton, M. E. Mrs.	Rej	Lynn	Barton, Isic Murphy	
Barton, Oliver P.	Rej	Washington	—	
Barton, Thomas E.	Rej	Fannin	—	
Bass, James	Rej	Nacogdoches	—	
Bass, John Bedell	Rej	Tom Green	—	
Bass, Richard	Rej	Hamilton	—	
Bassham, T. F.	Rej	Terry	—	
Bassham, T. J.	Rej	Kaufman	—	
Bates, G. E. Mrs.	Rej	Wise	—	
Bates, J. Y.	Rej	Navarro	—	
Bates, S. J. Mrs.	Rej	Shelby	Bates, John Hardy	
Bates, Simpson Smith	Rej	Bee	—	
Battaile, Sarah	Rej	McLennan	Battaile, Charles Robinson	
Batte, R. G.	Rej	Titus	—	
Batten, J. C.	Rej	Cherokee	—	
Battle, Levi Franklin	Rej	Brazos	—	
Batto, Ben	Rej	Bandera	—	
Baucom, Michel	Rej	Caldwell	Baucom, Thomas Martin	
Bauer, August Mrs.	Rej	Guadalupe	Bauer, August	
Baugh, Daniel A.	Rej	Bowie	—	
Baugh, Samuel Newton	Rej	Lamar	—	
Baumbach, George	Rej	Fayette	—	
Bayer, Berno	Rej	Colorado	—	
Bayless, Bettie	Rej	Randall	Bayless, Milton	
Baylor, Emily J.	Rej	Bexar	Baylor, John Robert	
Baylor, Henry W.	Rej	Bexar	—	
Baylor, Mary J.	Rej	Bee	Baylor, William L.	
Beackham, L. L.	RejM	Coryell	—	
Beadle, Samuel M.	Rej	Jack	—	
Beadle, Samuel Madison	Rej	Archer	—	
Beaird, A. L.	Rej	Titus	—	
Beakley, J. H.	Rej	Titus	—	
Beal, J. T., Sr	Rej	Smith	—	
Beall, Hezekiah	Rej	Freestone	—	

Index to Rejected Confederate Pension Applications

Name	Status	County	Veteran	Number
Beall, Mary A.	Rej	Hill	Beall, W. M.	
Beaman, Harriet Abney Hester	Rej	Orange	Beaman, William Green	
Bean, Robert	Rej	Dallas		
Bean, Sam	Rej	Tyler		
Bean, W. H.	Rej	Denton		
Beard, A. E. Mrs.	Rej	San Augustine	Beard, Benjamin Alexander	
Beard, Caroline	Rej	Jefferson	Beard, Anthony W.	
Beard, James Lafayette Mrs.	Rej	Ellis	Beard, James Lafayette	
Beard, Sarah H.	Rej	Tarrant	Beard, Nathaniel Champion	
Beasley, E. S.	RejM	San Jacinto		
Beasley, Marion	Rej	Montague		
Beasley, S. T.	Rej	Houston		
Beatty, Willie Agnes	Rej	Lubbock	Beatty, George L.	49717
Beau, Robert	RejM	Dallas		
Beau, W. H.	RejM	Denton		
Beauchamp, J. C.	Rej	Bowie		
Beauchamp, Sarah J.	Rej	Blanco	Beauchamp, A. J.	
Beaver, William Goodwin	Rej	Unknown		
Beavers, Mollie J.	Rej	Randall	Beavers, William Easley	
Beazley, Ellen E.	Rej	Harris	Beazley, Herbert Washington	
Becher, Anna	Rej	Harris	Becher, John	
Beck, Mary Elizabeth	Rej	Wise	Beck, Benjamin Franklin	
Beckham, L. L.	Rej	Coryell		
Beckham, Nancy E.	Rej	Parker	Beckham, W. C.	
Beckmann, Herman	Rej	Gillespie		
Beckner, Charles B.	Rej	Hall		
Bedell, Abner Whitfield Mrs.	Rej	Coleman	Bedell, Abner Whitfield	
Bedell, H. Mrs.	RejM	Galveston		
Bedell, William Harry	Rej	Galveston		
Bedford, Archabald	Rej	Knox		
Beene, Lem S.	Rej	Leon		
Behrens, Julius	Rej	Galveston		
Beissner, Bertha	Rej	Bexar	Beissner, Frederick Louis	
Belcher, Ada	Rej	Hill	Belcher, George Washington	
Belcher, Julia A.	Rej	Palo Pinto	Belcher, J. J.	
Bell, E. F. Mrs.	Rej	Titus	Bell, Robert William	
Bell, Hezekiah	RejM	Freestone		
Bell, J. P.	Rej	Parker		
Bell, J. T.	Rej	Nacogdoches		
Bell, M. L. Mrs.	Rej	Titus	Bell, L. B.	
Bell, Sallie	Rej	Shelby	Bell, John Freeman	16505
Bell, Sarah Annie E.	Rej	Walker	Bell, James H.	
Bell, W. V. Mrs.	Rej	Tarrant	Bell, Henry Clay	
Bellamy, A. F.	Rej	Van Zandt		
Benfer, Phillip	Rej	Bexar		
Benge, G. C.	Rej	Cherokee		
Benge, O. M.	Rej	Cherokee		
Benner, George	Rej	Wharton		
Bennett, E. C. Mrs.	Rej	Foard	Bennett, Abner Hill	22143
Bennett, Harrett N.	Rej	Brown	Bennett, Richard Barton	
Bennett, J. E. Mrs.	Rej	Tarrant	Bennett, John B.	05790
Bennett, J. P.	Rej	Callahan		
Bennett, M. L. Mrs.	Rej	Falls	Bennett, William Isaac	23281
Bennett, S. F.	Rej	Hopkins		
Bennett, W. A.	Rej	Young		
Bennett, William George	Rej	Tarrant		
Bennett, Wincy	Rej	Upshur	Bennett, Leroy	
Benson, W. C.	Rej	Coke		
Bentley, Martha Sophronia	Rej	Lamar	Bentley, Thomas Baker	

Index to Rejected Confederate Pension Applications

Bentley, Thomas Baker	Rej	Lamar	—	—
Benton, A. D.	Rej	Lamar	—	—
Benton, F. Mrs.	Rej	Trinity	Benton, F.	—
Benton, J.	Rej	Kaufman	—	—
Benton, Mattie D.	Rej	Morris	Benton, Peter Goodman	—
Bentoro, H. D.	RejM	Johnson	—	—
Berkley, W. H.	Rej	Montgomery	—	—
Berry, Charlie	Rej	Caldwell	—	—
Berry, E. T.	Rej	Van Zandt	—	—
Berry, J. W.	Rej	Nacogdoches	—	—
Berry, Lizzie	Rej	Jasper	Berry, William Green	—
Berry, Lou	RejM	Bastrop	—	—
Berry, Nancy Jane	Rej	Fannin	Berry, Joseph Nelson	—
Berry, Pierce	Rej	Jackson	—	—
Berry, R. W.	Rej	Sabine	—	—
Berry, S. H.	Rej	Washington	—	—
Berryhill, Miles	Rej	Liberty	—	—
Berryman, A. B.	Rej	Freestone	—	—
Berryman, Martha	Rej	Limestone	Berryman, H. C.	—
Berryman, William Larkin	Rej	Llano	—	—
Bertrand, F. O.	Rej	Webb	—	—
Beryman, Arch B.	Rej	Howard	—	—
Best, G. J.	Rej	Jones	—	—
Best, James	Rej	Houston	—	—
Bethea, James C.	Rej	Milam	—	—
Beville, A. A.	Rej	McLennan	—	—
Beville, W. T.	Rej	Cherokee	—	—
Bibb, Eli	Rej	Rains	—	—
Bickley, M. H. Mrs.	Rej	Sabine	Bickley, William Washington	—
Bielefeld, Minna	Rej	Austin	Bielefeld, Christian	—
Biggs, C. B. Mrs.	Rej	Henderson	Biggs, James	—
Biggs, C. B. Mrs.	RejM	Llano	—	—
Bigham, W. E.	RejM	Henderson	—	—
Billingby, John H.	Rej	Llano	—	—
Billingsley, Stacy Watson	Rej	Atascosa	Billingsley, Thomas	11788
Billingsly, Sarah	Rej	Lamar	Billingsly, Francis Marion	—
Bills, James M.	Rej	Fannin	—	—
Bills, Mary	Rej	Coleman	Bills, I. W.	—
Bins, F. L.	Rej	Bowie	—	—
Birdwell, May	Rej	Cooke	Birdwell, Andrew Russell	—
Birket, Elizabeth Haggard	Rej	Collin	Birket, James Patrick	—
Bishop, Charles Levi Mrs.	Rej	Kaufman	Bishop, Charles Levi	—
Bishop, J. D.	Rej	Coryell	—	—
Bishop, Lucien J.	Rej	Haskell	—	—
Bishop, Stephen Mrs.	Rej	Potter	Bishop, Stephen	—
Bishop, T. W.	Rej	Coleman	—	—
Black, Amelia Hays	Rej	Wichita	Black, John Wesley	—
Black, C. C.	Rej	Ward	—	—
Black, George Bogart	Rej	Comanche	—	—
Black, Henry F.	Rej	Coryell	—	—
Black, Henry Y.	Rej	Camp	—	—
Black, M. A.	Rej	Hopkins	—	—
Black, M. E. Mrs.	Rej	Clay	Black, Isaac	15728
Black, M. J. Mrs.	Rej	Dallas	Black, Sidney A.	—
Blackburn, E. J. Mrs.	RejM	Bowie	—	—
Blackburn, H. C. Mrs.	Rej	Grayson	Blackburn, Richard Baxter	—
Blackburn, Ida	Rej	Milam	Blackburn, John Wesley	—
Blackburn, Martha E.	Rej	Denton	Blackburn, W. J.	—
Blackburn, W. P.	Rej	Harris	—	—

Index to Rejected Confederate Pension Applications

Blacklidge, A. C.	Rej	Leon		
Blackstock, Sarah Ann	Rej	Lavaca	Blackstock, Thomas Newton	06629
Blackwell, Mary	Rej	Rusk	Blackwell, Wiley	
Blackwell, Sarah P.	Rej	Van Zandt	Blackwell, H. F.	
Blair, Adella C.	Rej	Taylor	Blair, John Herald	
Blair, C. H.	Rej	Limestone		
Blair, Charles C.	Rej	Erath		
Blair, Ewing	Rej	Nueces		
Blair, J. J.	Rej	Bell		
Blair, M. A. Mrs.	Rej	Hamilton	Blair, William	
Blair, William Clary	Rej	Fannin		
Blake, John L.	Rej	Potter		
Blake, Nancy C.	Rej	Dallas	Blake, John Henry	01274
Blakeley, James McVey	Rej	Lubbock		
Blakeney, W. M.	Rej	Freestone		
Blalock, Annie	Rej	Polk	Blalock, J. K. P.	14644
Blalock, C. D.	Rej	Harrison		
Blalock, G. D.	Rej	Wheeler		
Bland, William C.	Rej	Freestone		
Blankenship, A. J.	Rej	Erath		
Blankenship, W. A.	Rej	Hunt		
Blasienz, C. A.	Rej	Milam		
Blasingame, John	Rej	Henderson		
Blaunt, Thomas W.	RejM	San Augustine		
Bledsoe, Benjamin Franklin Mrs.	Rej	Mills	Bledsoe, Benjamin Franklin	
Bledsoe, Bettie	Rej	Johnson	Bledsoe, James Slaughter	
Bleike, Theresa	Rej	Harris	Bleike, Frederick P.	
Blewett, Theresa	RejM	Harris		
Blewett, W. R.	Rej	Collin		
Block, Mary A.	Rej	Orange	Block, Frederick William	
Blocker, J. M.	Rej	Hill		
Blocker, Nelson	Rej	Robertson		
Blocker, W. R.	RejM	Collin		
Blount, J. M.	RejM	Hill		
Bludworth, Benjamin P. Mrs.	Rej	Fayette	Bludworth, Benjamin Portinent	
Blue, B. W.	Rej	Van Zandt		
Blue, Emanuel	Rej	Tarrant		
Blue, M. E. Mrs.	Rej	Smith	Blue, Washington Mueller	
Blue, Moses Henry	Rej	Palo Pinto		
Blue, R. W.	RejM	Van Zandt		
Boales, A. H.	Rej	Edwards		
Board, S. A. Mrs.	Rej	Van Zandt	Board, Phillip William	
Boatman, Elizabeth E.	Rej	Cooke	Boatman, Jesse J.	
Boatright, Nancy Ann	Rej	Llano	Boatright, Martin	02876
Bobbitt, A. T. L.	Rej	San Augustine		
Bobo, I. G. L.	Rej	Live Oak		
Bockman, J. G.	Rej	Tom Green		
Bodenhamer, S. L.	Rej	Burnet		
Bogan, Green	Rej	Morris		
Bogg, J. V.	RejM	Wise		
Boggs, James W.	Rej	Edwards		
Boggs, Nannie J.	Rej	Zavala	Boggs, James Willis	
Boisseau, J. R.	Rej	Harrison		
Boisseau, Josephine	Rej	Harrison	Boisseau, James Rivers	
Bolding, J. A.	Rej	Kaufman		
Bolding, N. C. Mrs.	Rej	Franklin	Bolding, James Harrison	
Boles, C. G.	Rej	Cherokee		
Bolin, M. J. Mrs.	Rej	Orange	Bolin, William R.	
Bolton, Arch	Rej	Harris		

Index to Rejected Confederate Pension Applications

Bolton, F. E. Mrs.	Rej	Nueces	Bolton, John Wesley	—
Bolton, M. E. Mrs.	Rej	Camp	Bolton, E. P.	—
Bomar, J. R.	Rej	San Saba	—	—
Bomar, Sarah Catherine	Rej	Harrison	Bomar, William James	—
Bonds, Mittie	RejM	Bexar	—	—
Bonneau, Ella	Rej	Sabine	Bonneau, Arnoldus	20092
Bonneau, J. B.	Rej	Parker	—	—
Bonner, Ellen	Rej	Falls	Bonner, Christopher Columbus	—
Bonner, Mary Elizabeth	Rej	Fisher	Bonner, Newsome Sallee	—
Bonner, Willis	Rej	Navarro	—	—
Booker, William W.	Rej	Upshur	—	—
Boon, W. W.	Rej	Comanche	—	—
Boone, Jonathan Bailey	Rej	Grayson	—	—
Boquet, J. V.	Rej	Calhoun	—	—
Boren, M. A. Mrs.	Rej	San Augustine	Boren, Will Moultrie	—
Boroughs, Tom	RejM	Shelby	—	—
Borrows, Tom	Rej	San Augustine	—	—
Boss, Marcus Lafayette	Rej	Collingsworth	—	—
Bostick, Sion R.	Rej	San Saba	—	—
Bostick, Susie Ann	Rej	Cherokee	Bostick, Charles Westley	—
Boswell, John Walker Mrs.	Rej	Wichita	Boswell, John Walker	—
Bosworth, J. A.	Rej	Harris	—	—
Botto, Cecelia L.	Rej	Bexar	Botto, Louis Thomas	—
Boughman, F. M.	RejM	Archer	—	—
Bounds, Easter	RejM	Madison	—	—
Bounds, Isaac	Rej	Collingsworth	—	—
Bounds, Mary	Rej	Panola	Bounds, Pascal Lafayette	—
Bourgeois, Joseph D.	Rej	Montgomery	—	—
Bourguin, Edward	Rej	Medina	—	—
Bourguin, Theresa	Rej	Medina	Bourguin, Edward	—
Bourne, Nancy	Rej	Grayson	Bourne, Charles Thomas	—
Bowen, Emaline Mary	Rej	Bell	Bowen, James Tinsley	20891
Bowen, Samuel P.	Rej	California	—	—
Bower, S. A. Mrs.	Rej	Williamson	Bower, J. P.	—
Bowers, William A. Mrs.	Rej	Gregg	Bowers, William A.	—
Bowles, Elizabeth	Rej	Eastland	Bowles, Benjamin Franklin	—
Bowles, Rilla	Rej	Kaufman	Bowles, N. Lafayette	—
Bowles, William Augustus, Sr.	Rej	Uvalde	—	—
Bowman, George	Rej	Wichita	—	—
Bownds, Mattie	Rej	Lee	Bownds, William	—
Box, E. H. Mrs.	Rej	Red River	Box, John Wesley	—
Box, J. P.	Rej	Llano	—	—
Box, R. H.	Rej	Sterling	—	—
Boyce, Richard T.	Rej	Burnet	—	—
Boyd, A. E. Mrs.	Rej	Cass	Boyd, William Ellison	—
Boyd, Calvin V.	Rej	Collin	—	—
Boyd, James R.	Rej	Scurry	—	—
Boyd, John J.	Rej	Montague	—	—
Boyd, M. C.	Rej	Childress	—	—
Boyd, M. E. Mrs.	Rej	Wood	Boyd, Thomas Benton	13125
Boyd, Syrena A.	Rej	Hill	Boyd, William J.	—
Boyer, G. M.	Rej	Rains	—	—
Boyett, C. H.	Rej	Nolan	—	—
Boyett, Mary A.	Rej	Henderson	Boyett, Silas Lodwick (lodrick)	27998
Boyles, Mattie	Rej	Clay	Boyles, William Henry	—
Boynton, Winnie Jane	Rej	Wood	Boynton, Samuel	—
Bra, C. P.	RejM	Leon	—	—
Brachear, W. C.	RejM	Harris	—	—
Brack, Henderson F.	Rej	Newton	—	—

Index to Rejected Confederate Pension Applications

Brackeen, Albert James	Rej	Fannin		
Brackeen, John G.	Rej	Van Zandt		
Brackin, Asa Pardue Mrs.	Rej	Lubbock	Brackin, Asa Pardue	
Bradberry, John	Rej	Coryell		
Bradburn, C. C.	Rej	Van Zandt		
Braddock, A. M. Mrs.	RejM	Travis		
Bradfield, James O.	Rej	Harrison		
Bradford, Mary E.	Rej	Smith	Bradford, William A.	
Bradley, Henry	Rej	Freestone		
Bradley, Henry F.	Rej	Hamilton		
Bradley, Sarah D.	Rej	Lavaca	Bradley, Daw	
Bradshaw, Mary	Rej	Grayson	Bradshaw, J. T.	
Bradshaw, Mary E.	Rej	Smith	Bradshaw, P. G.	
Brady, Alfred E.	Rej	Milam		
Brady, King	Rej	Hood		
Brady, Susan C.	Rej	Denton	Brady, Phillip Gross	
Braley, Lena	Rej	Kimble	Braley, Erastus Asberry	07275
Braley, Mandy	Rej	Polk	Braley, James S.	
Bralley, Catherine B.	RejM	Fannin		
Bralley, Catherine L.	Rej	Cooke	Bralley, John	
Branan, Emma	Rej	Upshur	Branan, Jessie Turison	
Branan, I. J. Mrs.	Rej	Hopkins	Branan, Luther B.	
Branch, Dollie	Rej	Delta	Branch, Tom	
Branch, Henry	Rej	Cherokee		
Branch, Mary	Rej	Collin	Branch, Thomas Andrew	
Brand, D. P. M.	Rej	Somervell		
Brandon, William Jordan	Rej	Delta		
Brandt, H. A.	Rej	Fayette		
Brannon, G. B.	Rej	Titus		
Brannon, M. A. Mrs.	RejM	Hill		
Branom, William Jefferson Mrs.	Rej	Hopkins	Branom, William Jefferson	47365
Bransom, Martha E.	Rej	Anderson	Bransom, Stephen Allen	
Brantley, H. T. Mrs.	Rej	Collin	Brantley, Henry Taylor	40226
Branum, Thomas P.	Rej	Franklin		
Brashear, B. A.	RejM	Lever		
Brashear, C. P. Mrs.	Rej	Leon	Brashear, John Brazil	
Brashears, W. C.	Rej	Parker		
Braswell, B. A.	Rej	Lee		
Bratton, Lavinia N.	Rej	Tarrant	Bratton, Thomas	
Bray, James L.	Rej	Wise		
Brazzil, J. W.	Rej	Coryell		
Breecheen, Sophia	Rej	Wise	Breecheen, James M.	
Breeding, Nancy Jane	Rej	Callahan	Breeding, Francie Marion	
Breedlove, W. A.	Rej	Brewster		
Bremer, Henry	Rej	Fayette		
Brewer, Hardy	Rej	Wood		
Brewer, Martha Ann	Rej	Bowie	Brewer, Linson	
Brewer, W. J.	Rej	Navarro		
Brewier, N. A.	Rej	Nacogdoches		
Brice, J. W.	Rej	Nueces		
Bridges, Estaline	Rej	Tarrant	Bridges, Adam Henry	
Briggs, Mattie Virginia	Rej	Tarrant	Briggs, John Clinton	22579
Briggs, Washington	Rej	Hall		
Brimberry, L. A. Mrs.	Rej	Houston	Brimberry, Peter	
Brimberry, M. E. Mrs.	Rej	Houston	Brimberry, Elbert	
Brimer, N. A. Mrs.	Rej	Nacogdoches	Brimer, Harrison	
Bristow, J. A.	Rej	Henderson		
Britt, Josie	Rej	Milam	Britt, John	
Britton, George L.	Rej	Denton		

Index to Rejected Confederate Pension Applications

Britton, W. M.	Rej	Panola	—	—
Brock, F. M.	Rej	Tarrant	—	—
Brock, J. F.	Rej	Archer	—	—
Brock, Sarah	Rej	Dallas	Brock, Marion	—
Brodie, C. A. Mrs.	Rej	Johnson	Brodie, J. B.	—
Broers, Fannie	Rej	Bexar	Broers, Peter	—
Brooks, Belle	Rej	Madison	Brooks, Madison Decalv	—
Brooks, David	Rej	Hood	—	—
Brooks, J. B.	Rej	Cherokee	—	—
Brooks, J. H.	Rej	Limestone	—	—
Brooks, Jim	Rej	Gonzales	—	—
Brooks, John W.	Rej	Guadalupe	—	—
Brooks, Mary Veracruse	Rej	Walker	Brooks, Robert Logan	16913
Brooks, R. L.	Rej	Schleicher	—	—
Brooks, Rebecca E.	Rej	Bowie	Brooks, Napoleon B.	—
Brooks, Reding L.	Rej	Walker	—	—
Brooks, Sarah Ann	Rej	Lavaca	Brooks, John C.	—
Brooks, Weldon	Rej	Hill	—	—
Brooks, William Lunsford	Rej	Wilbarger	—	—
Brooks, William S.	Rej	Kaufman	—	—
Brooks, William T.	Rej	Henderson	—	—
Brotton, Elizer Mrs.	Rej	Morris	Brotton, Y. E.	—
Brown, A. E. Mrs.	Rej	Brown	Brown, William Lunceford	—
Brown, A. L.	Rej	Henderson	—	—
Brown, Alice	Rej	Tarrant	Brown, Francis Marion	—
Brown, Andrew J.	Rej	Parker	—	—
Brown, Andrew Jackson Mrs.	Rej	Shelby	Brown, Andrew Jackson	—
Brown, Benjamin Franklin	Rej	Bell	—	—
Brown, C. T.	Rej	Shelby	—	—
Brown, D. J.	Rej	Hamilton	—	—
Brown, E. B.	Rej	Llano	—	—
Brown, Ed M.	Rej	Navarro	—	—
Brown, G. H.	Rej	Clay	—	—
Brown, Georgia	Rej	Smith	Brown, Allen Charles	41863
Brown, Gordon Mrs.	Rej	Burnet	Brown, Gordon	35452
Brown, Heppie	Rej	Nolan	Brown, Samuel Sheilds	—
Brown, Ida	Rej	Kaufman	Brown, Thomas Jefferson	32034
Brown, J. D.	Rej	Titus	—	—
Brown, J. M.	Rej	Harris	—	—
Brown, J. P.	Rej	Eastland	—	—
Brown, J. P.	Rej	Lavaca	—	—
Brown, J. W.	Rej	Van Zandt	—	—
Brown, John	Rej	Jefferson	—	—
Brown, Lucinda Brown	Rej	Bexar	Brown, John	—
Brown, Lucinda E.	Rej	Coryell	Brown, James R.	—
Brown, Luticia A.	Rej	Rusk	Brown, George W.	—
Brown, Luvenia	Rej	Panola	Brown, Andrew Jackson	—
Brown, Martha	Rej	Hill	Brown, Frank M.	—
Brown, Martha A.	Rej	Nacogdoches	Brown, John O.	—
Brown, Martha Ann	Rej	Nacogdoches	Brown, Gilford Green	—
Brown, Mary	Rej	Shelby	Brown, Andrew Jackson	—
Brown, Mary	RejM	Travis	—	—
Brown, Mary E.	Rej	Montague	Brown, Lewis A.	—
Brown, Mary S.	Rej	Dallas	Brown, G. W.	—
Brown, Mattie L.	Rej	Freestone	Brown, Phillip Clark	—
Brown, Mildred	Rej	Concho	Brown, James Thomas	—
Brown, P. T.	Rej	Hill	—	—
Brown, Peter R.	Rej	Fisher	—	—
Brown, R. N.	Rej	Grayson	—	—

Index to Rejected Confederate Pension Applications

Name	Status	County	Veteran	Number
Brown, Rachel Rebecca	Rej	Hill	Brown, Perry Oliver	
Brown, Sam J.	Rej	Potter	—	
Brown, Sarah	Rej	Hall	Brown, Charles Lewis	
Brown, Sarah Angelina	Rej	Tarrant	Brown, Hyram	
Brown, T. A.	Rej	Collin	—	
Brown, Virgil S.	Rej	Freestone	—	
Brown, W. B.	Rej	Denton	—	
Brown, W. L.	Rej	Mills	—	
Brown, W. P.	Rej	Wise	—	
Brown, W. W.	Rej	McLennan	—	
Brown, William	Rej	Henderson	—	
Brown, William A.	Rej	Parker	—	
Brown, William C.	Rej	McMullen	—	
Brown, William H.	Rej	Wise	—	
Brown, William Harrison	Rej	Wise	—	
Brown, William Richard Mrs.	Rej	Dallas	Brown, William Richard	
Browne, John T.	Rej	Harris	—	
Brownfield, W. A.	Rej	Scurry	—	
Browning, Ida	Rej	Camp	Browning, Pleasant West	14803
Browning, J. V.	Rej	Milam	—	
Browning, John I.	Rej	Wood	—	
Browning, Peyton Graves	Rej	Lavaca	—	
Bruce, G. W.	Rej	Gonzales	—	
Bruce, M. Ellen Mrs.	Rej	Trinity	Bruce, John B.	
Bruns, Lisette	Rej	Fayette	Bruns, John Alberto	
Bruton, Nancy E.	Rej	Bandera	Bruton, James R.	
Bryan, J. T.	Rej	Lamar	—	
Bryan, Kittie Cate	Rej	Floyd	Cate, Jacob	
Bryan, Mary	Rej	San Augustine	Bryan, Seburn J.	
Bryant, Belle	Rej	Dallas	Bryant, Ben Newton	
Bryant, Frances Codelia	Rej	Hopkins	Bryant, Lucius Rhods	
Bryant, Frank	Rej	Limestone	—	
Bryant, Joe Eleck	Rej	Terry	—	
Bryant, M. M. Mrs.	Rej	Grimes	Bryant, Thomas Needham	
Bryant, Milian Mirandy	Rej	Leon	Bryant, David Washington	
Bryant, Samuel Alexander Mrs.	Rej	San Saba	Bryant, Samuel Alexander	
Bryant, T. N.	Rej	Grimes	—	
Bryant, Thomas R.	Rej	Fannin	—	
Brymer, John T.	Rej	Tarrant	—	
Bryson, Margreate Henrietta	Rej	McLennan	Bryson, William Wiley	
Buchanan, Fannie	Rej	Goliad	Buchanan, Samuel Beaty	
Buchanan, Marinda A.	Rej	Bastrop	Buchanan, William Alexander	12259
Buchanan, Mary Clark	Rej	Hunt	Buchanan, Henry Clay	43505
Buck, J. G. H.	Rej	Anderson	—	
Buckingham, C. S. Mann Mrs.	Rej	Denton	Mann, Brice William	
Buckow, Joe	Rej	Harris	—	
Buford, Edward	Rej	Van Zandt	—	
Bull, C. V. Mrs.	Rej	Coleman	Bull, John Campbell	
Bull, T. D.	Rej	Eastland	—	
Bullard, B. F.	Rej	Tarrant	—	
Bullard, Benjamin	Rej	Shelby	—	
Bullard, M.	RejM	Smith	—	
Bullard, Mary Ann	Rej	Real	Bullard, Christopher Columbus	
Bullard, N. A. H.	Rej	Wood	—	
Bullard, Sally E.	Rej	Collin	Bullard, William	
Bullard, Wiley M.	Rej	Smith	—	
Bullion, C. A. Mrs.	Rej	Mitchell	Bullion, George Wilson	
Bullock, William Lowery Mrs.	Rej	Dallas	Bullock, William Lowery	
Bundick, Martin W.	Rej	Guadalupe	—	

Index to Rejected Confederate Pension Applications

Bundren, John W.	Rej	Bexar	—	
Bundy, Martha	Rej	Williamson	Bundy, Zachery Taylor	
Bunn, Wiley	Rej	Dallas	—	
Bunton, John W.	Rej	Sutton	—	
Burditt, A. B. Mrs.	Rej	Atascosa	Burditt, Jessie F.	
Burge, T. F.	Rej	Denton	—	
Burger, Mary R.	RejM	Cherokee	—	
Burgess, A. S.	Rej	Henderson	—	
Burgess, F. J. Mrs.	Rej	Rains	Burgess, J. T.	
Burgess, T. B.	Rej	Shelby	—	
Burk, Elizabeth	Rej	Rusk	Burk, R. T.	
Burke, A. C. Mrs.	Rej	San Saba	Burke, James Polk	
Burke, Daniel	Rej	Harris	—	
Burke, David	RejM	Harris	—	
Burke, Francis A.	Rej	Guadalupe	—	
Burke, Francis M.	Rej	Upshur	—	
Burke, G. F.	RejM	Polk	—	
Burke, Tobias	Rej	Travis	—	
Burkehalter, Frances	Rej	Sabine	Burkehalter, James D.	
Burkhart, James McDonnal	Rej	McLennan	—	
Burkhart, Nancy White	Rej	Hopkins	Burkhart, Stephen Houston	
Burks, Benjamin F.	Rej	Polk	—	
Burks, Josephine	Rej	Polk	Burks, Benjamin Franklin	
Burks, Joshua	Rej	Bastrop	—	
Burks, M. J. Mrs.	Rej	Van Zandt	Burks, Maston Milton	
Burleson, J. A.	Rej	Fannin	—	
Burleson, John F.	Rej	Bastrop	—	
Burleson, Josephine Elizabeth	Rej	Mills	Burleson, William Harrison	
Burleson, Mary	Rej	Travis	Burleson, Jacob	
Burnes, Sarah Ann	Rej	Leon	Burnes, William Alexander	
Burnett, Jennie	Rej	Grayson	Burnett, Alexander Hamilton	22895
Burnett, M. A. Mrs.	Rej	Borden	Burnett, Isaac	
Burnett, N. P. Mrs.	Rej	Williamson	Burnett, J. L.	
Burnett, Nissie	Rej	Washington	Burnett, William S.	
Burnett, P. C.	Rej	Van Zandt	—	
Burnett, Sarah Margaret	Rej	Montague	Burnett, Robert Middleton	
Burns, Addie	Rej	Cass	Burns, John H.	23464
Burns, B. F.	RejM	Bexar	—	
Burns, C. C.	Rej	Caldwell	—	
Burns, D. S.	RejM	Grayson	—	
Burns, D. T.	Rej	Franklin	—	
Burns, Isham L.	Rej	Grayson	—	
Burns, John, Sr.	Rej	Karnes	—	
Burns, Louisa	RejM	Collin	—	
Burns, Nancy H.	Rej	Shelby	Burns, William Reece	
Burns, S. W. Mrs.	Rej	Grimes	Burns, Reason Robert	
Burrell, W. G.	Rej	Parker	—	
Burris, B. F.	Rej	Bexar	—	
Burrough, W. E.	Rej	Tarrant	—	
Burroughs, Tom	Rej	Shelby	—	
Burrow, B. C.	Rej	Lampasas	—	
Burrow, Catherine A.	Rej	Panola	Burrow, John Alexander	
Burt, Emma Garrett	Rej	Bell	Burt, Henry McGuire	
Burt, Henry M.	Rej	Bell	—	
Burton, Helen	Rej	Ellis	Burton, Zenas Leland Boggs	
Burton, L. E. Mrs.	Rej	Armstrong	Burton, William Franklin	
Burton, M. A. F. Mrs.	Rej	Shackelford	Burton, William Thomas Jarrell	
Burton, Sarah Elizabeth	Rej	Harrison	Burton, Nathaniel	
Busby, W. A.	Rej	Upshur	—	

Index to Rejected Confederate Pension Applications

Name	Status	County	Soldier	Number
Busby, William Henry Harrison	Rej	Sabine		
Bush, Ellie	Rej	Clay	Bush, William Rhodes	
Bussey, Annie L.	Rej	Dallas	Bussey, Charles Henry	
Butler, J. B.	Rej	Red River		
Butler, James	Rej	Mitchell		
Butler, Lizzie T.	Rej	Henderson	Butler, Marshal Neigh	12409
Butler, M. E. Mrs.	Rej	Morris	Butler, Solomon Anderson	
Butler, Virginia	Rej	Dallas	Butler, Joe W.	
Butterfield, William H.	Rej	Cass		
Buttfield, J. B.	Rej	Jefferson		
Byars, Euphrie S.	Rej	Bastrop	Byars, Charles Terrell	38374
Byerly, Stephen John	Rej	Fayette		
Bynum, Eliza	Rej	Ellis	Bynum, Asa	
Bynum, I. L.	Rej	Titus		
Bynum, M. B.	Rej	Lampasas		
Bynum, Nancy Catherine Wilson	Rej	Taylor	Wilson, Matt Frederick	
Bynum, R. L. Mrs.	Rej	Comanche	Bynum, Jesse Ellis	
Byram, John A.	Rej	Clay		
Byram, Sallie	Rej	Red River	Byram, Samuel M.	
Byrd, Evie Mae	Rej	Robertson	Byrd, Isaac Wilburn (bird)	49935
Byrd, F. C. Mrs.	Rej	Baylor	Byrd, Thomas S.	
Byrd, J. W.	Rej	Eastland		
Byrd, L. P. Mrs.	Rej	Smith	Byrd, Monroe Washington	31319
Byrd, M. A. Mrs.	Rej	Erath	Byrd, A. J.	
Byrne, Martha E. Walker	Rej	Falls	Walker, William E.	
Byrum, Mary A.	Rej	Coleman	Byrum, E. W.	
Byrun, T. C.	RejM	Titus		
Cabitt, John W.	RejM	Upshur		
Cable, J. H.	Rej	Collin		
Cabler, Gaston Davidson	Rej	Baylor		
Caddell, J. B.	Rej	McLennan		
Cadenhead, James M.	Rej	Camp		
Cadey, A. H.	Rej	Harris		
Caffall, Thomas	Rej	Karnes		
Caffey, Francis Elmira	Rej	Brown	Caffey, Abraham	
Cagle, Virginia Frances	Rej	Navarro	Cagle, James Pinkney	
Cain, A. J.	Rej	Upshur		
Cain, James A.	Rej	Limestone		
Cain, Martha	Rej	Henderson	Cain, Ferdinand C.	
Cain, Sarah A.	Rej	Freestone	Cain, William	
Cain, William	Rej	Freestone		
Caldwell, O. B.	Rej	Travis		
Caldwell, Selena	Rej	Dallas	Caldwell, William	
Caldwell, W. Emily	Rej	Van Zandt	Caldwell, Wylie Harrison	21675
Calhoun, J. M.	Rej	Coryell		
Calhoun, Lela G.	Rej	Jefferson	Calhoun, Benjamin Franklin	
Calhound, Martha E.	Rej	Travis	Calhound, William Henry	
Callaham, Benjamin G.	Rej	Bosque		
Callaway, J. I.	Rej	Limestone		
Callaway, Joe Anna	Rej	Houston	Callaway, Elijah Holcomb	
Callaway, Leona	Rej	Red River	Callaway, James A.	
Callaway, William J.	Rej	Brown		
Calley, J. M.	Rej	Comanche		
Callison, Alex	Rej	Colorado		
Calvery, William Johnson	Rej	Hill		
Cameron, Mollie	Rej	Bowie	Cameron, William Cannon	
Camp, Mary E.	Rej	Hunt	Camp, William Lafayette	22722
Campbell, A. C. Mrs.	Rej	Knox	Campbell, John Alexander	
Campbell, A. J. Mrs.	Rej	Harris	Campbell, Ephraim McLain	

Index to Rejected Confederate Pension Applications

Campbell, Charles	Rej	Walker	—	
Campbell, J. I.	Rej	Williamson	—	
Campbell, Mary F.	Rej	Mills	Campbell, Thomas Jefferson	—
Campbell, W. H.	Rej	Houston	—	
Campion, Mary Mc Tiernan	Rej	Nueces	Campion, William S.	—
Canard, Robert	Rej	Hopkins	—	
Canble, Nannie Mae	RejM	Hill	—	
Cannon, Della	Rej	Trinity	Cannon, David Crockett	—
Cannon, James William	Rej	Hunt	—	
Cannon, John L.	Rej	Hopkins	—	
Cantrell, Alexander C.	Rej	Coryell	—	
Cantrell, B. F.	Rej	Van Zandt	—	
Cantrell, J. C.	Rej	Henderson	—	
Cantrell, Miles	Rej	Travis	—	
Cantrell, Sarah F.	Rej	Coryell	Cantrell, Alexander C.	Rej
Cantrell, Shadrach	Rej	Anderson	—	
Capps, Elvira Ann Ligett	Rej	Dallas	Ligett, James	—
Caradine, R.	Rej	Childress	—	
Caraway, C. M.	RejM	Comanche	—	
Cardwell, A. F.	Rej	Childress	—	
Cargill, T. D.	Rej	Kinney	—	
Carlisle, John	Rej	Callahan	—	
Carlisle, Lawrence	Rej	Bee	—	
Carlton, N. A. Mrs.	Rej	Gregg	Carlton, Coleman Columbus	—
Carmichael, Flem	Rej	Orange	—	
Carner, James A.	Rej	Dimmit	—	
Carney, Rebecca	Rej	Wise	Carney, George W.	—
Carnoline, William	Rej	Angelina	—	
Caro, J. M.	Rej	Starr	—	
Carothers, A. M.	Rej	Travis	—	
Carpenter, Allen R.	Rej	Limestone	—	
Carpenter, Hattie	Rej	Dallas	Carpenter, John Robert	—
Carpenter, Mary	Rej	Bexar	Carpenter, Frank	—
Carpenter, N. J. Mrs.	Rej	Hunt	Carpenter, Owen Lovel	—
Carrier, Mary	Rej	Nacogdoches	Carrier, J. E.	—
Carroll, Ami Bass Mrs.	Rej	Harris	Carroll, Ami Bass	—
Carroll, B. A. Mrs.	Rej	Shelby	Carroll, John Jesse	—
Carroll, E. M.	RejM	Jackson	—	
Carroll, Emma B.	Rej	Freestone	Carroll, David Vinson	10085
Carroll, Josephine	Rej	McLennan	Carroll, John Giles	—
Carroll, L. E. Mrs.	Rej	Rusk	Carroll, J. C.	—
Carroll, W. H.	Rej	McLennan	—	
Carson, Mary A.	Rej	Madison	Carson, T. H.	—
Carson, Sarah M.	Rej	Collin	Carson, William Stewart	—
Carson, Seburn F.	Rej	Hemphill	—	
Carter, Alfred H.	Rej	Freestone	—	
Carter, Bernetie Hanah	Rej	Brown	Carter, Alexander Aulkie	—
Carter, Elizabeth	Rej	Parker	Carter, Joseph Wilson	—
Carter, F. M.	Rej	Angelina	—	
Carter, J. M.	Rej	Erath	—	
Carter, John Henry Mrs.	Rej	Eastland	Carter, John Henry	—
Carter, Susan M.	Rej	Shelby	Carter, Hubbard	—
Carter, Thomas J.	Rej	Delta	—	
Carter, Wade H.	Rej	Panola	—	
Carter, William Mrs.	Rej	Kinney	Carter, William	—
Cartwright, C. W.	Rej	Bastrop	—	
Cartwright, J. L.	Rej	Johnson	—	
Cartwright, Osa	Rej	Shelby	—	
Cartwright, William W.	Rej	Nacogdoches	—	

Index to Rejected Confederate Pension Applications

Name	Status	County	Veteran	Number
Caruthers, Elizabeth	Rej	Wise	Caruthers, Benjamin Newton	
Caruthers, Permelia	RejM	Kaufman		
Carvajal, Vincente F.	Rej	Wilson		
Casber, Millie E.	RejM	Shelby		
Casey, A. A.	Rej	Hood		
Casey, A. T.	Rej	Wise		
Cash, Benjamin R.	Rej	Wood		
Casper, Columbus H.	Rej	Lampasas		
Cassady, Elizabeth Jane	Rej	Leon	Cassady, Francis Marion	12034
Castanon, Rumalda	Rej	Atascosa	Castanon, Luis	
Castleberry, Ida Mae	Rej	Wilbarger	Castleberry, Archibald H.	
Castleberry, James	Rej	Gregg		
Cates, Rowena Hale	Rej	Wise	Cates, Charles Donahue	
Cathcart, J. F.	Rej	San Saba		
Catvery, W. J.	RejM	Hill		
Cauthen, John G.	Rej	Callahan		
Cavender, Helen	Rej	Parker	Cavender, John Calvin	
Cavitt, John W.	Rej	Upshur		
Cawthon, Fannie M.	Rej	McLennan	Cawthon, Nathan	
Cessna, Green K.	Rej	Fort Bend		
Chambers, Ella	Rej	Denton	Chambers, Joseph Taylor	
Chambers, Francis	Rej	Milam	Chambers, William	
Chambers, J. T.	Rej	Denton		
Chambers, Laura Ann	Rej	Taylor	Chambers, Henry Freeman	
Chambers, Maranda	Rej	Coryell	Chambers, S. A.	08268
Chambers, Taylor	Rej	Denton		
Chambles, H. F.	Rej	Karnes		
Chambles, Louise	Rej	Victoria	Chambles, Jackson	
Chambless, Eliza Amanda	Rej	Harris	Chambless, James Madison	
Chambless, Ephraim	Rej	Tyler		
Chambless, Hellen A.	Rej	Leon		
Chambless, J. A., Dr.	Rej	Red River		
Chambliss, Susan Ann	Rej	Lee	Chambliss, Joseph	
Chamness, Mattie	Rej	Panola	Chamness, Ben C.	
Champion, M. F. Mrs.	Rej	Brown	Champion, George Wesley	
Chance, D. H.	Rej	Hardin		
Chandler, Ann V.	Rej	Sabine	Chandler, John	
Chandler, George W.	Rej	Montgomery		
Chandler, Georgia	Rej	McLennan	Chandler, Joseph Alvin	
Chandler, H. M. Mrs.	Rej	Young	Chandler, John Lemuel	
Chandler, Hallan J.	Rej	Limestone		
Chandler, Isaac	Rej	Cass		
Chandler, J. N.	Rej	Hood		
Chandler, Thomas	Rej	Live Oak		
Chandler, Washington W.	Rej	Reeves		
Channell, H. J.	Rej	Cass		
Chapman, Al J.	Rej	Collin		
Chapman, F. T.	Rej	Uvalde		
Chapman, H. S. Mrs.	Rej	Harris	Chapman, Enoch Ordillo	
Chapman, Husie T.	Rej	Colorado	Chapman, David Madison	
Chapman, Lavina Ann	Rej	Williamson	Chapman, William	
Chapman, Sallie B.	Rej	Kaufman	Chapman, William Benjamin	
Chappell, M. E. Johnson Mrs.	Rej	Harris	Johnson, Henry Clay	
Charles, Mattie	Rej	Dallas	Charles, Joseph (joel) Barksdale	16174
Chatham, Martha Jane	Rej	Montgomery	Chatham, Andrew Singleton	
Cheek, C. S. Mrs.	Rej	Comanche	Cheek, Thomas Jackson	
Cheek, J. W.	Rej	Foard		
Chenault, M. E. Mrs.	Rej	Ellis	Chenault, James Monroe	22542
Chenault, Ruth Ann	Rej	Dallas	Chenault, William	

Index to Rejected Confederate Pension Applications

Cheney, W. C.	Rej	Comanche	—	
Chenoweth, T. J.	Rej	Grayson	—	
Cherry, J. E.	Rej	Milam	—	
Cherry, John Randolph	Rej	Hood	—	
Cherry, Sallie	Rej	Panola	Cherry, Joshua W.	
Cheshire, G. P.	Rej	Nolan	—	
Chester, J. C.	Rej	Hopkins	—	
Childress, F. M.	Rej	Red River	—	
Childress, James	Rej	Ellis	—	
Childress, Peyton Franklin Mrs.	Rej	Clay	Childress, Peyton Franklin	
Chiles, Maggie	Rej	Bowie	Chiles, Archibald Henry	
Choates, Mary J.	Rej	Kaufman	Choates, James Rufus	
Chrestman, Francis Lavisa	Rej	Terry	Chrestman, Thomas Jarrot	
Chrisman, M. L. Mrs.	Rej	Dallas	Chrisman, Wallace Alexander	
Christian, Adam	Rej	Morris	—	
Christian, Mary J.	Rej	Montgomery	Christian, James K.	
Christian, Peruvia	Rej	Hunt	Christian, James D.	
Christian, R. T.	Rej	Newton	—	
Christian, R. T.	Rej	Jasper	—	
Christian, W. A.	Rej	Milam	—	
Christopher, W. L.	Rej	Nacogdoches	—	
Christy, John	Rej	Angelina	—	
Church, Serene H.	Rej	Comal	Church, Caleb I.	
Churchwell, John M.	Rej	San Saba	—	
Ciprian, Cecilio	Rej	Webb	—	
Cissell, Vincent	Rej	Taylor	—	
Clack, M. R.	Rej	Rockwall	—	
Clack, Sallie	Rej	Wheeler	Clack, James Thomas	
Claiborne, Ethel	Rej	Grayson	Claiborne, John Harrison	15855
Claiborne, Holbert T.	Rej	Bastrop	—	
Clapp, Peter L.	Rej	Waller	—	
Clarie, E. F. Mrs.	RejM	Harris	—	
Clark, A. J.	Rej	Dallas	—	
Clark, Annie M.	Rej	Limestone	—	
Clark, Antonette Elizabeth	Rej	Caldwell	Clark, John	
Clark, B. B.	Rej	Taylor	—	
Clark, E. H.	Rej	Bowie	—	
Clark, Elizabeth Jane	Rej	Newton	Clark, Oliver Comistock	
Clark, F. N.	Rej	Dallas	—	
Clark, G. W.	Rej	Dallas	—	
Clark, J. K.	RejM	Williamson	—	
Clark, J. L.	Rej	Cooke	—	
Clark, James H.	Rej	Lubbock	—	
Clark, Jerry	Rej	Bowie	—	
Clark, Martha Ann	Rej	Hill	Clark, David Garrison	
Clark, Mary F.	Rej	Tarrant	Clark, Ephriam Elisha	
Clark, P. C.	Rej	Houston	—	
Clark, Sela Ann	Rej	Delta	Clark, Wellington	
Clark, Susan Ann	Rej	Houston	Clark, John Anderson	
Clark, W. A. Mrs.	Rej	Tom Green	Clark, W. A.	
Clark, William T. Mrs.	Rej	Navarro	Clark, William T.	
Clarke, I. V.	Rej	Harrison	—	
Clay, Jane	Rej	Wheeler	Clay, E. B.	
Clayton, John H.	Rej	Gonzales	—	
Clayton, Rosa	Rej	Hardin	Clayton, Josephus	
Clegg, S. A. E. Mrs.	Rej	Trinity	Clegg, William Owen	
Clements, Jesse	Rej	Cass	—	
Clements, Mildred Amanda	Rej	Smith	Clements, Jephthah S.	
Clements, S. J. Mrs.	Rej	Burleson	Clements, A. E.	

Index to Rejected Confederate Pension Applications

Clemons, Alice	Rej	Taylor	Clemons, David Godfrey	
Clepper, Sarah Ann	Rej	Waller	Clepper, Lorenzo D.	
Clevenger, Margaret M.	Rej	Angelina	Clevenger, William	
Click, John	Rej	Johnson		
Click, Rufus	Rej	Medina		
Clinton, D. M.	Rej	Smith		
Cloninger, Nancy L.	Rej	Cass	Cloninger, Amos B.	14824
Cloud, John Jefferson	Rej	Concho		
Cloud, Mary	RejM	Van Zandt		
Clough, Mary	Rej	Van Zandt	Clough, George W.	
Cobb, Alexander	Rej	Titus		
Cobb, Calvin L.	RejM	Fannin		
Cobb, Mary	Rej	San Augustine	Cobb, Elcona C.	
Cobb, Mary Jane Lewis	Rej	Jefferson	Lewis, Alexander	
Coble, Calvin Luther	Rej	Fannin		
Cobler, G. W.	Rej	Grayson		
Cochran, Emma A.	Rej	Young	Cochran, David Jackson	
Cochran, Fannie	Rej	Henderson	Cochran, David James	
Cochran, P. M. Mrs.	Rej	Williamson	Cochran, James	
Cockburn, James P.	Rej	Red River		
Cockerham, John David	Rej	Tarrant		
Cole, E. A. Mrs.	Rej	Hunt	Cole, John	
Cole, J. C.	Rej	Tarrant		
Cole, J. G.	Rej	Van Zandt		
Cole, J. H., Sr.	Rej	Van Zandt		
Cole, Larkin Granville	Rej	Terry		
Cole, M. S.	Rej	Cherokee		
Coleman, Albert	Rej	Harrison		
Coleman, J. C.	Rej	Denton		
Coleman, J. W.	Rej	Henderson		
Coleman, James H.	Rej	Bosque		
Coleman, Mittie A.	Rej	Dewitt	Coleman, Edward Perry	
Coleman, W. C.	Rej	Tarrant		
Collard, Mary Jane	Rej	Brazos	Collard, Joe Larrison	
Collier, A. J.	Rej	Jack		
Collier, J. W.	Rej	Tyler		
Collier, John J.	RejM	Cherokee		
Collier, Mary Alma	Rej	Bexar	Collier, John Joseph	
Collier, Mary Elizabeth	Rej	Montague	Collier, Johnathan	
Collier, W. B.	Rej	Kimble		
Collins, Alzena	Rej	Fannin	Collins, J. S.	
Collins, C. C.	Rej	Harrison		
Collins, Della	Rej	Hidalgo	Collins, James Rice	
Collins, Ida	Rej	Shelby	Collins, Arthur	
Collins, J. O.	Rej	Shelby		
Collins, Japhet	Rej			
Collins, Jessie O.	Rej	Foard	Collins, Thomas Luman	19578
Collins, Josiah M. Mrs.	Rej	Grayson	Collins, Josiah M.	
Collins, Levi F.	Rej	Taylor		
Collins, Romulus Madison Mrs.	Rej	Tom Green	Collins, Romulus Madison	
Collins, Thomas P.	Rej	Grayson		
Coltharp, A. B.	Rej	Henderson		
Coltharp, Maryetta	Rej	Henderson	Coltharp, Abel Bruce	
Colville, Mary D.	Rej	San Patricio	Colville, William Thomas	
Combs, Daniel W.	Rej	Burleson		
Combs, Sarah	Rej	Carson	Combs, Zur David	
Comer, Calvin Hampton Mrs.	Rej	Tarrant	Comer, Calvin Hampton	22418
Comer, Don	Rej	Harris		
Compton, T. P. Mrs.	Rej	Harris	Compton, John Perkins	27297

Index to Rejected Confederate Pension Applications

Cone, Maggie	Rej	Grimes	Cone, Henry Shrock	—
Cone, Mary F.	Rej	Hunt	Cone, W. C.	—
Congalton, John Alexander	Rej	Hill	—	—
Conn, J. G.	Rej	Madison	—	—
Conn, J. M.	Rej	Parker	—	—
Connally, Charles P.	Rej	Garza	—	—
Conner, Ellen	Rej	Washington	Conner, James Monroe	13007
Conner, James P.	Rej	Bailey	—	—
Conners, John	Rej	Hill	—	—
Connolly, S. J. Mrs.	Rej	Ellis	Connolly, Owen	—
Connon, James William	RejM	Hunt	—	—
Consford, J. T.	Rej	San Augustine	—	—
Cook, A. M.	Rej	Callahan	—	—
Cook, Alice	Rej	Atascosa	Cook, Caswell Washington	12729
Cook, Cynthia M.	Rej	Bexar	Cook, William Montgomery	—
Cook, D. J.	Rej	Madison	—	—
Cook, E. E. Mrs.	Rej	Titus	Cook, Jasper	—
Cook, Elizabeth	Rej	Upshur	Cook, David	—
Cook, Emily Jane	Rej	Henderson	Cook, George W.	—
Cook, H. A. Mrs.	Rej	Travis	Cook, Eli	—
Cook, James W. Mrs.	Rej	Harris	Cook, James W.	—
Cook, John Henry Mrs.	Rej	Fannin	Cook, John Henry	—
Cook, M. Mrs.	Rej	Erath	Cook, James Edward	—
Cook, Maggie	Rej	Bexar	Cook, James Franklin	—
Cook, Mahala	Rej	Travis	Cook, James Edward	—
Cook, Mary L.	Rej	Hamilton	Cook, William Washington	—
Cook, Richard F.	Rej	Lavaca	—	—
Cook, Viney Ragan	Rej	Houston	Ragan, Alfred Asa	13143
Cook, W. H.	Rej	Houston	—	—
Cook, W. H.	Rej	Knox	—	—
Cook, W. H.	Rej	Mitchell	—	—
Cook, W. W.	Rej	Camp	—	—
Cooke, George Martin Mrs.	Rej	Johnson	Cooke, George Martin	—
Cooksey, Sam	Rej	Mitchell	—	—
Coon, Leander W.	Rej	Burnet	—	—
Cooper, F. P. Mrs.	Rej	Bosque	Cooper, Benjamin Franklin	—
Cooper, Florence C.	Rej	Floyd	Cooper, Samuel Thomas	49052
Cooper, George A.	Rej	Nolan	—	—
Cooper, George W.	Rej	Menard	—	—
Cooper, Henry	Rej	Burleson	—	—
Cooper, Henry Payton	Rej	Bosque	—	—
Cooper, J. C.	Rej	Colorado	—	—
Cooper, James W.	Rej	Fannin	—	—
Cooper, Mary D.	Rej	Dallas	Cooper, John Maoy	—
Cooper, Mattie	Rej	Dallas	Cooper, William	—
Cooper, William	Rej	Collin	—	—
Coopwood, Martha	Rej	Bastrop	Coopwood, John	—
Coots, Caroline	Rej	Bexar	Coots, George W.	—
Cope, C. W.	Rej	Limestone	—	—
Copeland, Richard Marion	Rej	Bell	—	—
Coppedge, May	Rej	Hunt	Coppedge, James J.	—
Corder, Etna G.	Rej	Wichita	Corder, Joel Gillum	—
Cordway, Angela M.	Rej	Hidalgo	Cordway, J. C.	02368
Corley, Ruth	Rej	Henderson	Corley, L. A.	—
Cornelius, Emma	Rej	Parker	Cornelius, Warren Woodson	—
Corner, James A.	RejM	Dimmit	—	—
Cornwell, Josie	Rej	Eastland	Cornwell, George Washington	—
Corona, Pas	Rej	Webb	—	—
Corrigan, Thomas	Rej	Brazoria	—	—

Index to Rejected Confederate Pension Applications

Cosby, J. W.	Rej	Milam		
Costen, E. P.	Rej	Jack		
Cothran, J. C.	Rej	Lamar		
Cothran, Wiley Monroe	Rej	Leon		
Cotten, N. L. Mrs.	Rej	Henderson	Cotten, William Thomas	50312
Cotter, J. J.	Rej	Kimble		
Cottingham, Sophronia	Rej	Bexar	Cottingham, John Rowe	
Cotton, M. A. Mrs.	Rej	Hunt	Cotton, Allen	
Cotton, Shedrick M. Mrs.	Rej	Travis	Cotton, Shedrick M.	13422
Couch, J. Calvin	Rej	Hamilton		
Couch, Mary	Rej	Howard	Couch, Josiah Calvin	
Couling, H.	Rej	Duval		
Counts, Mary E.	Rej	Tarrant	Counts, William	
Court, Louise Mohl	Rej	Harris	Court, Charles	
Courtney, Ollie Matilda	Rej	Kerr	Courtney, Thomas Jefferson	
Couser, M. E. Mrs.	Rej	Collin	Couser, Marvin Alexander	
Covey, Maria M.	Rej	Val Verde	Covey, Joseph	
Covey, Thomas Jefferson Mrs.	Rej	Upshur	Covey, Thomas Jefferson	
Cowan, Eliza	Rej	Foard	Cowan, William Wallace	
Cowan, James Washington Mrs.	Rej	Bell	Cowan, James Washington	
Cowan, Mary	Rej	Grayson	Cowan, Maron C.	
Cowan, Mary	RejM	Collin		
Coward, Willis B.	Rej	Harris		
Cowart, A. C. Mrs.	Rej	Wood	Cowart, Andrew Jackson	17024
Cox, A. A. Mrs.	Rej	Wilson	Cox, Frank Marion	
Cox, C. B. Mrs.	Rej	Falls	Cox, John Marshal	
Cox, Eliza B.	Rej	Walker	Cox, James Rambean	
Cox, Elizabeth Louvicia	Rej	Tarrant	Cox, George	
Cox, James	Rej	Dallas		
Cox, John Wesley	Rej	Lampasas		
Cox, L. H. Mrs.	RejM	Hunt		
Cox, Mary	Rej	Wood	Cox, C. W.	
Cox, W. T.	Rej	Grayson		
Coyle, George Worthy	Rej	Ward		
Cozby, F. M. Mrs.	Rej	Cooke	Cozby, John Chatten Calhoun	11731
Crabb, J. D.	Rej	Wise		
Craig, Susan	Rej	Freestone	Craig, Samuel R.	
Craighead, Bytha E.	Rej	Dallas	Craighead, William E.	30909
Crain, Billy	Rej	Fannin		
Crain, J. D.	Rej	Matagorda		
Crain, W. W.	Rej	Fannin		
Crane, A. J.	Rej	Erath		
Crane, Eugene	Rej	Bexar		
Cranford, J. W.	Rej	Franklin		
Crawford, Eliza	Rej	Montgomery	Crawford, Francis Marion	
Crawford, George Andrew Mrs.	Rej	Coryell	Crawford, George Andrew	44032
Crawford, J. B.	Rej	Ellis		
Crawford, J. M.	Rej	Johnson		
Crawford, O. H. P.	Rej	Nacogdoches		
Crawford, R. H.	Rej	Brewster		
Crawford, S. L.	Rej	Comanche		
Crawford, William Hamilton	Rej	Bowie		
Crawson, Jennie	RejM	Fannin		
Creasy, M. C. Mrs.	Rej	Clay	Creasy, John Burton	
Crenshaw, Eula	Rej	McLennan	Crenshaw, John Benjamin	39484
Crenshaw, Sallie E.	Rej	Brazos	Crenshaw, Samuel Perry	
Crews, S. J. Mrs.	Rej	Tyler	Crews, John Jefferson	25490
Crick, Cornelia W.	Rej	Wichita	Crick, Charles Newton	
Criswell, J. H.	Rej	Colorado		

Index to Rejected Confederate Pension Applications

Cromer, S. H.	Rej	Wood	—	—
Crook, Georgia S.	Rej	McLennan	Crook, Samuel Joshua	—
Crook, Susan	Rej	Smith	Crook, Ruben Franklin	—
Cropper, J. S.	Rej	Hamilton	—	—
Cross, J. F.	Rej	Van Zandt	—	—
Cross, L. L.	Rej	Lamar	—	—
Cross, Mary P.	Rej	Hill	Cross, William J.	—
Crouch, Jane C.	Rej	Rusk	Crouch, Joseph C.	—
Crow, M. I.	Rej	Houston	—	—
Crow, Solomon	Rej	Parker	—	—
Crowder, G. W., Sr.	Rej	Harris	—	—
Crowder, S. M. Wood Mrs.	Rej	Hunt	Wood, Henry Clay	15548
Crowe, Josiah A.	Rej	Hardin	—	—
Crownover, Rachel Susie	Rej	Tarrant	Crownover, James Melton	—
Crowson, William L.	Rej	Hill	—	—
Crump, Cornelia Elizabeth	Rej	Shelby	Crump, William James	16548
Crump, Sallie	Rej	Morris	Crump, Winfield Scott	—
Crunk, Susan M.	Rej	Concho	Crunk, Jos W.	—
Cruse, N. H. Mrs.	Rej	Lamar	Cruse, William Richard	—
Cubit, Gilbert	Rej	Gonzales	—	—
Cude, George W.	Rej	Comanche	—	—
Cude, Kate	Rej	Bexar	—	—
Culbertson, Mildred H.	Rej	McLennan	James, Dr.	—
Culbertson, R. W.	Rej	Shelby	—	—
Culbesson, Elizabeth Ann	Rej	Hunt	Culbesson, Columbus Young	—
Culp, C. A. Mrs.	Rej	Comanche	Culp, Amos Franklin	—
Culwell, Sarah Belle	Rej	Parker	Culwell, Hezekiah	—
Cummings, Bridget	Rej	Anderson	Cummings, Thomas	—
Cummins, Minnie C.	Rej	El Paso	Cummins, William Fletcher	—
Cuniff, John	Rej	Jefferson	—	—
Cunningham, Daniel Mrs.	Rej	Childress	Cunningham, Daniel	—
Cunningham, David	Rej	Lamar	—	—
Cunningham, J. W.	Rej	Bee	—	—
Cunningham, Thomas Mabry Mrs.	Rej	Polk	Cunningham, Thomas Mabry	—
Curbella, Soloman	Rej	Bexar	—	—
Curbo, S. A. Mrs.	Rej	Rusk	Curbo, Thomas Benton	—
Currin, Addie Maroney	Rej	Hunt	Maroney, James	—
Currington, Lillie F.	Rej	Wilson	Currington, Joseph Green	32907
Curry, David Webster	Rej	Brown	—	—
Curry, John Pickney Mrs.	Rej	Hopkins	Curry, John Pickney	—
Curry, Margret	Rej	Jones	Curry, John Wiseman	—
Curry, Rebecca S.	Rej	Burnet	Curry, David Phillips	—
Curry, S. L. Mrs.	Rej	Brown	Curry, Benjamin Franklin	—
Curry, Thomas Jefferson Mrs.	Rej	Limestone	Curry, Thomas Jefferson	42904
Curry, William	RejM	Unknown	—	—
Custer, Rachel Elizabeth	Rej	Mason	Custer, Michael	—
Dailey, Henry	Rej	Guadalupe	—	—
Dale, Elizabeth	Rej	Mitchell	Dale, Edward	—
Dallar, J. W.	RejM	Collingsworth	—	—
Dalton, Charles Fox Mrs.	Rej	McLennan	Dalton, Charles Fox	—
Dalton, E. S. Mrs.	Rej	Denton	Dalton, Jeremiah	—
Dame, Valentine	Rej	Victoria	—	—
Dandridge, E. B. Mrs.	Rej	Hill	Dandridge, Joseph Robert	12417
Daniel, E.	RejM	Liberty	—	—
Daniel, Francis A. Mrs.	Rej	Johnson	Daniel, James Monroe	—
Daniel, J. F.	Rej	Potter	—	—
Daniel, J. W.	Rej	Matagorda	—	—
Daniel, John B.	Rej	Palo Pinto	—	—
Daniel, Mary Ann	Rej	Uvalde	Daniel, J. W.	—

Index to Rejected Confederate Pension Applications

Daniel, Thomas M.	Rej	Anderson		
Daniel, William	Rej	Wise		
Daniel, William Brown	Rej	Camp		
Daniel, William E.	Rej	Liberty		
Daniell, J. M.	Rej	Jones		
Daniell, L.	Rej	Bell		
Daniels, Reania	Rej	Cherokee	Daniels, John Mark	
Danley, Charles W.	Rej	Bell		
Dann, Jacob G.	Rej	Cherokee		
Dansby, S. A. Mrs.	Rej	Bosque	Dansby, Jonathan	
Darby, John Leeright	Rej	Hunt		
Darby, Mary Charity	Rej	Tarrant	Darby, Thomas Jefferson	26258
Darcy, S. A. Mrs.	Rej	Brazoria	Darcy, Jos	
Darden, Alfred Britton Mrs.	Rej	McLennan	Darden, Alfred Britton	
Darling, Delilah	Rej	Titus	Darling, Milas Madison	
Darling, Leonidas	Rej	Fannin		
Darnell, A. B. Mrs.	Rej	Morris	Darnell, Ugene Preston	
Darnell, Martha Jane Brown	Rej	Travis	Brown, Henry Jackson	40169
Dauchy, Annie E.	Rej	Bexar	Dauchy, Carey Cephus	
Daughtery, G. W., Jr.	Rej	Scurry		
Daughtery, L. H.	Rej	Kaufman		
Davenport, Martha E.	Rej	Bowie	Davenport, William J.	
Davidson, H. A.	Rej	Harris		
Davies, Susan A.	Rej	Travis	Davies, Anderson Dickson	
Davis, Adolphus	Rej	Tarrant		
Davis, Asariah	Rej	Hunt		
Davis, Benjamin	Rej	Cooke		
Davis, C. W.	Rej	Johnson		
Davis, C. W.	Rej	Collin		
Davis, Celia Elizabeth	Rej	Erath	Davis, Wallace Parks	
Davis, D. Tom	Rej	Tarrant		
Davis, David Crockett Mrs.	Rej	Dallas	Davis, David Crockett	
Davis, G. A.	Rej	Hunt		
Davis, George	Rej	Kaufman		
Davis, H. N. C.	Rej	Ellis		
Davis, Isaac W.	Rej	Cooke		
Davis, J. A.	Rej	Navarro		
Davis, J. B.	Rej	Foard		
Davis, J. B.	Rej	Parker		
Davis, J. C.	RejM	Freestone		
Davis, J. H.	Rej	Upton		
Davis, J. I.	Rej	Leon		
Davis, J. P.	RejM	Robertson		
Davis, J. S.	RejM	Leon		
Davis, J. W.	RejM	Navarro		
Davis, James B.	Rej	Dallas		
Davis, James J.	Rej	Erath		
Davis, James W.	Rej	Henderson		
Davis, John Mack	Rej	Wichita		
Davis, John S.	Rej	Travis		
Davis, Lucy Prudence	Rej	Terry	Davis, James Monroe	
Davis, M. A. Mrs.	Rej	Parker	Davis, Chancer Hine	
Davis, M. I.	Rej	Caldwell		
Davis, M. J. Mrs.	Rej	Bell	Davis, William	
Davis, Margaret Jenet	Rej	Upshur	Davis, William Allen	
Davis, Mary Ellen	Rej	Navarro	Davis, Andrew Jackson	
Davis, Mary J.	Rej	Jack	Davis, Nathan W.	
Davis, Mary P.	Rej	Presidio	Davis, James Joshua	
Davis, Nancy	Rej	Van Zandt	Davis, Lafayette	

Index to Rejected Confederate Pension Applications

Davis, Nesbit C.	Rej	Grayson		
Davis, O. C. Mrs.	Rej	Jones	Davis, W. R.	
Davis, Parilee	Rej	Parker	Davis, Adolphus	
Davis, R. A. Mrs.	Rej	Cass	Davis, John Jones	
Davis, R. L.	Rej	Shelby		
Davis, Richard W.	Rej	Bastrop		
Davis, Ruby	Rej	Jones	Davis, William	
Davis, T. A.	Rej	Kendall		
Davis, T. J.	Rej	Kent		
Davis, Thomas Murphy Mrs.	Rej	Medina	Davis, Thomas Murphy	
Davis, W. M.	Rej	McLennan		
Davis, W. P. Mrs.	Rej	Rusk	Davis, W. P.	
Davis, William	Rej	Gonzales		
Davlin, H.	Rej	Van Zandt		
Davlin, J. P.	Rej	Robertson		
Dawdy, William A.	Rej	Medina		
Dawson, A. M.	Rej	Red River		
Dawson, Annie	Rej	Marion	Dawson, G. W. L.	
Dawson, Arizona	Rej	Harris	Dawson, Benjamin Thomas	
Dawson, Charles Wesley Mrs.	Rej	Dallas	Dawson, Charles Wesley	
Dawson, Peter Thomas	Rej	Freestone		
Dawson, Susan	Rej	Parker	Dawson, Henry Frank	
Day, B. F.	Rej	Comanche		
Day, Christina H.	Rej	Wood	Day, Joseph Richard	
Day, Ethelbert Morgan Mrs.	Rej	Henderson	Day, Ethelbert Morgan	
Day, G. J.	Rej	Shelby		
Day, H. C.	Rej	Dallas		
Day, J. N.	Rej	Wood		
Day, James D.	Rej	Wichita		
Day, N. C. Mrs.	Rej	Collin	Day, James Marshall	
Day, Robert M.	Rej	Stephens		
Day, Thomas O.	Rej	Taylor		
Dean, Annie J.	Rej	Tyler	Dean, Jesse B.	12170
Dean, J. A.	Rej	Harrison		
Dean, James Laban Mrs.	Rej	Shelby	Dean, James Laban	
Dean, N.	RejM	Limestone		
Dean, Rachel (Sarah)	Rej	Grimes	Dean, Thomas Zacheria	
Dean, T. Z.	RejM	Grimes		
Dearcy, L. A. Mrs.	RejM	Brazoria		
Dearman, Rhoda L.	Rej	Goliad	Dearman, John	
Deaton, Annie M.	Rej	Eastland	Deaton, Frank Carl	23040
Deaton, J. C.	Rej	Palo Pinto		
Deaton, J. T., Sr.	Rej	Trinity		
Deaton, Rachel	Rej	Trinity	Deaton, James Turner	
Deaver, T. M. Mrs.	RejM	Houston		
Deberry, J. W.	Rej	Leon		
Deblanc, Charlotte	Rej	Liberty	Deblanc, Louis	
Deborah, J. L. P.	Rej	Lavaca		
Debord, John H.	Rej	Lavaca		
Defoor, J. R.	Rej	Palo Pinto		
Defriend, J. B. Mrs.	Rej	Shelby	Defriend, Phillip Henry	
Delesdernier, Eliza Granger	Rej	Harris	Delesdernier, Louis Frederick	
Delhis, M. Z. Mrs.	RejM	Kaufman		
Delhom, Jean Marie	Rej	Bexar		
Dellinger, A. M.	Rej	Marion	Dellinger, Mike	
Dellinger, Sophia	Rej	Bowie	Dellinger, Cepha Crooks	
Delno, M. H. Mrs.	Rej	Wharton	Delno, O. H.	
Deloney, Lewis H.	Rej	Dewitt		
Denby, John Henry Mrs.	Rej	Sabine	Denby, John Henry	25263

Index to Rejected Confederate Pension Applications

Denmark, J. W.	Rej	Newton		
Denney, Alice Sands Pannell	Rej	Tarrant	Pannell, Charles C.	
Dennis, Caleb B.	Rej	Fannin		
Dennis, S. E. Gregory Mrs.	Rej	Mills	Gregory, Riley Burvine	
Denson, A. D.	Rej	Bell		
Denson, Nelson	Rej	Falls		
Denson, Whitfield Watson	Rej	San Jacinto		
Denton, J. W.	RejM	Newton		
Derieux, George Lewis	Rej	Childress		
Derryberry, Chris W.	Rej	Cooke		
Despain, Joseph M.	Rej	Hopkins		
Devore, Emma	Rej	Liberty	Devore, Warren	
Dewberry, T. M.	Rej	Henderson		
Dewitt, Francis L.	Rej	Hill	Dewitt, Dewitt Clinton	
Dewitt, John E.	Rej	Erath		
Dezell, John T.	Rej	Leon		
Diamond, George W.	Rej	Grayson		
Dick, A. P.	Rej	Red River		
Dick, C. H.	RejM	Austin		
Dick, John	Rej	Galveston		
Dickard, M. A.	Rej	Harrison		
Dickerson, Lizzie	Rej	San Augustine	Dickerson, John Marshall	25907
Dickey, A. J.	Rej	Tarrant		
Dickey, M. A. Mrs.	Rej	Hunt	Dickey, J. J.	
Dickey, Mary	Rej	Knox	Dickey, Robert Andrew	
Dickey, Rufus James	Rej	San Patricio		
Dickey, W. N.	Rej	Jackson		
Dickson, Bud	Rej	Harrison		
Dickson, James Benton	Rej	Shelby		
Dickson, John Brantley	Rej	Shelby		
Dickson, W. H.	Rej	Red River		
Diedrich, Auguste Mrs.	Rej	Colorado	Diedrich, Henry W.	
Dielman, F.	Rej	Marion		
Dierlem, Elmira	Rej	Calhoun	Dierlem, Christian	08038
Dierlem, John, Sr.	Rej	Calhoun		
Diesing, William	Rej	Lampasas		
Dietrich, Jack	Rej	Matagorda		
Diggs, B. H.	Rej	Childress		
Dildy, E. Robert Mrs.	Rej	Coryell	Dildy, E. Robert	35889
Dill, Lou Murray	Rej	Bexar	Dill, Charles R.	
Dillann, E. Mrs.	RejM	Bowie		
Dillard, Allan B.	Rej	Uvalde		
Dillard, H. B. Mrs.	Rej	Limestone	Dillard, Edward M.	
Dillard, Margaret Wooley	Rej	Falls	Wooley, R. C.	
Dillard, S. A. Mrs.	Rej	Parker	Dillard, John Lovett	
Dillman, F.	RejM	Marion		
Dillman, John	RejM	Calhoun		
Dimmitt, Alamo A.	Rej	Guadalupe		
Dingler, J. P.	Rej	Comanche		
Dismuke, M. A. Mrs.	Rej	Henderson	Dismuke, Robert Mosley	
Dismukes, Cora	Rej	McLennan	Dismukes, Marcus Lavett	
Dittmor, August	Rej	Austin		
Ditto, J. S.	Rej	Tarrant		
Ditto, Sarah Jane Owens	Rej	Sterling	Owens, Joe	
Dixon, Eugenia Josephine	Rej	Van Zandt	Dixon, James Tillman	
Dixon, Mary H.	Rej	Parker	Dixon, Thomas	
Dixon, Mary P.	Rej	Panola	Dixon, John W.	
Doak, Mary A.	Rej	Hill	Doak, James B.	
Dobkins, William Calloway Mrs.	Rej	Tarrant	Dobkins, William Calloway	

Index to Rejected Confederate Pension Applications

Dobson, Mary Lou	Rej	Brown	Dobson, Marshall Melton	
Docharty, L. O.	Rej	Tarrant		
Docus, Maud	RejM	Montgomery		
Dodd, J. B.	Rej	Travis		
Dodd, Joseph Washington	Rej	Fannin		
Dodd, T. C.	Rej	Matagorda		
Dodgen, Dora	Rej	Dallam	Dodgen, James Harris	29949
Dodson, Alf	Rej	Ellis		
Dodson, Elizabeth J.	Rej	Rains	Dodson, George Hampton	
Dodson, Sarah Adaline	Rej	Comanche	Dodson, William Stephens	
Doherty, Sarah Elizabeth	Rej	Bexar	Doherty, George Patrick	
Dollar, J. W.	Rej	Collingsworth		
Donald, R. Q.	RejM	Wise		
Donelson, Charles	RejM	Galveston		
Donhoo, Calvin C.	Rej	Johnson		
Donnelson, Artimisa Elizabeth	Rej	Leon	Donnelson, James Henry	
Donnerberg, Bernhard	Rej	Comal		
Donohue, Charles	Rej	Palo Pinto		
Dooley, James Luther	Rej	Williamson		
Dooling, Mary J.	Rej	Upshur	Dooling, Pat	16798
Dorgon, Margaret	Rej	Marion	Dorgon, M. V.	
Dorough, E. A. Mrs.	Rej	Van Zandt	Dorough, James Willis	
Dosier, John R.	Rej	Hardin		
Doss, J. F.	Rej	Parker		
Doss, J. L.	Rej	Mitchell		
Doss, John P.	Rej	Hill		
Doss, M. L.	Rej	Burleson		
Dossett, Larry	Rej	Comanche		
Douglas, Dora	Rej	Anderson	Douglas, William Lipscomb	05264
Douglas, Linnie M.	Rej	Fannin	Douglas, John	
Douglass, Elisha F.	Rej	Tarrant		
Douglass, F. M.	Rej	Milam		
Douglass, J. C.	Rej	Karnes		
Douglass, James W.	Rej	McLennan		
Douglass, M. J. Mrs.	Rej	Grayson	Douglass, Elbridge Garey	
Douphrate, Kate	Rej	Upshur	Douphrate, J. W.	
Downer, W. A.	Rej	Wheeler		
Downs, D. N.	Rej	Harrison		
Downs, Elizabeth	Rej	Coryell	Downs, W. A.	
Downs, J. A.	Rej	Harrison		
Downs, John Wesley	Rej	McLennan		
Downs, Matilda	Rej	Van Zandt	Downs, Charles Mitchell	12713
Downs, W. A.	Rej	Harris		
Doyle, A. E. Mrs.	RejM	Lee		
Doyle, M. S. Mrs.	Rej	Eastland	Doyle, Albert B.	
Doyle, Mary A.	Rej	Travis	Doyle, Michael J.	
Doyle, Mary J.	Rej	Callahan	Doyle, Francis W. A.	
Doyle, R. E. Mrs.	Rej	Lee	Doyle, F. H.	
Drake, Aaron	Rej	Madison		
Drake, John A.	Rej	Trinity		
Drennen, William C.	Rej	Wise		
Dreyer, Josephine	Rej	Dewitt	Dreyer, Gideon	
Driggers, James L.	Rej	Henderson		
Drummond, Charles O.	Rej	Duval		
Drury, James H.	Rej	Hall		
Dubose, Wade (William) H. Mrs.	Rej	Titus	Dubose, Wade (william) Hampton	16691
Duce, Mark Gallespy	Rej	Bastrop		
Ducos, Jean	Rej	Bexar		
Dudley, Benjamin F.	Rej	Cooke		

Index to Rejected Confederate Pension Applications

Dudley, Mary Lou	Rej	Bexar	Dudley, William Agusta F.	
Dudley, William R.	Rej	Lamar		
Duease, Katie Lavene	Rej	Hill	Duease, George Buchanan	
Dugat, Ellen	Rej	Bee	Dugat, W. S.	
Dugat, Joseph A.	Rej	Uvalde		
Duggan, Susan Elizabeth	Rej	Eastland	Duggan, Benjamin Frederick	
Duke, E. K.	Rej	Anderson		
Duke, J. F.	Rej	Denton		
Dula, D. F.	Rej	Brown		
Dulaney, William Henry	Rej	Hardeman		
Dunagan, Alfred M.	Rej	Freestone		
Dunaway, Ida	Rej	Trinity	Dunaway, Elvin	19297
Dunaway, Rebecca Clara	Rej	Wichita	Dunaway, James Cicero	
Duncan, Idella	Rej	Ellis	Duncan, William Tucker (dunkin)	19024
Duncan, Jennie	Rej	Reagan	Duncan, William Moses (dick)	
Duncan, M. A. Mrs.	Rej	Eastland	Duncan, W. B.	
Duncan, Sarah	Rej	Gonzales	Duncan, Ashley Summerfield	
Dungan, Moses H.	Rej	Collin		
Dunham, Nancy Anne Bowdoin	Rej	Guadalupe	Bowdoin, Simeon Travis	
Dunlap, David Crockett	Rej	Trinity		
Dunlap, Vonie	Rej	Nolan	Dunlap, Robert M.	
Dunlap, W. C.	Rej	Cass		
Dunman, Kate	Rej	Cameron	Dunman, Daniel	
Dunn, G. W.	Rej	McLennan		
Dunn, G. W. Mrs.	RejM	Unknown		
Dunn, Leah A.	Rej	Lampasas	Dunn, Joseph T.	
Dunn, Louise Jane	Rej	Dallas	Dunn, Luke William	
Dunnam, Alzada M.	Rej	Trinity	Dunnam, Sidney H.	
Dunnam, Viola J.	Rej	Tarrant	Dunnam, James Wesley	18406
Dunning, J. E.	Rej	Wheeler		
Dunning, Roanzy	Rej	Gregg		
Dunton, Mary	Rej	Henderson	Dunton, William Henry	
Dupree, J. E.	RejM	Fannin		
Durham, Alice	Rej	Young	Durham, Rufus Edward	
Durham, Eliza S.	Rej	Coryell	Durham, Wiley M.	
Durham, Paulina	Rej	Trinity	Durham, H. L. T.	
Durrett, Hose	Rej	Cherokee		
Durrett, William J.	Rej	Cooke		
Dutton, Josie	Rej	Coryell	Dutton, A. J. (drew)	
Duvall, Martha	Rej	Johnson	Duvall, Joseph Dabney	
Dycus, N. C. Mrs.	Rej	Williamson	Dycus, E. H.	
Dyer, D. C.	Rej	Palo Pinto		
Dyer, W. A.	Rej	Comanche		
Dykes, M. V.	Rej	Bexar		
Dykes, Martin Van Buren	Rej	Hays		
Eads, Miles A.	Rej	Haskell		
Eads, William A.	Rej	Palo Pinto		
Eaker, M. H.	Rej	Mason		
Earnest, Ann Freeman	Rej	La Salle	Earnest, Edward Waugh	
Easley, J. C.	Rej	Anderson		
Easterling, A. E.	Rej	Hamilton		
Eaton, John	Rej	Limestone		
Eaton, Lafayette	Rej	Johnson		
Eaves, Dovie	Rej	Robertson	Eaves, James Wade	16322
Eaves, W. H.	Rej	Shelby		
Ebert, James	Rej	Polk		
Ebner, Amanda F.	Rej	Bexar	Ebner, Phillip Henry	
Echols, Ellen J.	Rej	Tarrant	Echols, George	
Echols, M. S. Mrs.	Rej	Gonzales	Echols, Redmond Durcent Lee	

Index to Rejected Confederate Pension Applications

Eckman, Daniel	Rej	Williamson	—	
Eddins, Tom	Rej	Shelby	—	
Eddleman, William C.	Rej	Hill	—	
Edens, Bitha J.	Rej	Bexar	Edens, Hugh Banister	—
Edgin, Martha Jane	Rej	Mills	Edgin, Thomas Preston	Rej
Edgin, Thomas Preston	Rej	Mills	—	
Edmond, John T.	RejM	Hunt	—	
Edmonds, Alice L.	Rej	Hunt	Edmonds, William B.	—
Edmonds, Laura M.	Rej	Collin	Edmonds, James William	—
Edmondson, C. J. Mrs.	Rej	Grimes	Edmondson, John Wellington	—
Edmondson, Richard H.	Rej	Travis	—	
Edmondson, T. J.	Rej	Red River	—	
Edmondson, William	Rej	Palo Pinto	—	
Edwards, J. R.	Rej	Shelby	—	
Edwards, Lewis Henry Mrs.	Rej	Hunt	Edwards, Lewis Henry	—
Edwards, Mary E.	Rej	Coryell	—	
Edwards, Mary E.	Rej	Coryell	Edwards, William Tinsley	—
Edwards, Mattie E.	Rej	Smith	Edwards, Edwin Gray	—
Edwards, Nora	Rej	Bastrop	Edwards, Henry Clay Ben	—
Edwards, Owen C.	Rej	Sabine	—	
Edwards, Pleasant Jackson	Rej	Kaufman	—	
Edwards, W. W.	Rej	Johnson	—	
Egan, Lou G.	Rej	McLennan	Egan, Thomas	—
Eggers, Maggie E.	Rej	Jackson	Eggers, Richard	—
Eickenroth, Minna	Rej	Fort Bend	Eickenroth, William	—
Eidelbach, Andrew	Rej	Fayette	—	
Eilenstein, Josephine M.	Rej	Anderson	Eilenstein, Bernard	—
Elder, John Allen	Rej	Dallas	—	
Elder, Mary Emma	Rej	Hill	Elder, Robert McInear	—
Elder, R. M.	Rej	Hill	—	
Elder, Sarah L.	Rej	Anderson	Elder, Ferdinand Tilman Saunders	—
Eldridge, Ann H.	Rej	Limestone	Eldridge, Caleb Baker	—
Eledge, James	Rej	Johnson	—	
Elenburg, John Henry	Rej	Robertson	—	
Elkins, Amelia	Rej	Burnet	Elkins, Benjamin Franklin	—
Elkins, Margaret	Rej	Bell	Elkins, Thomas Jasper	—
Elledge, Joseph	Rej	Robertson	—	
Eller, Margeret E.	Rej	Williamson	Eller, Robert Williamson	08799
Ellerd, America Jane	Rej	Lamb	Ellerd, Thomas Jefferson	08485
Elliott, James Marchall Mrs.	Rej	Dallas	Elliott, James Marchall	11370
Elliott, L. Mrs.	RejM	Cass	—	
Elliott, M. E. Mrs.	Rej	Hardeman	Elliott, Thomas Elliott	—
Elliott, Mary I.	Rej	Harris	Elliott, Frank Lee	—
Elliott, Mary M.	Rej	Grimes	Elliott, George	—
Elliott, Penn B.	Rej	Travis	—	
Elliott, Sarah E. (Ragsdale)	Rej	Hood	Elliott, John Thomas	11962
Elliott, William Jerome Mrs.	Rej	Cherokee	Elliott, William Jerome	—
Elliott, Z. F.	Rej	Franklin	—	
Ellis, C. W.	Rej	Houston	—	
Ellis, H. W.	Rej	Runnels	—	
Ellis, M. E. Mrs.	Rej	Angelina	Ellis, Spencer Decab	—
Ellis, Mary E.	Rej	Erath	Ellis, Joel Wade	—
Ellis, Nancy	Rej	Leon	Ellis, Garland W.	—
Ellis, S. M. Mrs.	Rej	Comanche	Ellis, Thomas Jefferson	—
Ellis, William M.	Rej	Panola	—	
Ellis, William S.	Rej	Bell	—	
Ellison, Celia E.	Rej	Hunt	Ellison, Thomas Dryden	—
Ellison, W. J.	Rej	Caldwell	—	
Elrod, John Tyler	Rej	Cass	—	

Index to Rejected Confederate Pension Applications

Elrod, N. T. Mrs.	Rej	Denton	Elrod, Bird Smith	
Elston, Sarah Elizabeth	Rej	Kaufman	Elston, David E.	
Emmons, G. B.	Rej	Shelby		
Emmons, Lizzie	Rej	Callahan	Emmons, James Holman	
Emmons, Martha L.	Rej	Parker	Emmons, Isaac	
Emond, John T.	Rej	Hunt		
Emry, M. M. Mrs.	Rej	Red River	Emry, William Louis	
Endsley, M. L. Mrs.	Rej	Somervell	Endsley, William Anderson	
Engledow, Harriet C.	Rej	Smith	Engledow, Robert	06650
English, L. R. Mrs.	Rej	Houston	English, Nathaniel Phillip	15616
English, S. A. Mrs.	Rej	Hays	English, Aron	
Enloe, Mary S.	Rej	Tyler	Enloe, David Curlee	
Ensey, E. L. A.	Rej	Wise		
Epley, Daniel	Rej	Mills		
Epperson, Elizabeth	Rej	Bell	Epperson, John L.	
Epperson, George L.	Rej	Llano		
Epperson, M. C.	Rej	Terry		
Epperson, Nannie E.	Rej	Coleman	Epperson, Romulous S.	
Eppler, Edwin R.	Rej	Hamilton		
Ernst, J. W.	Rej	Bexar		
Erskine, B. H., Sr.	Rej	Zavala		
Ervin, Dock	Rej	Austin		
Erwin, S. E. Mrs.	Rej	Parker	Erwin, J. R.	
Erwin, Sarah Craig	Rej	Travis	Erwin, Thomas Douthit	
Erwin, W. H.	Rej	Jack		
Eselick, Nancy L.	Rej	Limestone	Eselick, Richard	
Eslinger, G. L.	Rej	Jones		
Espitia, Felipa R. De	Rej	Victoria	Espitia, Fernandes	43197
Essary, Levi	Rej	Madison		
Estes, R. Y.	Rej	Bosque		
Etheridge, Alletha	Rej	Ellis	Etheridge, John Lewis	
Etheridge, J. H.	Rej	Rains		
Ethetton, T. A. Mrs.	Rej	Erath	Ethetton, Stephen	
Ethridge, N. J. Mrs.	Rej	Haskell	Ethridge, Burl	
Etter, Jacob	Rej	Medina		
Etter, Sue	Rej	McLennan	Etter, Charles Miller	
Eustace, William Tomlin	Rej	Henderson		
Evans, Bettie	Rej	Bexar	Evans, Silas Adwright	
Evans, F. M.	Rej	Leon		
Evans, J. T.	Rej	Brazos		
Evans, John D.	Rej	Cherokee		
Evans, Lorena	RejM	Brazos		
Evans, Phoebe	Rej	Dallas	Evans, John S.	
Evans, Sarah W.	Rej	Brazos	Evans, John Marion	
Evans, Sue A.	Rej	Hill	Samuel Taylor, Dr.	
Evans, Thomas Jackson Mrs.	Rej	Tyler	Evans, Thomas Jackson	
Evatt, Fred Newton Mrs.	Rej	Taylor	Evatt, Fred Newton	
Everett, T. A. Mrs.	Rej	Van Zandt	Everett, John Franklin	29730
Everitt, Mary L.	Rej	Angelina	Everitt, James C.	
Evrett, Isibel	Rej	Smith	Evrett, J. S.	
Ewell, C. W.	Rej	Comanche		
Ewing, Ella	Rej	Hunt	Ewing, Shedric N.	32918
Ezell, Gillum Merit	Rej	McLennan		
Ezell, R. A.	Rej	Bee		
Fair, Eva	Rej	Brown	Fair, George Fannin	09925
Faircloth, L. A. Mrs.	Rej	Erath	Faircloth, William Harrison	20773
Fallis, T. H.	Rej	Hopkins		
Farmer, A. D.	Rej	Tarrant		
Farmer, Henry	Rej	Wise		

Index to Rejected Confederate Pension Applications

Farmer, Joseph Webster	Rej	Burleson		
Farmer, Rebecca	Rej	Milam	Farmer, George W.	
Farmer, Sarah Jane	Rej	Navarro	Farmer, Joseph Calvin	
Farrar, W. S.	Rej	Falls		
Farrell, Hugh	Rej	Harris		
Farrington, Charles Lafayette	Rej	Walker		
Farrington, William C.	Rej	Denton		
Farwell, Henry	Rej	Goliad		
Faucett, S. J. Mrs.	Rej	Lamar	Faucett, M. E.	
Faulkner, Susan P.	Rej	Milam	Faulkner, Alex C.	
Fears, James Ramsey	Rej	Cass		
Featherston, J. H.	Rej	Van Zandt		
Feazel, I. S.	Rej	Bowie		
Fellows, Anna	Rej	Wichita	Fellows, Edwin Jackson	
Felps, Jasper Newton	Rej	Hardin		
Felton, Edwin	Rej	Hopkins		
Fender, Andrew J.	Rej	Rockwall		
Fenley, James Taylor	Rej	El Paso		
Fennell, Warren J.	Rej	Upshur		
Fergason, Nickolas K.	Rej	Tarrant		
Fergerson, Virginia Angeline	Rej	Hunt	Fergerson, William Mackton	
Ferguson, Bettie	Rej	Dallas	Ferguson, Frank	
Ferguson, Hannah	Rej	Bexar	Ferguson, Daniel	
Ferguson, P. E.	Rej	McLennan		
Ferguson, Rosalie	Rej	Howard	Ferguson, William Alphanso	
Ferguson, Sarah Ellen	Rej	Erath	Ferguson, Posey Munroe	26585
Ferrell, J. H.	Rej	Dallas		
Ferrell, M. O. Mrs.	Rej	Tarrant	Ferrell, Silas H.	13522
Fiedler, John A.	Rej	Marion		
Field, L. B. Mrs.	Rej	Frio	Field, Stonton Slaughter	
Fielder, Rutha Elizabeth	Rej	Limestone	Fielder, Richmond R.	
Fields, Eller O. Mrs.	Rej	Montgomery	Fields, J. M. B.	
Fields, Maria	Rej	Coke	Fields, Levi Westly	
Fields, Martha Ann	Rej	Navarro	Fields, David Fletcher	
Fillyan, A. A.	Rej	Jasper	Fillyan, C. G.	
Fincher, J. M.	Rej	Tarrant		
Findley, David Sigar Mrs.	Rej	Rusk	Findley, David Sigar	
Finkelstein, Abe	Rej	Lavaca		
Finkley, Lyda	Rej	Hopkins	Finkley, Griffin	
Finley, Harriett R.	RejM	Dallas		
Finn, Dennis	Rej	El Paso		
Fish, R. M.	Rej	Montague		
Fisher, Robert H.	Rej	Harris		
Fite, C. C.	Rej	Tom Green		
Fite, Joseph Hiram Mrs.	Rej	Tom Green	Fite, Joseph Hiram	51356
Fitts, E. M., Sr.	Rej	Cherokee		
Fitzgerald, J. K. P.	Rej	Limestone		
Fitzhugh, Mary Jane	Rej	Collin	Fitzhugh, William	
Flanagan, James Ervin Mrs.	Rej	Ector	Flanagan, James Ervin	
Flannery, J. F.	Rej	Grayson		
Fleming, Julia	Rej	Dewitt	Fleming, Adam	
Fleming, L. H. Moody Mrs.	Rej	Cameron	Moody, Andrew D.	
Fleming, Martha E.	Rej	Collin	Fleming, G. M.	
Fletcher, F. L. Mrs.	Rej	Scurry	Fletcher, Thomas	
Fletcher, Jennie	Rej	Childress	Fletcher, Jerry Washington	39660
Fletcher, Jeptha	Rej	Hopkins		
Fletcher, Nathan J.	Rej	Baylor		
Fletcher, Ollie O.	Rej	Comanche	Fletcher, Charley Maclemore	
Fletcher, Preston	Rej	Cherokee		

Index to Rejected Confederate Pension Applications

Name	Status	County	Soldier	Number
Fletcher, Richard	Rej	Tarrant		
Fletcher, Washington Brewster	Rej	Coke		
Flippen, Andrew J.	Rej	Colorado		
Flippin, M. B.	Rej	Taylor		
Florence, E.	RejM	Upshur		
Florence, Mary Rebecca	Rej	Upshur	Florence, Wiley E.	
Florence, Sam T.	Rej	Lubbock		
Florence, Wiley E.	Rej	Upshur		
Flournoy, W. F.	Rej	San Augustine		
Flowers, H. M.	Rej	Caldwell		
Flowers, J. C.	Rej	Rains		
Flowers, James T.	Rej	Hockley		
Flowers, Susan C.	Rej	Erath	Flowers, W. A.	
Floyd, Charles	Rej	Harris		
Floyd, J. H.	Rej	Upshur		
Foehner, Louisa	Rej	Washington	Foehner, Bernard	
Follis, Thomas Hays Mrs.	Rej	Hunt	Follis, Thomas Hays	
Followill, Catherine	Rej	Wise	Followill, Moses	
Folly, E. A. Mrs.	Rej	Parker	Folly, B. F.	
Fondren, Jesse	Rej	Jasper		
Fondren, Mary Mollie	Rej	Parker	Fondren, William Scott	
Fooshee, Salvina	Rej	Fannin	Fooshee, George Washington	
Forbes, Carey A.	Rej	Tarrant	Forbes, D. F.	
Forbes, R. C.	Rej	Uvalde		
Ford, David J.	Rej	San Saba		
Ford, Elizabeth C.	Rej	Gregg	Ford, George Berryman	
Ford, Evelyn S.	Rej	Jefferson	Ford, William Hamilton	
Ford, Nancy	Rej	Milam	Ford, J. W.	
Ford, Susan Elizabeth	Rej	Lamar	Ford, James D.	25174
Ford, W. M.	Rej	San Saba		
Fore, Laura Margaret	Rej	McLennan	Fore, Archie Monroe	49903
Foreman, C. E.	Rej	Clay		
Forgason, S. A. Mrs.	Rej	Johnson	Forgason, Dixon Allen	
Forman, Samuel T.	Rej	Limestone		
Forrester, G. W.	Rej	Caldwell		
Forrester, J. M.	Rej	Parker		
Forse, Lucinda B.	Rej	San Augustine	Forse, John Smith	
Fortenberry, T. E.	Rej	Milam		
Fortson, William Green	Rej	Panola		
Foster, Benjamin Jackson	Rej	Tarrant		
Foster, J. F.	Rej	Bowie		
Foster, Martha Ann	Rej	Shelby	Foster, Lewis Thomas	
Foster, Mary E.	Rej	Comanche	Foster, Andrew Boyd	
Foster, Mary Lee	Rej	Upshur	Foster, Crayton	
Foster, T. M.	Rej	Washington		
Foster, W. A.	Rej	Eastland		
Foster, W. H.	Rej	Gonzales		
Foster, William A.	Rej	Mitchell		
Foster, William Thomas Mrs.	Rej	Bell	Foster, William Thomas	
Fowler, Hattie	Rej	Marion	Fowler, George Houston	
Fowler, Josephine	Rej	Coleman	Fowler, Bailey Butler	
Fowler, Malinda	Rej	Ellis	Fowler, Wilson	
Fowler, W. J.	Rej	Gonzales		
Fox, B. F.	Rej	Travis		
Fox, Susan Jane	Rej	San Augustine	Fox, Robert Tonoel	
Fox, V. E. Mrs.	Rej	Harris	Fox, E. E.	
Foxworth, Liddia	Rej	Upshur	Foxworth, Levi	50955
Fralick, Henry	Rej	Harris		
Francis, J. H.	Rej	Hopkins		

Index to Rejected Confederate Pension Applications

Name	Status	County	Veteran	Number
Franck, Philip	Rej	Washington	—	
Franklin, N. J.	Rej	Comanche	—	
Franklin, William M.	Rej	Frio	—	
Franks, R. H.	Rej	Coryell	—	
Franks, W. D.	Rej	Wilson	—	
Franks, W. D.	Rej	Caldwell	—	
Fraweek, D. B.	RejM	Goliad	—	
Frazer, Maud	Rej	Fayette	Frazer, William Christopher	
Frazier, J. C.	Rej	Limestone	—	
Frazier, James M.	Rej	Morris	—	
Frazier, Martha E.	Rej	Van Zandt	Frazier, Elsberry S.	
Frazier, W. J.	Rej	Tyler	—	
Frazor, E.	Rej	Mitchell	—	
Freeman, E. C. Mrs.	Rej	Navarro	Freeman, Asa Grissom	
Freeman, Mollie J.	Rej	Titus	Freeman, John Littleberry	30179
Freeman, W. W.	Rej	Dallas	—	
French, H. J.	Rej	Leon	—	
French, M. E.	Rej	Milam	—	
French, Narcissa Adeline	Rej	McLennan	French, Ervin Derius	
French, W. G.	Rej	Madison	—	
French, Wiley	Rej	Hill	—	
Frezia, Cassie Jones	Rej	Jasper	Jones, David M.	10442
Frierson, Cynthia C.	Rej	Fayette	Frierson, George Parker	
Frischmeyer, Frank	Rej	Travis	—	
Frost, James	Rej	Bowie	—	
Fruger, Frozan	Rej	Liberty	—	
Fry, F. L. Mrs.	Rej	Titus	Fry, Andrew Jackson	
Fry, Jacob	Rej	Travis	—	
Fry, James M.	Rej	Van Zandt	—	
Fry, Richard J.	Rej	Taylor	—	
Fry, Willis P.	Rej	Fannin	—	
Fuchs, Caroline Julia	Rej	Kendall	Fuchs, Herman Theodor	
Fulford, S. J.	Rej	Erath	—	
Fuller, Eller Mrs.	Rej	Bexar	Fuller, George Washington	
Fuller, Zacherias Taylor	Rej	Bell	—	
Fulmer, Mary Alice	Rej	Tarrant	Fulmer, James Adams	
Fulton, Mary E.	Rej	Galveston	Fulton, Roger Lawson	
Fulton, William	Rej	Callahan	—	
Fultz, Delilah	Rej	Shelby	—	
Fulwiler, Roxie Ann	Rej	Bell	Fulwiler, Joseph Calvin	
Funderburgh, Charity A. Boggs	Rej	Eastland	Boggs, Thomas Boone	
Funkhouser, Alice	Rej	Nueces	Funkhouser, Luther David	
Funston, Thomas D.	Rej	Lamar	—	
Fuson, Jonas Calvin Mrs.	Rej	Denton	Fuson, Jonas Calvin	43282
Fussell, Joe	Rej	Titus	—	
Fusselman, Samuel P.	Rej	Medina	—	
Fuston, Gertrude Annie	Rej	McLennan	Fuston, George Washington	
Gaddy, William M.	Rej	Dallas	—	
Gage, Bettie	Rej	Bastrop	Gage, William	
Gage, James Monroe	Rej	Menard	—	
Gahagan, Joseph	Rej	Jack	—	
Gallagher, Charles Henry	Rej	Collin	—	
Gallaher, Emma	Rej	Bexar	Gallaher, Stephen	
Gallaway, E. M. Mrs.	Rej	Coryell	Gallaway, Joe A.	
Galloway, W. J.	Rej	Polk	—	
Galloway, William H.	Rej	Wood	—	
Gamble, Bob	Rej	Franklin	—	
Gandee, E. J. Mrs.	Rej	Palo Pinto	Gandee, William Alexander	
Gant, John J.	Rej	Wise	—	

Index to Rejected Confederate Pension Applications

Garcia, Crescencia R. De	Rej	Webb	Garcia, Jose Maria	
Garcia, Juana	Rej	Atascosa	Garcia, Mariano	
Garcia, Mary	Rej	Atascosa	Garcia, Jesus	
Gardener, Charles W.	Rej	Robertson		
Gardner, J. R.	Rej	Shackelford		
Gardner, Mary S.	Rej	Limestone	Gardner, Joseph	
Gardner, Sam K.	Rej	Colorado		
Gardner, William	Rej	Henderson		
Garland, Thomas Kimber	Rej	Fisher		
Garmon, William	Rej	Bosque		
Garner, B. F.	Rej	Milam		
Garner, Elizabeth E.	Rej	Houston	Garner, William J.	
Garner, Mary J.	Rej	Comanche	Garner, Joseph A.	07457
Garretson, Hattie	Rej	Titus	Garretson, William Walter	23948
Garretson, R. G. Mrs.	Rej	Titus	Garretson, W. A.	
Garrett, Frances	Rej	Bell	Garrett, Arch P.	
Garrett, L. A. Cooper Mrs.	Rej	Lamar	Cooper, Nophlet Harris	
Garrett, M. E. Mrs.	Rej	Johnson	Garrett, Joseph Madison	
Garrett, Mary	Rej	Jefferson	Garrett, Isaac Newton	
Garrett, Mary Etta	Rej	McLennan	Garrett, Tom Calhoun	
Garrett, Nancy J.	Rej	Lamar	Garrett, J. M.	
Garrett, W. D.	Rej	Hays		
Garrett, William A.	Rej	Dickens		
Garrison, Mollie E.	Rej	Hill	Garrison, D. Levi	
Garrison, W. P.	Rej	Red River		
Garza, Juan De La	Rej	Atascosa		
Garza, Simon	Rej	Bexar		
Garza, Ygnacio	Rej	Atascosa		
Gaston, Laura J.	Rej	Cooke	Gaston, Edward Baxter	
Gatling, C. B. Mrs.	Rej	San Augustine	Gatling, George E.	
Gatling, George E.	Rej	San Augustine		
Gault, Bettie	Rej	Navarro	Gault, Samuel Bryson	
Gauntt, John W.	Rej	Henderson		
Gay, T. A.	Rej	Montgomery		
Gayle, James C.	Rej	Montgomery		
Gayler, R. T.	Rej	Fannin		
Gazler, Edwin T.	Rej	Live Oak		
Gebbert, Regina	Rej	Galveston	Gebbert, Ford	
Gee, Dora	Rej	Camp	Gee, Robert B.	13650
Gehring, Elizabeth	Rej	Harris	Gehring, Frederick William	
Gentry, G. T.	Rej	Falls		
Gentry, Jesse	Rej	Orange		
Gentry, Kinnie	Rej	Harris	Gentry, Lewis	
Gentry, M. A. Mrs.	Rej	Hardin	Gentry, Neely Wilson	
Gentry, S. E. Mrs.	Rej	Jones	Gentry, William	15809
Gentz, Lizzie	Rej	Jefferson	Gentz, Fred	
George, Charles Robert	Rej	Fort Bend		
George, E. B. Mrs.	RejM	Erath		
George, Jerusha Moffett	Rej	Bexar	George, Bowen Knox	
George, Mary M.	Rej	Hunt	George, John	
George, Thomas F.	Rej	Dallas		
George, W. R.	Rej	McLennan		
Getton, William	Rej	Dallas		
Gibbs, John M.	Rej	Wise		
Gibson, A. C. Peden Mrs.	Rej	Parker	Peden, James Knox	
Gibson, Amos	Rej	Trinity		
Gibson, H. A.	RejM	Parker		
Gibson, J. S.	Rej	Smith		
Gibson, R. P.	Rej	Uvalde		

Index to Rejected Confederate Pension Applications

Name	Status	County	Veteran	Number
Gibson, William M.	Rej	Trinity	—	—
Gidden, J. W.	Rej	Donley	—	—
Gideon, W. W.	Rej	Eastland	—	—
Giese, Hermann	Rej	Milam	—	—
Giesler, George	Rej	Uvalde	—	—
Gifford, Malinda J.	Rej	Cherokee	Gifford, Americus	—
Gilbert, A. W.	Rej	Cass	—	—
Gilbreath, Polly Ann	Rej	Cottle	Gilbreath, William David	—
Giles, Angeline	Rej	Sabine	Giles, Clark	—
Giles, James Albert	Rej	Taylor	—	—
Gill, Edmond Pressley Mrs.	Rej	Liberty	Gill, Edmond Pressley	27457
Gill, Grace	Rej	McLennan	Gill, Alexander James	—
Gill, John William	Rej	Tarrant	—	—
Gill, Martha	Rej	Fannin	Gill, Edwin Smith	—
Gill, William E.	Rej	Dallam	—	—
Gilleland, Elizabeth R.	Rej	Wood	Gilleland, John B.	—
Gillentine, M. A. Mrs.	Rej	Hamilton	Gillentine, Spencer Parker	—
Gillespie, E. A. Mrs.	Rej	Camp	Gillespie, Travis Lawry	—
Gillespie, Groves L.	Rej	Camp	—	—
Gillespie, James E.	Rej	Collin	—	—
Gillespie, Vertina	Rej	Upshur	Gillespie, Alixander T.	—
Gillespie, W. A. C.	Rej	Dallas	—	—
Gilliam, Mary A.	Rej	Cooke	Gilliam, Charles Daniel	05837
Gilliland, Henry Clay	Rej	Parker	—	—
Gilliland, J. C.	Rej	Johnson	—	—
Gilmore, Alex	Rej	Lamar	—	—
Gilmore, Sarah Ellen	Rej	Live Oak	Gilmore, Thomas Ingram	—
Gilpin, George W.	Rej	Titus	—	—
Gilpin, S. A. Mrs.	Rej	Titus	Gilpin, George Washington	—
Gipson, Jency M.	Rej	Potter	Gipson, John Leroy	08034
Gipson, Joseph Miller Mrs.	Rej	Jefferson	Gipson, Joseph Miller	—
Gipson, Matilda C.	Rej	Coke	Gipson, Jim	—
Givens, N.	Rej	Ellis	—	—
Glaeser, E.	Rej	Bexar	—	—
Glakeler, Cornelia	Rej	Jack	Glakeler, Thomas Jefferson	—
Glasgow, S. F. Mrs.	Rej	Nolan	Glasgow, T. L.	46936
Glass, Elizabeth A.	Rej	Hill	Glass, Ryman	39235
Glass, James	Rej	Brown	—	—
Glass, M. A. Mrs.	RejM	Cass	—	—
Glass, Nancy Jane	Rej	Dallas	Glass, William Josephus	—
Glass, W. F.	Rej	Coryell	—	—
Glaze, Lydia A.	Rej	Montgomery	Glaze, John Foster	—
Gleaser, E.	RejM	Bexar	—	—
Gleghorn, Abram (Dock)	Rej	Gonzales	—	—
Gleghorn, J. H.	Rej	Scurry	—	—
Glenn, W. H.	Rej	Grayson	—	—
Glover, John C.	Rej	Leon	—	—
Glover, John William	Rej	Gonzales	—	—
Glover, L. T.	Rej	Bexar	—	—
Glover, P. T.	Rej	Shackelford	—	—
Glover, W. F.	Rej	Sabine	—	—
Goad, J. O.	Rej	Clay	—	—
Godley, Martha Alice	Rej	Anderson	Godley, John Lawrence	—
Goen, Sarah Jane	Rej	Cherokee	Goen, Levi Sterling	—
Gofford, M. A. Mrs.	Rej	Jack	Gofford, James	—
Gohlke, Augusta	Rej	Dewitt	Gohlke, Fritz Rudolph	—
Golden, E.	Rej	Grayson	—	—
Golden, G. A.	Rej	McLennan	—	—
Golding, N. C.	Rej	Montgomery	—	—

Index to Rejected Confederate Pension Applications

Applicant	Status	County	Veteran	Number
Golding, Nannie D.	Rej	Montgomery	Golding, John Madison	
Gollihar, Charles Ashley	Rej	Nueces		
Gondee, W. A.	Rej	Johnson		
Gonzales, Grejonio	Rej	Cameron		
Gonzales, Martin	Rej	Webb		
Gonzales, Petra N.	Rej	Bexar	Gonzales, Santos	
Gooch, Lou G. Mrs.	Rej	Hunt	Gooch, Granville Pierce	20116
Gooch, Sarah F.	Rej	Dallas	Gooch, Nicholas	
Good, D. J.	Rej	Callahan		
Goode, A. J.	Rej	Franklin		
Goode, S. H.	Rej	Hunt		
Goodman, J. W.	Rej	Cass		
Goodman, John Claud	Rej	Nacogdoches		
Goodman, John S.	Rej	Kimble		
Goodman, Josephine Bassham	Rej	Upshur	Bassham, Leroy Filey	
Goodman, S. J. Mrs.	Rej	Cass	Goodman, Jesse Wellington	
Goodman, Sauson Rose	Rej	Jefferson	Rose, James	
Goodrum, Reuben	Rej	Waller		
Goodson, Addie	Rej	Montgomery	Goodson, James	
Goodwin, A. C. Mrs.	Rej	Fannin	Goodwin, G. H.	
Goodwin, A. M. Mrs.	Rej	Bowie	Goodwin, John	
Goodwin, Isaiah	Rej	Ellis		
Goodwin, J. G.	RejM	Rusk		
Goodwin, John Mrs.	Rej	Bowie	Goodwin, John	
Goodwin, Malissa	Rej	Houston	Goodwin, James W.	39728
Goodwin, Sarah J.	Rej	Upshur	Goodwin, J. W.	
Goolsby, G. C.	Rej	Marion		
Goolsby, Lucindy C.	Rej	Upshur	Goolsby, John David	
Gorden, A. J.	Rej	Upshur		
Gordon, Charles	Rej	Tarrant		
Gordon, James W. Mrs.	Rej	Anderson	Gordon, James W.	
Gordon, Margarett P.	Rej	Grayson	Gordon, William Alexander	
Gordon, Prairie Lee	Rej	Bexar	Gordon, John Holden	
Gore, John T.	Rej	Knox		
Gorham, Douglas G. Mrs.	Rej	Dallas	Gorham, James Calvin	
Gorham, James Cresswell Mrs.	Rej	Dallas	Gorham, James Cresswell	
Gorman, C. A.	Rej	El Paso		
Gorman, Sam	Rej	Leon		
Gorrsen, Henry	Rej	Galveston		
Goskey, J. W.	Rej	Hunt		
Gough, Frank V.	Rej	Young		
Grace, Elizabeth	Rej	Floyd	Grace, James Mathews	
Grady, Martha Jane	Rej	Wichita	Grady, Dennis Jackson	
Gragg, Eliza Ann	Rej	Gray	Gragg, Leeandsen Smith	
Graham, C. F.	Rej	San Augustine		
Graham, Charles Barton	Rej	Coryell		
Graham, E. G.	Rej	Leon		
Graham, J. H.	Rej	Lamar		
Graham, J. W.	Rej	Foard		
Graham, Jane	Rej	Brazos	Graham, George Washington	
Graham, M. C.	Rej	Jack		
Graham, S. A. Mrs.	Rej	Ellis	Graham, John Lewis	
Graves, Anna	Rej	Erath	Graves, William Dickerson	
Graves, H. B.	Rej	Hunt		
Graves, Houston Bartlett Mrs.	Rej	Tarrant	Graves, Houston Bartlett	23585
Graves, Martha Ellen	Rej	Wood	Graves, Joseph Kirkland	
Graves, Mary F.	Rej	Hopkins	Graves, John E.	
Graves, Nathaniel T. B. Mrs.	Rej	Childress	Graves, Nathaniel T. B.	
Graves, Nelson M.	Rej	Gonzales		

Index to Rejected Confederate Pension Applications

Graves, W. A.	Rej	Limestone	—	
Graves, W. A.	Rej	Taylor	—	
Gray, I. S.	Rej	Bexar	—	
Gray, Jesse S.	Rej	Cooke	—	
Gray, John	Rej	Coleman	—	
Gray, Sarah L.	Rej	Van Zandt	Gray, W. M.	
Gray, William J.	Rej	Wise	—	
Gray, William James	Rej	El Paso	—	
Gray, William T.	Rej	Tarrant	—	
Green, Aaron	Rej	Bexar	—	
Green, B. E.	Rej	Parker	—	
Green, C. E. Mrs.	Rej	Wise	Green, James	
Green, Caroline	Rej	Trinity	Green, William Perry	
Green, Elias	Rej	McLennan	—	
Green, Etta	Rej	Parker	Green, Posie Wesley G.	27443
Green, J. A.	Rej	Stonewall	—	
Green, J. M. Mrs.	Rej	Erath	Green, George Kerr	
Green, J. W.	Rej	Walker	—	
Green, Jacob T.	Rej	Upshur	—	
Green, James	Rej	Williamson	—	
Green, Lillian	Rej	Howard	Green, James Powell	
Green, Lundy T.	Rej	Nacogdoches	Green, F. P.	
Green, Sarah	Rej	Jack	Green, Seburn	08741
Green, Sarah K.	Rej	Knox	Green, John G.	
Green, T. A.	Rej	Harrison	—	
Green, William A.	Rej	Burleson	—	
Green, William A.	Rej	Parker	—	
Greene, J. I.	Rej	Scurry	—	
Greene, Sarah A.	Rej	Dallas	Greene, James T.	
Greenup, Nancy	Rej	Eastland	Greenup, William M.	
Greenwood, Edwin W.	Rej	Lampasas	—	
Greer, Emma	Rej	Wood	Greer, Young Taylor	
Greer, J. N.	Rej	Comanche	—	
Gregg, M. A. Mrs.	Rej	Guadalupe	Gregg, Oliver Hans	
Gregg, Silas	Rej	Eastland	—	
Gregory, A. D.	Rej	Lavaca	—	
Gregson, John Mrs.	Rej	Cooke	Gregson, John	
Grell, John O.	Rej	Medina	—	
Greshaw, J. H.	Rej	Nacogdoches	—	
Greshaw, J. H.	Rej	Tarrant	—	
Greve, Cladia	Rej	Brazoria	Greve, Henry	
Grice, John J.	Rej	Upshur	—	
Grice, Lewis Mrs.	Rej	Kent	Grice, Lewis	
Grier, Martha E.	Rej	Angelina	Grier, John A.	
Griffin, A. P. Mrs.	Rej	Liberty	Griffin, James Wilson	22780
Griffin, Artie	Rej	Collin	Griffin, James P.	
Griffin, Eliza Jane	Rej	Fannin	Griffin, Michael	
Griffin, F. M.	Rej	Burleson	—	
Griffin, Georgia	Rej	Gregg	Griffin, Jonas	
Griffin, J. J.	Rej	Coleman	—	
Griffin, John W. Mrs.	Rej	Jones	Griffin, John W.	20396
Griffin, L. O. Mrs.	Rej	Johnson	Griffin, Logan Monroe	19059
Griffin, Leila B.	Rej	Tarrant	Griffin, James Benjamin	
Griffin, Martha	Rej	Harris	Griffin, Joseph Ezekel	
Griffin, Mary Ann	Rej	Medina	Griffin, Henry	
Griffin, Mattie	Rej	Potter	Griffin, John R.	
Griffin, Noah	Rej	Leon	—	
Griffith, Hey B.	Rej	Liberty	—	
Griffith, M. C. Mrs.	Rej	Anderson	Griffith, Willis Marion	

Index to Rejected Confederate Pension Applications

Grigg, E. T.	Rej	Grayson		
Griggs, Annie S.	Rej	Ellis	Griggs, Charles Jordan	
Griggs, Mary A.	Rej	Williamson	Griggs, Squire Shedrick	
Grimes, Ellen	Rej	Red River	Grimes, Granville	
Grimes, George Green	Rej	Gregg		
Grimes, Hawood (Hayward) P. Mrs.	Rej	McLennan	Grimes, Hawood(ward) Pinkney	12986
Grimes, J. F.	Rej	Lamar		
Grimes, John	Rej	Parker		
Grimm, Fritz	Rej	Austin		
Grinder, Alice A.	Rej	Lamar	Grinder, Willis	
Griner, Mary M.	Rej	Newton	Griner, T. M.	
Grisham, J. W.	Rej	Cottle		
Grisham, John H.	Rej	Falls		
Grisham, T. J.	Rej	Montague		
Grissom, George W.	Rej	Cherokee		
Grissom, H. B.	Rej	Wilson		
Grissom, John L.	Rej	Rusk		
Grissom, W. B.	Rej	Titus		
Griswell, J. I.	Rej	Tarrant		
Griswold, Cora C. Smith	Rej	Bell	Smith, Hugh	
Grizzle, Sam H.	Rej	Tarrant		
Groff, Elizabeth Lemon	Rej	Medina	Lemon, Joseph	
Groner, Tillie Gilchrist	Rej	Young	Groner, William Christopher	34886
Groschke, Dora	Rej	Harris	Groschke, Emil	
Groschke, F. E.	Rej	Harris		
Groves, S. J. Mrs.	Rej	Brown	Groves, William Finley	
Grubb, Samantha	Rej	Robertson	Grubb, Ira William	08895
Grubbs, Columbus Hamilton	Rej	Orange		
Guest, M. B.	Rej	Erath		
Guest, Martin V.	Rej	Stonewall		
Guinn, Bird H.	Rej	Panola		
Guinn, Susan	Rej	Travis	Guinn, Daniel	
Gundy, Martha Malinda	Rej	Mills	Gundy, James Priestly	
Gunn, F.	Rej	Hill		
Gunter, Adelia Rhodes	Rej	Parker	Rhodes, Andrew Washington	
Gunter, Elizabeth Catherine	Rej	Freestone	Simmons, George Washington	
Gunter, John L.	Rej	Hill		
Gurley, J. A. Mrs.	Rej	Red River	Gurley, John William	
Guthrie, S. M.	Rej	Dewitt		
Gwyn, H. F.	Rej	Fisher		
Hacker, Christopher Columbus	Rej	Tarrant		
Haddox, Alexander	Rej	Wilson		
Haddox, Oliver King Mrs.	Rej	Burleson	Haddox, Oliver King	
Haden, Susan C.	Rej	Tarrant	Haden, William Alexander	
Hadley, J. M.	Rej	Bosque		
Haegelin, Joe	Rej	Medina		
Hagar, J. D.	Rej	San Saba		
Hagerman, Max	Rej	Colorado		
Haggard, James Mason	Rej	Denton		
Hagood, Eugene Chamberlain	Rej	Galveston		
Hagood, Eugene Chamberlain Mrs.	Rej	Galveston	Hagood, Eugene Chamberlain	Rej
Hahn, Jacob	Rej	Colorado		
Haidusek, August	Rej	Fayette		
Hairgrove, J. M.	Rej	Shelby		
Halbert, Phebe	Rej	Sabine	Halbert, James	
Haldy, Benjamin	Rej	Bexar		
Hale, John C. Dade Mrs.	Rej	Tarrant	Dade, Morris Horatio	
Hale, John W.	Rej	Collin		
Hale, Jonathan	Rej	Coryell		

Index to Rejected Confederate Pension Applications

Hale, Lida C.	Rej	Bosque	Hale, William Dickson	—
Hale, Minerva J.	Rej	Lampasas	Hale, Jonathan	—
Hale, R. P.	Rej	Menard	—	—
Hale, William C.	Rej	Robertson	—	—
Hales, A. D.	Rej	San Jacinto	—	—
Hales, Amanda Jane	Rej	Wichita	Hales, Warren Robert	—
Haley, Polk	Rej	Van Zandt	—	—
Haley, S. L. Mrs.	Rej	Leon	Haley, Charles Metlock	—
Haley, Thomas B.	Rej	Angelina	—	—
Haley, Thomas E.	Rej	Hill	—	—
Hall, B. C. R.	Rej	Brown	—	—
Hall, C. J. Mrs.	Rej	Cooke	Hall, Robert H.	—
Hall, C. M.	Rej	Palo Pinto	—	—
Hall, Charles	RejM	Grayson	—	—
Hall, D. W.	Rej	Williamson	—	—
Hall, Elizabeth	Rej	Harrison	Hall, William W.	—
Hall, G. H.	Rej	Cass	—	—
Hall, G. W. T.	Rej	Hamilton	—	—
Hall, J. F.	Rej	Wheeler	—	—
Hall, J. G.	Rej	Grayson	—	—
Hall, Marcus	Rej	Montgomery	—	—
Hall, Nancy	Rej	Grayson	Hall, John Garnett	—
Hall, Nancy Koon	Rej	Upshur	Koon, John Jacob	17780
Hall, Param T.	Rej	San Saba	—	—
Hall, Polly Ann	Rej	Collin	Hall, Joseph M.	—
Hall, S. D. Mrs.	Rej	Dallas	Hall, Martin	—
Hall, S. M. Mrs.	Rej	Van Zandt	Hall, Hugh Crockett	—
Hall, Sarah Samantha	Rej	Bowie	Hall, David S.	—
Hall, W. L.	Rej	Tarrant	—	—
Hall, William Alexander	Rej	Bosque	—	—
Hall, William L.	Rej	Grimes	—	—
Hall, Yancy David Mrs.	Rej	Stephens	Hall, Yancy David	—
Hallmark, T. A. Mrs.	Rej	Hardin	Hallmark, J. M.	—
Hambrick, Martha	Rej	Angelina	Ham(b)rick, John Harreson	36707
Hambright, A. E. J. Mrs.	Rej	Hamilton	Hambright, F. A.	—
Hamer, Mary D.	Rej	Fannin	Hamer, Daniel Jarman	—
Hamic, Sarah Josephine	Rej	Somervell	Hamic, Thomas Jefferson	42771
Hamilton, A. G. Mrs.	Rej	Hunt	Hamilton, Gustavas	—
Hamilton, C. J. Mrs.	Rej	Harris	Hamilton, Willis Prescott	—
Hamilton, J. C.	Rej	Tarrant	—	—
Hamilton, J. J.	Rej	Smith	—	—
Hamilton, Julia Jackson	Rej	Anderson	Jackson, Andrew Kendrick	—
Hamilton, Margaret P.	Rej	Bell	Hamilton, William	—
Hamilton, Mary E.	Rej	Cooke	Hamilton, John Ervin	26977
Hamilton, Mollie	Rej	Johnson	Hamilton, James Miles	—
Hammer, Lorena	Rej	Henderson	Hammer, Isaac	—
Hammers, Isaac	Rej	Hunt	—	—
Hammers, S. M.	RejM	Travis	—	—
Hammers, S. N.	RejM	Travis	—	—
Hammett, A. B.	Rej	Delta	—	—
Hammett, Sarah E.	Rej	Coryell	Hammett, James Calvin	—
Hammett, W. H.	Rej	Hunt	—	—
Hammock, A. D.	Rej	Fannin	—	—
Hammock, James	Rej	Crosby	—	—
Hammons, J. Henry	Rej	Bowie	—	—
Hamner, S. N.	Rej	Travis	—	—
Hamner, Sam A.	Rej	Waller	—	—
Hampil, Lila Fordtran	Rej	Gonzales	Hampil, Charles William	—
Hampton, W. G.	Rej	Cass	—	—

Index to Rejected Confederate Pension Applications

Hampton, Wade	Rej	Bexar	—	—
Hancock, J. M.	Rej	Jasper	—	—
Hancock, Levi	Rej	Callahan	—	—
Hancock, Mollie E.	Rej	Bexar	Hancock, William Henry	—
Hand, J. B.	Rej	Bandera	—	—
Handcock, Mary J.	Rej	Wichita	Handcock, James	—
Hanes, J. J.	Rej	Hunt	—	—
Haney, Malinda	Rej	Fort Bend	Haney, Jim	—
Hankens, E.	Rej	Arkansas	—	—
Hanna, E. C. Mrs.	Rej	Floyd	Hanna, Nathaniel Green	—
Hanna, E. J. Mrs.	Rej	Grayson	Hanna, W. S.	—
Hanns, J. W.	RejM	Shackelford	—	—
Hannum, O. E.	Rej	Brewster	—	—
Hanson, Lucinda	Rej	Tom Green	Hanson, A. Q.	—
Harbour, I.	Rej	Unknown	—	—
Harbour, Mintia C.	Rej	Wilbarger	Harbour, Obed Wesley	—
Hardaway, R. A. Mrs.	Rej	Franklin	Hardaway, J. T.	—
Hardcastle, S. B.	Rej	Milam	Hardcastle, Eli	—
Hardee, Bettie	Rej	Leon	Hardee, T. H.	—
Hardee, Isaiah Mrs.	Rej	Harris	Hardee, Isaiah	—
Hardegree, E. E. Mrs.	Rej	Van Zandt	Hardegree, H. L.	—
Hardegree, J. H.	Rej	Sterling	—	—
Hardin, Ben F.	Rej	Travis	—	—
Hardin, N. L. Mrs.	Rej	Archer	Hardin, Carroll	—
Harding, Thomas C.	Rej	Goliad	—	—
Hardt, Mary	Rej	Medina	Hardt, Henry	—
Hardwick, J. H., Sr.	Rej	Navarro	—	—
Hardwick, Mattie	Rej	Denton	Hardwick, Robert Joseph	—
Hardy, C. W.	Rej	Harris	—	—
Hardy, M. E. Mrs.	Rej	Houston	Hardy, John Henry	—
Hardy, Maliccie Elviny	Rej	San Augustine	Hardy, Bevley Dotson	—
Hardy, Mattie M.	Rej	Stephens	Hardy, George Washington	33167
Hare, A. R.	Rej	Morris	—	—
Hargraves, J. V.	Rej	Jefferson	—	—
Hargrove, J. M.	RejM	Shelby	—	—
Hargrove, W. D.	Rej	Travis	—	—
Hargrove, W. R.	Rej	Harrison	—	—
Harkrider, S. C. Mrs.	Rej	Titus	Harkrider, Henry	—
Harlas, W. M.	Rej	Martin	—	—
Harman, B. A.	Rej	Montgomery	—	—
Harman, J. D. P.	Rej	Montgomery	—	—
Harmon, Margaret Jane	Rej	McLennan	Harmon, William C.	—
Harp, John	Rej	Karnes	—	—
Harper, Ellen Gordon	Rej	Burleson	Harper, William Henry	—
Harper, W. R.	Rej	Tarrant	—	—
Harper, Wiley Mangrum Mrs.	Rej	Limestone	Harper, Wiley Mangrum	28054
Harral, Hugh	Rej	Lamar	—	—
Harrell, Abigail	Rej	Upshur	Harrell, Miles	—
Harrell, Mary E.	Rej	Milam	Harrell, James Abner	—
Harrington, John A.	RejM	Cass	—	—
Harrington, Mary J. H.	Rej	Bexar	Harrington, John Absolom	—
Harrington, Robert Gibson Mrs.	Rej	Randall	Harrington, Robert Gibson	—
Harris, Abraham	Rej	Tarrant	—	—
Harris, Alford	Rej	Orange	—	—
Harris, Charles Woodson	Rej	Shelby	—	—
Harris, Elizabeth	Rej	Parker	Harris, William	—
Harris, Frank M.	Rej	Angelina	—	—
Harris, Frederick Bailey Mrs.	Rej	Hale	Harris, Frederick Bailey	—
Harris, G. C.	Rej	Alabama	—	—

Index to Rejected Confederate Pension Applications

Harris, Hiram Woodward Mrs.	Rej	Stephens	Harris, Hiram Woodward	—
Harris, J. F.	Rej	Gregg	—	—
Harris, J. J.	Rej	Lee	—	—
Harris, J. R.	Rej	Wise	—	—
Harris, John F. Mrs.	Rej	Gregg	Harris, John F.	—
Harris, Joseph Henry	Rej	Lampasas	—	—
Harris, Ludie	Rej	Denton	Harris, Lewis Gray	32555
Harris, Mary Jane	Rej	San Jacinto	Harris, Wright	—
Harris, Mary Jane Beck	Rej	Montague	Beck, William James	—
Harris, N. C. Mrs.	Rej	Johnson	Harris, John	—
Harris, Naomi Isabelle	Rej	San Saba	Harris, Charles Buchanan	—
Harris, Nellie J.	Rej	Jackson	Harris, Henry Clay	41843
Harris, Richard	Rej	San Patricio	—	—
Harris, Sarah Elizabeth	Rej	Palo Pinto	Harris, Peter Eldridge	—
Harris, Thomas J.	Rej	Matagorda	—	—
Harris, Waller Fosgate Mrs.	Rej	Harris	Harris, Waller Fosgate	—
Harris, William Thomas	Rej	Edwards	—	—
Harris, William Thomas Mrs.	Rej	Denton	Harris, William Thomas	—
Harrison, Emma	Rej	Lampasas	Harrison, James H.	—
Harrison, G. W.	Rej	Lynn	—	—
Harrison, Harriett H.	Rej	Upshur	Harrison, Abram	—
Harrison, Ira Hubbard	Rej	Hopkins	—	—
Harrison, Reuben	Rej	Harris	—	—
Harrison, Sallie W.	Rej	Eastland	Harrison, Andrew Jackson	—
Harrison, Sarah Eveline	Rej	Cottle	Harrison, Robert Dennis	—
Harrison, William B.	Rej	Austin	—	—
Harry, Nancy Ann	Rej	Hopkins	Harry, John Thomas	—
Hart, Aron	Rej	Grayson	—	—
Hart, Emily L.	Rej	Hall	Hart, William Harrison	—
Hart, J. C. Mrs.	Rej	Hunt	Hart, Richard Syrus	—
Hart, Kate	Rej	Harris	Hart, Henry	—
Hart, Margaret V.	Rej	Robertson	Hart, C. C.	—
Hart, Rosa Arbelle	Rej	Collin	Hart, George Russell	39709
Hart, Stephen C.	Rej	Foard	—	—
Hart, William A.	Rej	Mason	—	—
Hart, Zachary Taylor Mrs.	Rej	Harris	Hart, Zachary Taylor	—
Hartley, Abigail	Rej	Limestone	Hartley, James	—
Hartley, W. C.	Rej	Tom Green	—	—
Harvey, S. J. Mrs.	Rej	Freestone	Harvey, A. S.	—
Harvey, William	Rej	Titus	—	—
Harvin, R. A.	Rej	Brazoria	—	—
Harwell, A. C.	Rej	Denton	—	—
Hash, B. H.	Rej	Dickens	—	—
Haskins, T. E.	Rej	Leon	—	—
Hassell, Joseph D. Mrs.	Rej	Childress	Hassell, Joseph D.	—
Hatch, Joseph A.	Rej	Bexar	—	—
Hatchel, H. G.	Rej	Bowie	—	—
Hatcher, Darling Greene	Rej	Caldwell	—	—
Hatcher, Stephen	Rej	Jefferson	—	—
Hatfield, Ephraim	Rej	Grayson	—	—
Hathorne, M. A.	Rej	Trinity	—	—
Hatter, N. A. Mrs.	Rej	Freestone	Hatter, John Lewis	—
Hatton, Laura	Rej	Van Zandt	Hatton, Markus Lafayette	11775
Hauenstein, J. J.	Rej	Harrison	—	—
Hawes, Magdalene Cook	Rej	Smith	Cook, Abraham James	28038
Hawkins, E. P. Mrs.	Rej	Clay	Hawkins, L. N.	—
Hawkins, Evaline	Rej	Grayson	Hawkins, Andrew	—
Hawkins, Louiza Prudence	Rej	Collingsworth	Hawkins, Lee N.	—
Hawkins, Margaret Ellen	Rej	Travis	Hawkins, Robert Brown	25839

Index to Rejected Confederate Pension Applications

Hawkins, Rachael Rebecca	Rej	Hill	Hawkins, Perry Oliver	—
Hawkins, Richard G.	Rej	Harris	—	—
Hay, Katie	Rej	Stonewall	Hay, Thomas Crawford	—
Hayes, Emma	Rej	Robertson	Hayes, Allen Anderson	—
Haygood, Jennie E.	Rej	Titus	Haygood, George Henry	18424
Haynes, G. W.	Rej	Jasper	—	—
Haynes, Robert H.	Rej	Kaufman	—	—
Haynes, S. J. Mrs.	Rej	Wheeler	Haynes, Jessie Franklin	—
Hays, D. A.	Rej	Childress	—	—
Hays, Elizabeth White	Rej	Tom Green	White, Robert	—
Hays, John M. Mrs.	Rej	Rusk	Hays, John M.	—
Hays, Mary A. Lowe	Rej	Wilbarger	Lowe, Benjamin Franklin	—
Hays, Mary C.	Rej	Denton	Hays, George Madison	02924 Missing
Hays, Ophelia	Rej	Bowie	Hays, Daniel	—
Hays, Sarah T.	Rej	Tarrant	Hays, William Jordan	—
Hays, W. S.	Rej	Henderson	—	—
Hays, William	Rej	Jefferson	—	—
Head, Fannie A.	Rej	Limestone	Head, J. R.	—
Head, L. M.	Rej	Johnson	—	—
Headen, Benjamin Franklin	Rej	McLennan	—	—
Heard, Demarius Virginia	Rej	Orange	Heard, John William	—
Heard, G. S.	Rej	Hardin	—	—
Heard, Hattie	Rej	Callahan	Heard, Autrey Washington	—
Heard, P. M.	Rej	Kaufman	—	—
Hearne, George	Rej	Shelby	—	—
Hearne, James Alford	Rej	Tarrant	—	—
Heath, Annie	Rej	Rusk	Heath, W. C.	—
Heath, Cora B.	Rej	Montague	Heath, Samuel Franklin	—
Heatley, Coleman	Rej	Stephens	—	—
Hedgpeth, M. L. Mrs.	Rej	Grayson	Hedgpeth, Robert Franklin	—
Heflen, Lizzie	Rej	Chambers	Heflen, Joe	21344
Heflin, M. L.	Rej	Sutton	—	—
Hefner, J. L.	Rej	Young	—	—
Hein, Sophie	Rej	Bexar	Hein, Ferdinand	—
Heins, Theodore E.	Rej	Gonzales	—	—
Helm, Indiana	Rej	Parker	Helm, William Newton	39885
Helmke, Fritz	Rej	Comal	—	—
Helms, Missouri Catherine	Rej	Erath	Helms, William Jacob	—
Helton, C. R. A. Mrs.	Rej	Tarrant	Helton, Joseph	—
Helton, J. N.	Rej	Bosque	—	—
Helton, James Counts	Rej	Cottle	—	—
Helton, James Counts Mrs.	Rej	Crosby	Helton, James Counts	Rej
Helton, Peter	Rej	Ellis	—	—
Henck, Fred	Rej	Galveston	—	—
Henderson, A. C. Mrs.	Rej	Freestone	Henderson, William Henry	—
Henderson, Huston	Rej	Limestone	—	—
Henderson, J. F.	Rej	Erath	—	—
Hendley, Joshua	Rej	Henderson	—	—
Hendley, Mary E.	Rej	Smith	Hendley, William Riley	21806
Hendrick, Thomas A.	Rej	Bastrop	—	—
Hendricks, Abe S.	Rej	Jefferson	—	—
Hendricks, William	Rej	Coke	—	—
Hendrix, George W.	Rej	Polk	—	—
Hendrix, Susan M.	Rej	Grayson	Hendrix, Jesse Elvis	—
Henley, Haseltine	Rej	Van Zandt	Henley, Licurgus	—
Henley, James A.	Rej	Brown	—	—
Henry, Andrew	Rej	Red River	—	—
Henry, Anna H.	Rej	Hardin	Henry, John Sampson	08059

Index to Rejected Confederate Pension Applications

Henry, W. F.	Rej	Coryell	—	—
Henshaw, John	Rej	Bexar	—	—
Henslee, Mary E.	Rej	Dallas	Henslee, William George	—
Hensley, George	Rej	Red River	—	—
Henson, Ellen Strawn	Rej	Delta	Strawn, Andrew Jackson	—
Henson, Isiah	Rej	Sabine	—	—
Herbert, J. H.	Rej	Tom Green	—	—
Herod, Elvira	Rej	Limestone	Herod, Thomas Jefferson	—
Herod, G. I.	Rej	Limestone	—	—
Herran, Margaret E.	Rej	Dallas	Herran, George Alexander	—
Herrera, Natividad	Rej	Webb	—	—
Herrin, S. W.	Rej	Hamilton	—	—
Herring, Absolum White	Rej	Motley	—	—
Herring, H. L.	Rej	Limestone	—	—
Herring, Mary Etter	Rej	Palo Pinto	Herring, Benjamin Timmins	—
Herrington, Catherine	Rej	Angelina	Herrington, James	—
Herrington, M. L. Mrs.	Rej	Anderson	Herrington, James Jasper	—
Herrington, Susannah	Rej	Anderson	Herrington, Allen Lafayette	—
Herrod, Robert McDaniel Mrs.	Rej	Johnson	Herrod, Robert McDaniel (herod)	21811
Hertz, Louis W.	Rej	Harris	—	—
Hester, Ida Qualls	Rej	Harris	Qualls, George Shaffer	—
Hester, James P.	Rej	Brown	—	—
Hester, Sarah Elizabeth	Rej	Mills	Hester, William Richard	—
Hewett, George Walton	Rej	McLennan	—	—
Hewitt, W. M.	Rej	Hill	—	—
Hibbitts, Wagie	Rej	Brown	Hibbitts, Luther Thomas	—
Hickey, Levi O. T.	Rej	Tarrant	—	—
Hickman, Katy	Rej	San Jacinto	Hickman, William Martin	—
Hickman, M. E. Mrs.	Rej	Harris	Hickman, James Reily	—
Hickman, R. D.	RejM	Rains	—	—
Hicks, I. M.	Rej	Bowie	—	—
Hicks, J. M.	Rej	Cass	—	—
Hicks, John McFarland Mrs.	Rej	Cass	Hicks, John McFarland	—
Hicks, Lydia	Rej	Shelby	Hicks, Edward Stephens	—
Hicks, Mary	Rej	Erath	Hicks, Robert William	25046
Hicks, T. N.	Rej	Grayson	—	—
Higdon, Thomas	Rej	Dallas	—	—
Higginbotham, Laura J.	Rej	Anderson	Higginbotham, William Franklin	31106
Higginbotham, S. R.	Rej	Hill	—	—
Higgins, Ephfum	Rej	Red River	—	—
Higgins, James Bright Mrs.	Rej	Ellis	Higgins, James Bright	—
Higgins, James E.	Rej	Hill	—	—
High, Ella Reid	Rej	Navarro	High, Robert Alford	35997
Highsmith, Catherine	Rej	Kimble	Highsmith, William	—
Highsmith, Francis E.	Rej	Bastrop	Highsmith, M. B.	—
Hight, J. H.	Rej	Harris	—	—
Hightower, K. H. Mrs.	Rej	Grayson	Hightower, W. C.	—
Hightower, Virginia N.	Rej	Rusk	Hightower, R. D.	—
Hignett, Mary	Rej	El Paso	Hignett, James	—
Hilbun, E. B.	Rej	Taylor	—	—
Hildebrandt, Dora	Rej	Dewitt	Hildebrandt, Edward Emil	—
Hildreth, J. D.	Rej	Lamar	—	—
Hill, C. F. Mrs.	Rej	Lamar	Hill, William Sanders	25702
Hill, Dosia Jane	Rej	Harrison	Hill, John Thomas	43183
Hill, Finis Campbell	Rej	Parker	—	—
Hill, G. B.	Rej	Cass	—	—
Hill, J. A.	Rej	Clay	—	—
Hill, James Martin	Rej	Ellis	—	—
Hill, Jesse E.	Rej	Fisher	—	—

Index to Rejected Confederate Pension Applications

Hill, John N.	Rej	Bell	—	—
Hill, L. L.	Rej	Rusk	—	—
Hill, Mary	Rej	Wise	Hill, Henry Harry	23173
Hill, Mary M.	Rej	Montague	Hill, Jacob Warren	—
Hill, S. P. Mrs.	Rej	Donley	Hill, Green Washington	—
Hill, Sarah W.	Rej	Harris	Hill, John Edwin	—
Hill, Thomas	Rej	Kaufman	—	—
Hill, W. H.	Rej	Harris	—	—
Hilley, Thomas Jefferson Mrs.	Rej	Dallas	Hilley, Thomas Jefferson	—
Hilliard, Harriet T.	Rej	Tarrant	Hilliard, Levi Napoleon Boneparte	—
Hillis, Sarah D.	Rej	Tom Green	Hillis, Stephen H.	—
Hines, H. E.	Rej	Lamar	—	—
Hines, J. M.	Rej	San Augustine	—	—
Hines, L. Mrs.	Rej	Limestone	Hines, James Hightower	—
Hinnard, L. S.	Rej	Coleman	—	—
Hinson, Annie	Rej	Brewster	Hinson, William Wallace	—
Hinson, S.	Rej	Trinity	—	—
Hinyard, Rufus	Rej	San Saba	—	—
Hitt, Amanda M.	Rej	McLennan	Hitt, Samuel James	—
Hittson, Eliza	Rej	Eastland	Hittson, William Daniel	—
Hobbs, Jesse C.	Rej	Parker	—	—
Hocker, Lillian	Rej	Caldwell	Hocker, Obe R.	00634
Hodge, Agnes P.	Rej	Fannin	Hodge, Thomas Garrett	—
Hodge, J. M.	Rej	Hopkins	—	—
Hodge, W. W. Edwards Mrs.	Rej	Erath	Edwards, James Allen	—
Hodges, Bettie	Rej	Stephens	Hodges, Riley Jordan	—
Hodges, Emily C.	Rej	Hunt	Hodges, Alfred Johnson	—
Hodges, H. C.	Rej	Henderson	—	—
Hodges, James R.	Rej	Harrison	—	—
Hodges, L. H.	Rej	Hall	—	—
Hodges, Soloman G.	Rej	Motley	—	—
Hodnett, John Foster Mrs.	Rej	Scurry	Hodnett, John Foster	—
Hoffman, Matilda	Rej	Harris	Hoffman, John Christopher	—
Hohle, Mathias	Rej	Austin	—	—
Hokett, J. H.	Rej	Parker	—	—
Holbert, Phebe	RejM	Sabine	—	—
Holbrook, Mary I.	Rej	Gregg	Holbrook, Milo Franklin	—
Holbrook, Treasey Ann	Rej	Smith	Holbrook, Jesse	—
Holcomb, W. T.	Rej	Hill	—	—
Holcombe, M. E. Mrs.	Rej	Wilson	Holcombe, Eli B.	26749
Holcount, J. H.	RejM	Houston	—	—
Holcount, W. T.	RejM	Hill	—	—
Holcroft, Nora	Rej	Dallas	Holcroft, Robert N.	18908
Holden, Emily E.	Rej	McLennan	Holden, Daniel Webster	36144
Holden, James	Rej	Tarrant	—	—
Holder, James Madison Mrs.	Rej	Travis	Holder, James Madison	—
Holder, Noah	Rej	Dallas	—	—
Holder, Rachel	RejM	Orange	—	—
Holder, W. Henry	Rej	Anderson	—	—
Holdredge, M. W. Mrs.	Rej	Scurry	Holdredge, George Washington	—
Holland, D. R.	Rej	Hemphill	—	—
Holland, M. P. Mrs.	Rej	Cass	Holland, James Madison	—
Holland, M. W.	Rej	Leon	—	—
Holland, Martha J.	Rej	Brown	Holland, John William	—
Holland, Mary T.	Rej	Bell	Holland, James Reuben	—
Holland, Thomas Taylor	Rej	Henderson	—	—
Hollaway, P. A.	Rej	Tyler	—	—
Hollaway, Sarah E.	RejM	Navarro	—	—
Holley, J. H.	Rej	Mitchell	—	—

Index to Rejected Confederate Pension Applications

Hollingsworth, M. M. Mrs.	Rej	Uvalde	Hollingsworth, Daniel	
Hollingsworth, W. M.	Rej	Potter	—	
Hollis, Malissa	Rej	Wood	Hollis, John Robinson	
Holloway, Fay	Rej	Hill	Holloway, John Vinson	
Holloway, John P.	Rej	Callahan	—	
Holloway, Joseph Silas	Rej	Gonzales	—	
Holly, Polk	RejM	Van Zandt	—	
Holly, W. G.	Rej	Marion	—	
Holman, Henrietta	Rej	San Augustine	Holman, Monroe	
Holmes, A. J.	Rej	Leon	—	
Holmes, E. W.	Rej	Travis	—	
Holmes, Elizabeth F.	Rej	Palo Pinto	Holmes, Robert	
Holmes, J. C.	Rej	Brazos	—	
Holmes, Mary E.	Rej	Somervell	Holmes, William Kensey	
Holmes, W. F.	Rej	Tyler	—	
Holt, Charles	Rej	Grayson	—	
Holt, Elenora Elvira Doyle	Rej	Lubbock	Holt, Constance (constant) William	25280
Holt, Jadie	Rej	Camp	Holt, Oliver Tate	
Holt, Mary Rushia	Rej	Lamar	Holt, John Evert	
Holton, L.	Rej	Goliad	—	
Honacker, Rosa	Rej	Hunt	Honacker, Patrick	
Hood, Leila Evans	Rej	Tarrant	Hood, William Jordan	
Hood, Sarah Jane	Rej	Austin	Hood, Perry C.	
Hooker, Lewis William	Rej	Eastland	—	
Hookett	RejM	Parker	—	
Hooks, Fannie	Rej	Gregg	Hooks, John Wesly	24270
Hooks, Hannah	Rej	Wood	Hooks, Joseph Thomas	
Hooks, J. F.	Rej	Hill	—	
Hooks, James Carroll Mrs.	Rej	Falls	Hooks, James Carroll	
Hooks, N. B.	Rej	Tyler	—	
Hooper, E. M.	Rej	Lee	—	
Hooper, Joseph Monroe Mrs.	Rej	Delta	Hooper, Joseph Monroe	
Hoover, Sarah	Rej	Upshur	Hoover, George Jefferson	
Hopkins, H. B.	Rej	Runnels	—	
Hopkins, J. S.	Rej	Sabine	—	
Hopkins, L. H.	Rej	Kaufman	—	
Hopper, E. M.	RejM	Lee	—	
Hopson, Louisa J.	Rej	Brown	Hopson, Wiley Martin	
Horn, Harriet	Rej	Jasper	Horn, John A. M.	
Horn, James	Rej	Leon	—	
Horne, Jane	Rej	Taylor	Horne, Thomas S.	
Horne, Robert M.	Rej	Potter	—	
Horne, T. J.	Rej	Orange	—	
Horton, Eda Rawls	Rej	San Augustine	Rawls, Dan	
Horton, James Graham Mrs.	Rej	Real	Horton, James Graham	
Horton, Jane	Rej	Montgomery	Horton, William	
Horton, M. P. Mrs.	Rej	Delta	Horton, John Elmore	
Horton, Roena Mayberry	Rej	McLennan	Mayberry, Josua Patterson	
Horton, S. H.	Rej	Dallas	—	
Horton, Thomas	Rej	Angelina	—	
Houchin, William A.	Rej	Johnson	—	
House, Elizabeth Catherine	Rej	Collin	House, William Richard	
House, Fred Mrs.	Rej	Medina	House, Fred	
House, J. H.	Rej	Mitchell	—	
House, Jane	RejM	Taylor	—	
House, Larnch	Rej	Tarrant	—	
House, Levina Emaline	Rej	Tarrant	House, Peter Martin	
Houshell, Abbie	Rej	Brown	Houshell, Martin V.	
Houston, A. L.	Rej	Travis	—	

Index to Rejected Confederate Pension Applications

Houston, J. T.	Rej	Clay	—	—
Howard, Elizabeth Rebecca	Rej	Anderson	Howard, James Edward	—
Howard, J. W.	Rej	San Jacinto	—	—
Howard, L. C.	Rej	Brown	—	—
Howard, M.	Rej	Hardeman	—	—
Howard, R. W.	Rej	Nolan	—	—
Howard, Sarah J.	Rej	Wilbarger	Howard, Madison	—
Howard, W. J.	Rej	Kaufman	—	—
Howard, W. M.	Rej	Tarrant	—	—
Howard, W. R.	Rej	Waller	—	—
Howell, A. C.	RejM	Tarrant	—	—
Howell, Amanda M.	Rej	Collin	Howell, J. P.	—
Howell, Elizabeth	Rej	Fisher	Howell, William David	—
Howell, H. W.	Rej	Coryell	—	—
Howell, Joe	Rej	Hays	—	—
Howell, Sarah	RejM	Upshur	—	—
Howell, Sarah Shain	Rej	Collin	Howell, John Edward	—
Howell, Setha Jane	Rej	Tarrant	Howell, D. T.	—
Howeth, Thomas Wesley	Rej	Freestone	—	—
Howland, Thomas Jefferson	Rej	Bexar	—	—
Hudgins, J. C.	Rej	Tarrant	—	—
Hudman, B. T.	Rej	Coke	—	—
Hudman, Lucindia	Rej	Travis	Hudman, Henry Alvin Harrison	—
Hudman, Susan M.	Rej	Kaufman	Hudman, Joseph J.	—
Hudson, Francis Jane	Rej	Delta	Hudson, H. H.	—
Hudson, Joe Decen Mrs.	Rej	Anderson	Hudson, Joe Decen	27376
Hudson, S. H.	Rej	Karnes	—	—
Hudson, Z. T.	Rej	Foard	—	—
Hudspeth, Mary E.	Rej	Harrison	Hudspeth, Thomas H.	—
Huebner, Henrietta E.	Rej	Harris	Huebner, Philip	—
Huegele, Regina	Rej	Medina	Huegele, Albert	—
Huff, John H.	Rej	McCulloch	—	—
Huff, Kate Jane	Rej	Hemphill	Huff, Ransom Frances	—
Huff, O. N. Mrs.	Rej	Sutton	Huff, J. B.	—
Huff, R. J.	Rej	Palo Pinto	—	—
Huff, S. M. D.	Rej	Nolan	—	—
Huffman, Elizabeth Jane	Rej	Lipscomb	Huffman, James Erastmus	—
Huffman, J. F.	Rej	Hunt	—	—
Huffor, G. A.	Rej	Gonzales	—	—
Huggins, M. E.	Rej	Hood	—	—
Huggins, R. J. Mrs.	Rej	Brown	Huggins, W. B.	—
Huggins, W. J.	Rej	Smith	—	—
Hughes, Anna Belle	Rej	Cass	Hughes, James Wilkins	—
Hughes, Ida V.	Rej	Lamar	Hughes, Byron	10956
Hughes, J. G.	Rej	Edwards	—	—
Hughes, Margaret I.	Rej	Hunt	Hughes, R. M.	—
Hughes, Minnie G.	Rej	Trinity	Hughes, John Allen	—
Hughes, Oins	Rej	Dewitt	—	—
Hughes, Robert Newton	Rej	Fisher	—	—
Hughes, Sallie Eliza	Rej	Shelby	Hughes, Leonard Vinson	—
Hughston, W. P.	Rej	Red River	—	—
Huling, Mary G.	Rej	Tom Green	Huling, George Sterling	—
Hull, Matt O.	Rej	Mills	—	—
Hull, Micaja Lewis	Rej	Sterling	—	—
Hullett, Sarah J.	Rej	Wise	Hullett, Benjamin Eaton	—
Hulon, Jennie	Rej	Montgomery	Hulon, James William	—
Hulzler, Martin	RejM	Medina	—	—
Humberson, Francis Abbygail	Rej	Erath	Humberson, Andrew Welton	—
Humphreys, Emma	Rej	Tom Green	Humphreys, James Polk	—

Index to Rejected Confederate Pension Applications

Humphreys, P. G.	Rej	Wood	
Humphries, Charles S.	Rej	Baylor	
Humphries, I. L. Mrs.	Rej	Hunt	Humphries, Thomas Johnson
Humphries, Mattie	Rej	Comanche	Humphries, Charles Burton ... 43837
Humphries, Permelia A.	Rej	Bowie	Humphries, Zacriah Taylor
Humphries, Sarah S.	Rej	Live Oak	Humphries, Henry Jackson
Hunley, W. L.	Rej	Tom Green	
Hunt, A. B.	Rej	Bexar	
Hunt, H. M.	Rej	Hardin	
Hunter, Edward A.	Rej	Dallas	
Hunter, James M.	Rej	Edwards	
Hunter, John H.	Rej	Harris	
Hunter, Judson	Rej	Jones	
Hunter, Mary L.	RejM	Dallas	
Hunter, William Alston	Rej	McLennan	
Husbands, Narcissa	Rej	Newton	Husbands, William Penington
Hutcheson, Matthew Franklin	Rej	Grayson	
Hutcheson, R. M.	Rej	Tom Green	
Hutchings, Stockely	RejM	Unknown	
Hutchinson, A.	Rej	Nacogdoches	
Hutchinson, Mary Lehmann	Rej	Bexar	Lehmann, Joseph
Hutto, Angeline	Rej	Trinity	Hutto, James Asberry
Hutzler, Martin	Rej	Medina	
Hyatt, Sarah Margaret	Rej	Lubbock	Hyatt, J. C.
Hyatte, John	Rej	Bowie	
Hyde, Ephraim P.	Rej	Grimes	
Hyles, E. A.	Rej	Grayson	
Inglehart, C. C. Mrs.	Rej	Matagorda	Inglehart, Edward Julius
Ingraham, Sallie	Rej	Cass	Ingraham, John Spencer
Ingram, C. A. Mrs.	Rej	Lamar	Ingram, T. R.
Ingram, Fannie	Rej	Limestone	Ingram, Samuel Columbus
Ingram, J. B.	Rej	Parker	
Ingram, M. A. Mrs.	Rej	Baylor	Ingram, John Thomas
Inman, Francis	Rej	Clay	Inman, William Joseph
Inman, James Benjamin	Rej	Trinity	
Ireson, Maggie E.	Rej	Wharton	Ireson, Lansford Orville
Irvin, Bettie M.	Rej	Grayson	Irvin, A. G.
Irving, E. V. Mrs.	Rej	Kerr	Irving, Richard Jones
Irwin, Sarah Cook	Rej	Bexar	Cook, Calvin Clark
Isaacks, Wesley Carroll	Rej	Bastrop	
Isbell, Richard Monroe	Rej	Upshur	
Isham, Rosey	Rej	Tarrant	Isham, Washington Marion
Ivey, Alexander Campbell	Rej	Travis	
Ivy, Mahaza R. A.	Rej	Navarro	Ivy, John W.
Ivy, Quitman	Rej	Nolan	
Jackson, B. J.	Rej	Grayson	
Jackson, J. A.	Rej	Leon	
Jackson, James T.	Rej	Henderson	
Jackson, John Adams	Rej	Denton	
Jackson, Levi	Rej	Coryell	
Jackson, M. J. Cammack Mrs.	Rej	Bosque	Cammack, James Curelton
Jackson, Mary E.	Rej	Delta	Jackson, James Washington
Jackson, Rebecca J.	Rej	Smith	Jackson, William A.
Jackson, Rufus	Rej	Jefferson	
Jackson, William A.	Rej	Goliad	
Jacobs, William	Rej	Van Zandt	
Jamasch, John	Rej	Galveston	
Jamerson, J. W.	Rej	Bosque	
James, A. J.	Rej	Grayson	

Index to Rejected Confederate Pension Applications

Name	Status	County	Veteran	Number
James, E. J. Mrs.	Rej	Harris	James, John W.	
Janisch, H.	Rej	Harris		
Janszen, Anna	Rej	Fayette	Janszen, Friedrich August	
Jarratt, Frankie	Rej	Ellis		
Jarratt, N. C. Mrs.	Rej	Cherokee	Jarratt, Henry Morris	
Jarrell, William Millner	Rej	Fannin		
Jarvis, G. W.	Rej	Bowie		
Jasper, William	RejM	Wilbarger		
Jay, Julia Hines	Rej	Carson	Hines, Pinkney Littleberry	
Jeffers, Martin V.	Rej	El Paso		
Jefferson, Sy, Sr.	Rej	Ellis		
Jenkins, J. W.	Rej	Brown		
Jenkins, Roxie	Rej	Bell	Jenkins, Thomas Jefferson	
Jennings, G. W.	Rej	Wise		
Jennings, Isham R.	Rej	McLennan		
Jennings, Mandy E.	Rej	Van Zandt	Jennings, Stephens Allen	
Jennings, Mollie	Rej	Knox	Jennings, S. R.	
Jennings, Sanford	Rej	Blanco		
Jennings, T. M.	Rej	McLennan		
Jennings, William R.	Rej	Grayson		
Jergins, Elizabeth	Rej	Walker	Jergins, Jesse J.	
Jergins, Jesse J.	Rej	Walker		
Jernigan, Mary Davis	Rej	Armstrong	Jernigan, George Washington	
Jernigan, W. A.	Rej	Trinity		
Jett, James B.	Rej	Collin		
Jetton, Samuel B.	Rej	Montague		
Jinkins, Matilda	Rej	Hardeman	Jinkins, Jasper	
Jirou, Mary	Rej	Hardin	Jirou, Joseph	
Jirou, Mollie	Rej	Harris	Jirou, Joseph	
Johnson, A. A. Mrs.	Rej	Rusk	Johnson, A. A.	
Johnson, Addison	Rej	San Jacinto		
Johnson, Amanda E.	Rej	Hopkins	Johnson, John Olliver	
Johnson, Dud	Rej	Henderson		
Johnson, E. W.	Rej	Travis		
Johnson, Elisha Cook Mrs.	Rej	Hill	Johnson, Elisha Cook	
Johnson, Francis	Rej	Kaufman	Johnson, Felix Robert	
Johnson, Frank E.	Rej	Cooke		
Johnson, G. W.	Rej	Bosque		
Johnson, Hellen	Rej	Young	Johnson, William	
Johnson, Iasham Allen	Rej	Bailey		
Johnson, J. B.	Rej	Harris		
Johnson, J. F.	RejM	Eastland		
Johnson, J. H.	Rej	Kaufman		
Johnson, Jack	Rej	Upshur		
Johnson, James P.	Rej	Lubbock		
Johnson, John Numun, Sr. Mrs.	Rej	Cherokee	John Numun, Sr.	23680
Johnson, Josephine	Rej	Galveston	Johnson, Benjamin Franklin	
Johnson, Kitty	Rej	Bosque	Johnson, Houston Bruten	
Johnson, L. E. Mrs.	Rej	Anderson	Johnson, John William	
Johnson, M. W.	Rej	Denton		
Johnson, Marinda	Rej	Donley	Johnson, Nehemiah	
Johnson, Mary Angeline	Rej	Delta	Johnson, George Walker	
Johnson, Mary E.	Rej	Harris	Johnson, J. W.	
Johnson, Mary M.	RejM	Johnson		
Johnson, Miles L.	Rej	El Paso		
Johnson, Nancy Adaline	Rej	Camp	Johnson, Linton Zadock	
Johnson, Nancy Caroline	Rej	Haskell	Johnson, William Riley	
Johnson, Nancy Elizabeth	Rej	Cass	Johnson, Jacob David	
Johnson, R. R.	Rej	Tom Green		

Index to Rejected Confederate Pension Applications

Johnson, R. W.	Rej	Bowie	—	—
Johnson, Renney	Rej	Nolan	—	—
Johnson, S. E. Mrs.	Rej	Cherokee	Johnson, Benjamin Alexander	—
Johnson, Sarah Harris	Rej	Brown	Johnson, William Green	—
Johnson, Silas B.	Rej	Stonewall	—	—
Johnson, T. P.	Rej	Grayson	—	—
Johnson, Telithia	Rej	Bosque	Johnson, John Henry	—
Johnson, W. A.	Rej	Eastland	—	—
Johnson, W. L.	Rej	Comanche	—	—
Johnson, William	Rej	McCulloch	—	—
Johnson, William S.	Rej	Travis	—	—
Johnson, William T. G.	Rej	Stephens	—	—
Johnston, A. W.	Rej	Jack	—	—
Johnston, Albert Monroe	Rej	Scurry	—	—
Johnston, Frank M.	Rej	Navarro	—	—
Johnston, Henry F.	Rej	Burleson	—	—
Johnston, J. J.	Rej	Hunt	—	—
Johnston, James	Rej	Houston	—	—
Johnston, James Jasper Mrs.	Rej	Tarrant	Johnston, James Jasper	—
Johnston, M. A. Mrs.	Rej	Trinity	Johnston, Samuel Rufus	—
Johnston, M. J.	Rej	Irion	—	—
Johnston, Margaret	Rej	Dallas	Johnston, Jasper J.	—
Johnston, S. A. Mrs.	Rej	Cherokee	Johnston, Stephens R.	—
Johnston, Sue M.	Rej	Lamar	Johnston, James Byron	—
Johnston, W. A.	Rej	Milam	—	—
Joiner, Angeline	Rej	Bell	Joiner, Daniel E.	—
Jolly, Ellen Victoria	Rej	Wichita	Jolly, William S.	—
Jolly, Martha	Rej	Bowie	Jolly, D. Andrew J.	—
Jones, A.	Rej	San Augustine	—	—
Jones, A. H.	Rej	Van Zandt	—	—
Jones, Annie	Rej	Erath	Jones, Arch Clumbis	—
Jones, C. C.	Rej	Wise	—	—
Jones, C. W.	Rej	Hopkins	—	—
Jones, E. J. Hatch Mrs.	Rej	Fayette	Hatch, Edward Williams	—
Jones, E. Samuel	Rej	Wise	—	—
Jones, Emily Jane	Rej	Bexar	Jones, Peter Parsons	—
Jones, Francis Ruth	Rej	Coleman	Jones, Russell Benjamin	—
Jones, Frank R.	Rej	Harris	—	—
Jones, J. F.	Rej	McLennan	—	—
Jones, J. R.	Rej	Panola	—	—
Jones, J. Ras	Rej	Panola	—	—
Jones, J. W.	Rej	Hunt	—	—
Jones, James	Rej	San Saba	—	—
Jones, John J.	Rej	Wood	—	—
Jones, M. H.	Rej	Erath	—	—
Jones, Mahala	Rej	Wilbarger	Jones, John Joseph	—
Jones, Martha	Rej	Jones	Jones, Robert Singleton	—
Jones, Mary	Rej	Grayson	Jones, Moses	—
Jones, Mary E.	Rej	Harrison	Jones, Daniel McClain	—
Jones, Mary Elizabeth	Rej	Mills	Jones, Christopher C.	—
Jones, Mary F.	Rej	Eastland	Jones, Crawford Francis	—
Jones, Mildred Reid	Rej	Bell	Jones, Isaac Van Zandt	—
Jones, Mittie	Rej	Bell	Jones, James	—
Jones, Pinkney Rhodes Mrs.	Rej	Cherokee	Jones, Pinkney Rhodes	32219
Jones, R. F.	Rej	Tarrant	—	—
Jones, R. M.	Rej	Grayson	—	—
Jones, Rebecca	Rej	Bell	Jones, Asberry Capers	—
Jones, Robert Isaac	Rej	Cass	—	—
Jones, S. H.	Rej	Panola	—	—

Index to Rejected Confederate Pension Applications

Name	Status	County	Veteran	Number
Jones, Sarah A.	Rej	Kerr	Jones, E. F.	
Jones, Sophronia	Rej	Anderson	Jones, H. P.	
Jones, Stephen	Rej	Rusk		
Jones, Thomas A.	Rej	Navarro		
Jones, Thomas Long	Rej	Jones		
Jones, Tommie	Rej	Rusk	Jones, Milton	
Jones, W. A.	Rej	Eastland		
Jones, W. L.	Rej	Travis		
Jones, Watts R.	Rej	Young		
Jones, William A.	Rej	Callahan		
Jones, William B.	Rej	Tom Green		
Jordan, A. L. Mrs.	Rej	Navarro	Jordan, James Ida	
Jordan, Bettie	Rej	Bosque	Jordan, John Plesant	
Jordan, E.	Rej	Limestone		
Jordan, Emily	Rej	Franklin	Jordan, Samuel J.	
Jordan, F. L. Mrs.	Rej	Navarro	Jordan, John Wesley	
Jordan, J. F.	Rej	Hill		
Jordan, Kate	Rej	Tarrant	Jordan, Thomas Sutherland	
Jordan, Ruth C.	Rej	Falls	Jordan, William Britton	
Joyce, Tennessee C.	Rej	Bell	Joyce, Little Berry William	
Juarez, Isabel Salinas De	Rej	Webb	Antonio, Sr.	16952
Juarez, Trindad L. De	Rej	Webb	Juarez, Ildefonzo	
Judkins, Eliza	Rej	Newton	Judkins, Charley Roundtree	
Judkins, Martha J.	Rej	Llano	Judkins, John	
Kabela, Joseph	Rej	McLennan		
Kaiser, Jennie	Rej	Fannin	Kaiser, Julius	
Kamplain, Jim Shaw	Rej	Mills		
Kane, Eliza	Rej	Harris	Kane, James Edward	
Karbach, Gustavus A.	Rej	Travis		
Kaufman, Pairlee Blackwell	Rej	Mason	Blackwell, John	
Kay, Sarah Jane	Rej	Comal	Kay, Andrew Jackson	
Keahey, Rutha	Rej	Erath	Keahey, James Edward	
Kearley, W. G.	Rej	Collin		
Keasler, J. H.	Rej	Cass		
Keese, Jane W.	Rej	Comanche	Keese, George Washington	
Keesee, T. J.	Rej	Ellis		
Keeton, Alexander A.	Rej	Cooke		
Keilberg, Otto	Rej	Bastrop		
Keith, D. N.	Rej	Titus		
Keith, Henry	Rej	Tarrant		
Keith, J. F.	Rej	Tarrant		
Keith, M. E. Mrs.	Rej	Brazos	Keith, John Bunion	03857
Keller, Tennessee Forrest	Rej	Tarrant	Keller, Isaac Thomas	
Kelley, Daniel	Rej	Jasper		
Kelley, M. L.	Rej	Jasper		
Kelley, M. M.	Rej	Fannin		
Kelley, Tyra Alexander Mrs.	Rej	Gregg	Kelley, Tyra Alexander	31889
Kelly, J. J.	Rej	Erath		
Kelly, James	Rej	Harris		
Kelly, L. S.	Rej	Gregg		
Kelly, William Robert	Rej	Montague		
Kelsay, Curtis William	Rej	Wise		
Kelsay, Curtis William Mrs.	Rej	Wise	Kelsay, Curtis William	Rej
Kelso, D. E. Mrs.	Rej	Travis	Kelso, Leroy	
Kemp, Barney B.	Rej	Mills		
Kemp, Eliza Ann	Rej	Johnson	Kemp, John W.	
Kemp, Sarah E.	Rej	Collin	Kemp, Andrew Jackson	
Kemper, Elizabeth H.	Rej	Harris	Kemper, John Splan	
Kemper, Granville Garrett	Rej	Hopkins		

Index to Rejected Confederate Pension Applications

Kemper, Granville Garrett Mrs.	Rej	Hopkins	Kemper, Granville Garrett	Rej
Kendall, Mary Edith	Rej	El Paso	Kendall, William Edward	
Kendrick, S. A. Mrs.	Rej	Wise	Kendrick, J. R.	
Keng, Herman	Rej	Lee		
Kennedy, J. F.	Rej	Harrison		
Kennedy, M. A. Mrs.	Rej	Wise	Kennedy, Samuel Banard	
Kennedy, R. E.	Rej	Grayson		
Kennedy, Samuel P.	Rej	Cass		
Kennedy, T. J. Knight Mrs.	Rej	Anderson	Knight, John Marion	
Kenner, Judith Sims	Rej	Harris	Kenner, Howson Calhoun	01793
Kenney, Henry B.	Rej	Bowie		
Kent, S. W.	Rej	Palo Pinto		
Kerley, M. F. Mrs.	Rej	Limestone	Kerley, Joseph Washington	
Kern, C.	Rej	Denton		
Kerr, J. G.	Rej	Clay		
Kerr, S. E. Mrs.	Rej	Clay	Kerr, William Archibald	
Kersh, Hattie G.	Rej	Tarrant	Kersh, John Washington	
Keuhn, J. W.	RejM	Travis		
Key, Lizzie	Rej	Sabine	Key, Enoch	
Key, R. M.	Rej	Randall		
Kibler, Andrew Jack	Rej	Coleman		
Kidd, J. A.	Rej	Stonewall		
Kieler, Alvina Zbitowsky	Rej	Dallas	Zbitowsky, Frank	
Kiesling, Karoline	Rej	Harris	Kiesling, John August	
Kiker, H. L. Mrs.	Rej	Erath	Kiker, Newton P.	
Kilgore, Jerry M.	Rej	Harris		
Kilgore, Sandy C.	Rej	Grayson		
Kimbell, D. F.	Rej	Titus		
Kimberlin, O. P. Mrs.	Rej	Hunt	Kimberlin, Jacob Abriham	05586
Kimble, C. C., Sr.	Rej	Burnet		
Kimmey, Julia A.	Rej	Upshur	Kimmey, Frances D. Larue	34075
Kincheloe, Mary	Rej	Hamilton	Kincheloe, George Haines	
Kindly, William Franklin	Rej	Panola		
Kindred, Joseph Colston	Rej	Colorado		
King, A. D. Mrs.	RejM	Nacogdoches		
King, Duncan	Rej	Falls		
King, Granville Millington Mrs.	Rej	Bastrop	King, Granville Millington	
King, H. J. Mrs.	Rej	Hamilton	King, Edward J.	
King, Ida	Rej	Smith	King, H. Robert	10773
King, M. E. McCullough Mrs.	Rej	Mitchell	McCullough, John Wesley	
King, P. B.	Rej	Titus		
King, Robert B.	Rej	Cottle		
King, Ruth Marold	Rej	Bexar	Marold, George Theo	
King, Selma E.	RejM	Nacogdoches		
King, Thomas B.	Rej	Austin		
King, Thomas W.	Rej	Callahan		
King, W. C.	Rej	Lamar		
Kinman, Sanford G.	Rej	Menard		
Kinnison, Amanda T.	Rej	Fort Bend	Kinnison, Simon English	
Kirby, James Lafayette Mrs.	Rej	Bexar	Kirby, James Lafayette	
Kirby, Julia J.	Rej	Robertson	Kirby, William Jackson	
Kirby, Mary Ellen	Rej	Johnson	Kirby, George Washington	28383
Kirby, William	Rej	Uvalde		
Kireshing, Karoline	RejM	Harris		
Kirkendall, B. F.	Rej	Hardin		
Kirkham, J. S.	Rej	Brazos		
Kirkley, W. M.	Rej	Smith		
Kirkpatrick, Isaac	Rej	Cherokee		
Kirkpatrick, Richard W.	Rej	Hood		

Index to Rejected Confederate Pension Applications

Kiser, W. E.	Rej	Hunt		
Kitchens, D. M.	Rej	Mitchell		
Kitchens, Sarah Rodicy	Rej	Mitchell	Kitchens, Bray Coleman	
Kite, Stephen	Rej	Lavaca		
Kizer, J. K.	Rej	Jack		
Klaeden, Emma A.	Rej	Washington	Klaeden, C. William	
Kline, John F.	Rej	Jefferson		
Klipper, J. A.	Rej	Harris		
Knight, M. T.	Rej	Smith		
Knight, Margaret A.	Rej	Leon	Knight, William Washington	
Knight, Mary Rebecca	Rej	Bell	Knight, Andrew	
Knight, Mattie	Rej	Dallas	Knight, John	46349
Knight, Reuben B.	Rej	Palo Pinto		
Knowles, Elijah Rogers	Rej	Bosque		
Knowles, Jefferson Troupe	Rej	Haskell		
Knowles, William Henry	Rej	Lamar		
Knox, Lula	Rej	Anderson	Knox, Marion Anderson	
Knox, Sam H. Mrs.	Rej	Houston	Knox, Sam H.	34750
Knudson, K.	Rej	Bosque		
Knuple, Sam	RejM	Gray		
Koening, August	Rej	Wharton		
Kornegay, Robert Arnold	Rej	Milam		
Kraulick, John	Rej	Austin		
Kritser, John S.	Rej	Williamson		
Kuehn, J. W.	Rej	Travis		
Kuehne, August	Rej	Bexar		
Kuhlmann, Henry	Rej	Bexar		
Kunkel, Sam	Rej	Gray		
Kupferschmidt, Katherine	Rej	Caldwell	Kupferschmidt, Heinrich	
Kuykendal, J. C.	Rej	Gonzales		
Laas, Marie	Rej	Lee	Laas, Charles William	
Lackendye, Jane	Rej	Rusk	Lackendye, Henry	
Lackey, John	Rej	Wharton		
Lackland, J. A.	Rej	Anderson		
Lacy, E. J. Mrs.	Rej	Bosque	Lacy, Warren	
Lafour, Martha	Rej	Chambers	Lafour, Joseph	
Lagrone, J. E.	Rej	Shelby		
Lagrone, M. K. Mrs.	Rej	Leon	Lagrone, Adam	
Laird, E. F. Mrs.	Rej	Wise	Laird, William Turner	06835
Laird, Sydney Mrs.	Rej	Bastrop	Laird, John Egbert Bell	
Laman, George Allen	Rej	Concho		
Lamance	RejM	Henderson		
Lamb, Hiram	Rej	Coke		
Lamb, John I.	Rej	Coryell		
Lambert, James R.	Rej	Wood		
Lambright, W. S.	Rej	Shelby		
Lancaster, A. J. Mrs.	Rej	Rusk	Lancaster, John Wheeler	
Lancaster, Eva	Rej	Bexar	Lancaster, Joseph	
Land, Ellen Rosa	Rej	Gray	Land, Thomas Franklin	
Land, Henry C.	Rej	Erath		
Landers, L. D.	Rej	McLennan		
Landrum, Willis J.	Rej	Montgomery		
Lane, Bettie	Rej	Hunt	Lane, William	
Lane, Christiana	Rej	Nacogdoches	Lane, Thomas Grover	
Lane, J. S.	Rej	Falls		
Lane, M. E. Mrs.	Rej	Williamson	Lane, I. W.	
Lane, Mary Emma	Rej	Fisher	Lane, Leroy Wilcus	
Lane, S. C.	Rej	Freestone		
Laney, Robert O.	Rej	Morris		

Index to Rejected Confederate Pension Applications

Lang, Charles R., Sr.	Rej	Walker	—	—
Lang, John Anderson	Rej	Wilbarger	—	—
Lange, Helmuth G. L.	Rej	Mason	—	—
Langford, Agnes Malissia	Rej	Stephens	Langford, George Augustus	19956
Langford, Tennessee	Rej	Upshur	Langford, Francis F.	04063
Langhlin, J. M.	RejM	Dallas	—	—
Langley, Robert L.	Rej	Parker	—	—
Langley, W. J.	Rej	Parker	—	—
Langston, M. D.	Rej	Potter	—	—
Langston, Phemy	Rej	Angelina	Langston, John M.	14157
Lankford, Young M.	Rej	Upshur	—	—
Lansdale, Sarah Jane	Rej	Upshur	Lansdale, George G.	16813
Lansford, Cassie	Rej	Knox	Lansford, George Washington	—
Lansford, Wyatt	RejM	Lampasas	—	—
Lara, Feliciano	Rej	Travis	—	—
Largent, J. P.	Rej	Anderson	—	—
Largent, Nannie B.	Rej	Howard	Largent, Walter	—
Largin, L. T. Mrs.	Rej	Dallas	Largin, Robert H.	—
Lary, J. E.	Rej	Grayson	—	—
Lary, Stephen D'jalma	Rej	Tarrant	—	—
Lasater, Benjamin F.	Rej	Tarrant	—	—
Lashley, E. F.	Rej	Tarrant	—	—
Lastinger, Georgia A.	Rej	McLennan	Lastinger, William H.	—
Laswell, G. C.	Rej	Coke	—	—
Latch, Louis Anderson	Rej	Upshur	—	—
Lattimore, S. C. Mrs.	Rej	Erath	Lattimore, John Lee	—
Laughlin, J. N.	Rej	Dallas	—	—
Law, G. A.	Rej	Travis	—	—
Lawler, Elizabeth	Rej	Burnet	Lawler, Newton	—
Lawley, T. R.	Rej	Grayson	—	—
Lawrence, A. R.	Rej	Dewitt	—	—
Lawrence, Ann	Rej	Coleman	Lawrence, Mills	—
Lawrence, G. W.	Rej	Runnels	—	—
Lawrence, J. W.	Rej	Gregg	—	—
Lawrence, Mary	Rej	Mills	Lawrence, Joseph Benjamin	—
Lawrence, William H.	Rej	Tarrant	—	—
Lawson, E. J. Mrs.	Rej	Red River	Lawson, Isiah Marion	—
Lawson, Eugene	Rej	Dewitt	—	—
Laymance, Amande E.	Rej	Henderson	Laymance, Jacob Reagan	—
Layne, E.	Rej	Smith	—	—
Layton, William K.	Rej	Bowie	—	—
Lea, Mary A.	Rej	Real	Lea, Edward Payon	—
Leach, J. G.	Rej	Jack	—	—
Leach, W. J.	Rej	Parker	—	—
Leary, Nettie P.	Rej	Hays	Leary, John Lemuel	—
Leatherwood, John M.	Rej	Jack	—	—
Ledbetter, James P.	Rej	McLennan	—	—
Ledbetter, James Peacock Mrs.	Rej	Travis	Ledbetter, James Peacock	—
Ledbetter, W. M.	Rej	Grayson	—	—
Lee, A. G.	Rej	Freestone	—	—
Lee, Baldwin P.	Rej	Mills	—	—
Lee, Fannie	Rej	Cass	Lee, William B.	—
Lee, Jos E.	Rej	Jones	—	—
Lee, L. M. Mrs.	Rej	Montague	Lee, Henry Burton	—
Lee, M. M.	Rej	Williamson	—	—
Lee, R. A.	Rej	Knox	—	—
Lee, Sarah C.	Rej	Cooke	Lee, James Chester	—
Lee, W. A.	Rej	Dallas	—	—
Lee, W. H.	Rej	Freestone	—	—

Index to Rejected Confederate Pension Applications

Lee, William H. Mrs.	Rej	Limestone	Lee, William H.	06749
Leeder, Harriet O.	Rej	Edwards	Leeder, William Arther	—
Leggett, A.	Rej	Hunt	—	—
Legrand, Petronia O.	Rej	Parker	Legrand, Peter Gower	—
Lehman, John	Rej	Lee	—	—
Lehman, Joseph	Rej	McLennan	—	—
Lemmon, Isaac	Rej	Cass	—	—
Lemmon, J. P.	Rej	Cass	—	—
Lemmon, James	RejM	Rusk	—	—
Lemmond, John L.	Rej	Young	—	—
Lemons, Mary D.	Rej	Terrell	Lemons, Joseph Francis	—
Lenderman, Mary M.	Rej	Somervell	Lenderman, Lemuel L.	—
Lentz, Sarah Elizabeth Milling	Rej	Lamar	Milling, William Alexander	—
Leroy, Sarah	Rej	Upshur	Leroy, Gilbert	—
Leslie, H. L. A.	Rej	Shelby	—	—
Lessing, William H.	Rej	Tarrant	—	—
Lester, C. M.	Rej	Nacogdoches	—	—
Lester, John	Rej	Hall	—	—
Levington, S. H.	Rej	Orange	—	—
Levy, M. H.	Rej	Bowie	—	—
Levyson, Fannie	Rej	Bexar	Levyson, Paul	—
Lewis, D. H.	Rej	Hunt	—	—
Lewis, G.	Rej	Trinity	—	—
Lewis, J. H.	Rej	Dallas	—	—
Lewis, James L.	Rej	Burleson	—	—
Lewis, John	Rej	Dewitt	—	—
Lewis, John D.	Rej	Smith	—	—
Lewis, L. L. Mrs.	Rej	Hill	Lewis, Henry Clay	—
Lewis, M. J. Mrs.	Rej	Cherokee	Lewis, W. W.	—
Lewis, Martin Vanburen	Rej	Haskell	—	—
Lewis, Matilda Jane	Rej	Milam	Lewis, William H.	—
Lewis, Meranay	Rej	Somervell	Lewis, George Washington	37573
Lewis, P. A. Mrs.	Rej	Milam	Lewis, William	—
Lewis, Rosalie	Rej	Kaufman	Lewis, Ed	—
Lewis, Viney	Rej	San Augustine	Lewis, William	—
Lewis, William	Rej	Dallas	—	—
Lewis, William	Rej	Parker	—	—
Lewis, William	Rej	Hardeman	—	—
Lewis, Willis Andrew Jackson Mrs.	Rej	Morris	Lewis, Willis Andrew Jackson	13013
Liles, H. C.	Rej	Smith	—	—
Liles, J. B.	Rej	San Jacinto	—	—
Liles, Richard	RejM	Stonewall	—	—
Lillard, John K.	Rej	Dallas	—	—
Lillard, Julia A.	Rej	Bexar	Lillard, William C.	—
Lincecum, B. D.	Rej	Caldwell	—	—
Lincecum, C. W.	Rej	Red River	—	—
Linch, D. W.	Rej	Bosque	—	—
Lindley, J. A.	Rej	Hopkins	—	—
Lindly, B. W.	Rej	Hopkins	—	—
Lindsay, George B.	Rej	Grayson	—	—
Lindsay, Lavina G.	RejM	Rockwall	—	—
Lindsay, William	Rej	Mason	—	—
Lindsey, Albert	Rej	Travis	—	—
Lindsey, Amanda	Rej	Washington	Lindsey, W. H.	—
Lindsey, Elijah	Rej	Cass	—	—
Lindsey, James E.	Rej	San Patricio	—	—
Lindsey, Orlena	Rej	Taylor	Lindsey, James Evans	—
Lindsey, William M. Mrs.	Rej	Milam	Lindsey, William M.	38260
Linebarger, John	Rej	Hamilton	—	—

Index to Rejected Confederate Pension Applications

Linemiller, Frank	Rej	Galveston	—	—
Linnartz, Peter P.	Rej	Bexar	—	—
Linzy, John	Rej	Bexar	—	—
Lipp, J. A.	Rej	Palo Pinto	—	—
Lippard, Allie Lee	Rej	Eastland	Lippard, Leonidus Bonaparte	20610
Lipscomb, Elizabeth	Rej	Hunt	Lipscomb, John Thomas	—
Lisenbee, Mary M.	Rej	Jefferson	Lisenbee, Worthington Gibbs	—
Little, Mary C. Bryan	Rej	Chambers	Bryan, Sydney Berwick	—
Littlejohn, Elbrige Gerry Mrs.	Rej	Smith	Littlejohn, Elbrige Gerry	—
Littlejohn, L. W. Mrs.	Rej	Lamar	Littlejohn, C. P.	—
Livingston, Joseph Henry	Rej	Falls	—	—
Lloyd, Margaret	Rej	Nacogdoches	Lloyd, T. C.	—
Lloyd, W. G.	Rej	Limestone	—	—
Loader, Thomas F.	Rej	Bosque	—	—
Loche, L. M. Mrs.	Rej	Bowie	Loche, W. B.	—
Lock, Frances	Rej	Palo Pinto	Lock, William Brandon	—
Lock, M. E. Mrs.	Rej	Van Zandt	Lock, James Dickerson	—
Locke, Francis Mrs.	Rej	Palo Pinto	Locke, Francis	—
Locke, Mary Allie	RejM	Dallas	—	—
Lockett, Caroline Henrietta	Rej	Walker	Lockett, Benjamin Franklin	—
Lockett, Mary E.	RejM	Bosque	—	—
Lockhart, Malissie L.	Rej	Tyler	Lockhart, Charley	—
Loflin, S. C. Mrs.	Rej	Coleman	Loflin, Joshias Y.	—
Loftis, Matilda J.	Rej	Wilbarger	Loftis, James Monroe	28774
Logan, Vina J.	Rej	Parker	Logan, Samuel W.	—
Logsdon, J. J.	Rej	Van Zandt	—	—
Lomax, Susan Frances	Rej	Bosque	Lomax, James Avery	—
London, J. G.	Rej	Johnson	—	—
Long, C. A. Mrs.	Rej	Titus	Long, Kenny	—
Long, E. A. Mrs.	Rej	Houston	Long, James S.	—
Long, Emma	Rej	Parker	Long, George Cathey	—
Long, I. F.	Rej	Robertson	—	—
Long, Isaac M.	Rej	Haskell	—	—
Long, J. C.	Rej	Williamson	—	—
Long, J. H.	Rej	Nacogdoches	—	—
Long, James A. S.	Rej	Gregg	—	—
Long, Jane	Rej	Bastrop	Long, Henry Travis	—
Long, John A.	RejM	Wilbarger	—	—
Long, John M.	Rej	Upshur	—	—
Long, L. J. Young Mrs.	Rej	Mills	Young, James Anderson	—
Long, Mathew S.	Rej	Upshur	—	—
Long, Tabatha	Rej	Caldwell	Long, Tobias	—
Longuemare, Palmyra	Rej	El Paso	Longuemare, Charles	—
Looney, Rosalie	Rej	Dallas	Looney, James K.	—
Loper, George B.	Rej	Callahan	—	—
Loper, Peter B.	Rej	Callahan	—	—
Lord, Samuel Jackson	Rej	Kaufman	—	—
Lott, Absolam	Rej	Trinity	—	—
Lott, Mary D.	Rej	Gonzales	Lott, William	—
Lott, Nellie	Rej	Bexar	Lott, Andrew Jackson	24830
Louden, Joseph V.	Rej	Bastrop	—	—
Love, J. H.	Rej	Angelina	—	—
Love, John I.	Rej	Jack	—	—
Love, M. C. Mrs.	Rej	Gregg	Love, Francis Marion	27491
Love, Martha A.	Rej	Anderson	Love, William Wilson	—
Love, Mattie	Rej	Erath	Love, Francis Marion	—
Love, Mildred	Rej	Harrison	Love, K. J.	—
Love, T. O.	Rej	Comanche	—	—
Lovin, J. T.	Rej	Robertson	—	—

Index to Rejected Confederate Pension Applications

Low, J. H.	Rej	Jones		
Lowe, Artie	Rej	Navarro	Lowe, Phillip Sublet	
Lowe, C. H.	Rej	Angelina		
Lowe, David M.	Rej	Navarro		
Lowe, Sidney	Rej	Shelby	Lowe, Jesse	
Lowe, W. L.	Rej	Sabine		
Lowery, Easter Ann	Rej	Falls	Lowery, Theophilus Daniel	
Lowery, M. S. P.	Rej	Limestone		
Lowrance, A. R.	Rej	Dewitt		
Lowrance, M. L. Mrs.	Rej	Kerr	Lowrance, Cain	
Lowrey, J. C.	Rej	Colorado		
Lucas, E. A. Mrs.	Rej	Hill	Lucas, P. F. M.	
Lucas, L.	Rej	Anderson		
Luckett, Joseph Ward Mrs.	Rej	Anderson	Luckett, Joseph Ward	26915
Luckey, S. S.	Rej	Lamar		
Luna, James M.	Rej	Grayson		
Lundy, H. S.	Rej	Colorado		
Lunsford, Lula	Rej	Rusk	Lunsford, Isaac Lee Hillard	22924
Lunsford, Sciron	Rej	Panola		
Lunsford, W. R.	Rej	Titus		
Lunsford, Wyatt	Rej	Lampasas		
Luque, Sarah	Rej	San Patricio	Luque, Michael	
Luttrell, Catherene	Rej	Fisher	Luttrell, Jacob G.	
Lynch, Martha	Rej	Johnson	Lynch, Edward Greene	
Lynn, Clarissa	Rej	Bexar	Lynn, Louis	
Lyons, A. B.	Rej	Orange		
Lyons, Catherine Amelia	Rej	Harris	Lyons, Thomas L.	
Lyons, John R.	Rej	Red River		
Lytle, Nancy R.	Rej	Smith	Lytle, Trevelon Lockrage	
Mabin, T. J.	Rej	Tarrant		
Mabray, Joseph	Rej	Hardin		
Mabrey, Jeff	Rej	Hopkins		
Mabry, William Patrick	Rej	Montague		
Machen, J. H.	Rej	Baylor		
Mack, J. H.	Rej	Dallas		
Mackey, George	Rej	Travis		
Mackey, M. E. F. Nixon Mrs.	Rej	Lamar	Nixon, Thomas Canter Fletcher	
Mackey, M. L. Mrs.	Rej	Hill	Mackey, William Ransom	
Madden, R. A. Mrs.	Rej	Bell	Madden, S. H.	
Maddox, Cornelia A.	Rej	Collingsworth	Maddox, Bryant L.	
Maddox, John	Rej	Hunt		
Madling, J. M.	RejM	Hays		
Madry, Ida Kennedy	Rej	Tarrant	Madry, John William	
Maher, Patrick	Rej	Dallas		
Maigne, Louise V.	Rej	Harris	Maigne, Charles Henry Chantilott	
Maines, E. B.	Rej	Montgomery		
Major, Eura P.	Rej	Erath	Major, Warren Thompson	
Maley, W. B.	Rej	Cameron		
Malicoat, Hamilton	Rej	Bell		
Mallow, Marion	Rej	Collin	Mallow, Armstead Conway	
Mallow, W. A. Mrs.	RejM	Brown		
Malone, Desire	Rej	Scurry	Malone, Solomon	
Malone, G. W.	Rej	Van Zandt		
Malone, M. J. Mrs.	Rej	Wood	Malone, Marion Jones	15175
Malone, S. M.	Rej	Hamilton		
Maloney, Margaret	Rej	Ellis	Maloney, James Madison	
Maloney, S. W.	Rej	Hunt		
Maness, J. A.	Rej	Trinity		
Manis, Mattie	Rej	Bexar	Manis, Cameron A.	

Index to Rejected Confederate Pension Applications

Mankin, Emma	Rej	Lampasas	Mankin, William J.	
Mann, E. D. Mrs.	Rej	Bowie	Mann, W. M.	
Mann, Elizabeth	Rej	Wichita	Mann, Joel Turner	
Mann, John H.	Rej	Wise		
Mann, Lemuel	Rej	San Patricio		
Mann, M. A. Mrs.	Rej	Titus	Mann, Thomas Louis	
Mann, W. B.	RejM	Hardeman		
Mannahan, James F.	Rej	Collingsworth		
Manning, B.	Rej	Dewitt		
Manning, L. A.	Rej	Clay		
Manning, Martha	Rej	Madison	Manning, John Williamson	06054
Manning, Thomas	Rej	Tarrant		
Mansfield, Emeline	RejM	Gaines		
Mansinger, Sarah	Rej	Rusk	Mansinger, John	
Maples, Martha	Rej	Fannin	Maples, E. F.	
Maples, Moses	Rej	Lamar		
Maples, R. A.	Rej	Bell		
Marett, John B.	Rej	Van Zandt		
Marion, Robert H.	Rej	Navarro		
Markintale, Joe Mrs.	Rej	Liberty	Markintale, Joe	
Marney, W. R.	Rej	Harrison		
Marrs, L. J. Mrs.	Rej	Hood	Marrs, William McDonald	
Marrs, W. B.	Rej	Hardeman		
Marsh, M. E. Mrs.	Rej	Grimes	Marsh, George Edward	24928
Marshall, B. T.	Rej	Mason		
Marshall, Caroline	Rej	Bexar	Marshall, Jacob G.	
Marshall, Delitha	Rej	Uvalde	Marshall, John James	
Marshall, Eliva	Rej	Navarro	Marshall, Joseph Taylor	
Marshall, Joseph W.	Rej	Angelina		
Marshall, Susan F.	Rej	Dallas	Marshall, Thomas Benton	
Marshall, T. C.	Rej	Red River		
Marshburn, J. J.	Rej	San Augustine		
Mart, Clemons Mrs.	RejM	Nacogdoches		
Martin, A. A. Mrs.	RejM	Delta		
Martin, A. G.	Rej	Trinity		
Martin, A. P.	Rej	Cherokee		
Martin, Alexander Corruth	Rej	Collin		
Martin, Alonzo E.	Rej	Angelina		
Martin, Amanda M.	Rej	Madison	Martin, William Thomas	
Martin, Cynthia A.	Rej	Panola	Daniel, Jr.	
Martin, Darthula D.	Rej	Dallas	Martin, Z. W.	
Martin, E. A.	Rej	Montague		
Martin, E. A.	Rej	Camp		
Martin, Elizabeth Frances	Rej	Callahan	Martin, Absalom Parks	
Martin, Hardy	Rej	Guadalupe		
Martin, Hattie	Rej	Galveston	Martin, John Henry	
Martin, Henry	Rej	Galveston		
Martin, J. J.	Rej	Hopkins		
Martin, J. L.	Rej	Camp		
Martin, J. S.	Rej	Freestone		
Martin, Joseph J.	Rej	Delta		
Martin, Josephine	Rej	Montgomery	Martin, John	
Martin, Lucy	Rej	Collin	Martin, John Walter	
Martin, M. H.	Rej	Somervell		
Martin, Mary A.	Rej	Cherokee	Martin, James M.	
Martin, Mary Amelia	Rej	Brazoria	Martin, Thomas D.	
Martin, Mary Jane	Rej	Gonzales	Martin, John Irving	
Martin, Miles M.	Rej	San Saba		
Martin, Nancy E.	Rej	Montague	Martin, Elisha Austin	

Index to Rejected Confederate Pension Applications

Martin, Nora A.	Rej	Delta	Martin, N. J.
Martin, Terry T.	Rej	Bowie	
Martin, W. F.	Rej	Sabine	
Martin, W. N. Mrs.	RejM	Lee	
Martin, Wiley	Rej	Fannin	
Martin, William F.	Rej	Jones	
Martinez, Erlinda Esquibel De	Rej	Bexar	Martinez, Jose (joseph) ... 06229
Martinez, Isabel Salinas De	Rej	Webb	Martinez, Antonio Juarez
Martinez, Marcos	Rej	Webb	
Mashburn, Ella H.	Rej	Knox	Mashburn, Charles
Mashburn, J. A.	Rej	Coryell	
Mashone, Fred Mrs.	RejM	Wise	Mashone, Fred
Masinger, Sarah	RejM	Rusk	
Mason, J. B.	Rej	Atascosa	
Mason, Mary M.	Rej	Rockwall	Mason, Mallory Sidney
Mason, Susan	Rej	Sabine	Mason, James Governor
Mason, W. W.	Rej	Brown	
Mass, Louisa Ellen	RejM	Palo Pinto	
Massengale, Alford A.	Rej	Henderson	
Massey, E.	Rej	Bandera	
Massey, Henderson	Rej	Harris	
Massey, Kansas	Rej	Dallas	Massey, Andrew Jackson
Massey, M. E. Mrs.	Rej	Reeves	Massey, Joel Vincent
Mast, Clemons	Rej	Nacogdoches	Mast, Andrew Jackson
Masters, M. E. Mrs.	Rej	Hopkins	Masters, William Jackson
Mathers, William Henry	Rej	Bastrop	
Mathews, George Richard Mrs.	Rej	Tarrant	Mathews, George Richard
Mathews, Mary	Rej	Hopkins	Mathews, Michael ... 26595
Mathias, Andreas	Rej	Fayette	
Mathis, C. C.	Rej	Hill	
Mathis, H. T.	Rej	Eastland	
Mathis, James	Rej	Upshur	
Matlock, Elizabeth	Rej	Taylor	Matlock, Stephen West
Matlock, Louis J.	Rej	Rusk	
Matlock, Nancy C.	Rej	Cooke	Matlock, George Monroe
Matthews, C. J.	Rej	Harris	
Matthews, Clara E. Canarian	Rej	Orange	Matthews, Adam
Matthews, Geogia	Rej	Hunt	Matthews, Alfred Gatlin
Matthews, James Antony	Rej	Hunt	
Matthews, John G.	Rej	Stonewall	
Matthews, Martha Evelyn	Rej	Wichita	Matthews, Asberry Hilliard
Matthews, Martha Jane	Rej	Collin	Matthews, James
Mattox, John W.	Rej	Wood	
Maupin, Margaret	Rej	Young	Maupin, Patrick
Maxcy, J. M.	Rej	Cass	
Maxey, Belle	Rej	Camp	Maxey, David Strong
Maxwell, Francis Marion	Rej	Waller	
Maxwell, Robert Thomas	Rej	Upshur	
Maxwell, Sallie	Rej	McLennan	Maxwell, William Stephenson
Maxwell, Sarah Frances	Rej	Lamar	Maxwell, Newton Thomas
Maxwell, T. M.	RejM	Waller	
May, Alice Am	Rej	Grayson	May, Benjamin Carey
May, M. E. Mrs.	Rej	Wise	May, Soliman Gillmore
May, N. F. Mrs.	Rej	Bee	May, Hugh
May, William	Rej	Shelby	
Mayberry, Susie D.	Rej	Uvalde	Mayberry, James Monroe
Mayer, V. J.	Rej	Jasper	
Mayes, C. S.	Rej	Hunt	
Mayes, George E.	Rej	Fort Bend	

Index to Rejected Confederate Pension Applications

Mayfield, Anna M. Scarlett	Rej	Stephens	Scarlett, Minor	
Mayfield, Gertrude Howard	Rej	Tom Green	Mayfield, John Elbert	
Mayfield, M. E. Mrs.	Rej	Lamar	Mayfield, J. P.	
Mayfield, Neppie	Rej	Karnes	Mayfield, George S.	
Mayfield, Omie	Rej	Kinney	Mayfield, Luke	
Mayo, John Louis	Rej	El Paso		
Mays, D. H.	Rej	Bell		
Mayson, Archy L.	Rej	Waller		
Maywald, Amanda	Rej	Grimes	Maywald, Frederick Gustus	
McAdams, I. F.	Rej	Dallas		
McAdams, J. H.	Rej	Leon		
McAdams, Lucius M.	Rej	Wichita		
McAdams, Mattie	Rej	Eastland	McAdams, William Jesse	
McAfee, M. J. Mrs.	Rej	Grayson	McAfee, Robert Garland	
McAlister, R. P.	Rej	Grayson		
McAllister, J. B. Mrs.	Rej	San Saba	McAllister, Daniel Barr	
McAlpine, D. A.	Rej	Bell		
McAlpine, Mary	Rej	Waller	McAlpine, Dugald Anderson	
McArthurn, W.	Rej	Jones		
McBrayer, A. J.	Rej	Franklin		
McBrayer, Elizabeth	Rej	Deaf Smith	McBrayer, Andrew Jackson	
McBrayer, G. W.	Rej	McLennan		
McBufe, Thomas	RejM	Rockwall		
McCaa, Isaac Newton	Rej	Freestone		
McCaffey, J. W. Mrs.	RejM			
McCain, J. C.	Rej	Cass		
McCain, Jesse E.	Rej	Tarrant		
McCall, Sallie Jemina Ball	Rej	Bexar	McCall, Robert Jefferson	
McCalla, James A.	Rej	Dallas		
McCallister, P. T.	Rej	Bell		
McCamb, W. H.	Rej	Houston		
McCamy, Rebecca	Rej	Hood	McCamy, Merriman	
McCane, G. H.	Rej	Colorado		
McCann, J. F.	Rej	Williamson		
McCann, T. S.	Rej	Angelina		
McCarthy, Mary Elizabeth	Rej	Galveston	McCarthy, Thomas Reynolds	15235
McCarty, B. F.	Rej	Donley		
McCarty, Ira C.	Rej	Callahan		
McCarty, J. D.	Rej	Parker		
McCarty, J. K.	RejM	Smith		
McCaskill, J. D.	Rej	Dewitt		
McCaskill, John	Rej	Cherokee		
McCaskill, Sarah	Rej	Bexar	McCaskill, James Marion	
McCasland, J. A.	Rej	Parker		
McCauley, Katherine	Rej	Titus	McCauley, Samuel Franklin	24361
McCauley, Louis Vance	Rej	Shelby		
McCaw, Narcissa Jane	Rej	Jack	McCaw, Robert Nelson	
McChristian, James M.	RejM	Bandera		
McClain, J. H.	Rej	Wharton		
McClain, J. P.	Rej	Wood		
McClain, Josie	Rej	Hardeman	McClain, William Browning	
McClain, Ruth	Rej	McLennan	McClain, James W.	
McClasland, J. A.	RejM	Parker		
McClellan, Sarah Eliz McDonald	Rej	Ellis	McDonald, John Robert	
McClelland, William	Rej	Tom Green		
McClellen, M. R. Mrs.	Rej	Van Zandt	McClellen, James	
McClendon, A. J.	RejM	Bastrop		
McClendon, J. C.	RejM	Henderson		
McClendon, James	RejM	Callahan		

Index to Rejected Confederate Pension Applications

McClendon, Joseph S.	Rej	Callahan		
McClintock, J. F.	Rej	Navarro		
McClung, D. L.	Rej	Hopkins		
McClure, S. D.	Rej	Hill		
McClusky, Joseph	Rej	Hardin		
McCoghren, W. G.	Rej	Polk		
McCollum, J. J.	Rej	Hunt		
McCollum, John J.	Rej	Delta		
McComb, W. H.	RejM	Houston		
McCombs, John Cameron	Rej	El Paso		
McCombs, M. M. Mrs.	Rej	Grayson	McCombs, W. W.	
McConnell, Isaac	Rej	Parker		
McConnico, Cora	Rej	McLennan	McConnico, Charles Timothy	
McCord, James M.	Rej	Lavaca		
McCorkle, E. J. Mrs.	RejM	Polk		
McCorwick, E. J. Mrs.	RejM	Polk		
McCory, J. W.	Rej	Shelby		
McCown, Jennie	Rej	Jones	McCown, James Davis	
McCoy, J. W.	RejM	Shelby		
McCoy, Lowry S.	Rej	Gonzales		
McCracken, C. C.	Rej	Coryell		
McCracken, John M.	Rej	Harris		
McCrary, Stoton P. Mrs.	Rej	Shelby	McCrary, William Erwin	
McCravey, Martha	Rej	Johnson	McCravey, William Cicero	
McCrow, Narcisso Jane	RejM	Jack		
McCuistion, J. T.	Rej	Llano		
McCuistion, James M.	Rej	Bandera		
McCuiston, Mary A.	Rej	Lamar	McCuistion, Harrison Montgomery	
McCuiston, Charley M.	RejM	Knox		
McCulloch, John M.	Rej	Brown		
McCulloch, L. C.	Rej	Bexar		
McCullough, Hugh G.	Rej	Upshur		
McCullough, Jasper	Rej	Taylor		
McCullough, L. F. Mrs.	Rej	Hunt	McCullough, Newton	
McCune, Mary H.	Rej	Grimes	McCune, James Perry	
McCurdy, John	Rej	Upshur		
McCurry, J. O.	Rej	Grimes		
McCurry, Richard M.	Rej	Collingsworth		
McDangle, J. U. S.	RejM	Collin		
McDaniel, Alice	Rej	Orange	McDaniel, Alex	43855
McDaniel, Eliza A.	Rej	Robertson	McDaniel, James S.	
McDaniel, H. C. McAdoo Mrs.	Rej	Taylor	McAdoo, Barnett Murphy	
McDaniel, H. L.	Rej	Callahan		
McDaniel, J. C.	Rej	Tarrant		
McDaniel, Joe Sire	Rej	Howard		
McDaniel, Rosettie	Rej	Wise	McDaniel, Marcus Silvester	
McDaniel, S. A.	Rej	Ellis		
McDaniels, Lenora Graves	Rej	Freestone	Graves, Charles M.	
McDavid, J. E.	Rej	Taylor		
McDermett, Leona	Rej	Dallas	McDermett, William B.	
McDonald, Alice	Rej	Hardin	McDonald, William Harrison	11934
McDonald, Lucile	Rej	Limestone	McDonald, James Russell	47840
McDonald, Nannie	Rej	Lamar	McDonald, George Washington	
McDonald, S. A. Mrs.	Rej	Bastrop	McDonald, N. P.	
McDonell, D.	Rej	Stonewall		
McDougal, John Washington	Rej	Collin		
McDougall, Sinil A. B.	Rej	Lubbock		
McDougle, Johanna	Rej	Harris	McDougle, James Ellison	
McDowell, Victoria	Rej	Hall	McDowell, James K.	

Index to Rejected Confederate Pension Applications

McDowell, W. M.	Rej	Harris		
McElhaney, Mose L.	Rej	Stonewall		
McElroy, J. A.	Rej	Ellis		
McElroy, John	Rej	Floyd		
McFadden, J. M.	Rej	Kaufman		
McFadden, Nancy Jane	Rej	Palo Pinto	McFadden, John Pennington	
McFadin, A. B.	Rej	Hill		
McFarland, Mary	Rej	Shelby	McFarland, Charles Baldwin	
McFarlane, Sallie J.	Rej	Anderson	McFarlane, Reuben Callaway	
McGaffey, John Wyatt Mrs.	Rej	Caldwell	McGaffey, John Wyatt	51238
McGee, Elslia	RejM	Houston		
McGee, G. W.	Rej	Polk		
McGee, J. L.	Rej	Young		
McGee, Mary J.	Rej	Wise	McGee, John F.	
McGill, R. V.	Rej	Hopkins		
McGill, Robert	Rej	Hopkins		
McGinnis, E.	Rej	Harris		
McGowan, Eliza Cadwell	Rej	Williamson	Cadwell, Daniel	
McGown, John F.	Rej	Sabine		
McGuire, Eliza A.	Rej	Falls	McGuire, James Monroe	
McGuire, Mary Ann	Rej	Mills	McGuire, William Jackson	
McGuire, Minerva	Rej	Tarrant	McGuire, Charles Louis	
McGuire, Seaborn Mrs.	Rej	Walker	McGuire, Seaborn	
McGuyer, C. B.	Rej	Delta		
McIlrain, Sarah A.	Rej	Liberty	McIlrain, Gilbert	
McIntosh, Charles Albert	Rej	Upshur		
McIntyre, Martin M.	Rej	Upshur		
McIver, Margarett Ann	Rej	San Augustine	McIver, Murdock	
McKay, C. E. Mrs.	Rej	Rains	McKay, J. E.	
McKay, S. E. Mrs.	Rej	Mason	McKay, Thomas	
McKee, Calvin	Rej	Howard		
McKee, R. R.	Rej	Cooke		
McKenney, Mary	Rej	Sherman	McKenney, William Thomas	
McKibbin, Robert Emmet Mrs.	Rej	Montgomery	McKibbin, Robert Emmet	
McKinley, R. A.	Rej	Camp		
McKinney, Harriett Emaline Borden	Rej	Montague	Borden, Benjamin Franklin	
McKinney, James S. Mrs.	Rej	Tarrant	McKinney, James S.	19722
McKinney, Jennie E.	Rej	Grayson	McKinney, James Stone	
McKinney, S. W. S.	Rej	Hunt		
McKinney, William	Rej	Denton		
McKinzie, N. A.	Rej	Shelby		
McKnight, C. F.	Rej	Gregg		
McKnight, H. B.	Rej	Madison		
McLain, Nathan W.	Rej	Hill		
McLauchlin, Edward	Rej	Henderson		
McLaurin, Talula	Rej	Bell	McLaurin, John Robert Melvin	28562
McLemore, John A.	Rej	McLennan		
McLendon, J. C.	Rej	Henderson		
McLendon, Sarah F.	Rej	Hunt	McLendon, Jacob Holcomb	
McLeod, Robert Pax Robbins Mrs.	Rej	Houston	Robbins, Robert Paxton	
McLeroy, M. J. Mrs.	Rej	Wood	McLeroy, Francis Jackson	
McMakin, Jefferson Berry Mrs.	Rej	Grayson	McMakin, Jefferson Berry	
McManera, Dawson	Rej	Trinity		
McMaster, William	Rej	Bexar		
McMayon, Isabell	Rej	Madison	McMayon, William	
McMichael, Mary Jane	Rej	Morris	McMichael, James Nelson	
McMillam, James	Rej	Van Zandt		
McMillan, Mary Z.	Rej	Harris	McMillan, Henry Clay	
McMillon, Elizabeth Reagan	Rej	Eastland	McMillon, Francis Marion	

Index to Rejected Confederate Pension Applications

Applicant	Status	County	Veteran	No.
McMinn, E. A. Mrs.	Rej	Montague	McMinn, Joseph G.	
McMinn, Frances C.	Rej	Hunt	McMinn, Milton Polk	
McMordie, F.	Rej	Hardeman		
McMurrian, Alice	Rej	Atascosa	McMurrian, Green Berry	
McNeal, James	Rej	Lamar		
McNeel, T. W.	Rej	Robertson		
McNeely, Elizabeth	Rej	Ellis	McNeely, Thomas G.	13300
McNeese, Alice	Rej	Brazos	McNeese, Henry J.	38515
McNeill, M. J.	Rej	Denton		
McNiece, Henry Jackson Mrs.	Rej	Madison	McNiece, Henry Jackson	
McNutt, J. M.	Rej	Comanche		
McNutt, W. P.	Rej	Hardeman		
McNutt, W. W.	Rej	Tarrant		
McNutt, William	Rej	Tarrant		
McPhail, H. N.	Rej	Van Zandt		
McPherson, Jennie L.	Rej	Tarrant	McPherson, Isaac	
McPherson, R. A. Mrs.	Rej	Cass	McPherson, Rodrick Randum	
McPherson, William W.	Rej	Tarrant		
McQueen, Rosanna J.	Rej	Fannin	McQueen, N. N.	
McQueen, S. B.	Rej	Milam		
McQuerry, A. A.	Rej	Jack		
McRae, Norman Harlow	Rej	Kaufman		
McRae, Sallie (Sarah)	Rej	Kaufman	McRae, Norman Harlow	Rej
McRee, J. L.	Rej	Eastland		
McShaw, W. A.	Rej	Runnels		
McSorley, James	Rej	Bexar		
McSpadden, T. S.	Rej	Wise		
McVea, John M.	Rej	Gonzales		
McWaters, Pellie	Rej	Tarrant	McWaters, William Thomas	
McWhirter, Mary Ann	Rej	Bexar	McWhirter, Irvin	
McWhorter, Mary C. Davis	Rej	Denton	Davis, William T.	
McWilliams, John H.	Rej	Van Zandt		
McWilliams, Martin	Rej	Bowie		
Meador, Martha Elizabeth	Rej	Motley	Meador, William Ellsberry	
Meadors, M. L. Mrs.	Rej	Dickens	Meadors, Soloman C.	
Meadows, Eliza Ann	Rej	Gregg	Meadows, James Kenchion	
Means, Ellen M.	Rej	Brewster	Means, Napoleon Bonaparte	
Means, Martha J.	Rej	Dallas	Means, Benjamin F.	
Mechling, William Thompson Mrs.	Rej	Bexar	Mechling, William Thompson	
Mecom, H. H.	Rej	Bell		
Medlin, Anna	Rej	Bexar	Medlin, John Coleman	46683
Medlin, Mildred C.	Rej	Motley	Medlin, Thomas Franklin	
Meelear, P. E. Mrs.	Rej	Upshur	Meelear, William	
Meeton, W. P.	RejM	Shackelford		
Mehrens, G.	Rej	Colorado		
Meier, W.	Rej	Harris		
Melton, J. C. Mrs.	Rej	Henderson	Melton, Elijah	
Melton, S. J.	Rej	Tarrant		
Menard, Alfred B.	Rej	Harris		
Menefee, Alex L.	Rej	Rusk		
Menefee, W. O.	Rej	Johnson		
Menefee, William	Rej	Fayette		
Menielle, Emile Mrs.	Rej	Tom Green	Menielle, Emile	
Mensch, Andrew J.	Rej	Bastrop		
Mercer, H. J.	Rej	Bowie		
Mercer, Joe Ann	Rej	Gregg	Mercer, Marion	
Mercer, Sarah B.	Rej	Tom Green	Mercer, Levi	
Merck, Mary	Rej	Terry	Merck, Samuel Nelson	
Meredith, L. A. Mrs.	Rej	Hill	Meredith, Elisha	

Index to Rejected Confederate Pension Applications

Merkin, Henry	Rej	Fayette		
Mershon, Fred L. Mrs.	Rej	Wise	Mershon, Fred L.	
Mersman, William	Rej	Austin		
Messer, America	Rej	Hall	Messer, Thomas Jefferson	
Metcalf, Sarah	Rej	Shelby	Metcalf, Jeremiah	
Metcalf, T. J.	Rej	Upshur		
Metz, August	Rej	Comal		
Metz, Redden	Rej	Llano		
Meyers, F. C.	RejM	Orange		
Michel, R. E. Mrs.	Rej	Harris	Michel, Maximillian	32490
Michels, Susannah	Rej	Hutchinson	Michels, Frank	
Middleton, W. T.	Rej	Calhoun		
Mikesha	Rej	Austin		
Mikeska, John	Rej	Austin		
Milam, Caroline	Rej	Anderson	Milam, Bartley Yeager	19876
Milam, H. P.	Rej	Dallas		
Mileford, L. J. Mrs.	Rej	Shelby	Mileford, Joseph Jameson	
Miles, Anna	Rej	Smith	Miles, James Lafayette	
Miles, G. F.	Rej	Cherokee		
Miller, A. F.	Rej	Morris		
Miller, Andrew Jackson	Rej	Bastrop		
Miller, Anna	Rej	Tarrant	Miller, John Michael	
Miller, Auguste Mrs.	RejM	Washington		
Miller, Benjamin F.	Rej	Young		
Miller, G. E.	Rej	Travis		
Miller, Hannah	RejM	Williamson		
Miller, J. J.	Rej	Titus		
Miller, J. L.	Rej	Fannin		
Miller, J. L.	Rej	Collin		
Miller, James Wilburn	Rej	Henderson		
Miller, John Lewis	Rej	Henderson		
Miller, M. E. Mrs.	Rej	Callahan	Miller, A. L.	
Miller, Maud Chestina	Rej	Fort Bend	Miller, Warren	
Miller, Mike C.	Rej	Hopkins		
Miller, Morris	Rej	Nolan		
Miller, Nannie	Rej	Panola	Miller, William Lee	
Miller, S. Mrs.	Rej	McCulloch	Miller, Peter	
Miller, S. P.	Rej	Atascosa		
Miller, Sarah	Rej	Eastland	Miller, John Crawford	
Miller, Sarah J.	Rej	Tarrant	Miller, Samuel Eli	
Miller, Thomas Milton Mrs.	Rej	Tarrant	Miller, Thomas Milton	
Miller, Victory	Rej	San Augustine	Miller, William Theophiolous	
Miller, W. T.	Rej	Rockwall		
Miller, Wilburn	RejM	Henderson		
Miller, William	Rej	Guadalupe		
Miller, William Elbert Mrs.	Rej	Potter	Miller, William Elbert	
Miller, William M.	Rej	San Patricio		
Miller, Zack	Rej	Lamar		
Millhollen, Sarah J.	RejM	Brown		
Millican, Laura J.	Rej	Tarrant	Millican, James Knox	
Milligan, Henry Richard	Rej	Trinity		
Million, Kate	Rej	Angelina	Million, Milledge	
Milliorn, James Monroe	Rej	Ward		
Mills, B. B.	Rej	Houston		
Mills, David L.	Rej	McLennan		
Mills, Elum Samuel	Rej	Taylor		
Mills, Gideon	Rej	Mitchell		
Mills, Seth Phineas Mrs.	Rej	Travis	Mills, Seth Phineas	
Mills, T. J.	RejM	Henderson		

Index to Rejected Confederate Pension Applications

Mills, W. S.	Rej	Armstrong		
Millsaps, Virginia N.	Rej	Jefferson	Millsaps, Hiram	
Milner, Ruth A.	Rej	Anderson	Milner, George W.	
Milton, William	Rej	Hill		
Mimms, Henry	Rej	San Jacinto		
Mims, Elizabeth	Rej	Marion	Mims, John Wesley	
Minifee, Dan	Rej	San Augustine		
Minnear, A. E. Mrs.	Rej	Grayson	Minnear, Moses B.	
Minter, S. A.	Rej	Hopkins		
Minton, Elizabeth J.	Rej	Denton	Minton, Wilson W.	
Misenhimer, W. L.	Rej	Johnson		
Mitchell, Andrew J.	Rej	Lamar		
Mitchell, B. B.	Rej	Johnson		
Mitchell, Betty Ollie	Rej	Hopkins	Mitchell, Winfield Scott	47835
Mitchell, Clara Laura	Rej	Ellis	Mitchell, Silas Americus	
Mitchell, James Harrison Mrs.	Rej	Titus	Mitchell, James Harrison	
Mitchell, John C.	Rej	Hopkins		
Mitchell, Levi F.	Rej	Eastland		
Mitchell, Mary Jane	Rej	Fisher	Mitchell, William L.	
Mitchell, P. A. Mrs.	Rej	Eastland	Mitchell, L. F.	
Mitchell, Purety E.	Rej	Panola	Mitchell, Josiah	
Mitchell, R. M.	Rej	Harris		
Mitchell, S. E. Mrs.	Rej	Johnson	Mitchell, Thomas Jefferson	
Mitchell, Sue	Rej	Tom Green	Mitchell, William Edward	
Mitchell, Susan Elizabeth	Rej	Harris	Mitchell, Thomas Jefferson	
Mitchem, E. J. Mrs.	Rej	Hunt	Mitchem, James Nathaniel	
Mixon, Early Charles	Rej	Knox		
Mixon, J. J.	Rej	Polk		
Mixson, Enna	Rej	Grayson	Mixson, Adrian Worth	41335
Mobley, A. M.	Rej	Archer		
Mobley, Jonathan	Rej	Coke		
Mobley, Zeb	Rej	Johnson		
Mobray, Joseph	Rej	Hardin		
Modgling, Ann P.	Rej	Brown	Modgling, Elijah	
Moezygemba, John	Rej	Bexar		
Moffit, Joseph Madison	Rej	Henderson		
Moffitt, Thomas Jefferson	Rej	Bell		
Moncrief, J. M.	Rej	McLennan		
Monday, Willie Narcissus	Rej	Kaufman	Monday, William Hampton	
Mongham, S. P.	RejM	Upshur		
Monk, M. M. Mrs.	Rej	Cherokee	Monk, C. H.	
Monkhouse, Alice C.	Rej	Caldwell	Monkhouse, John Fortner	
Monkres, Robert Pope	Rej	Wilbarger		
Monroe, M. L.	Rej	Leon		
Montgomery, M. L. Mrs.	Rej	Fisher	Montgomery, Joseph Haynes	26303
Montgomery, Martha	Rej	Tarrant	Montgomery, Samuel Asbury	
Montgomery, Mary A.	Rej	Cooke	Montgomery, Jefferson C.	09187
Montgomery, T. J.	Rej	Nolan		
Montgomery, W. F.	Rej	Crosby		
Moon, J. N. Mrs.	Rej	Hill	Moon, William Bookout	09237
Moon, W. B.	Rej	Leon		
Mooney, M. B.	Rej	Tarrant		
Mooneyham, J. L.	Rej	Hunt		
Moore, Benjamin Crow	Rej	El Paso		
Moore, Charles R.	Rej	Hood		
Moore, Delila	Rej	Smith	Moore, Richard	
Moore, Eliza Ann	Rej	Freestone	Moore, James Hosea	
Moore, Enola	Rej	Comanche	Moore, James Barnett	
Moore, Franklin Monroe Mrs.	Rej	Hopkins	Moore, Franklin Monroe	30019

Index to Rejected Confederate Pension Applications

Moore, H. C.	RejM	Dallas	—	—
Moore, H. H.	Rej	Runnels	—	—
Moore, J. A.	Rej	Tarrant	—	—
Moore, J. P.	Rej	Dallas	—	—
Moore, J. W., Sr.	Rej	Hamilton	—	—
Moore, James	Rej	Travis	—	—
Moore, John B. Mrs.	Rej	Tarrant	Moore, John B.	—
Moore, Kate	Rej	Parker	Moore, Joseph C.	—
Moore, L. C.	Rej	Dallas	—	—
Moore, L. M.	Rej	Dewitt	—	—
Moore, L. M. Mrs.	Rej	Waller	Moore, L. M.	—
Moore, M.	Rej	Galveston	—	—
Moore, M. C. Mrs.	Rej	Tarrant	Moore, Joseph Atlas	—
Moore, Martha Ann	Rej	Dallas	Moore, James John	—
Moore, Mattie	Rej	San Saba	Moore, Rollie Vanburan	—
Moore, N. A. Mrs.	Rej	Fannin	Moore, Joseph Redmond	—
Moore, N. E. Stewart Mrs.	Rej	Bexar	Stewart, John	—
Moore, P. C. Mrs.	Rej	Lamar	Moore, Sandy	—
Moore, P. L.	Rej	Hunt	—	—
Moore, Phillip M.	Rej	Delta	—	—
Moore, R. C. Mrs.	Rej	Cherokee	Moore, David	—
Moore, R. R.	Rej	Jack	—	—
Moore, S. D.	Rej	McLennan	—	—
Moore, S. T. Mrs.	RejM	Johnson	—	—
Moore, Sallie	Rej	Johnson	Moore, Henry Pope	02982
Moore, Sallie F.	Rej	Lampasas	Moore, John William	—
Moore, Samuel	Rej	Bexar	—	—
Moore, Susan A.	RejM	Bowie	—	—
Moore, W. C.	Rej	Falls	—	—
Moore, William H.	Rej	Concho	—	—
Moore, William T.	Rej	Hill	—	—
Moorhead, Frances Anne	Rej	Montgomery	Moorhead, Newton Jasper	—
Moose, A. C.	Rej	Kerr	—	—
Moose, L. J. Mrs.	Rej	Bexar	Moose, W. Andrew	—
Morehead, J. L.	Rej	Hopkins	—	—
Morehead, John L.	Rej	Delta	—	—
Moreman, C. R.	Rej	Deaf Smith	—	—
Moren, Permelia	Rej	Fannin	Moren, Robert	—
Moreno, Helena T. De	Rej	Webb	Moreno, Lejundo	—
Moreno, Victoriana J. De	Rej	Webb	Moreno, Bartolo	—
Moresnau, C. R.	RejM	Deaf Smith	—	—
Morgan, D. M.	Rej	Henderson	—	—
Morgan, Eliza	Rej	Fayette	Morgan, Levi	—
Morgan, Emeline	Rej	Collin	Morgan, Joseph	—
Morgan, Eva	Rej	Johnson	Morgan, John Little	—
Morgan, Isaac N.	Rej	Navarro	—	—
Morgan, J. A. Mrs.	Rej	Smith	Morgan, James A.	20899
Morgan, J. P.	Rej	Grayson	—	—
Morgan, John W.	Rej	Lamar	—	—
Morgan, Louisa	Rej	Bastrop	Morgan, Renal Edward	—
Morgan, M. E. Mrs.	Rej	San Jacinto	Morgan, David Daniel	—
Morgan, Martha Jane	Rej	Jefferson	Morgan, Charles	—
Morgan, Nathaniel	Rej	Bowie	—	—
Morgan, Oliver Alvin	Rej	Jefferson	—	—
Morgan, Permelia	RejM	Fannin	—	—
Morgan, Sam	Rej	Trinity	—	—
Morgan, Thomas P.	Rej	Milam	—	—
Morris, A. P. Mrs.	Rej	Grayson	Morris, Joseph	—
Morris, Ann	Rej	Franklin	Morris, Benjamin Franklin	—

Index to Rejected Confederate Pension Applications

Morris, Benjamin Franklin	Rej	Sabine		
Morris, David Ewing Mrs.	Rej	Dickens	Morris, David Ewing	
Morris, Enoch	Rej	Travis		
Morris, Fairie I.	Rej	Randall	Morris, Thomas Jefferson	
Morris, Francis M.	Rej	Dallas		
Morris, John Thomas Mrs.	Rej	Hamilton	Morris, John Thomas	14247
Morris, Julia A.	Rej	Brown	Morris, William	
Morris, Lizzie Slone	Rej	Coryell	Slone, John	
Morris, Marion E.	Rej	Jones	Morris, C. Parks	
Morris, R. B. Mrs.	Rej	Freestone	Morris, James	
Morris, W. G.	Rej	Hood		
Morrison, Francis Marion	Rej	Taylor		
Morrison, Susan A.	Rej	Wichita	Morrison, William Jasper	
Morrow, A. M.	Rej	Houston		
Morrow, Mary Catherine	Rej	Collin	Morrow, John G. Burkhardt	
Morrow, Robert	Rej	Tarrant		
Morse, E. J. Mrs.	Rej	Hunt	Morse, Ebinezer Steward	Rej
Morse, Ebinezer Steward	Rej	Hunt		
Moseley, Joe Mrs.	Rej	Navarro	Moseley, Mat Martin	
Moseley, Marelda Jane	Rej	Atascosa	Moseley, Mark Nathaniel	25300
Moses, William G.	Rej	Wise		
Mosley, Benjamin F.	Rej	Dallas		
Mosley, E. B.	Rej	Ellis		
Mosley, H. P.	Rej	Henderson		
Mosley, J. T.	Rej	Shelby		
Mosley, Noah	Rej	Tarrant		
Moss, Benjamin F.	Rej	Medina		
Moss, Eliza	Rej	Bosque	Moss, James Milton	
Moss, J. M.	Rej	Grayson		
Moss, John D.	Rej	Van Zandt		
Moss, Louisa Ellen	Rej	Palo Pinto	Moss, John Gaston	
Mote, Jennie	Rej	Hopkins	Mote, Franklin	15520
Mott, Jim M.	Rej	Madison		
Mott, Joseph	Rej	Galveston		
Mott, L. E. Mrs.	Rej	Cass	Mott, Thomas	
Moughon, S. P.	Rej	Upshur		
Mounger, Kate	Rej	Grayson	Mounger, Peter Marcus	
Mouser, Henry	Rej	Blanco		
Mowrey, M. A. Mrs.	Rej	Cooke	Mowrey, Robert Armstrong	
Moxley, Minnie	Rej	Erath	Moxley, Thomas	24833
Muckleroy, Anthony	Rej	Dewitt		
Mueller, Auguste Mrs.	Rej	Washington	Mueller, August	
Mulder, Harve	Rej	Grayson		
Mulhousen, Frank	RejM	Harrison		
Mulhousen, William	Rej	Harrison		
Muller, P. E. Mrs.	Rej	Upshur	Muller, William Marion	
Mullins, Fannie A.	Rej	Mills	Mullins, Daugherty Dandridge	
Mullins, Frank M.	RejM	Medina		
Mullins, Vincent	Rej	Lamar		
Mullins, W. J.	Rej	Denton		
Mullins, William	Rej	Medina		
Munger, Hiram Runnels	Rej	Liberty		
Munn, Annie	Rej	Eastland	Munn, Green Duncan	
Murchison, Murdock Mrs.	Rej	Harris	Murchison, Murdock	
Murdock, Rebecca	Rej	Dallas	Murdock, Adam	
Murphey, John	Rej	Anderson		
Murphey, R. K.	Rej	Henderson		
Murphy, Anna	Rej	Smith	Murphy, Sandy	47793
Murphy, G. W.	RejM	Hunt		

Index to Rejected Confederate Pension Applications

Murphy, J. T.	Rej	Rockwall	—	—
Murphy, Jesse	Rej	Dallas	—	—
Murphy, Jesse J.	Rej	Johnson	—	—
Murphy, Margaret E.	Rej	Cass	Murphy, J. B.	—
Murphy, S.	Rej	Parker	—	—
Murphy, W. A.	Rej	Tarrant	—	—
Murray, James K. P.	Rej	Bexar	—	—
Murray, John Watts	Rej	Crosby	—	—
Murray, Thomas P.	Rej	Bexar	—	—
Murray, William W.	Rej	Menard	—	—
Murrell, George W.	Rej	Upshur	—	—
Murry, W. J.	Rej	Rusk	—	—
Murtschin, Auges	RejM	Lee	—	—
Muse, Elisa Jane Josephine	Rej	Cherokee	Muse, Joseph William	—
Mutz, Mary	Rej	Wilson	Mutz, Lawrence	—
Myers, B. I. Mrs.	Rej	Tarrant	Myers, Charles Lafayette	22310
Myers, E. M. Mrs.	Rej	Angelina	Myers, R. M.	14580
Myers, Frank C.	Rej	Orange	—	—
Myers, George	RejM	Coryell	—	—
Myers, George W.	Rej	Hill	—	—
Myers, Joel H.	Rej	Hill	—	—
Myers, M. M.	Rej	Burleson	—	—
Myers, Robert C.	Rej	Orange	—	—
Myers, T. C.	RejM	Orange	—	—
Nabors, H. A.	Rej	Delta	—	—
Naegelin, Joseph	Rej	Medina	—	—
Nale, R. L.	Rej	Lamar	—	—
Nance, E.	Rej	Knox	—	—
Nance, Henry Hamilton	Rej	Fannin	—	—
Nance, Sophie Jane	Rej	Comanche	Nance, William Bascom	—
Nance, T. A.	RejM	Tarrant	—	—
Nantz, J. T.	Rej	Jasper	—	—
Nash, B. H.	Rej	Montgomery	—	—
Nash, Cenie	Rej	Trinity	Nash, Emanuel	—
Nash, J. T.	Rej	Denton	—	—
Nations, Lavicy	Rej	Mills	Nations, L. Isaace	—
Navarro, Celso	Rej	Bexar	—	—
Navarro, Corsenciano	Rej	Bexar	—	—
Navarro, Escolastica Goda De	Rej	Zapata	Navarro, Antonio	—
Neace, T. A.	Rej	Tarrant	—	—
Neal, A. J. Mrs.	Rej	Red River	Neal, Benjamin Franklin	19575
Neal, Harvey C.	Rej	Bexar	—	—
Neal, J. M.	Rej	Karnes	—	—
Neal, James E.	Rej	Montgomery	—	—
Neal, Sarah J.	Rej	Burleson	Neal, Pinckney Green	—
Neal, T. M.	Rej	Somervell	—	—
Neatherlin, P. M.	Rej	Uvalde	—	—
Neathery, John	Rej	Red River	—	—
Neel, Margaret	Rej	Tarrant	Neel, James Mack	—
Neeley, M. E. Mrs.	Rej	Rockwall	Neeley, John	—
Neeley, Willis	Rej	Grimes	—	—
Neelly, Louise P.	Rej	Tarrant	Neelly, George Washington	—
Neely, H. L.	Rej	Hood	—	—
Neely, R. B.	Rej	Erath	—	—
Neidlinger, S. M. Mrs.	Rej	Trinity	Neidlinger, J. G.	—
Neighbors, I.	Rej	Crosby	—	—
Neil, B. H. Mrs.	Rej	Eastland	Neil, B. H.	33333
Neil, James P. Mrs.	Rej	Hill	Neil, James P.	—
Neil, Margaret	RejM	Tarrant	—	—

Index to Rejected Confederate Pension Applications

Neill, E. J. Mrs.	Rej	Grayson	Neill, James Thomas Lafayette
Neill, J. M.	Rej	Smith	
Neily, M. E. Mrs.	RejM	Rockwall	
Nelins, Curtis	Rej	Gonzales	
Nelson, George W.	Rej	Palo Pinto	
Nelson, J. W.	Rej	Navarro	
Nelson, Jane C.	Rej	Navarro	Nelson, Jefferson Wise
Nelson, S. R.	Rej	Hunt	
Nelson, S. W.	Rej	Wood	
Neugent, Eliza	Rej	Bowie	Neugent, Terence
Nevills, Mary A.	Rej	Rusk	Nevills, Thomas Griffin
Newkirk, James H.	Rej	Archer	
Newman, A. M. Mrs.	Rej	Stephens	Newman, Simpson
Newman, G. H.	Rej	Nacogdoches	
Newman, Henrietta	Rej	Falls	Newman, Edward Peter
Newman, L. R.	Rej	Bexar	
Newman, Rebecca Jane	Rej	Harrison	Newman, W. D.
Newman, Susan O.	Rej	Austin	Newman, Greer J.
Newsom, E. T. Mrs.	Rej	Freestone	Newsom, Joel
Newton, J. S.	Rej	Madison	
Newton, M. E. Mrs.	Rej	Bexar	Newton, D. C.
Newton, W. A.	Rej	McLennan	
Nicholas, Thomas	Rej	Rusk	
Nichols, George	Rej	Bexar	
Nichols, James W.	Rej	Van Zandt	
Nichols, James Warren Mrs.	Rej	Navarro	Nichols, James Warren
Nichols, Jonathan B.	Rej	Mills	
Nichols, Mallie	Rej	Floyd	Nichols, Washington Columbus 47634
Nichols, R. H.	Rej	San Augustine	
Nicholson, J. L.	Rej	Grayson	
Nickerson, E. T.	Rej	Madison	
Nix, J. N.	Rej	Burleson	
Nix, Mary P. Hudman	Rej	Panola	Hudman, James T.
Nix, W. H.	Rej	Montague	
Noble, G. O.	Rej	Williamson	
Noble, J. R.	RejM	Henderson	
Noble, Mary Coffey	Rej	Victoria	Noble, Albert Edwards
Nobles, B. E. Mrs.	Rej	Limestone	Nobles, Joseph Goodrich
Noland, W. T.	Rej	Anderson	
Noles, J. A.	Rej	Johnson	
Norfleet, Jasper Holmes Benton	Rej	Coke	
Norfleet, Mary A.	Rej	Randall	Norfleet, Jasper Holmes Benton .... Rej
Norman, John M.	Rej	Bexar	
Norman, William Ervin Mrs.	Rej	Hood	Norman, William Ervin
Norris, Fannie L.	Rej	Taylor	Thomas, Dr.
Norris, J. H.	Rej	Hunt	
Norton, James W.	Rej	Coryell	
Norvell, Mattie Elizabeth	Rej	Hall	Norvell, David A.
Norvell, Samuel Johnson Mrs.	Rej	Navarro	Norvell, Samuel Johnson 16175
Norvill, Mary Jane	Rej	Burleson	Norvill, Andrew Jackson
Norwood, B. C.	Rej	Bandera	
Norwood, Elmira	Rej	Jefferson	Norwood, James Daniel
Nowell, Mary E.	Rej	Burleson	Nowell, Reuben
Nugent, Alfred	Rej	Liberty	
Nuner, Luvicy J. B.	Rej	Montgomery	Nuner, John Barber
O'Banion, Mary Elizabeth	Rej	Harris	O'Banion, Jesse Lee 16527
O'Docharty, L.	Rej	Tarrant	
Ogle, Laura Frances	Rej	Tarrant	Ogle, Franklin
Ogles, Harkless	Rej	Tarrant	

Index to Rejected Confederate Pension Applications

Oglesby, Elisha C.	Rej	Grayson	—	—
Ojeman, John	Rej	Harris	—	—
Oliver, Emma Virginia	Rej	Bowie	Oliver, John Alfred	—
Oliver, F. N. B.	Rej	Wilson	—	—
Oliver, J. H.	Rej	Crosby	—	—
Oliver, Kisiar Caroline	Rej	McLennan	Oliver, Benjamin P.	—
Oliver, Lue	Rej	Johnson	Oliver, John W.	47598
Oliver, Mattie A.	Rej	Bowie	Oliver, Joseph Wynn	00486
Oliver, Nancy	Rej	Upshur	Oliver, James Bryant	—
O'Neal, Andrew J.	Rej	Nueces	—	—
O'Neal, G. R.	Rej	Stonewall	—	—
O'Neal, H. M.	Rej	Hill	—	—
O'Neal, M. J. Mrs.	Rej	Dawson	O'Neal, James Richard	—
O'Neal, M. J. Mrs.	Rej	McLennan	O'Neal, Hiram Marion	—
O'Neill, E. A. Mrs.	Rej	Frio	O'Neill, William	—
O'Quinn, John A.	Rej	Angelina	—	—
O'Rear, Emma	Rej	Marion	O'Rear, James (Joseph) Addison	23381
Orme, T. M.	Rej	Hunt	—	—
Orrell, Bettie	Rej	Real	Orrell, R. P.	—
Orrick, Lillie	Rej	Ellis	Orrick, William David	42565
Orsburn, Elizabeth J.	Rej	Upshur	Orsburn, William H.	—
Ortiz, Mariana R. De	Rej	Bexar	Ortiz, Monico	Rej
Ortiz, Monico	Rej	Bexar	—	—
Ortmann, Justina Louisa	Rej	Bexar	Ortmann, William	—
Osborn, George S.	Rej	Palo Pinto	—	—
Osborn, S. H.	Rej	Coryell	—	—
Osburn, Hattie	Rej	Tarrant	Osburn, William Thompson	—
Osteen, Newton	Rej	Denton	—	—
Oswalt, Francis	Rej	Bell	Oswalt, Lebury	—
Oteman, John	RejM	Harris	—	—
Overall, Ella B.	Rej	Bexar	Overall, Isaac Rudolphus	—
Overton, J. E.	Rej	Van Zandt	—	—
Owen, E. M.	Rej	Brown	—	—
Owen, H. E.	Rej	Kaufman	—	—
Owen, Henrietta	Rej	Ellis	Owen, Zebbie Dee	—
Owen, Henry J.	Rej	Hill	—	—
Owen, J. M.	Rej	Falls	—	—
Owen, S. W.	Rej	McLennan	—	—
Owen, William Henry Mrs.	Rej	Galveston	Owen, William Henry	—
Owens, Amanda	Rej	Tom Green	Owens, John R.	—
Owens, Lillie W.	Rej	Shelby	Owens, James William	22292
Owens, Mary F.	Rej	Coke	Owens, William Riley	—
Owens, Minnie	Rej	Dawson	Owens, John Thomas	—
Ownbey, Ava	Rej	Bosque	Ownbey, James Lafayette	—
Oxford, S. O.	Rej	Bandera	—	—
Pace, Florence	Rej	Harrison	Pace, John William	47356
Pace, G. R.	Rej	Comanche	—	—
Pace, R. M.	Rej	Nacogdoches	—	—
Padgett, J. W.	Rej	Mitchell	—	—
Padgett, John B.	Rej	Coryell	—	—
Page, John D.	Rej	San Saba	—	—
Paine, Columbia	Rej	Montague	Paine, T. P.	—
Painpare, Oscar	Rej	Tarrant	—	—
Palm, William	Rej	Dallas	—	—
Palmer, A. W. Mrs.	Rej	Bexar	Palmer, Christopher Columbus	—
Palmer, Bettie Eugenia	Rej	Wichita	Palmer, James Asa	—
Palmer, S. E.	Rej	Freestone	—	—
Palmer, Susan	Rej	Williamson	Palmer, Isaiah Tyson	—
Pangle, J. F.	Rej	Burnet	—	—

Index to Rejected Confederate Pension Applications

Parchman, Martin V.	Rej	Caldwell		
Pardue, L. B. Mrs.	Rej	Lamar	Pardue, Joseph Alexander	
Pardue, Mary E.	Rej	Comanche	Pardue, John N.	
Parish, J. W.	Rej	Delta		
Parish, Lucien B.	Rej	Freestone		
Park, J. L.	Rej	Ellis		
Park, John T.	Rej	Madison		
Park, Nathan H.	Rej	Madison		
Parker, A. C.	Rej	Leon		
Parker, B. F. Mrs.	Rej	Houston	Parker, B. F.	
Parker, Cora	Rej	Cass	Parker, John Jacob	49426
Parker, E.	Rej	Cass		
Parker, Ester	Rej	Navarro	Parker, John B.	
Parker, George M.	Rej	Rockwall		
Parker, Harris	Rej	Upshur		
Parker, J. M.	Rej	Taylor		
Parker, Joseph	Rej	Parker		
Parker, Lucindia	Rej	Mills	Parker, Sam	
Parker, M. D. Mrs.	Rej	Hunt	Parker, Jackson F.	
Parker, Mandy E.	Rej	Shelby	Parker, William Fisher	16523
Parker, Margaret Ann	Rej	Bastrop	Parker, Job Henry	
Parker, Nancy Ann	Rej	Houston	Parker, Josephus	
Parks, John Dudley	Rej	Denton		
Parnell, Nancy Emily	Rej	Dallas	Parnell, William	
Parr, F. C.	Rej	Dallas		
Parris, John	Rej	Bosque		
Parrish, S. D. Mrs.	Rej	Jack	Parrish, John Buckhamon	
Parrish, T. J.	Rej	Grayson		
Parshall, J. G.	Rej	Bosque		
Parsons, M. J.	Rej	Limestone		
Parsons, Serepta	Rej	Parker	Parsons, Amsley	26604
Partin, Elizabeth	Rej	Henderson	Partin, Samuel	
Pascoe, Letha	Rej	Galveston	Pascoe, William H.	
Passons, Milton Brocket	Rej	Dallas		
Passons, W. M.	Rej	Kaufman		
Pate, James W.	Rej	Montague		
Pate, W. F.	Rej	Henderson		
Paterson, Frances P.	Rej	Galveston	Paterson, Robert	
Patrick, George L.	Rej	Grayson		
Patrick, M. A. Mrs.	Rej	Waller	Patrick, Edward	
Patrick, Thomas A.	Rej	Hopkins		
Patterson, Aseneith	Rej	Travis	Patterson, Oliver H.	
Patterson, G. R.	Rej	Hamilton		
Patterson, John	Rej	Limestone		
Patton, George Washington	Rej	Midland		
Patton, James M.	Rej	Travis		
Patton, M. J.	Rej	Erath		
Patton, Sophronie	Rej	Caldwell	Patton, Dorn	
Paul, M.	Rej	Coryell		
Paulett, J. S.	Rej	Cass		
Paulson, Leonard G.	Rej	Smith		
Payne, Alvah	Rej	Brazos		
Payne, G. W.	Rej	Coke		
Payne, John L.	Rej	Palo Pinto		
Payne, M. L.	Rej	Ellis		
Payne, T. J.	Rej	Montague		
Payne, W. H., Sr.	Rej	Grayson		
Payton, Kate V.	Rej	Harris	Payton, Charles S.	
Pearce, C. M. Mrs.	Rej	Dimmit	Pearce, J. S.	

Index to Rejected Confederate Pension Applications

Pearce, L. J.	RejM	Coryell	—	—
Pearce, Sarah A.	Rej	Walker	Pearce, Luizy C.	—
Pearson, J. M.	Rej	Hopkins	—	—
Pearson, Jennie	Rej	Fannin	Pearson, Thomas Prigmore	—
Pearson, Joe Mrs.	Rej	Grimes	Pearson, Joe	30375
Pearson, L. J.	RejM	Coryell	—	—
Pearson, L. J. Mrs.	Rej	Lampasas	Pearson, Richard Marion	—
Pearson, M. V.	Rej	Sterling	—	—
Pearson, William Smith	Rej	Travis	—	—
Pease, Madena	Rej	Shelby	Pease, Blackburn	—
Peavy, Mary M.	Rej	Marion	Peavy, G. L.	—
Peck, Joseph	RejM	Red River	—	—
Peck, M. W.	Rej	Anderson	—	—
Peden, W. M.	Rej	Wood	—	—
Pedigo, Charles H.	Rej	Bell	—	—
Peek, Nancy	Rej	Red River	Peek, J. N.	—
Peevy, George W.	Rej	Leon	—	—
Pefferling, Christina	Rej	Bexar	Pefferling, Edward	—
Pegues, James Alston Mrs.	Rej	Smith	Pegues, James Alston	—
Pela, Victor	Rej	Victoria	—	—
Pendergast, Annie	Rej	Tarrant	Pendergast, John Thomas	—
Pendergrass, John W.	Rej	Bexar	—	—
Pendergrass, Mary E.	Rej	Comanche	Pendergrass, William Thomas	—
Pendleton, James Knox	Rej	Travis	—	—
Pennell, E. L. Mrs.	Rej	Clay	Pennell, Bluford W.	—
Penney, Emory Hartwell	Rej	Washington	—	—
Pennington, G. W. Cummings Mrs.	Rej	Trinity	Cummings, William Jones	—
Peoples, G. W.	Rej	Nacogdoches	—	—
Perdue, Melissa Ann	Rej	Knox	Perdue, John Daniel	26088
Perez, Alejo Encarnacion	Rej	Bexar	—	—
Perez, Florence E.	Rej	Bexar	Perez, Alejo Encarnacion	Rej
Perkins, John B.	Rej	Bexar	—	—
Perkins, John P.	Rej	Comanche	—	—
Perkins, Lee F.	Rej	Hill	—	—
Perkins, Nancy L.	Rej	Comanche	Perkins, Richard Sharp	—
Perkins, Susan	Rej	Coryell	Perkins, James Washington	33285
Perkins, W. B.	Rej	Goliad	—	—
Perry, F. S.	Rej	Wise	—	—
Perry, J. C. Mrs.	Rej	Comanche	Perry, Henry	—
Perry, J. H.	Rej	Bosque	—	—
Perry, L. L. Mrs.	Rej	Collingsworth	Perry, Franklin Sanford	—
Perry, Thomas Jackson	Rej	Henderson	—	—
Perryman, Louise	Rej	Bexar	Perryman, Edward	—
Pese, Andrew	Rej	Lee	—	—
Peteet, Richard	Rej	Upshur	—	—
Peteete, Nancy Camellas	Rej	Grimes	Peteete, Thomas Henderson	—
Peters, Elijah A.	Rej	Falls	—	—
Peters, Tom B.	Rej	Navarro	—	—
Pettigrew, Clara	Rej	Tarrant	Pettigrew, Green Jordan	—
Petty, Dave	Rej	Leon	—	—
Petty, Elisha	Rej	Limestone	—	—
Petty, Jasper Sevier	Rej	Navarro	—	—
Petty, Josha L.	Rej	McLennan	—	—
Petty, Samuel Houston	Rej	Hill	—	—
Petty, W. F. Mrs.	Rej	Van Zandt	Petty, W. F.	24857
Pevehouse, Dora	Rej	Limestone	Pevehouse, John	12584
Peveto, Sarah	Rej	Orange	Peveto, John	—
Pevoto, Robert	Rej	Orange	—	—
Pewitt, M. J. Mrs.	Rej	Wise	Pewitt, Joseph Andes	—

Index to Rejected Confederate Pension Applications

Peyton, John R.	Rej	Brazos		
Pfiffer, Ernst	Rej	Austin		
Phelps, T. B.	Rej	Jones		
Philips, R. R.	Rej	Cherokee		
Phillips, C. B. Mrs.	Rej	Dewitt	Phillips, C. B.	
Phillips, G. W.	Rej	Kaufman		
Phillips, Gabriel Jones	Rej	Montgomery		
Phillips, John F.	Rej	Wilson		
Phillips, John L.	Rej	Rusk		
Phillips, L. P. Mrs.	Rej	Nacogdoches	Phillips, Elijah	
Phillips, M. R.	Rej	Brazos		
Phillips, Whit	Rej	Hopkins		
Philpot, Joe W.	Rej	Gonzales		
Phipps, William C.	Rej	Freestone		
Pickard, Charles E.	Rej	Lamar		
Pickard, J. A.	Rej	Shelby		
Pickens, H. T.	Rej	Cherokee		
Pickett, Clara	Rej	Washington	Pickett, George Washington	
Pickett, J. D.	Rej	Hardeman		
Pierce, Francis Ann Victory	Rej	Van Zandt	Pierce, Rickerson C.	
Pierce, John Brown	Rej	Wilbarger		
Pierce, John C.	Rej	Bandera		
Pierce, William C.	Rej	Leon		
Piercey, John W.	Rej	Dallas		
Pierson, N. M. Mrs.	Rej	Swisher	Pierson, Richmond	
Pigot, Dominique	Rej	Bexar		
Pike, John	Rej	Tarrant		
Pilgrim, S. E. Mrs.	Rej	Camp	Pilgrim, Isaac Tims	
Pinkerton, Elizabeth F.	Rej	Wichita	Pinkerton, Thomas Urban	
Pinkerton, John P.	Rej	Rusk		
Pinkerton, N. J. Mrs.	Rej	Van Zandt	Pinkerton, James Calvin	
Pinson, Amanda Adeline	Rej	Ellis	Pinson, William Harrison	
Piper, Bertha	Rej	Milam	Piper, F. H.	18128M
Piper, James Alexander	Rej	Burnet		
Piper, Margaret A.	Rej	Wilbarger	Piper, Leonidas Zebedee	
Piper, Sam Mrs.	Rej	Haskell	Piper, Sam	
Pitman, R.	Rej	Harris		
Pitts, G. W.	Rej	Johnson		
Pitts, J. C.	Rej	Harris		
Pitts, P. M.	Rej	Lamar		
Pitts, R. H.	Rej	Wise		
Plummer, Cordalean	Rej	Shackelford	Plummer, Allison Richard	
Plunket, M. E. Mrs.	Rej	Hunt	Plunket, C. J.	
Podesta, Joseph	Rej	Harris		
Poe, Andrew J.	Rej	Travis		
Pogue, J. W.	Rej	Ellis		
Poindexter, Henderson Owen	Rej	Hunt		
Poindexter, Joe S.	Rej	Fort Bend		
Polk, Israel E.	Rej	Hunt		
Polk, James K.	Rej	Fisher		
Polk, James Monroe	Rej	Travis		
Polk, Mary	Rej	San Augustine	Polk, John Kenneth	
Pollard, J. L.	Rej	Dallas		
Polster, Catherine	Rej	McLennan	Polster, George	
Ponder, John Washington Mrs.	Rej	Nacogdoches	Ponder, John Washington	
Ponder, Lucy A. T.	Rej	Houston	Ponder, S. M.	
Pool, John A., Sr.	Rej	Presidio		
Pool, Malinda	Rej	Smith	Pool, John Attmon	23984
Pope, E. W.	Rej	Panola		

Index to Rejected Confederate Pension Applications

Name	Status	County	Veteran	Number
Pope, George C.	Rej	Williamson	—	
Pope, George Washington Mrs.	Rej	Grayson	Pope, George Washington	
Pope, W. A.	Rej	Dallas	—	
Popejoy, Simon M.	Rej	Stephens	—	
Porter, E. N. Mrs.	Rej	Shelby	Porter, Amos	
Porter, G. A.	Rej	Hood	—	
Porter, J. H.	Rej	Bell	—	
Porter, James H.	Rej	Parker	—	
Porter, Mary E.	Rej	Grayson	Porter, William J.	
Porter, William M.	Rej	Haskell	—	
Post, M. M. Mrs.	Rej	Haskell	—	
Post, M. M. Mrs.	Rej	Haskell	Post, John S.	23267
Potter, E. B., Dr.	Rej	Eastland	—	
Potter, E. J.	Rej	Smith	—	
Potts, W. B.	Rej	Angelina	—	
Powell, Bridgett	Rej	Coryell	Powell, John I.	
Powell, C. P. A.	Rej	Cass	—	
Powell, Charles Ford	Rej	Wheeler	—	
Powell, F. Marion	Rej	Freestone	—	
Powell, J. J.	Rej	Van Zandt	—	
Powell, Mary Jane	Rej	Bexar	Powell, William Moses	
Powell, W. D.	Rej	Harrison	—	
Powell, W. M.	Rej	Bexar	—	
Powell, William	Rej	Cass	—	
Power, Jake G.	Rej	Mills	—	
Power, John Isaac	Rej	Tom Green	—	
Powers, John Preston	Rej	Dallas	—	
Powers, Josephine Williams	Rej	Cooke	Williams, John Morrison	
Prater, M. E. Mrs.	Rej	Johnson	Prater, Robert Joseph	38684
Prator, J. H.	Rej	Cass	—	
Pratt, Lenard Allen	Rej	Morris	—	
Pratt, T. M.	Rej	Bell	—	
Preslar, William Joshua Mrs.	Rej	Midland	Preslar, William Joshua	
Pressley, Charles Alexander Mrs.	Rej	Garza	Pressley, Charles Alexander	23679
Pressley, Ophelia	Rej	Burleson	Pressley, Julius Joseph	30320
Prestridge, Usebia J.	Rej	Johnson	Prestridge, Benjamin Bagley	
Preusser, Joe	Rej	Reeves	—	
Price, David	Rej	Leon	—	
Price, Elizabeth	Rej	Upshur	Price, George Washington	
Price, Elizabeth	Rej	Leon	Price, David	
Price, Emily	Rej	Hardeman	Price, Emory Black	09495
Price, F. M.	Rej	Delta	—	
Price, G. N.	Rej	Eastland	—	
Price, Isaac	Rej	Young	—	
Price, James A.	Rej	Henderson	—	
Price, Levi L.	Rej	Lamar	—	
Price, Margaret	RejM	Burnet	—	
Price, Nancy Ann Rebecca	Rej	Jefferson	Price, Peter William	
Price, Nancy D.	Rej	Anderson	Able, Sr.	14546
Price, William H.	Rej	Unknown	—	
Prichard, Anderson	Rej	Cass	—	
Prince, Margaret J.	Rej	Burnet	Prince, Henry Franklin	
Priour, Julian John M., Sr Mrs.	Rej	Nueces	Julian John Marie, Sr.	
Pritchard, Sarah E.	Rej	Young	Pritchard, William Benton	
Pritchard, W. H.	Rej	Harrison	—	
Pritchett, Benjamin F.	Rej	Cherokee	—	
Pritchett, Sarah Hoyt	Rej	Hill	Pritchett, Elias Frank	
Privitt, Ann E.	Rej	Wise	Privitt, Frank Merion	
Prock, W. R.	Rej	Briscoe	—	

Index to Rejected Confederate Pension Applications

Proctor, George W.	Rej	Bell		
Proctor, S. E. Mrs.	Rej	Leon	Proctor, John Thomas	
Provence, A. M. Mrs.	Rej	Wise	Provence, Thomas Marion	
Pruett, M. A. Mrs.	Rej	Frio	Pruett, Daniel Lippan Lafayette	
Pruett, W. S.	Rej	Bosque		
Pruitt, B. H.	Rej	Jack		
Pruitt, Jane	Rej	Leon	Pruitt, George Thomas	
Puckett, Mary R.	Rej	Tarrant	Puckett, Jackson	
Puckett, Samuel M.	Rej	Dallas		
Pue, Edward B.	Rej	Bexar		
Pugh, Lassiephine	Rej	Freestone	Pugh, Aladen Lester	
Pujo, Dominique	Rej	Bexar		
Pullen, Charles	Rej	Nacogdoches		
Pullen, J. G.	Rej	Collin		
Pullen, J. R.	Rej	Rockwall		
Pulley, John William	Rej	Bell		
Pulliam, Bettie	Rej	Harris	Pulliam, John Standford	
Punchard, Samuel W.	Rej	Bell		
Purcell, A. J. Mrs.	Rej	Bastrop	Purcell, Charles M.	
Purcell, Maria Elizabeth	Rej	Goliad	Purcell, Ruben Cadmel	
Purswell, W. S.	Rej	Montgomery		
Purvis, A. L.	Rej	Gray		
Pyle, M. S.	Rej	Cherokee		
Pynes, Christopher Columbus Mrs.	Rej	Franklin	Pynes, Christopher Columbus	15171
Pyron, Octavia	Rej	Bexar	Pyron, Charles L.	
Quedy, Isabel	Rej	Bexar	Quedy, John	
Quintero, Thomas	Rej	Bexar		
Quirk, Mary Reily	Rej	Navarro	Reily, William	
Radford, Robert Rutherford	Rej	Red River		
Ragan, John W.	Rej	Hunt		
Ragan, R. A. Mrs.	RejM	Houston		
Ragland, Alice	Rej	Trinity	Ragland, William Wilson	
Ragland, M. A. Mrs.	Rej	Scurry	Ragland, Peyton	
Ragon, John Wilson	Rej	Haskell		
Ragsdale, J. C.	Rej	Travis		
Ragsdale, James Edward	Rej	Lamar		
Ragsdale, Samuel A.	Rej	Grayson		
Rainer, A.	Rej	Kent		
Rainer, H. K.	Rej	Collin		
Rainey, W. A.	Rej	Wise		
Rainey, William Smith Mrs.	Rej	Tarrant	Rainey, William Smith	
Rainwater, Amanda Adeline	Rej	Jones	Rainwater, Benjamin Franklin	
Ralph, A. M.	Rej	Montague		
Ralston, Eliza	Rej	McLennan	Ralston, Luther Whitfield	
Ramsey, E. J. Mrs.	Rej	Navarro	Ramsey, S. T.	
Ramsey, Jennie	Rej	Brown	Ramsey, William Henry	
Ramsey, John A.	Rej	Red River		
Ranbe, F.	Rej	Austin		
Randolph, J. N.	Rej	Bowie		
Rankin, John W.	Rej	Dallas		
Rankin, Lucinda	Rej	Bexar	Rankin, James	
Ransom, Bettie	Rej	Madison	Ransom, James Roe	
Ransom, Eugene Albert Mrs.	Rej	Baylor	Ransom, Eugene Albert	
Ransom, Jacob Henry Mrs.	Rej	Harris	Ransom, Jacob Henry	38843
Ransom, William	Rej	Bexar		
Rape, Belle	Rej	Upshur	Rape, William David	
Rash, S. A.	Rej	Hood		
Ratcliff, J. H.	Rej	Houston		
Ratcliff, J. T.	Rej	Bowie		

Index to Rejected Confederate Pension Applications

Raticin, James Jefferson Mrs.	Rej	Hopkins	Raticin, James Jefferson	
Ratliff, Ann Eliza	Rej	Erath	Ratliff, Luther Judson	
Ratliff, R. E. Mrs.	Rej	Montgomery	Ratliff, J. R.	
Rattan, Rosetta	Rej	Hunt	Rattan, John	
Rawlins, Joseph Robert	Rej	Knox		
Rawls, John C.	Rej	Wilson		
Rawls, Margaret	Rej	Tom Green	Rawls, J. T.	
Rawls, Richard Henry	Rej	San Saba		
Rawls, Willie Anna	Rej	Lamar	Rawls, John Boyd	06017
Ray, A. J. Mrs.	Rej	Callahan	Ray, James Samuel	26412
Ray, A. L.	Rej	Kent		
Ray, Frank	Rej	Matagorda		
Ray, James K.	Rej	Grayson		
Read, Emma	Rej	Houston	Read, John	17882
Reader, N. J. Mrs.	Rej	Karnes	Reader, Thomas Jefferson	
Reagan, Thomas	Rej	Lavaca		
Reardon, Hartwell Spain	Rej	Camp		
Reardon, M. R. Mrs.	Rej	Camp	Reardon, Hartwell Spain	Rej
Reaves, Angelina	Rej	Marion	Reaves, David	
Rector, Mary S.	Rej	Caldwell	Rector, James W.	
Red, Marshack	Rej	Uvalde		
Redd, Theodore B.	Rej	Tarrant		
Redden, William Robison	Rej	Bell		
Reddick, William	Rej	Gregg		
Redding, Francis M.	Rej	Harris		
Redding, Leona	Rej	Milam	Redding, David Franklin	24387
Redding, Thomas Crocker	Rej	Taylor		
Redick, John	Rej	Grayson		
Redus, Blewett S.	Rej	San Augustine		
Redus, Leah	Rej	Medina	Redus, James	
Redus, M. S.	RejM	San Patricio		
Redus, Samuel G.	Rej	Fisher		
Redwine, M. M.	Rej	Lynn		
Redwine, W. H.	Rej	Montague		
Redwood, Callie	Rej	Grayson	Redwood, George Edward	
Reece, S. M. Mrs.	Rej	Comanche	Reece, J. W.	
Reed, Emma	RejM	Houston		
Reed, G. W.	Rej	Kaufman		
Reed, Jennie	Rej	Shelby	Reed, Ira	
Reed, Lou	Rej	Leon	Reed, John Patrick	
Reed, Mary B.	Rej	Morris	Reed, John T.	
Reeder, Army T.	Rej	Dallas	Reeder, Thomas Benton	
Reeds, J. M.	Rej	Lee		
Reese, B. W. Mrs.	Rej	Jasper	Reese, Henry Clay	
Reese, Cuthbert	Rej	Jasper		
Reese, Emanuel	Rej	Austin		
Reeves, Addie E.	Rej	Coke	Reeves, Andrew Jackson	
Reeves, Andrew Washington Mrs.	Rej	Fayette	Reeves, Andrew Washington	38404
Reeves, Jacob Franklin	Rej	Eastland		
Reeves, John L.	Rej	Wichita		
Reid, John Tom	Rej	Bastrop		
Reifel, C. R.	Rej	Galveston	Reifel, William Nicholas	
Reiger, Mary	Rej	Matagorda		
Reil, McDuffin Mrs.	Rej	Erath	Reil, McDuffin	
Rembert, T. A.	Rej	Robertson		
Renfro, George	Rej	Shelby		
Renfro, James R.	Rej	San Augustine		
Renfro, Peter	Rej	Chambers		
Rettig, Paul	Rej	Rusk		

Index to Rejected Confederate Pension Applications

Revell, Hennie E.	Rej	El Paso	Revell, Joseph	
Revier, Margaret	Rej	Johnson	Revier, John Francis	
Revill, Matt L.	Rej	Upshur	—	
Reynolds, Isaac	Rej	Bandera	—	
Reynolds, John	Rej	Falls	—	
Reynolds, Joseph E.	Rej	Hardeman	—	
Reynolds, Margaret	Rej	Shelby	Reynolds, Henry H.	
Rhea, Thomas Jeff Ritchie Mrs.	Rej	Scurry	Rhea, Thomas Jefferson Ritchie	50136
Rhodes, James C.	Rej	Shelby	—	
Rhodes, M. V. Mrs.	Rej	Bowie	Rhodes, William Thomas	
Rhodes, Ruth	Rej	Tyler	Rhodes, Arnold	
Rhodus, Amelia	Rej	Bexar	Rhodus, Henry M.	11212
Rhubottom, Amelia	Rej	Chambers	Rhubottom, Charles Foster	
Rhyne, D. A. Mrs.	Rej	Cass	Rhyne, Jacob G.	
Ribble, Harvey W.	Rej	Van Zandt	—	
Rice, J. D.	Rej	Caldwell	—	
Rice, Joseph Mrs.	Rej	Houston	Rice, Joseph	24770
Rice, S. A. Davis Mrs.	Rej	Falls	Davis, George Thedore	
Rice, S. J.	Rej	Rains	—	
Rich, M. L. Mrs.	Rej	Jack	Rich, Thomas J.	
Richards, Anna Bell	Rej	Hill	Richards, David Winchester	
Richards, E. E. Mrs.	RejM	Dallas	—	
Richards, N.	Rej	Houston	—	
Richards, Nancy J.	Rej	San Jacinto	Richards, John Pruitt	
Richardson, A. J.	Rej	Anderson	—	
Richardson, A. V.	Rej	Henderson	—	
Richardson, Alice W.	Rej	Hall	Richardson, Thomas Presley	
Richardson, E. E. Massingill Mrs.	Rej	Dallas	Massingill, George Washington	
Richardson, G. L.	Rej	Navarro	—	
Richardson, Henry	Rej	Hays	—	
Richardson, Jennie A.	Rej	Medina	Richardson, Allie O.	
Richardson, John	RejM	Hall	—	
Richardson, M. A. Mrs.	Rej	Mitchell	Richardson, George H.	
Richardson, Maggie	Rej	Tarrant	Richardson, John C.	
Richardson, Moses	Rej	Cherokee	—	
Richardson, R. M.	Rej	Erath	—	
Richardson, Stephen Austin	Rej	Hardin	—	
Richey, Daniel Boone	Rej	Falls	—	
Richey, Martha W.	Rej	Orange	Richey, Thomas Cope	
Richter, Mary L.	Rej	Harris	Richter, Herman	
Rickard, George A.	Rej	Bosque	—	
Riddle, Annie	Rej	Tarrant	Riddle, William Nelson	
Riddle, T. W.	Rej	Van Zandt	—	
Rider, Henry	Rej	Panola	—	
Ridling, William Washington	Rej	Stephens	—	
Riemenschneider, Lorenz	Rej	Goliad	—	
Riffe, Dora	Rej	Brazoria	Riffe, Chris	
Riffe, Parmelia	Rej	Lampasas	Riffe, John	
Riggs, D. A.	Rej	Burnet	—	
Riggs, Leonidas	Rej	San Patricio	—	
Rikard, A. B. Wheeler Mrs.	Rej	Travis	Wheeler, John Wesley	
Riley, G. H.	Rej	Cass	—	
Riley, Janie Elizabeth	Rej	Hardeman	Riley, William Bishop	
Riley, Sylvester	Rej	Wise	—	
Riley, W. T.	Rej	Harrison	—	
Ring, Mary Ann	Rej	Hall	Ring, William	Rej
Ring, William	Rej	Hall	—	
Ringwald, C. F.	Rej	Red River	—	
Rinker, A. F.	Rej	Fisher	—	

Index to Rejected Confederate Pension Applications

Rion, Lessie Connor	Rej	Harris	Rion, Augustus Thomas	—
Risenhover, L. H.	Rej	Kaufman	—	—
Ritter, M. A. Mrs.	Rej	Clay	Ritter, William	—
Rivers, M. M.	Rej	Hill	—	—
Rives, C. S.	Rej	McLennan	—	—
Riviere, John Kirk	Rej	McLennan	—	—
Roach, David Henry	Rej	Hardin	—	—
Roach, Henry	Rej	Tyler	—	—
Roach, Joseph Daniel Mrs.	Rej	Hunt	Roach, Joseph Daniel	—
Roach, Mary F.	Rej	Hopkins	Roach, Thomas Norman	—
Roark, Isaac M.	Rej	Hansford	—	—
Robbins, Daniel Monroe	Rej	Wood	—	—
Robbins, George W.	Rej	San Saba	—	—
Robbins, M. E. Mrs.	Rej	McCulloch	Robbins, Milton Clay	33279
Robbins, S. J. Mrs.	Rej	Tarrant	Robbins, G. J.	24222
Robbins, Thomas Jefferson Mrs.	Rej	Eastland	Robbins, Thomas Jefferson	—
Roberson, E. D.	Rej	Van Zandt	—	—
Roberson, Eugene	Rej	Reeves	—	—
Roberson, J. H.	Rej	Karnes	—	—
Roberts, A. C.	Rej	Anderson	—	—
Roberts, Brownlee	Rej	San Saba	—	—
Roberts, J. H.	Rej	Bexar	—	—
Roberts, J. J.	Rej	Dallas	—	—
Roberts, Jiles Jackson	Rej	Atascosa	—	—
Roberts, Josephine A.	Rej	Brown	Roberts, Joshua T.	—
Roberts, Leonora	Rej	Burleson	Roberts, Jonathan	—
Roberts, Martin M.	Rej	Haskell	—	—
Roberts, Mary R.	Rej	Wharton	Roberts, Thomas Jefferson	—
Roberts, Nannie E.	Rej	Ellis	Roberts, William Henry	—
Roberts, S. E.	Rej	Fannin	—	—
Roberts, Turner Ingram	Rej	Sabine	—	—
Roberts, Victoria	Rej	Dallas	Roberts, John Jefferson	—
Roberts, W. L.	Rej	Cass	—	—
Roberts, William A.	Rej	Parker	—	—
Robertson, Arabella	Rej	Waller	Robertson, James Noah	—
Robertson, E. C.	Rej	Mitchell	—	—
Robertson, E. D. Mrs.	Rej	Dallas	Robertson, Richard Henry	—
Robertson, Edna Lysanious	Rej	Uvalde	Robertson, Amos Hezekiah	34736
Robertson, F. E. Mrs.	Rej	Robertson	Robertson, E. G. S.	—
Robertson, George Washington	Rej	Hale	—	—
Robertson, H. O.	Rej	Washington	—	—
Robertson, James Edward	Rej	Jones	—	—
Robertson, Laura B.	Rej	Bexar	Robertson, Thomas Lofton	—
Robertson, M. A. Mrs.	Rej	Tarrant	Robertson, N. P.	—
Robertson, O. P. Mrs.	Rej	Harris	Robertson, Zedoc Franklin	—
Robinson, Belle	Rej	Cass	Robinson, J. M.	30492
Robinson, Braxton	Rej	Milam	—	—
Robinson, Elizabeth	Rej	Hardeman	Robinson, Francis Marion	—
Robinson, J. E. Mrs.	Rej	Lee	Robinson, Robert Locke	—
Robinson, J. I.	Rej	Comanche	—	—
Robinson, J. M. Mrs.	Rej	Cass	Robinson, J. M.	—
Robinson, J. N.	Rej	Dallas	—	—
Robinson, Jennie E.	Rej	Lee	Robinson, Rober L.	—
Robinson, L. C.	Rej	Rusk	—	—
Robinson, Lucinda	Rej	Tarrant	Robinson, R. R.	—
Robinson, Reuben R.	Rej	Young	—	—
Robinson, Sam	Rej	Franklin	—	—
Robinson, W. F.	Rej	Coryell	—	—
Robinson, W. F.	Rej	Taylor	—	—

Index to Rejected Confederate Pension Applications

Name	Status	County	Veteran	Number
Robinson, W. W.	Rej	Jack		
Robison, F. A.	Rej	Jack		
Robison, H. V.	Rej	Montgomery		
Robison, J. R.	Rej	Blanco		
Robison, Lewellen	Rej	Blanco		
Rochester, Mary P.	Rej	Wichita	Rochester, R. S.	
Roden, W. A.	Rej	Angelina		
Rodgers, Geneva A.	Rej	Ellis	Rodgers, James Alexander	25443
Rodgers, John W.	Rej	Gonzales		
Rodgers, M. F. Mrs.	Rej	Harris	Rodgers, Victor W.	
Rodgers, Mary A.	Rej	Kaufman	Rodgers, John W.	
Rodgers, Mary Isabel	Rej	Jefferson	Rodgers, Jesse Moore	
Rodgers, Phillip	Rej	Upshur		
Rodgers, W. E.	Rej	Nolan		
Rodgers, W. H.	Rej	Coke		
Rodman, H. M.	Rej	Hill		
Rodriguez, Jesus	Rej	Webb		
Rodriguez, Lucinda	Rej	Bexar	Rodriguez, Juan Manuel	
Roeber, W. Mrs.	Rej	Bosque	Roeber, Albrecht Alexander	
Rogers, A. J.	Rej	Limestone		
Rogers, Allie	Rej	Polk	Rogers, William Pinckney	
Rogers, E. C. Mrs.	Rej	Hidalgo	Rogers, Paul Hamilton	12404
Rogers, E. Pomeroy	Rej	Parker		
Rogers, Francis M.	Rej	Titus		
Rogers, Henry Dodson	Rej	Dallam		
Rogers, J. M.	Rej	San Augustine		
Rogers, J. M. Mrs.	Rej	San Augustine	Rogers, James Madison	
Rogers, Jim M.	Rej	Erath		
Rogers, John N.	RejM	Gonzales		
Rogers, Mattie	Rej	Washington	Rogers, Benjamin Sion	
Rogers, Moses Columbus Mrs.	Rej	Clay	Rogers, Moses Columbus	
Rogers, Spires Alexander	Rej	Burleson		
Rogers, W. F.	Rej	Titus		
Rogers, W. R.	Rej	Freestone		
Rogerson, William	Rej	Waller		
Roman, Sam	Rej	Wise		
Roman, Sam	Rej	Wise		
Rome, Clara A. (Alcena C.)	Rej	Walker	Rome, William Booth	
Rome, Clara A. (Alcena C.)	Rej	Walker	Rome, William Booth	
Rook, J. R.	Rej	Walker		
Rook, J. R.	Rej	Walker		
Rooks, Harrison T.	Rej	Lamar		
Rooks, Harrison T.	Rej	Lamar		
Roomell, John	Rej	Guadalupe		
Roop, B. J.	Rej	Bell		
Roper, Charles	Rej	Fannin		
Rosa, William Guillermor De La	Rej	Bexar		
Roscoe, A. L.	RejM	Panola		
Roscoe, Solom	RejM	Limestone		
Rose, John	Rej	Harris		
Rose, Louisie	Rej	Freestone	Rose, John Lincy	
Rose, Malinda	Rej	Van Zandt	Rose, John Henry	04849
Rose, Robert	Rej	Wilson		
Rosell, C. E.	Rej	Dallas		
Ross, Dan W.	Rej	Comanche		
Ross, David A. C.	Rej	Burleson		
Ross, F. S.	Rej	Cherokee		
Ross, G. W.	Rej	Montague		
Ross, Mary S.	Rej	Parker	Ross, John Henry	

Index to Rejected Confederate Pension Applications

Name	Status	County	Veteran	Number
Ross, W. F.	Rej	Denton	—	—
Rosson, G. W.	Rej	Bell	—	—
Rosson, John Ellis	Rej	Taylor	—	—
Rosson, Joseph Gains	Rej	Montague	—	—
Rounsavall, A. M.	Rej	Henderson	—	—
Rounsavall, W. A.	Rej	Titus	—	—
Roussau, Travis	Rej	Rusk	—	—
Rouswell, Mary E.	Rej	Baylor	Rouswell, Simon B.	—
Routh, Amasira	Rej	Uvalde	—	—
Routon, Louisa Calhoun	Rej	Bell	Routon, John	—
Rowin, Abe	Rej	Angelina	—	—
Rowland, James R.	Rej	Smith	—	—
Rowland, John P.	Rej	Wood	—	—
Rowsey, T. S.	Rej	Hunt	—	—
Rowzee, T. J.	Rej	Travis	—	—
Royal, George H.	Rej	Lampasas	—	—
Rubio, Franzisco	Rej	Bexar	—	—
Rucker, Thomas H.	Rej	Hunt	—	—
Ruckwardt, Susan A.	Rej	Harris	Ruckwardt, Robert	—
Rudasill, Levi L.	Rej	Bee	—	—
Rugeley, Frank	Rej	Smith	—	—
Ruiz, Juan Antonio	Rej	Atascosa	—	—
Rumph, David Maltravers	Rej	Tarrant	—	—
Rundell, Mary Jane	Rej	Upshur	Rundell, Samuel	—
Runnells, Jason S.	Rej	Angelina	—	—
Runnels, Elizabeth	Rej	San Augustine	Runnels, Francis Marion	06644
Runnels, Joseph	Rej	Shelby	—	—
Rusher, Daniel	Rej	Houston	—	—
Rushton, J. C.	Rej	Angelina	—	—
Rushton, Jospeph Clifton	Rej	Rusk	—	—
Russell, J. J.	Rej	Nacogdoches	—	—
Russell, John L.	Rej	Fannin	—	—
Russell, Joseph	Rej	Burnet	—	—
Russell, Nancy	Rej	Angelina	Russell, John Jackson	—
Russell, Robert Franklin	Rej	Cherokee	—	—
Russell, W. M.	Rej	Johnson	—	—
Russell, William L.	Rej	Red River	—	—
Russell, Zona	Rej	Crosby	Russell, John Weldon	—
Rutcliff, J. H.	RejM	Houston	—	—
Rutherford, George S.	Rej	Robertson	—	—
Rutherford, J. W.	Rej	Ellis	—	—
Rutherford, Mary Etta	Rej	Tom Green	Rutherford, James McCullough	—
Rutledge, Andrew Jackson	Rej	Travis	—	—
Rutledge, S. A. Mrs.	Rej	Wise	Rutledge, Robert G.	—
Ryan, Ada J.	Rej	Palo Pinto	Ryan, James William	—
Ryan, John F.	Rej	Angelina	—	—
Rylander, G. E.	Rej	Hays	—	—
Ryon, M. R.	Rej	Burleson	—	—
Sachtleban, Charles	Rej	Comal	—	—
Sadberry, Irene	Rej	Comanche	Sadberry, Ivey	—
Sagray, Charles	Rej	Bexar	—	—
Sailors, Alfred Luther	Rej	Hopkins	—	—
Salyer, Jennie	Rej	Galveston	Salyer, Dave Jasper	08218
Salziger, Godfrey	Rej	Comal	—	—
Samaniego, E. Manuel	Rej	Bexar	—	—
Samaniego, Virginia S.	Rej	Zavala	Samaniego, Juan	—
Samford, J. K.	Rej	Shelby	—	—
Samples, Manerva	Rej	Wichita	Samples, John	—
Sampson, Johnson	Rej	Kaufman	—	—

Index to Rejected Confederate Pension Applications

Sams, Nancy J. A.	Rej	Castro	Sams, James L.	
Samuel, Bessie	Rej	Bexar	Samuel, Desoto	
Samuels, Eliza J.	Rej	Walker	Samuels, Newman Jackson (samuel)	24336
Sandel, Jack	Rej	Walker		
Sanderford, M. J. Mrs.	Rej	Bell	Sanderford, William Elisha	25481
Sanders, Alexander	Rej	Kent		
Sanders, Amanda	Rej	Palo Pinto	Sanders, John	
Sanders, Annie	Rej	Rusk	Sanders, John Andrew	27102
Sanders, Joshua	Rej	Knox		
Sanders, Julius	Rej	Newton		
Sanders, L. W.	Rej	Brown		
Sanders, Lula	Rej	Comanche	Sanders, Green Berry	
Sanders, Mary Willis Swayne	Rej	Bell	Sanders, Sarge Prentiss	
Sanders, N. E. Mrs.	Rej	Lynn	Sanders, Arden Dallas	
Sanders, Sam	Rej	Mason		
Sanders, W. M.	Rej	Robertson		
Sandifer, J. M.	Rej	Hopkins		
Sandlin, Clara Emeline	Rej	Somervell	Sandlin, Joseph	03752
Sandlin, William M. Mrs.	Rej	Stonewall	Sandlin, William M.	
Sandmann, Christian	Rej	Harris		
Sanford, M. J. Mrs.	RejM	Bell		
Sanford, Mary A.	Rej	Travis	Sanford, William D.	
Sargent, Lizzie	Rej	Kaufman	Sargent, William Blake	
Sasser, J. F.	Rej	Red River		
Sauls, Emily Sophia	Rej	Wichita	Sauls, Henry Robert	15484
Saunders, A. W. Mrs.	Rej	Guadalupe	Saunders, Richard E.	
Savage, Bettie A.	Rej	Nolan	Savage, John Wesley	
Savage, D. C.	Rej	Dallas		
Sawyers, James B.	Rej	Hill		
Sayers, L. A. Mrs.	Rej	Tarrant	Sayers, John Thomas	
Scarborough, Tamer	Rej	Smith	Scarborough, P. D.	
Schlick, F. A.	Rej	Gonzales		
Schmidt, Henriette	Rej	Harris	Schmidt, Frank	09477
Schmidt, Jacob	Rej	Austin		
Schmidt, Katherine	Rej	Dewitt	Schmidt, Frederick William	
Schneider, Dorthea	Rej	Medina	Schneider, Joseph	
Schneider, Nancy	Rej	Houston	Schneider, Charles	
Schriwsher, Jackson	Rej	Coryell		
Schroeder, E. J.	Rej	Lee		
Schroeder, Miner	Rej	Fayette	Schroeder, G. H.	
Schultea, Minnie	Rej	Lavaca	Schultea, Joseph	
Schultz, Charles	Rej	Goliad		
Schulwick, John	RejM	Leon		
Schwartz, C. A.	Rej	Colorado		
Scoggin, J. W.	Rej	Grayson		
Scott, Amanda	Rej	Madison	Scott, William Allen	
Scott, Eliza B.	Rej	Tarrant	Scott, James Chambers	
Scott, H. E. Mrs.	Rej	Van Zandt	Scott, T. F.	
Scott, H. E. Mrs.	Rej	Newton	Scott, F. G.	24025
Scott, J. A.	Rej	Hall		
Scott, J. E.	Rej	Leon		
Scott, J. E. Mrs.	RejM	Bexar		
Scott, James A.	Rej	Brown		
Scott, James Monroe Mrs.	Rej	Bosque	Scott, James Monroe	
Scott, Kate	Rej	Tarrant	Scott, Augustus Faust	
Scott, M. E. Mrs.	Rej	Johnson	Scott, John Coleman Burris	
Scott, M. M. Mrs.	Rej	Hill	Scott, Alexander E.	
Scott, Mary J.	Rej	Robertson	Scott, Reuben G.	
Scott, Melinda J.	Rej	Lamar	Scott, Milton Montgomery	

Index to Rejected Confederate Pension Applications

Scott, N. L. Mrs.	Rej	Comanche	Scott, Thomas J.	
Scott, Parkes	Rej	Frio	—	
Scott, Pete (R. L.)	Rej	Bosque	—	
Scott, Simeon	Rej	Bosque	—	
Scott, Timothy	Rej	Mason	—	
Scott, Walter	Rej	Harris	—	
Scrivner, John J.	Rej	Hill	—	
Scroggins, Anderson Aaron	Rej	Travis	—	
Scruggs, D. D.	Rej	Brazoria	—	
Scruggs, L. R.	Rej	Dallas	—	
Scruggs, M. J. Mrs.	Rej	Bexar	Scruggs, Levi Smith	
Scruggs, S. E. Mrs.	Rej	Shelby	Scruggs, H. M.	
Scurlock, W. L.	Rej	Polk	—	
Searcy, Emmett M.	Rej	Panola	—	
Searcy, N. A. Mrs.	Rej	Hood	Searcy, W. D.	
Seat, Martha Ann	Rej	Anderson	Seat, John Bruce	
Seaton, Joseph M.	Rej	Wood	—	
Seawell, Henry W.	Rej	Galveston	—	
Seay, M. E. Mrs.	Rej	Motley	Seay, R. A.	
Sebesta, John	Rej	Burleson	—	
Secrest, M. E. Mrs.	Rej	Lamar	Secrest, Isaac Newton	
Sedberry, Fannie (Francis)	Rej	McLennan	Sedberry, John Wesley	
Seely, Marion W.	Rej	Henderson	—	
Seely, Sue	Rej	Wise	Seely, William E.	
Self, D. P.	Rej	Cherokee	—	
Self, E. F. Mrs.	Rej	Anderson	Self, Chestley	
Sellers, A. R.	Rej	San Jacinto	—	
Sellers, Eliza	Rej	Nacogdoches	Sellers, Madison	
Sellers, M. L. Mrs.	Rej	Calhoun	Sellers, James Calhoun	
Sessums, Mary	Rej	Hill	Sessums, Cedar	
Sessums, P. T.	Rej	Madison	—	
Seward, Marion F.	Rej	Bexar	—	
Sewell, J. A.	Rej	Smith	—	
Sewell, Sarah	Rej	Burleson	Sewell, Joe Ivenes	
Sewell, Sarah V.	Rej	Jefferson	Sewell, John W. A.	
Sext, Sarah Jane Rebeca	Rej	Marion	Sext, Jacob	
Sexton, Henry McKenny Mrs.	Rej	Burleson	Sexton, Henry McKenny	
Shaddock, W. H.	Rej	Gregg	—	
Shadle, M. J.	RejM	Parker	—	
Shamburger, Edwin	Rej	Wood	—	
Shannon, J. T.	Rej	Atascosa	—	
Shannon, J. W.	Rej	Young	—	
Shannon, M. J. Mrs.	Rej	Stonewall	Shannon, Lihue Marion	
Sharp, Enoch Asberry Mrs.	Rej	Leon	Sharp, Enoch Asberry	19861
Sharp, F. J. Mrs.	Rej	Morris	Sharp, John Richard	
Sharp, J. R.	Rej	Morris	—	
Sharp, James	Rej	Fannin	—	
Sharp, William	Rej	Dallas	—	
Sharples, Roxana	Rej	Uvalde	Sharples, James Alexander	
Shaver, Alex	Rej	Houston	—	
Shaver, John S.	Rej	Newton	—	
Shaver, Laura	Rej	Madison	Shaver, Jasper	09570
Shaver, W. J.	Rej	Anderson	—	
Shaw, Cornelius H.	Rej	Knox	—	
Shaw, D. B.	Rej	Erath	—	
Shaw, George Mark	Rej	Hopkins	—	
Shaw, Hugh Jasper	Rej	Wise	—	
Shaw, J. W.	Rej	Atascosa	—	
Shaw, James M.	Rej	Bell	—	

Index to Rejected Confederate Pension Applications

Name	Status	County	Veteran	No.
Shaw, Mary Ellen	Rej	Travis	Shaw, Robert Burns	—
Shaw, W. G.	Rej	San Saba	—	—
Shean, Harriet	Rej	Galveston	Shean, Pat	—
Shelby, Alfred	Rej	Guadalupe	—	—
Shelby, George M.	Rej	Delta	—	—
Sheldon, Lillie A. Partain	Rej	Hamilton	Partain, William H	—
Shelton, Jeremiah M.	Rej	Red River	—	—
Shelton, Mary E.	Rej	Donley	Shelton, John Milton	—
Shelton, Parthena	Rej	Bexar	Shelton, Marcus	—
Shephard, G. W.	Rej	Leon	—	—
Shepherd, H. G.	Rej	Lamar	—	—
Shepherd, Mattie Jane	Rej	Angelina	Shepherd, Thomas Jefferson	24093
Sheppard, Alline	Rej	Bosque	Sheppard, Neal Floyd	25733
Sheppard, Mary J.	Rej	Montague	Sheppard, Martin Vanburen	—
Sheppard, Newton A.	Rej	Bandera	—	—
Sheppard, William A., Sr.	Rej	Bandera	—	—
Sheridan, Laura D.	Rej	Houston	Sheridan, John H.	—
Sherrill, Alice	Rej	Archer	Sherrill, James Thomas	30718
Shipley, J. C.	Rej	Tarrant	—	—
Shipman, R. E.	Rej	Edwards	—	—
Shipman, W. M.	Rej	Erath	—	—
Shires, Henrietta	Rej	Harris	Shires, Peter	—
Shirey, S. H.	RejM	Unknown	—	—
Shirley, F. E. Mrs.	Rej	Parker	Shirley, Robert Alexander	—
Shivers, Dona	Rej	Dallas	Shivers, William Henry	—
Shockley, A. M. Mrs.	Rej	Bowie	Shockley, James Marion	—
Shook, J. A.	Rej	Jack	—	—
Shook, J. P.	Rej	Nolan	—	—
Shoults, G. W.	Rej	Panola	—	—
Shows, Bertha Geneva	Rej	Swisher	Shows, James Benjamin	—
Shows, E. F. Mrs.	Rej	Brazos	Shows, John	—
Shropshire, E. Love	Rej	Wood	—	—
Shropshire, Lola	Rej	Johnson	Shropshire, David Naman	30719
Shuler, A. M.	Rej	Mills	—	—
Shurman, T. T.	Rej	Leon	—	—
Sidney, Ella May	Rej	Stephens	Sidney, David	—
Sierra, Juan	Rej	Atascosa	—	—
Sifford, Belle	Rej	Henderson	Sifford, Samuel Washington	—
Simmons, J. C.	Rej	Montgomery	—	—
Simmons, Julia Achsah	Rej	Cass	Simmons, Thomas R.	—
Simmons, Martha Bourgeois	Rej	Dallas	Bourgeois, Jules	—
Simmons, Mary D.	Rej	Hopkins	Simmons, Thomas Madison	—
Simons, H. M. Mrs.	Rej	Leon	Simons, Robert Porter	—
Simpson, D. H.	Rej	Llano	—	—
Simpson, E. L.	Rej	Houston	—	—
Simpson, John D.	Rej	Delta	—	—
Simpson, John Randolph	Rej	Cherokee	—	—
Simpson, W. H.	Rej	Hardeman	—	—
Sims, Allen T.	Rej	Wood	—	—
Sims, Ann L.	Rej	Grayson	Sims, Edward B.	—
Sims, E. G.	Rej	Hardin	—	—
Sims, E. M. Mrs.	Rej	Hill	Sims, William Argia	—
Sims, J. W.	Rej	Childress	—	—
Sims, James L.	Rej	Angelina	—	—
Sims, John L.	RejM	Grayson	—	—
Sims, Lena Gibson	Rej	Bell	Sims, William Humpreys	—
Sims, M. G.	Rej	Baylor	—	—
Sims, T. S.	Rej	Grayson	—	—
Sims, W. F.	Rej	Frio	—	—

Index to Rejected Confederate Pension Applications

Sims, W. R.	Rej	Ellis	—	
Sinclair, Alexander	Rej	Comanche	—	
Singletary, J. B.	Rej	Cherokee	—	
Singleton, F. C.	Rej	Travis	—	
Sisson, E. J.	RejM	Van Zandt	—	
Sitterle, Blaise	Rej	Victoria	—	
Skeeters, David Caufman	Rej	Cherokee	—	
Skelton, W. M.	Rej	Trinity	—	
Skinner, J. F.	Rej	Lampasas	—	
Skinner, M. T.	Rej	Hill	—	
Skinner, Miles S.	Rej	Comanche	—	
Slaven, James	Rej	Harris	—	
Slavin, E. C. Mrs.	Rej	Grayson	Slavin, J. B.	—
Slavin, G. A.	Rej	Ochiltree	—	
Slider, J. R.	Rej	Rains	—	
Smart, A. A. Mrs.	Rej	Wood	Smart, Charles H.	22076
Smart, Martha J.	Rej	Upshur	Smart, S. A.	—
Smart, Nathanial	Rej	Upshur	—	
Smart, Silas Americus	Rej	Upshur	—	
Smith, A. B.	Rej	Colorado	—	
Smith, A. J.	Rej	Bexar	—	
Smith, A. J.	Rej	Cass	—	
Smith, A. L. Mrs.	Rej	Hopkins	Smith, John Fleming	47153
Smith, A. O.	Rej	Rusk	—	
Smith, B. F.	Rej	Johnson	—	
Smith, B. W.	Rej	Callahan	—	
Smith, Byron Walker Mrs.	Rej	Bexar	Smith, Byron Walker	—
Smith, C. A.	Rej	Travis	—	
Smith, C. E.	Rej	Montgomery	—	
Smith, C. E.	Rej	Sabine	—	
Smith, C. R.	Rej	Collin	—	
Smith, Charles Edward Mrs.	Rej	Scurry	Smith, Charles Edward	07873
Smith, Clay P. Stones Mrs.	Rej	Washington	Stones, Henry Napier	—
Smith, D. C.	Rej	Hopkins	—	
Smith, D. W. C.	Rej	Dallas	—	
Smith, Daniel Hale Mrs.	Rej	Crosby	Smith, Daniel Hale	—
Smith, Dolly A.	Rej	Tarrant	Smith, A. P.	—
Smith, E. A. Mrs.	Rej	Jasper	Smith, Green Barnwell	15741
Smith, E. C. Mrs.	Rej	Wood	Smith, Thomas Dixon	—
Smith, E. Mrs.	Rej	Brown	Smith, William Giles	—
Smith, Eliza S.	Rej	Hopkins	Smith, John Thomas	—
Smith, Elizabeth	Rej	Wood	Smith, Joseph A.	—
Smith, Elizabeth	Rej	Jefferson	Smith, Presley Edward	—
Smith, Elizabeth	Rej	Burleson	Smith, James Rhett	—
Smith, Elizabeth A.	Rej	Scurry	Smith, John M.	—
Smith, Elizabeth C.	Rej	Dallas	Smith, William Lockhart	—
Smith, Fannie	Rej	Bell	Smith, Thomas W.	05174
Smith, Francis Tipton	Rej	Jefferson	—	
Smith, G. M.	Rej	Dallas	—	
Smith, George Washington	Rej	Mills	—	
Smith, Griffin	Rej	Hunt	—	
Smith, Gussie	Rej	Grayson	Smith, John Bransford	—
Smith, H. T. Mrs.	Rej	Ellis	Smith, Nathan C.	24794
Smith, Henry L. Mrs.	RejM	Runnels	Smith, Henry L.	—
Smith, Irena	Rej	Houston	Smith, Bee	—
Smith, Isaac	Rej	Fannin	—	
Smith, J. A.	Rej	Cass	—	
Smith, J. B.	Rej	Camp	—	
Smith, J. D.	Rej	Milam	—	

Index to Rejected Confederate Pension Applications

Name	Status	County	Veteran	Number
Smith, J. F.	Rej	Galveston	—	—
Smith, J. F.	Rej	Eastland	—	—
Smith, J. H.	Rej	Brown	—	—
Smith, J. H.	Rej	Grayson	—	—
Smith, J. W.	Rej	Crosby	—	—
Smith, James F.	Rej	Jasper	—	—
Smith, James K.	Rej	Robertson	—	—
Smith, James Z. T.	Rej	Bell	—	—
Smith, Jane Elizabeth	Rej	Nacogdoches	Smith, Alvin Dean	—
Smith, Jennie	Rej	Trinity	Smith, Tom S.	30177
Smith, Jim (James)	Rej	Navarro	—	—
Smith, Joe H.	Rej	Cooke	—	—
Smith, Joe N.	Rej	Travis	—	—
Smith, John M.	Rej	Mason	—	—
Smith, John N.	Rej	Newton	—	—
Smith, Joseph Hillery	Rej	Henderson	—	—
Smith, L. S.	Rej	Erath	—	—
Smith, M. A.	RejM	Wise	—	—
Smith, M. A. Mrs.	Rej	Dallas	Smith, Robert Pinkney	—
Smith, M. A. Mrs.	Rej	Hale	Smith, James Dekalb	—
Smith, M. J. Mrs.	Rej	Denton	Smith, James Alford	24565
Smith, M. L. Mrs.	Rej	Tarrant	Smith, John	—
Smith, Margaret	Rej	Shelby	Smith, Charles Ratcliff	—
Smith, Martha Ann	Rej	Henderson	Smith, Zacariah Jefferson	—
Smith, Martha L.	Rej	Robertson	Smith, Jeptha L.	—
Smith, Martha Phillips	Rej	Fayette	Smith, Henry Edwin	—
Smith, Mary	Rej	Parker	Smith, Robert Alexander	—
Smith, Mary Ann	Rej	Burleson	Smith, Ellis D.	—
Smith, Mary Ann	Rej	Sabine	Smith, Henry C.	—
Smith, Mary Ann Patrick	Rej	Sabine	Patrick, Henry	—
Smith, Mary J.	Rej	Lampasas	Smith, Phillip	—
Smith, Mary Jane	Rej	Coleman	Smith, William B.	—
Smith, Matilda	Rej	Franklin	Smith, Thomas Jefferson	—
Smith, Nathanial	RejM	Upshur	—	—
Smith, Nicholas G.	Rej	Kaufman	—	—
Smith, P. W. Mrs.	Rej	Erath	Smith, E. B.	—
Smith, Parish	Rej	Houston	—	—
Smith, Ples	Rej	Bell	—	—
Smith, Presley E.	Rej	Callahan	—	—
Smith, R. E. J.	RejM	Karnes	—	—
Smith, R. W.	Rej	Parker	—	—
Smith, R. W.	Rej	Guadalupe	—	—
Smith, Rebecca M.	Rej	Dallas	Smith, George Davis	—
Smith, Robert Reno	Rej	Travis	—	—
Smith, S. A. Mrs.	Rej	Titus	Smith, H. G.	—
Smith, S. C. Mrs.	Rej	Van Zandt	Smith, Harvey	—
Smith, S. E. Mrs.	Rej	Schleicher	Smith, J. M.	—
Smith, S. L.	Rej	Cherokee	—	—
Smith, Salina A.	Rej	Harrison	Smith, William Alexander	—
Smith, Sallie L.	Rej	Milam	Smith, James W.	—
Smith, Sarah	RejM	Houston	—	—
Smith, Sarah A.	Rej	Grayson	Smith, Robert Polk	—
Smith, Sarah E.	Rej	Coleman	Smith, Ebenezer	—
Smith, Sarah Elizabeth	Rej	Jack	Smith, William Harrison	—
Smith, Sarah Elizabeth	Rej	Garza	Smith, William Patton	—
Smith, Sue H.	Rej	Parker	Smith, Joseph Albert	—
Smith, T. A.	Rej	Dallas	—	—
Smith, Tempy	Rej	McLennan	Smith, William Russell	—
Smith, W. A.	Rej	Wise	—	—

Index to Rejected Confederate Pension Applications

Name	Status	County	Veteran	No.
Smith, W. A. Mrs.	RejM	Henderson		
Smith, W. D.	Rej	Parker		
Smith, W. L.	Rej	Lampasas		
Smith, W. M.	Rej	Shelby		
Smith, W. M.	RejM	Robertson		
Smith, W. P.	Rej	Carson		
Smith, W. S. N. Mrs.	Rej	Polk	Smith, W. S. N.	21599
Smith, W. W.	Rej	Hardin		
Smith, William	Rej	Gonzales		
Smith, William A.	Rej	Van Zandt		
Smith, William Archer Mrs.	Rej	Walker	Smith, William Archer	
Smith, William M.	Rej	McLennan		
Smith, William R.	Rej	Fannin		
Smith, William Thomas	Rej	Stephens		
Smith, Wyley C.	Rej	Marion	Smith, Henry Alexander	28728
Smythia, Loveisa Jane	Rej	Erath	Smythia, Hosea Merrett	
Sneed, Sam	Rej	Coryell		
Snell, Ida Haggerty	Rej	New York	Snell, John James	
Snellings, J. A.	Rej	Borden		
Snider, Amanda	Rej	Tom Green	Snider, Chester	
Snider, Annie	Rej	Montague	Snider, Samuel Copeland	11300
Snider, F. M.	Rej	Cottle		
Snider, S. M.	Rej	Shelby		
Snigleton, J. C.	RejM	Travis		
Snipes, George W.	Rej	Cass		
Snodgrass, Thomas Alexander	Rej	Hunt		
Snow, Jack	Rej	Leon		
Snow, Mary J.	Rej	Tarrant	Snow, Zacariah A.	
Solomon, P. H.	Rej	Hays		
Southall, Emma	Rej	Rockwall	Southall, Levi Cornelius	
Southwell, S. E. Mrs.	Rej	Bexar	Southwell, John Thomas	
Sowell, W. N.	Rej	Guadalupe		
Spain, M. E.	Rej	Travis		
Spaith, Leopoldine	Rej	Harris	Spaith, David	
Spalding, George	Rej	Brown		
Sparkman, J. B.	Rej	Hopkins		
Sparks, J. M.	Rej	Hale		
Sparks, Mary Caroline	Rej	Franklin	Sparks, Daniel	
Sparks, Susan P.	Rej	Collin	Sparks, Moses	
Sparks, U. J.	Rej	Archer		
Sparrow, Mary Ann	Rej	Goliad	Sparrow, Josephus	
Speckels, Gerhard Eilert Mrs.	Rej	Fayette	Speckels, Gerhard Eilert	
Speegle, E. J. Mrs.	Rej	Eastland	Speegle, Samuel Jefferson	
Speer, Mary A.	Rej	Hopkins	Speer, James Milton	
Speer, Thomas Alfred Mrs.	Rej	Bell	Speer, Thomas Alfred	
Spence, Marindy	Rej	Kaufman	Spence, John James	
Spence, Mary	Rej	Gillespie	Spence, George McDuffey	
Spencer, D. S.	Rej	Hopkins		
Spencer, John W.	Rej	Dallas		
Spencer, Samuel F.	Rej	Dallas		
Spiller, George	Rej	Jack		
Spillers, H. C.	Rej	Dallas		
Spinks, Francis Marion	Rej	Henderson		
Spring, Willie	Rej	Trinity	Spring, Jeremiah Hennon	
Sprinkle, Codie Bell	Rej	Tarrant	Sprinkle, William Henry	
Sprinkle, Codie Bell Hill	Rej	Tarrant	Hill, Edwin Harrison	
Sprinkles, F. M.	Rej	Kerr		
Sprott, James D.	Rej	Travis		
Sprouse, Addie	Rej	Denton	Sprouse, John Adams Crain	

Index to Rejected Confederate Pension Applications

Name	Status	County	Veteran	Number
Sprouse, Susan	Rej	Van Zandt	Sprouse, John	
Srygley, Maude	Rej	Tarrant	Srygley, James Milton	
St. John, Joan	Rej	Bexar	St. John, William Milton	
Staats, N. W.	Rej	Clay		
Stacey, Margaret Bawcum	Rej	Grimes	Stacey, William Warren	
Stafford, James L.	Rej	Angelina		
Stafford, William Henry	Rej	Colorado		
Stalcup, Margaret	Rej	Collin	Stalcup, Joseph	
Stallings, H. P.	Rej	Cherokee		
Stallings, J. M.	Rej	Montague		
Stallings, Joe	Rej	Callahan		
Stanfield, Martha J.	Rej	Falls	Stanfield, John Logan	
Stanford, John H.	Rej	Stephens		
Stanford, Mattie	Rej	Limestone	Stanford, Simon Allen	
Stanford, N. A. Mrs.	Rej	Real	Stanford, C. C.	
Stanford, S. A.	Rej	Limestone		
Stanford, Sarah Malinda	Rej	Wise	Stanford, James Franklin	
Stanford, William C. Mrs.	Rej	Lamb	Stanford, William C.	
Stanton, Mell Merth	Rej	Bell		
Stapp, Delaney A.	Rej	Harris	Stapp, Larkin S.	
Stapp, Samuel N.	Rej	Fannin		
Starkey, T. J.	Rej	Cherokee		
Starnes, E. J. Mrs.	Rej	Coleman	Starnes, Joseph W.	
Starrett, J. S.	Rej	Young		
Statcup, Margaret	RejM	Collin		
Stautzenberger, Susanna	Rej	Bexar	Stautzenberger, Andrew	17073
Stayton, Nannie B.	Rej	Rockwall	Stayton, James Insley	
Steagall, Lenora	Rej	Navarro	Steagall, Thomas Gardner	
Stedman, B. B.	Rej	Anderson		
Stedman, Kate M.	Rej	Dallas	Stedman, Edward Bernard	
Stedman, Thomas Ragland	Rej	Ellis		
Steed, Dovie Whitehurst	Rej	Wood	Whitehurst, Hilliard Montier	
Steed, R. W.	Rej	Cass		
Steel, R. L. Mrs.	Rej	Stephens	Steel, George Washington	42813
Steele, Hampton	Rej	Limestone		
Steelman, Joseph F.	Rej	Bowie		
Stegall, Permelia Ann	Rej	Tarrant	Stegall, John William	
Stephens, Emma	Rej	Comanche	Stephens, John Washington	26025
Stephens, Julia Ann	Rej	Smith	Stephens, Joseph Milton	
Stephens, M. E. Mrs.	Rej	Eastland	Stephens, Samuel Goodson	
Stephens, N. J. Mrs.	Rej	Taylor	Stephens, Marshal Henry	
Stephens, Peter	Rej	McLennan		
Stephenson, Alice R.	Rej	Dallas	Stephenson, James A.	08601
Stephenson, J. M.	Rej	Freestone		
Stephenson, Leonora	Rej	Lubbock	Stephenson, Leonidas Elihu	
Stephenson, Mary A. Shaw	Rej	Nueces	Stephenson, John A.	
Stephenson, W. S.	Rej	Comanche		
Sterling, John	Rej	Tyler		
Sterling, W. H.	Rej	Polk		
Stevens, M. E. Mrs.	RejM	Eastland		
Stevens, Malinda Catherine	Rej	Kaufman	Stevens, Thomas Fletcher	
Stevens, S. M. Mrs.	Rej	Montague	Stevens, Henry Walker	
Stevens, William Oscar	Rej	Fannin		
Stevens, William Oscar Mrs.	Rej	McCulloch	Stevens, William Oscar	Rej
Steward, Stout	Rej	Cherokee		
Stewart, Cathrine Jane	Rej	Hood	Stewart, Isaac	
Stewart, Henry	Rej	Henderson		
Stewart, J. A.	Rej	Hamilton		
Stewart, Jemima	RejM	Cass		

Index to Rejected Confederate Pension Applications

Stewart, John Waller	Rej	Jones		
Stewart, L. W. Tyson Mrs.	Rej	Galveston	Tyson, Henry Lyons	
Stewart, Letha	Rej	Upshur	Stewart, R. A.	
Stewart, Martha W.	Rej	Lamar	Stewart, H. S.	
Stewart, Nannie	Rej	Haskell	Stewart, David Isaah	22736
Stewart, Othella Richards	Rej	Red River	Richards, Burl Hill	
Stewart, R. F.	Rej	Edwards		
Stewart, Rufus M.	Rej	Cass		
Stewart, William P.	Rej	Bell		
Stidham, Zachariah	Rej	Irion		
Stiles, Leander Reno Mrs.	Rej	Fannin	Stiles, Leander Reno	
Still, H. C.	Rej	Harris		
Still, Mary E.	Rej	Young	Still, John William	22334
Stinnett, Mollie Clay	Rej	Matagorda	Stinnett, William Henry	
Stitt, Sarah Elizabeth	Rej	Limestone	Stitt, John Thomas	
Stobb, Augusta	Rej	Wilson		
Stockett, Mary A.	Rej	Tarrant	Stockett, Joseph Smith	
Stocks, T. H.	Rej	Franklin		
Stockton, Ella	Rej	Jones	Stockton, Augustine Partnership	
Stockton, W. R.	Rej	Hopkins		
Stoddard, Henry Bates	Rej	Brazos		
Stokes, J. K. P.	Rej	Trinity		
Stone, A. W.	Rej	Falls		
Stone, G. W.	Rej	Tarrant		
Stone, Mary C.	Rej	Dallas	Stone, Henry Bideman	
Stone, William	Rej	Rusk		
Stooksberry, M. E. Mrs.	Rej	Delta	Stooksberry, J. S.	
Storey, James	Rej	Harris		
Stork, Gertrude	Rej	Milam	Stork, Jacob	
Story, William	Rej	Dallas		
Stott, J. T.	Rej	Sabine		
Stout, E. L. Mrs.	Rej	Montague	Stout, Charles W.	33536
Stout, Elizabeth	Rej	Aransas	Stout, Joseph	
Stovall, Andrew Jackson Mrs.	Rej	Hardin	Stovall, Andrew Jackson	30933
Stovall, John R.	Rej	Montgomery		
Strader, W. L.	Rej	Milam		
Strahan, Mary R.	Rej	Nacogdoches	Strahan, Manuel	
Strain, Ellen Tabitha Palmertree	Rej	Runnels	Palmertree, George Washington	
Strait, Christopher Columbus	Rej	Matagorda		
Strange, Sallie	Rej	Nacogdoches	Strange, Samuel Edmond	
Strange, W. M.	Rej	Upshur		
Strather, B. P.	Rej	Hopkins		
Strawn, M. A. Mrs.	Rej	Grayson	Strawn, James Washington	
Street, J. K.	Rej	Dallas		
Streich, Martha L.	Rej	Lavaca	Streich, Theodore H.	
Stringer, Daniel T.	Rej	Bosque		
Stringfellow, M. E. Mrs.	Rej	Bowie	Stringfellow, John Johnson	
Stripling, W. C.	Rej	Franklin		
Strother, Belton	Rej	Freestone		
Strother, Margaret M.	Rej	Freestone	Strother, Samuel N.	
Stuart, J. W.	Rej	Freestone		
Stuart, P. C.	Rej	Kaufman		
Stubbeman, D.	Rej	Dewitt		
Stubblefield, G. W.	Rej	Clay		
Stubblefield, Lucy A.	Rej	Bosque	Stubblefield, William Jones	
Stubbs, Lillie D.	Rej	Freestone	Stubbs, John James	50140
Stuckert, W. A.	Rej	Washington		
Stutsman, A. T.	Rej	Fannin		
Sue, F. W.	Rej	Hood		

Index to Rejected Confederate Pension Applications

Suhr, Elizabeth	Rej	Austin	Suhr, Joachim	
Sullivan, J. W.	Rej	Caldwell	—	
Sullivan, Mary L.	Rej	Kaufman	Sullivan, Reson Fowler	
Sullivent, G. W.	Rej	Jack	—	
Summers, Sallie F.	Rej	Houston	Summers, Caly G.	12920
Sumner, John	Rej	Karnes	—	
Sumners, Susan S.	Rej	Dewitt	Sumners, A. M.	
Surratt, M. E. Mrs.	Rej	Franklin	Surratt, James Monroe	
Sutherlin, Francis Marion	Rej	Sterling	—	
Sutphen, Saphronia Ann	Rej	Stephens	Sutphen, Samuel C.	
Suttle, Annie	Rej	McLennan	Suttle, Thomas Dixon	
Suttle, H. M.	Rej	Leon	—	
Suttle, James J.	Rej	Callahan	—	
Sutton, Theopilus	Rej	Lamar	—	
Sutton, William	Rej	Coke	—	
Swain, Elvira Jane (Jennie E)	Rej	El Paso	Swain, Henry Clay	
Swan, W. M.	RejM	Rusk	—	
Swaner, Francis Marion	Rej	Falls	—	
Swann, M. C. Mrs.	Rej	Smith	Swann, T. M.	
Swartz, Charles A.	Rej	Victoria	—	
Swenson, Otto	Rej	Bosque	—	
Swift, E. J. Mrs.	Rej	Erath	Swift, William Henry	
Swinburn, Mary Ann	Rej	Sutton	Swinburn, John	
Swinford, Bettie	Rej	Tarrant	Swinford, Sam L.	
Swinney, Ella	Rej	Rusk	Swinney, Thomas Jefferson	
Swinney, Sarah A.	Rej	Lampasas	Swinney, Wilson Ransom	
Swords, Mary	Rej	Dallas	Swords, Thomas Williamson	
Sydow, Freidreika	Rej	Fort Bend	Sydow, Johan F.	
Sypert, Ada Frances	Rej	Bell	Sypert, William Rufus	
Talley, Bettie Horton	Rej	Freestone	Horton, Moses Dodson	
Talley, James Franklin	Rej	Dallas	—	
Talley, M. W.	Rej	Franklin	—	
Talley, Margarett Ann	Rej	Montague	Talley, Louis Lee	
Talley, Moses Watson	Rej	Hopkins	—	
Talley, William S.	Rej	Collin	—	
Tamplin, Alec	Rej	Shelby	—	
Tankersley, John H.	Rej	Harris	—	
Tankersley, Martin Walker Mrs.	Rej	Taylor	Tankersley, Martin Walker	43335
Tankersley, Merrill	Rej	Frio	—	
Tannehill, Frank R.	Rej	Unknown	—	
Tanner, Henry Alice	Rej	Tarrant	Tanner, Edmon Dennyan	
Tanner, Isaack L.	Rej	Jefferson	—	
Tanner, N. J. Mrs.	Rej	Trinity	Tanner, Pleasant Thomas	
Tanton, Gip	Rej	Hardin	—	
Tapp, Hugh	Rej	Kaufman	—	
Tarpley, Susan	Rej	Fannin	Tarpley, Henry Lindsey	28250
Tarter, William M.	Rej	Johnson	—	
Tarver, Wells	Rej	Kaufman	—	
Tarwater, Margaret	Rej	Tarrant	Tarwater, John Clinton	
Tate, C. C.	Rej	Harris	—	
Tate, Maria L.	Rej	Young	Tate, John Scott	
Tate, Robert Lions Hars	Rej	Franklin	—	
Tatum, H. S.	Rej	Tarrant	—	
Tatum, H. S.	RejM	Parmer	—	
Taylor, A. F.	Rej	Ellis	—	
Taylor, D. S. Mrs.	Rej	Falls	Taylor, D. S.	
Taylor, E. P.	Rej	Grayson	—	
Taylor, George R.	Rej	El Paso	—	
Taylor, H. L.	Rej	Bowie	—	

Index to Rejected Confederate Pension Applications

Taylor, J. A.	Rej	Delta		
Taylor, J. G. L.	Rej	Harris		
Taylor, J. M. Mrs.	Rej	Limestone	Taylor, J. M.	31396
Taylor, James	Rej	Atascosa		
Taylor, James F.	Rej	Shelby		
Taylor, John	Rej	McLennan		
Taylor, John M.	Rej	Hardin		
Taylor, Martha J.	Rej	Rusk	Taylor, J. Thomas	12968
Taylor, Mary E.	Rej	Burnet	Taylor, William Washington	
Taylor, Mary James	Rej	El Paso	Taylor, Henry Mills	
Taylor, Mattie Sue	Rej	Morris	Taylor, Henry Harrison	
Taylor, Milledge	Rej	Floyd		
Taylor, N. E. Mrs.	Rej	Grayson	Taylor, William Marion	
Taylor, O. C.	Rej	Cherokee		
Taylor, P. H.	Rej	Lampasas		
Taylor, S. A. Mrs.	Rej	Travis	Taylor, James William	
Taylor, Sallie Ann	Rej	Wichita	Taylor, John	
Taylor, Sally Elizabeth	Rej	Houston	Taylor, Baldy Washington	
Taylor, Susan A.	Rej	Bosque	Taylor, N. H.	
Taylor, W. J.	Rej	Polk		
Taylor, W. J.	Rej	Callahan		
Teague, Jesse Mrs.	Rej	Tarrant	Teague, Jesse	
Teal, T. A.	RejM	Brown		
Teal, Tennie	Rej	Dickens	Teal, Edward	
Teel, Robert J.	Rej	Medina		
Teer, William Alexander Mrs.	Rej	McLennan	Teer, William Alexander	
Templin, B. F.	Rej	Hopkins		
Templin, Benjamin Franklin	Rej	Shelby		
Tenney, Samuel Fisher	Rej	Houston		
Tennstett, C.	Rej	Harris		
Terrell, David	Rej	Canada		
Terrell, Francis M.	Rej	Hunt		
Terry, Cyrus	Rej	San Saba		
Terry, F. M.	Rej	Smith		
Terry, J. L.	Rej	Shackelford		
Terry, William Harrison	Rej	Coleman		
Tevis, John W.	Rej	Parker		
Thackston, Margaret A.	Rej	Dewitt	Thackston, Thomas Jefferson	
Thamm, Ernestine	Rej	Dewitt	Thamm, Arthur Emil	
Tharp, J. A.	RejM	Marion		
Theall, Eureka	Rej	Matagorda	Theall, Joseph	
Thomahley, S. L. Mrs.	RejM	Van Zandt		
Thomas, Bird P.	Rej	Waller		
Thomas, C. R. Mrs.	Rej	Wood	Thomas, Mathis Newton	
Thomas, Calvin Morgan Mrs.	Rej	Lamar	Thomas, Calvin Morgan	
Thomas, F. J. C. Mrs.	Rej	Ellis	Thomas, Albert	
Thomas, J. J.	Rej	Williamson		
Thomas, Jasper Jefferson	Rej	Leon		
Thomas, John Allen	Rej	Houston		
Thomas, Lane	Rej	Milam		
Thomas, M. E. Mrs.	Rej	Orange	Thomas, Benjamin B.	
Thomas, Martha Isabella	Rej	El Paso	Thomas, Francis Marion	
Thomas, Mittie Francis	Rej	Hardeman	Thomas, Isham Randal	
Thomas, N. E. Mrs.	Rej	Bowie	Thomas, Hiram Benjamin	
Thomas, Nancy	Rej	Shelby	Thomas, William Marion	
Thomas, Sarah Ann Appling	Rej	Walker	Appling, John Loyal	
Thomas, Sarah Ann Appling	RejM	San Saba	Appling, John Loyal	
Thomas, Sarah E.	Rej	Bosque	Thomas, Joseph C.	44095
Thomas, Sena	Rej	Collin	Thomas, James Marsh	

Index to Rejected Confederate Pension Applications

Thomason, Celia	Rej	McLennan	Thomason, Tom White	24946
Thomason, S. C. Mrs.	Rej	Cherokee	Thomason, George Washington	
Thompson, Alonzo	Rej	Howard		
Thompson, D. B.	Rej	Dallas		
Thompson, E.	Rej	Erath		
Thompson, E. A. Mrs.	Rej	Houston	Thompson, Nimrod Ogilsby	
Thompson, Ellen C.	RejM	Bell		
Thompson, Frank	Rej	Hopkins		
Thompson, Henry E.	Rej	Montague		
Thompson, J. C.	Rej	Unknown		
Thompson, J. F.	Rej	Tarrant		
Thompson, James P.	Rej	Cherokee		
Thompson, Jesse A.	Rej	Hill		
Thompson, John Madison Mrs.	Rej	Henderson	Thompson, John Madison	15432
Thompson, John W.	Rej	Collin		
Thompson, L. B. Mrs.	Rej	Hill	Thompson, John William	
Thompson, Lucinda M.	Rej	Travis	Thompson, James A.	
Thompson, Martha Jane	Rej	Jefferson	Thompson, William Jackson	
Thompson, Mary	Rej	Hemphill	Thompson, Wiley	
Thompson, Mary A.	Rej	Van Zandt	Thompson, Thomas M.	
Thompson, Mary Francis	Rej	Collin	Thompson, Archibal	
Thompson, Matilda M.	Rej	Scurry	Thompson, Ed	
Thompson, Sudie M. Pruitt	Rej	Bell	Pruitt, Spencer Howard	
Thompson, T. G.	Rej	Van Zandt		
Thompson, William L.	Rej	Jefferson		
Thompson, Witiam P. Mrs.	Rej	Hill	Thompson, Witiam P.	
Thomson, Ellen Clay	Rej	Bell	Thomson, Jasper McDonald	11801
Thorn, Mollie	Rej	Smith	Thorn, John Willis	
Thornton, F. E. Mrs.	Rej	San Saba	Thornton, Seaborn Jefferson	
Thornton, M. A. Mrs.	Rej	Cherokee	Thornton, Burrus Morgan	
Thornton, William James	Rej	Collin		
Thrasher, Genie M.	Rej	Dallas	Thrasher, William Benjamin	22119
Threadgill, Tom	Rej	Montague		
Thurber, H. E.	Rej	Menard		
Thurston, W. H.	Rej	Nacogdoches		
Tidwell, A. J.	Rej	Rains		
Tidwell, Daniel W.	Rej	Mitchell		
Tidwell, Elender T.	Rej	Smith	Tidwell, Josiah Jefferson	
Tidwell, Samuel M.	Rej	Tarrant		
Tiley, J. T.	Rej	Hill		
Till, Meredith D.	Rej	Henderson		
Tillerson, W. J.	Rej	Concho		
Tillery, R. C.	Rej	Runnels		
Tillman, J. E. Martin Mrs.	Rej	Angelina	Martin, John	
Tillman, Nancy E.	Rej	Lampasas	Tillman, George Luther	
Tilman, Mary P.	Rej	Hunt	Tilman, Stephen D.	
Tilman, S. S.	Rej	Franklin		
Tilton, Benjamin Wesley	Rej	Chambers		
Timms, G. W.	Rej	Ellis		
Tindall, Thomas R.	Rej	Erath		
Tindle, Robert	Rej	Tyler		
Tiner, J. M.	RejM	Brazoria		
Tiner, Nancy	Rej	Johnson	Tiner, Lewis Jackson	
Tinkle, J. F. Mrs.	Rej	Nacogdoches	Tinkle, William Stanley	
Tinkler, J. W.	Rej	Harris		
Tinnin, J. A.	Rej	Rains		
Tinsley, J. M.	Rej	Brazoria		
Tinsley, Mahala Ellen	Rej	Brazoria	Tinsley, Samuel Preston	
Tipps, George W.	Rej	Cooke		

Index to Rejected Confederate Pension Applications

Applicant	Status	County	Veteran	Number
Tipton, Ruth L.	Rej	Wise	Tipton, Samuel Pleasant	—
Tipton, Sarah Ann	Rej	Wichita	Tipton, Phylander S.	—
Tisdale, Florence	Rej	Bexar	Tisdale, James Smith	—
Todd, Davidson	Rej	Cherokee	—	—
Todd, Elizabeth R.	Rej	Bell	Todd, Felix Franklin	—
Tolson, Joseph W.	Rej	Hopkins	—	—
Tolson, Julia A.	RejM	Madison	—	—
Tomlinson, Mary E.	Rej	Panola	Tomlinson, Samuel M.	—
Tooke, Ishaw	Rej	Coleman	—	—
Toole, James	Rej	Harris	—	—
Tow, Rube	Rej	Mills	—	—
Towns, S. A. Mrs.	Rej	Gonzales	Towns, Addison Pleasant	—
Townsend, A. B.	Rej	Williamson	—	—
Townsend, J. C.	Rej	Young	—	—
Townsend, Lilly Laura	Rej	Medina	Townsend, James Thomas	—
Townsend, Margaret J.	Rej	Bexar	Townsend, William Wallace	—
Townzen, J. E.	Rej	Baylor	—	—
Trafton, E. B.	Rej	Gonzales	—	—
Trail, E. J. Mrs.	Rej	Kaufman	Trail, William Henry	—
Trammell, L. L.	Rej	Coryell	—	—
Trammell, T. J.	Rej	Blanco	—	—
Trammell, W. T.	Rej	Harris	—	—
Trantham, J. A.	Rej	Arkansas	—	—
Trapp, Eugene Mrs.	Rej	Dallas	Trapp, Eugene	—
Traugott, Caroline	Rej	Travis	Traugott, Joseph M.	09908
Travis, Joseph	Rej	Montgomery	—	—
Travis, M. A. Mrs.	Rej	Van Zandt	Travis, Elbert D.	—
Traweek, M. A. Mrs.	Rej	Sutton	Traweek, R. C.	—
Treadwell, James	Rej	Angelina	—	—
Treadwell, W. A.	Rej	Throckmorton	—	—
Tribble, E. C. Mrs.	Rej	Robertson	Tribble, J. B.	—
Tribble, Lean	Rej	Milam	Tribble, Albert Gibson	—
Tribout, Clementina C.	Rej	Galveston	Tribout, Charles	—
Trimble, L. W.	RejM	Travis	—	—
Trimble, Milton	Rej	Somervell	—	—
Triplett, Perry Commodore	Rej	Cooke	—	—
Tripp, William H. H.	Rej	Dallas	—	—
Trisler, Mollie	Rej	Henderson	Trisler, William Harrison	—
Trotter, E. N.	Rej	Grayson	—	—
Tubb, J. W.	Rej	Runnels	—	—
Tucker, Emma	Rej	Tarrant	Tucker, Joseph Burns	22727
Tucker, Hillery	Rej	Lavaca	—	—
Tucker, James Milton	Rej	Coke	—	—
Tucker, James Milton	RejM	Gonzales	—	—
Tucker, James Thomas	Rej	Wichita	—	—
Tucker, Jennie	Rej	Dallas	Tucker, George Washington	31202
Tucker, John	Rej	Jefferson	—	—
Tucker, John	Rej	Harrison	—	—
Tucker, Milton A.	Rej	Limestone	—	—
Tucker, P. R. Mrs.	Rej	Haskell	Tucker, J. M.	—
Tucker, Simeon J.	Rej	Upshur	—	—
Tulley, A. H. Welch Mrs.	Rej	Bowie	Welch, John Daniel	—
Tunstall, Thomas B.	Rej	Houston	—	—
Turman, William	Rej	Fannin	—	—
Turnbow, J. H.	Rej	Erath	—	—
Turnbow, James	Rej	Erath	—	—
Turner, Anna Webb	Rej	Kaufman	Turner, William Harvey	—
Turner, C. H.	Rej	Harris	—	—
Turner, E. W.	Rej	Harris	—	—

Index to Rejected Confederate Pension Applications

Turner, Isabella Caroline	Rej	San Jacinto	Turner, James Gipson	—
Turner, J. H.	Rej	Freestone	—	—
Turner, James G.	Rej	San Jacinto	—	—
Turner, Joseph O.	Rej	Dallas	—	—
Turner, L. A.	Rej	Bastrop	—	—
Turner, Lemuel Amaziah Mrs.	Rej	Bastrop	Turner, Lemuel Amaziah	—
Turner, M. C. Mrs.	Rej	Milam	Turner, F. M.	—
Turner, S. J. Mrs.	Rej	Nacogdoches	Turner, James Mickleberry	—
Turner, Sarah Elizabeth	Rej	Nacogdoches	Turner, James Madison	05566
Turner, Thomas E. Mrs.	Rej	Limestone	Turner, Thomas E.	—
Turner, Thomas Jerry	Rej	Tarrant	—	—
Turney, H. I.	Rej	Brown	—	—
Tweedle, W. H.	Rej	Bell	—	—
Tyer, George L.	Rej	Houston	—	—
Tyner, Lewis T.	Rej	Bastrop	—	—
Tynes, Samuel	Rej	Nacogdoches	—	—
Umbarger, S. G.	Rej	Randall	—	—
Underhill, Stephen Edward Monaghan	Rej	Travis	—	—
Underwood, Callie	Rej	Victoria	Underwood, Andrew	—
Underwood, Clara	Rej	Harris	Underwood, George E.	—
Upton, Bessie	Rej	Tarrant	Upton, George Washington	—
Ussery, Sarah Jane	Rej	Caldwell	Ussery, Mastin	—
Utzman, Jacob	Rej	Gregg	—	—
Vaden, L.	Rej	Hopkins	—	—
Vaden, L.	RejM	Trinity	—	—
Valdez, Apolonia	Rej	Bexar	Valdez, Jose Maria	—
Valentine, John	Rej	Pecos	—	—
Valverde, Mary	Rej	Gillespie	Valverde, John	—
Van Dyke, J. E.	Rej	Red River	—	—
Vance, Mary P.	Rej	King	Vance, J. G.	—
Vancleave, Corteous	Rej	Zavala	—	—
Vancleave, Will G.	Rej	Hunt	—	—
Vanhagen, John Bryant	Rej	Grimes	—	—
Vann, J. H.	Rej	Travis	—	—
Vanschoubrock, Alice	Rej	San Augustine	Vanschoubrock, Silas Henry	18317
Vansickle, M. E. Mrs.	Rej	Hunt	Vansickle, Thomas Jefferson	05603
Vardeman, E. Mrs.	Rej	Robertson	Vardeman, John B.	—
Vaughan, Annie A.	Rej	Bowie	Vaughan, Josiah Judson	—
Vaughan, Francis M.	Rej	Grayson	—	—
Vaughan, G. L.	Rej	Upshur	—	—
Vaughan, James P.	Rej	Freestone	—	—
Vaughan, S. M. Mrs.	Rej	Cass	Vaughan, H. I.	06451
Vaughn, James B.	Rej	Wise	—	—
Veale, Dora Henry	Rej	Fisher	Veale, Christopher Columbus	18732
Veale, Henry C.	Rej	Stephens	—	—
Venable, Isaac H. H.	Rej	Van Zandt	—	—
Venable, Peyton Smith	Rej	Archer	—	—
Vermillion, Diapa	Rej	Milam	Vermillion, Robert Aiken	Rej
Vermillion, Robert Aiken	Rej	Bastrop	—	—
Vernon, Isaac Newton	Rej	Rockwall	—	—
Vesey, F. W.	Rej	McLennan	—	—
Vick, C. H.	Rej	Austin	—	—
Vick, Ida M.	Rej	Scurry	Vick, Walter Calvin	—
Vickers, Joshua	Rej	Jones	—	—
Vickers, N. R. Mrs.	Rej	Coke	Vickers, William M.	—
Vickery, J. V.	Rej	Liberty	—	—
Vickery, Udora	Rej	San Jacinto	Vickery, Vance	—
Villastrigo, Tomas	Rej	Webb	—	—
Vineyard, Catherine	Rej	Montague	Vineyard, George Washington	—

Index to Rejected Confederate Pension Applications

Vineyard, Hattie Adaline Doss	Rej	Bell	Doss, Christopher Columbus	—
Vining, Matthew Cole	Rej	Travis	—	—
Vinson, Van Buren Mrs.	Rej	Harris	Vinson, Van Buren	—
Vogelsong, C.	Rej	Washington	—	—
Voorhies, James David	Rej	Dallas	—	—
Votaw, Landon Jackson Mrs.	Rej	Fayette	Votaw, Landon Jackson	—
Waddell, N. A.	Rej	Young	—	—
Wade, A. J.	Rej	San Augustine	—	—
Wade, J. W.	Rej	Hill	—	—
Wade, Sam Houston	Rej	Hill	—	—
Wadkins, H. M.	Rej	Freestone	—	—
Wadlington, E. V. E. Mrs.	Rej	Harrison	Wadlington, William Spencer	—
Waits, J. R.	Rej	Rusk	—	—
Waldemore, Julia	Rej	Dallas	Waldemore, Albert Wm. Schlidear	—
Waldermore, A. W.	Rej	Tarrant	—	—
Waldon, Susan E.	Rej	Limestone	Waldon, James	—
Waldrep, John	Rej	Polk	—	—
Waldrom, C. E.	Rej	Henderson	—	—
Waldrop, F. P.	Rej	Lee	—	—
Walker, E. J.	Rej	Trinity	—	—
Walker, Henry	Rej	Gonzales	—	—
Walker, J. M.	Rej	Milam	—	—
Walker, John William Mrs.	Rej	Jones	Walker, John William	—
Walker, Lavinia	Rej	Dallas	Walker, Albert A.	—
Walker, Lucinda Coombs	Rej	Grimes	Walker, John Grimes	32501
Walker, M. E. Wright Mrs.	Rej	Hamilton	Wright, Thomas Benton	—
Walker, Martha F.	Rej	Wilson	Walker, Robert Wilson	35115
Walker, N. B.	Rej	Ellis	—	—
Walker, R. L. Mrs.	Rej	Smith	Walker, Andrew Dorroty	09116
Walker, R. M.	Rej	Orange	—	—
Walker, Sarah	Rej	Polk	Walker, William Jackson	—
Walker, Sarah	Rej	Upshur	Walker, Robert W.	—
Walker, William Hampton	Rej	Montague	—	—
Wall, Donnie Lue	Rej	Stephens	Wall, Joseph Wylie	36970
Wall, Eunice J.	Rej	Uvalde	Wall, George Allen	24142
Wall, Frances Mrs.	Rej	Hunt	Wall, William Hugh	—
Wallace, Clifton Pope Mrs.	Rej	Nacogdoches	Wallace, Clifton Pope	—
Wallace, D. H.	Rej	Anderson	—	—
Wallace, Evander	Rej	Harris	—	—
Wallace, J. W.	Rej	Edwards	—	—
Wallace, Joel S.	Rej	Wise	—	—
Wallace, John	Rej	Menard	—	—
Wallace, John J.	Rej	Rains	—	—
Wallace, John W.	Rej	Zavala	—	—
Wallace, Laura	Rej	Comanche	Wallace, Robert Craddock	—
Wallace, Luna	Rej	El Paso	Wallace, Alfred Dashiel	—
Wallace, Malvina L.	Rej	Blanco	Wallace, John Lee	—
Wallace, Mary Francis	Rej	Bowie	Wallace, Thomas Benton	24209
Wallace, N. E. Mrs.	Rej	Grayson	Wallace, Samuel Lewis	—
Wallace, Vann	Rej	Harris	—	—
Wallace, William B. Mrs.	Rej	Nacogdoches	Wallace, William B.	—
Wallen, Geneva	Rej	Val Verde	Wallen, Calvin	—
Waller, George W.	Rej	Dallas	—	—
Waller, Gertha	Rej	Baylor	Waller, William Richard	14656
Waller, Josephine	Rej	Ellis	Waller, Nathaniel Lewis	—
Walling, James K.	Rej	Potter	—	—
Walling, Jesse T.	Rej	Taylor	—	—
Walling, Vance	Rej	Uvalde	—	—
Wallingford, Thomas G.	Rej	Uvalde	—	—

Index to Rejected Confederate Pension Applications

Applicant	Status	County	Soldier	No.
Wallis, Reuben Harry Mrs.	Rej	Cameron	Wallis, Reuben Harry	
Walpole, Ann Henry	Rej	Lamar	Walpole, James Lewis	
Walpole, Mary Josephine	Rej	Van Zandt	Walpole, James Harris	
Walraven, Amanda	Rej	Johnson	Walraven, Anderson	
Walston, Joshua Henry Asbury	Rej	Milam		
Walter, Fred	Rej	Bexar		
Walter, Nancy Elizabeth Leopard	Rej	Bexar	Leopard, George	
Walters, E. A.	Rej	Van Zandt		
Walters, James M.	Rej	Hill		
Walters, M.	RejM	Nacogdoches		
Walton, M. G.	Rej	Williamson		
Wantz, Xavier	Rej	Unknown		
Ward, Bettie	Rej	Bexar	Ward, Thomas	
Ward, H. W.	Rej	Leon		
Ward, J. W.	Rej	Hood		
Ward, L. D.	Rej	Burleson		
Ward, Mary A.	Rej	Red River	Ward, Samuel Harrison	
Ward, R. J. Mrs.	Rej	Williamson	Ward, James	
Ward, Simeon Leonidas	Rej	Fannin		
Ward, William	Rej	Hamilton		
Warden, Susanah V. Brundage	Rej	Dallas	Brundage, John C.	
Ware, William Jasper	Rej	Wilbarger		
Warner, Brady Riley Mrs.	Rej	Harris	Warner, Brady Riley	
Warner, Joe	Rej	Grimes		
Warren, Angie L.	Rej	Grayson	Warren, Jacob R.	
Warren, Benjamin Hamson Mrs.	Rej	Johnson	Warren, Benjamin Hamson	
Warren, Calvin W.	Rej	Angelina		
Warren, Jacob R.	RejM	Grayson		
Warren, Jane E.	Rej	Titus	Warren, Jesse C.	
Warren, John	Rej	Midland		
Warren, M. E. Mrs.	Rej	Hidalgo	Warren, George Pennington	
Warren, Mary Frankie	Rej	Runnels	Warren, John Avery	
Wasburn, J. A.	RejM	Coryell		
Washburn, E. E.	Rej	Caldwell		
Wassermann, Gustave	Rej	Dewitt		
Waters, Daniel D.	Rej	Cass		
Wathen, Benjamin Southern	Rej	Dallas		
Watkins, Betty	Rej	Wilson	Watkins, Zadok Bird	
Watkins, Katie	Rej	Lubbock	Watkins, Micajah L.	
Watkins, Maggie A.	Rej	Jackson	Watkins, Thomas Emmet	
Watkins, Mattie E.	Rej	Hays	Watkins, Calvert	35506
Watkins, W. W.	Rej	Mason		
Watkins, William Brutus H. Mrs.	Rej	Van Zandt	Watkins, William Brutus Howard	
Watson, Belle	Rej	Hunt	Watson, John	21113
Watson, David M.	Rej	Wise		
Watson, Idella M.	Rej	Van Zandt	Watson, William Pinckney	29936
Watson, Jerry	Rej	Harris		
Watson, John	Rej	Hunt		
Watson, M.	Rej	Grayson		
Watson, Mary E.	Rej	Ellis	Watson, Charlie Oscar	
Watson, Mary S.	Rej	Colorado	Watson, Clement S.	
Watson, Mary T.	Rej	Angelina	Watson, William	
Watson, P. W.	Rej	Bowie		
Watson, Robert Anderson	Rej	Wise		
Watson, S. H. Mrs.	Rej	Coryell	Watson, Wells	
Watson, Sarah Ann	Rej	Edwards	Watson, J. W.	
Watson, Thomas Henry Mrs.	Rej	Wise	Watson, Thomas Henry	
Watson, W. H.	Rej	Palo Pinto		
Watson, W. P. Mrs.	RejM	Van Zandt		

Index to Rejected Confederate Pension Applications

Watterson, J. L.	Rej	Navarro		
Watts, R. F.	Rej	Rusk		
Wear, Hugh Andrew	Rej	Bell		
Weatherall, M. C. Mrs.	Rej	Cass	Weatherall, Joseph Dickson	
Weatherford, J. C. Mrs.	Rej	Polk	Weatherford, Mack	
Weatherly, J.	Rej	Henderson		
Weathers, J. P.	Rej	Falls		
Weathersbee, H. W.	Rej	San Jacinto		
Weaver, Alexander A.	Rej	Victoria		
Weaver, John	RejM	Kendall		
Weaver, John Thomas	Rej	Upshur		
Weaver, L. C.	Rej	Angelina		
Weaver, Larkin C.	Rej	Angelina		
Weaver, T. M.	Rej	Henderson		
Weaver, W. H.	Rej	Comanche		
Weaver, William B.	Rej	Chambers		
Webb, D. L.	Rej	Hill		
Webb, Felix T.	Rej	Clay		
Webb, George M. Troup	Rej	Fayette		
Webb, Isaac J.	Rej	Dimmit		
Webb, W. A.	RejM	Bastrop		
Webster, M. P. Mrs.	Rej	Blanco	Webster, Daniel Bradley	04927
Webster, Minnie C.	Rej	Navarro	Webster, Abram Perry	42202
Wedgeworth, J. T.	Rej	Shelby		
Weed, John	Rej	Bee		
Weeks, J. W.	Rej	Angelina		
Weeks, Wiley F.	Rej	Angelina		
Weems, J. B.	Rej	Harris		
Weems, Stannie	Rej	Johnson	Weems, John Bartholomew	
Weikle, Adam	Rej	Lamar		
Weil, Henry	Rej	Comal		
Weir, Albert	Rej	Hays		
Welch, Caroline	Rej	Limestone	Welch, John	
Welch, J. S.	Rej	Angelina		
Welch, J. T.	Rej	Bexar		
Welch, John	Rej	Madison		
Welch, Stephen E.	Rej	Mitchell		
Welch, Thomas A.	Rej	Erath		
Wells, B. I.	Rej	Navarro		
Wells, Berryman W.	Rej	Travis		
Wells, F. M.	Rej	Montgomery		
Wells, H. T.	Rej	Rusk		
Wells, Henry A.	Rej	Irion		
Wells, Mary	Rej	Ellis	Wells, William	
Wells, Mary M.	Rej	Rockwall	Wells, James H.	
Wells, N. C. Mrs.	Rej	Jack	Wells, William Riley	
Welsh, M. H.	Rej	Cass	Welsh, Howell Marion	
Welty, John	Rej	Brown		
Welty, Joseph	Rej	Brown		
Wendel, George	Rej	Dewitt		
Werner, John	Rej	Kendall		
West, Benjamin F.	Rej	Montague		
West, Demcy F.	Rej	Bell		
West, Euclideas J.	Rej	Henderson		
West, H. W.	Rej	Leon		
West, John M.	Rej	Tom Green		
Westbrook, Frank	Rej	Robertson		
Westbrook, William B.	Rej	Newton		
Westbrooks, Nancy	Rej	Anderson	Westbrooks, William Bazzell	

Index to Rejected Confederate Pension Applications

Name	Status	County	Veteran	Number
Whaley, J. C.	Rej	Dallas		
Whaley, Kate	Rej	Limestone	Whaley, Milton J.	
Whatley, Bird	Rej	Eastland		
Wheeler, A. G.	Rej	Travis		
Wheeler, G. W.	Rej	Red River		
Wheeler, Isaac Newton	Rej	Travis		
Wheeler, Martha Ann	Rej	Erath	Wheeler, W. Marion	
Wheeler, W. H.	Rej	Angelina		
Wheeler, Walter	Rej	Dallas		
Whillock, J. H.	RejM	Robertson		
Whisenant, J. N.	Rej	Hays		
Whisenant, Margaret Martin	Rej	Gregg	Whisenant, Christopher Columbus	
Whisenant, S. A. Mrs.	Rej	Smith	Whisenant, John Dill	
Whitaker, America	Rej	Lampasas	Whitaker, O.	
Whitaker, Madison Franklin	Rej	Nacogdoches		
Whitaker, Martha	Rej	Jack	Whitaker, George Patillo	
White, Andrew Ashby	Rej	Bexar		
White, B. N.	Rej	Van Zandt		
White, Charles B.	Rej	Upshur		
White, E. J.	Rej	Sabine		
White, Edward W.	Rej	Harris		
White, Edwin	Rej	Madison		
White, Emma	Rej	Howard	White, Hunley V.	
White, Frances	Rej	Grayson	White, Stephen	
White, Henry Kirk Mrs.	Rej	Brazos	White, Henry Kirk	
White, Henry Lawson	Rej	Tarrant		
White, J. D.	Rej	Victoria		
White, J. M.	Rej	Franklin		
White, James Simmons	Rej	Bowie		
White, James Simmons	Rej	Smith		
White, John J.	Rej	Jefferson		
White, John Oldham Mrs.	Rej	Harris	White, John Oldham	
White, M. E. Mrs.	Rej	Llano	White, William M.	
White, Martha	Rej	Travis	White, John C.	
White, Mary E.	Rej	Angelina	White, Henry Harrison	
White, Mary Lizzie	Rej	Bell	White, Joseph M. Jackson	
White, Mattie	Rej	Tarrant	White, John Washington	
White, Mollie	Rej	Anderson	White, William Ellis	
White, Peter S.	Rej	Lamar		
White, Robert M.	Rej	Callahan		
White, Samuel	Rej	Hunt		
White, Sarah C.	Rej	Bowie	White, Richard McGee	22496
White, Sue	Rej	Tarrant	White, William Samuel	
White, Susie	Rej	Dewitt	White, William Watt	
White, Tennessee	Rej	Scurry	White, Matthew	
White, Thomas W.	Rej	Coleman		
White, W. A.	Rej	Hamilton		
White, W. A.	Rej	Montague		
White, W. L.	RejM	Tarrant		
White, William Alexander	Rej	Bell		
White, William F.	Rej	Franklin		
White, William L.	Rej	Denton		
Whitehead, Eugene Magee	Rej	Denton		
Whitehead, Sarah Caroline	Rej	Brown	Whitehead, William Tuzwell	
Whitehead, William W.	Rej	Angelina		
Whitehurst, Joe	Rej	Lubbock		
Whitescarver, John L.	Rej	Houston		
Whitfield, Ada	Rej	Lavaca	Whitfield, William Robert	
Whitley, E.	Rej	Madison		

Index to Rejected Confederate Pension Applications

Name	Status	County	Veteran	Number
Whitley, N. J.	Rej	Harris		
Whitley, R. S.	Rej	Dallas		
Whitley, Verlindia Jane	Rej	Bosque	Whitley, Jonas Marrion	
Whitlock, A. B.	Rej	Bastrop		
Whitman, Mary W.	Rej	Montgomery	Whitman, Edward Doak	
Whitmire, Nancy Jane	Rej	San Jacinto	Whitmire, Jesse W.	
Whitson, J. T.	Rej	Nueces		
Whittaker, George	Rej	Harris		
Whittington, John Williams	Rej	Dallas		
Wichman, Harry	Rej	Jefferson		
Wickersham, Henry W.	Rej	Palo Pinto		
Wiebush, George W.	Rej	Falls		
Wiggins, Addie	Rej	Montgomery	Wiggins, Uriah Jasper	
Wiggins, R. F. Mrs.	Rej	Houston		
Wiggins, S. C. Mrs.	Rej	Lubbock	Wiggins, Seaborn Lawrence	
Wiggins, William	Rej	Tyler		
Wiginton, Fannie	Rej	Hall	Wiginton, Levy Marion (wigginton)	25768
Wilburn, Perry	Rej	Nacogdoches		
Wilburn, W. M.	Rej	Shelby		
Wilcox, Mollie	Rej	Upshur	Wilcox, Wash	16837
Wilcoxson, J. T.	Rej	Collin		
Wilcoxson, R. M.	Rej	Hunt		
Wiley, Charles Reed	Rej	Sterling		
Wiley, James O.	Rej	Walker		
Wilkening, Henry L.	RejM	Lampasas		
Wilkerson, George W.	Rej	Harris		
Wilkerson, William T.	Rej	Milam		
Wilkes, Mary Ann	Rej	Dallas	Wilkes, C. B.	
Wilkins, J. G.	Rej	Denton		
Wilkins, John Taylor Mrs.	Rej	Dallas	Wilkins, John Taylor	23708
Wilkinson, E. B.	Rej	Tarrant		
Wilkinson, Lorina	Rej	Hunt	Wilkinson, John Overby	
Wilkinson, Mary E.	Rej	Bell	Wilkinson, Albert Galliton	
Willbanks, Elizabeth A.	Rej	Dallas	Willbanks, George Baxter	
Willbern, Alfred Reagan	Rej	Karnes		
Wille, Lucy	Rej	Guadalupe	Wille, Christian	
Willhoite, Nannie	Rej	Delta	Willhoite, John	
Williams, A. M. Mrs.	Rej	Harrison	Williams, Robert Pinkney	
Williams, Andrew Jackson Mrs.	Rej	Washington	Williams, Andrew Jackson	
Williams, Ann S.	Rej	Tarrant	Williams, George Washington	
Williams, Armanda L.	Rej	Kaufman	Williams, Thomas Whitfield	
Williams, C. J. Mrs.	RejM	Ellis	Williams, John B.	
Williams, C. L.	Rej	Dallas		
Williams, Eliza J.	Rej	San Saba	Williams, Edward J.	
Williams, F. S.	Rej	Lavaca		
Williams, G. K.	Rej	Limestone		
Williams, G. L.	Rej	Bowie		
Williams, G. M., Sr.	Rej	Wood		
Williams, George	Rej	Dewitt		
Williams, George W.	Rej	Wood		
Williams, H. W.	RejM	Harrison		
Williams, Ida	Rej	Red River	Williams, W. A.	04839
Williams, J. C.	Rej	El Paso		
Williams, J. E. Mrs.	RejM	Franklin		
Williams, J. H.	Rej	Colorado		
Williams, J. I.	Rej	Foard		
Williams, James T.	Rej	Robertson		
Williams, Jesse J.	Rej	Parmer		
Williams, John L.	Rej	Bosque		

Index to Rejected Confederate Pension Applications

Name	Status	County	Veteran	Number
Williams, Joseph P.	Rej	Robertson	—	
Williams, Josie	Rej	Cherokee	Williams, Levi W.	
Williams, Lee M.	Rej	McLennan	—	
Williams, Louisa	Rej	Caldwell	Williams, William Jefferson	
Williams, M. A. Martin Mrs.	Rej	Lampasas	Martin, John	
Williams, M. C.	Rej	Goliad	—	
Williams, Martin Davenport	Rej	Trinity	—	
Williams, Mary	Rej	Rusk	Williams, John Arnold	
Williams, Mary E.	Rej	Limestone	Williams, Philip	
Williams, Matilda	Rej	Hill	Williams, Stephen	
Williams, Neely	Rej	Comanche	Williams, John Calvin	
Williams, Richard James	Rej	Jasper	—	
Williams, S. E. Mrs.	Rej	Van Zandt	Williams, James Westley	
Williams, Samuel	Rej	Sabine	—	
Williams, Samuel, Sr.	Rej	San Augustine	—	
Williams, W. B.	Rej	Harris	—	
Williams, W. W.	Rej	Hopkins	—	
Williamson, E. O. Mrs.	Rej	Palo Pinto	Williamson, Zachry Taylor	32560
Williamson, F. V. Mrs.	Rej	Rockwall	Williamson, Robert Bruce	
Williamson, George	Rej	Liberty	—	
Williamson, Jim C.	Rej	Hood	—	
Williamson, John H.	Rej	Montgomery	—	
Williamson, Judge	Rej	Freestone	—	
Williamson, Mary J.	Rej	Anderson	Williamson, W. D.	14556
Williamson, Susan Nancy	Rej	Coleman	Williamson, Joseph	
Williamson, W. B.	Rej	Hopkins	—	
Williamson, W. C.	Rej	Freestone	—	
Williamson, William	Rej	Orange	—	
Willingham, Alfred J.	Rej	Washington	—	
Willingham, Thomas	Rej	Leon	—	
Willis, Anna	Rej	Liberty	Willis, Alfred Augusta	
Willis, Carter I.	Rej	Shelby	—	
Willis, E. C.	Rej	Jack	—	
Willis, Edward Ambler	Rej	Kimble	—	
Willis, G. W.	RejM	Wise	—	
Willis, Isam	Rej	Van Zandt	—	
Willis, M. E. Mrs.	Rej	Van Zandt	Willis, Isam	Rej
Wills, Finis Colby Mrs.	Rej	Van Zandt	Wills, Finis Colby	
Wilson, Andy	Rej	Kimble	—	
Wilson, C. H.	Rej	Clay	—	
Wilson, Edward Henderson	Rej	Chambers	—	
Wilson, Edward Henderson Mrs.	RejM	Chambers	Wilson, Edward Henderson	
Wilson, Elizabeth	Rej	Collin	Wilson, John C.	
Wilson, Elizabeth	Rej	Cass	Wilson, Charles H.	05819
Wilson, Elizabeth	Rej	Tarrant	Wilson, James D.	
Wilson, Elizabeth H.	Rej	Dewitt	Wilson, W. J.	
Wilson, Etta E.	Rej	Collin	Wilson, Thomas Benton	
Wilson, Fannie E.	Rej	Titus	Wilson, James M.	
Wilson, James C.	Rej	Shelby	—	
Wilson, James R.	Rej	Milam	—	
Wilson, John H.	Rej	Van Zandt	—	
Wilson, Lizzie	Rej	Chambers	Wilson, James	
Wilson, M. A. Mrs.	Rej	Gonzales	Wilson, Charles William	
Wilson, Margaret	Rej	Eastland	Wilson, John G.	
Wilson, Margaret Ann	Rej	Archer	Wilson, Charles McDuff	
Wilson, Mary C.	Rej	Hunt	Wilson, Jackson	
Wilson, Mary C.	Rej	Williamson	Wilson, Nathaniel Hogg	
Wilson, Mary E.	Rej	Eastland	Wilson, Elliott Keith	
Wilson, Mary L.	Rej	Kaufman	Wilson, Richard Israel	

Index to Rejected Confederate Pension Applications

Name	Status	County	Veteran	No.
Wilson, Mattie W.	Rej	McLennan	Wilson, Robert B.	—
Wilson, Nola Hill	Rej	Hill	Wilson, James Henry	—
Wilson, Rebecca Francis	Rej	Lamar	Wilson, Philix Griffin	—
Wilson, Robert Henry	Rej	Lamar	—	—
Wilson, Sarah E.	Rej	Hopkins	Wilson, Hineard E.	—
Wilson, T. A.	Rej	Collin	—	—
Wilson, W. J.	Rej	Hall	—	—
Wilson, W. P.	Rej	Dallas	—	—
Wilson, William	Rej	Newton	—	—
Wilson, William	RejM	Milam	—	—
Wimberley, P.	Rej	Guadalupe	—	—
Wimberly, R. C.	Rej	Limestone	—	—
Winburn, Emalina Cureton	Rej	Hill	Cureton, James Everette	—
Windett, T. J.	RejM	Bell	—	—
Windham, W. Pierce	Rej	Newton	—	—
Wing, Susan	Rej	Harris	Wing, William	—
Wingate, R. P.	Rej	Orange	—	—
Wingfield, Jane A.	Rej	Jackson	Wingfield, Joel H.	—
Winkler, Anna	Rej	Comal	Winkler, Niclaus	—
Winslett, F. A. Mrs.	Rej	Hood	Winslett, Jesse Coleman	—
Wiseman, John William	Rej	Madison	—	—
Wiseman, John William Mrs.	Rej	Bexar	Wiseman, John William	Rej
Withers, Peter Clay	Rej	Denton	—	—
Witherspoon, W. C.	Rej	Panola	—	—
Witt, Eli	RejM	Collingsworth	—	—
Witt, Wade Hampton	Rej	El Paso	—	—
Wofford, Malon Mrs.	Rej	Real	Wofford, Malon	—
Wofford, Mary Edna	Rej	Dickens	Wofford, Green Berry	47635
Wolf, W. L.	Rej	Freestone	—	—
Wolfenberger, H. M.	RejM	Parker	—	—
Wolff, W. C.	Rej	Dallas	—	—
Wolkarte, Charles J.	Rej	Harris	—	—
Wolston, J. H. A.	RejM	Milam	—	—
Womack, E. C.	Rej	Brown	—	—
Womack, E. W.	Rej	Bosque	—	—
Womack, John Albert	Rej	Freestone	—	—
Womack, Nannie	RejM	Unknown	—	—
Wommack, James William Mrs.	Rej	Cass	Wommack, James William	—
Wood, Alonzo C.	Rej	Wood	—	—
Wood, C. J. Mrs.	Rej	Harris	Wood, William Barnes	—
Wood, D. A.	Rej	Dallas	—	—
Wood, E. E. Perry Mrs.	Rej	Cherokee	Perry, William	—
Wood, I. T.	Rej	Coleman	—	—
Wood, J. H.	Rej	Kimble	—	—
Wood, James Franklin Mrs.	Rej	Brewster	Wood, James Franklin	—
Wood, John	Rej	Zavala	—	—
Wood, John M.	Rej	Panola	—	—
Wood, John W.	Rej	Rusk	—	—
Wood, Joseph	Rej	Dallas	—	—
Wood, Nannie E.	Rej	Brown	Wood, Thomas Kemsey	—
Wood, Priscilla Ann Elizabeth	Rej	Bell	Wood, Hiriam Marian	—
Wood, S. J. Mrs.	Rej	Erath	Wood, J. W.	—
Wood, William	Rej	Trinity	—	—
Woodard, Maude	Rej	Houston	Woodard, Franklin Columbus	—
Woodburn, Sam	Rej	Burleson	—	—
Woodley, George M.	Rej	Houston	—	—
Woodruff, Eliza Elizabeth	Rej	Jones	Woodruff, James Pinckney	—
Woodruff, Lucretia E.	Rej	Hunt	Woodruff, James Thomas	—
Woods, James S.	Rej	Kaufman	—	—

Index to Rejected Confederate Pension Applications

Name	Status	County	Veteran	Number
Woods, Mary	Rej	Gonzales	Woods, John A.	
Woods, Milo	Rej	Shelby		
Woodson, Charles	Rej	Dallas		
Woodward, Andrew C.	Rej	Donley		
Woodworth, Sarah E.	Rej	Williamson	Woodworth, Silas Franklin	
Wook, I. T.	RejM	Coleman		
Wooldridge, C. J.	Rej	Navarro		
Wooldridge, Catherine E.	Rej	Montgomery	Wooldridge, Samuel D.	
Wooldridge, E. D. T.	Rej	Montgomery		
Woolsey, Stephen M.	Rej	Cooke		
Woolverton, T. E.	Rej	Cooke		
Wooten, Francis M.	Rej	Robertson		
Wooten, Mattie Lloyd	Rej	Denton	Wooten, Charles	
Wooten, W. R.	Rej	Navarro		
Wooton, Janett (Darky J.)	Rej	Eastland	Wooton, James	01206
Worden, Henry	Rej	Bell		
Worley, J. W.	Rej	Delta		
Wormack, M. J. Mrs.	Rej	Morris	Wormack, Josiah Duncan	
Worthington, Joseph C.	Rej	Rains		
Wray, Sarah Pernelia	Rej	Howard	Wray, Thomas Jefferson	
Wright, C. L.	Rej	Wharton		
Wright, Crawford	Rej	Wood		
Wright, J. E.	Rej	Dallas		
Wright, J. F.	Rej	Gregg		
Wright, J. W.	Rej	Parker		
Wright, John S.	Rej	Dallas		
Wright, L.	Rej	Kimble		
Wright, Lucy	Rej	Wood	Wright, John Joseph Terry	
Wright, Maggie E.	Rej	Houston	Wright, William L.	
Wright, Marmaduke G. Mrs.	Rej	Hopkins	Wright, Marmaduke Gillewater	13402
Wright, N. M. Mrs.	Rej	Denton	Wright, Samuel Charles	
Wright, Robert Franklin	Rej	Harris		
Wright, W. G.	Rej	Rusk		
Wuest, Dorothea	Rej	Blanco	Wuest, August	
Wurz, Gebke	Rej	Dewitt	Wurz, Joseph Paul	
Wyatt, Abner	Rej	San Jacinto		
Wyatt, C. D.	Rej	Lampasas		
Wyatt, J. J.	RejM	Eastland		
Wyatt, J. T.	RejM	Bowie		
Wyatt, M. A. Mrs.	Rej	Brazos	Wyatt, Henry Clay	
Wyatt, Tom	Rej	Austin		
Wylie, John Marshall	Rej	Erath		
Wynn, Amanda	Rej	Dallas	Wynn, W. O.	11131
Wynn, Elizabeth L.	Rej	Williamson	Wynn, George F.	
Wynn, J. J.	Rej	Eastland		
Wynne, J. T.	Rej	Bowie		
Yancy, W. H. C.	Rej	Parker		
Yantis, Elizabeth	Rej	Comanche	Yantis, James Lapsley	
Yarbrough, James G.	Rej	Hardin		
Yarbrough, Thomas Jackson	Rej	McLennan		
Yarbrough, William J.	Rej	Cherokee		
Yates, J. S.	Rej	Parker		
Yates, Mary L.	Rej	Runnels	Yates, David A.	
Yeager, J. F.	Rej	Lee		
Yoast, J. F.	Rej	Menard		
Yocum, J. N.	Rej	Stephens		
York, H. G.	Rej	Hopkins		
York, L. D.	Rej	Calhoun	York, Armstead Neuman	
York, Robert J.	RejM	Comanche		

Index to Rejected Confederate Pension Applications

Yother, Jackson V.	Rej	Collin	—
Young, Catherine M.	Rej	Grayson	Young, Daniel Augustus
Young, E. G.	Rej	Bowie	—
Young, Ella Holt	Rej	Tarrant	Young, James Beasley
Young, Evaline V.	Rej	Upshur	Young, Thomas J.
Young, G. A. Mrs.	Rej	Jack	Young, T. G.
Young, Hinchea	Rej	Ellis	—
Young, Jefferson George	Rej	Brown	—
Young, John B.	Rej	Austin	—
Young, L. D.	Rej	Bailey	—
Young, Mary E.	Rej	Presidio	Young, William Fairfase
Young, Susan J.	Rej	Travis	Young, William H.
Youngblood, E. J.	Rej	Waller	—
Youngblood, Francis Marion	Rej	Parker	—
Zachry, Amelia C.	Rej	Clay	Zachry, A. D.
Zuniga, Felipa Flores De	Rej	Webb	Zuniga, Alejandro

Index to Confederate Pension Applications

Name	No.	County	Veteran	No.
Aaron, A. M. Mrs.	31459	Bexar	Aaron, Martin	24458
Aaron, Fred	02236	Jackson	—	—
Aaron, Jane C.	10313	Atascosa	Aaron, William	00410
Aaron, Martin	29458	Bexar	—	—
Aaron, Tennessee Mrs.	04034	Upshur	Aaron, William Henry	—
Aaron, William	00410	Bexar	—	—
Abbe, David Greenberry	13370	Howard	—	—
Abbe, John C.	30423	Van Zandt	—	—
Abbe, M. S. I. (Mrs.)	45270	Van Zandt	Abbe, John C.	30423
Abbey, William D.	11308	Travis	—	—
Abbott, Emily Hayden	49479	Montgomery	Hayden, Samuel Turner	—
Abbott, Emma Ophelia Berkley	41623	Brewster	Berkley, Benjamin Franklin	—
Abbott, Henry H.	31011	Ellis	—	—
Abbott, J. B.	43228	Parker	—	—
Abbott, J. S. A.	26536	Limestone	—	—
Abbott, J. W.	09556	Newton	—	—
Abbott, Joshua	01772	Harris	—	—
Abbott, L. A. Mrs.	07050	Robertson	Abbott, John B.	—
Abbott, L. J.	23220	Hopkins	—	—
Abbott, Mary Catherine	21076	Harris	Abbott, John	—
Abbott, Matthew Johnson	46168	Henderson	—	—
Abbott, S. B.	06191	Caldwell	—	—
Abbott, S. M. Mrs.	36096	Parker	Abbott, Theodore Freeling	23221
Abbott, Sarah E.	50353	Henderson	Abbott, Matthew Johnson	46168
Abbott, Solomon	12113	Robertson	—	—
Abbott, Theodore Freeling	23221	Parker	—	—
Abbott, Thomas J.	25900	Stonewall	—	—
Abbott, W. H.	22719	Jones	—	—
Abell, R. A.	22350	Colorado	—	—
Abendroth, Louise	51263	Fort Bend	Abendroth, Carl	—
Abercrombie, Albert Galiton	30180	Hopkins	—	—
Abercrombie, M. S. Mrs.	45401	Hopkins	Abercrombie, Albert Galiton	30180
Abernathy, D. F.	17353	Bosque	—	—
Abernathy, G. A. Mrs.	14825	Cass	Abernathy, Marshall Rufus	—
Abernathy, Ida	15824	Kaufman	Abernathy, John Wesley	—
Abernathy, James M.	16901	Walker	—	—
Abernathy, Laban	12217	Young	—	—
Abernathy, Lucy Roberts	43816	Collin	Abernathy, William Meshack	—
Abernathy, M. V.	03777	Tarrant	—	—
Abernathy, Mary A.	18226	Palo Pinto	Abernathy, Jesse L.	—
Abernathy, Mattie	51803	Fort Bend	Abernathy, Thomas Clayton	—
Abernathy, S. E. Mrs.	15329	Grimes	Abernathy, Sterling Howard	—
Abernathy, S. J. S.	22198	Palo Pinto	—	—
Abernathy, T. C.	Rej	Harris	—	—
Abernathy, Thomas Elbert	35635	Grimes	—	—
Abernathy, Thomas Elbert Mrs.	37093	Grimes	Abernathy, Thomas Elbert	35635
Able, James Milton	17514	Concho	—	—
Able, James Milton Mrs.	51424	McCulloch	Able, James Milton	17514
Ables, Emma C.	41889	Tarrant	Ables, Thomas Spottswood	22990
Ables, Emma M.	00360	Bexar	Ables, Joseph M.	—
Ables, Etta	46217	Erath	Ables, William R.	15098
Ables, L. V. Mrs.	29233	Rusk	Ables, John D.	—
Ables, Thomas Spottswood	22990	Tarrant	—	—
Ables, William R.	15098	Erath	—	—
Abney, George P.	32647	Brazoria	—	—

Index to Confederate Pension Applications

Name	Number	County	Veteran	Vet. Number
Abney, James A.	47699	Brown	—	—
Abolos, Juan	09109	Travis	—	—
Absher, G. W.	25513	Mills	—	—
Absher, Henry Alexander	39047	Mills	—	—
Absher, John	02489	Lampasas	—	—
Abshire, Easom	22672	Lamar	—	—
Abshire, Matilda Catherine	02695	Limestone	Abshire, William Jackson	—
Abshire, Nannie	34706	Lamar	Abshire, Easom	22672
Acker, A. L. Mrs.	20324	Johnson	Acker, John	—
Acker, Bayless Grace, Sr. Mrs.	45566	Cherokee	Bayless Grace, Sr.	—
Acker, George Washington	39853	Hunt	—	—
Acker, Joe	20677	Cherokee	—	—
Acker, Sarah	03675	Smith	Acker, William P.	—
Acker, Sarah A.	41830	Hunt	Acker, George Washington	39853
Acker, W. A.	13268	Cherokee	—	—
Acker, Walter, Sr.	39400	Harris	—	—
Acker, Winder H.	19738	Eastland	—	—
Ackerman, James	28937	Childress	—	—
Acord, Margaret	39074	Harris	Acord, John	—
Acosta, Bill	Rej	Bexar	—	—
Acosta, Domingo	06085	Travis	—	—
Acosta, Mary	36639	Travis	Acosta, Domingo	06085
Acree, Alfred W.	Rej	Waller	—	—
Acrey, Abner	14881	Cherokee	—	—
Acrey, Albert Newton	12780	Cherokee	—	—
Acrey, Harriet	32959	Cherokee	Acrey, Abner	14881
Acrey, M. A. Mrs.	32008	Ellis	Acrey, Albert Newton	12780
Acrey, M. E. Mrs.	25421	Nacogdoches	Acrey, James	—
Acton, F. E.	22335	Brazoria	—	—
Acton, S. N.	18437	Tom Green	—	—
Acuff, J. M. W.	Rej	Gregg	—	—
Adair, Blanche	51873	Fisher	Adair, James K.	51242
Adair, H. G.	12430	Hopkins	—	—
Adair, James K.	51242	Fisher	—	—
Adair, James Robert Dillard Mrs.	33768	Bell	Adair, James Robert Dillard	—
Adair, Lizzie	45380	Lynn	Adair, Richard Harding	—
Adair, Lucy F.	45552	Wichita	Adair, Elisha Young	—
Adair, M. E. Mrs.	08368M	Hunt	—	—
Adair, S. R. Mrs.	21625	Wise	Adair, James Robert	—
Adamietz, Constantine	30874	Bandera	Adamietz, John	—
Adams, A. J.	11588	Navarro	—	—
Adams, A. Mrs.	00266	Bell	Adams, Benjaman	—
Adams, Adam	23155	Stephens	—	—
Adams, Albert S.	12331	Dallas	—	—
Adams, Alexander	34478	Llano	—	—
Adams, Amanda	34264	Dallas	Adams, James Louis	—
Adams, Amanda I.	41030	Bexar	Adams, George Foster	—
Adams, Amanda J.	07917	Mills	Adams, David	—
Adams, Anjaline	19668	McCulloch	Adams, Benjamin	12610
Adams, Archibald Gray Mrs.	41166	Harrison	Adams, Archibald Gray	—
Adams, Archie	19594	Houston	—	—
Adams, B. P.	30287	Henderson	—	—
Adams, Benjamin	12610	San Saba	—	—
Adams, Benjamin Franklin	23989	Harrison	—	—
Adams, Benjamin Manning	06695	Henderson	—	—
Adams, Caroline	07174	Coke	Adams, Sylvester	—
Adams, Carrie M.	15998	McLennan	Adams, Edwin Wesley	—
Adams, Carry	18212	Newton	Adams, Thomas Faban	—
Adams, Catherine A.	20333	Hopkins	Adams, Pleasant Newton	11489

Index to Confederate Pension Applications

Adams, Cerro G.	51609	Dallas	Adams, John Quincy	
Adams, Charles I.	16193	Newton		
Adams, Collin	Rej	Tarrant		
Adams, Cyntha I.	27610	Johnson	Adams, William Lewis	15794
Adams, D. W.	07005	Hill		
Adams, David	06914	Hamilton		
Adams, Dicy A.	25187	Navarro	Adams, Fredric Leanear	
Adams, Dudley	09701	Grayson		
Adams, E. C. Mrs.	25662	Smith	Adams, Rufus Barton	
Adams, E. V. Mrs.	25615	Van Zandt	Adams, James Allen	
Adams, Earle	47753	Houston		
Adams, Eliza	00193	Bastrop	Adams, Allen A.	
Adams, Elizabeth	Rej	Red River	Adams, William	
Adams, Elizabeth E.	12816	Dimmit	Adams, Francis Marion	10822
Adams, Ella	43781	Lavaca	William F., Sr.	07889
Adams, Ellen	34355	McLennan	Adams, John Mathew	
Adams, Emma	40061	Grayson	Adams, Theodore Hugh	10906
Adams, Emma	48055	Houston	Adams, Earle	47753
Adams, Emma Olive	50370	Hall	Adams, William R.	45210
Adams, F. E. Mrs.	19842	Cherokee	Adams, James Franklin	09171
Adams, F. F. Mrs.	Rej	Rusk	Adams, Samuel	
Adams, F. M.	17354	Bosque		
Adams, F. M.	21621	Travis		
Adams, Fannie	30213	Rusk	Adams, Samuel	
Adams, Fannie	33393	Bexar	Adams, George Washington	
Adams, Fannie Tiberius	RejM	Brown	Adams, Zachariah Burges	
Adams, Frances Emma	49710	Polk	Adams, William Andrew	37541
Adams, Francis Andrews	01255	Ellis		
Adams, Francis Andrews Mrs.	36618	Ellis	Adams, Francis Andrews	01255
Adams, Francis Madison	26697	Grayson		
Adams, Francis Marion	10822	Bee		
Adams, G. W.	Rej	Nolan		
Adams, G. W.	09732	Milam		
Adams, G. W.	26580	Grayson		
Adams, Gay	50627	McLennan	Adams, Thomas Edward	42139
Adams, George T.	20334	Marion		
Adams, George V.	05469	Henderson		
Adams, H.	45014	Madison		
Adams, H. A. Mrs.	19199	Polk	Adams, Isham	
Adams, H. R. S. Mrs.	06105	Tarrant	Adams, J. F.	
Adams, Hannah L.	34968	Lubbock	Adams, Dudley	09701
Adams, Henriette	49232	Guadalupe	Adams, Jacob	
Adams, Isaac B.	33678	Erath		
Adams, Isaac G.	08255	Comanche		
Adams, Isaac Newton Mrs.	49158	Baylor	Adams, Isaac Newton	
Adams, J. A.	24715	Red River		
Adams, J. A.	40150	Van Zandt		
Adams, J. Calvin	41307	Parker		
Adams, J. L.	01066	Dallas		
Adams, J. M.	00146	Bandera		
Adams, J. M.	00487	Bowie		
Adams, J. Q.	06284	Hopkins		
Adams, J. Q.	27701	Navarro		
Adams, J. R.	Rej	Montague		
Adams, J. T.	01402	Fannin		
Adams, J. T.	02948	Milam		
Adams, J. W. P.	23207	Nacogdoches		
Adams, James A.	25373	Parker		
Adams, James Allen	Rej	Kaufman		

Index to Confederate Pension Applications

Name	No.	County	Soldier	No.
Adams, James Franklin	09171	Cherokee	—	
Adams, James G.	00461	Bosque	—	
Adams, James M.	05118	Tom Green	—	
Adams, James Warren	26327	Frio	—	
Adams, James Warren	47355	Bexar	—	
Adams, Joe	18077	Madison	—	
Adams, John B.	15880	Lavaca	—	
Adams, John D.	19551	Edwards	—	
Adams, John Daniel	Rej	Edwards	—	
Adams, John F.	16546	Shelby	—	
Adams, John H. B.	21623	Johnson	—	
Adams, John Nonce	23273	Newton	—	
Adams, John W.	25565	Collin	—	
Adams, John William	20009	Young	—	
Adams, Jonathan	21620	Shelby	—	
Adams, Josie	49572	Bell	Adams, Richard Wesley	
Adams, Julia A.	35466	Titus	Adams, Samuel Patterson	
Adams, Julius J.	47163	Bell	—	
Adams, L. A. Mrs.	14879	Cherokee	Adams, Newton Cannon	
Adams, L. A. Mrs.	23410	Ellis	Adams, Samuel Dudley	
Adams, L. C.	20211	Tarrant	—	
Adams, L. C. Mrs.	19930	Waller	Adams, Edwin Thompson	
Adams, L. Ellen	46405	Taylor	Adams, William Thomas	
Adams, L. H.	36364	Palo Pinto	Adams, Adam	23155
Adams, L. P. Mrs.	42430	Rains	McAlpin, John Thomas	
Adams, Laura Mansfield	46961	Hardin	Adams, Lewis Gratis	
Adams, Laura W.	32636	Milam	Adams, Willis Franklin	
Adams, Lemuel George	30519	Smith	—	
Adams, Lucinda	24675	Comanche	Adams, Isaac G.	08255
Adams, M. A. Mrs.	45715	McLennan	Adams, Charles Calib	
Adams, M. C. Mrs.	37805	Bosque	Adams, William Henderson	17355
Adams, M. E. Mrs.	Rej	Freestone	Adams, John Lumpkin Lamberth	
Adams, M. F. Mrs.	40983	Taylor	Adams, Hugh Kerens	
Adams, M. M.	20950	Polk	—	
Adams, M. M. Mrs.	09795	Bosque	Adams, W. J.	
Adams, M. T.	36417	Shackelford	—	
Adams, M. V. Mrs.	Rej	Hopkins	Adams, J. M. D.	
Adams, Margaret	47668	Erath	Adams, Andrew Jackson	
Adams, Margaret E.	22482	Lavaca	Adams, Hodge R.	
Adams, Margaret L.	08051	Nacogdoches	Adams, William V.	
Adams, Martha	36344	Smith	Adams, Lemuel George	30519
Adams, Martha Ann	46612	Wise	Adams, Marvin	
Adams, Martha Caroline	09567	Travis	Adams, Benjamin Theodore	
Adams, Mary	04390	Williamson	Adams, George	
Adams, Mary	16194	Newton	Adams, Blackshear	
Adams, Mary	46877	Bexar	Anton M., Sr.	
Adams, Mary A.	09288	Milam	Adams, J. T.	02948
Adams, Mary A.	25637	Harrison	Adams, Benjamin Franklin	23989
Adams, Mary Ann	11135	Sutton	Adams, John Q.	
Adams, Mary Ann	14698	Bexar	Adams, W. C.	
Adams, Mary C.	34707	Hall	Adams, Willliam Cicero	
Adams, Mary J.	04035	Upshur	Adams, William W.	
Adams, Mattie S.	47934	Tarrant	Adams, James William	
Adams, Moses	18867	Cherokee	—	
Adams, N. E. Mrs.	18630	Smith	Adams, Nathaniel Lafayette	13512
Adams, N. E. Mrs.	30255	Dallas	Adams, James	
Adams, N. J. Mrs.	45371	Llano	Adams, Alexander	34478
Adams, N. N. Mrs.	17722	Gregg	Adams, William Russell	
Adams, N. R. Mrs.	Rej	Llano	Adams, Alexander	34478

Index to Confederate Pension Applications

Applicant	No.	County	Veteran	No.
Adams, Nancy J.	30589	Rockwall	Adams, Thomas Leroy	—
Adams, Nannie	19084	Lavaca	Adams, John Bullock	—
Adams, Naoma V.	Rej	Panola	Adams, Lorenzo Harris	—
Adams, Nathaniel Lafayette	13512	Smith	—	
Adams, O. V. Mrs.	51687	Leon	Adams, Joe	18077
Adams, Olivia	42726	Travis	Adams, William Darsey	32953
Adams, P. C. Mrs.	15951	Madison	Adams, John Quincy	—
Adams, Pleasant Newton	11489	Hopkins	—	
Adams, Q. J. Mrs.	21622	Cherokee	Adams, Isaac Joseph	—
Adams, R. A. Mrs.	17620	Erath	Adams, John A.	—
Adams, Rachel E.	32545	Smith	Adams, William Washington	—
Adams, Renie	Rej	Leon	Adams, Joe	—
Adams, Richard H.	09666	Bexar	—	
Adams, Robert F.	23834	Anderson	—	
Adams, Robert S.	17112	Johnson	—	
Adams, S. A. Mrs.	Rej	Robertson	Adams, Robert Hamlin	—
Adams, S. A. Mrs.	29555	Houston	Adams, Archie	19594
Adams, S. H.	Rej	Lubbock	—	
Adams, S. J. Mrs.	12066	Milam	Adams, G. W.	09732
Adams, Sallie	16619	Smith	Adams, Wilson	—
Adams, Samuel B.	13456	Montgomery	—	
Adams, Samuel Owens	47361	Floyd	—	
Adams, Samuel Wadkins	28228	Jefferson	—	
Adams, Sarah	30853	Nacogdoches	Adams, Washington Franklin	10711
Adams, Sarah	33144	Jefferson	Adams, Samuel Wadkins	28228
Adams, Sarah Jane	26644	Shelby	Adams, John Bickerton	—
Adams, Sarah P.	35655	Young	Adams, John William	20009
Adams, Smith Sample	06762	McLennan	—	
Adams, Susan A.	51494	Wilson	Adams, William Monroe	11930
Adams, Susan N.	08344M	Henderson	—	
Adams, T. E. Mrs.	24837	Hunt	Adams, William Bennett	15626
Adams, T. J.	23217	Colorado	—	
Adams, Tabitha Goodwin	38153	Angelina	Goodwin, Ike	—
Adams, Theodore Hugh	10906	Denton	—	
Adams, Thomas Edward	42139	McLennan	—	
Adams, Virginia	52021	Travis	Adams, James McEwen	—
Adams, Virginia N.	22742	Robertson	Adams, Joseph Ross	—
Adams, W. F.	Rej	San Augustine	—	
Adams, W. H.	00489	Bowie	—	
Adams, Washington Franklin	10711	Nacogdoches	—	
Adams, Wiley	21018	Williamson	—	
Adams, William	27932	Grimes	—	
Adams, William Andrew	37541	Polk	—	
Adams, William B.	31966	Scurry	—	
Adams, William B.	41130	Lamar	—	
Adams, William Bennett	15626	Hunt	—	
Adams, William Darsey	32953	Kaufman	—	
Adams, William F., Sr.	07889	Lavaca	—	
Adams, William Henderson	17355	Bosque	—	
Adams, William Lewis	15794	Johnson	—	
Adams, William M.	Rej	Brazoria	—	
Adams, William Monroe	11930	Guadalupe	—	
Adams, William R.	45210	Hall	—	
Adams, Z. T.	31267	Hunt	—	
Adamson, Alice Catharine	23721	Taylor	Adamson, Simon Granville	—
Adamson, Amelia J.	16051	Mitchell	Adamson, Lawson P.	—
Adamson, Maggie	16235	Denton	Adamson, L. H.	—
Adamson, Margaret E.	05370	Grayson	Adamson, Johnathan	—
Adamson, Mary M.	41129	Smith	Adamson, Bluford Wells	—

Index to Confederate Pension Applications

Name	No.	County	Related	No.
Adare, M. V. Mrs.	39027	Hays	Adare, William Branch	25739
Adare, Samuel Jurden	25738	Hays		
Adare, William Branch	25739	Hays		
Adcock, E. V. Mrs.	47411	Jeff Davis	Adcock, James Goodwin	
Adcock, John	11218	Guadalupe		
Adcock, Lewis	08934	Guadalupe		
Adcock, R. L.	10570	Jefferson		
Adcock, Ransom Jefferson	47371	Taylor		
Adcock, S. C. Mrs.	34535	Callahan	Adcock, John	11218
Adcock, Samuel	Rej.	Cherokee		
Adcock, Y. F.	23529	Jones		
Addington, Elizabeth	46128	Bexar	Addington, Jason Andrew	17326
Addington, Jason Andrew	17326	Bexar		
Addington, Mollie A.	39052	Caldwell	Addington, David	
Addison, A. J.	Rej.	Milam		
Addison, Andrew Jackson	29036	Cherokee		
Addison, Britton	04638	Angelina		
Addison, John K.	13711	Bexar		
Addison, M. A. Mrs.	43748	Lamar	Addison, Andrew Jackson	29036
Aderhold, A. C.	17823	Hill		
Aderholt, Amanda	37857	Lubbock	Aderholt, Emanuel M.	
Adkins, Charles	15138	Fannin		
Adkins, Charley Mrs.	26976	Tarrant	Adkins, Charley	15138
Adkins, Emma Lavina	46130	Tarrant	Adkins, Thomas Hillery	24615
Adkins, G. F.	16890	Van Zandt		
Adkins, Harriet L.	18946	Fannin	Adkins, John Williams	
Adkins, Judith A.	25543	Bell	Adkins, William Anderson	04389
Adkins, Mary A.	38950	Eastland	Adkins, Samuel	10209
Adkins, Mary Elizabeth	43168	Bee	Adkins, Joel Walker	
Adkins, Rufus G.	13814	Freestone		
Adkins, Samuel	10209	Taylor		
Adkins, Sarah Julia	31690	Freestone	Adkins, Agrippa	
Adkins, Spencer	16219	Palo Pinto		
Adkins, Thomas Hillery	24615	Smith		
Adkins, William Anderson	04389	Williamson		
Adkinson, John J.	19472	Panola		
Adkisson, Duncan Rodolph	31027	Navarro		
Adkisson, Duncan Rodolph Mrs.	34393	Navarro	Adkisson, Duncan Rodolph	31027
Adkisson, Nancy Ordella	31673	Erath	Adkisson, Thomas Hamilton	01329
Adkisson, Thomas Hamilton	01329	Erath		
Adley, John	26255	Madison		
Adney, Elizabeth	07976	Tom Green	Adney, W. A.	
Adrain, M. E. Mrs.	17220	Wood	Adrain, William Harvey	
Adrian, D. W.	23409	Gregg		
Adrian, E. V. Mrs.	37183	Gregg	Adrian, D. W.	23409
Adrian, Emma Anna	50542	Kerr	Adrian, John Cass	46329
Adrian, James Fowler	26658	Wood		
Adrian, John Cass	46329	Kerr		
Adrian, Sarah Elizabeth	35534	Wood	Adrian, James Fowler	26658
Affleck, Isaac Dunbar	21271	Washington		
Affleck, Mary Hunt	35828	Washington	Affleck, Isaac Dunbar	21271
Agee, Daniel Henderson	15527	Hopkins		
Agee, Emily V.	51326	Angelina	Agee, R. E.	28968
Agee, George Marion	24904	Fannin		
Agee, Jonathan F.	21139	Tarrant		
Agee, Narcissus C.	38964	Hamilton	Agee, William A.	30228
Agee, R. E.	28968	Angelina		
Agee, S. A. Mrs.	20848	Hopkins	Agee, Daniel Henderson	15527
Agee, William A.	30228	Hamilton		

Index to Confederate Pension Applications

Agee, William J.	05676	Coleman	—	
Agnese, Mary S.	41155	Bexar	Agnese, Arthur M.	
Agnew, Elizabeth	05436	Gregg	Agnew, Sam A.	
Agnew, Nancy E.	08726	Hill	Agnew, Allen	
Agnew, S. W.	12775	Cherokee	—	
Aguilar, Estefana M. De	04451	Wilson	Aguilar, Neponnseno	
Aguilar, Jesus	04957	Bexar	—	
Aguilar, Librado	04308	Webb	—	
Aguilar, Visitacion G. De	52056	Bexar	Aguilar, Guadalupe	
Ahlbrecht, Margarett	41319	Brazoria	Ahlbrecht, William (Wilhelm)	
Aiken, John W.	28812	Callahan	—	
Aiken, Lewis Lawrence	03514	Rusk	—	
Aiken, M. E. Mrs.	16395	Rusk	Aiken, Lewis Lawrence	03514
Aikin, J. F.	Rej	Marion	—	
Aikin, M. E. Mrs.	Rej	Red River	Aikin, Jacob Willis	
Aikin, Samuel	14190	Dallas	—	
Aills, S. A. Mrs.	25902	Upshur	Aills, Thomas Payne	04033
Aills, Thomas Payne	04033	Upshur	—	
Ainsworth, Elizabeth	10860	Chambers	Ainsworth, Daniel Godias	08599
Ainsworth, Daniel Godias	08599	Chambers	—	
Ainsworth, J. G.	Rej	Limestone	—	
Ainsworth, J. L.	31547	Trinity	—	
Ainsworth, J. P.	05898	Mason	—	
Ainsworth, James Wilson	25604	Limestone	—	
Ainsworth, Joe T.	23677	Dallas	—	
Ainsworth, Leo	RejM	Callahan	—	
Ainsworth, Leven	09161	Callahan	—	
Ainsworth, Lucy Helen	43392	Limestone	Ainsworth, James Wilson	25604
Ainsworth, Mary	35679	Delta	Ainsworth, Leven	09161
Ainsworth, Matilda	10915	Eastland	Ainsworth, Hiram G.	
Ainsworth, Sallie	50048	Travis	Ainsworth, Spencer Montague	
Airheart, Amanda R.	30774	Kaufman	Airheart, Leander Frazier	22931
Airheart, H. T.	14649	Bosque	—	
Airheart, Henry Reagan	35826	Potter	—	
Airheart, Henry Reagan Mrs.	42408	Johnson	Airheart, Henry Reagan	35826
Airheart, Leander Frazier	22931	Kaufman	—	
Airheart, M. J. Mrs.	27933	Limestone	Airheart, Henry Columbus	
Akard, Ben W.	47592	Parker	—	
Ake, Amanda	18883	Coke	Ake, William Raleigh	
Ake, Bobbie	39810	El Paso	Ake, Thomas Jefferson	02766
Ake, Thomas Jefferson	02766	Mason	—	
Aker, J. M.	Rej	Johnson	—	
Aker, Jefferson Mitchell Mrs.	50797	Johnson	Aker, Jefferson Mitchell	
Akers, J. H.	Rej	Parker	—	
Akers, M. T. Mrs.	30140	Tarrant	Akers, William Parks	
Akin, Annie	49034	Stephens	Akin, Edward P.	
Akin, David	26792	Howard	—	
Akin, Elizabeth H.	15297	Gregg	Akin, Thomas Green	01663
Akin, John D.	13497	Rusk	—	
Akin, Kate	15403	Harrison	Akin, George Washington	
Akin, M. R. Mrs.	15402	Harrison	Akin, Joseph Bonaparte	
Akin, Polly T.	22786	Cameron	Akin, Isom	
Akin, Susan Arabel	30875	Bowie	Akin, William Collin	
Akin, Susan T.	26294	Wilbarger	Akin, Robert Jasper	
Akin, Thomas Green	01663	Gregg	—	
Akin, W. C.	Home	Bowie	—	
Akin, W. D.	23342	Marion	—	
Akins, Henry K.	34782	Wood	—	
Akins, James A.	34491	Dallas	—	

Index to Confederate Pension Applications

Name	App. No.	County	Veteran	Vet. App. No.
Akins, John	10969	Harris		
Akins, Joseph F.	13426	Marion		
Akins, Martha M.	45929	Nacogdoches	Akins, John David Riley	
Akins, Ophelia E.	Rej	Dallas	Akins, John J.	
Akins, P. D.	46144	Collin		
Akins, T. M.	28995	Hood		
Akridge, Harriet	25588	Fannin	Akridge, Cicero Virgie	
Alafila, Francisca Baco De	04307	Webb	Alafila, Mateo	
Alagood, E. T.	49015	Cooke		
Albert, E. T.	02289	Johnson		
Albert, Emeline	03493	Runnels	Albert, Matthew	
Albert, J. H.	02290	Johnson		
Albert, Laura A.	Rej	Harris	Albert, Jules	
Albert, Mary V.	07879	Johnson	Albert, E. T.	
Albertson, Annie D.	33985	Travis	Albertson, William Henry	
Albertson, Catherine E.	37247	Grimes	Albertson, John Joseph	21315
Albertson, Elif Mrs.	41229	Smith	Albertson, Elif	
Albertson, F. M.	15330	Grimes		
Albertson, John Joseph	21315	Grimes		
Albertson, Lorenzo Wood	35050	Bell		
Albertson, Mary Augusta	38488	Bell	Albertson, Lorenzo Wood	35050
Albright, James Thomas	39373	Coleman		
Albright, Lorindia	45299	Coleman	Albright, James Thomas	39373
Albright, M. C. Mrs.	22741	Tarrant	Albright, Wilburn	
Albritton, Allen Kendrick	23514	Navarro		
Albritton, Asa T.	Rej	Wise		
Albritton, J. R.	05242	Navarro		
Albritton, M. P. Mrs.	25808	Smith	Albritton, Matthew Ford	
Albritton, Mary E.	34436	Navarro	Albritton, Allen Kendrick	23514
Albritton, T. M. Mrs.	34345	Angelina	Albritton, George Washington	
Alcorn, Sallie Howard	41285	Washington	Alcorn, John Hodge	
Alderette, Ramona	14007	Tom Green	Alderette, Pablo	
Alderman, Amos K.	21630	Henderson		
Alderman, Daniel	15912	Leon		
Alderman, Margaret Catherine	50499	Comal	Alderman, Amos K.	21630
Alders, D. F. Mrs.	20981	Nacogdoches	Alders, William Montgomery	
Alders, Mary E.	18186	Nacogdoches	Alders, James Singleton	
Alderson, Elizabeth S.	15137	Fannin	Alderson, William Edward	
Alderson, Emily	14626	Bastrop	Alderson, Joseph Kyser	
Aldredge, D. F.	Rej	Camp		
Aldrich, A. A., Sr.	13861	Houston		
Aldrich, Julia	38482	Houston	Aldrich, Collin	
Aldridge, Cleopatra	21140	Fannin	Aldridge, William Jasper	13305
Aldridge, J. C.	33344	Comanche		
Aldridge, J. L.	25899	Cooke		
Aldridge, James K. Polk	22488	Grayson		
Aldridge, Louisa S.	18615	Galveston	Aldridge, William Henry	07065
Aldridge, M. A. E. Mrs.	01521	Freestone	Aldridge, James W.	
Aldridge, M. M. Mrs.	36160	Grayson	Aldridge, James K. Polk	22488
Aldridge, Martha	40407	Fannin	Aldridge, William Watson	
Aldridge, Mary A.	37222	Ector	Aldridge, Marcus De Lafayette	
Aldridge, Nancy Ann Eliza	01774	Harris	Aldridge, Lewis Madison	
Aldridge, Robert J.	04516	Wood		
Aldridge, William Henry	07065	Galveston		
Aldridge, William Jasper	13305	Fannin		
Alegria, Jesusa Gonzalez De	32583	Webb	Alegria, Lucas	
Alegria, Lucas	06256	Webb		
Alewine, B. J.	10502	Victoria		
Alewine, William H.	35323	Ellis		

Index to Confederate Pension Applications

Alexander, A. A. Mrs.	26428	Caldwell	Alexander, George Leander	00633
Alexander, Amanda	43680	Jefferson	Alexander, Amos Madison	—
Alexander, Angus Chism	19584	Van Zandt	—	—
Alexander, Aurelia Alpha	Rej	Taylor	Alexander, Henry Bennett	—
Alexander, B. A. Mrs.	34253	Caldwell	Alexander, James	26078
Alexander, Bandey M.	29505	Wilbarger	—	—
Alexander, Buena Vista	15038	Delta	Alexander, Henry B.	—
Alexander, C. P. Mrs.	36792	Lampasas	Alexander, William Riley	—
Alexander, Carolota D. De	Rej	Webb	Alexander, William J.	—
Alexander, Cirene Rebbecca	47765	Erath	Alexander, James Boyd	—
Alexander, Daniel L.	12860	Grayson	—	—
Alexander, E. A. Mrs.	09980	Bell	Alexander, John R.	06298
Alexander, E. C. Mrs.	27282	Bowie	Alexander, William Patton	11827
Alexander, E. D.	25382	Wilson	—	—
Alexander, E. R.	43569	Ellis	—	—
Alexander, E. T. Mrs.	32809	Johnson	Alexander, Robert Parks	—
Alexander, E. Z.	27651	Red River	—	—
Alexander, Edwin H.	45837	Llano	—	—
Alexander, Eliza Jane	03249	Panola	Alexander, J. A.	—
Alexander, Elizabeth J.	Rej	Van Zandt	Alexander, John Marion	—
Alexander, Ellen	39774	Grayson	Alexander, James Madison	05831
Alexander, Emily M.	32381	Camp	Alexander, William A.	—
Alexander, Emma L.	37809	Van Zandt	Alexander, Angus Chism	19584
Alexander, Emma Virginia	36674	Nolan	Alexander, John Adam	33130
Alexander, F.	06919	Rusk	—	—
Alexander, Francis R.	45056	Tom Green	Alexander, J. P.	39162
Alexander, Franklin Calloway	12363	Franklin	—	—
Alexander, G. M.	Rej	Dewitt	—	—
Alexander, George	14625	Bastrop	—	—
Alexander, George Leander	00633	Caldwell	—	—
Alexander, Isa	46838	Stephens	Alexander, James Marshall	—
Alexander, Isaac Pinkney	32868	Franklin	—	—
Alexander, J. E. Mrs.	17529	Coryell	Alexander, Paul	—
Alexander, J. M.	29984	Polk	—	—
Alexander, J. P.	39162	Midland	—	—
Alexander, Jake	Rej	Webb	—	—
Alexander, James	26078	Caldwell	—	—
Alexander, James Madison	05831	Collin	—	—
Alexander, Jason B.	08438M	Panola	—	—
Alexander, Jerry R.	17208	Panola	—	—
Alexander, John A.	30195	Titus	—	—
Alexander, John Adam	33130	Coleman	—	—
Alexander, John C.	21631	McLennan	—	—
Alexander, John Johnson	09742	Panola	—	—
Alexander, John R.	06298	Bell	—	—
Alexander, L. A. Mrs.	20022M	Titus	—	—
Alexander, Laura C.	04292	Washington	Alexander, William	—
Alexander, Lucindy	18762	Franklin	Alexander, Franklin Calloway	12363
Alexander, M. C. Mrs.	18583	Cherokee	Alexander, Patrick Fountain	00776
Alexander, M. E. Mrs.	33551	Erath	Alexander, John	—
Alexander, M. J. Mrs.	01238	Ellis	Alexander, J. R.	—
Alexander, M. J. Mrs.	04154	Van Zandt	Alexander, John	—
Alexander, Madora	50474	Knox	Alexander, Thomas Brooks	—
Alexander, Martha Ann	49357	Hunt	Alexander, Thomas Carroll	39010
Alexander, Martha Jane	37432	Grayson	Alexander, Daniel L.	12860
Alexander, Martha Luvenia	42613A	Titus	Alexander, John Anthony	—
Alexander, Mary	49032	Stephens	Alexander, Alford Dewit	—
Alexander, Mary E.	49412	Burnet	Alexander, Frank	—
Alexander, Mary Marinda	50643	Trinity	Alexander, Joseph	—

Index to Confederate Pension Applications

Alexander, Mecie	50862	McLennan	Alexander, John Newton	—
Alexander, N. W.	10581	Archer	—	—
Alexander, Patrick Fountain	00776	Cherokee	—	—
Alexander, R. M.	Rej	Dallas	—	—
Alexander, Rena Cimeon	Rej	Kerr	—	—
Alexander, Richard Marion	36767	Knox	—	—
Alexander, Richard Marion Mrs.	41250	Knox	Alexander, Richard Marion	36767
Alexander, Robert Grandison	17096	Harrison	—	—
Alexander, Robert Grandison Mrs.	38124	Harrison	Alexander, Robert Grandison	17096
Alexander, Sam B.	11208	Ellis	—	—
Alexander, Sarah Saphronia	38224	Franklin	Alexander, Isaac Pinkney	32868
Alexander, Sophie	Rej	Potter	Alexander, James E.	—
Alexander, Susan M.	47858	Dewitt	Alexander, G. M. (Tip)	—
Alexander, Texana	19991	Hopkins	Alexander, John Stephenson	—
Alexander, Thomas Carroll	39010	Hunt	—	—
Alexander, Thomas J.	14558	Angelina	—	—
Alexander, Thomas W.	07612	Hill	—	—
Alexander, W. A.	30211	McLennan	—	—
Alexander, W. H.	27479	Hill	—	—
Alexander, W. J. Mrs.	29095	Grayson	Alexander, Philander	—
Alexander, W. W.	Rej	Leon	—	—
Alexander, W. W.	Rej	Freestone	—	—
Alexander, Wiley P.	09578	Wood	—	—
Alexander, William M.	00174	Bastrop	—	—
Alexander, William N.	19737	Coleman	—	—
Alexander, William P.	14324	McLennan	—	—
Alexander, William Patton	11827	Bowie	—	—
Alford, Aaron R.	30150	Hamilton	—	—
Alford, Addie	42242	Harrison	Alford, Josiah Perry	—
Alford, Allen Josiah	16522	Shelby	—	—
Alford, Amelia B.	49217	Young	Alford, James Hamilton	—
Alford, Augustus Orion Mrs.	45485	Rusk	Alford, Augustus Orion	—
Alford, Charles Nielson	21385	Johnson	—	—
Alford, E. L.	Rej	Harrison	—	—
Alford, Edmond Lafayette Mrs.	39767	Tarrant	Alford, Edmond Lafayette	—
Alford, Georgia Hellena	21626	Shelby	Alford, John Allen	11121
Alford, J. C.	18167	Morris	—	—
Alford, J. P.	Rej	Harris	—	—
Alford, J. R.	42691	Hamilton	—	—
Alford, Jackson	03446	Robertson	—	—
Alford, James F.	Rej	Fisher	—	—
Alford, James M.	21632	Shelby	—	—
Alford, John Allen	11121	Shelby	—	—
Alford, Julius Caeser	Rej	Liberty	—	—
Alford, Lizzie	43824	Hamilton	Alford, Aaron R.	30150
Alford, M. E. Mrs.	32382	Johnson	Alford, Charles Nelson	21385
Alford, Maryann Sims	38544	Shelby	Alford, James M.	21632
Alford, Nancie Ellen	32571	San Augustine	Alford, John Harrison	—
Alford, Nannie L.	39193	Shelby	Alford, Allen Josiah	16522
Alford, S. A. Mrs.	19926	Grayson	Alford, Artimus Salithel	—
Alford, Samantha M.	07370	Shelby	Alford, W. H.	—
Alford, Sarah Ann	26326	Young	Alford, Jacob L.	—
Alford, Shird	14603	Atascosa	—	—
Alford, Thaddie C.	39241	Henderson	Alford, Albert Nelson	—
Alford, Thomas	28367	Hardeman	—	—
Alford, Verona Elizabeth	43785	Hamilton	Alford, J. R.	42691
Alison, Mary	41252	Dallas	Alison, Cusack	—
Alison, Robert D.	Rej	Collin	—	—
Allard, Edward	11000	Johnson	—	—

Index to Confederate Pension Applications

Name	No.	County	Related	Related No.
Allard, George Washington	47915	Clay	—	—
Allard, Sallie	Rej	Clay	Allard, George Washington	47915
Allbright, Jacob Franklin	15621	Houston	—	—
Allbright, Jacob Franklin Mrs.	35480	Houston	Allbright, Jacob Franklin	15621
Allbright, M. A. Mrs.	33876	Leon	Allbright, Allen Dune	—
Allbright, William N., Sr. Mrs.	40595	Hays	William Nelson, Sr.	—
Allbritton, George W.	00054	Angelina	—	—
Allbritton, John	13692	Angelina	—	—
Allbritton, M. T. Mrs.	14882	Cherokee	Allbritton, Washington Wiggins	—
Allbritton, Mary Ann	39800	Angelina	Allbritton, Elam M.	—
Allbritton, Ruth	38779	Angelina	Allbritton, John	13692
Allbritton, Sara C.	02565	Lee	Allbritton, W. A.	—
Allcorn, E. A. Mrs.	29001	McCulloch	Allcorn, Elijah Hodge	21452
Allcorn, Elijah Hodge	21452	McCulloch	—	—
Allcorn, Elizabeth	00568	Burleson	Allcorn, John H.	—
Allcorn, John Caldwell	41289	Brown	—	—
Allcorn, Mary Elizabeth	50553	Brown	Allcorn, John Caldwell	41289
Allcorn, Sallie H.	Rej	Washington	Allcorn, John H.	—
Alldredge, Martin V.	23525	Angelina	—	—
Alldredge, Mary J.	37899	Angelina	Alldredge, Martin V.	23525
Allee, Bettie	21629	Parker	Allee, Andrew Lafayette	—
Allee, M. J. Mrs.	Rej	Houston	Allee, William Mylus	05196
Allee, William Mylus	05196	Houston	—	—
Allegre, S. F. Mrs.	49774	Freestone	Allegre, Warren	—
Allen, A. A.	Rej	Collin	—	—
Allen, A. L.	39329	Hall	—	—
Allen, A. T. Mrs.	17020	Wood	Allen, Dewitt Clinton	—
Allen, Abraham B.	08644	Collin	—	—
Allen, Abraham Biln	00405	Bexar	—	—
Allen, Addie	20360	Williamson	Allen, George Washington	19336
Allen, Addie M.	36054	Williamson	Allen, Richard Ellis	—
Allen, Albert Luther	35879	Travis	—	—
Allen, Alexander	18842	Bowie	—	—
Allen, Amanda	00290	Bell	Allen, William	—
Allen, Amie	49771	Smith	Allen, John Watson	—
Allen, Anna	41012	Lamar	Allen, Drewery Wilkins	15857
Allen, Annie May	39771	Tarrant	Allen, George Robert	20889
Allen, Armstrong	50933	Fannin	—	—
Allen, B. S.	11321	Van Zandt	—	—
Allen, Barbara C.	37650	Sterling	Allen, Bitham	35196
Allen, Benjamin	13606	Tarrant	—	—
Allen, Benjamin Richard	19290	Travis	—	—
Allen, Bettie	42628	Tarrant	Allen, Benjamin	13606
Allen, Bettie Lou	52072	Travis	Allen, Orcenith Fisher	—
Allen, Bitham	35196	Sterling	—	—
Allen, C. M. Mrs.	41749	Hopkins	Allen, John L.	—
Allen, C. W.	06338	Henderson	—	—
Allen, Callie Mrs.	15856	Lamar	Allen, James Almsrine	—
Allen, Charlotte C.	04153	Van Zandt	Allen, John A.	—
Allen, D. Evan	10044	Dallas	—	—
Allen, D. P.	34956	Jack	—	—
Allen, Drewery Wilkins	15857	Lamar	—	—
Allen, E. N.	09250	Hunt	—	—
Allen, E. P.	11329	Anderson	—	—
Allen, E. T.	02070	Houston	—	—
Allen, Eldridge Washington, Dr.	22743	Milam	—	—
Allen, Elijah Sherwood	16620	Smith	—	—
Allen, Elizabeth	11587	Navarro	Allen, George	—
Allen, Ellen J.	47575	Coryell	Allen, Luther M.	—

Index to Confederate Pension Applications

Allen, Emily	19929	Madison	Allen, Abraham B.	
Allen, Emily M.	32507	Williamson	Allen, Robert Russell	22811
Allen, Eunice F.	50658	Bell	Allen, Lewis Carlton	32513
Allen, Ezra	12583	Robertson		
Allen, F. M.	02564	Lee		
Allen, Fannie K.	40874	Milam	Allen, John Louie	
Allen, Fannie Thomason	Rej	McLennan	Thomason, Robert Henry	
Allen, Fredrick Lowery Mrs.	46886	Travis	Allen, Fredrick Lowery	
Allen, G. H.	Rej	Hopkins		
Allen, G. W.	06997	Erath		
Allen, George	03943	Travis		
Allen, George Chapel	09073	McLennan		
Allen, George Robert	20889	Tarrant		
Allen, George T.	20264	Austin		
Allen, George Walker	16919	Waller		
Allen, George Washington	19336	Williamson		
Allen, Georgia	22512	Rains	Allen, Leroy Moore	17209
Allen, H.	Rej	Bosque		
Allen, H. D.	35325	Kimble		
Allen, H. H.	Rej	Van Zandt		
Allen, H. H.	25330	Angelina		
Allen, H. P.	23274	Coleman		
Allen, H. W.	07255	Houston		
Allen, Hannah R.	49653	Collin	Allen, Charles Fauntleroy	
Allen, Henry Clay	50517	Hill		
Allen, Hiram	08058	Burleson		
Allen, I. B.	31026	Grayson		
Allen, Isaac H.	01372	Falls		
Allen, Isabella	40491	Red River	Allen, Robert Anderson	
Allen, J. A.	02430M	Lamar		
Allen, J. A.	10450	Parker		
Allen, J. A.	14880	Cherokee		
Allen, J. B.	17062	Young		
Allen, J. E.	02071	Houston		
Allen, J. E. Mrs.	15867	Lampasas	Allen, Hiram	08058
Allen, J. G.	15482	Hill		
Allen, J. G.	29506	Tyler		
Allen, J. G. Mrs.	45208	Tyler	Allen, J. G.	29506
Allen, J. L.	Rej	Mason		
Allen, J. M.	23523	Rusk		
Allen, J. R.	Rej	Fayette		
Allen, J. T.	21628	Comanche		
Allen, James A.	23148	Red River		
Allen, James L.	23218	Coleman		
Allen, James Marion	17021	Wood		
Allen, James V.	32760	Hardeman		
Allen, James W.	09934	Mills		
Allen, Jane	09486	Houston	Allen, J. E.	02071
Allen, Jane C.	29922	Smith	Allen, William Camp	
Allen, Jeremiah Hilliard	23243	Cass		
Allen, Jerimiah Hilliard Mrs.	39889	Cass	Allen, Jerimiah Hilliard	23243
Allen, Jessie	37046	Milam	Eldridge Washington, Dr.	22743
Allen, Jessie A.	40596	Young		
Allen, John B.	14559	Angelina		
Allen, John H.	01293	Erath		
Allen, John Hudson, Sr.	26462	Mills		
Allen, John L.	13758	Collin		
Allen, John R.	Rej	Lampasas		
Allen, John T.	Rej	Cherokee		

Index to Confederate Pension Applications

Name	No.	County	Veteran	Vet. No.
Allen, John W.	11751	Franklin	—	
Allen, John W. Mrs.	Rej	Falls	Allen, John W.	
Allen, Jonathan Yarborough	17081	Coryell	—	
Allen, Jonathan Yarborough Mrs.	36647	Coryell	Allen, Jonathan Yarborough	17081
Allen, Joseph	08678	Falls	—	
Allen, Julia M.	21307	Smith	Allen, Elijah Sherwood	16620
Allen, Katie	28362	Freestone	Allen, James Wilson	
Allen, L. C. Mrs.	19445	Cherokee	Allen, A. Judson	
Allen, L. T.	04152	Van Zandt	—	
Allen, Laura E.	47005	Bell	Allen, Benjamin Franklin	
Allen, Laura Eleanor	32960	Wichita	Allen, Virgil Stanley	
Allen, Leroy Moore	17209	Rains	—	
Allen, Lewis Carlton	32513	Matagorda	—	
Allen, Lorena	50498	Cass	Allen, William Alexander	33766
Allen, Lou Mrs.	15097	Erath	Allen, Isaac H.	01372
Allen, Louisa S.	26725	Navarro	Allen, Joseph Negus	
Allen, Louise E.	47822	Potter	Allen, Hugh Ewing	
Allen, Lucy F.	40814	Fayette	Allen, James Russell	
Allen, M. A. Mrs.	00685	Cass	Allen, William	
Allen, M. C. Mrs.	43921	Franklin	Crumpler, John (James) Wesley	04523
Allen, M. E. Mrs.	16436	Sabine	Allen, James Thomas	
Allen, M. E. Mrs.	47758	Smith	Allen, David Crockett	
Allen, M. J. Mrs.	RejM	Houston	—	
Allen, M. J. Mrs.	36954	Smith	Allen, Robert Isiah	13185
Allen, M. M.	RejM	Williamson	—	
Allen, M. S. Mrs.	31242	Fisher	Allen, Henry Cyrus	
Allen, Madeline Louisa	41172	Grayson	Allen, William Riley	
Allen, Maggie Davis	43829	Smith	Allen, John Seaburn	
Allen, Margaret	43818	Burnet	Allen, Albert Luther	35879
Allen, Martha	51501	Hill	Allen, Henry Clay	50517
Allen, Martha A.	37862	Grayson	Allen, Thomas Newton	
Allen, Martha Jane	43923	Bosque	Allen, Hanable	
Allen, Martha Melvina	49704	Wichita	Allen, Cary Crawford	
Allen, Martin R.	19927	Bexar	—	
Allen, Mary A.	15999	McLennan	Allen, George Chapel	09073
Allen, Mary C.	02914	Medina	Allen, William	
Allen, Mary E.	Rej	Tarrant	Allen, Joseph B.	
Allen, Mary E.	28259	Wilson	Allen, Thomas Jefferson	12208
Allen, Mary Hamilton	43892	Falls	Allen, John William	
Allen, Mary Jane	51431	Upshur	Allen, William Green	
Allen, Mary L.	42117	McLennan	Allen, William Origen	18612
Allen, Mary Louise	41744	Van Zandt	Allen, William Alexander	38240
Allen, Mat	Rej	Burnet	—	
Allen, Mattie	47714	Cass	Allen, Thomas Simms	
Allen, Mattie	51972	Fannin	Allen, Armstrong	50933
Allen, Mattie V.	18013	Lee	Allen, Robert Emil	
Allen, Mollie	51546	Young	Allen, Jessie A.	40596
Allen, Moses M.	Rej	Sterling	—	
Allen, Moses Mrs.	28597	Tarrant	Allen, Moses	
Allen, N.	07355	Palo Pinto	—	
Allen, N. J. Mrs.	12639	Taylor	Allen, James W.	
Allen, Nellie	Rej	Wichita	Allen, Virgil Stanley	
Allen, Nelson H.	18840	Bosque	—	
Allen, O. C.	09853	Smith	—	
Allen, O. H.	34185	Dallas	—	
Allen, Ophelia Mrs.	04514	Wood	Allen, J. C.	
Allen, Ozais C.	03674	Smith	—	
Allen, Perency Ann	40597	Grimes	Allen, George Anderson	
Allen, Phillip Tropwell Mrs.	Rej	Johnson	Allen, Phillip Tropwell	

Index to Confederate Pension Applications

Name	App. No.	County	Veteran	Vet. No.
Allen, Pinkney Pike	11577	Nacogdoches		
Allen, R. E. Mrs.	42079	Tarrant	Allen, Rufus Perry	31028
Allen, Rachel C.	20495	Waller	Allen, George Walker	16919
Allen, Rebecca	14048	Williamson	Allen, W. G.	
Allen, Rebecca Elizabeth	27139	Jones	Allen, Thomas	
Allen, Rebecca J.	13957	Mills	Allen, James W.	09934
Allen, Richard	12642	Travis		
Allen, Robert Isiah	13185	Smith		
Allen, Robert Russell	22811	Williamson		
Allen, Rosa	Rej	Tarrant	Allen, Moses A.	
Allen, Rufus Perry	31028	Tarrant		
Allen, S. A. Mrs.	16683	Titus	Allen, George Hunt	
Allen, S. A. Mrs.	27304	Camp	Allen, George W.	
Allen, S. C. Mrs.	35901	Harrison	Allen, Ab	
Allen, S. E. Mrs.	21021	Donley	Allen, Abraham Biln	00405
Allen, S. M. Mrs.	19235	Rusk	Allen, Franklin Jefferson	
Allen, S. M. Mrs.	34040	Bosque	Allen, Nelson H.	18840
Allen, S. P. Mrs.	28630	McCulloch	Allen, William Stone	
Allen, S. Safrony	28934	Wood	Allen, James Marion	17021
Allen, S. Y.	13899	Panola		
Allen, Sallie A.	21576	McCulloch	Allen, John W.	
Allen, Sallie C.	Rej	Wise	Allen, J. T.	
Allen, Sallie S.	29485	Hood	Allen, John Henry	
Allen, Sarah	01260	Ellis	Allen, Joel	
Allen, Sarah E.	Rej	Donley	Allen, Abraham B.	
Allen, Sarah J.	12455	Hunt	Allen, E. N.	09250
Allen, Sarah Jane	Rej	McLennan	Allen, John Woodson	
Allen, Susan A.	23149	Collin	Allen, Patrick Henry	
Allen, Susan Mildred	42418	Lamar	Allen, Edward Claiborne	
Allen, T. H.	23164	Hunt		
Allen, T. J.	Rej	Bell		
Allen, T. P.	04407	Williamson		
Allen, T. S.	Rej	Cass		
Allen, Tabitha	47263	Young	Allen, Andrew Jackson	
Allen, Tabitha F.	06344	Kaufman	Allen, David	
Allen, Theodocia Ernest	49075	Tarrant	Allen, William Terry	
Allen, Thomas Jefferson	12208	Wilson		
Allen, Thomas R.	38093	Denton		
Allen, V. F. Mrs.	27060	Rusk	Allen, William Elisha	
Allen, V. S.	29774	Tarrant		
Allen, W. A.	19471	Houston		
Allen, W. J.	Rej	Hill		
Allen, W. N.	28975	Hays		
Allen, W. S.	21030	Comal		
Allen, W. W.	Rej	Williamson		
Allen, William	04479	Wise		
Allen, William Alexander	33766	Cass		
Allen, William Alexander	38240	Van Zandt		
Allen, William Calvin	07909	Montague		
Allen, William E.	22633	Rusk		
Allen, William H.	29262	Fannin		
Allen, William J.	Rej	Tarrant		
Allen, William Origen	18612	McLennan		
Allen, William R.	18334	San Saba		
Allen, William V.	45744	Jack		
Allen, Z. Ella	26338	Falls	Allen, John Wesly	
Allender, James Atwood	31241	Hill		
Allensworth, J. F.	31750	Hardeman		
Alley, Elijah Stover	20886	Reeves		

Index to Confederate Pension Applications

Name	No.	County	Veteran	No.
Alley, G. R.	06277	Kaufman		
Alley, John R.	29491	Colorado		
Alley, John R. Mrs.	41722	Colorado	Alley, John R.	29491
Alley, M. H. Mrs.	39356	Marion	Alley, Daniel Nelson	
Alley, Mary E.	02947	Milam	Alley, John H.	
Alley, Rhoda Thornton	49010	Fannin	Thornton, Aaron Brantley	
Alley, T. J. Mrs.	18783	Grimes	Alley, W. T.	05298
Alley, W. T.	05298	Grimes		
Allgood, William J.	31380	Hunt		
Allin, Emma	43879	Harris	Allin, Green Taylor	
Allis, T. H. Mrs.	35088	Nueces	Allis, Melvin Hall	
Allison, D. K.	40233	Travis		
Allison, Eleanor Rebecca	40048	Caldwell	Allison, George Lafayette	
Allison, Elizabeth	Rej	Wise	Allison, James William	
Allison, Elizabeth Ann	51342	Wichita	Allison, Samuel Hinton	
Allison, Epsibeth	36053	Tyler	Allison, Joseph Faircloth	
Allison, Faraba S.	25544	Edwards	Allison, Lorenzo Dow	18926
Allison, G. A.	Rej	Bowie		
Allison, Henry Hamilton	30138	Taylor		
Allison, Isabella Q.	18682	Lamar	Allison, William G.	13404
Allison, John	11446	Foard		
Allison, John	20953	Red River		
Allison, John Thomas	28672	Leon		
Allison, John Thomas Mrs.	51432	Leon	Allison, John Thomas	28672
Allison, Julius C.	18017	Leon		
Allison, K. J. Mrs.	39254	Wise	Allison, Samuel Gillaspie	
Allison, Lorinzo Dow	18926	Edwards		
Allison, Louisa Freestone	49057	Bexar	Allison, William Mack	
Allison, Louisa J.	40316	Taylor	Allison, Henry Hamilton	30138
Allison, Martha J.	47128	Travis	Allison, Jerome Houston	
Allison, Mary J.	00271	Bell	Allison, Thomas J.	
Allison, Missouri	45973	Hopkins	Allison, William Madison	41083
Allison, N. L. Mrs.	34854	Erath	Allison, James Washington	
Allison, Rachel V.	03776	Tarrant	Allison, William Morgan	
Allison, Robert Socrates	20512	Panola		
Allison, Sallie J.	33019	Panola	Allison, Robert Socrates	20512
Allison, Sam Houston Mrs.	39911	Houston	Allison, Sam Houston	
Allison, Scott	47450	Collin		
Allison, Sophia	01225	Ellis	Allison, James	
Allison, Thomas R.	17541	Dallas		
Allison, William G.	13404	Lamar		
Allison, William M.	43606	Titus		
Allison, William Madison	41083	Hopkins		
Allison, William W.	25663	Collin		
Allman, Kitty	49546	Brown	Allman, Nelson Atkinson	
Allman, Margaret C.	34708	Limestone	Allman, Joseph	
Allphin, B. S.	11244	Madison		
Allred, Alfred	01759	Hamilton		
Allred, B. K.	23153	Upshur		
Allred, Lavina	30368	San Patricio	Allred, Alfred	01759
Allred, Mary Luranie	33326	Smith	Allred, Starling Roberts	
Allred, T. J.	15795	Johnson		
Allred, Violet Jane	29644	Cherokee	Allred, Seymore	
Allston, Amelia	20101	Harrison	Allston, Peter J.	17785
Allston, Peter J.	17785	Harrison		
Allsup, Clara H.	43148	Harris	Allsup, William H.	31751
Allsup, Thomas Henry	27015	Hays		
Allsup, William H.	31751	Galveston		
Allums, Addie	51020	Panola	Allums, John A.	16234

Index to Confederate Pension Applications

Name	Number	County	Related	Related Number
Allums, John A.	16234	Panola		
Almon, J. L.	22374	Hunt		
Almond, Anna Greig	51337	Harris	Almond, Steven A.	42544
Almond, Steven A.	42544	Harris		
Almond, W. G.	37437	Angelina		
Alonzo, Peter	Rej	Milam		
Alphin, R. J.	35528	Navarro		
Alsabrooks, G. M.	Rej	Cass		
Alsobrook, J. M.	02431	Lamar		
Alsobrook, N. C. Mrs.	19629	Lamar	Alsobrook, J. M.	02431
Alsobrook, W. M.	13531	Taylor		
Alsobrooks, Mary A.	Rej	Cass	Alsobrooks, George	
Alston, C. F.	23150	Wood		
Alston, Henry Franklin	21059	Bexar		
Alston, J. Mrs.	19659	Trinity	Alston, Willis Wilson	04004
Alston, Thomas Franklin Mrs.	32943	Dallas	Alston, Thomas Franklin	
Alston, Thomas J.	Rej	Smith		
Alston, W. P.	Rej	Bandera		
Alston, Willis Wilson	04004	Trinity		
Alsup, Henry Anderson	22826	Ellis		
Alsup, John Anderson Mrs.	22874	Panola	Alsup, John Anderson	
Alsup, Sarah E.	Rej	Milam	Alsup, William E.	
Alsup, Thomas Houston	22288	Ellis		
Alsworth, C. W.	30611	Harris		
Altizer, Louisa Jane	19571	San Saba	Altizer, David Riley	
Altman, D. H.	05169	Bell		
Altman, Eliza	49117	Lampasas	Altman, John Israel	
Altman, M. A. Mrs.	21105	Mitchell	Altman, Bradford Henderson	
Altman, W. A. Mrs.	32359	Lampasas	Altman, Josiah	
Altman, William H.	46368	Hardeman		
Altwein, Gustave	Rej	Guadalupe		
Altwein, Marie	44093	Comal	Altwein, Edward	
Alverson, William C.	00515	Brazos		
Alvis, Charles Jefferson	41060	Kaufman		
Alvis, D. H.	05521	Hopkins		
Alvis, Isabella	45036	Kaufman	Alvis, Charles Jefferson	41060
Alvis, William W.	11061	Nacogdoches		
Alwood, Richard Henry	Rej	Cooke		
Alwood, Richard Henry Mrs.	Rej	Cooke	Alwood, Richard Henry	
Amador, Jose Marcia	04948	Bexar		
Aman, Malinda E.	22199	Limestone	Aman, John	
Amarine, D. E.	23259	Mason		
Amason, Jesse James	16002	McLennan		
Amason, Pollie	20825	Shelby	Amason, Hiram	
Amason, W. T.	07189	Dewitt		
Ament, Anthony Gholson	35324	McLennan		
Ament, Ellen Idel	35662	Angelina	Ament, Anthoney Gholson	35324
Ames, Mary S. L.	22966	Parker	Ames, James Henry	
Amick, Alvin	10188	Rockwall		
Amick, Nancy	27931	Grimes	Amick, Thomas Brooks	
Amidon, Almedia	Rej	Williamson	Amidon, Dwight Calvert	38436
Amidon, Dwight Calvert	38436	Travis		
Ammons, Francina	16150	Nacogdoches	Ammons, Thaddens H.	04824
Ammons, Thaddens H.	04824	Nacogdoches		
Amos, John	11190	Camp		
Amos, William W.	36438	Jefferson		
Amsler, Julia	45591	Harris	Amsler, Charles	
Amsler, Sophia	20049	Lavaca	Amsler, Louis Philip	
Amthor, Mary	43774	Austin	Amthor, Otto	

Index to Confederate Pension Applications

Name	App#	County	Soldier	Soldier App#
Anders, Henry L.	Rej	Delta		
Anders, Henry L.	17899	Hunt		
Anders, J. H. Mrs.	32796	Hunt	Anders, John B.	31568
Anders, J. W.	26689	Montgomery		
Anders, John B.	31568	Hunt		
Anders, L. J.	45127	Van Zandt		
Anders, L. J. Mrs.	Rej	Van Zandt	Anders, L. J.	45127
Anders, Lucy	03097	Navarro	Anders, Watt	
Anders, Rebecca R.	16856	Van Zandt	Anders, William	
Anderson, A. E. Mrs.	34168	Collin	Anderson, Grant James	24136
Anderson, A. J.	Rej	Montgomery		
Anderson, A. J.	00291	Bell		
Anderson, A. J. Mrs.	41315	Shackelford	Anderson, William Henry	22636
Anderson, Albert A.	26196	Denton		
Anderson, Albert Byron	23147	Lavaca		
Anderson, Alvin H.	04151	Van Zandt		
Anderson, Andrew Jackson	38520	Jefferson		
Anderson, Annie	31030	Panola	Anderson, Matthew Earl	
Anderson, Antha Mrs.	00263	Bell	Anderson, David	
Anderson, Archibald English	13893	Panola		
Anderson, Archibald English Mrs.	16236	Panola	Anderson, Archibald English	13893
Anderson, Artie	34785	Terrell	Anderson, John Floyd	30205
Anderson, Asa Green	17249	Freestone		
Anderson, B. F.	18523	Wharton		
Anderson, B. M.	Rej	Lavaca		
Anderson, Bailey J.	19966	Martin		
Anderson, Ben	Rej	San Augustine		
Anderson, Boon	18040	Limestone		
Anderson, C. E.	43723	Jefferson		
Anderson, C. J. Mrs.	02432	Lamar	Anderson, W. M.	
Anderson, C. P. Mrs.	05229	Kimble	Anderson, T. D.	
Anderson, Caroline E.	07450	Callahan	Anderson, George K.	
Anderson, Catherine	02946	Milam	Anderson, William P.	
Anderson, Charles C.	19217	Rusk		
Anderson, Cordelia	16643	Tarrant	Anderson, Joseph Gude	
Anderson, Daniel Smoot	26971	Fannin		
Anderson, Diana	21633	Potter	Anderson, Willis Pinkney	
Anderson, Dorinda	03248	Panola	Anderson, John C.	
Anderson, E. A. Mrs.	43559	Lubbock	Anderson, William Henry	
Anderson, E. L.	35563	Erath		
Anderson, Eliza	Rej	Harris	Anderson, Matterson	
Anderson, Eliza Ann	35711	Falls	Anderson, Maben Calaway	31997
Anderson, Elizabeth	09819	Tom Green	Anderson, J. W.	03886
Anderson, Elizabeth S.	50899	Travis	Anderson, Alfred Washington	
Anderson, Elizabeth W.	13876	Nacogdoches	Anderson, D. A.	
Anderson, Ella	15627	Hunt	Anderson, Nathan	
Anderson, Ellen	02235	Jackson	Anderson, George W.	
Anderson, Ellen Crim	43239	Lee	Anderson, George McDuffie	
Anderson, Emma	43753	Parker	Anderson, James Jefferson	
Anderson, Erathmus	23205	Erath		
Anderson, Etta B.	50164	Liberty	Anderson, Andrew Jackson	38520
Anderson, Fannie E.	45265	Bell	Anderson, Leonidas Wren	23222
Anderson, Fannie L.	36691	Freestone	Anderson, Asa Green	17249
Anderson, Florence Virginia	49504	Bexar	Anderson, William Boyd	
Anderson, Francis Marion	20385	Van Zandt		
Anderson, Francis Marion	38300	Tyler		
Anderson, Francis Marion Mrs.	27594	Limestone	Anderson, Francis Marion	
Anderson, Frank M.	Rej	Limestone		
Anderson, George Washington	27127	Jones		

Index to Confederate Pension Applications

Anderson, George Washington	38027	Wheeler		
Anderson, Grant James	24136	Collin		
Anderson, H. H.	11378	Cherokee		
Anderson, H. H.	37606	Collingsworth		
Anderson, H. J.	02072	Houston		
Anderson, Hillon Luvicy	23515	Panola	Anderson, Gregg	
Anderson, Hugh Stewart	03093	Motley		
Anderson, Hugh Stewart Mrs.	Rej	Motley	Anderson, Hugh Stewart	03093
Anderson, I. B.	Rej	Throckmorton		
Anderson, I. E.	Rej	Harrison		
Anderson, Ida	39779	Limestone	Anderson, Boon	18040
Anderson, Ike	35463	Haskell		
Anderson, Isaac	02522	Lavaca		
Anderson, Isaac Hamilton	06795	Galveston		
Anderson, J. A.	17084	Dallas		
Anderson, J. C.	07445	Bell		
Anderson, J. I.	Rej	Leon		
Anderson, J. K. P.	13453	Montgomery		
Anderson, J. M.	09437	Bosque		
Anderson, J. W.	03886	Tom Green		
Anderson, J. W.	12006	Lamar		
Anderson, J. W.	15070	Ellis		
Anderson, J. W.	21469	Falls		
Anderson, James	47985	Bell		
Anderson, James E., Capt.	30439	Leon		
Anderson, Jane	47115	Trinity	Anderson, John Byron	
Anderson, Jane Gillian	34216	San Patricio	Anderson, Balus Earl	
Anderson, Jennie	21300	Jones	Anderson, Samuel Joseph	
Anderson, Jennie	22963	Matagorda	Anderson, Wayne	
Anderson, Jesse Columbus	18963	Freestone		
Anderson, John	10741	Shelby		
Anderson, John	10952	Grayson		
Anderson, John	14418	Somervell		
Anderson, John	29570	Rusk		
Anderson, John Duncan	47168	Guadalupe		
Anderson, John E.	Rej	Falls		
Anderson, John Floyd	30205	Terrell		
Anderson, John L.	Rej	Harris		
Anderson, John Mrs.	45905	Rusk	Anderson, John	29570
Anderson, John Rudolphus	23208	Fannin		
Anderson, John Rudolphus Mrs.	37717	Fannin	Anderson, John Rudolphus	23208
Anderson, John W.	25501	Taylor		
Anderson, John Walker	21418	Taylor		
Anderson, Josephine R.	23146	Taylor	Anderson, George Washington	
Anderson, L. A. Mrs.	Rej	Van Zandt	Anderson, Elijah B.	
Anderson, L. E. Mrs.	41936	Hunt	Anderson, Emanuel C. C.	
Anderson, Laura	43323	Collin	Anderson, Joseph Alexander	
Anderson, Lee	Rej	Motley		
Anderson, Lennie Evelyn	29229	Harris	Anderson, John Stow	
Anderson, Leonadus Wren	23222	Bell		
Anderson, Luranie	51368	Tyler	Anderson, Francis Marion	38300
Anderson, M. A. Mrs.	07997	Taylor	Anderson, J. C.	
Anderson, M. B.	08777	Navarro		
Anderson, M. C. Mrs.	Rej	Montague	Anderson, Isaac Franklin	
Anderson, M. E. Mrs.	16394	Rusk	Anderson, Franklin Shuba	
Anderson, M. J. Mrs.	22914	Ellis	Anderson, Isaac Hamilton	06795
Anderson, M. J. Mrs.	35954	Lavaca	Anderson, Albert Byron	23147
Anderson, M. M. Mrs.	29502	Upshur	Anderson, George Washington	
Anderson, M. V.	16855	Van Zandt		

Index to Confederate Pension Applications

Name	No.	County	Veteran	No.
Anderson, Maben Calaway	31997	Falls		
Anderson, Malinda E.	10555	Williamson	Anderson, John M.	
Anderson, Margaret C.	26044	Collin	Anderson, William C.	
Anderson, Maria	05249	Panola	Anderson, Wyatt	
Anderson, Martha	21400	Tarrant	Anderson, Thomas Bryant	
Anderson, Martha	49830	Guadalupe	Anderson, John Duncan	47168
Anderson, Martha E.	23428	Henderson	Anderson, George Washington	
Anderson, Martha Elizabeth	27718	Houston	Anderson, George Washington	
Anderson, Martha J.	22565	Van Zandt	Anderson, Francis Marion	20385
Anderson, Martha Jane	48038	Lamar	Anderson, Jonathan	
Anderson, Martha L.	39609	Potter	Anderson, David Jordon	
Anderson, Martha M.	38258	Fisher	Anderson, Vachel Hobbs	18951
Anderson, Mary	16283	Potter	Anderson, Newton Rufus	
Anderson, Mary	39029	Martin	Anderson, Bailey Jack	
Anderson, Mary	43617	Coryell	Anderson, William Jasper	
Anderson, Mary Ann	47624	Coleman	Bills, Isaac Walker	00842
Anderson, Mary Caroline	50998	Erath	Anderson, Wilburn Lafayette	27029
Anderson, Mary Elizabeth	41819	El Paso	Anderson, William Walker	
Anderson, Mary Elizabeth	47832	Lubbock	Anderson, Thomas Leaborn	28177
Anderson, Mary Ellen	49732	Jones	Anderson, Hugh Allen	
Anderson, Mary J.	06481	Johnson	Anderson, A. B.	
Anderson, Mary J.	36562	Erath	Anderson, Erathmus	23205
Anderson, Mary Jane	32264	Jones	Anderson, George Washington	27127
Anderson, Mary M.	15341	Guadalupe	Anderson, Henry Minor	
Anderson, Michael H.	12263	Bell		
Anderson, Mollie	Rej	Martin	Anderson, Bailey J.	19966
Anderson, N., Capt.	09636	Hunt		
Anderson, Nathan	Rej	Grayson		
Anderson, O. E. Mrs.	26885	Nacogdoches	Anderson, James Allen	
Anderson, Parlee Jane	01903	Hill	Anderson, James I.	
Anderson, Pinckney	05245	Navarro		
Anderson, Rebecca Frances	51176	Johnson	Anderson, Calvin Henry	
Anderson, Rebecca V.	38428	Bell	Anderson, Michael H.	12263
Anderson, Richard Barkley Mrs.	46697	Denton	Anderson, Richard Barkley	
Anderson, Robert J.	22601	Bastrop		
Anderson, Rubin Bishop	04636	Angelina		
Anderson, S. H.	04676	Gonzales		
Anderson, S. J.	Rej	Hunt		
Anderson, S. J. Mrs.	42161	Donley	Anderson, George Washington	38027
Anderson, S. R.	27115	Cooke		
Anderson, Samuel B.	21419	Smith		
Anderson, Samuel H.	42128	Dallas		
Anderson, Sarah	09252	Jack	Anderson, W. J.	02196
Anderson, Sarah Allice	26324	Taylor	Anderson, Stephen Jones	
Anderson, Sarah E.	21322	Johnson	Anderson, Wesley Benton	10897
Anderson, Sarah H.	29870	Fannin	Anderson, Thomas Jefferson	
Anderson, Sarah M.	10521	Victoria	Anderson, Isaac	02522
Anderson, Susan E.	28030	Kaufman	Anderson, John Smith	
Anderson, Susan J. Windham	Rej	Kaufman	Windham, Benjamin B.	
Anderson, Susan L.	20419	Panola	Anderson, Wilson Livingston	
Anderson, T. A.	46773	Grayson		
Anderson, T. D. W.	01042	Dallas		
Anderson, T. M. Mrs.	40091	Menard	Anderson, Thomas	
Anderson, Thomas	19444	McLennan		
Anderson, Thomas B.	46791	Ward		
Anderson, Thomas H.	40343	Williamson		
Anderson, Thomas Jefferson	Rej	Taylor		
Anderson, Thomas Leaborn	28177	Denton		
Anderson, Thomas Lee	21434	Panola		

Index to Confederate Pension Applications

Anderson, Thomas Lee Mrs.	23880	Panola	Anderson, Thomas Lee	21434
Anderson, Tisie	36032	Hopkins	Anderson, William	—
Anderson, Vachel Hobbs	18951	Fisher	—	
Anderson, W. B. Mrs.	36756	Grimes	Anderson, William Bryan	—
Anderson, W. Carroll	23517	Lampasas		
Anderson, W. J.	Rej	Hunt		
Anderson, W. J.	02196	Jack		
Anderson, W. P.	Rej	Shelby		
Anderson, W. R.	27100	Burnet		
Anderson, W. R.	32168	Johnson		
Anderson, W. T.	14031	Tyler		
Anderson, W. V.	15528	Hopkins		
Anderson, Wesley Benton	10897	Dallas		
Anderson, Wilburn Lafayette	27029	Erath		
Anderson, William D. G.	40667	McCulloch		
Anderson, William Daton	51031	Robertson		
Anderson, William Henry	22636	Shackelford		
Anderson, William Wallace	Rej	Randall		
Anderson, Zachariah J.	20445	Dallas		
Anderton, N. E. Mrs.	03778	Tarrant	Anderton, T. D.	—
Anderwald, Anton	18819	Bandera		
Anderwald, Katherine	35821	Bandera	Anderwald, Anton	18819
Andress, Elizabeth B.	13389	Johnson	Andress, H. M.	00276
Andress, Emma O.	50725	Dallas	Andress, William Thomas	—
Andress, H. M.	00276	Bell		
Andrew, Irene	51411	Shelby	Andrew, Samuel David	—
Andrew, Sarah Jane	Rej	Palo Pinto	Andrew, William	—
Andrews, A. R.	01627	Grayson		
Andrews, Ann	40830	Madison	Andrews, William M.	—
Andrews, Carrie M.	30768	Kaufman	Andrews, Arthur Washington	—
Andrews, Charles W.	10489	Travis		
Andrews, Cyrus M.	12803	Dallas		
Andrews, Della	Rej	Johnson	Andrews, John Calvin	—
Andrews, Emma L.	35795	Grayson	Andrews, Mark Henry	34144
Andrews, Francis Marion	13571	Washington		
Andrews, George P.	26204	Titus		
Andrews, J. D.	23204	McLennan		
Andrews, Jochu Lee	34067	Stephens		
Andrews, Jochu Lee Mrs.	36787	Shackelford	Andrews, Jochu Lee	34067
Andrews, John N.	04673	Rockwall		
Andrews, Julia A.	18281	Rockwall	Andrews, John N.	04673
Andrews, L. E. Mrs.	23219	Hill	Andrews, Thomas Warren	—
Andrews, M. E. Mrs.	42041	Taylor	Andrews, Francis Marion	13571
Andrews, M. J. Mrs.	17993	Lamar	Andrews, Gustavus Adolphus	—
Andrews, Mark Henry	34144	Grayson		
Andrews, Mary Agatha	46434	Galveston	Andrews, William Morgan	—
Andrews, Mollie E.	15282	Grayson	Andrews, Edwin J.	—
Andrews, Narcissa Caroline	01773	Harris	Andrews, Wade Lafayette	—
Andrews, O. S.	06349	Mitchell		
Andrews, R. H.	07198	Eastland		
Andrews, R. W.	00612	Caldwell		
Andrews, Sam R.	11854	Collin		
Andrews, Sarah	21221	Rusk	Andrews, John Bell	—
Andrews, Sarah J.	38185	Brown	Andrews, Wade Anderson	—
Andrews, W. W.	Rej	Hill		
Andrews, William	Rej	Kaufman		
Andrews, William Gaston	02809	McLennan		
Andrus, Emily E.	26375	Cherokee	Andrus, Lewis Theophilis	—
Andrus, V. E. Mrs.	18084	Madison	Andrus, Louis	—

Index to Confederate Pension Applications

Name	App#	County	Veteran	Vet App#
Andruss, Margaret E.	33999	Montague	Andruss, Harvey Adolphus	—
Angel, George W.	25901	Scurry	—	—
Angell, M. L. Mrs.	38828	Angelina	Angell, James Wilbur	—
Angerhoffer, Mary C.	46401	Galveston	Angerhoffer, Charles Alexander	—
Angermueller, Simon	10957	Guadalupe	—	—
Anglin, Bettie E.	39591	Lamar	Anglin, William Francis	—
Anglin, Eliza J.	37530	Collin	Anglin, William Thomas	—
Anglin, Mary Green	34041	Cameron	Anglin, Andrew Lawson	—
Anglin, Permelia	46555	Milam	Anglin, James Madison	—
Anglin, S. H.	13108	Van Zandt	—	—
Anglino, Flora A.	41224	Red River	Anglino, Thaddeus Augustus	—
Annan, William R.	Rej	Wilson	—	—
Annis, Sarah F.	25800	Taylor	Annis, Jerome Thomas Latimer	—
Ansley, Eudora M.	38301	Gregg	Ansley, Wesley S.	32291
Ansley, Frances K.	41588	Smith	Ansley, Jeremiah	—
Ansley, George S.	24868	Aransas	—	—
Ansley, J. C.	05708	Erath	—	—
Ansley, James Nickoles	31029	Robertson	—	—
Ansley, James Thomas	23172	Gregg	—	—
Ansley, Mary E.	43647	Aransas	Ansley, George S.	24868
Ansley, O. F.	42610	Dallas	—	—
Ansley, Princess	35186	Robertson	Ansley, James Nickoles	31029
Ansley, Wesley S.	32291	Gregg	—	—
Anthony, Annie E.	Rej	Moore	Anthony, Samuel Wesley	—
Anthony, Bersheba	32835	Victoria	Anthony, Robert Henry	—
Anthony, Charity E.	22181	Hall	Anthony, William Eli	—
Anthony, George L.	33372	Reeves	—	—
Anthony, John S.	13066	Shelby	—	—
Anthony, Margaret F.	16030	Milam	Milton, Dr.	—
Anthony, Mary	40875	Newton	Anthony, Thomas B.	06923
Anthony, Nancy Elizabeth	37426	Nacogdoches	Anthony, William Franklin	19517
Anthony, Stephen	Rej	Atascosa	—	—
Anthony, Thomas B.	06923	Sabine	—	—
Anthony, William	02111	Hunt	—	—
Anthony, William E. R.	Rej	Hall	—	—
Anthony, William Franklin	19517	San Augustine	—	—
Antonio, Myra	49681	Bexar	Antonio, Charles	—
Apel, M. E. Mrs.	31229	Wood	Apel, Williams M.	—
Appel, August Mrs.	Rej	Bexar	Appel, August	—
Appell, Sophia A.	03779	Tarrant	Appell, Francis Phillip	—
Apperson, John Thomas	34637	Erath	—	—
Apperson, Joseph	Rej	Cherokee	—	—
Apperson, S. J. Mrs.	38277	Erath	Apperson, John Thomas	34637
Apple, George W.	20137	Dallas	—	—
Appleby, S. J. Mrs.	14646	Bosque	Appleby, Andrew Thomas	—
Appleton, A. M. Mrs.	42618	Tarrant	Appleton, Oliver	23151
Appleton, James	09104	Tarrant	—	—
Appleton, Oliver	23151	Tarrant	—	—
Appleton, Samansie C.	Rej	Tarrant	Appleton, James	09104
Applewhite, Annie Elizabeth	47342	Comanche	Applewhite, John Woody	—
Applewhite, James Bloodworth	18001	Lampasas	—	—
Applewhite, M. E. Mrs.	42706	Mills	Applewhite, James Bloodworth	18001
Applin, Margret E.	14183	Coryell	Applin, John J.	—
Applin, Mattie	39840	Milam	Applin, John Marion	—
Appling, A. A. Simpson Mrs.	38575	Wilson	Simpson, Timothy Sears	—
Appling, Amaricus Columbus	47363	Hays	—	—
Appling, Mary Virginia	47550	Hays	Appling, Amaricus Columbus	47363
Arant, Lavisa	40551	Lubbock	Arant, James K. Polk	—
Arbogast, Amanda Butcher	43726	Hill	Arbogast, Paul McNeil	—

Index to Confederate Pension Applications

Name	Number	County	Related	Related Number
Arbuckle, James K. Polk	29303	Bell		
Arbuckle, Lucy	32235	Bell	Arbuckle, James K. Polk	29303
Archer, John	30819	Montague		
Archer, John M.	Rej	Hutchinson		
Archer, M. E. Mrs.	50651	Nolan	Archer, Benjamin Franklin	
Archer, Marian M.	07838	Harris	Archer, Robert	
Archer, Mattie G.	27002	Harris	Archer, Rufus L.	
Archer, Nancy Elizabeth	51771	Hood	Archer, Joel Crawford	
Archer, Nancy J.	Rej	Limestone	Archer, William J.	32997
Archer, Nancy M.	50692	Hansford	Archer, John M.	Rej
Archer, Peterson Clark	19624	Walker		
Archer, R. W.	26715	Tarrant		
Archer, Rosa M.	15378	Harris	Archer, William Eggleston	
Archer, S. E. Mrs.	16086	Morris	Archer, Judson Merces	
Archer, Sallie M. Mrs.	05038	Wood	Archer, David B.	
Archer, Sarah L.	21147	Walker	Archer, Peterson Clark	19624
Archer, W. B.	26923	Hopkins		
Archer, William J.	32997	Limestone		
Archey, D. T.	17999	Lampasas		
Archibald, Edwin L.	11035	Limestone		
Archinard, Samuel	Rej	Harris		
Ard, D. A.	50314	Henderson		
Ard, John	Rej	Hopkins		
Ard, Laura	51542	Henderson	Ard, D. A.	50314
Ardis, S. J. Mrs.	17721	Gregg	Ardis, Thomas Archibald	
Ardoin, Miranda Woodruff	36326	El Paso	Ardoin, Serand	34492
Ardoin, Serand	34492	El Paso		
Arendale, Rosa Lee	39927	Travis	Arendale, William Moses	
Aresmendes, Sabino	07681	Wilson		
Argabright, John Henry	42748	Coryell		
Argabright, Lizzie	43149	Coryell	Argabright, John Henry	42748
Arganbright, E. H.	08002	Van Zandt		
Argo, Mary	27824	Denton	Argo, David	
Ariola, Gray	06633	Madison		
Arledge, I. M. Mrs.	17133	Milam	Arledge, John Hugh Hew	
Arledge, John	12761	Callahan		
Arledge, Martha Bernice	45074	Montague	Arledge, Garrett Longmarr	
Armentrant, M. A. Mrs.	26240	San Saba	Armentrant, George Pogue	
Armer, Sarah	17216	Waller	Armer, Thomas	
Armes, F. H.	Rej	Van Zandt		
Armes, Mary A.	30740	Mason	Armes, John English	
Armitage, S. B. Mrs.	Rej	Trinity	Armitage, Wilbur Fisk	
Armitage, Wilber Fisk	Rej	Madison		
Armontrout, Harriett	50619	Hamilton	Armontrout, George Washington	
Armor, Annie	19512	McCulloch	Armor, G. G.	05003
Armor, G. G.	05003	McCulloch		
Arms, Marion	11267	Smith		
Arms, Martha	06113AM	Blanco		
Arms, Mary E.	16575	Smith	Arms, Marion	
Arms, Nancy Ellen	17508	Comanche	Arms, Nathan	06113
Arms, Nathan	06113	Blanco		
Armstrong, A. E. Mrs.	19539	Rusk	Armstrong, Thomas E.	
Armstrong, A. E. Mrs.	22549	Shelby	Armstrong, James Boucher	
Armstrong, Ann Almena	38717	Cherokee	Armstrong, Martin Wiley	
Armstrong, Annette F.	49668	Bexar	Armstrong, John William	
Armstrong, Benjamin Joshua	30234	Tarrant		
Armstrong, Burrell Green	14226	Freestone		
Armstrong, Burrell Green Mrs.	35960	Freestone	Armstrong, Burrell Green	14226
Armstrong, Corinne A.	40138	Dallas	Armstrong, John Bell	01040

Index to Confederate Pension Applications

Armstrong, D. H.	03898	Travis		
Armstrong, D. M.	40806	San Augustine		
Armstrong, Edmond	01041	Dallas		
Armstrong, Edmond Mrs.	17565	Dallas	Armstrong, Edmond	01041
Armstrong, Elizabeth	12590	Rusk	Armstrong, W. A. J.	
Armstrong, F. M.	46776	Collin		
Armstrong, George Hamilton	00816	Childress		
Armstrong, George W.	09350	Travis		
Armstrong, H. A. Mrs.	35469	Tarrant	Armstrong, Benjamin Joshua	30234
Armstrong, Hannibal	42053	Harris		
Armstrong, Hugh	01428	Fannin		
Armstrong, Isaac Taylor	47805	Taylor		
Armstrong, J. A. Mrs.	26219	Milam	Armstrong, Martin	
Armstrong, J. H.	21094	Morris		
Armstrong, J. J.	22175	Erath		
Armstrong, J. L.	25176	Hunt		
Armstrong, J. W.	41881	Tarrant		
Armstrong, James B. F.	09992	Bexar		
Armstrong, James Houston	02112	Hunt		
Armstrong, Jo M.	08551	Hunt		
Armstrong, John Bell, Sr.	01040	Dallas		
Armstrong, John Burke	32842	Hays		
Armstrong, John J.	33900	Colorado		
Armstrong, John Sayers	10742	Smith		
Armstrong, Julia F.	10761	Travis	Armstrong, D. H.	03898
Armstrong, L. P. Mrs.	37431	Johnson	Armstrong, William Hamilton	28716
Armstrong, Leonora	Rej	Tarrant	Armstrong, Ramsey Clarke	50711
Armstrong, Levi Wilson	23299	Ellis		
Armstrong, M. E. Mrs.	41438	Taylor	Armstrong, Alfred Monroe	
Armstrong, M. L. V. Mrs.	39196	Upshur	Armstrong, James Watson	
Armstrong, Martha	50130	Freestone	Armstrong, Thomas Dorman	42935
Armstrong, Mary A.	45140	Hays	Armstrong, John Burke	32842
Armstrong, Mary Elizabeth	34805	Eastland	Armstrong, Samuel Wesley	10364
Armstrong, Mary Francis	20088	Stephens	Armstrong, William W.	03382
Armstrong, Mary Gertrude	36626	Baylor	Armstrong, William P.	
Armstrong, N. I.	27034	Franklin		
Armstrong, N. J. Mrs.	33663	Smith	Armstrong, John Sayers (Sealus)	10742
Armstrong, Nancy C.	43158	Harris	Armstrong, Hannibal	42053
Armstrong, Nancy Elizabeth	42476	Brown	Armstrong, Stephen Francis	
Armstrong, R. C. McDonough Mrs.	51310	Tarrant	McDonough, James Stanford	07373
Armstrong, R. J. Mrs.	50057	Hood	Armstrong, William Smith	
Armstrong, Ramsey Clarke	50711	Tarrant		
Armstrong, Samuel Wesley	10364	Eastland		
Armstrong, Sarah	39970	Tom Green	Armstrong, Alfred William	
Armstrong, Sarah A.	49040	Ellis	Armstrong, Thomas B.	
Armstrong, Sarah Jane	38626	Young	Armstrong, John Bryant	
Armstrong, Thomas Dorman	42935	Navarro		
Armstrong, Turner	38653	Franklin		
Armstrong, V. M.	26694	Lampasas		
Armstrong, William Hamilton	28716	Somervell		
Armstrong, William J.	Rej	Live Oak		
Armstrong, William Louis, Sr.	22470	Tarrant		
Armstrong, William Martin Mrs.	44083	Taylor	Armstrong, William Martin	
Armstrong, William N.	14065	Eastland		
Armstrong, William Smith	45962	Hood		
Armstrong, William W.	03382	Rains		
Arnall, E. Mrs.	20851	Travis	Arnall, James Andrew	
Arnett, Alonzo	28390	Tom Green		
Arnett, Alonzo Mrs.	36380	Tom Green	Arnett, Alonzo	28390

Index to Confederate Pension Applications

Arnett, Belle Kennedy	50690	Limestone	Arnett, Sandridge Thomas	
Arnett, David Nathan	49599	Mitchell	—	
Arnett, John Franklin	14310	Leon	—	
Arnett, Ophelia	51395	Mitchell	Arnett, David Nathan	49599
Arnett, Phebe	50021	Limestone	Arnett, Hansford	
Arnim, Julius E.	08833	Lavaca	—	
Arnold, Abner E.	28657	Victoria	—	
Arnold, Alfred Z.	25875	Lamar	—	
Arnold, Alice	34202	Tarrant	Arnold, John	12948
Arnold, Amanda	29007	Panola	Arnold, James Isaah	
Arnold, Ann	02683	Limestone	Arnold, William E.	
Arnold, Ann P.	00298	Bell	Arnold, M. D.	
Arnold, Arminda	35226	Upshur	Arnold, Jordon B.	23152
Arnold, Belle	29167	Harris	Arnold, John Bills	
Arnold, Benjamin Vinson	25425	Milam	—	
Arnold, Caroline	47738	Coleman	Arnold, Richard A.	
Arnold, Clara	45860	Dallas	Arnold, Joel Turnham	24978
Arnold, Cora Elliott	35285	Jones	Arnold, Francis Marion	23403
Arnold, D. D.	16038	Milam	—	
Arnold, E. L.	30132	Waller	—	
Arnold, E. L. Mrs.	32572	Brown	Arnold, William F.	
Arnold, Elizabeth	33952	Bexar	Arnold, Henry Allen	27539
Arnold, Emily J.	38161	Uvalde	Arnold, James Madison	19617
Arnold, F. M.	41215	Briscoe	—	
Arnold, Francis Marion	23403	Jones	—	
Arnold, George M., Sr.	19270	Smith	—	
Arnold, H.	09261	Johnson	—	
Arnold, Hattie	Rej	Tarrant	Arnold, John Wesley	41417
Arnold, Henry Allen	27539	Bexar	—	
Arnold, Hiram	19928	Denton	—	
Arnold, Isadore	10255	Galveston	—	
Arnold, J. W.	30059	Lamar	—	
Arnold, James Buchanan Mrs.	35213	Bosque	Arnold, James Buchanan	
Arnold, James M.	46934	Nacogdoches	—	
Arnold, James Madison	19617	Bandera	—	
Arnold, James Mitchum	Rej	Briscoe	—	
Arnold, Joel Turnham	24978	Dallas	—	
Arnold, John	12948	Kaufman	—	
Arnold, John Wesley	41417	Tarrant	—	
Arnold, Jonathan Hewett	22888	Trinity	—	
Arnold, Jordon B.	23152	Upshur	—	
Arnold, Kate	41541	Milam	Arnold, Joseph Clairbourne	
Arnold, Laurela J.	51354	Hunt	Arnold, Marcellus M.	47015
Arnold, Lewis Trent	21024	Nueces	—	
Arnold, Lydia	49726	Cherokee	Arnold, William A.	36122
Arnold, M. C. Mrs.	30398	Bosque	Arnold, Berryman	
Arnold, Malissa	30842	Rusk	Arnold, Moses	
Arnold, Marcellus M.	47015	Hunt	—	
Arnold, Margaret	23368	Hunt	Arnold, James Henry	
Arnold, Marie Ann	33834	Galveston	Arnold, Isadore	10255
Arnold, Martha Ann	50995	Angelina	Arnold, James Benjamin	
Arnold, Mary Frances	41117	Delta	Arnold, Ralph	
Arnold, Minnie C.	45333	Briscoe	Arnold, F. M.	41215
Arnold, Mollie	35547	Coryell	Arnold, Henry Summerfield	
Arnold, N. C. Mrs.	31621	Comanche	Arnold, Lidwell Taylor	
Arnold, Peter Hawkins	12287	Brazoria	—	
Arnold, Price	33131	Tarrant	—	
Arnold, Rankin	15622	Houston	—	
Arnold, Robert P.	33668	Callahan	—	

Index to Confederate Pension Applications

Name	App. No.	County	Veteran	Vet. No.
Arnold, Rosa E.	34939	Milam	Arnold, Benjamin Vinson	25425
Arnold, S. E. Mrs.	33310	Brazoria	Arnold, Peter Hawkins	
Arnold, Sallie Ann	Rej	Lynn	Arnold, Edward Dorell	
Arnold, T. J. Mrs.	36983	Trinity	Arnold, Johnathan Hewett	22888
Arnold, T. W.	16618	Smith		
Arnold, Thomas J.	07501	Hunt		
Arnold, W. H.	01043	Dallas		
Arnold, W. L.	29114	Rusk		
Arnold, William	22759	Angelina		
Arnold, William A.	36122	Cherokee		
Arnold, William Butler	Rej	Harris		
Arnold, William H.	08749	Lampasas		
Arnold, William M.	19488	Harrison		
Arnold, William McNutt	39638	Grayson		
Arnold, William Osborne	25755	Fannin		
Arnold, William Thomas Mrs.	Rej	Harrison	Arnold, William Thomas	
Arnspiger, J. H.	38898	Grayson		
Arnspiger, Mollie	50772	Grayson	Arnspiger, J. H.	38898
Arnwine, Ida	30901	Cherokee	Arnwine, William	00016
Arnwine, Mary Elizabeth	29388	Cherokee	Arnwine, Alfred William	
Arnwine, William	00016	Anderson		
Arocha, John N.	00345	Bexar		
Arons, Henry Clay Mrs.	Rej	Limestone	Arons, Henry Clay	
Arredondo, Guadalupe	33962	Wilson	Arredondo, Joaquin	06428
Arredondo, Joaquin	06428	Wilson		
Arrendale, Elizabeth Price	34893	Erath	Arrendale, Franklin Lafayette	
Arrington, Charles Thomas	08569	Hood		
Arrington, Georgia V.	38128	Houston	Arrington, Bennett B.	
Arrington, J. T.	39303	Franklin		
Arrington, Mary	27381	Johnson	Arrington, Charles Thomas	08569
Arrington, Nancy	22740	Angelina	Arrington, Sterling James	
Arrington, Sallie A.	Rej	Brazos	Arrington, Pinkney Henderson	
Arrington, Sarah C.	50103	Hemphill	Arrington, George Washington	
Arrington, T. W.	Rej	Denton		
Arrington, Thomas W.	25362	Kaufman		
Arrowood, Elizabeth	32265	Tom Green	Arrowood, McDaniel	26891
Arrowood, Hillman	14970	Coryell		
Arrowood, Mary A.	20874	Coryell	Arrowood, Hillman	14970
Arrowood, McDaniel	26891	Tom Green		
Arther, W. H.	43616	Eastland		
Arthur, Benjamin F.	22739	Milam		
Arthur, Eliza Jane	32037	Tom Green	Arthur, Steven Dexter	
Arthur, Elizabeth Jane	43629	Nacogdoches	Arthur, William Henry	22638
Arthur, Emma A.	23213	Hopkins	Arthur, John Thomas	
Arthur, Fannie L.	34284	Wichita	Arthur, William Goodman	
Arthur, J. P.	20210	Smith		
Arthur, James	Rej	Anderson		
Arthur, Julia	40167	Erath	Arthur, Charles Lewis	
Arthur, Matthew Tolbert	02810	McLennan		
Arthur, Rebecca	04683	Shackelford	Arthur, George P.	
Arthur, Sarah	37485	Baylor	Arthur, Matthew Tolbert	02810
Arthur, William Henry	22638	Nacogdoches		
Artzt, Gustav	36371	Comal		
Arvin, Sallie A.	46344	Brown	Arvin, Jameson Alexander	
Asberry, Jesse	27533	Falls		
Asbury, Florence Ann	42306	Cameron	Asbury, Joseph Alexander	
Asbury, Nancy L.	45832	Falls	Asbury, John Thomas	
Asbury, Thomas	10765	Travis		
Aschen, Henry F.	19477	Fayette		

Index to Confederate Pension Applications

Name	No.	County	Veteran	No.
Aschenbeck, Margaret	42780	Milam	Aschenbeck, John Henry	
Ascue, R. B.	Rej	Brown		
Ash, Dora	47959	Harris	Ash, Gerage	
Ash, J. F.	Rej	Rusk		
Ash, J. S.	01008	Coryell		
Ash, M. E. Mrs.	19165	Nacogdoches	Ash, James Franklin	
Ash, Maggie R.	49061	Runnels	Ash, William H.	
Ashabranner, W. H.	04406	Williamson		
Ashburn, Leona Gertrude	06941	Limestone	Ashburn, Davis Collins Bell	
Ashby, E. J. Mrs.	23396	Milam	Ashby, Titus Green Fare	
Ashby, J. A.	02944	Milam		
Ashby, M. A. Mrs.	14313	Liberty	Ashby, William K.	
Ashcraft, Jessie	50935	McLennan	Ashcraft, Sam A.	
Ashcraft, Sallie Ray	42712	Bell	Ashcraft, William James	27766
Ashcraft, William James	27766	Bell		
Asher, Annie Vaughan	41081	Dallas	Vaughan, Stephen H.	
Asher, Frank	12726	Bandera		
Asher, Nellie	51254	Uvalde	Asher, John Henry	
Ashford, Eva	Rej	Foard	Ashford, James	20678
Ashford, James	20678	Foard		
Ashford, Joseph L.	28939	Waller		
Ashford, Mary	20743	Smith	Ashford, William Thomas	
Ashford, Montgomery Paton	Rej	Tarrant		
Ashford, Montgomery Paton Mrs.	Rej	Motley	Ashford, Montgomery Paton	Rej
Ashford, Virginia Adilade	49641	Potter	Ashford, Charlie Stewart	
Ashill, Sallie	28404	Hopkins	Ashill, John Allen	
Ashley, C. C. Mrs.	08950	Anderson	Ashley, Ezekial	
Ashley, E. J.	27955	Fort Bend		
Ashley, Eliza	26376	Haskell	Ashley, John Hale	
Ashley, George Holloman	02812	McLennan		
Ashley, Hannah	09539	Coleman	Ashley, Mark C.	
Ashley, J. F.	RejM	Rusk		
Ashley, J. R.	01371	Falls		
Ashley, Jessie Garrett	Rej	Hill		
Ashley, M. E. Mrs.	Rej	Hunt	Ashley, Moses Samuel McDuffey	
Ashley, Malinda	Rej	Cooke	Ashley, Thomas S.	
Ashley, Mary	45083	Anderson	Ashley, Henry Clay	
Ashley, Nancy	43160	McLennan	Ashley, George Holloman	02812
Ashley, Robert	Rej	Denton		
Ashley, Robert A.	16039	Milam		
Ashley, S. C. Mrs.	42096	Donley	Ashley, James Alexander	
Ashley, T. G.	RejM	Hill		
Ashley, Thomas S.	02811	McLennan		
Ashley, William A.	34426	Milam		
Ashlock, W. F.	12070	Montague		
Ashmore, A. C.	RejM	Navarro		
Ashmore, E. A. Mrs.	18787	Houston	Ashmore, Ebenezer Lewellen	17883
Ashmore, Ebenezer Lewellen	17883	Houston		
Ashmore, Hattie C.	12087	Navarro	Ashmore, Andrew J.	
Ashmore, M. J. Mrs.	08739	Hopkins	Ashmore, Amus	
Ashmore, Margaret E.	15619	Houston	Ashmore, Joseph Henry	
Ashmore, Nancy B.	Rej	Travis	Ashmore, John Bloomer	
Ashmore, W. J.	07497	Houston		
Ashton, B. F.	05324	Montague		
Ashton, Hugh L.	21337	Cooke		
Ashworth, Carlton	42889	Van Zandt		
Ashworth, Cevena	RejM	Trinity		
Ashworth, Henrietta	00042	Angelina	Ashworth, Eli	
Ashworth, J. M.	46517	Reeves		

Index to Confederate Pension Applications

Ashworth, Joshua Harrison	29002	Angelina	—	
Ashworth, M. C. Mrs.	37645	Van Zandt	Ashworth, John	
Ashworth, Rachel Elizabeth	45055	Van Zandt	Ashworth, Carlton	42889
Ashworth, Sub	12251	Angelina	—	
Ashworth, U. V. Mrs.	41832	Angelina	Ashworth, Joshua Harrison	29002
Askew, Charles W.	11691	Waller	—	
Askew, Dortha Ann	50047	Anderson	Askew, John Dykes	
Askew, Isabella	01987	Hopkins	Askew, Richard L.	
Askew, Lucius Q. C. Mrs.	34285	Smith	Askew, Lucius Quinby Cincinnattus	14267
Askew, Lucius Quinby Cincinnattus	14267	Henderson	—	
Askew, Mollie C.	46822	Milam	Askew, William Henry	
Askew, Nancy Elizabeth	49251	Eastland	Askew, Paskel Clark	
Askew, Sarah Elizabeth	47227	Travis	Askew, Henry Garrison	
Askew, Sarah H.	Rej	Llano	Askew, George Christian	
Askew, William Henry Mrs.	28905	Tarrant	Askew, William Henry	
Askey, James Harrison	38868	Swisher	—	
Askey, Sarah	42016	Swisher	Askey, James Harrison	38868
Askins, Cordelia Caledonia	34759	Taylor	Askins, Joseph Gantt	30079
Askins, Francis Marion	09663	Medina	—	
Askins, Frank (Francis) M. Mrs.	40014	Atascosa	Askins, Frank (Francis) Marion	09663
Askins, Joseph Gantt	30079	Taylor	—	
Aslin, Charles F.	17539	Dallas	—	
Aston, Annie	50909	Terry	Aston, John Monroe	
Aston, Isabelle	06714	Comanche	Aston, Celsa D.	
Aston, W. E. Mrs.	Rej	Scurry	Aston, John Monroe	
Aswell, James Robert	16576	Smith	—	
Aswell, Sue	21515	Smith	Aswell, James Robert	16576
Atchison, A. W.	23215	Bosque	—	
Atchison, Bettie	39321	Llano	Atchison, John Surguen	
Atchison, David Monroe	26698	Rusk	—	
Atchison, James W.	39829	Parker	—	
Atchley, D. P.	05785	Dallas	—	
Atchley, Martha	01988	Hopkins	Atchley, J. C.	
Ater, Frances Isabel	Rej	Burnet	Ater, Albert Melvin	
Athey, Emeline V.	18248	Parker	Athey, James	
Athey, James H.	12981	Limestone	—	
Athey, W. W.	Rej	Van Zandt	—	
Athey, William Wesley Mrs.	46209	Angelina	Athey, William Wesley	
Atkins, Elizabeth C.	31914	Brazos	Atkins, James Polk	
Atkins, Ella	36561	Potter	Atkins, William	33807
Atkins, G. H. McMillan Mrs.	Rej	Dallas	McMillan, John Thomas	
Atkins, Haywood Augustus	15139	Fannin	—	
Atkins, John B.	35471	Bee	—	
Atkins, John L.	41206	Brown	—	
Atkins, Julia Bowles	34013	Bee	Atkins, Thomas Ragsdale	28635
Atkins, Lorenzo Dow	29264	Bee	—	
Atkins, Mary	06472	Johnson	Atkins, W. A.	
Atkins, Mary A.	45122	Bee	Atkins, Lorenzo Dow	29264
Atkins, Thomas Ragsdale	28635	Bee	—	
Atkins, Tom M.	Rej	Hood	—	
Atkins, Virginia	20423	Fannin	Atkins, Haywood Augustus	15139
Atkins, William	33807	Tarrant	—	
Atkins, William T., Sr.	41354	Marion	—	
Atkinson, Alonzo	05807	Mills	—	
Atkinson, Ann P.	15620	Houston	Atkinson, Daniel	
Atkinson, Carrie L.	Rej	Nueces	Atkinson, Edward	33339
Atkinson, Catherine M.	35268	Nueces	Atkinson, Jeremiah	
Atkinson, Edward	33339	Nueces	—	
Atkinson, Elisha Anderson	01468	Fayette	—	

Index to Confederate Pension Applications

Atkinson, Eliza	27322	Burnet	Atkinson, Albert	
Atkinson, H. C. Mrs.	17889	Houston	Atkinson, Louis	
Atkinson, I. M. Mrs.	47660	Smith	Atkinson, Eli	
Atkinson, J. G.	06500	Camp		
Atkinson, Jeremiah M.	05024	Nueces		
Atkinson, John H.	26095	Tarrant		
Atkinson, John Wilkins	03058	Montgomery		
Atkinson, Lafayet	07462	Cherokee		
Atkinson, M. C. Mrs.	23411	Upshur	Atkinson, Richard Andrews	
Atkinson, Margaret	33330	Nueces	Atkinson, Frank	
Atkinson, Mary A.	26831	Montgomery	Atkinson, John Wilkins	03058
Atkinson, Mary E.	10607	Cherokee	Atkinson, Lafayette	
Atkinson, Mary G.	43746	Mills	Atkinson, Henry Alfred	
Atkinson, Mary Jane	51756	Gonzales	Atkinson, William Mayo	46126
Atkinson, Nancy	18912	Dallas	Atkinson, Henry	
Atkinson, Parlee	42554	Leon	Atkinson, William C.	18049
Atkinson, Q. V. Mrs.	32612	Trinity	Atkinson, Elias	
Atkinson, Rebecca	21239	Austin	Atkinson, Soloman	
Atkinson, Rebecca	40798	Milam	Atkinson, Elliott Decatur	
Atkinson, Sarah E.	15937	Karnes	Atkinson, U. N.	02366
Atkinson, T. R. Mrs.	17888	Houston	Atkinson, John	
Atkinson, U. N.	02366	Karnes		
Atkinson, William C.	18049	Leon		
Atkinson, William J.	13029	Panola		
Atkinson, William Mayo	46126	Gonzales		
Atmar, Joseph Yates	19556	Freestone		
Atmar, S. E. Mrs.	34309	Freestone	Atmar, Joseph Yates	19556
Attaway, James David	31527	Hunt		
Attaway, Laura	37414	Wood	Attaway, Benjamin Franklin	
Attaway, Martha Elvie	40239	Hunt	Attaway, James David	31527
Attaway, Martha Jane	21627	Wood	Attaway, Green E.	
Attaway, Martha L.	29529	Panola	Attaway, Isaah	
Attaway, William W.	35794	Dallas		
Atteberry, Elizabeth	22757	Hunt	Atteberry, Church	
Atwell, Helen	02245	Jasper	Atwell, William	
Atwell, Joseph L.	49992	Runnels		
Atwood, Catherine	43241	Ellis	Atwood, A. C.	
Atwood, J. C.	01832	Harrison		
Atwood, Luther Oliver	12937	Johnson		
Atwood, Mary	00274	Bell	Atwood, Thomas	
Atwood, Mary I.	06697	Henderson	Atwood, B. A.	
Atwood, P. B.	16642	Tarrant		
Atwood, Rufus Marion Mrs.	49604	Smith	Atwood, Rufus Marion	
Atwood, Sallie P.	09881	Harrison	Atwood, J. C.	01832
Atwood, Sarah E.	41848	Navarro	Atwood, Luther Oliver	12937
Atwood, W. H.	09850	Montague		
Atwood, William M.	08356M	Hood		
Atzenhofer, Bertha	43471	Dewitt	Atzenhofer, Charles	39217
Atzenhofer, Charles	39217	Dewitt		
Auding, S.	00043	Angelina		
Auding, W. R.	15457	Henderson		
Audrain, Lucy Margaret	47306	Clay	Audrain, Samuel Kiethly	
Auerback, Frank	33880	Colorado		
Aughtry, James E.	25903	Cooke		
Aulsop, Eliza	00195	Bastrop	Aulsop, Joel	
Ault, James B.	11758	Stephens		
Aultman, Emma M.	17022	Wood	Aultman, James W.	04515
Aultman, James W.	04515	Wood		
Austell, C. C.	20480	Henderson		

Index to Confederate Pension Applications

Austell, George W.	42233	Henderson		
Austell, Josephine	43416	Henderson	Austell, George W.	42233
Austin, H. P.	20519	Dawson		
Austin, J. M.	15377	Harris		
Austin, John William	23206	Denton		
Austin, Mary F.	23154	Hale	Austin, Henry Mier	
Austin, Minerva	20169	Navarro	Austin, Moses	13475
Austin, Moses	13475	Navarro		
Austin, N. L. Mrs.	08905	Van Zandt	Austin, D. M.	
Austin, N. S. Mrs.	34769	Denton	Austin, John Willliam	23206
Austin, S. F. Mrs.	38026	Tarrant	Austin, Hezekiah Hollaman	
Austin, W. R.	37673	Tarrant		
Austin, W. W.	19106	Mason		
Autrey, Bird Griffin	23209	Coryell		
Autrey, Eliza Ann	02291	Johnson	Autrey, Jacob Clinton	
Autrey, James	Rej	Tarrant		
Autrey, James L.	Rej	Bexar		
Autrey, M. O. Mrs.	38123	Coryell	Autrey, Bird Griffin	23209
Autrey, Margarite	41776	Bowie	Autrey, Henry Duke	
Autrey, Martha	34104	Bexar	Autrey, James Larry	
Autrey, Matthew	03991	Trinity		
Autrey, Robert Martin	21624	Bowie		
Autrey, Sarah Jane (Smytha)	45827	Bowie	Autrey, Robert Martin	21624
Autrey, William Taylor Mrs.	50227	Denton	Autrey, William Taylor	
Autry, A. E. Mrs.	12945	Karnes	Autry, G. M.	Rej
Autry, G. M.	Rej	Karnes		
Autry, Nancy	46070	Hill	William Perry, Sr.	28654
Autry, William Perry, Sr.	28654	Hill		
Autry, Winnie M.	Rej	Jack	Autry, J. A.	
Avance, Caldonia	25389	Delta	Avants, James I.	01102
Avance, Nancy Mary	36008	Lamar	Avants, John George	17577
Avance, Sam M.	Rej	Delta		
Avant, Alice	41145	Jefferson	Avant, Thomas	
Avant, L. W.	07130	Anderson		
Avant, Mattie	45081	Atascosa	Avant, Abner	
Avant, Narsisa E.	51223	Anderson	Avant, Mason Simpson	
Avant, W. W.	49719	Robertson		
Avants (Avance), James I.	01102	Delta		
Avants (Avance), John George	17577	Delta		
Aven, A. J.	Rej	Hale		
Aven, Alonzo Jutson	51216	Lubbock		
Aven, Frances Henderson	42617	Hunt		
Aven, Jennie	49941	Hunt	Aven, Frances Henderson	42617
Avent, Bettie Simmons	12201	Williamson	Avent, J. L.	
Avent, G. W.	42195	Randall		
Avera, James, Sr.	10231	Waller		
Avera, Sallie	17237	Hopkins	Avera, James Walton	
Avery, Anthony Holloway	32802	Medina		
Avery, E. V. Mrs.	37272	Wilson	Avery, Anthony Holloway	32802
Avery, Jeannette C.	42739	Llano	Avery, John Calvin	39611
Avery, John Calvin	39611	Llano		
Avery, Martha J.	20866	Stonewall	Avery, Sanders	
Avery, Needham	09855	Bastrop		
Avery, Virginia W.	46865	Potter	Avery, Vincent Robert Coleman	
Avery, William T.	38220	Dimmit		
Avirett, Mary E.	14645	Bosque	Avirett, Robert Alexander	
Avrett, Margaret S.	46745	Milam	Avrett, William A.	
Avriett, Dulcina	31031	Henderson	Avriett, James	
Avrritt, W. J.	02945	Milam		

Index to Confederate Pension Applications

Name	App#	County	Veteran	Vet App#
Awalt, Martha Ann	43412	Tarrant	Awalt, William Joseph	—
Awalt, William Quinn	12200	Williamson	—	—
Awalt, William Quinn Mrs.	43116	Williamson	Awalt, William Quinn	12200
Awbrey, Julia Ann	43302	Brown	Awbrey, Thomas Jefferson	05661
Awbrey, M. T.	10186	Red River	—	—
Awbrey, Martha Francis	46601	Grimes	Awbrey, Benjamin Young	—
Awbrey, Thomas Jefferson	05661	Burleson	—	—
Awinger, Nannie	19051	Hunt	Awinger, Middleton Davis	—
Awtrey, Francis Adelia	37367	Grayson	Awtrey, Thomas Jefferson	—
Awtrey, M. A. Mrs.	32346	Parker	Awtrey, William Eldridge	—
Axley, Elizabeth	23511	Lampasas	Axley, John	—
Aycock, A. D. Mrs.	35556	Taylor	Aycock, John Magness	23928
Aycock, Aaron	38238	Harrison	—	—
Aycock, B. L.	35557	Hardin	—	—
Aycock, Joel	26747	Denton	—	—
Aycock, John Magness	23928	Callahan	—	—
Aycock, Mattie	21634	Lamar	Aycock, Willis Monroe	19554
Aycock, Richard W.	26613	Bosque	—	—
Aycock, Willis Monroe	19554	Howard	—	—
Ayer, Susan	28781	Shackelford	Ayer, David	—
Aynew, Jane P.	Rej	Eastland	Aynew, A. J.	—
Ayres, B. O.	17804	Henderson	—	—
Ayres, Clara Henry	49395	Montague	Ayres, James Arthur	—
Ayres, Daniel M.	11399	Coryell	—	—
Ayres, James Knox Mrs.	46445	Harris	Ayres, James Knox	—
Ayres, Jennie	51037	Coryell	Ayres, Daniel M.	11399
Ayres, Joeseph	19513	Nacogdoches	—	—
Ayres, John T.	18504	Victoria	—	—
Ayres, M. J. Mrs.	31691	Coryell	Ayres, Robert H.	10356
Ayres, Mark A. Mrs.	50087	Grayson	Ayres, Mark A.	—
Ayres, Mary Elizabeth	41674	Matagorda	Ayres, James Franklin	—
Ayres, Minnie Higdon	50173	Dallas	Ayres, Samuel	—
Ayres, Robert H.	10356	Coryell	—	—

B

Name	App#	County	Veteran	Vet App#
Babb, Buna	Rej	Bowie	Babb, Daniel Harrison	—
Babb, D. H.	Rej	Bowie	—	—
Babb, M. Susan	37079	Parker	Babb, William Marion	—
Babb, Mary Ann Davidson	42082	Falls	Davidson, Andrew Jackson	—
Babb, S. E. Mrs.	06898	Dallas	—	—
Babbit, R. T. Mrs.	07597	Grayson	Babbit, Harrison P.	—
Babbitt, Sarah E.	18833	Bexar	Babbitt, Jefferson Allen	—
Babcock, H. M.	12687	Calhoun	—	—
Babcock, James E.	47916	Lampasas	—	—
Baber, S. J.	22882	Erath	—	—
Babers, Ben Joseph	29541	Cherokee	—	—
Baccus, George William	51269	Llano	—	—
Bachman, Mary E.	47684	Red River	Bachman, Archibald T.	—
Bachman, W. F.	19615	Dallas	—	—
Back, Caroline	23237	Gray	Back, William	—
Backus, Mournen	36910	Brown	Backus, Thomas Jefferson	—
Bacon, Ellen M.	14514	Anderson	Bacon, John Andrew	—
Bacon, Georgia V.	05063	Waller	Bacon, Thomas	—
Bacon, Jennie M.	18458	Travis	Bacon, Robbert Stafford	—
Bacon, John	Rej	Denton	—	—
Bacon, John Harrison	43554	Collin	—	—
Bacot, Francis Josephine	37085	Fisher	Bacot, William Calhoun	34450
Bacot, Pensurela Helen	38774	Travis	Bacot, Thomas Wright	—

Index to Confederate Pension Applications

Name	No.	County	Soldier	No.
Bacot, William Calhoun	34450	Fisher		
Badger, Charles Wallace	16719	Travis		
Badger, Sallie M.	27693	Travis	Badger, Charles Wallace	16719
Badgett, J. R.	27619	Kaufman		
Badgett, Kate	16162	Navarro	Badgett, Burrell Freeman	
Badgett, R. S.	Rej	Wharton		
Badgett, S. H.	33917	Grayson		
Bagby, A. P.	27946	Lavaca		
Bagby, Elmira L.	18413	Tarrant	Bagby, Thomas Madison	
Bagby, Mary B.	27579	Harris	Bagby, Richard Hobson	13840
Bagby, Richard Hobson	13840	Harris		
Baggerly, Isiah Joseph	06667	Burleson		
Baggerly, Matilda	38040	Milam	Baggerly, Isiah Joseph	06667
Baggett, B. H.	26086	San Jacinto		
Baggett, Barton	02949	Milam		
Baggett, Jane	31643	Archer	Baggett, Silas	30233
Baggett, Julia A.	33549	Potter	Baggett, Hiram W.	
Baggett, Mary Ann	29578	Freestone	Baggett, Silas Messer	
Baggett, Mary Elizabeth	06638	San Augustine	Baggett, John Gaston	
Baggett, Mollie	47895	Matagorda	Baggett, Benjamin Hogan	
Baggett, Neal	02950	Milam		
Baggett, Oma	51450	Donley	Baggett, Henry Preston	
Baggett, Silas	30233	Archer		
Baggett, W. J.	Rej	Runnels		
Baggett, W. J.	Rej	Milam		
Bagley, Annie	40832	Hays	Bagley, Charles Hamilton	14785
Bagley, Charles Hamilton	14785	Caldwell		
Bagley, H. C. Mrs.	46391	Nolan	Bagley, Morgan	
Bagley, J. G.	14903	Cherokee		
Bagley, John Roundtree	29503	Harrison		
Bagley, Josephine	32705	Hays	Bagley, Maribeau Lamar	
Bagley, Margaret Tennessee	36825	Hays	Bagley, David Ross	
Bagley, Mary A. Clayton	51400	Hays	Bagley, Lindsey Burleson	
Bagley, Thomas J.	36250	Brown		
Bagwell, Berry Judson	31607	Rusk		
Bagwell, Nancy Ellen	25954	Wise	Bagwell, William Anderson	
Bagwell, Sarah E.	05046	Red River	Bagwell, Nathaniel R.	
Bailey, A. C. Mrs.	04163	Van Zandt	Bailey, Butler	
Bailey, A. E.	05434	Camp		
Bailey, A. E. Mrs.	18559	Wise	Bailey, Horace Coleman	09369
Bailey, A. L.	Rej	Harris		
Bailey, Ada	Rej	Nacogdoches	Bailey, John	
Bailey, Alonzo B.	30746	San Jacinto		
Bailey, Anne A.	04520	Wood	Bailey, J. J.	
Bailey, Annie E.	37580	Hopkins	Bailey, John Wyley	17669
Bailey, Artimisa	40664	Trinity	Bailey, David Hayne	08679
Bailey, Bryan Whitfield	06108	Panola		
Bailey, C. F.	28090	Grayson		
Bailey, C. H.	13471	Navarro		
Bailey, C. H. Mrs.	35897	Tarrant	Bailey, C. H.	13471
Bailey, Caroline	38813	Polk	Bailey, Thomas A.	
Bailey, Charles M.	11685	Walker		
Bailey, Crucie	23737	Fannin	Bailey, James Madison	09543
Bailey, D.	12487	McCulloch		
Bailey, David Hayne	08679	Falls		
Bailey, Dena	42122	Collin	Bailey, Earl Thomas	
Bailey, E. M. Mrs.	04765	Brazos	Bailey, J. M.	
Bailey, Eliza C.	07394	Wood	Bailey, Thomas B.	
Bailey, Elizabeth	51198	Walker	Bailey, Charles M.	11685

Index to Confederate Pension Applications

Name	No.	County	Veteran	No.
Bailey, Ellen L.	36031	Grayson	Bailey, Joseph Edward	10867
Bailey, Emilie C.	23276	Collin	Bailey, William Porter	—
Bailey, Fannie D.	19979	Hopkins	Bailey, Zacheriah W.	—
Bailey, Frances	20437	Waller	Bailey, Bryant Whitfield	06108
Bailey, Frances Marion	25410	Harris		
Bailey, Francis M.	41293	Palo Pinto		
Bailey, Frederick Augustus	28569	Burnet		
Bailey, Frederick Augustus Mrs.	38563	Harris	Bailey, Frederick Augustus	28569
Bailey, George Washington	08326	Grimes		
Bailey, Horace Coleman	09369	Wise		
Bailey, Hulda Manervie	40881	Camp	Bailey, Stephen Pinkney	17408
Bailey, Ida	45404	Travis	Bailey, James E.	22465
Bailey, J. R.	38642	Milam		
Bailey, James Alfred	33974	Henderson		
Bailey, James E.	22465	Travis		
Bailey, James Madison	09543	Fannin		
Bailey, Joe M.	45104	Coryell		
Bailey, John Benjamin	11010	Kaufman		
Bailey, John G.	Rej	Van Zandt		
Bailey, John T.	Rej	Bexar		
Bailey, John W.	01518	Freestone		
Bailey, John William	23716	Shelby		
Bailey, John William Mrs.	38132	Shelby	Bailey, John William	23716
Bailey, John Wyley	17669	Franklin		
Bailey, Joseph Edward	10867	Cherokee		
Bailey, Josephus	Rej	Wise		
Bailey, L. C. Mrs.	Rej	Denton	Bailey, James Marshall	—
Bailey, Lou E.	31587	Milam	Bailey, William Henderson	—
Bailey, M. A. Mrs.	18522	Washington	Bailey, Robert C.	—
Bailey, M. A. Mrs.	28577	Kaufman	Bailey, James	—
Bailey, Maggie	41560	Donley	Bailey, Allison M.	—
Bailey, Margaret Ann	35683	El Paso	Bailey, William Washington	—
Bailey, Margaret Francis	31523	Hopkins	Bailey, Master N.	—
Bailey, Martha A.	00334	Bexar	Bailey, William B.	—
Bailey, Martin Howard	02951	Milam		
Bailey, Mary Elizabeth	04920	Bastrop	Bailey, Burrell	—
Bailey, Mary J.	32836	Tarrant	Bailey, Robert Wesley	—
Bailey, Mary J.	42482	Fannin	Bailey, Braxton Bryant	—
Bailey, Mary L.	23399	Harris	Bailey, Pitser Miller	—
Bailey, Minerva C.	21636	Shelby	Bailey, Williams M.	—
Bailey, Nancy L.	07904	Montague	Bailey, James M.	—
Bailey, Nannie	32860	Madison	Bailey, Ira Webb	—
Bailey, Osman F.	09529	Aransas		
Bailey, P. R.	18766	Kerr		
Bailey, Peter James	17483	Collin		
Bailey, Peter James Mrs.	Rej	Freestone	Bailey, Peter James	17483
Bailey, Rebecca M.	18558	Wise	Bailey, Josephus	—
Bailey, Rufus K.	47803	Hill		
Bailey, S. P. Mrs.	24870	Harris	Bailey, Haman Lewis	—
Bailey, Sallie	52040	Navarro	Bailey, George Dargan Williamson	—
Bailey, Sarah Carrie	51119	Harris	Bailey, Thomas S.	—
Bailey, Sarah Francis	38326	Henderson	Bailey, James Alfred	33974
Bailey, Sarah M.	Rej	McLennan	Bailey, William Bennett	—
Bailey, Stephen Pinkney	17408	Camp		
Bailey, Tabitha	Rej	Stephens		
Bailey, Texas J. Mrs.	14441	Tarrant	Bailey, H. E.	—
Bailey, Thomas A.	00855	Clay		
Bailey, W. F.	18548	Wise		
Bailey, W. H.	38727	Dallas		

Index to Confederate Pension Applications

Name	App#	County	Soldier	Soldier App#
Bailiff, A. J.	Rej	Van Zandt		
Bailiff, Silas N.	00565	Burleson		
Bailiff, W. R.	21639	Fisher		
Baillio, Helene	02662	Liberty	Baillio, S. P.	
Baily, James A.	06072	Harris		
Bain, Annie	14979	Coryell	Bain, S. McNeil	
Bain, Benjamin	04028	Upshur		
Bain, L. R. Mrs.	12656	Upshur	Bain, Benjamin	04028
Bain, Sarah A.	29951	Freestone	Bain, Harvey Allison	
Bain, Susan Caroline	50053	Wichita	Bain, William Samuel	
Baines, Mary	33650	Eastland	Baines, Alexander	
Baines, Ruth Amit	39145	Blanco	Baines, John Wilson	
Bains, Sallie J.	18062	Limestone	Bains, Benton Buchanan	
Baird, B. H.	00989	Coryell		
Baird, Berta	49366	Ellis	Baird, William Alfred	
Baird, C. B.	07567	Coryell		
Baird, Franklin J.	07185	Comanche		
Baird, George W.	00663	Camp		
Baird, J. W.	09154	Brazos		
Baird, John	07227	Harris		
Baird, M. E. Mrs.	10039	Coryell	Baird, B. H.	00989
Baird, Mary D.	39127	Lampasas	Baird, William Cleveland	27749
Baird, Mary E.	20807	Polk	Baird, James Chambers	
Baird, Mattie R.	14804	Camp	Baird, George W.	00663
Baird, R. H. Mrs.	33033	Comanche	Baird, Franklin J.	07185
Baird, William Cleveland	27749	Bell		
Baisden, Permelia Caroline	42871	Ellis	Baisden, Richard R.	
Baits, Martha Jane	Rej	Wise	Baits, George Edward	
Baker, A. H. (Bert)	45142	Panola		
Baker, A. V.	20998	Callahan		
Baker, A. V. Mrs.	07330	Montgomery	Baker, G. W.	
Baker, Albert William	01472	Fayette		
Baker, Alexander Stevenson	29664	Milam		
Baker, Alice	50661	Tyler	Baker, George Washington	30401
Baker, Amanda	Rej	Caldwell	Baker, John White	18859
Baker, Andrew Jackson	20112	Wise		
Baker, Annie Elizabeth	23522	Cherokee	Baker, Green Benjamin	04162
Baker, Annie Thomas	45120	Bell	Baker, Joseph N.	
Baker, Aurelia	21610	Howard	Baker, Joel	
Baker, B. T.	11672	Upshur		
Baker, Ben F.	27430	Montgomery		
Baker, Catherine (Katie)	Rej	Liberty	Baker, John	
Baker, Charles	12631	Tarrant		
Baker, Charles Eugene	31916	Nacogdoches		
Baker, Charles Eugene Mrs.	33780	Nacogdoches	Baker, Charles Eugene	31916
Baker, Cornelia C.	31044	Red River	Baker, David Alexander	
Baker, D. A.	18272	Red River		
Baker, Daniel Asbury	35082	San Patricio		
Baker, David Giles	37527	Van Zandt		
Baker, Deliliah I.	15800	Johnson	Baker, William H.	
Baker, E. C.	21566	Nacogdoches		
Baker, E. M. Mrs.	25403	Madison	Baker, Fountain S.	09725
Baker, E. R. Mrs.	21637	Fayette	Baker, Joseph Harrison	17654
Baker, Eli Wesley	28070	Dimmit		
Baker, Eliza	10131	Lampasas	Baker, C. G.	
Baker, Eliza J.	50666	Bandera	Baker, W. B.	27484
Baker, Elizabeth	33569	Lamar	Baker, John Armstrong	29777
Baker, Elvira	51779	Milam	Baker, Alexander Stevenson	29664
Baker, F. M.	27347	Smith		

Index to Confederate Pension Applications

Baker, Fountain S.	09725	Leon		
Baker, Frank C.	47700	Hall		
Baker, George C.	22308	Hays		
Baker, George C., Sr.	29116	Fort Bend		
Baker, George W.	40594	Parker		
Baker, George Washington	30401	Tyler		
Baker, Green Benjamin	04162	Van Zandt		
Baker, Hamilton Hampton	30139	Wood		
Baker, Helen M.	51049	Lamar	Baker, Isaac Fiske	
Baker, Henry	00132	Austin		
Baker, Henry Franklin Mrs.	38447	Hamilton	Baker, Henry Franklin	
Baker, Isaac	25896	Fannin		
Baker, Isaac William	39809	Cherokee		
Baker, Isham Lee	09466	Gonzales		
Baker, J. A.	Rej	Lamar		
Baker, J. C.	29086	Tyler		
Baker, J. H.	02433	Lamar		
Baker, J. M.	05798	Jack		
Baker, J. S.	01655	Gregg		
Baker, J. W.	20605	Red River		
Baker, J. W. Mrs.	20086	Falls	Baker, John Geter	
Baker, Jackson	11969	Houston		
Baker, James	37876	Taylor		
Baker, James A.	03228	Palo Pinto		
Baker, James D.	14033	Walker		
Baker, James Franklin	04411	Williamson		
Baker, Janetta	47210	Harris	Baker, William H.	
Baker, John Armstrong	29777	Lamar		
Baker, John F.	Rej	Bexar		
Baker, John M.	02114	Hunt		
Baker, John R.	11096	Potter		
Baker, John W.	Rej	Delta		
Baker, John W.	34340	Potter		
Baker, John White	18859	Caldwell		
Baker, Joseph Echols	11444	Fayette		
Baker, Joseph Hardy	09135	Bandera		
Baker, Joseph Harrison	17654	Fayette		
Baker, Joshua P.	10021	Cass		
Baker, Julia A.	39068	Bexar	Baker, Augustus Loel	
Baker, Julia E.	22897	Smith	Baker, James Lyons Sanford	
Baker, L. E. Mrs.	12446	Hunt	Baker, John M.	02114
Baker, Lizzie	Rej	Cooke	Baker, George W.	
Baker, Lou Mrs.	00319	Bell	Baker, John A.	
Baker, Louisa Phenolia	Rej	Brown	Baker, Henry	
Baker, M. A. Mrs.	33720	Nacogdoches	Baker, Thomas Hamilton	
Baker, M. C. Mrs.	27308	McCulloch	Baker, John Ranscelor	
Baker, M. C. Mrs.	30693	McLennan	Baker, William Richard	20136
Baker, M. E. Mrs.	25773	Hill	Baker, James Franklin	04411
Baker, M. E. Mrs.	36881	Wood	Baker, Hamilton Hampton	30139
Baker, M. J. Mrs.	04801	Red River	Baker, M.	
Baker, M. J. Mrs.	06326	Henderson	Baker, John A.	
Baker, M. J. Mrs.	14716	Bowie	Baker, Allen Johnson	
Baker, M. Mrs.	00466	Bosque	Baker, W. P.	
Baker, Maggie Jane	39064	Gonzales	Baker, Joseph Hardy	09135
Baker, Malissa	38793	Van Zandt	Baker, David Giles	37527
Baker, Martha	27900	Wise	Baker, Andrew Jackson	20112
Baker, Martha Ann	22572	Palo Pinto	Baker, James Allen	
Baker, Martha Ann	47114	Taylor	Baker, Andrew Alexander	
Baker, Martha Ann Johnson	Rej	Cherokee	Johnson, J. N., Sr.	23680

Index to Confederate Pension Applications

Baker, Mary	Rej	Caldwell	Baker, Green	
Baker, Mary	15914	Leon	Baker, J. P.	
Baker, Mary A.	15117	Falls	Baker, E.	
Baker, Mary Ella	43947	Cherokee	Baker, Isaac William	39809
Baker, Mary J.	Rej	Bowie	Baker, A. J.	
Baker, Mary Nancy	20856	Taylor	Baker, Robert	
Baker, Mary R.	31853	Leon	Baker, Robert	
Baker, Mathi A. Mrs.	41297	Travis	Baker, John A.	
Baker, Minnie E.	44017	Lamar	Baker, Murdock McIntosh	
Baker, Minta	46342	San Patricio	Baker, Daniel Asbury	35082
Baker, Myra L. Greenwade	49706	Hill	Greenwade, Palmer Moses	
Baker, N. A. Mrs.	05173	Bell	Baker, W. W.	
Baker, Nancy	07396	Williamson	Baker, S. W.	
Baker, Octavia P.	49583	Harris	Baker, John Berrian	
Baker, Patti	17658	Fayette	Baker, Joseph Echols	11444
Baker, R. E. Mrs.	15427	Henderson	Baker, Abraham	
Baker, R. J. Mrs.	09064	Lamar	Baker, J. H.	02433
Baker, Rebecca Ann	45957	Jones	Baker, Samuel Bryant	
Baker, Rebecca E.	21638	Brazos	Baker, William Batts	05253
Baker, Robert A.	33345	Hamilton		
Baker, Robert A. Mrs.	40093	Hamilton	Baker, Robert A.	33345
Baker, Robert Watt Mrs.	35053	Brown	Baker, Robert Watt	
Baker, Rosalia	46895	Dallas	Baker, Madison Pinkney	
Baker, Rufus F.	14963	Cooke		
Baker, S. F. A.	11154	Tyler		
Baker, Sarah	39240	Parker	Baker, Allen	
Baker, Solena	35306	Bowie	Baker, Joshua P.	10021
Baker, Solomon M.	11222	Hamilton		
Baker, Sorona R.	45115	Van Zandt	Baker, William Jefferson	17173
Baker, Susan	38649	Collin	Baker, John Wakefield	
Baker, T. V.	03614	Shackelford		
Baker, W. B.	27484	Bandera		
Baker, W. R.	21446	Nacogdoches		
Baker, W. S.	30738	Wood		
Baker, William	Rej	Houston		
Baker, William	26065	Grayson		
Baker, William Batts	05253	Brazos		
Baker, William E.	22150	Rusk		
Baker, William Jefferson	17173	Van Zandt		
Baker, William Richard	20136	McLennan		
Balades, Sicilia	04453	Wilson	Balades, Francisco	
Balansuela, Encarnacion	00391	Bexar		
Balch, Samuel P.	10536	Coryell		
Baldree, Fannie	06639	San Augustine	Baldree, J. H.	
Baldree, Jim Marion	26089	Sabine		
Baldree, Mary Elizabeth	39667	Sabine	Baldree, Jim Marion	26089
Baldridge, J. A.	01045	Dallas		
Baldridge, J. L.	15488	Hill		
Baldridge, M. E. Mrs.	32876	Denton	Baldridge, Robert James	
Baldwin, A. M. Mrs.	Rej	Harrison	Baldwin, Benjamin Harris	42429
Baldwin, Benjamin Harris	42429	Harrison		
Baldwin, Cuff Fitzpatrick	38777	Harrison		
Baldwin, Daniel M.	28591	Delta		
Baldwin, Elizabeth Jane	42410	Walker	Baldwin, William Franklin	19400
Baldwin, F. M.	03295	Parker		
Baldwin, Fannie C.	Rej	Red River	Baldwin, George Scott	
Baldwin, Francis Gardner Mrs.	41076	Dallas	Baldwin, Francis Gardner	
Baldwin, H. C.	26139	Erath		
Baldwin, J. G.	14393	Runnels		

Index to Confederate Pension Applications

Name	No.	County	Veteran	No.
Baldwin, J. G. Mrs.	45383	Wichita	Baldwin, J. G.	14393
Baldwin, Peter T.	20764	Kerr	—	—
Baldwin, Sarah E.	26378	Kaufman	Baldwin, Charles Simpson	—
Baldwin, Susan Jane	43546	Dallas	Baldwin, James Hiram	—
Baldwin, William Franklin	19400	Walker	—	—
Bales, B. Z. Mrs.	29359	Johnson	Bales, Jesse Wallace	—
Bales, W. H.	23455	Llano	—	—
Balke, Amanda	39466	Austin	Balke, Christian	—
Ball, A. J.	38281	Dallas	—	—
Ball, Benjamin F.	47190	Dallas	—	—
Ball, George J.	41572	Milam	—	—
Ball, Henderson A.	Rej	Tarrant	—	—
Ball, Henry Washington	07880	Kaufman	—	—
Ball, J. M.	06675	Collin	—	—
Ball, John Lewis	49626	Johnson	—	—
Ball, Margaret Elizabeth	07732	Wise	Ball, Benjamin Jackson	—
Ball, Margaret J.	22645	Cherokee	Ball, Elias Tidwell	—
Ball, Martha A.	22745	Cherokee	Ball, Taudy	—
Ball, Mary Jane	43456	Kaufman	Ball, Henry Washington	07880
Ball, Peter Marion	21640	Grayson	—	—
Ball, Ruth E.	42080	Denton	Ball, Andrew Thomas	—
Ball, Sarah	07875	Jack	Ball, William J.	—
Ball, Thomas T.	22611	Tarrant	—	—
Ball, Venetia C.	42867	Bowie	Ball, Kennedy Wade	—
Ball, William Lee	Rej	Bowie	—	—
Ballard, A. E. Mrs.	Rej	Kaufman	Ballard, John Wesley	—
Ballard, A. L.	08320	Grayson	—	—
Ballard, Adeline	05495	Henderson	Ballard, Euphronius Franklin	—
Ballard, Anna	37444	Dallas	Ballard, John Rogers	29292
Ballard, Annie	51934	Tarrant	Ballard, James Dan	—
Ballard, C. B. Mrs.	22673	Ellis	Ballard, Thomas Daniel	—
Ballard, C. Matilda	46647	Anderson	Ballard, Andrew Jackson	—
Ballard, David Berry	10894	Dallas	—	—
Ballard, E. A. Mrs.	01044	Dallas	Ballard, A. J.	—
Ballard, Elijah	13030	Panola	—	—
Ballard, Eliza	36328	Panola	Ballard, Elijah	13030
Ballard, F. M.	10146	Menard	—	—
Ballard, James M.	Rej	Red River	—	—
Ballard, John Jackson	07266	Jefferson	—	—
Ballard, John Rogers	29292	Johnson	—	—
Ballard, Josie	46480	Rockwall	Ballard, Louis Jefferson	14184
Ballard, Laura	17907	Hunt	Ballard, Timothy C.	—
Ballard, Louis Jefferson	14184	Coryell	—	—
Ballard, Louisa	07999	Van Zandt	Ballard, Joshua	—
Ballard, M. A. K. Mrs.	18695	Howard	Ballard, Elijah Jasper	—
Ballard, Martha A.	Rej	Bexar	Ballard, Christopher A.	—
Ballard, Mary Francis	43057	Dickens	Ballard, William Curtis	—
Ballard, Mary L.	35016	Karnes	Ballard, Soloman	—
Ballard, N. L.	19787	Tarrant	—	—
Ballard, N. M.	04674	Rockwall	—	—
Ballard, Nannie Carolina	Rej	Bell	Ballard, Leonard	—
Ballard, Sallie E.	46135	Grayson	Ballard, William G.	—
Ballard, Savanah Isabella	38127	Nacogdoches	Ballard, Samuel W.	—
Ballard, Theodosia E.	27642	Jefferson	Ballard, John Jackson	07266
Ballard, Thomas Elbert	13027	Palo Pinto	—	—
Ballard, W. H.	25351	Jones	—	—
Ballard, W. R.	09759	Throckmorton	—	—
Balle, Locario	04311	Webb	—	—
Ballew, Elizabeth A.	10672	Kerr	Ballew, R. T.	—

Index to Confederate Pension Applications

Ballew, George Edward	32954	Tarrant	—	
Ballew, Mary R.	33646	Tarrant	Ballew, George Edward	32954
Ballew, Sarah J.	01138	Denton	Ballew, William	
Ballinger, John L.	36179	Fannin	—	
Ballinger, Mary Scott	43354	Dallas	Ballinger, James Micheal	
Ballman, M. E. Pool Mrs.	38928	Wilbarger	Pool, George Washington	
Ballon, Lugenio	20751	McCulloch	—	
Ballou, Blanch M.	50962	McCulloch	Ballou, Lugenio	20751
Ballou, Seth T.	47086	Hamilton	—	
Ballou, William Harry Mrs.	Rej	Taylor	Ballou, William Harry	
Balthrop, Jennie	35918	Travis	Balthrop, Thomas T.	11668
Balthrop, Thomas T.	11668	Travis	—	
Balthrop, Wilie R.	Rej	Hunt	—	
Bancone, Michael Mrs.	RejM	Caldwell	Bancone, Michael	
Bandy, Aliff Mrs.	20709	Bandera	Bandy, John Jefferson	Rej
Bandy, John Jefferson	Rej	Bandera	—	
Bandy, P.	00714	Cass	—	
Bandy, Sarah E. Jones	Rej	Brewster	Jones, Bewford Whittington	
Banes, James Kenneth	34219	Tarrant	—	
Banes, James Kenneth Mrs.	39008	Tarrant	Banes, James Kenneth	34219
Banister, Margaret	03419	Red River	Banister, B.	
Banister, William L.	32586	Marion	—	
Bankhead, Georgia Ann	36760	Parker	Bankhead, Gardner Jarrett	
Bankhead, M. C. Mrs.	43035	Parker	Bankhead, George Greer	
Bankhead, Susan Alcinda	49923	Lamar	Bankhead, Leander Jackson	
Banks, Andrew H.	28982	Wise	—	
Banks, Andrew H. Mrs.	31875	Wise	Banks, Andrew H.	28982
Banks, C. B.	13489	Polk	—	
Banks, David Dickerson	38094	Cherokee	—	
Banks, David Dickerson Mrs.	45228	Cherokee	Banks, David Dickerson	38094
Banks, E. F. Mrs.	16147	Nacogdoches	Banks, Joseph Thomas	
Banks, Eliza H.	11450	Franklin	Banks, Peter S.	
Banks, James Anderson	23682	Knox	—	
Banks, Josiphine	Rej	Titus	Banks, John	
Banks, L. F.	18565	Wood	—	
Banks, Lila Edwards	46312	Bexar	Banks, Edwin Gray	
Banks, M. A. Mrs.	28546	Johnson	Banks, William Clarendon	
Banks, Martha Jane	40277	Navarro	Banks, Thomas Jefferson	28876
Banks, Mittie L.	45546	Nueces	Banks, William Lewis	34696
Banks, R. P.	Rej	Titus	—	
Banks, R. W.	17849	Hopkins	—	
Banks, Sallie Townsend	48019	Scurry	Townsend, Charles Newton	
Banks, Sarah A.	35549	Johnson	Banks, Solomon Jasper	
Banks, Thomas	29316	Bastrop	—	
Banks, Thomas Jefferson	28876	Navarro	—	
Banks, W. W.	Rej	Cherokee	—	
Banks, William	51518	Galveston	—	
Banks, William Lewis	34696	Dimmit	—	
Banks, William W.	17359	Bowie	—	
Bankston, Jane	15086	El Paso	Bankston, Aaron	
Bankston, Levi	03944	Travis	—	
Bankston, R. S.	05439	Hardin	—	
Bankston, Willis Jasper	25973	Bosque	—	
Banner, Thomas Jefferson	Rej	Terrell	—	
Banta, D. B.	Rej	Kerr	—	
Banta, Daniel Jefferson	13920	Kerr	—	
Banta, David R.	10012	Burnet	—	
Banta, G. Wilson	43904	Bandera	—	
Banta, John	02417	Kerr	—	

Index to Confederate Pension Applications

Name	No.	County	Veteran	No.
Barb, G. H.	23317	Tarrant		
Barbary, James Henry	24129	Hunt		
Barbary, R. E. Mrs.	30691	Hunt	Barbary, James Henry	24129
Barbee, Addie	42318	Grayson	Barbee, John Calvin	
Barbee, Cordelia	45509	Hays	Barbee, John Jones	
Barbee, E. J. Mrs.	17827	Hill	Barbee, John T.	
Barbee, Fannie E.	01361	Falls	Barbee, Wylie Edward	
Barbee, M.	41403	Runnels		
Barbee, Martha Louise	36239	Bosque	Barbee, Joseph Samuel	
Barbee, Mollie	01641	Grayson	Barbee, James H.	
Barbee, Napoleon B.	21523	Houston		
Barbee, Sallie	26472M	Hays		
Barbee, Sarah	39039	Palo Pinto	Barbee, Willis Munroe	
Barbee, Sophronia	03786	Tarrant	Barbee, Henry	
Barbee, Tennie	19180	Orange	Barbee, Joseph Hamilton	
Barbee, W. M.	05464	Hamilton		
Barber, Alice	32650	Panola	Barber, Cullen Andrew	16226
Barber, Caladoina C.	37128	Fannin	Barber, George W.	18942
Barber, Cullen Andrew	16226	Panola		
Barber, D. A. Mrs.	03250	Panola	Barber, J. A.	
Barber, G. C.	11843	Cass		
Barber, George W.	18942	Fannin		
Barber, Isam Washington	23520	Hood		
Barber, J. L.	03849	Titus		
Barber, John Murphy	22599	Dallas		
Barber, Joseph Addison	08246	Chambers		
Barber, M. A. Mrs.	25570	Hood	Barber, Isam Washington	23520
Barber, M. E. Mrs.	18708	Cherokee	Barber, Jeams Jackson	
Barber, Margaret L.	38129	Dallas	Barber, John Murphy	22599
Barber, N. G.	01904	Hill		
Barber, Nat J.	22750	Harrison		
Barber, P. B.	29827	Gregg		
Barber, P. W.	04856	Nacogdoches		
Barber, R. J.	06632	Madison		
Barber, Robert V.	45567	Dallas		
Barber, Sallie	09228	Hill	Barber, N. G.	01904
Barber, W. H.	45047	Hardin		
Barbour, John Thomas	32200	Johnson		
Barbour, John Thomas Mrs.	38085	Johnson	Barbour, John Thomas	32200
Barclay, Ellen	34942	Tyler	Robert B., Sr.	19396
Barclay, Hugh W.	12936	Johnson		
Barclay, J. H.	Rej	Hopkins		
Barclay, J. K. P.	Rej	Milam		
Barclay, James Knox Polk Mrs.	46392	Milam	Barclay, James Knox Polk	
Barclay, John Bunion	19924	Williamson		
Barclay, M. E. Mrs.	15500	Hopkins	Barclay, Joseph Hugh	
Barclay, Martha	41982	Williamson	Barclay, John Bunion	19924
Barclay, Mary E.	16270	Polk	Barclay, W. W.	14069
Barclay, Mary J.	16767	Tyler	Barclay, Anderson Edward	
Barclay, Mary Jane	03447	Robertson	Barclay, David	
Barclay, Robert B., Sr.	19396	Tyler		
Barclay, W. W.	14069	Hardin		
Barcroft, James D. Mrs.	41059	Comanche	Barcroft, James D.	
Barcroft, Sarah A.	30586	Hardeman	Barcroft, Lorenzo Overall	
Bard, Benjamin Franklin	25001	Madison		
Bard, Martha Virginia	38607	Madison	Bard, Benjamin Franklin	25001
Bardin, D. C.	27040	Fayette		
Bardin, Lavenia	43448	Tarrant	Bardin, John Christopher	
Bardin, S. D.	02878	Llano		

Index to Confederate Pension Applications

Barefield, Ellen	45090	Grimes	Barefield, Francis Marion	32503
Barefield, Francis Marion	32503	Grimes	—	—
Barefield, John C.	Rej	McLennan	—	—
Barefield, S. J. Mrs.	29517	Jasper	Barefield, Henry D.	—
Barefoot, J. W.	12762	Callahan	—	—
Barentine, Mary D.	10616	Cooke	Barentine, H. L.	—
Barfield, A. R. M. Mrs.	05734	Gregg	Barfield, Samuel P.	—
Barfield, Alice	39871	Van Zandt	Barfield, Charles Lewis	—
Barfield, B. T.	Rej	Dallas	—	—
Barfield, Elcy	04982	Williamson	—	—
Barfield, James C.	15487	Hill	—	—
Barfield, James H.	28032	Kaufman	—	—
Barfield, Lewis Solomn	14352	Nacogdoches	—	—
Barfield, Lydia M.	49537	Van Zandt	Barfield, John Fletcher	—
Barfield, Macon	13451	Montgomery	—	—
Barfield, Margaret Tabitha	39088	Walker	Barfield, William	12675
Barfield, Mary Jane	42592	Travis	Barfield, James H.	28032
Barfield, Rit Barto Mrs.	46059	Bowie	Barfield, Rit Barto	—
Barfield, S. M. Mrs.	31593	Polk	Barfield, Henry Lawrence	—
Barfield, William	12675	Walker	—	—
Barfoot, Aaron Warren	49332	Scurry	—	—
Barfoot, L. J. Mrs.	49684	Scurry	Barfoot, Aaron Warren	49332
Bargsley, Andrew J.	28353	Stephens	—	—
Barham, Joel Hamlet Mrs.	46950	Nacogdoches	Barham, Joel Hamlet	—
Barham, Stephen Hamlet Mrs.	27399	Rusk	Barham, Stephen Hamlet	—
Barineau, Hattie	36375	Hunt	Barineau, John Edward	15322
Barineau, John Edward	15322	Grimes	—	—
Baring, Johanna	27280	Colorado	Baring, Albert Ernest	—
Barker, A. M.	42613	Comanche	—	—
Barker, Ann	Rej	Parker	Barker, J. J.	—
Barker, Annie E.	28269	Parker	Barker, James Jasper	—
Barker, Catherine Powell	50567	Cherokee	Powell, James Thomas Lafayette	—
Barker, D. D.	45822	Concho	—	—
Barker, David	45144	Tom Green	—	—
Barker, E. J. Mrs.	40562	Polk	Barker, Joseph William	13490
Barker, E. M. Mrs.	38712	Kent	Barker, Marcellus	—
Barker, Elizabeth M.	50653	Johnson	Barker, Joseph Gilham	40447
Barker, Emily C.	34855	Mills	Barker, Henry	—
Barker, Eveline A.	39974	Nacogdoches	Barker, Thomas Braxton	25904
Barker, Gussie	35825	Johnson	Barker, Usher Freeland	—
Barker, I. M.	Rej	Llano	—	—
Barker, James William	14210	Erath	—	—
Barker, Jesse C.	32083	Wichita	—	—
Barker, John	42308	Tom Green	—	—
Barker, John Christopher Columbus	19485	Howard	—	—
Barker, John Mrs.	43846	Tom Green	Barker, John	42308
Barker, Joseph G.	Rej	Hill	—	—
Barker, Joseph Gilham	40447	Johnson	—	—
Barker, Joseph William	13490	Polk	—	—
Barker, L. C.	45972	Hamilton	—	—
Barker, Leah	43525	Bexar	Barker, Emory Crawford	—
Barker, Lou E.	Rej	Eastland	Barker, Thomas Hensie	—
Barker, Martha E.	41110	Comanche	Barker, John Christopher Columbus	19485
Barker, Ophelia	17131	McLennan	Barker, Thomas	—
Barker, Perpeturia	29321	McLennan	Barker, Reuben Benton	12490
Barker, R. B.	Rej	Williamson	—	—
Barker, Reuben Benton	12490	McLennan	—	—
Barker, S. C. Mrs.	12154	Tom Green	Barker, William	11696
Barker, Sarah Ada	34203	Hood	Barker, Napoleon	—

Index to Confederate Pension Applications

Barker, T. C. Mrs.	23262	Hunt	Barker, Joseph Franklin	
Barker, Thomas	Rej	Limestone		
Barker, Thomas Braxton	25904	Nacogdoches		
Barker, William	11696	Wilbarger		
Barker, William H.	26887	McLennan		
Barkley, J. M. Mrs.	36290	Dewitt	Barkley, Robert Upton	12855
Barkley, John L.	02352	Jones		
Barkley, Robert Upton	12855	Gonzales		
Barkley, William Cathcart Mrs.	42471	Leon	Barkley, William Cathcart	
Barksdale, Americus C.	29037	Rusk		
Barksdale, Americus C. Mrs.	37480	Rusk	Barksdale, Americus C.	29037
Barksdale, Louis F.	20430	Edwards		
Barksdale, M. M.	28275	Rusk		
Barksdale, Nannie B.	01077	Dallas	Barksdale, Hickerson	
Barksdale, Nathaniel	30951	Johnson		
Barkwell, Marcellus E.	Rej	Limestone		
Barlow, Alice Ray	Rej	El Paso	Barlow, John E.	
Barlow, Darling	41916	Harris		
Barlow, George	25654	McLennan		
Barlow, Joseph F.	03599	San Saba		
Barlow, Sharlotie	16227	Panola	Barlow, De J.	
Barmore, James Sebert, Sr.	05259	Milam		
Barmore, Margaret M.	27949	Milam	James Sebert, Sr.	05259
Barmore, Mary C.	19132	Milam	Barmore, William Bryant	
Barnard, Benjamin Franklin	27514	Callahan		
Barnard, George	35179	Coryell		
Barnard, I. Nace	23241	Wharton		
Barnard, Mary E.	45201	Travis	Barnard, Levi Madison	
Barnard, P. A. Mrs.	34536	Callahan	Barnard, Benjamin Franklin	27514
Barnes, A. A.	17450	Cherokee		
Barnes, A. D. Mrs.	36033	Hopkins	Barnes, Joseph Frederick	15566
Barnes, A. M.	05509M	Hopkins		
Barnes, Albert L.	Rej	San Augustine		
Barnes, Andrew Black	28284	Grayson		
Barnes, Andrew Black Mrs.	38257	McLennan	Barnes, Andrew Black	28284
Barnes, Andrew Jackson	29331	Navarro		
Barnes, Annie	30502	Brazos	Barnes, Williams S.	00518
Barnes, Augustus Marion	08273	Dallas		
Barnes, B. F.	24865	Jones		
Barnes, Celestia A.	35017	Dallas	Barnes, William Reeves	25748
Barnes, D. Mrs.	32493	Bexar	Barnes, John	
Barnes, Delila	07556	Bexar	Barnes, Frederick	
Barnes, Edwin	27678	Navarro		
Barnes, Elizabeth H.	14807	Camp	Barnes, Warren Riley	
Barnes, F. F. Mrs.	Rej	Erath	Barnes, John Burgess	
Barnes, Fannie	49538	Bexar	Barnes, Thomas Benton	
Barnes, George W.	45288	Falls		
Barnes, H. H.	07060	Galveston		
Barnes, Hugh P.	31752	Johnson		
Barnes, J. A.	17810	Henderson		
Barnes, J. E.	Rej	Fannin		
Barnes, J. J.	09172	Clay		
Barnes, J. V.	34145	San Augustine		
Barnes, James	49746	Eastland		
Barnes, James H.	22746	Ellis		
Barnes, James Jasper	16768	Tyler		
Barnes, James Jasper Mrs.	38028	Tyler	Barnes, James Jasper	16768
Barnes, James L.	14119	Bell		
Barnes, James R.	29024	Travis		

Index to Confederate Pension Applications

Barnes, John F.	34582	McLennan	—	—
Barnes, John L.	19917	Hill	—	—
Barnes, Joseph Frederick	15566	Hopkins	—	—
Barnes, Kathrine	Rej	Wharton	Barnes, Fredrick C.	—
Barnes, L. A. Mrs.	47240	Collin	Barnes, James G.	—
Barnes, Lucy Ann	07190	Erath	Barnes, William Hubbard	—
Barnes, Lucy P.	29942	Navarro	Barnes, Andrew Jackson	29331
Barnes, M. J.	Rej	Archer	—	—
Barnes, Manerva	Rej	Montague	Barnes, J. G.	—
Barnes, Mary A.	35719	Dallas	Barnes, Augustus Marion	08273
Barnes, Mary J.	41165	McLennan	Barnes, John F.	34582
Barnes, Mattie L.	43833	Robertson	Barnes, Richard Joseph	41553
Barnes, Minerva	08406	Marion	—	—
Barnes, Mollie	28465	Houston	Barnes, Francis Marion	—
Barnes, Patterson Columbus Mrs.	43949	Travis	Barnes, Patterson Columbus	—
Barnes, R. B.	05415	Hill	—	—
Barnes, Richard Joseph	41553	Robertson	—	—
Barnes, Robert Henry	50248	Throckmorton	—	—
Barnes, Robert T.	09229	Hill	—	—
Barnes, Sallie	40992	Grimes	Barnes, William Riley	—
Barnes, Sarah E.	31692	Polk	Barnes, John Robert Calvin	—
Barnes, Stephen	11283	Walker	—	—
Barnes, Thomas Jefferson Mrs.	38174	Collin	Barnes, Thomas Jefferson	—
Barnes, W. A.	50364	Milam	—	—
Barnes, W. B.	04156	Van Zandt	—	—
Barnes, W. T.	30674	Camp	—	—
Barnes, William A., Sr	Rej	Kaufman	—	—
Barnes, William G.	10037	Collin	—	—
Barnes, William Reeves	25748	Dallas	—	—
Barnes, William S.	00518	Brazos	—	—
Barnes, William Thomas	41580	Robertson	—	—
Barnes, Willis	00730	Chambers	—	—
Barnett, A. E. Mrs.	Rej	Wharton	Barnett, Wood Fork	—
Barnett, A. J. Mrs.	21218	Val Verde	Barnett, John Lafayette Monroe	20066
Barnett, A. L. Mrs.	Rej	Wise	Barnett, John Abb	—
Barnett, Albert McCann	17608	El Paso	—	—
Barnett, C. A. Mrs.	35714	Panola	Barnett, John Crawford	28449
Barnett, Elisha Green	45914	Wise	—	—
Barnett, Emily Frances	43441	Palo Pinto	Barnett, Alford J.	—
Barnett, Emma V.	51330	Scurry	Barnett, John Wesley	—
Barnett, F. M. Mrs.	38661	Wise	Barnett, William H.	25085
Barnett, Flora	06386	Ellis	Barnett, W. F. D.	—
Barnett, Florence A.	44051	Parker	Barnett, George Franklin	—
Barnett, Francis Marion	18566	Wood	—	—
Barnett, G. W.	12147	Tarrant	—	—
Barnett, George Alison	31033	Eastland	—	—
Barnett, Georgia Ann	21257	Grimes	Barnett, John Calhoun	15327
Barnett, H. S.	28278	Comanche	—	—
Barnett, Henry Clay	23294	Wood	—	—
Barnett, Isabel J.	35656	Wood	Barnett, Henry Clay	23294
Barnett, J. H.	34573	Hamilton	—	—
Barnett, J. W.	03227	Palo Pinto	—	—
Barnett, James A.	31833	Collin	—	—
Barnett, James Alfred	31917	Matagorda	—	—
Barnett, James Alfred Mrs.	47280	Wharton	Barnett, James Alfred	31917
Barnett, James Hartwell	42506	Williamson	—	—
Barnett, James Madison	50034	Parker	—	—
Barnett, James W.	10646	Harris	—	—
Barnett, John	06845	Wise	—	—

Index to Confederate Pension Applications

Barnett, John Calhoun	15327	Grimes	—	
Barnett, John Clark	18853	Burleson	—	
Barnett, John Crawford	28449	Panola	—	
Barnett, John Lafayette Monroe	20066	Val Verde	—	
Barnett, L. B.	02663	Liberty	—	
Barnett, Lila	45948	Collin	Barnett, Thomas Barton	
Barnett, Lucy Ann	Rej	Williamson	Barnett, John Perry	
Barnett, M. A. Mrs.	40289	Nacogdoches	Barnett, Robert Donald	
Barnett, M. A. V. Mrs.	01905	Hill	Barnett, F. M.	
Barnett, M. D.	Rej	Kent	—	
Barnett, M. F. Mrs.	49600	Williamson	Mason, John Perry	
Barnett, M. J. Mrs.	Rej	Coleman	Barnett, Rine	
Barnett, Margaret Reese Thornton	47621	El Paso	Thornton, Edward Quinn	
Barnett, Martha E.	23132	Bexar	Barnett, Francis Marion	18566
Barnett, Mary C.	34894	Burleson	Barnett, John Clark	18853
Barnett, Mary D.	24842	Jack	Barnett, David Harrison	—
Barnett, Mary V.	43603	Williamson	Barnett, James Hartwell	42506
Barnett, Mattie A.	50235	Parker	Barnett, James Madison	50034
Barnett, Minnie T.	45558	Hill	Barnett, Albert Graham	—
Barnett, N. P.	Rej	Jasper	—	
Barnett, Nancy V.	25468	Stephens	Barnett, Marcus McKinley	—
Barnett, Pearl	Rej	Rusk	Barnett, (henry) Thomas	41004
Barnett, R. A. Mrs.	02604	Leon	Barnett, Albert	
Barnett, Rial Mrs.	40646	Runnels	Barnett, Rial	
Barnett, S. A. Mrs.	05350	Grayson	Barnett, J. J.	
Barnett, Thomas	41004	Panola	—	
Barnett, W. H.	12551	Nacogdoches	—	
Barnett, William H.	25085	Wise	—	
Barnhart, Annie	27830	Travis	Barnhart, John Strickler	—
Barnhart, Henry M.	11765	Henderson	—	
Barnhill, F. F.	Rej	Montague	—	
Barnhill, Florence	16004	McLennan	Barnhill, John Bayliss	01465
Barnhill, John Bayliss	01465	Fayette	—	
Barnhill, John D.	01436	Fannin	—	
Barnhill, Sarah C.	17650	Fannin	Barnhill, John D.	01436
Barnwell, Elizabeth	14806	Camp	Barnwell, Joseph Edmond	—
Barnwell, L. C. Mrs.	17179	Camp	Barnwell, Sam Morgan	
Barnwell, M. L. Mrs.	06452	Cass	Barnwell, W. J.	
Barnwell, Mary	49338	Red River	Barnwell, M. W.	
Baron, Thomas	08455M	Robertson	—	
Barr, G. W.	25602	Jones	—	
Barr, H. E. Mrs.	29008	Denton	Barr, Thomas R. C.	—
Barr, James	42909	Hill	—	
Barr, James L.	06851	Wise	—	
Barr, John	03976	Travis	—	
Barr, M. E. Mrs.	38062	Henderson	Barr, Paschall Crawford	31569
Barr, Minnie A.	46173	McLennan	Barr, James	—
Barr, Paschall Crawford	31569	Henderson	—	
Barr, William	37892	Tarrant	—	
Barret, James M.	23022	McLennan	—	
Barrett, A. E. Mrs.	34356	Grayson	Barrett, James Harris	—
Barrett, Abram B.	17895	Hunt	—	
Barrett, B. C.	31034	Milam	—	
Barrett, D. A.	40483	Madison	—	
Barrett, D. E.	11183	Bell	—	
Barrett, Elizabeth	01499	Franklin	Barrett, B. J.	—
Barrett, Elizabeth	47866	Dallas	Barrett, Patrick Francis	—
Barrett, Emma M.	37579	Titus	Barrett, James Burrell	—
Barrett, F. P.	27446	Liberty	—	

Index to Confederate Pension Applications

Applicant	No.	County	Veteran	No.
Barrett, Frances E.	05389	Hill	Barrett, Richard F.	
Barrett, J. H.	29731	Grayson	—	
Barrett, John	Rej	Hood	—	
Barrett, John	23526	Hood	—	
Barrett, Josephine Lavinia	32644	McLennan	Barrett, Franklin Rush	
Barrett, Joshua D.	04698	Freestone	—	
Barrett, M. J. Mrs.	Rej	Franklin	Barrett, William Satterwhite	
Barrett, M. P. Mrs.	36875	Hill	Barrett, John Parks	
Barrett, Nancy J.	17624	Erath	Barrett, Willis T.	
Barrett, S. E.	Rej	Rains	—	
Barrett, Sarah E.	23307	Parker	Barrett, Milton Reeves	
Barrett, Sarah V.	40390	Delta	Barrett, Howard Welcome	
Barrett, William	00992	Coryell	—	
Barrett, William M.	11213	Fannin	—	
Barrier, F. M.	11651	Tarrant	—	
Barrier, Rebecca C.	Rej	Titus	Barrier, Mike T.	
Barrier, S. A. Mrs.	04980	Williamson	Barrier, C. R.	
Barrineau, Edwin Martin	23356	Bowie	—	
Barrineau, Mary	34895	Bowie	Barrineau, Edwin Martin	23356
Barringer, Calvin Lafayette	28229	Fannin	—	
Barringer, Calvin Lafayette Mrs.	43602	Bexar	Barringer, Calvin Lafayette	28229
Barrington, L. V. Mrs.	39148	Guadalupe	Barrington, Perry Charles	33477
Barrington, Manley Mrs.	19658	Tarrant	Barrington, Manley	
Barrington, Manly	00246	Bell	—	
Barrington, Mary E.	26081	San Saba	Barrington, William Thomas	11039
Barrington, Perry Charles	33477	Guadalupe	—	
Barrington, W. W.	16966	Williamson	—	
Barrington, William Thomas	11039	Llano	—	
Barron, Addie Franklin	32325	Harris	Barron, Thomas	08455M
Barron, Annie	21519	Camp	Barron, James Wiley	17407
Barron, Edna Addielaid	49167	Cass	Barron, Joseph	
Barron, Etta	49697	Fisher	Barron, Sam	33818
Barron, Georgia A.	28874	Smith	Barron, Isaac Newton	21253
Barron, Isaac Newton	21253	Smith	—	
Barron, J. S.	16599	Smith	—	
Barron, James Henry Miles	20093	Haskell	—	
Barron, James L.	00477	Bowie	—	
Barron, James Wiley	17407	Camp	—	
Barron, Jasper Mrs.	15394	Harris	Barron, Jasper	
Barron, John W.	38937	Bowie	—	
Barron, Louisa Ann	28789	McLennan	Barron, Virgil Aaron	
Barron, Lucy Elizabeth	36412	Haskell	Barron, James Henry Miles	20093
Barron, Lucy H.	22184	Dallas	Barron, William Marion	
Barron, Mary F.	Rej	Dallas	Barron, James Powell	
Barron, Mary Jane	31622	Shelby	Barron, John Alfred	
Barron, Ola (Martha Ola)	46673	Kaufman	Barron, Thompson	
Barron, Robert	Rej	Rockwall	—	
Barron, Robert	26581	Collin	—	
Barron, Sam	25656	Nacogdoches	—	
Barron, Sam	33818	Fisher	—	
Barron, Sarah M.	43056	Bowie	Barron, John W.	38937
Barron, Virginia	47772	Collin	Barron, James Madison	
Barrow, Benjamin S.	20127	Chambers	—	
Barrow, Cordelia	33877	Jasper	Barrow, Daniel	17916
Barrow, Daniel	17916	Jasper	—	
Barrow, E. J. Mrs.	16137	Nacogdoches	Barrow, James Turmon	
Barrow, Hannah	20574	Liberty	Barrow, Benjamin Franklin	
Barrow, Henry Vincent	19588	Matagorda	—	
Barrow, I. N.	18453	Travis	—	

Index to Confederate Pension Applications

Name	App. No.	County	Soldier/Related	No.
Barrow, John	04610	Liberty	—	—
Barrow, John	21635	Chambers	—	—
Barrow, L. J.	Rej	Hardin	—	—
Barrow, Levy Joseph	29411	Hardin	—	—
Barrow, Levy Joseph Mrs.	30854	Hardin	Barrow, Levy Joseph	29411
Barrow, M. A. Mrs.	29395	Caldwell	Barrow, Seth L.	—
Barrow, Martha	30279	Goliad	Barrow, Henry Vincent	19588
Barrow, Richard Vincent	Rej	Galveston	—	—
Barrow, Sarah P.	49874	Tarrant	Barrow, James Goodman	—
Barrow, Sidney M.	45681	Chambers	Barrow, Benjamin S.	20127
Barry, Celestia R.	23140	McLennan	Barry, Claudus Ceasar	—
Barry, Grace Ware	51543	Erath	Barry, Thomas Patrick	49609
Barry, J. W.	35289	Milam	—	—
Barry, John Newton, Sr.	02880	Llano	—	—
Barry, Louis Howard	42906	Grimes	—	—
Barry, R. A. Mrs.	49316	Harris	Barry, Murrel	—
Barry, Sallie	28219	Fannin	Barry, John	—
Barry, Thomas Patrick	49609	Erath	—	—
Barry, William T.	Rej	Williamson	—	—
Bars, F. A. Mrs.	06202	Anderson	Bars, G. W.	—
Bartee, E. B. Mrs.	43435	Baylor	Bartee, James Samuel	—
Bartee, Elizabeth	31693	San Jacinto	Bartee, John Overton	—
Bartee, Elizabeth Ann	14290	Houston	Bartee, James W.	12915
Bartee, F. E. Mrs.	Rej	San Jacinto	Bartee, John Overton	—
Bartee, James W.	12915	Houston	—	—
Bartee, Martha W.	08698	Grayson	Bartee, J. H.	—
Bartee, S. A. Mrs.	40185	Houston	Bartee, Robert Ballard	—
Bartels, Charles	02566	Lee	—	—
Barthold, Virginia G.	51995	Parker	Barthold, Edward	—
Bartholomew, G. D.	05668	Coleman	—	—
Bartles, M. A. Mrs.	10591	Bell	Bart(t)les, S. M.	00273
Bartlett, Addie	45538	Wise	Bartlett, J. L.	34119
Bartlett, Celia	46597	Hopkins	Bartlett, Henry Thomas	14284
Bartlett, D. W.	08818	Cass	—	—
Bartlett, E. J. Ivien	45624	Dawson	—	—
Bartlett, Henry Thomas	14284	Hopkins	—	—
Bartlett, J. L.	34119	Wise	—	—
Bartlett, J. P.	19337	Wilson	—	—
Bartlett, James E.	41502	Coleman	—	—
Bartlett, Linnie B.	47673	Brown	Bartlett, James Edward	—
Bartlett, Mary Ann	47943	Bell	Bartlett, John Thomas	—
Bartlett, Nancy Helen Cruce	Rej	Jones	Cruce, John William Richard	—
Bartlett, S. A. Mrs.	Rej	Travis	Bartlett, Otho Francis	—
Bartlett, Sarah Catherine	51936	McLennan	Bartlett, Appless	—
Bartley, Nancy C.	51520	Smith	Bartley, Samuel A.	—
Bartley, Nancy J.	29330	Smith	Bartley, William Whenery	—
Bartley, Pernetta Madora Shipman	45166	Somervell	Shipman, William Malcom	43094
Barton, Amelia	35578	Hood	Barton, Joshua	07251
Barton, B. A. Mrs.	40879	Franklin	Barton, David T.	12177
Barton, Bailey Anderson	15059	Eastland	—	—
Barton, Clara	47146	Val Verde	Barton, Summerfield Harrison	—
Barton, Clark Gilbert	35054	Hill	—	—
Barton, Columbus	28195	Howard	—	—
Barton, David O.	42679	Bosque	—	—
Barton, David T.	12177	Upshur	—	—
Barton, Francis Elizabeth	38845	Burnet	Barton, Columbus	28195
Barton, Garland Walker	42991	Concho	—	—
Barton, Hiram	Rej	Upshur	—	—
Barton, J. J.	23301	Nacogdoches	—	—

Index to Confederate Pension Applications

Name	No.	County	Veteran	No.
Barton, J. L.	Rej	Wood		
Barton, Jacob H.	14515	Anderson		
Barton, James G.	13235	Bowie		
Barton, James Henry	06465	Johnson		
Barton, Joshua	07251	Hood		
Barton, Lavinia V.	14439	Tarrant	Barton, Martin Van Buren	
Barton, Lem	03448	Robertson		
Barton, Louisa	39656	Jefferson	Barton, William John	
Barton, Lucy C.	36398	Hill	Barton, Clark Gilbert	35054
Barton, M. E. Mrs.	Rej	Lynn	Barton, Isic Murphy	
Barton, M. R.	12685	Baylor		
Barton, M. R.	20920	Bowie		
Barton, Marguerite Caroline	22900	Palo Pinto	Barton, Bailey Anderson	15059
Barton, Mary A.	17080	Cooke	Barton, James Henry	06465
Barton, Mary S.	12653	Upshur	Barton, Hiram	
Barton, Melvinia	30590	Franklin	Barton, James Henry	
Barton, N. J. Mrs.	43830	Lynn	Barton, Garland Walker	42991
Barton, Oliver P.	Rej	Washington		
Barton, Richard Oliver G.	35149	Hill		
Barton, Robert M.	30446	Rusk		
Barton, S. C. Mrs.	07017	Hill	Barton, Alfred M.	
Barton, S. C. Mrs.	35895	Hill	Barton, Richard Oliver	35149
Barton, Susan A.	30776	Anderson	Barton, Jacob H.	14515
Barton, Thomas E.	Rej	Fannin		
Barton, Thomas J.	29761	Denton		
Barton, Thomas K.	18609	Upshur		
Barton, Tom L.	35148	Hill		
Barton, William F.	06015	Somervell		
Barton, Y. H.	11009	Kaufman		
Barttles (Bartles), S. M.	00273	Bell		
Barwick, Flora A.	04031	Upshur	Barwick, William B.	
Barzack, Stephen	00127	Austin		
Basden, Martha A.	40993	Tarrant	Basden, John Henry	
Basden, Sarah Matilda	33700	Lamar	Basden, William Right	
Basey, Elizabeth	51612	Wichita	Basey, William	
Basey, James	10214	Travis		
Basham, C. J.	30614	Coryell		
Bashum, William Riley	27510	Eastland		
Basinger, Fannie	27868	Cooke	Basinger, Martin M.	
Basinger, G. W.	14902	Cherokee		
Baskerville, Richard H.	38566	Wilbarger		
Baskett, E. J. Mrs.	23278	Smith	Baskett, John Lewis	
Baskin, Eliza C.	08181	Bexar	Baskin, John N.	
Baskin, George Baxter	41602	Mills		
Baskin, J. J.	24988	Knox		
Baskin, John C.	35032	Hamilton		
Baskin, John N.	00355	Bexar		
Baskin, Rosa Ella	49365	Mills	Baskin, George Baxter	41602
Baskin, William S.	23314	Henderson		
Basquez, Seberano	08845	Bexar		
Bass, Alice	30511	Nacogdoches	Bass, E. C.	
Bass, Amanda	28580	Dallas	Bass, Drury Washington	15027
Bass, Areline	37630	Trinity	Bass, Thomas Wade	
Bass, Bennett	04007	Tyler		
Bass, Bennett	04013	Tyler		
Bass, Drury Washington	15027	Dallas		
Bass, E.	00756	Cherokee		
Bass, E. J. Mrs.	21425	Bowie	Bass, James Uriah	
Bass, James	Rej	Nacogdoches		

Index to Confederate Pension Applications

Bass, James F.	07846	Hill	—	
Bass, James M.	13347	Harris	—	
Bass, James Uriah	06130	Tyler	—	
Bass, Jesse Newton	25705	Cooke	—	
Bass, John Bedell	Rej	Tom Green	—	
Bass, Julia Helen	50776	Bexar	Bass, Napoleon Arthur	
Bass, Laura L.	51472	Bosque	Bass, Enos Kendall	
Bass, Mary A.	19378	Tyler	Bass, James Uriah	06130
Bass, Melvina	34042	Cooke	Bass, Jesse Newton	25705
Bass, Moses Windham	31515	Shelby	—	
Bass, P. A. Mrs.	32293	Atascosa	Bass, Elihu Holcomb	
Bass, Richard	Rej	Hamilton	—	
Bass, S. A. Mrs.	16705	Tom Green	Bass, Sumner Harney	
Bass, S. M. Mrs.	16598	Smith	Bass, Tully Ingram	
Bass, Sallie	10572	Johnson	Bass, James F.	07846
Bass, Susan E.	28088	Harrison	Bass, Benjamin Redwick	
Bass, Tilman	05838	Cooke	—	
Bass, W. W.	18434	Tom Green	—	
Bassett, Burrel E.	08193	Milam	—	
Bassett, M. E. Mrs.	46234	Eastland	Bassett, Isaac	
Bassett, M. J. Mrs.	43184	Hill	Bassett, Thomas Jefferson	
Bassett, Nancy E.	17865	Hopkins	Bassett, Lisander Wallace	
Bassett, Sarah Scott	01564	Galveston	Bassett, Robert Houston	
Bassett, William Parnell Mrs.	31694	Rusk	Bassett, William Parnell	
Bassham, Rosena	33223	Kaufman	Bassham, Thomas Jefferson	
Bassham, T. F.	Rej	Terry	—	
Bassham, T. J.	Rej	Kaufman	—	
Bassinger, Sarah Jane	47211	Ellis	Bassinger, William Marion	
Batchelor, Francis Marion	17185	Dewitt	—	
Batchelor, M. E. Mrs.	21642	Red River	Batchelor, Roberto Means	
Batchelor, Mary	34310	Jackson	Batchelor, Francis Marion	17185
Batchelor, Rispy Ann	23024	Foard	Batchelor, Hilliard Austin	
Batchelor, Thomas Jefferson	39697	Freestone	—	
Batchelor, Tillie	51290	Freestone	Batchelor, Thomas Jefferson	39697
Bate, W. W.	19239	San Augustine	—	
Bateman, B. H.	21349	Jefferson	—	
Bateman, E. A. Mrs.	23676	Cass	Bateman, William Jason	
Bateman, J. M.	08733	Hopkins	—	
Bateman, J. N.	31608	Red River	—	
Bateman, M. L. Mrs.	20968	Hunt	Bateman, Nathaniel M.	
Bates, Amy Nulas	51095	Montague	Bates, Elbert	50960
Bates, Daniel C.	22828	Brown	—	
Bates, Dinnitia W. Mrs.	06455	Johnson	Bates, Isaac	
Bates, E. F. Mrs.	11032	Limestone	Bates, C. S.	
Bates, Ebenezer Houston	50391	Robertson	—	
Bates, Elbert	50960	Montague	—	
Bates, Elihu	23467	Jones	—	
Bates, Ellen Howard	33690	Burleson	Bates, James Monroe	11359
Bates, Finis C., Sr.	03609	Schleicher	—	
Bates, G. E. Mrs.	Rej	Wise	—	
Bates, J. Y.	Rej	Navarro	—	
Bates, James	29345	Tarrant	—	
Bates, James Monroe	11359	Burleson	—	
Bates, John M.	04573	Travis	—	
Bates, Joseph Carson	39985	Upshur	—	
Bates, Joseph Carson Mrs.	42510	Upshur	Bates, Joseph Carson	39985
Bates, Julia	51247	Robertson	Bates, Ebenezer Houston	50391
Bates, Laura Chambliss	47151	Shelby	Chambliss, Littleton Marion	12616
Bates, Lelia A. Hyams	43284	Coryell	Hyams, Issac Smith	

Index to Confederate Pension Applications

Bates, Margaret	43246	Terry	Bates, Jeams Harvey	—
Bates, Martha M.	19776	Limestone	Bates, Lawrence Franklin	—
Bates, Mary	34533	Brown	Bates, Daniel C.	22828
Bates, Mary Ellen	29539	Dallas	Bates, James Robert	—
Bates, Mary M.	51573	Tom Green	Bates, Reubin Columbus	20752
Bates, N. A. Mrs.	39992	Limestone	Bates, Thomas Jefferson	—
Bates, Nannie	41177	Navarro	Uriah Mat, Jr.	18201
Bates, P. A. Mrs.	22377	Denton	Bates, Reuben H.	—
Bates, Reubin Columbus	20752	Tom Green	—	—
Bates, Robert F.	16829	Upshur	—	—
Bates, Rufus R.	12844	Frio	—	—
Bates, S. A. Mrs.	34105	Limestone	Bates, John Edward	—
Bates, S. J. Mrs.	Rej	Shelby	Bates, John Hardy	—
Bates, Sarah A.	01375	Falls	Bates, Robert M.	—
Bates, Simon Smith	40244	McMullen	—	—
Bates, Simpson Smith	Rej	Bee	—	—
Bates, Sue	32103	Travis	Bates, William Marshall	—
Bates, Susan J.	27470	Shelby	Bates, John	—
Bates, T. J.	04651	Panola	—	—
Bates, Thomas A.	23012	Clay	—	—
Bates, Uriah Mat, Jr.	18201	Navarro	—	—
Bates, W. J.	09945	Rusk	—	—
Bates, William A.	14980	Coryell	—	—
Bates, William W.	13028	Panola	—	—
Batot, Rosa	50408	Bexar	Batot, Bernhardt	—
Batsell, Charles William	29469	Cameron	—	—
Batsell, Martha A.	41732	Tarrant	Batsell, John Felix	—
Batsell, Rosa Florence	34896	Cameron	Batsell, Charles William	29469
Batson, A. E. Mrs.	15955	Madison	Batson, Seth	—
Batson, R. G.	31422	Bell	—	—
Battaile, Aaron White	25397	McLennan	—	—
Battaile, E. J. Mrs.	04409	Williamson	Battaile, I. F.	—
Battaile, Nannie	34720	McLennan	Battaile, Aaron White	25397
Battaile, Sarah	Rej	McLennan	Battaile, Charles Robinson	—
Batte, Angie Pinkston	25387	Ellis	Batte, Gardner	—
Batte, Louisa Hatton	17791	Harrison	Batte, Daniel Edward	—
Batte, R. G.	Rej	Titus	—	—
Batten, J. C.	Rej	Cherokee	—	—
Batterton, Baker Allen	37223	McCulloch	—	—
Batterton, Jonas	34451	Grayson	—	—
Batterton, L. A. Mrs.	51885	McCulloch	Batterton, Baker Allen	37223
Battle, A. J.	12284	Brazos	—	—
Battle, George Mrs.	45771	Karnes	Battle, George	—
Battle, Levi Franklin	Rej	Brazos	—	—
Battle, M. A. Mrs.	20828	Hopkins	Battle, William Henry	05515
Battle, Sallie Ann	21339	Brazos	Battle, Levi Franklin	Rej
Battle, William Henry	05515	Hopkins	—	—
Battles, A.	23468	Hill	—	—
Battles, J. K.	41626	Scurry	—	—
Battles, Rebecca C.	50852	Van Zandt	Battles, Thomas Jefferson	29594
Battles, Thomas Jefferson	29594	Van Zandt	—	—
Batto (Batot), Rosa	50408	Bexar	Batto (Batot), Bernhardt	—
Batto, Ben	Rej	Bandera	—	—
Batton, Sarah Francis	37058	Travis	Batton, Samuel Hall	—
Baty, Elizabeth Ann	34159	Fayette	Baty, John Wesley	31844
Baty, James	39608	Eastland	—	—
Baty, John Wesley	31844	Bosque	—	—
Baty, John Wilson	20166	Hood	—	—
Baty, S. E. Mrs.	50430	Harris	Baty, William Francis Marion	—

Index to Confederate Pension Applications

Name	No.	County	Veteran	Vet. No.
Baucom, Michel	Rej	Caldwell	Baucom, Thomas Martin	
Baucom, Nancy E.	41434	Parker	Baucom, William Mack	
Bauer, Anton	12815	Dewitt		
Bauer, August Mrs.	Rej	Guadalupe	Bauer, August	
Bauer, Carl E.	01462	Fayette		
Bauer, H.	08508M	Victoria		
Bauer, John	13819	Gonzales		
Bauer, Kate	13109	Victoria	Bauer, Herman	
Bauer, Louise	43359	Fayette	Bauer, John	13819
Baugh, A. G.	20346	Wise		
Baugh, Daniel A.	Rej	Bowie		
Baugh, Francis Elizabeth	49016	Brown	Baugh, Levin Powell	
Baugh, J. E. Mrs.	27712	Haskell	Baugh, J. K. P.	23229
Baugh, J. K. P.	23229	Haskell		
Baugh, L. L. Mrs.	06512	Parker	Baugh, D. H.	
Baugh, Loving H.	40267	Dallas		
Baugh, Luther Neander	51495	Tarrant		
Baugh, Michael V.	16148	Nacogdoches		
Baugh, N. J. Mrs.	09257	Johnson	Baugh, J. A.	
Baugh, Samuel Newton	Rej	Lamar		
Baugh, William Polk	37343	Bexar		
Baughman, Augusta	40668	Rusk	Baughman, William C.	18308
Baughman, Charles Washington	09637	Hunt		
Baughman, F. M.	00104	Archer		
Baughman, M. A. Mrs.	37396	Van Zandt	Baughman, Charles Washington	09637
Baughman, William C.	18308	Rusk		
Baughn, Susan J.	45574	Lamar	Baughn, George Calvin	
Bauguss, John Warren	17316	Bell		
Bauguss, Mary Angie Cameron	51767	Bell	Bauguss, John Warren	17316
Baum, Daniel	42085	Potter		
Baumbach, George	Rej	Fayette		
Baumbach, John Friederich	20906	Fayette		
Baumbach, Kate	34897	Fayette	Baumbach, John Friederich	20906
Bawcom, J. C.	10015	Burnet		
Bawcom, Mary Jane	46122	Garza	Bawcom, David Brittan	
Baxley, A. A. Mrs.	09712	Hopkins	Baxley, John	
Baxley, Ann E.	02073	Houston	Baxley, R. W. F.	
Baxley, Henrietta	31038	Lamar	Baxley, James Abbott	
Baxley, Willie Creagh	42307	Dallas	Baxley, Andrew Jackson	
Baxter, Clara	45498	Palo Pinto	Baxter, Jerome N.	32132
Baxter, David H.	18715	Gregg		
Baxter, Fannie	38466	Gregg	Baxter, Richard H.	15301
Baxter, George	00098	Archer		
Baxter, J. D. Mrs.	13855	Houston	Baxter, Joseph D.	
Baxter, Jerome N.	32132	Erath		
Baxter, L. D. Mrs.	17128	Mason	Baxter, William Francis	02767
Baxter, M. E. Mrs.	46948	Lamar	Baxter, William Isaac	
Baxter, Martha Francis	37397	Dimmit	Baxter, John Fletcher	
Baxter, Nancy C.	36212	Coleman	Baxter, William Sanders	
Baxter, Rachel E.	41790	Brown	Baxter, John A.	
Baxter, Richard H.	15301	Gregg		
Baxter, S. J. Mrs.	30326	Ellis	Baxter, Thomas	15083
Baxter, Tabitha	43121	Hopkins	Baxter, William Stanlow	
Baxter, Thomas	15083	Ellis		
Baxter, Thomas M.	23309	Jones		
Baxter, William Francis	02767	Mason		
Baxter, William P.	13775	Denton		
Bayer, Berno	Rej	Colorado		
Bayles, A. P.	06897	Dallas		

Index to Confederate Pension Applications

Name	App#	County	Veteran	Vet#
Bayless, Bettie	Rej	Randall	Bayless, Milton	
Bayless, John H.	39431	Taylor		
Bayliss, Henretta Clardy	46215	Johnson	Bayliss, Samuel Moody	40733
Bayliss, Samuel Moody	40733	Johnson		
Baylor, A. I. Mrs.	38606	Bastrop	Baylor, George Wyth	
Baylor, Emily J.	Rej	Bexar	Baylor, John Robert	
Baylor, George Wythe	28182	Bexar		
Baylor, Henry W.	Rej	Bexar		
Baylor, Mary J.	Rej	Bee	Baylor, William L.	
Baylor, R. Carrie	43812	Bexar	Baylor, Walker Keith	37340
Baylor, Walker Keith	37340	Bexar		
Bayne, F. H.	47087	Houston		
Bayne, S. L. Mrs.	33394	Donley	Bayne, Matthias T.	
Baynham, Hillary O.	50757	Clay		
Bays, Joseph	31022	Knox		
Bays, Joseph Mrs.	32494	Knox	Bays, Joseph	31022
Bays, Lucy Brooks	24963	Lamar	Bays, William Alexander	
Baze, William Jasper Mrs.	29031	Tarrant	Baze, William Jasper	
Bazemore, Ira Blount	39977	Travis		
Bazemore, Ira Blount Mrs.	45271	Travis	Bazemore, Ira Blount	39977
Bazer, I. E.	11266	Shelby		
Bazwell, Mary J.	27751	Harrison	Bazwell, Burrell R.	
Beach, Benjamin	27444	Donley		
Beach, Benjamin Franklin Mrs.	49552	Erath	Beach, Benjamin Franklin	
Beach, Charlotte Amelia	21568	Throckmorton	Beach, George Marion	13083
Beach, George Marion	13083	Throckmorton		
Beackham, L. L.	RejM	Coryell		
Beadle, Samuel M.	Rej	Jack		
Beadle, Samuel Madison	Rej	Archer		
Beadles, Francis Isabelle	46511	Erath	Beadles, Dallas Polk	
Beadles, Nancy Ann	07640	Morris	Beadles, Ben	
Beaird, A. L.	Rej	Titus		
Beaird, J. L.	09558	Panola		
Beaird, Mary Elizabeth	51730	Burleson	Beaird, Thomas Jefferson	49849
Beaird, Thomas Jefferson	49849	Burleson		
Beaird, William C.	23200	Brown		
Beakley, J. H.	Rej	Titus		
Beal, Fanie L.	43368	McLennan	Beal, Ewel	
Beal, H. M. Mrs.	04933	Brown	Beal, Albert	
Beal, J. T., Sr	Rej	Smith		
Beal, Rufus Gebhard Mrs.	46149	Johnson	Gebhard, Lewis H.	
Beale, Richard H.	01989	Hopkins		
Beall, Adolphus M.	01163	Dewitt		
Beall, Anna C.	01153	Denton	Beall, M. A.	
Beall, Elias Neal	18314	Sabine		
Beall, Elitha Heby	38621	Young	Beall, Benjamin Holland	
Beall, Fannie E.	21005	Sabine	Beall, Elias Neal	18314
Beall, George W.	04161	Van Zandt		
Beall, Hezekiah	Rej	Freestone		
Beall, John Frank	37067	Cherokee		
Beall, John Lumpkin Mrs.	50584	Hunt	Beall, John Lumpkin	
Beall, Martha Ann	43269	Hopkins	Beall, James Thomas	
Beall, Mary A.	Rej	Hill	Beall, W. M.	
Beall, Mary C.	51358	Cherokee	Beall, John Frank	37067
Beall, Mary L.	14463	Van Zandt	Beall, George A.	
Beall, O. B.	42745	Kendall		
Beall, O. D.	13478	Nolan		
Beam, D. L.	24812	Comanche		
Beam, D. P. Mrs.	06144	Grayson	Beam, D. P.	

Index to Confederate Pension Applications

Beam, Mary A.	04157	Van Zandt	Beam, R. E.	—
Beaman, Harriet Abney Hester	Rej	Orange	Beaman, William Green	—
Beaman, S. E. Mrs.	27027	Wise	Beaman, Uriah	—
Bean, Annie Fields	36327	Lee	Bean, Charles Hill	—
Bean, C. H.	06619	Hunt	—	—
Bean, Elwood M.	09612	Milam	—	—
Bean, Julia	50465	Lampasas	Bean, William D.	—
Bean, Melinda Francis	40365	Navarro	Bean, Leroy Pickens	—
Bean, Robert	Rej	Dallas	—	—
Bean, Sam	Rej	Tyler	—	—
Bean, V. B. Mrs.	32713	Tarrant	Bean, Orlando Whitford	—
Bean, W. H.	Rej	Denton	—	—
Beane, Harriet	15270	Gonzales	Beane, Jasper	—
Bear, Elizabeth	26625	Lampasas	Bear, William	17998
Bear, William	17998	Lampasas	—	—
Beard, A. E. Mrs.	Rej	San Augustine	Beard, Benjamin Alexander	—
Beard, A. E. Mrs.	18124	Medina	Beard, Green	—
Beard, C. J. Mrs.	21643	Runnels	Beard, Franklin Carson	—
Beard, Callie	40851	Travis	Beard, John Taylor	30121
Beard, Callie	44080	Harris	Beard, Travis Rufus	—
Beard, Caroline	Rej	Jefferson	Beard, Anthony W.	—
Beard, Cynthia Ellen	14516	Anderson	Beard, John	—
Beard, Ellen	30876	Limestone	Beard, Barney Washington	—
Beard, Fannie Elizabeth	30561	Ellis	Beard, James Lafayette	—
Beard, J. A.	23335	Milam	—	—
Beard, J. A. Mrs.	00762	Cherokee	Beard, William S.	—
Beard, J. T.	14744	Brazos	—	—
Beard, James A.	00057	Angelina	—	—
Beard, James Lafayette Mrs.	Rej	Ellis	Beard, James Lafayette	—
Beard, James M.	37404	Jackson	—	—
Beard, John A.	37675	Brazos	—	—
Beard, John Taylor	30121	Burnet	—	—
Beard, Joseph Monroe	30697	Wood	—	—
Beard, Joseph Monroe Mrs.	42220	Wood	Beard, Joseph Monroe	30697
Beard, Louisa A.	18133	Milam	Beard, Coleman Campbell	—
Beard, Mary Ann	07538	Travis	Beard, Alexander	—
Beard, S. J. Mrs.	23236	Gray	Beard, James Henry	—
Beard, S. M. Mrs.	17457	Cherokee	Beard, John Wily	—
Beard, Sarah H.	Rej	Tarrant	Beard, Nathaniel Champion	—
Beard, T. L. Mrs.	29256	Limestone	Beard, James Rose	—
Beard, William	27629	Rusk	—	—
Bearde, A. Jack	41657	Runnels	—	—
Bearde, Andrew J.	38472	Coleman	—	—
Bearden, Christopher P. Mrs.	51964	Eastland	Bearden, Christopher Pinkney	41443
Bearden, Christopher Pinkney	41443	Eastland	—	—
Bearden, Elizabeth M.	21092	Harris	Bearden, John Major	—
Bearden, J. P.	45522	Shelby	—	—
Bearden, John W.	18869	Cherokee	—	—
Bearden, Louisa M.	18213	Newton	Bearden, Jonathan	—
Bearden, Mary J. A.	13604	Rusk	Bearden, A. B.	—
Bearden, Mary Virginia	32655	Hunt	Bearden, Willis Calvin	11981
Bearden, Richard Eldrick	25132	Eastland	—	—
Bearden, S. Mrs.	15486	Hill	—	—
Bearden, Sophronia H.	28480	Eastland	Bearden, Richard Eldrick	25132
Bearden, Willis Calvin	11981	Hunt	—	—
Bearfield, James Andrew	33502	Tom Green	—	—
Bearfield, Tabitha	42514	Tom Green	Bearfield, James Andrew	33502
Beasley, E. A.	28568	Angelina	—	—
Beasley, E. J. Mrs.	18431	Titus	Beasley, Zacariah Richard	—

Index to Confederate Pension Applications

Beasley, E. S.	RejM	San Jacinto		
Beasley, Georgia	46324	Dallas	Beasley, Matt	
Beasley, Isaac Newton	03622	Shelby		
Beasley, Joseph Mitchell	36271	Wheeler		
Beasley, Lemuel	19298	Trinity		
Beasley, Marion	Rej	Montague		
Beasley, Martha C.	36744	Wheeler	Beasley, Joseph Mitchell	36271
Beasley, Martha Emma	28227	Rusk	Beasley, William Lennon	23005
Beasley, Mary	31037	Angelina	Beasley, E. A.	28568
Beasley, Mary Elizabeth	06336	Henderson	Beasley, Wyat S.	
Beasley, Mary M.	45277	Grayson	Beasley, William Harris	31035
Beasley, Matilda C.	21192	Robertson	Beasley, Joseph Thompson	
Beasley, Nancy America	35307	Shelby	Beasley, Isaac Newton	03622
Beasley, S. T.	Rej	Houston		
Beasley, Samuel H.	36279	Jackson		
Beasley, Sarah F. Stallings	50773	Montague	Stallings, James Andrew	
Beasley, Stephen Thomas Mrs.	39832	Houston	Beasley, Stephen Thomas	
Beasley, William Harris	31035	Grayson		
Beasley, William Lennon	23005	Rusk		
Beasly, Thomas	02353	Jones		
Beat, Nancy J.	19919	Tarrant	Beat, Frederick Shesser	
Beatty, George L.	49717	Lubbock		
Beatty, Willie Agnes	Rej	Lubbock	Beatty, George L.	49717
Beaty, Charles W.	50100	McLennan		
Beaty, Henry M.	19465M	Collin		
Beaty, James E.	41687	Palo Pinto		
Beaty, James Perry	28510	Gonzales		
Beaty, Lee T.	50717	Caldwell		
Beaty, Martha A.	10455	Polk	Beaty, Warren J.	
Beaty, Mary Ann	23333	Donley	Beaty, William Jasper	
Beaty, Mary Jane	39238	Denton	Beaty, John Alexander	
Beaty, Mary Lewis	49083	Tyler	Beaty, Thomas Boston	47018
Beaty, Pollie	51422	Gonzales	Beaty, James Perry	28510
Beaty, S. A. Mrs.	17509	Comanche	Beaty, James W.	
Beaty, S. S.	10904	Denton		
Beaty, Sallie A.	17786	Harrison	Beaty, Alfred Newell	
Beaty, T. J.	11778	Van Zandt		
Beaty, Thomas Boston	47018	Tyler		
Beau, Robert	RejM	Dallas		
Beau, W. H.	RejM	Denton		
Beaucham, Philip Dallas	12231	Mason		
Beauchamp, A. R. Mrs.	15350	Harris	Beauchamp, Green McCullough	
Beauchamp, Ada A.	41513	Ellis	Beauchamp, Jerry Downing	17599
Beauchamp, Belle	17648	Fannin	Beauchamp, Joseph Moore	01404
Beauchamp, Dell Meta Mrs.	43038	Johnson	Beauchamp, Dell Meta	
Beauchamp, Elijah P.	27744	Tarrant		
Beauchamp, Elijah P. Mrs.	34840	Tarrant	Beauchamp, Elijah P.	27744
Beauchamp, J. C.	Rej	Bowie		
Beauchamp, J. S.	12347	Erath		
Beauchamp, Jerry Downing	17599	Ellis		
Beauchamp, Joseph Moore	01404	Fannin		
Beauchamp, Josie Easter Mrs.	34286	Lamar	Beauchamp, Jesse Denson	
Beauchamp, Margaret E.	38395	Freestone	Beauchamp, William Hamil	
Beauchamp, Payton G.	41275	Wichita		
Beauchamp, Sarah J.	Rej	Blanco	Beauchamp, A. J.	
Beaumont, Emily L.	15055	Dewitt	Beaumont, David Greenleaf	
Beaumont, Gabriel B.	47466	Coleman		
Beaumont, Gulielmus Henry, Dr.	07155	Brown		
Beaumont, Jacob K.	02269	Jefferson		

Index to Confederate Pension Applications

Beaumont, Nannie D.	51299	Coleman	Beaumont, Gabriel Boothroyd	—
Beaumont, Sarah L.	27286	Uvalde	Beaumont, William Henry	—
Beavens, Louisa Arms	20897	Harris	Beavens, Christopher Columbus	—
Beaver, Cynthia Arabella	47078	Williamson	Beaver, Ambrose Clarke	—
Beaver, M. E. Mrs.	23319	Ellis	Beaver, William Goodwin	—
Beaver, Mary Julia Pyron	09433	Bexar	Pyron, James William	—
Beaver, Nathan	46264	Hamilton	—	
Beaver, Thomas Henry	17088	Freestone	—	
Beaver, William Goodwin	Rej	Unknown	—	
Beavers, A. C.	04816	Nacogdoches	—	
Beavers, Columbus Stephens	15163	Franklin	—	
Beavers, E. J. Mrs.	31049	Hill	Beavers, Jesse Mercer	—
Beavers, Elizabeth	08591	Montague	Beavers, W. H.	—
Beavers, Emma	52073	Dallas	Beavers, John Alvin	—
Beavers, L. C. Mrs.	16827	Upshur	Beavers, William Washington	—
Beavers, Lavina	13465	Nacogdoches	Beavers, A. C.	04816
Beavers, Lillian V.	49808	Milam	Beavers, Joseph Edward	—
Beavers, M. A. Mrs.	38256	Kaufman	Beavers, S. Z.	38212
Beavers, Mary A.	19069	Jones	Beavers, Washington Lafayette	—
Beavers, Mary F.	21364	Franklin	Beavers, Columbus Stephens	15163
Beavers, Mollie J.	Rej	Randall	Beavers, William Easley	—
Beavers, R. N.	00999	Coryell	—	
Beavers, Rosa Ann	25898	Lamar	Beavers, Silas James	—
Beavers, S. Z.	38212	Concho	—	
Beavers, Spence M.	09256	Jefferson	—	
Beazley, Ellen E.	Rej	Harris	Beazley, Herbert Washington	—
Beazley, Eugenie S.	50988	Polk	Beazley, William Hubert	30073
Beazley, James Harvey Mrs.	47631	Houston	Beazley, James Harvey	—
Beazley, William Hubert	30073	San Jacinto	—	
Bebe, Sallie P.	41734	Comanche	Bebe, Bluford Sanford	—
Becher, Anna	Rej	Harris	Becher, John	—
Bechtold, Elizabeth	28402	Harrison	Bechtold, Joseph	—
Beck, A. A. Mrs.	19158	Nacogdoches	Beck, Alexander	—
Beck, D. M.	00548	Brown	—	
Beck, Elizabeth	25895	Grayson	Beck, James Redmond	11452
Beck, Ellen	05573	Kaufman	Beck, A. J.	—
Beck, Hulda	25971	Bell	Beck, Vivian Johnathan	00297
Beck, Irene Matilda	27872	Rockwall	Beck, David	—
Beck, Jacob Alexander	06092	Travis	—	
Beck, James Mrs.	27247	Somervell	Beck, James	—
Beck, James Redmond	11452	Freestone	—	
Beck, Jesse Bryant	16503	Shelby	—	
Beck, Lee R.	43968	Bexar	Beck, Josiah Edwin	—
Beck, M. M. Mrs.	01494	Franklin	Beck, M. L.	—
Beck, Martha A.	17820	Henderson	Beck, William Henry	05481
Beck, Martin Monroe Mrs.	27047	Upshur	Beck, Martin Monroe	—
Beck, Mary E. S.	10344	Cherokee	Beck, Elijah	—
Beck, Mary Elizabeth	Rej	Wise	Beck, Benjamin Franklin	—
Beck, Pettie	40082	Wheeler	Beck, William	—
Beck, S. E. Mrs.	47741	Collin	Beck, Samuel J.	—
Beck, Sarah A.	33065	Dewitt	Beck, Richard	—
Beck, Sarah J.	21043	Shelby	Beck, Jesse Bryant	16503
Beck, Vivian Johnathan	00297	Bell	—	
Beck, William Henry	05481	Henderson	—	
Becke, Elizabeth	35187	Cooke	Becke, William A.	31423
Becke, William H.	31423	Cooke	—	
Becker, Henrietta	45057	Washington	Becker, Edward F.	—
Becker, William	14020	Travis	—	
Beckett, Mary R.	48067	Bexar	Beckett, Richard Capel	—

Index to Confederate Pension Applications

Beckham, Bettie F.	37638	Henderson	Beckham, Henry Herbert	30392
Beckham, F. A.	12916	Houston	—	—
Beckham, Henry Herbert	30392	Henderson	—	—
Beckham, J. J.	26643	Shelby	—	—
Beckham, John L.	15425	Henderson	—	—
Beckham, Joseph Murrah Mrs.	34137	Robertson	Beckham, Joseph Murrah	—
Beckham, L. L.	Rej	Coryell	—	—
Beckham, M. G.	45069	Shelby	—	—
Beckham, Meranda	17860	Hopkins	Beckham, William Reily	—
Beckham, Nancy E.	Rej	Parker	Beckham, W. C.	—
Beckham, P. H. Mrs.	43996	Henderson	Beckham, John L.	15425
Beckham, Peter	23253	Van Zandt	—	—
Beckham, S. E. Mrs.	06285	Hopkins	Beckham, J. S.	—
Beckham, W. A.	20436	Fayette	—	—
Beckham, William James	26174	Tarrant	—	—
Beckham, William James Mrs.	35089	Tarrant	Beckham, William James	26174
Beckley, Sallie F.	47082	Lamar	Beckley, John Simpson	—
Beckmann, Herman	Rej	Gillespie	—	—
Beckner, Charles B.	Rej	Hall	—	—
Beckner, Henry D.	19569	Johnson	—	—
Beckwith, Georgeana	07775	Chambers	—	—
Beckwith, James A.	00731	Chambers	—	—
Beckwith, Sarah Cornelia	39062	Harris	Beckwith, Frances Marion	—
Beckworth, Isaac	26381	Henderson	—	—
Becton, L. S. Mrs.	28437	Hopkins	Becton, John Allen	—
Bedell, Abner Whitfield Mrs.	Rej	Coleman	Bedell, Abner Whitfield	—
Bedell, H. D.	Home	Travis	—	—
Bedell, H. Mrs.	RejM	Galveston	—	—
Bedell, Mary C.	37499	Colorado	Bedell, John Wesley	—
Bedell, W. H.	51416	Dallas	—	—
Bedell, William Harry	Rej	Galveston	—	—
Bedford, Ann S.	01186	Eastland	Bedford, Jonas M.	—
Bedford, Archabald	Rej	Knox	—	—
Bedford, David Roughton Mrs.	26574	Tarrant	Bedford, David Roughton	—
Bedford, H. G.	27849	Winkler	—	—
Bedford, J. M.	08882	Parker	—	—
Bedford, James Holleell	49672	Mitchell	—	—
Bedford, Lou J.	51352	Mitchell	Bedford, James Holleell	49672
Bedford, Sarah E.	49019	Runnels	Bedford, William Gordon	—
Bedgood, Sarah Elizabeth Daves	51018	Palo Pinto	Daves, John Nuton	—
Bedichek, Lucretia	46356	McLennan	Bedichek, James Madison	—
Bedingfield, C. L. Mrs.	17534	Crosby	Bedingfield, John Davis	—
Bedwell, M. A. Mrs.	43322	Scurry	Bedwell, Leroy Polk	—
Bee, Mildred Tarver	00367	Bexar	Bee, Hamilton P.	—
Beebe, John	01767	Hardeman	—	—
Beebe, John	20177	Hardeman	—	—
Beecher, Annie	29941	Harris	Beecher, John	—
Beeker, John C.	00966	Cooke	—	—
Beeland, Edward Whitfield	24852	Collin	—	—
Beeland, S. F. Mrs.	34357	Collin	Beeland, Edward Whitfield	24852
Beeman, Gerald Alonzo	42545	Comanche	—	—
Beeman, M. E. Mrs.	29132	Houston	Beeman, James H.	—
Beeman, Mary	46414	Wichita	Beeman, Samuel H.	—
Beeman, Mattie	34806	Potter	Beeman, Charles Wesley	—
Beeman, Sam M.	39535	Mitchell	—	—
Beene, Emily N.	17944	Jones	Beene, James K. Polk	—
Beene, Garrett K.	33139	Freestone	—	—
Beene, J. S.	23339	Hunt	—	—
Beene, Lem S.	Rej	Leon	—	—

Index to Confederate Pension Applications

Name	No.	County	Veteran	No.
Beene, Lucial Shelton	23701	Leon		
Beene, Mary Elizabeth	23300	Freestone	Beene, Obadiah Franklin	
Beene, Nancy K.	34335	Leon	Beene, Lucial Shelton	23701
Beene, Sallie T.	45830	Coryell	Beene, Franklin Terry	
Beene, Thomas A.	28201	Rockwall		
Beesley, James P.	30820	Gonzales		
Beeson, John Stuart	16844	Uvalde		
Beeson, Mary Y.	47543	Limestone	Beeson, David William	
Beeson, S. F. Mrs.	31042	Uvalde	Beeson, John Stuart	16844
Beeson, S. P. Mrs.	15597	Houston	Beeson, Jehu	
Beetley, Samuel Zebedee J. Mrs.	32348	Aransas	Beetley, Samuel Zebedee Joines	
Beggs, James W.	16851	Van Zandt		
Beggs, W. R.	21646	Burnet		
Begley, Mary Catherine Goodwin	49853	Fannin	Goodwin, William Thomas	
Beheler, William T.	49425	McLennan		
Beheller, Jennie	14605	Angelina	Beheller, Marshall B.	
Behrens, Julius	Rej	Galveston		
Behrns, Johann Heinrich	01533	Gillespie		
Beimer, Lucy	45076	Falls	Beimer, Herman	
Beinhorn, Mary	15355	Harris	Beinhorn, Christian	
Beissner, Bertha	Rej	Bexar	Beissner, Frederick Louis	
Belch, Frances	37882	Galveston	Belch, William Joseph	34484
Belch, William Joseph	34484	Galveston		
Belcher, Ada	Rej	Hill	Belcher, George Washington	
Belcher, Benjamin Arthur	13788	Ellis		
Belcher, Cornelia Frances	43618	Robertson	Belcher, Wyatte Newton	
Belcher, James L.	23306	Bosque		
Belcher, Julia A.	Rej	Palo Pinto	Belcher, J. J.	
Belcher, L. C. Mrs.	49632	Johnson	Belcher, Thomas H.	
Belcher, Loucrecia	49647	Tom Green	Belcher, Thomas	
Belcher, Mary A.	37727	Bosque	Belcher, John M.	
Belcher, Robert, Sr.	16600	Smith		
Belcher, William Henry Mrs.	51966	Bexar	Belcher, William Henry	
Belden, Martha Ann	09815	Orange	Belden, John C.	
Beler, Nancy	42593	Travis	Beler, William Haskell	
Beler, W. H.	07662	Smith		
Beleu, James J.	25368	Parker		
Belew, Sallie E.	27649	Parker	Belew, James J.	25368
Belew, V. J. Mrs.	39954	Collin	Belew, William Madison	38342
Belew, William	10322	Bexar		
Belew, William L.	10048	Dallas		
Belew, William Madison	38342	Collin		
Belew, Zacariah T.	17990	Knox		
Belk, Adaline R.	46112	Coryell	Belk, Elijah K.	
Belk, J. F.	31753	Nacogdoches		
Bell, A. J.	30612	Archer		
Bell, Abner J.	38722	Hale		
Bell, Addie	49421	Titus	Bell, James Polk	42404
Bell, Alpheus Houston	09867	Cherokee		
Bell, Armenta Jane	43700	Wilson	Bell, Rufus Drake	
Bell, Bettie	39891	Navarro	Bell, Thomas	12785
Bell, C. C.	08421M	Navarro		
Bell, C. C. Mrs.	49149	Denton	Bell, Charles C.	46072
Bell, Catharine	51344	Robertson	Bell, James Gerard	
Bell, Charles C.	46072	Denton		
Bell, E. F. Mrs.	Rej	Titus	Bell, Robert William	
Bell, Elijah	28286	Real		
Bell, Eliza	06586	Tarrant	Bell, James C.	
Bell, Elizabeth	17709	Grayson	Bell, James Preston	05339

Index to Confederate Pension Applications

Name	App#	County	Veteran	Vet App#
Bell, Elizabeth	47412	Gonzales	Bell, John Milton	
Bell, Elizabeth A.	14687	Bell	Bell, James Knox	13214
Bell, Elizabeth C.	50596	Harris	Bell, George Pinkney	
Bell, Ezekial Lemuel	26153	Navarro		
Bell, Ezekial Lemuel Mrs.	41460	Navarro	Bell, Ezekial Lemuel	26153
Bell, H. E.	30200	Jefferson		
Bell, Hezekiah	RejM	Freestone		
Bell, I. H.	24816	Midland		
Bell, J. H.	22311	Deaf Smith		
Bell, J. P.	Rej	Parker		
Bell, J. T.	Rej	Nacogdoches		
Bell, J. W.	11034	Limestone		
Bell, J. W.	25712	Ellis		
Bell, James Augustus	11537	Limestone		
Bell, James Knox	13214	Bell		
Bell, James Polk	42404	Titus		
Bell, James Preston	05339	Grayson		
Bell, James Robert	38140	Navarro		
Bell, Jesse W.	25558	Nacogdoches		
Bell, Joan	22200	Grayson	Bell, Thomas Wilson	
Bell, John F.	08952	Angelina		
Bell, John Freeman	16505	Shelby		
Bell, John M.	42435	Wilson		
Bell, John Newton Mrs.	32446	Tarrant	Bell, John Newton	
Bell, John P.	33447	Tom Green		
Bell, John Thomas	12207	Wilson		
Bell, Joseph Athel	10584	Austin		
Bell, Joseph Henry	49430	Brown		
Bell, Joseph Robertson	04809	Nacogdoches		
Bell, Joseph T.	29107	Wood		
Bell, Josh P.	45869	Panola		
Bell, Kate	17570	Dallas	Bell, Bushrod W.	
Bell, Leonard L.	10621	Dimmit		
Bell, Lucy	22180	Smith	Bell, Leonidas Theodore	
Bell, M. E. Mrs.	Home	Travis	Bell, Joseph Athel	10584
Bell, M. F. Mrs.	18667	Titus	Bell, Stephen Thomas	
Bell, M. L. Mrs.	Rej	Titus	Bell, L. B.	
Bell, M. S. Mrs.	19204	Red River	Bell, Thomas Henry	
Bell, Mahala	38787	Rusk	Bell, Osborn	
Bell, Marion Davis	10623	Dimmit		
Bell, Martha	37348	Angelina	Bell, Mathew	03283
Bell, Martha E.	03516	Rusk	Bell, John C.	
Bell, Martha F.	13468	Nacogdoches	Bell, Joseph Robertson	04809
Bell, Martha L.	10758	Travis	Bell, George	
Bell, Martha L.	43608	Parker	Bell, Francis Marion	
Bell, Mary Ann	19726	Henderson	Bell, George Donald	
Bell, Mary Ann Elizabeth	50425	Wilson	Bell, John M.	42435
Bell, Mary E.	26522	McLennan	Bell, James Berry	
Bell, Mary J.	17341	Bexar	Bell, James Archibald	
Bell, Mary W.	10185	Red River	Bell, John N.	
Bell, Mathew	03283	Panola		
Bell, May	50319	Burleson	Bell, Emmett Broaddus	
Bell, N. F. Mrs.	40581	Freestone	Bell, George Washington	
Bell, Nancy J.	05634	Erath	Bell, Joshua	
Bell, Nancy L.	30985	Anderson	Bell, Uriah Jasper	17273
Bell, Nena	26123	Fort Bend	Bell, Francis Tetra Lafayette	
Bell, R. A. V. Mrs.	39438	Navarro	Bell, James Robert	38140
Bell, R. E. Mrs.	28653	Rusk	Bell, Zachariah M.	
Bell, R. E. Mrs.	40455	Dallas	Bell, Charles Alexander	

Index to Confederate Pension Applications

Name	App #	County	Soldier	Soldier App #
Bell, Richard Jackson	20069	Cherokee		
Bell, Richard Jackson Mrs.	51731	Smith	Bell, Richard Jackson	20069
Bell, Ruth	27540	Mitchell	Bell, McCollum	
Bell, S. A. Mrs.	11228	Henderson	Bell, John	
Bell, Sallie	Rej	Shelby	Bell, John Freeman	16505
Bell, Sallie	34346	Dimmit	Bell, Marion Davis	10623
Bell, Sarah Ann	35072	Bell	Bell, Alexander	
Bell, Sarah Annie E.	Rej	Walker	Bell, James H.	
Bell, Sarah E.	26474	Hays	Bell, Rufus Lafayette	
Bell, Sarah Elizabeth	45045	Dallas	Bell, Madison Levi	
Bell, Susan R.	33417	Parker	Bell, Joseph Perry	
Bell, Susan S.	11401	Dallas	Bell, R. P.	
Bell, T. J.	33289	Burnet		
Bell, Thomas	12785	Cherokee		
Bell, Thomas J.	03867	Titus		
Bell, Thomas J.	22157	Goliad		
Bell, Uriah	12414	Hill		
Bell, Uriah Jasper	17273	Anderson		
Bell, W. P.	25822	Travis		
Bell, W. T.	23404	Milam		
Bell, W. V. Mrs.	Rej	Tarrant	Bell, Henry Clay	
Bell, Watson Warren Mrs.	29759	Hopkins	Bell, Watson Warren	
Bell, William M.	21644	Baylor		
Bell, William Rufus	33929	Lamar		
Bell, William V.	10622	Dimmit		
Bell, Z.	07433	Bandera		
Bellah, Henry	01072	Dallas		
Bellah, Nancy	35326	Dallas	Bellah, Andrew Jackson	
Bellah, Samuel H.	10148	Menard		
Bellamy, A. F.	Rej	Van Zandt		
Bellamy, A. F.	11110	Rusk		
Bellamy, A. N.	21645	Gonzales		
Bellamy, Asbury Jackson	21618	Bastrop		
Bellamy, Elizabeth A.	00601	Caldwell	Bellamy, Asa R.	
Bellamy, Georgia W.	34038	Bastrop	Bellamy, Asbury Jackson	21618
Bellar, Antoine	13935	Liberty		
Belle, J. T.	10166	Nacogdoches		
Bellenger, Moore F.	39561	Parker		
Bellew, Armelia	32428	McLennan	Bellew, Valentine Roger	
Bellinger, John	32225	Falls		
Bellmyer, Marcella King	50984	Collin	King, John	
Bellows, Fannie M.	47545	Collin	Bellows, Appleton Allen	
Bellows, Nettie	36969	Montague	Bellows, John Tabor	
Bellows, William R.	14085	Montague		
Bellune, Charlotte A.	12696	Harris	Bellune, James T.	
Belote, Allen	32598	Marion		
Belote, C. A.	49878	Grayson		
Belsha, John E.	19386	Shelby		
Belt, J. W.	05235	Navarro		
Belt, Mollie Julia Pierce	50922	Ellis	Belt, Daniel Lee	
Belton, Carrie Watkins	49488	McLennan	Watkins, William S.	
Belyen, Berry	06278	Kaufman		
Belyen, David N.	18636	Tarrant		
Belyen, R. J. Mrs.	07082	Williamson	Belyen, W. F.	
Belyen, Richard	12471	Kaufman		
Belyen, Ruth	34649	Kaufman	Belyen, Richard	12471
Benbow, James Richard	47666	Dewitt		
Benbow, James Richard Mrs.	52047	Dewitt	Benbow, James Richard	47666
Bendy, Harry W.	23279	Tyler		

Index to Confederate Pension Applications

Name	No.	County	Veteran	No.
Bendy, M. M. Mrs.	33963	Tyler	Bendy, James Hall	
Benefield, B. J.	41450	Marion	—	
Benefield, E. J. Mrs.	19586	Van Zandt	Benefield, Hyram Hampton	04160
Benefield, Emma	26794	Harrison	Benefield, William M.	
Benefield, Hyram Hampton	04160	Van Zandt	—	
Benevides, Estevan	08857	Webb	—	
Benfer, Phillip	Rej	Bexar	—	
Benge, Agnes	30569	Cherokee	Benge, Obadiah Martin	
Benge, Clarissa	12305	Cherokee	Benge, H. L.	
Benge, G. C.	Rej	Cherokee	—	
Benge, Margaret Catherine	29634	Cherokee	Benge, William Cummings	
Benge, O. M.	Rej	Cherokee	—	
Benge, R. F.	12307	Cherokee	—	
Benge, Sophie Young	20824	Concho	Benge, Robert Titus	
Benge, Thomas J.	16329	Robertson	—	
Benham, Benjamin Franklin	22544	Caldwell	—	
Benham, John D.	40356	San Saba	—	
Benner, George	Rej	Wharton	—	
Bennett, Abner Hill	22143	Hunt	—	
Bennett, Cherry	25060	Haskell	Bennett, James Monroe	
Bennett, David W.	09074	Medina	—	
Bennett, E. C. Mrs.	Rej	Foard	Bennett, Abner Hill	22143
Bennett, Elijah Jasper	47597	Hill	—	
Bennett, Ellen	40842	Grayson	Bennett, William Coleman	
Bennett, G. M.	13012	Montgomery	—	
Bennett, George Henry	03899	Travis	—	
Bennett, George Henry	09778	Guadalupe	—	
Bennett, H. C. Mrs.	00914	Comanche	Bennett, Legro	
Bennett, Harrett N.	Rej	Brown	Bennett, Richard Barton	
Bennett, Isabella	08292	Eastland	Bennett, Lee G.	
Bennett, Isham H.	11130	Smith	—	
Bennett, J. C.	22789	Dallas	—	
Bennett, J. E. Mrs.	Rej	Tarrant	Bennett, John B.	05790
Bennett, J. P.	Rej	Callahan	—	
Bennett, James Jackson	09711	Hopkins	—	
Bennett, Joel	15164	Franklin	—	
Bennett, John B.	05790	Dallas	—	
Bennett, John T.	17307	Bastrop	—	
Bennett, L. E. Mrs.	02292	Johnson	Bennett, John T.	
Bennett, L. E. Mrs.	15187	Freestone	Bennett, Daniel Pink	
Bennett, L. G.	01189	Eastland	—	
Bennett, L. H. Mrs.	26058	Harris	Bennett, Theodore George	
Bennett, Laura	40199	Anderson	Bennett, Miles	
Bennett, M. J. Mrs.	14798	Callahan	Bennett, John Pinkston	
Bennett, M. L. Mrs.	Rej	Falls	Bennett, William Isaac	23281
Bennett, Martha J.	32065	Parker	Bennett, Thomas	
Bennett, Mary	31458	Denton	Bennett, James Alexander	
Bennett, Mary Elizabeth	35598	Hays	Bennett, George Henry	09778
Bennett, Mary Lillian	49093	Fisher	Bennett, Armon Capers	
Bennett, Matilda F.	03621	Shelby	Bennett, John	
Bennett, Nancy M.	34856	Tarrant	Bennett, Elijah Berry	
Bennett, Orlena	50089	Navarro	Bennett, Francis Marion	
Bennett, R. G.	40152	Baylor	—	
Bennett, S.	04480	Wise	—	
Bennett, S. A. Mrs.	40582	Marion	Bennett, James Jackson	09711
Bennett, S. F.	Rej	Hopkins	—	
Bennett, Sallie Francis	50927	Tarrant	Bennett, William George	
Bennett, Sarah	23316	Parker	Bennett, Jacob Samuel	
Bennett, Sarah F.	19294	Travis	Bennett, Frank R.	

Index to Confederate Pension Applications

Name	App#	County	Veteran	Vet App#
Bennett, Sarah F.	33030	Travis	Bennett, George Henry	03899
Bennett, Sarah Jane	14411	Smith	Bennett, I. H.	11130
Bennett, Sarah Jane	14450	Trinity	Bennett, Richard Oliver	
Bennett, W. A.	Rej	Young		
Bennett, W. J.	05034	Upshur		
Bennett, William George	Rej	Tarrant		
Bennett, William Isaac	23281	Falls		
Bennett, Wincy	Rej	Upshur	Bennett, Leroy	
Bennick, A. R.	25968	Tyler		
Bennick, Jacob J.	06053	Walker		
Bennick, Susan	00829	Coke	Bennick, Isreal Martin	
Bennington, Martha Ann	22468	Delta	Bennington, James Thomas	
Bennington, W. J.	02435	Lamar		
Benson, Alice E.	33158	Bastrop	Benson, Willis Key	
Benson, George J.	31400	Lampasas		
Benson, J. R.	26245	Sutton		
Benson, J. W.	13922	Lamar		
Benson, James McDonald	09183	Cooke		
Benson, Jane	50318	Houston	Benson, Edward Paul	
Benson, John	28101	Harris		
Benson, John W.	02490	Lampasas		
Benson, Margaret	01412	Fannin	Benson, George	
Benson, Margaret Ann	41994	Harris	Benson, John	28101
Benson, Martha Jane	11204	Eastland	Benson, Spencer	
Benson, Mary E.	04769	Clay	Benson, William W.	
Benson, Mary E.	22425	Cooke	Benson, James McDonald	09183
Benson, Nancy Isabellia	13317	Gillespie	Benson, William Thomas	11545
Benson, Nannie C.	33813	Travis	Benson, John Wesley	
Benson, S. H.	01775	Harris		
Benson, Sallie R.	34196	Lampasas	Benson, George J.	31400
Benson, Sarah J.	08486M	Titus		
Benson, W. C.	Rej	Coke		
Benson, W. F.	08768	Mitchell		
Benson, William Thomas	11545	Llano		
Benthall, W. T.	13937	Limestone		
Bentley, Alice G.	51279	Taylor	Bentley, Henry Lewis	47186
Bentley, E. J. Mrs.	31857	Coryell	Bentley, Jesse H.	
Bentley, Henry Lewis	47186	Taylor		
Bentley, James Franklin	37240	McCulloch		
Bentley, John H.	25025	Nacogdoches		
Bentley, Joseph L.	03781	Tarrant		
Bentley, M. A. Mrs.	04164	Van Zandt	Bentley, A. J.	
Bentley, Margret	28523	Bowie	Bentley, James Benjamin	
Bentley, Martha Sophronia	Rej	Lamar	Bentley, Thomas Baker	
Bentley, Mattie	36073	Jack	Bentley, Thomas Jefferson	24986
Bentley, Samuel Z. J.	08956	Aransas		
Bentley, Thomas Baker	Rej	Lamar		
Bentley, Thomas Jefferson	24986	Jack		
Benton, A. C.	05893	Grayson		
Benton, A. D.	Rej	Lamar		
Benton, Edmund Daniel	12861	Grayson		
Benton, Emuel	05483	Henderson		
Benton, F. Mrs.	Rej	Trinity	Benton, F.	
Benton, H. A. Mrs.	31415	Trinity	Benton, Dack F.	
Benton, J.	Rej	Kaufman		
Benton, John Newton	03301	Parker		
Benton, L. J. Mrs.	04519	Wood	Benton, T. F.	
Benton, Mariah	20595	Parker	Benton, John Newton	03301
Benton, Mark	31484	Stonewall		

Index to Confederate Pension Applications

Benton, Martha Elizabeth	47526	Montague	Benton, Philip Jasper	—
Benton, Mary E.	28639	Fannin	Benton, Edmond Houston	—
Benton, Mary Elizabeth	35486	Sutton	Benton, Mark	—
Benton, Mattie D.	Rej	Morris	Benton, Peter Goodman	—
Benton, Sarah Ann	35018	Wilson	Benton, William Hays	04455
Benton, Sarah B.	19699	Grayson	Benton, Edmund Daniel	12861
Benton, Susan	46381	Navarro	Benton, Thomas H.	—
Benton, William Franklin	24896	Schleicher	—	—
Benton, William Hays	04455	Wilson	—	—
Bentoro, H. D.	RejM	Johnson	—	—
Berger, Anton Louis	02407	Kendall	—	—
Berger, Jake C.	12309	Cherokee	—	—
Berger, Mary R.	45347	Cherokee	Berger, Jake C.	12309
Berger, Thomas	29258	Panola	—	—
Bergeron, M. F. Mrs.	47002	Robertson	Bergeron, Louis Alce	—
Bergin, O. M.	15351	Harris	—	—
Berkley, W. H.	Rej	Montgomery	—	—
Bernal, Leonardo	04452	Wilson	—	—
Bernhard, Joseph	09761	Williamson	—	—
Berrigan, A. E. Mrs.	34224	Cottle	Berrigan, Peter	—
Berry, Allen Griffin	13591	Grayson	—	—
Berry, Andrew Jackson	23519	Cherokee	—	—
Berry, Ann E.	08763	McLennan	Berry, W. C.	—
Berry, Anna V.	46294	Johnson	Berry, Jesse Polk	—
Berry, B. A. Mrs.	16861	Van Zandt	Berry, Elisha Tunnell	—
Berry, Charlie	Rej	Caldwell	—	—
Berry, Clara Frances	13563	Uvalde	Berry, Walker W.	—
Berry, Colombus M.	07939	Parker	—	—
Berry, Cornelia E.	03678	Smith	Berry, Elisha	—
Berry, Cynthia	46841	Collin	Berry, William Willis	—
Berry, Delila	35160	Coryell	Berry, Emanuel	—
Berry, E. T.	Rej	Van Zandt	—	—
Berry, Eliza J.	20357	Rusk	Berry, John G.	16389
Berry, Elizabeth	32147	Bell	Berry, Thomas Rountree	—
Berry, Ellen	50203	Fayette	Berry, William Thomas	—
Berry, Elvania E.	09805	Dallas	Berry, John F.	—
Berry, Emanuel	06107	Bandera	—	—
Berry, Emma	36193	Bastrop	Berry, James Madison	20913
Berry, Fannie	47638	Eastland	Berry, James Alexander	—
Berry, Flora Emily	42253	Palo Pinto	Berry, Hugh Mose M.	37370
Berry, Georgia A.	30616	Washington	Berry, Stanley H.	—
Berry, Hugh A.	28829	Comanche	—	—
Berry, Hugh Mose M.	37370	Palo Pinto	—	—
Berry, J. W.	Rej	Nacogdoches	—	—
Berry, James H.	42043	Bell	—	—
Berry, James H. Mrs.	51514	Bell	Berry, James H.	42043
Berry, James Madison	20913	Scurry	—	—
Berry, James T.	26241	Cooke	—	—
Berry, James W.	25752	Bowie	—	—
Berry, John	10670	Kendall	—	—
Berry, John G.	16389	Rusk	—	—
Berry, John James	24702	Coleman	—	—
Berry, Joseph	02788	Matagorda	—	—
Berry, Josiah Montgomery	31596	Hill	—	—
Berry, L. R. Mrs.	33083	Grayson	Berry, James T.	26241
Berry, Lizzie	Rej	Jasper	Berry, William Green	—
Berry, Lou	RejM	Bastrop	—	—
Berry, Lucy A.	09118	Victoria	Berry, William J.	04259
Berry, M. A.	21459	Ellis	—	—

Index to Confederate Pension Applications

Name	App#	County	Veteran	Vet App#
Berry, M. A. Mrs.	31040	Van Zandt	Berry, Andrew Vestle	
Berry, M. E. Mrs.	50748	Cherokee	Berry, Andrew Jackson	23519
Berry, Margaret Alice	45370	Hill	Berry, Josiah Montgomery	31596
Berry, Mary Ann	40526	Grayson	Berry, Allen Griffin	13591
Berry, Mary C.	06199	Anderson	Berry, Darius	
Berry, Mary Catherine	51507	Callahan	Berry, Andrew Jackson	
Berry, Mary J.	35235	Lamar	Berry, William Tollie	27315
Berry, Matilda	03517	Rusk	Berry, Henry H.	
Berry, N. C. Mrs.	28118	Tarrant	Berry, William Grant	
Berry, Nancy Jane	Rej	Fannin	Berry, Joseph Nelson	
Berry, Nancy Jane	21012	Rusk	Berry, Silas Joseph	
Berry, Nannie	32204	Coleman	Berry, John James	24702
Berry, Pamla Ann	45739	Dallas	Berry, James Clifton	
Berry, Pierce	Rej	Jackson		
Berry, R. W.	Rej	Sabine		
Berry, S. H.	Rej	Washington		
Berry, Sarah Demandy	27910	Cherokee	Berry, George Washington	
Berry, Sarah E.	37529	Angelina	Berry, W. M.	
Berry, Tom Newton	38940	Mills		
Berry, W. C.	07892	McLennan		
Berry, William Henry Mrs.	45376	Navarro	Berry, William Henry	
Berry, William J.	04259	Victoria		
Berry, William T.	01746	Guadalupe		
Berry, William Tollie	27315	Lamar		
Berry, William Wesley	15868	Lampasas		
Berryhill, Ida	52027	Liberty	Berryhill, Miles F.	
Berryhill, James Carl	26662	Wood		
Berryhill, James Carl Mrs.	41712	Wood	Berryhill, James Carl	26662
Berryhill, Lydia Ann	19834	Nacogdoches	Berryhill, Thomas B.	16134
Berryhill, Miles	Rej	Liberty		
Berryhill, Thomas B.	16134	Nacogdoches		
Berryhill, Thomas F.	23471	Fannin		
Berryman, A. B.	Rej	Freestone		
Berryman, Annie	25978	Limestone	Berryman, Henry Clay	
Berryman, J. M.	43161	Tom Green		
Berryman, Jackson	00628	Caldwell		
Berryman, Martha	Rej	Limestone	Berryman, H. C.	
Berryman, William	06912	Grimes		
Berryman, William Larkin	Rej	Llano		
Bertling, Henry	33627	Gonzales		
Bertrand, F. O.	Rej	Webb		
Bertrand, F. O.	04310	Webb		
Bertrand, Mary F.	46410	Coryell	Bertrand, John Raney	
Berwick, Mary S.	28777	Orange	Berwick, Gilbert	
Berwick, Zelpha	31048	Jefferson	Berwick, Eli	
Beryman, Arch B.	Rej	Howard		
Besing, Henry R.	20583	Potter		
Bess, Frances	01692	Grimes	Bess, Christopher	
Bessent, Abraham Benjamin	21647	Calhoun		
Bessent, Nancy Ann Rebecca	30856	Calhoun	Bessent, Abraham Benjamin	21647
Best, Alice Manning	35555	Galveston	Best, Max	
Best, G. J.	Rej	Jones		
Best, James	Rej	Houston		
Best, Jane	27695	Tyler	Best, Julius Jasper	
Best, Olivia E.	32318	Matagorda	Best, Samuel Rainey	
Best, S. M. Mrs.	27378	Houston	Best, James	
Bethea, James C.	Rej	Milam		
Bethea, Louisa A.	40802	Brazos	Bethea, Cade	
Bethell, A. P. Mrs.	01222	Ellis	Bethell, W. R. E.	

Index to Confederate Pension Applications

Name	No.	County	Veteran	No.
Bethell, E. Z. Mrs.	21358	Hunt	Bethell, James Monroe	
Bethell, Lucinda C.	20428	Palo Pinto	Bethell, William Parson	08867
Bethell, William Parson	08867	Hunt		
Bethurum, Elizabeth Jane	47102	Dallas	Bethurum, Robert Porter	
Betterton, A. D.	06771	Nacogdoches		
Betterton, Z. L. Mrs.	05825	Cass	Betterton, Jesse	
Bettis, Carrie E.	40548	Montague	Bettis, Alfred Young	
Bettis, Henry W.	41393	Burleson		
Bettis, John B.	27135	Erath		
Bettis, John B. Mrs.	43192	Mitchell	Bettis, John B.	27135
Bettis, N. O. Mrs.	21521	Fannin	Bettis, Moses W.	
Betts, Eva R.	41046	Donley	Betts, William Elijah	
Betts, Frances Jane	24753	Anderson	Betts, James M.	20685
Betts, I. R.	20544	Freestone		
Betts, J. B.	24071	Cass		
Betts, James M.	20685	Leon		
Betts, Susanna J.	37298	Jackson	William Powell, Sr.	25683
Betts, William Powell, Sr.	25683	Jackson		
Bevel, Eliza	00669	Camp	Bevel, R. H.	
Beverly, M. S. Mrs.	30877	Tyler	Beverly, Richard Stafford	
Bevil, M. E. Mrs.	18267	Rains	Bevil, William Thomas	
Bevil, Margaret J.	12462	Jasper	Bevil, George S.	
Bevil, William T.	16287	Rains		
Bevill, B. J.	19252	San Saba		
Bevill, Martha J.	31695	Travis	Bevill, Francis Marion	
Bevill, R. E.	23502	Parker		
Bevill, R. W.	30974	Limestone		
Beville, A. A.	Rej	McLennan		
Beville, W. T.	Rej	Cherokee		
Bexley, J. D.	15165	Franklin		
Bibb, Eli	Rej	Rains		
Bibb, L. D. Mrs.	19921	Callahan	Bibb, Henry H.	
Bibb, Thomas B.	14461	Val Verde		
Bibby, Hester M.	41762	Smith	Bibby, James Hardy	23359
Bibby, James Hardy	23359	Hopkins		
Bible, Eliza I.	12743	Bosque		
Bice, H. E. Mrs.	34169	Hamilton	Bice, John Thomas	
Bice, L.	00758	Cherokee		
Bickham, Mollie	29557	Mills	Bickham, William Thomas	
Bickley, Eudora Pauline	45908	Anderson	Bickley, S. J. (Rock)	
Bickley, George Samuel	14407	Smith		
Bickley, H. M. Mrs.	36777	Smith	Bickley, George Samuel	14407
Bickley, J. S.	14093	Sabine		
Bickley, J. S.	26436	Sabine		
Bickley, M. H. Mrs.	Rej	Sabine	Bickley, William Washington	
Bickley, M. J. Mrs.	45727	Collin	Bickley, Joseph Polsol	
Bickley, William Washington Mrs.	28739	Sabine	Bickley, William Washington	
Biddle, M. A. Mrs.	07213	Gonzales	Biddle, Thomas C.	
Biddy, William	01505	Franklin		
Bidwell, E. B.	17521	Coryell		
Bidwell, Mattie Myra	30837	Coryell	Bidwell, E. B.	17521
Bielefeld, Minna	Rej	Austin	Bielefeld, Christian	
Bielstein, Minnie	32383	Victoria	Bielstein, August	
Bieschwale, Betsy	23312	Kendall	Bieschwale, Henry	
Biffle, James M.	00468	Bosque		
Biffle, Nancy L.	31367	Tarrant	Biffle, Nathan Fletcher	
Bigbee, R. A. Mrs.	22800	Grayson	Bigbee, Lewellen Washington	
Bigbee, Sally	20081	Milam	Bigbee, Thomas Mortimus	10428
Bigbee, Thomas Mortimus	10428	Milam		

Index to Confederate Pension Applications

Name	App. No.	County	Veteran	Vet. No.
Biggers, Isom	39584	Shelby		
Biggers, Mozel Price	49955	Fannin	Price, James Olive	
Biggerstaff, Sallie	35037	Fannin	Biggerstaff, John Milton	
Biggerstaff, Z. O. Mrs.	49043	Fannin	Biggerstaff, William Owen	
Biggio, Rebecca M.	47212	Webb	Biggio, William	
Biggs, Benjamin Franklin	01346	Erath		
Biggs, C. B. Mrs.	Rej	Henderson	Biggs, James	
Biggs, C. B. Mrs.	RejM	Llano		
Biggs, James	14099	Camp		
Biggs, James Harvey	11116	Shackelford		
Biggs, Joseph E.	18227	Panola		
Biggs, M. E. Mrs.	09009	Ellis	Biggs, Henry	
Biggs, Mary Clemmie	46644	Marion	Biggs, Davis	
Biggs, Mary R.	19495	Fannin	Biggs, John McClure	
Biggs, Narcissa Jane	41386	El Paso	Biggs, Benjamin Franklin	
Biggs, Pattie Dallam	50533	Cameron	Biggs, William Henry Harrison	47094
Biggs, Sarah J.	29329	Shackelford	Biggs, James Harvey	11116
Biggs, Thomas	48076	Camp		
Biggs, William Henry Harrison	47094	Cameron		
Bigham, Hannah E.	01906	Hill	Bigham, Thomas F.	
Bigham, John S.	43093	Bell		
Bigham, Laura Ann	39654	Hill	Bigham, W. L.	32781
Bigham, W. E.	RejM	Henderson		
Bigham, W. L.	32781	Hill		
Bigham, William T.	22885	Fannin		
Bighorn, R. J. Mrs.	06296	Bell	Bighorn, M. S.	
Bilberry, M. Monroe	10879	Comanche		
Bilbo, Ephreham Hughey	01315	Erath		
Bilbo, J. L. Mrs.	21648	Tarrant	Bilbo, Ephreham Hughey	01315
Bilbo, P. H.	23261	Polk		
Bilbro, Annie	21649	Montague	Bilbro, William Henry	
Bilderback, William J.	13826	Grayson		
Biles, Rebecca	32919	Camp	Biles, W. S.	18632
Biles, W. S.	18632	Camp		
Billingby, John H.	Rej	Llano		
Billings, E. S.	40785	Matagorda		
Billingslea, W. H.	06903	Johnson		
Billingsley, Benjamin Franklin	26932	Parker		
Billingsley, Catherine C.	43943	Clay	Billingsley, Benjamin Franklin	26932
Billingsley, F. J.	05910	Taylor		
Billingsley, F. L. Mrs.	33145	Johnson	Billingsley, Grandison	02293
Billingsley, George W. Mrs.	33422	Bexar	Billingsley, George Washington	22976
Billingsley, George Washington	22976	Bexar		
Billingsley, Grandison	02293	Johnson		
Billingsley, J. C.	38971	Collin		
Billingsley, John	09398	Somervell		
Billingsley, John S.	10487	Travis		
Billingsley, Joseph Smallwood	38341	Collin		
Billingsley, Joseph W.	22419	Stephens		
Billingsley, Mary	17159	Shelby	Billingsley, William Manning	
Billingsley, Mary A.	32148	Parker	Billingsley, John Fowler	
Billingsley, Mary Belle	43589	Childress	Billingsley, Joseph Smallwood	38341
Billingsley, Stacy Watson	Rej	Atascosa	Billingsley, Thomas	11788
Billingsley, Thomas	11788	Atascosa		
Billingsley, William Franklin	09264	Kerr		
Billingsly, D. D. Mrs.	17117	Kerr	Billingsly, William Franklin	09264
Billingsly, L. K.	28062	Jefferson		
Billingsly, Mary J.	17196	Lamar	Billingsly, William P.	
Billingsly, Sarah	Rej	Lamar	Billingsly, Francis Marion	

Index to Confederate Pension Applications

Name	Number	County	Related	Related #
Bills, D. B.	05392	Hill		
Bills, G. C.	07166	Caldwell		
Bills, Isaac Walker	00842	Coleman		
Bills, James M.	Rej	Fannin		
Bills, John Aquilla	18924	Eastland		
Bills, Mary	Rej	Coleman	Bills, I. W.	
Bills, Mary Betsy	45653	Johnson	Bills, George Washington	
Bills, Mollie M.	28332	Eastland	Bills, John Aquilla	18924
Bills, O. C.	38049A	Hood		
Bills, Sarah J.	40469	Denton	Bills, Wilson Persis	
Binford, Benjamin Ingraham	14470	Waller		
Binford, S. A. Mrs.	50132	Bexar	Binford, John Henry	
Bingham, Addie	45244	Henderson	Bingham, William Ezekial	41134
Bingham, Jennie B.	10946	Galveston	Bingham, Charles O.	
Bingham, John William	11743	Tyler		
Bingham, L. A. Mrs.	00307	Bell	Bingham, James	
Bingham, Lou Mrs.	21421	Tyler	Bingham, John William	11743
Bingham, Lucindy	29378	Uvalde	Bingham, Harmon	
Bingham, Mary F.	17200	Madison	Bingham, Frank Enlisses	
Bingham, Rebecca Snider	45912	Jones	Bingham, Alfred Gains	
Bingham, Thomas M.	32546	Erath		
Bingham, Thomas Sidney	22899	Comanche		
Bingham, Victoria	51203	Comanche	Bingham, Thomas Sidney	22899
Bingham, William Ezekial	41134	Henderson		
Bingle, Christian	28760	Harris		
Bingle, J. C. (Charles)	17439	Chambers		
Bingle, Martha	33641	Harris	Bingle, Christian	28760
Binion, E. C. Mrs.	29852	Angelina	Binion, Algernon Hamilton	
Binion, E. W. Mrs.	32429	Upshur	Binion, Milton Booker	17171
Binion, Ella	29905	Titus	Binion, Monroe Whitfield	
Binion, Milton Booker	17171	Upshur		
Binnion, Eliza	32308	Bastrop	Binnion, Thomas Steward	
Bins, F. L.	Rej	Bowie		
Bins, Lidia	04742	Waller	Bins, George W.	
Binyon, James Richard Mrs.	33606	Tarrant	Binyon, James Richard	
Birch, A. L. Mrs.	40878	Polk	Birch, W. H.	23228
Birch, Thomas F.	34026	Polk		
Birch, W. H.	23228	Polk		
Birchfield, D. P.	28321	Trinity		
Birchfield, H. K. Mrs.	38738	Wood	Bi(or u)rchfield, Geo. Washington	35034
Bird, Abraham	50068	Robertson		
Bird, Catherine	05870	Falls	Bird, Lafayette	
Bird, Francis Richmond	16164	Navarro		
Bird, George Yell Mrs.	47611	Cooke	Bird, George Yell	
Bird, Issac W.	49935	Robertson		
Bird, J. L.	32983	Erath		
Bird, M. J. Mrs.	34969	Jasper	Bird, William Augustus	27793
Bird, Martha A.	49730	Lubbock	Bird, William Jasper	
Bird, Mary E.	36378	Panola	Bird, John Montgomery	
Bird, Melissa S.	36854	Brown	Bird, Francis Richmond	16164
Bird, P. D.	10094	Hamilton		
Bird, S. C. Mrs.	17221	Wood	Bird, Joseph W.	
Bird, William Augustus	27793	Jasper		
Birdsell, Lockwood	06497	Aransas		
Birdsong, Miles Jefferson	09092	Panola		
Birdsong, Miles Jefferson Mrs.	17141	Panola	Birdsong, Miles Jefferson	09092
Birdwell, Adaline B.	23296	Nacogdoches	Birdwell, John C.	
Birdwell, George Preston	22848	Cherokee		
Birdwell, J. A.	17154	Sabine		

Index to Confederate Pension Applications

Name	No.	County	Veteran	No.
Birdwell, J. F.	10873	Collin	—	—
Birdwell, Laura F.	17152	Rusk	Birdwell, Benjamin Franklin	—
Birdwell, M. M. Mrs.	45530	Cooke	Birdwell, Andrew Russell	—
Birdwell, Malinda	37639	Nacogdoches	Birdwell, Robert Randolph	—
Birdwell, May	Rej	Cooke	Birdwell, Andrew Russell	—
Birdwell, Samuel Lafayette	21397	Henderson	—	—
Birdwell, Sarah Ellen	46178	Smith	Birdwell, Samuel Lafayette	21397
Birdwell, Texana E.	28010	Nacogdoches	Birdwell, William	—
Birket, Elizabeth Haggard	Rej	Collin	Birket, James Patrick	—
Birmingham, Martha Jane	40657	Panola	Birmingham, Thomas	—
Birney, Simon Foster Mrs.	49493	Falls	Birney, Simon Foster	—
Bishop, A. H. Mrs.	19800	Johnson	Bishop, John Thomas	—
Bishop, Anna	37412	Harris	Bishop, Lewis	—
Bishop, Benjamin Franklin	17190	Grimes	—	—
Bishop, C. D.	30152	Hamilton	—	—
Bishop, C. D. Mrs.	38659	Hamilton	Bishop, C. D.	30152
Bishop, Charles Levi Mrs.	Rej	Kaufman	Bishop, Charles Levi	—
Bishop, Delphia Ann	34265	Kaufman	Bishop, Benjamin Franklin	—
Bishop, E. A. Mrs.	45001	Palo Pinto	Bishop, Zackariah R.	—
Bishop, Elizabeth	02523	Lavaca	Bishop, Philip	—
Bishop, Fannie L.	38083	Grimes	Bishop, Benjamin Franklin	17190
Bishop, George W.	07945	Rains	—	—
Bishop, Isaac	17488	Collin	—	—
Bishop, Isabelle	35327	Limestone	Bishop, John	12031
Bishop, J. C.	08957	Atascosa	—	—
Bishop, J. D.	Rej	Coryell	—	—
Bishop, J. L.	12950	Kimble	—	—
Bishop, James Richard	20454	Nolan	—	—
Bishop, John	12031	Limestone	—	—
Bishop, Jonathan	06242	Eastland	—	—
Bishop, Joseph Goodman	37592	Navarro	—	—
Bishop, L. E. Mrs.	21320	Hunt	Bishop, Thomas Wesby	17194
Bishop, Lavinia	07801	Eastland	Bishop, Jonathan	06242
Bishop, Lucien J.	Rej	Haskell	—	—
Bishop, Martha A.	35019	Wilson	Bishop, Robert	25108
Bishop, Mary	25635	Rusk	Bishop, Philip J.	—
Bishop, Mary	43414	Navarro	Bishop, Joseph Goodman	37592
Bishop, Mary A.	08192	Mason	Bishop, Andrew J.	—
Bishop, Mary Salome	46816	Nolan	Bishop, James Richard	20454
Bishop, Minerva J.	43882	Wood	Bishop, C.	—
Bishop, R. S.	07002	Hill	—	—
Bishop, Rachel Lee	49683	Bell	Bishop, Jacob	—
Bishop, Robert	25108	Wilson	—	—
Bishop, Stephen Mrs.	Rej	Potter	Bishop, Stephen	—
Bishop, T. W.	Rej	Coleman	—	—
Bishop, Thomas Wesby	17194	Hunt	—	—
Bishop, W. W.	20455	Johnson	—	—
Biskamp, Elizabeth A.	02247	Jasper	Biskamp, William Flowers	—
Bissett, Samuel	29573	Brewster	—	—
Bittel, John	08760	McCulloch	—	—
Bitterman, Levi Mrs.	49919	Nueces	Bitterman, Levi	—
Bittick, Belle	22201	Shelby	Bittick, Henry W. Conway	12615
Bittick, Henry W. Conway	12615	Shelby	—	—
Bittick, Jasper Newton Mrs.	21067	Taylor	Bittick, Jasper Newton	—
Bius, Ferdinand L.	10596	Bowie	—	—
Bius, Sarah	39775	Bowie	Bius, Ferdinand L.	10596
Bivens, E. G.	23537	Montague	—	—
Bivens, Fannie	41665	Montague	Bivens, E. G.	23537
Bivings, Edward Augusta Mrs.	47609	Ellis	Bivings, Edward Augusta	—

Index to Confederate Pension Applications

Name	No.	County	Veteran	Vet. No.
Bivins, E. C. Mrs.	36236	Lampasas	Bivins, Thomas C.	06760
Bivins, James K. Mrs.	46558	Gregg	Bivins, James K.	
Bivins, Mat	11071	Newton		
Bivins, Ruth	33748	Lampasas	Bivins, Elias	
Bivins, S. E. Mrs.	06932	Limestone	Bivins, James	
Bivins, Thomas C.	06760	Lampasas		
Bizzell, David James	26243	Fannin		
Bizzell, Frank M.	08732	Hopkins		
Bizzell, William	13991	Somervell		
Black, A. W.	29788	Johnson		
Black, Agnes Adeline	41171	Lampasas	Black, William	
Black, Alfred Prince	25827	Montague		
Black, Amelia Hays	Rej	Wichita	Black, John Wesley	
Black, Benjamin Franklin	17180	Camp		
Black, Benjamin P.	21650	Lee		
Black, C. C.	Rej	Ward		
Black, C. C.	33503	Ward		
Black, Charles Asbury	13670	Travis		
Black, Charles S.	46069	Fannin		
Black, Cordelia F.	33979	Williamson	Black, John Winters	28570
Black, Corene Francis	40864	Mills	Black, William Sheridan	
Black, E. P. Mrs.	26105	Midland	Black, Benjamin Franklin	
Black, E. V. Mrs.	20635	Tyler	Black, Thomas Daniel	11155
Black, Edward Madison	34633	Ward		
Black, Fannie Douglas	11888	Donley	Black, S. A.	
Black, Frances	19963	Hopkins	Black, Calvin Morgan	
Black, Frances S.	22881	Colorado	Black, William James	
Black, George Bogart	Rej	Comanche		
Black, George Hayes	23318	Upshur		
Black, H. A.	13197	Angelina		
Black, H. C. Mrs.	28646	Concho	Black, William Pinckney	04932
Black, H. F.	28935	Jack		
Black, Henry C.	13833	Harris		
Black, Henry F.	Rej	Coryell		
Black, Henry Y.	Rej	Camp		
Black, Isaac	15728	Jack		
Black, James Maddison	04518	Wood		
Black, Jane C.	11475	Harrison	Black, T. M.	01833
Black, Jennie	33721	Montague	Black, Alfred Prince	25827
Black, John R.	13275	Collin		
Black, John Winters	28570	Williamson		
Black, Joseph Albert	18666	Nueces		
Black, Joseph Albert Mrs.	32412	Nueces	Black, Joseph Albert	18666
Black, Josiah	39793	Coryell		
Black, Lillie	30114	Harris	Black, William Dunlap	
Black, M. A.	Rej	Hopkins		
Black, M. E. Mrs.	Rej	Clay	Black, Isaac	15728
Black, M. J. Mrs.	Rej	Dallas	Black, Sidney A.	
Black, M. M. Mrs.	30396	Lee	Black, Benjamin Pearson	
Black, Margaret A.	00168	Bastrop	Black, John B.	
Black, Margaret B.	28006	Titus	Black, Joseph D.	
Black, Mark Anthony Mrs.	49435	Uvalde	Black, Mark Anthony	
Black, Mary A.	28807	Childress	Black, Erastus Mathew	
Black, Mary Ann	01991	Hopkins	Black, Robert W.	
Black, Mary C.	36225	Anderson	Black, John Adams	
Black, Mary G.	45403	Camp	Black, Ben Franklin	17180
Black, Mary Isabell	47733	Cass	Black, John Adam	
Black, Mattie A.	36891	Ward	Black, Edward Madison	34633
Black, Nora	32447	Fannin	Black, John Sparks	

Index to Confederate Pension Applications

Name	Number	County	Soldier	Soldier #
Black, O. F.	31243	Upshur	Black, George Hayes	23318
Black, R. C. Mrs.	32430	Tarrant	Black, Temple Thomas	—
Black, Rachel	41965	Hill	Black, William Henry Harrison	—
Black, Sallie E.	16166	Navarro	Black, James R.	—
Black, Sarah E.	30692	Wood	Black, James Maddison	04518
Black, Susan Elizabeth	33323	Travis	Black, William Wheaton	—
Black, T. M.	01833	Harrison	—	—
Black, Texanna	20860	Taylor	Black, James	—
Black, Thomas A.	26278	San Jacinto	—	—
Black, Thomas Daniel	11155	Tyler	—	—
Black, Thomas M.	12804	Dallas	—	—
Black, William C.	02814	McLennan	—	—
Black, William Henry Mrs.	29487	Tarrant	Black, William Henry	—
Black, William N.	16630	Sterling	—	—
Black, William Pinckney	04932	Brown	—	—
Blackburn, Albert Arnimus	22886	Grayson	—	—
Blackburn, Bertha	28920	Dallas	Blackburn, James Lafayette	—
Blackburn, C. J. Mrs.	28261	Grayson	Blackburn, Albert Arnimus	22886
Blackburn, E. J. Mrs.	RejM	Bowie	—	—
Blackburn, Elizabeth	04811	Nacogdoches	Blackburn, James G.	—
Blackburn, Elizabeth	26253	McLennan	Blackburn, James Henry	—
Blackburn, G. W.	09628	Erath	—	—
Blackburn, H. C. Mrs.	Rej	Grayson	Blackburn, Richard Baxter	—
Blackburn, Helen J.	11487	Hill	Blackburn, Robert	—
Blackburn, Ida	Rej	Milam	Blackburn, John Wesley	—
Blackburn, James Monroe	23351	Taylor	—	—
Blackburn, Jane	07296	Menard	Blackburn, Elija	—
Blackburn, John	12459	Hunt	—	—
Blackburn, John G.	19767	Bell	—	—
Blackburn, Martha E.	Rej	Denton	Blackburn, W. J.	—
Blackburn, Mary	51675	Taylor	Blackburn, James Monroe	23351
Blackburn, Mary J.	04862	Nacogdoches	Blackburn, Robert B.	—
Blackburn, N. F. Mrs.	08578	Hill	Blackburn, J. C.	—
Blackburn, N. M. Mrs.	03850	Titus	Blackburn, J. D.	—
Blackburn, Richard P.	47169	Cooke	—	—
Blackburn, S. A. R. Mrs.	13702	Bell	Blackburn, W. L. H.	—
Blackburn, Samuel	10456	Red River	—	—
Blackburn, Sara Elizabeth	31559	McLennan	Blackburn, David Murray	—
Blackburn, T. J.	12883	Harrison	—	—
Blackburn, W. P.	Rej	Harris	—	—
Blackburn, William J.	08039	Denton	—	—
Blackerby, Sarah	26523	Parker	Blackerby, Elijah	—
Blackley, A. P.	43036	Taylor	—	—
Blacklidge, A. C.	Rej	Leon	—	—
Blacklock, Benjamin Thomas	09833	Coryell	—	—
Blacklock, M. E. Mrs.	18756	Tarrant	Blacklock, Benjamin Thomas	09833
Blackman, Cynthia E.	09568	Travis	Blackman, George J.	—
Blackman, G. J.	04410	Williamson	—	—
Blackman, Harriet E.	02953	Milam	Blackman, William M.	—
Blackman, Isaac J.	08901	Robertson	—	—
Blackman, James	11567	Montgomery	—	—
Blackman, Jesse H.	23548	Franklin	—	—
Blackman, M. A. Mrs.	39540	Houston	Blackman, Isiah	—
Blackman, Martha E.	14301	Jones	Blackman, Isaac J.	08901
Blackman, Mary C.	18245	Parker	Blackman, Thomas	—
Blackman, Mary Jane	19176	Nolan	Blackman, Henry Hanson	—
Blackman, Susan A.	36912	Throckmorton	McDaniel, John Watson	—
Blackmon, Dillon	02607	Leon	—	—
Blackmon, Effie Ann	37841	Navarro	Blackmon, Dillon	02607

Index to Confederate Pension Applications

Name	App#	County	Spouse/Veteran	Ref#
Blackmon, Harmon C.	46093	Limestone		
Blackmon, Janie (Eliza Jane)	43496	Bowie	Blackmon, Benjamin J.	
Blackmon, L. G.	26547	Leon		
Blackmon, Levi	15169	Franklin		
Blackmon, Samuel	09641	Robertson		
Blackmon, Sarah C.	05051	Upshur	Blackmon, Franklin F.	
Blackmon, Solomon B.	18288	Robertson		
Blackmon, Stephen R.	40978	Henderson		
Blackmon, T.	03339	Parker		
Blackmon, William Sparks	46624	McLennan		
Blackshear, E. A.	15757	Jasper		
Blackshear, James I.	34278	Madison		
Blackstock, B. B.	45554	Camp		
Blackstock, John F.	17028	Wood		
Blackstock, Sarah Ann	Rej	Lavaca	Blackstock, Thomas Newton	06629
Blackstock, Thomas Newton	06629	Lavaca		
Blackstone, Lula Rose Griffin	51951	Dallas	Blackstone, John Fuller H.	
Blackstone, M. J. Mrs.	09535	Brown	Blackstone, John H.	
Blackstone, William H.	23542	Upshur		
Blackwelder, John S.	25037	Denton		
Blackwelder, Margaret S.	29350	Denton	Blackwelder, John S.	25037
Blackwell, E. J. Mrs.	31047	Young	Blackwell, Joseph	
Blackwell, Elias High Mrs.	31696	Johnson	Blackwell, Elias High	
Blackwell, Georgia Ana	29061	Cass	Blackwell, David	
Blackwell, Henry Clay	45853	Travis		
Blackwell, J. M. V.	03300	Parker		
Blackwell, James Marion	22202	McLennan		
Blackwell, James Marion Mrs.	24639	McLennan	Blackwell, James Marion	22202
Blackwell, Jesse	36108	Fayette		
Blackwell, Joel W.	38528	Dickens		
Blackwell, John Tarleton	07847	Hill		
Blackwell, L. A. Mrs.	18411	Tarrant	Blackwell, Jocab Soloman	
Blackwell, L. H. Mrs.	22902	Falls	Blackwell, John Tarleton	07847
Blackwell, M. L. Mrs.	36067	Houston	Steadman, Eli Townsend	
Blackwell, Mary	Rej	Rusk	Blackwell, Wiley	
Blackwell, Mary Jane	30698	Wood	Blackwell, Reuben Bradley	
Blackwell, Mary L.	16614	Smith	Blackwell, Hamilton Wiley	
Blackwell, Rebecca	46222	McCulloch	Blackwell, Richard	
Blackwell, Rebecca C.	16628	Somervell	Blackwell, Francis Marion	
Blackwell, Sarah P.	Rej	Van Zandt	Blackwell, H. F.	
Blackwell, Synthia Caroline	50159	Lampasas	Blackwell, John Milton	
Blackwood, John Milton	13388	Johnson		
Blackwood, Sarah Ann	40030	Burnet	Blackwood, Columbus Jefferson	
Blagge, Caroline E.	13315	Galveston	Blagge, Harry W.	
Blagge, Hamilton	12845	Galveston		
Blain, Catherine A.	29845	Jefferson	Blain, William S.	
Blain, Doralee	45307	Grayson	Blain, John Marlin	31032
Blain, Emma	02425	Kimble		
Blain, John Marlin	31032	Grayson		
Blain, Martha A.	30811	Grayson	Blain, James C.	
Blaine, John L.	13736	Caldwell		
Blair, Adella C.	Rej	Taylor	Blair, John Herald	
Blair, C. H.	Rej	Limestone		
Blair, Charles C.	Rej	Erath		
Blair, E. B.	08629	Brown		
Blair, Emily E.	14661	Bell		
Blair, Ewing	Rej	Nueces		
Blair, Fannie C.	50540	Dallas	Blair, George W.	46778
Blair, George W.	27068	Denton		

Index to Confederate Pension Applications

Name	No.	County	Veteran	No.
Blair, George W.	46778	Dallas	—	
Blair, Greene Washington	26067	Johnson	—	
Blair, J. D.	00296	Bell	—	
Blair, J. J.	Rej	Bell	—	
Blair, J. M.	03229	Palo Pinto	—	
Blair, James Robert	32761	Navarro	—	
Blair, James Robert Mrs.	39464	Navarro	Blair, James Robert	32761
Blair, Jessamine M.	18817	Archer	Blair, James Monroe	
Blair, John F.	11426	Erath	—	
Blair, M. A. Mrs.	Rej	Hamilton	Blair, William	
Blair, M. E. Cowan Mrs.	38605	Delta	Cowan, William Thomas	
Blair, M. E. Mrs.	01167	Dewitt	Blair, George W.	
Blair, Martha L.	23521	Ellis	Blair, James Wesley	
Blair, Mary E.	19443	Dallam	Blair, George Powell	
Blair, Mattie Clark	41847	Brown	Blair, David Joseph	
Blair, Mattie E.	35634	Jefferson	Blair, Wiley	
Blair, Meeky	31271	Erath	Blair, Charles C.	
Blair, Richard	46375	Cherokee	—	
Blair, S. E.	32856	Erath	—	
Blair, S. J. Mrs.	33722	Johnson	Blair, Greene Washington	26067
Blair, Samuel H.	28426	Fort Bend	—	
Blair, Sarah C.	31305	Parker	Blair, John Nickolson	
Blair, William Clary	Rej	Fannin	—	
Blake, A. M.	01489	Franklin	—	
Blake, Asa	00317	Bell	—	
Blake, Christopher C.	05720	Collin	—	
Blake, Elizabeth A.	34807	Gregg	Blake, Jesse Columbus	15296
Blake, Hester	33888	Jasper	Blake, William Wales	
Blake, J. C.	07691	Collin	—	
Blake, James H.	47174	Navarro	—	
Blake, Jesse Columbus	15296	Gregg	—	
Blake, John	28082	Smith	—	
Blake, John Henry	01274	Ellis	—	
Blake, John Henry Mrs.	41663	Harris	Blake, John Henry	
Blake, John L.	Rej	Potter	—	
Blake, Julia Upshaw	36480	Dallas	Blake, Samuel Reece	
Blake, L. M.	08304	Franklin	—	
Blake, M. J. Mrs.	08839	Bell	Blake, Asa	00317
Blake, Margaret E.	11217	Grayson	Blake, Allen	
Blake, Nancy C.	Rej	Dallas	Blake, John Henry	01274
Blake, S. E. Mrs.	34941	Bexar	Blake, Robert Bruce	
Blake, W. H.	06125	Hardin	—	
Blakeley, Gertrude	19135	Mitchell	Blakeley, Samuel Thomas	
Blakeley, James McVey	Rej	Lubbock	—	
Blakely, N. H. Mrs.	27841	Hamilton	Blakely, James Daniel	
Blakely, S. L.	07012	Hill	—	
Blakemore, Edwin D.	47039	Hunt	—	
Blakemore, John Thomas	03034	Mitchell	—	
Blakemore, M. E. Mrs.	12156	Tom Green	Blakemore, John Thomas	03034
Blakemore, Mary Curtis	33723	Cherokee	Blakemore, William White	
Blakeney, John C.	30617	Ellis	—	
Blakeney, John William	12131	San Saba	—	
Blakeney, Lizzie Ann	50419	Freestone	Blakeney, William	
Blakeney, Lue	38310	Ellis	Blakeney, John C.	30617
Blakeney, Mary Jane	05471	Henderson	Blakeney, Robert James	
Blakeney, Nannie	47259	Dallas	Blakeney, George W.	
Blakeney, Sophia	39634	Bexar	Blakeney, John William	12131
Blakeney, W. M.	Rej	Freestone	—	
Blakenship, Mary F.	38079	Montague	Blakenship, Levi	

Index to Confederate Pension Applications

Blakeway, Mary Sue	38860	Houston	Blakeway, William M.	15598
Blakeway, William M.	15598	Houston	—	—
Blakey, Lillian	47437	Ellis	Blakey, Josiah Thomas	—
Blakey, Paleoligus Adolphus	37000	Franklin	—	—
Blakney, J. E.	25168	Parker	—	—
Blalock, A. P.	35659	Cherokee	—	—
Blalock, Ann A.	39955	Collin	Blalock, Thomas Hart Benton	27482
Blalock, Annie	Rej	Polk	Blalock, J. K. P.	14644
Blalock, C. D.	Rej	Harrison	—	—
Blalock, G. D.	Rej	Wheeler	—	—
Blalock, George Robert	03677	Smith	—	—
Blalock, J. K. P.	14644	Bosque	—	—
Blalock, J. R.	23238	Gray	—	—
Blalock, Lottie Louise	37772	Wood	Blalock, William Richard	30903
Blalock, Mary	45506	Cass	Blalock, Henry King	—
Blalock, Mary E.	20141	Smith	Blalock, George Robert	03677
Blalock, Matilda E.	25126	Hopkins	Blalock, Thomas Newton	15501
Blalock, Mattie M.	34311	Harrison	Blalock, Charles Stewart	—
Blalock, Thomas Hart Benton	27482	Collin	—	—
Blalock, Thomas Newton	15501	Hopkins	—	—
Blalock, W. I.	31616	Cass	—	—
Blalock, W. P.	29050	Cass	—	—
Blalock, William Richard	30903	Wood	—	—
Blanca, Santos	04969	Bexar	—	—
Blanchard, Belle Glass	40284	Coryell	Glass, Richard Johnson	—
Blanchard, Robert	07620	Lamar	—	—
Bland, Amanda	11432	Falls	Bland, Gideon	—
Bland, David	34625	Orange	—	—
Bland, George A.	17847	Hopkins	—	—
Bland, J. Thomas	46614	Henderson	—	—
Bland, M. C. Mrs.	20080	Coryell	Bland, George	—
Bland, Mary S.	15599	Houston	Bland, Benjamin F.	—
Bland, W. Calvin	12141	Tarrant	—	—
Bland, William C.	Rej	Freestone	—	—
Blankenship, A. J.	Rej	Erath	—	—
Blankenship, E. A. Mrs.	47678	Bowie	Blankenship, A. J.	—
Blankenship, Francis Marion	14118	Bell	—	—
Blankenship, Susan E.	16036	Milam	Blankenship, Francis Marion	14118
Blankenship, W. A.	Rej	Hunt	—	—
Blankinship, W. A.	14502	Knox	—	—
Blankinship, W. Robert	13752	Cherokee	—	—
Blanks, Christopher Columbus	03783	Tarrant	—	—
Blanks, Dixie	33664	Cooke	Blanks, Joseph Thompson	28238
Blanks, Joseph Thompson	28238	Cooke	—	—
Blanks, Laura J.	16646	Tarrant	Blanks, Christopher Columbus	03783
Blanks, William Henry	23263	Tom Green	—	—
Blanton, Amanda Catherine	49662	Young	Blanton, James Herod	—
Blanton, B. F.	47468	Grayson	—	—
Blanton, Benjamin	33819	Johnson	—	—
Blanton, Elihu P.	33820	Johnson	—	—
Blanton, J. A. Mrs.	29251	Johnson	Blanton, John Martin	—
Blanton, J. O.	02813	McLennan	—	—
Blanton, Jacob Davidson	24477	Cherokee	—	—
Blanton, Julia	51568	Grayson	Blanton, B. F.	47468
Blanton, M. E. Mrs.	36034	Knox	Blanton, Benjamin	33819
Blanton, Mary E.	38870	Carson	Blanton, Nelson Ransom	25743
Blanton, Mildred A.	16146	Nacogdoches	Blanton, James Harvey	—
Blanton, Nancy Jane	42266	Collin	Blanton, James Wesley	—
Blanton, Nelson Ransom	25743	Williamson	—	—

Index to Confederate Pension Applications

Blanton, S. Lizzie	49971	Coleman	Blanton, Charles Guinn	
Blanton, Sarah Tabitha	43782	Tarrant	Blanton, James Elijah	
Blanton, Susan F.	16115	Nacogdoches	Blanton, Melvin Geter	
Blanton, W. R.	10837	Bexar		
Blanton, W. W. Mrs.	30769	Bexar	Blanton, Walton Wilkins	04454
Blanton, Walton Wilkins	04454	Wilson		
Blasienz, C. A.	Rej	Milam		
Blasienz, Lizzie	46460	Milam	Blasienz, C. Albert	
Blasingame, James I.	39197	Hunt		
Blasingame, John	Rej	Henderson		
Blasingame, Louisa Adeloid	30347	Lee	Blasingame, Joseph	
Blasingame, Martha W.	36736	Van Zandt	Blasingame, Silas Alexander	19312
Blasingame, Silas Alexander	19312	Van Zandt		
Blassingame, John David Mrs.	49322	Grayson	Blassingame, John David	
Blassingame, Mary Jane	49886	Tarrant	Blassingame, Winn Gowen	
Blassingame, William W.	45010	Tarrant		
Blaunt, Thomas W.	RejM	San Augustine		
Blaylock, Rebecca C.	49011	Titus	Blaylock, Albert Taylor	
Blaylock, Richard Avery	25491	Bell		
Blaylock, Richard Avery Mrs.	48056	Bell	Blaylock, Richard Avery	25491
Bledsoe, Benjamin Franklin Mrs.	Rej	Mills	Bledsoe, Benjamin Franklin	
Bledsoe, Bettie	Rej	Johnson	Bledsoe, James Slaughter	
Bledsoe, Bettie	33906	Comanche	Bledsoe, George Washington	00549
Bledsoe, Carrie	23303	Parker	Bledsoe, Isaac Curd	
Bledsoe, E. W. Mrs.	04293	Washington	Bledsoe, John	
Bledsoe, Fleming G.	15022	Dallas		
Bledsoe, George Washington	00549	Brown		
Bledsoe, Jesse	37605	Hunt		
Bledsoe, John Talley	24961	Coleman		
Bledsoe, John Talley Mrs.	38425	Coleman	Bledsoe, John Talley	24961
Bledsoe, N. J. Mrs.	35707	Montgomery	Bledsoe, R. M.	13412
Bledsoe, R. M.	13412	Leon		
Bledsoe, Sallie A.	33203	Wichita	Bledsoe, Caleb Bailey	
Bledsoe, Willis A.	13648	Tarrant		
Bleike, Theresa	Rej	Harris	Bleike, Frederick P.	
Blessing, Soloman Thomas	42615	Dallas		
Blessington, Joseph Palmer Mrs.	18625	Harris	Blessington, Joseph Palmer	
Blevins, Arps	32826	Garza		
Blevins, C. E. Mrs.	17466	Clay	Blevins, Robert	
Blevins, Dedrick	42686	Garza		
Blevins, E. J.	04590	Tarrant		
Blevins, L. P. Mrs.	35642	Young	Blevins, Squire Echols	34427
Blevins, Louisa	43198	Tarrant	Blevins, William	38013
Blevins, Sarah Ann	41045	Tarrant	Blevins, Louis	
Blevins, Squire Echols	34427	Young		
Blevins, Sue O.	47824	Dallas	Blevins, David Crockett	
Blevins, Virginia C.	10422	Medina	Blevins, William Riley	
Blevins, William	38013	Tarrant		
Blew, Martha Omella	40036	Burnet	Blew, James A.	
Blewett, Theresa	RejM	Harris		
Blewett, W. R.	Rej	Collin		
Blisard, E. A. Mrs.	45290A	Red River	Blisard, William Thomas	04840
Blisard, William Thomas	04840	Red River		
Bliss, Daniel	01776	Harris		
Blissett, Sarah C.	27525	Navarro	Blissett, Samuel Carter	
Blocher, N. J. Mrs.	23465	Hill	Blocher, James Michael	
Block, Frederick William	03203	Orange		
Block, Louisa	39559	Orange	Block, Charles Lewis	
Block, Mary A.	Rej	Orange	Block, Frederick William	

Index to Confederate Pension Applications

Name	Number	County	Related	Related Number
Blocker, Fannie	40735	Milam	Blocker, James Robert	28890
Blocker, J. M.	Rej	Hill	—	
Blocker, J. R.	16035	Milam	—	
Blocker, James Robert	28890	Milam	—	
Blocker, Martha A.	30615	Galveston	Blocker, Robert H.	—
Blocker, Martha H.	14762	Burleson	Blocker, John Cole	—
Blocker, Mason Acker	38372	Palo Pinto	Blocker, William Leander	33808
Blocker, Nelson	Rej	Robertson	—	
Blocker, W. R.	RejM	Collin	—	
Blocker, William Leander	33808	Palo Pinto	—	
Bloodworth, Lucy A.	07891	McLennan	Bloodworth, Francis M.	—
Bloomfield, E. M. Mrs.	29374	Walker	Bloomfield, Robert Homes	—
Bloomfield, L.	23545	Angelina	—	
Bloomfield, Nannie	37181	Angelina	Bloomfield, L.	23545
Blossom, Bertha	26500	Matagorda	Blossom, Joseph	—
Blount, Alfred John	20652	Bell	—	
Blount, Byrd W.	01114	Delta	—	
Blount, Eliza A.	13449	Montgomery	Blount, Green Albert	—
Blount, Green Jackson	01992	Hopkins	—	
Blount, J. K.	08860	Bandera	—	
Blount, J. M.	RejM	Hill	—	
Blount, M. A. Mrs.	17864	Hopkins	Blount, Green Jackson	01992
Blount, M. L. Mrs.	16689	Titus	Blount, E. Alex	—
Blount, Rebecca B.	23552	Limestone	Blount, Luther Whitfield	—
Blount, Thomas W.	46927	San Augustine	—	
Bloxom, Leslie	28037	Falls	—	
Bludworth, Benjamin P. Mrs.	Rej	Fayette	Bludworth, Benjamin Portinent	—
Bludworth, Mary	43655	Galveston	Bludworth, Benard Leonard	—
Blue, B. W.	Rej	Van Zandt	—	
Blue, Emanuel	Rej	Tarrant	—	
Blue, Helen	20936	Washington	Blue, James H.	08010
Blue, James H.	08010	Washington	—	
Blue, M. E. Mrs.	Rej	Smith	Blue, Washington Mueller	—
Blue, Moses Henry	Rej	Palo Pinto	—	
Blue, Nancy L.	31039	Van Zandt	Blue, John Henry	—
Blue, R. W.	RejM	Van Zandt	—	
Blue, W. G.	17015	Wood	—	
Blum, Johanna	31927	Hays	Blum, Casper Fredrich	—
Blumberg, Harmon	16920	Waller	—	
Blumberg, Katharine	35005	Waller	Blumberg, Harmon	16920
Blume, Darling Pinkney	10806	Brazos	—	
Blume, Darling Pinkney Mrs.	35883	Brazos	Blume, Darling Pinkney	10806
Blume, John Henry	18743	Chambers	—	
Blume, Phoebe	34970	Chambers	Blume, John Henry	18743
Blundell, John Adam	05884	Franklin	—	
Blundell, Mary E.	17027	Wood	Blundell, John Adam	05884
Blunt, P. W.	23240	Wood	—	
Blythe, Elizabeth A.	01993	Hopkins	Blythe, William T.	—
Boales, A. H.	Rej	Edwards	—	
Boales, James A., Sr.	06888	Uvalde	—	
Boales, Lovina	20361	Edwards	James A., Sr.	06888
Boals, Mary J.	21651	Tarrant	Boals, Robert Franklin	—
Board, Robert Milton	21655	Collin	—	
Board, S. A. Mrs.	Rej	Van Zandt	Board, Phillip William	—
Boase, W. J.	03848	Titus	—	
Boatman, Andrew B.	08911	Jack	—	
Boatman, Elizabeth E.	Rej	Cooke	Boatman, Jesse J.	—
Boatman, John M.	10974	Henderson	—	
Boatman, N. C. Mrs.	04818	Nacogdoches	Boatman, J. R.	—

Index to Confederate Pension Applications

Name	App. No.	County	Veteran/Spouse	Vet. No.
Boatman, Poly	50603	Burnet	Boatman, Andrew B.	08911
Boatner, E.	03515	Rusk	—	—
Boatner, Ezekiel G.	23329	Brazoria	—	—
Boatright, Anna	32993	Travis	Boatright, James B.	16718
Boatright, Charles	08316	Gonzales	—	—
Boatright, G. D.	17246	Rusk	—	—
Boatright, James B.	16718	Travis	—	—
Boatright, John B.	19633	Val Verde	—	—
Boatright, Martin	02876	Llano	—	—
Boatright, Mary A.	18457	Travis	Boatright, Charles	08316
Boatright, Nancy Ann	Rej	Llano	Boatright, Martin	02876
Boatright, Rebecca	02877	Llano	Boatright, John	—
Boatwright, B. P.	22715	Grayson	—	—
Boaz, Elizabeth (M. E.) Barrow	27328	Smith	Boaz, Thomas Benton	—
Boaz, Ellis R.	23226	Smith	—	—
Boaz, Sue E.	29283	Smith	Boaz, Ellis R.	23226
Boaz, Viola M.	50026	Tarrant	Boaz, David	—
Boazman, Nancy Alice	38576	Tarrant	Boazman, Joseph Wallace	—
Bobbett, M. G.	23840	Kaufman	—	—
Bobbitt, A. T. L.	Rej	San Augustine	—	—
Bobbitt, B. L.	09883	Houston	—	—
Bobbitt, Francis	34593	Houston	Bobbitt, B. L.	09883
Bobbitt, George R.	14343	Montgomery	—	—
Bobbitt, J. T.	25005	Hill	—	—
Bobbitt, Jim L.	10247	Cherokee	—	—
Bobbitt, Maredon Gentry	24115	Kaufman	—	—
Bobbitt, Uriah R.	30316	San Augustine	—	—
Bobbitt, Virginia	34943	Kaufman	Bobbitt, Maredon Gentry	24115
Bobo, I. G. L.	Rej	Live Oak	—	—
Bobo, James Edward	30445	Lamar	—	—
Bobo, Lee Ann	34524	Hood	Bobo, Andrew Jackson	—
Bobo, M. A. Mrs.	23349	Hood	Bobo, Andrew Green	—
Bobo, Mary E.	49069	Johnson	Bobo, Elijah B.	—
Bobo, P. A. Mrs.	25979	Cass	Bobo, James W.	—
Bobo, Rebecca	46251	Delta	Bobo, James Edward	30445
Bockman, J. G.	Rej	Tom Green	—	—
Bockman, M. A. Mrs.	27674	Morris	Bockman, John C.	—
Boddeker, Frank	32012	Galveston	—	—
Bodenhamer, Christian Shiares	10234	Wharton	—	—
Bodenhamer, David S.	28146	Ellis	—	—
Bodenhamer, Elizabeth Gilchrist	26116	Harris	Bodenhamer, Christian Shiares	10234
Bodenhamer, Ida Mae	45124	Dallas	Bodenhamer, David S.	28146
Bodenhamer, S. L.	Rej	Burnet	—	—
Bodenhamer, William W.	01907	Hill	—	—
Bodiford, A. G.	05313	Montague	—	—
Bodiford, James Leroy	14503	Wood	—	—
Bodiford, Josephine Petteway	51957	Robertson	Petteway, Michael Micajah	—
Bodiford, Margarett A.	35350	Wood	Bodiford, James Leroy	14503
Bodiford, Peter V.	12508	Milam	—	—
Bodine, Attillia	37468	San Augustine	Bodine, John	—
Boecler, Paul	01456	Fayette	—	—
Boehme, Gottlob	00895	Colorado	—	—
Boerner, Louisa	27919	Nueces	Boerner, Hermann	—
Boese, Kate	24984	Milam	Boese, Charles	—
Bogan, Green	Rej	Morris	—	—
Bogard, Thomas Washington	10703	Montague	—	—
Bogg, J. V.	RejM	Wise	—	—
Boggess, Barbra A.	49775	Montague	Boggess, Irby Holt	—
Boggess, Brazzilla Bryan	20212	Rusk	—	—

Index to Confederate Pension Applications

Boggess, Laura Owen	47414	Dallas	Boggess, Rush Welborn	
Boggess, Mariah Parr	21526	Rusk	Boggess, Brazzilla Bryan	20212
Boggess, Nannie J.	19077	Kaufman	Boggess, Henry Jills	
Boggs, James Robert	10749	Tarrant		
Boggs, James Robert Mrs.	20071	Tarrant	Boggs, James Robert	10749
Boggs, James W.	Rej	Edwards		
Boggs, Mary E.	17231	Cherokee	Boggs, C. W.	
Boggs, Nannie J.	Rej	Zavala	Boggs, James Willis	
Boggs, Sallie	23547	Anderson	Boggs, Alva Devotie	
Boggs, Zenas L.	13074	Tarrant		
Boggus, E. L.	01198	Eastland		
Boggus, J. H.	03787	Tarrant		
Boggus, M. E. Mrs.	14778	Caldwell	Boggus, James Carter	
Boggus, Robert Thomas	40674	Palo Pinto		
Boggus, William H.	18846	Brazos		
Bogue, Richard E.	30904	Van Zandt		
Bogy, Joseph Vetoe	16983	Wise		
Bogy, Ruth V.	29231	Wise	Bogy, Joseph Vetoe	16983
Bohannon, C. A. Mrs.	23049	Cass	Bohannon, William Chadwell	05818
Bohannon, Maria	50183	Dallas	Bohannon, Alexander Campbell	
Bohannon, Nancy	08003	Van Zandt	Bohannon, J. M.	
Bohannon, William Chadwell	05818	Cass		
Bohler, A. J. Mrs.	18793	Marion	Bohler, Christopher Columbus	01834
Bohler, Christopher Columbus	01834	Harrison		
Bohm, Emilie	35803	Guadalupe	Bohm, Henry William	
Boisseau, J. R.	Rej	Harrison		
Boisseau, Josephine	Rej	Harrison	Boisseau, James Rivers	
Boland, Josiah Ashberry	27375	Nueces		
Boland, Susan A. M.	37382	Bexar	Boland, Josiah Ashberry	27375
Bolding, Cynthia	35533	Val Verde	Bolding, James A.	23350
Bolding, F. G.	12715	Williamson		
Bolding, J. A.	Rej	Kaufman		
Bolding, James Alison	23350	Tom Green		
Bolding, M. C. Mrs.	13643	Harrison	Bolding, O. W.	
Bolding, Mary E.	13603	Rusk	Bolding, George W.	
Bolding, N. C. Mrs.	Rej	Franklin	Bolding, James Harrison	
Bolding, Parthenia	11291	Harrison	Bolding, William R.	
Bolen, Mathias Edmond	11541	Limestone		
Bolen, Sarah H.	20170	Limestone	Bolen, Mathias Edmond	11541
Boles, Ax	05482	Henderson		
Boles, C. G.	Rej	Cherokee		
Boles, P. A. Mrs.	39901	Potter	Boles, William	29336
Boles, Virginia	30210	Stephens	Boles, John Ashley	
Boles, William	29336	Collin		
Boley, George Lewis	22429	Parker		
Boley, L. A. Mrs.	45545	Parker	Boley, George Lewis	22429
Bolin, Francis Wright	37385	Morris		
Bolin, L. E. Mrs.	43611	Morris	Bolin, Francis Wright	37385
Bolin, M. J. Mrs.	Rej	Orange	Bolin, William R.	
Bolin, Mary Isabell	43987	Dallas	Bolin, William	
Bolin, Sanford W.	10348	Collin		
Bolin, William R.	21281	Orange		
Boling, M. E. Mrs.	37379	Grayson	Boling, Marshall L.	17706
Boling, M. E. Mrs.	51437	Comanche	Boling, Wilford Farris Hampton	
Boling, Marshall L.	17706	Grayson		
Boling, Sarah F.	23783	Bosque	Boling, William H.	11818
Boling, William H.	11818	Bosque		
Bolles, Charles E.	05060	Upshur		
Bolles, James H.	23935	Jackson		

Index to Confederate Pension Applications

Name	App#	County	Related	Related#
Bolleter, Julia	42292	Dallas	Bolleter, Julius	—
Bolling, Cornelia A.	11644	Tarrant	Bolling, J. H.	10482
Bolling, J. H.	10482	Tarrant	—	—
Bolling, Margaret	42015	Erath	Bolling, William Green	41301
Bolling, William Green	41301	Erath	—	—
Bollmeyer, Elizabeth	01463	Fayette	Bollmeyer, William	—
Bolls, Isibelle	09520	Upshur	—	—
Bolmes, Edward A.	35438	Harris	—	—
Bolt, Martin Jasper	08630	Burnet	—	—
Bolt, Mary Jane	43967	Burnet	Bolt, Martin Jasper	08630
Bolton, Arch	Rej	Harris	—	—
Bolton, Daniel E.	19043	Hunt	—	—
Bolton, E.	11375	Cherokee	—	—
Bolton, F. E. Mrs.	Rej	Nueces	Bolton, John Wesley	—
Bolton, J. W.	03282	Panola	—	—
Bolton, J. W.	22969	Somervell	—	—
Bolton, James Alexander	30613	Cherokee	—	—
Bolton, Jasper N.	09370	Wise	—	—
Bolton, Julia A.	36847	Cherokee	Bolton, James Alexander	30613
Bolton, L. F. Mrs.	06708	Cass	Bolton, Bryant R.	—
Bolton, M. E. Mrs.	Rej	Camp	Bolton, E. P.	—
Bolton, M. M. Mrs.	35757	Rusk	Bolton, Wade Austin	30199
Bolton, Maggie	41647	Caldwell	Bolton, Matthew Perryman	30108
Bolton, Matthew Perryman	30108	Caldwell	—	—
Bolton, R. L. Mrs.	19799	Hunt	Bolton, Daniel E.	19043
Bolton, Susie McDonald	45153	Dallas	McDonald, Thomas Benton	—
Bolton, Wade Austin	30199	Rusk	—	—
Bomar, E. J. Mrs.	43965	Hunt	Bomar, John Calvin	—
Bomar, J. R.	Rej	San Saba	—	—
Bomar, Josie	23493	Foard	Bomar, Reuben Clark	—
Bomar, P. R.	46920	Collin	—	—
Bomar, Sarah Catherine	Rej	Harrison	Bomar, William James	—
Bomar, Thomas H.	32697	Reeves	—	—
Bond, J. A.	28251	Ellis	—	—
Bond, J. D.	00876	Collingsworth	—	—
Bond, J. M.	17415	Cass	—	—
Bond, James Morgan	23315	Parker	—	—
Bond, James R.	50924	Kaufman	—	—
Bond, Josie	31903	Parker	Bond, James Morgan	23315
Bond, Miles	40623	Foard	—	—
Bond, Morris L.	26975	Jefferson	—	—
Bond, N. A. Mrs.	44063	Blanco	Bond, Solomon Lafayette	—
Bond, Rebecca W.	46393	Foard	Bond, Miles	40623
Bond, S. A. Mrs.	14736	Brazos	Bond, J. M.	—
Bonds, A. B.	04371	Wharton	—	—
Bonds, Dorcas	03284	Panola	—	—
Bonds, Easter	45719	Madison	Bonds, Carroll	—
Bonds, Mittie	RejM	Bexar	—	—
Bonds, Nancy C.	25165	Jones	Bonds, William Merideth	—
Bonds, Sarah R.	22787	Walker	Bonds, Robert Richard	—
Bone, Francis M.	16475	San Saba	—	—
Bone, Martha Ann	28172	Lamar	Bone, John Bell	—
Bone, Sarah J.	11909	Fisher	Bone, Thomas J.	—
Boney, Martha Jane	46467	Madison	Boney, William James	—
Boney, Z.	10293	Harris	—	—
Bonham, Joseph K.	17641	Fannin	—	—
Bonham, M. L.	10170	Navarro	—	—
Bonham, Samuel	11462	Grayson	—	—
Bonham, Sarah L.	12871	Hardin	Bonham, Milledge L.	—

Index to Confederate Pension Applications

Name	No.	County	Related	No.
Bonin, Gertrude	29521	Harris	Bonin, Telesphere	17756
Bonin, O.	15393	Harris	—	—
Bonin, Telesphere	17756	Harris	—	—
Bonknight, David H. E.	05052	Upshur	—	—
Bonn, Kate	07054	Galveston	Bonn, Henry E.	—
Bonneau, Arnoldus	20092	Harris	—	—
Bonneau, Ella	Rej	Sabine	Bonneau, Arnoldus	20092
Bonneau, H. S.	08562	Sabine	—	—
Bonneau, J. B.	Rej	Parker	—	—
Bonner, Annie F.	35118	Smith	Bonner, Joseph Baker	27212
Bonner, Annie L.	47810	Navarro	Bonner, Joseph Elisha	—
Bonner, Bettie	23246	Cherokee	Bonner, Augustus Henry	—
Bonner, Clara Bell Moore	52004	Cass	Bonner, Francis James	—
Bonner, D. H. L.	21653	Smith	—	—
Bonner, Dempsey Dekalb	18447	Travis	—	—
Bonner, Ellen	Rej	Falls	Bonner, Christopher Columbus	—
Bonner, Emma Green	40880	Parker	Bonner, Robert Willis	31036
Bonner, Emma V.	20627	Travis	Bonner, Dempsey Dekalb	18447
Bonner, John Calvin	07442	Bell	—	—
Bonner, John Henry	38796	Smith	—	—
Bonner, John Henry Mrs.	47612	Smith	Bonner, John Henry	38796
Bonner, Joseph	01835	Harrison	—	—
Bonner, Joseph Baker	27212	Smith	—	—
Bonner, Laura J.	41389	Travis	Bonner, John Columbus	—
Bonner, Martha A.	34820	Caldwell	Bonner, Samuel A.	17396
Bonner, Mary Elizabeth	Rej	Fisher	Bonner, Newsome Sallee	—
Bonner, Mary Jane	16504	Shelby	Bonner, Andrew Jackson	—
Bonner, Mattie F.	19550	Upshur	Bonner, William Decotor	04029
Bonner, Moses J.	47914	Tarrant	—	—
Bonner, Oliver A.	36521	Freestone	—	—
Bonner, Persis Ann	09613	Milam	Bonner, John Calvin	07442
Bonner, Robert Willis	31036	Parker	—	—
Bonner, Samuel A.	17396	Caldwell	—	—
Bonner, William Decotor	04029	Upshur	—	—
Bonner, Willis	Rej	Navarro	—	—
Bonnett, Ella	41251	Dallas	Bonnett, Foster A.	30962
Bonnett, Foster A.	30962	Dallas	—	—
Bonney, C. L.	30366	Caldwell	—	—
Booher, Mary Elizabeth	38104	Montague	Booher, Dory	—
Booker, George Lincoln Mrs.	45050	Somervell	Booker, George Lincoln	—
Booker, Henry	03298	Parker	—	—
Booker, James L.	13037	Rains	—	—
Booker, Martha J. Mrs.	00703	Cass	Booker, G. W.	—
Booker, Mary C.	26450	Rains	Booker, James L.	13037
Booker, Minerva	12099	Parker	Booker, Henry	03298
Booker, Robert S.	37664	Washington	—	—
Booker, William W.	Rej	Upshur	—	—
Bookman, P. E.	10287	Van Zandt	—	—
Bookman, S. E. Mrs.	37674	Grimes	Bookman, Paul Evans	—
Boon, Green Myrack	11583	Navarro	—	—
Boon, John	37193	Tarrant	—	—
Boon, Mary Ann	40486	Falls	Boon, William	—
Boon, N. A.	06463	Johnson	—	—
Boon, Thomas Jefferson	40865	Navarro	—	—
Boon, Thomas Jefferson Mrs.	51148	Navarro	Boon, Thomas Jefferson	40865
Boon, W. W.	Rej	Comanche	—	—
Boone, (James) Henry	09406	Travis	—	—
Boone, B. H.	04370	Wharton	—	—
Boone, Benjamin Howard	21135	Cooke	—	—

Index to Confederate Pension Applications

Name	No.	County	Veteran	No.
Boone, C. E. Mrs.	44073	Cherokee	Boone, John Bliss	
Boone, C. N.	42662	Real		
Boone, D. G.	37698	Wilson		
Boone, Daniel T.	05742	Knox		
Boone, E. F.	22883	Tarrant		
Boone, J. W.	02421	Kimble		
Boone, Jane	39059	Fort Bend	Boone, James Henry	09406
Boone, John Lawrence	31602	Johnson		
Boone, Jonathan Bailey	Rej	Grayson		
Boone, Lacy	30905	Calhoun		
Boone, M. M. Mrs.	09897	Nacogdoches	Boone, S. N.	
Boone, Martha S.	05774	Dallas	Boone, J. B. F.	
Boone, Mary	47894	Tarrant	Boone, Daniel	
Boone, Mary E.	38125	Johnson	Boone, John Lawrence	31602
Boone, Sorata N.	47080	Cameron	Boone, Squire Larkin	39024
Boone, Squire Larkin	39024	Cameron		
Boone, Susan	41840	Cooke	Boone, Benjamin Howard	21135
Boone, Susan L.	02815	McLennan	Boone, Mordecai	
Boone, T. J.	08673	Eastland		
Boone, Thomas W.	30403	Fort Bend		
Boone, William Alonzo	42524	Denton		
Boone, William Alonzo Mrs.	43592	Denton	Boone, William Alonzo	42524
Boone, William R.	09069	Llano		
Booth, E. C. Mrs.	04391	Williamson	Booth, George R.	
Booth, E. T. Mrs.	05164	Brazoria	Booth, W. R.	
Booth, Eliza A.	19442	Bell	Booth, Joseph A.	
Booth, Ella Blanche	33857	Harris	Booth, Charles Monroe	
Booth, Henry Forley James Madison	42732	Johnson		
Booth, J. R. L.	11404	Dallas		
Booth, John Tapley	32972	Jefferson		
Booth, M. A. Mrs.	14509	Eastland	Booth, Q.	05913
Booth, M. E. Mrs.	46540	Johnson	Booth, (Henry Forley) Jas. Madison	42732
Booth, Mollie	38689	Tarrant	Booth, John Tapley	32972
Booth, Q.	05913	Taylor		
Booth, S. A. Mrs.	45129	Callahan	Booth, Abril William	
Booth, Sarah	17574	Dallas	Booth, Charles Thomas	
Booth, Sarah E.	46263	Brazoria	Booth, William	
Booth, Shelbey	12716	Limestone		
Booth, Sheppard Walter Mrs.	35328	Camp	Booth, Sheppard Walter	
Booth, William Le Grand	11958	Hill		
Booth, William Porter	10266	Hill		
Boothe, James S. F.	08842	Bell		
Boothe, Mary Ann	38972	Gonzales	Boothe, George Jefferson	
Boothe, Parolee Anna	47707	Dewitt	Boothe, William Nathaniel	
Boothe, Sarah J.	39715	Milam	Boothe, William Thompson	
Boozer, Christopher Columbus	40961	Morris		
Boozer, Emma	38245	Shelby	Boozer, Jesse Carter	19997
Boozer, G. W.	26515	Morris		
Boozer, Harriett	42823	Morris	Boozer, Christopher Columbus	40961
Boozer, J. O. Mrs.	31681	Burnet	Boozer, Hugh Dickson	
Boozer, Jesse Carter	19997	Shelby		
Boquet, J. V.	Rej	Calhoun		
Borah, Mary F.	51744	Dallas	Borah, William Joshua	
Bordeaux, Rebecca Priscilla	00011	Anderson	Bordeaux, John J.	
Borden, Anna	30870	Jack	Borden, Joe	30189
Borden, Clara V.	47671	Galveston	Borden, James Cochran	
Borden, Eli	07041	Robertson		
Borden, Fannie Q.	49544	Bexar	Borden, Guy	
Borden, Jack W.	33412	Tarrant		

Index to Confederate Pension Applications

Name	Number	County	Veteran	Vet. Number
Borden, Joe	30189	Jack	—	—
Borden, M. J. Mrs.	13649	Limestone	Borden, Eli	07041
Borden, Nannie Denton Elliott	51883A	Tarrant	Denton, John Burnard	08250
Border, Clara	50475	Lubbock	Border, Wade	38343
Border, Sid	04369	Wharton	—	—
Border, Wade	38343	Travis	—	—
Borders, R. D. Mrs.	38662	Gregg	Borders, William Roberts	29027
Borders, William Roberts	29027	Rusk	—	—
Boren, Alexander B.	49021	Montague	—	—
Boren, C. M.	26878	Fannin	—	—
Boren, Camillus Uriah	29497	Tarrant	—	—
Boren, Elizabeth	37553	Tarrant	Boren, Camillus Uriah	29497
Boren, Hattie O.	46852	Ellis	Boren, Joseph S.	—
Boren, Katherine	01994	Hopkins	Boren, Bennett	—
Boren, M. A. Mrs.	Rej	San Augustine	Boren, Will Moultrie	—
Boren, Marium Elizabeth	51798	Montague	Boren, Alexander B.	49021
Boren, Martha	45711	Ellis	Boren, William Milton	—
Boren, Sarah	05750	Mills	Boren, James	—
Boren, Susan	41903	Upshur	Boren, William Lemmons	29794
Boren, William Lemmons	29794	Upshur	—	—
Borge, A. C. Mrs.	26018	Angelina	Borge, Calson McKeiner	—
Bornefeld, Hermania	47967	Victoria	Bornefeld, Julius Albert	—
Bornon, M. C.	35752	Smith	—	—
Boroughs, Tom	RejM	Shelby	—	—
Borrows, Tom	Rej	San Augustine	—	—
Bort, John W.	40256	Real	—	—
Bort, Mary T.	45409	Edwards	Bort, John W.	40256
Borum, Amanda A.	51859	Collin	Borum, Ransom Tucker	33868
Borum, Andrew	43221	Harris	—	—
Borum, Ransom Tucker	33868	Collin	—	—
Borum, William Virgil	26027	Bastrop	—	—
Bose, Julius	00369	Bexar	—	—
Bosley, Sallie	02606	Leon	Bosley, William	—
Boss, John Thomas	06009	Morris	—	—
Boss, Marcus Lafayette	Rej	Collingsworth	—	—
Bost, J. H.	37101	Caldwell	—	—
Bost, L. S.	05433	Caldwell	—	—
Bost, Myrta Manson	51531	Rockwall	Manson, Henry Walker	—
Bost, Susanah	21652	Rockwall	Bost, Jacob	—
Bostian, James Calvin	13718	Bowie	—	—
Bostian, N. E. Mrs.	37369	Bowie	Bostian, James Calvin	13718
Bostick, J. H.	16766	Tyler	—	—
Bostick, Katie T.	50428	Tarrant	Bostick, John	—
Bostick, Martha M.	03680	Smith	Bostick, James M.	—
Bostick, S. E. Mrs.	18503	Van Zandt	Bostick, William	—
Bostick, Sam G.	30349	Harrison	—	—
Bostick, Sarah I.	39821	Jasper	Bostick, William Kyle	15756
Bostick, Sion R.	Rej	San Saba	—	—
Bostick, Susie Ann	Rej	Cherokee	Bostick, Charles Westley	—
Bostick, William Kyle	15756	Jasper	—	—
Bostick, William W.	28226	Harrison	—	—
Boston, J. M.	01638	Grayson	—	—
Boston, Mary	09840	Grayson	Boston, J. M.	01638
Bostwick, Emma	51468	McLennan	Bostwick, Harmon Gilbert	—
Boswell, Elbert	11771	Madison	—	—
Boswell, Hartwell	45620	Dallas	—	—
Boswell, J. L. C.	41526	Hill	—	—
Boswell, James M.	05505	Hopkins	—	—
Boswell, James Polk	22986	Van Zandt	—	—

Index to Confederate Pension Applications

Boswell, James Polk Mrs.	45215	Van Zandt	Boswell, James Polk	22986
Boswell, John Walker Mrs.	Rej	Wichita	Boswell, John Walker	
Boswell, Joseph L.	10093	Hale		
Boswell, Lillie	50639	Dallas	Boswell, Hartwell	45620
Boswell, Rosa F.	40517	Dallas	Boswell, John Jay	
Boswell, Sallie Eugenia	49720	Robertson	Boswell, Richard Pinkney	
Boswell, W. A.	08810	Wheeler		
Boswell, William Mrs.	23338	Tarrant	Boswell, William	
Bosworth, J. A.	Rej	Harris		
Bosworth, Josephine	45793	Lavaca	Bosworth, James Augustus	
Botello, Antonia Gonzales De	04309	Webb	Victor, Sr.	
Botello, Carlota	19338	Wilson	Botello, Victor	
Botello, Concepcion	04314	Webb		
Botello, Ignacia S. De	04312	Webb	Botello, Antonio	
Botello, Matilde	04313	Webb		
Bothwell, Bridget	04954	Bexar	Bothwell, E. H.	
Bott, F. A.	11422	Ellis		
Botter, Annie	34457	Cass	Botter, Jacob Black	
Botto, Cecelia L.	Rej	Bexar	Botto, Louis Thomas	
Bottoms, H. M. Smith Mrs.	38640	Hill	Smith, James Albert	
Bottoms, Reuben H.	04027	Upshur		
Boucher, Lucy A.	41954	McLennan	Boucher, Lewis Alexander	
Bouchillon, Sallie E.	15118	Falls	Bouchillon, Benjamin Franklin	
Boud, Sarah J.	20520	Hunt	Boud, James Monroe	
Boughman, F. M.	RejM	Archer		
Bouknight, E. J. Mrs.	36023	Upshur	Bouknight, James Logan	16796
Bouknight, James L.	16796	Upshur		
Bouknight, Josie	42501	Montague	Bouknight, Milledge Porter	30112
Bouknight, Milledge Porter	30112	Montague		
Boulden, Bettie	04748	El Paso	Boulden, Henry Clay	
Bouldin, Jessie	47241	Gonzales	Bouldin, James Augustus	
Boulter, Alvina J.	51854	Runnels	Boulter, Young Lacy	
Boulter, Anderson B.	40228	Smith		
Boulter, Margaret	50369	Smith	Boulter, Anderson B.	40228
Boultinghouse, John	28234	Burnet		
Boulton, Isaac Goodall	27284	Mills		
Boulware, Martha Elmira	22842	Liberty	Boulware, James Franklin	
Boulware, Thomas P.	17093	Grimes		
Bounds, Benjamin H., Rev.	15723	Hunt		
Bounds, Easter	RejM	Madison		
Bounds, F. M.	35381	Collin		
Bounds, Isaac	Rej	Collingsworth		
Bounds, J. C.	27268	Newton		
Bounds, J. C.	33740	Hardin		
Bounds, L. J. Mrs.	17623	Erath	Bounds, John Wesley	
Bounds, Leonard Rush	28865	Navarro		
Bounds, Lucy Ann	39315	Aransas	Bounds, William Jackson	
Bounds, Mary	Rej	Panola	Bounds, Pascal Lafayette	
Bounds, Mary L.	03623	Shelby	Bounds, Thomas R.	
Bounds, Michael M.	39044	Midland		
Bounds, Nancy J.	33243	Navarro	Bounds, Leonard Rush	28865
Bounds, R. V. Mrs.	49628	Freestone	Bounds, Thomas Allen	
Bounds, Rachel E.	20794	Grimes	Bounds, William Alexander	01681
Bounds, S. C. Mrs.	20473	Hunt	Bounds, Benjamin H.	15723
Bounds, William Alexander	01681	Grimes		
Bourgeois, Joseph D.	Rej	Montgomery		
Bourguin, Edward	Rej	Medina		
Bourguin, Theresa	Rej	Medina	Bourguin, Edward	
Bourland, E. E. Mrs.	34650	Eastland	Bourland, Francis Marion	07802

Index to Confederate Pension Applications

Name	App. No.	County	Veteran	Vet. App. No.
Bourland, Eugenia Loggins	49591	Jasper	Loggins, Arguyle G.	
Bourland, Francis Marion	07802	Eastland		
Bourland, Mary S.	49356	Donley	Bourland, William Reece	
Bourland, Zilpha	50340	Montague	Bourland, Samuel Robert	
Bourn, Mary	50160	Brown	Bourn, Tuck	
Bourne, Nancy	Rej	Grayson	Bourne, Charles Thomas	
Bousmann, Jacob	06705	Bosque		
Boutwell, Alfred R.	03977	Travis		
Boutwell, Mary Jane	34014	Travis	Boutwell, Alfred R.	03977
Bouyer, John Marc	16256	Parker		
Bouyer, Mary C.	36556	Parker	Bouyer, John Marc	16256
Bowden, Charles W.	40077	Brown		
Bowden, D. E. Mrs.	30208	Brown	Bowden, William Sebastian	
Bowden, E. M.	09289	Milam		
Bowden, E. R.	37734	Harris		
Bowden, Henry A.	19453	Walker		
Bowden, John T.	10211	Travis		
Bowden, John W.	30072	Coryell		
Bowden, John W. Mrs.	50949	Bosque	Bowden, John W.	30072
Bowden, Mary J.	45095	Brown	Bowden, Charles W.	40077
Bowden, Samuel B.	06848	Wise		
Bowden, W. S.	26420	Eastland		
Bowden, William Acey	40927	Lamar		
Bowden, William R.	20481	Brown		
Bowdoin, Julia A.	35091	Bowie	Bowdoin, Morris Watts	
Bowe, Henry	11858	Colorado		
Bowen, Alice	40273	Bexar		
Bowen, Cathorine E.	33004	Johnson	Bowen, Samuel Hardeman	32504
Bowen, E.	15499	Hopkins		
Bowen, Elizabeth	18860	Caldwell	Bowen, Joseph Thomas	02524
Bowen, Elizabeth Rebecca	39142	Wharton	Bowen, John Rankin	34178
Bowen, Emaline Mary	Rej	Bell	Bowen, James Tinsley	20891
Bowen, F. E.	27188	Williamson		
Bowen, George H.	22524	McLennan		
Bowen, H. B.	50382	Jack		
Bowen, James Tinsley	20891	Bell		
Bowen, Jasper Newton	27851	Callahan		
Bowen, John Rankin	34178	Wharton		
Bowen, John W.	22647	Clay		
Bowen, John W. Mrs.	37660	Clay	Bowen, John W.	22647
Bowen, Joseph Thomas	02524	Lavaca		
Bowen, Joshua	11670	Tyler		
Bowen, Julia C.	05115	Fannin	Bowen, John A.	
Bowen, Julia O.	14820	Cass	Bowen, William Asberry	
Bowen, Mahala	32149	Dewitt	Bowen, William M.	10601
Bowen, Margaret	30340	Callahan	Bowen, Jasper Newton	27851
Bowen, Martha C.	17309	Bastrop	Bowen, Hiram Cox	
Bowen, Nancy Ellen	51888	Collingsworth	Bowen, Reese	
Bowen, S. A. Mrs.	19328	Wharton	Bowen, William Roe	
Bowen, S. F.	04155	Van Zandt		
Bowen, Samuel Hardeman	32504	Johnson		
Bowen, Samuel P.	Rej	California		
Bowen, Selah E.	14517	Anderson	Bowen, Wiley Henton	
Bowen, T. C.	07639	Montague		
Bowen, W. R.	46658	Bexar		
Bowen, William Jefferson	13624	Johnson		
Bowen, William Jefferson Mrs.	31345	Johnson	Bowen, William Jefferson	13624
Bowen, William M.	10601	Caldwell		
Bowen, William Woodson	13589	Dallas		

Index to Confederate Pension Applications

Bowen, William Woodson Mrs.	41621	Oldham	Bowen, William Woodson	13589
Bower, Christopher John	35451	Limestone	—	—
Bower, Emily V.	50509	Dallas	Bower, Edwin G.	—
Bower, Mahala	43025	Callahan	Bower, Christopher John	35451
Bower, P. C. Mrs.	18729	Limestone	Bower, John Jacob	—
Bower, S. A. Mrs.	Rej	Williamson	Bower, J. P.	—
Bowers, Abraham	40193	Armstrong	—	—
Bowers, Addie	45784	Harris	Bowers, Phillip Rower	17949
Bowers, Alfred Maxey	12939	Johnson	—	—
Bowers, C. Mrs.	44013	Montague	Bowers, Joseph H.	—
Bowers, Clara	52074	Panola	Bowers, Giles	50362
Bowers, Dolly	47403	Falls	Bowers, Sugars	—
Bowers, Emoline	13537	Travis	Bowers, Alfred Maxey	12939
Bowers, Francis Marion Mrs.	50572	Crosby	Bowers, Francis Marion	—
Bowers, George Robert	26876	Dallas	—	—
Bowers, Giles	50362	Panola	—	—
Bowers, Hattie	35092	Johnson	Bowers, Young Philomon	15791
Bowers, James P.	36324	Bandera	—	—
Bowers, John	34146	Wise	—	—
Bowers, John Robert	08459	Collin	—	—
Bowers, Martha Ann	42379	Johnson	Bowers, James W.	—
Bowers, Mary A.	36289	Dallas	Bowers, George Robert	26876
Bowers, Mary Ann	21656	Jefferson	Bowers, John R.	—
Bowers, Phillip Rower	17949	Jefferson	—	—
Bowers, Thomas M.	11828	Bowie	—	—
Bowers, William A. Mrs.	Rej	Gregg	Bowers, William A.	—
Bowers, Young Philomon	15791	Johnson	—	—
Bowlden, Annie	50936	Dallas	Bowlden, Frederick James	42260
Bowlden, Frederick James	42260	Dallas	—	—
Bowles, A. R. Mrs.	39395	Montague	Bowles, George James	—
Bowles, Amanda Parker	35681	Maverick	Bowles, Greenville	—
Bowles, Elizabeth	Rej	Eastland	Bowles, Benjamin Franklin	—
Bowles, Green Berry	Home	Travis	—	—
Bowles, John R.	18945	Fannin	—	—
Bowles, M. E. Mrs.	20946	Travis	Bowles, John Salinas	—
Bowles, M. W.	18976	Grayson	—	—
Bowles, Martha A.	03822	Tarrant	Bowles, Henry S.	—
Bowles, Rilla	Rej	Kaufman	Bowles, N. Lafayette	—
Bowles, Virginia C.	24854	Eastland	Bowles, Boliver	—
Bowles, William Augustus, Sr.	Rej	Uvalde	—	—
Bowlin, Catherine	39946	Jasper	Bowlin, Robert James	—
Bowlin, Elizabeth	18353	Shelby	Bowlin, William Marion	—
Bowlin, J. W.	05777	Dallas	—	—
Bowlin, Joseph Henry	18403	Tarrant	—	—
Bowlin, Julia A.	38393	Tarrant	Bowlin, Joseph Henry	18403
Bowlin, M. M. Mrs.	43468	Wise	Bowlin, Newton Rhea	—
Bowlin, Susan M.	31854	Collin	Bowlin, Solomon	—
Bowling, George W.	46626	Bexar	—	—
Bowling, James Alexander	30163	Kaufman	—	—
Bowling, James W.	06524	Wood	—	—
Bowling, M. J. Mrs.	14876	Cherokee	Bowling, Larkin Sanders	—
Bowling, Martha A.	31999	Wood	Bowling, James W.	06524
Bowling, Mary Alice	47396	Travis	Bowling, William Riley	—
Bowling, Sallie B.	32455	Kaufman	Bowling, James Alexander	30163
Bowling, William J.	20695	Donley	—	—
Bowls, George F.	12469	Kaufman	—	—
Bowman, Brina E.	48062	Collin	Bowman, George Washington	—
Bowman, E. E. Mrs.	36215	Grayson	Bowman, James Redford	—
Bowman, Elizabeth	51787	Bexar	Bowman, Tyre (Tira)	—

Index to Confederate Pension Applications

Name	App #	County	Veteran	Vet App #
Bowman, Fannie A.	43337	Bexar	Bowman, James Holly	
Bowman, George	Rej	Wichita		
Bowman, H. D.	14384	Robertson		
Bowman, Henry	05833	Cooke		
Bowman, John	40987	Bosque		
Bowman, John Hester	30246	Johnson		
Bowman, John Hester Mrs.	38600	Johnson	Bowman, John Hester	30246
Bowman, Josephine	33894	Medina	Bowman, Jackson	
Bowman, Margaret L.	36152	Cooke	Bowman, Henry	05833
Bowman, Martha Jane	31561	Hunt	Bowman, Alfred De Lafayette	
Bowman, Mary J.	49284	Travis	Bowman, Thornton Hardie	
Bowman, Sam Houston	32169	Childress		
Bowman, Samuel J.	28102	Taylor		
Bowman, Sarah J.	35490	Childress	Bowman, Sam Houston	32169
Bowman, William H.	00523	Brazos		
Bownds, Mattie	Rej	Lee	Bownds, William	
Bowser, Alida	49293	Dallas	Bowser, Benjamin Franklin	
Box, Andrew Jackson	30568	Kaufman		
Box, Ann L.	09165	Cherokee	Box, Severe D.	
Box, Bell P.	18828	Bell	Box, Francis Soloman	
Box, E. H. Mrs.	Rej	Red River	Box, John Wesley	
Box, Eliza A.	39119	Cameron	Box, Frank M.	
Box, Ellen	19231	Rusk	Box, Benjamin Barton	
Box, Emeline	21658	Runnels	Box, George Washington	
Box, J. P.	Rej	Llano		
Box, James Rubin Mrs.	34469	Van Zandt	Box, James Rubin	
Box, John Jasper Wesley	15596	Houston		
Box, Josie	49008	Hill	Box, William Floyd	
Box, Laura Jane	39870	Montague	Box, Milow R.	
Box, Lottie	32105	Kaufman	Box, Andrew Jackson	30568
Box, Louisa	41569	Hidalgo	Box, Lina Helen	
Box, R. H.	Rej	Sterling		
Box, Robert D.	43202	Anderson		
Box, S. E. Mrs.	31381	Tarrant	Box, M. D. Lafayette	
Box, Sarah C.	43122	Van Zandt	Box, William A.	39808
Box, Sarah J.	15593	Houston	Box, William Henderson	
Box, Susan Adeline	32413	Cherokee	Box, John Jasper Wesley	15596
Box, William A.	39808	Van Zandt		
Boxley, Elizabeth Virginia	35981	Brazos	Boxley, Richard Henry Lee	
Boyce, Henry W.	10852	Burnet		
Boyce, John Brandon	26761	McLennan		
Boyce, Lucy Margaret	28326	Travis	Boyce, James Orville	
Boyce, Mary A.	49004	Uvalde	Boyce, Milton Carroll	25173
Boyce, Mary F.	07839	Harris	Boyce, R. P.	
Boyce, Mary O. S.	47068	Travis	Boyce, William	
Boyce, Milton Carroll	25173	Uvalde		
Boyce, Richard T.	Rej	Burnet		
Boyce, Sarah Elizabeth	23453	Dallas	Boyce, Richard Thomas	
Boyd, A. B. Mrs.	42350	Parker	Boyd, Franklin Marion	
Boyd, A. E. Mrs.	Rej	Cass	Boyd, William Ellison	
Boyd, A. E. Prichard Mrs.	25600	Cass	Prichard, Anderson	
Boyd, Amanda H.	18170	Morris	Boyd, Oliver P.	03087
Boyd, B. F.	18019	Leon		
Boyd, Bradford Martin	15472	Hill		
Boyd, Bradford Martin Mrs.	35093	Hill	Boyd, Bradford Martin	15472
Boyd, C. T. Mrs.	05201	Delta	Boyd, E. W.	
Boyd, Calvin V.	Rej	Collin		
Boyd, David	11589	Navarro		
Boyd, Eliza	05421	Hill	Boyd, John	

Index to Confederate Pension Applications

Boyd, Eliza	42490	Wise	Boyd, Thomas	39417
Boyd, Eugenia Gertrude	50249	Hidalgo	Boyd, Robert Cleveland	—
Boyd, Eva	45219	Bell	Boyd, William Daniel	—
Boyd, Fannie	49974	Archer	Boyd, John Allen	—
Boyd, Felix Young Mrs.	43383	Bell	Boyd, Felix Young	—
Boyd, Francis M.	10699	McLennan	—	—
Boyd, Henry Thomas	35000	Hill	—	—
Boyd, Hugh Dunlap	15023	Dallas	—	—
Boyd, Isaac Alexander Mrs.	46146	Lubbock	Boyd, Isaac Alexander	—
Boyd, J. C.	24729	Hopkins	—	—
Boyd, J. J.	13311	Freestone	—	—
Boyd, J. J.	22908	Titus	—	—
Boyd, J. S.	26451	Williamson	—	—
Boyd, James	20271	Travis	—	—
Boyd, James	26166	Bell	—	—
Boyd, James A.	28511	Navarro	—	—
Boyd, James Mrs.	34898	Tom Green	Boyd, James	26166
Boyd, James R.	Rej	Scurry	—	—
Boyd, Jane	25469	Henderson	Boyd, William	—
Boyd, John	34638	Lavaca	—	—
Boyd, John A. Mrs.	38667	Tarrant	Boyd, John A.	—
Boyd, John J.	Rej	Montague	—	—
Boyd, M. A. Mrs.	43858	Burnet	Boyd, James	20271
Boyd, M. C.	Rej	Childress	—	—
Boyd, M. E. Mrs.	Rej	Wood	Boyd, Thomas Benton	13125
Boyd, M. V.	03294	Parker	—	—
Boyd, Martha E.	43344	Bell	Boyd, Isaac	—
Boyd, Martha Josephine	47067	El Paso	Boyd, James Gordon Davis	—
Boyd, Mary R.	18899	Comanche	Boyd, Larkin Madison	—
Boyd, Millie Jane	38058	Potter	Boyd, Moses Ervin	—
Boyd, Oliver P.	03087	Morris	—	—
Boyd, Robert Ross	30843	Anderson	—	—
Boyd, Sallie E.	30285	Henderson	Boyd, Andrew Emmett	—
Boyd, Sarah F.	10816	Austin	Boyd, Thomas W.	—
Boyd, Sarah K.	39669	Dallas	Boyd, Hugh Dunlap	15023
Boyd, Sarah Rebecca	31354	Anderson	Boyd, Robert Ross	30843
Boyd, Syrena A.	Rej	Hill	Boyd, William J.	—
Boyd, T. D. Mrs.	42568	Tom Green	Boyd, Theodore D.	36712
Boyd, Theodore D.	36712	Tom Green	—	—
Boyd, Thomas	39417	Wise	—	—
Boyd, Thomas Benton	13125	Wood	—	—
Boyd, W. E.	36370	Cass	—	—
Boyd, W. W.	45012	Johnson	—	—
Boyd, William	14677	Bell	—	—
Boyd, William H.	07600	Grayson	—	—
Boyd, William J.	05418	Hill	—	—
Boyd, William J.	46400	Falls	—	—
Boyd, Willie Mrs.	16323	Robertson	Boyd, James Boyce	—
Boyd, Willis Woodward	08932	Bell	—	—
Boyd, Willis Woodward Mrs.	34456	Bell	Boyd, Willis Woodward	08932
Boydston, B. F., Sr.	07702	Marion	—	—
Boydstun, John D.	42259	Callahan	—	—
Boyer, Dan	42702	Anderson	—	—
Boyer, G. M.	Rej	Rains	—	—
Boyer, George Melville	41187	Cooke	—	—
Boyer, Jennie	45580	Fannin	Boyer, George Melville	41187
Boyer, Stephen	10565	Bexar	—	—
Boyet, Elzie	16153	Nacogdoches	—	—
Boyet, Sarah Allen	19843	Nacogdoches	Boyet, Elzie	16153

Index to Confederate Pension Applications

Name	Number	County	Veteran	Vet. No.
Boyet, William	06642	San Augustine	—	
Boyett, C. H.	Rej	Nolan	—	
Boyett, Elijah Walkup	12392	Harris	—	
Boyett, Jefferson Mrs.	34043	Nacogdoches	Boyett, Jefferson	
Boyett, M. E. Mrs.	20827	Wise	Boyett, James Elijah	
Boyett, Mary A.	Rej	Henderson	Boyett, Silas Lodwick (lodrick)	27998
Boyett, Silas Lodrick	27998	Henderson	—	
Boyett, William B. Mrs.	34204	Nacogdoches	Boyett, William B.	
Boykin, Ebb Mrs.	47825	Runnels	Boykin, Ebb	
Boykin, Edna A.	42027	Parker	Boykin, James Wilburn	11087
Boykin, Elbe R.	29952	Jones	Boykin, Starling Ray	
Boykin, Eliza Jane	09002	Dewitt	Boykin, W. J.	01171
Boykin, Francis Marion	27235	Concho	—	
Boykin, J. E.	08674	Eastland	—	
Boykin, James Wilburn	11087	Parker	—	
Boykin, John	02074	Houston	—	
Boykin, Martha E.	22370	Comanche	Boykin, William Alfred	
Boykin, Martha Jane	45721	Bexar	Boykin, Francis Marion	27235
Boykin, Mollie Ann	31041	Van Zandt	Boykin, Robert Sanford	
Boykin, Sarah A.	02605	Leon	Boykin, James A.	
Boykin, Susan	17290	Angelina	Boykin, William Y.	
Boykin, T. J.	05692	Erath	—	
Boykin, W. J.	01171	Dewitt	—	
Boyle, George Curling	23584	Young	—	
Boyle, J. W. W.	22887	Brown	—	
Boyle, Martha T.	21657	Bexar	Boyle(s), John	03900
Boyle, Mary Francis	35654	Young	Boyle, George Curling	23584
Boyle, Thomas	02789	Matagorda	—	
Boyles, Ann Eliza	14468	Van Zandt	Boyle)s, William P.	12669
Boyles, D. H.	45465	Falls	—	
Boyles, Gabriel Hardin	43566	Parker	—	
Boyles, Johnnie	03900	Travis	—	
Boyles, Mary E.	43591	Parker	Boyles, Gabriel Hardin	43566
Boyles, Mattie	Rej	Clay	Boyles, William Henry	
Boyls, Mary Catherine	30013	Wilson	Boyls, Sylvester	
Boyls, William P.	12669	Van Zandt	—	
Boynton, G. M.	23810	Lynn	—	
Boynton, M. E. Mrs.	19232	Rusk	Boynton, Andrew Jackson	
Boynton, Winnie Jane	Rej	Wood	Boynton, Samuel	
Boyter, Fannie J.	43214	Parker	Boyter, James Levi	
Boze, Eliza	50979	Fannin	Boze, Josiah	49674
Boze, Josiah	49674	Fannin	—	
Boze, Martha Mirandy	37868	Ellis	Boze, William George	
Bozeman, A. C.	26186	Jefferson	—	
Bozeman, J. R.	Home	Travis	—	
Bozeman, Joseph Hill	23304	Limestone	—	
Bozeman, Joseph Hill Mrs.	42566	Limestone	Bozeman, Joseph Hill	23304
Bozeman, Sarah A.	22753	Milam	Bozeman, William Morris	
Bozzell, E. H. Mrs.	16218	Palo Pinto	Bozzell, William	
Bozzell, Joseph Arch	43805	Palo Pinto	—	
Bozzell, Martha Rena	46302	Palo Pinto	Bozzell, Joseph Arch	43805
Bra, C. P.	RejM	Leon	—	
Brabson, Ann	47999	Parker	Brabson, Thomas M.	
Brace, James	02817	McLennan	—	
Bracewell, M. E. Mrs.	18991	Grimes	Bracewell, Joseph Marion	
Brachear, W. C.	RejM	Harris	—	
Brack, Edward Dargan	45165	Wichita	—	
Brack, H. F.	08432M	Newton	—	
Brack, Henderson F.	Rej	Newton	—	

Index to Confederate Pension Applications

Brack, Joseph	41108	Grayson		
Brack, Joseph Mrs.	41981	Grayson	Brack, Joseph	41108
Brack, S. C. Mrs.	30473	Angelina	Brack, Robert Toombs	
Brack, Susanna	40288	Wichita	Brack, William Bolding	
Brackeen, Albert James	Rej	Fannin		
Brackeen, H. I. Mrs.	26690	Hunt	Brackeen, Nathaniel Terry	
Brackeen, Hiram Alonzo	35033	Taylor		
Brackeen, John G.	Rej	Van Zandt		
Brackeen, L. J. Mrs.	34620	Hopkins	Brackeen, William C.	28998
Brackeen, Lucy Jane	51627	Motley	Brackeen, Allen Hill	
Brackeen, Mary Francis	49606	Wichita	Brackeen, Hiram Alonzo	35033
Brackeen, William C.	28998	Hopkins		
Brackeer, E. J.	07986	Delta		
Brackenridge, Lavina A.	22409	Kaufman	Brackenridge, Thomas Emerson	14467
Brackenridge, Thomas Emerson	14467	Van Zandt		
Brackin, Asa Pardue Mrs.	Rej	Lubbock	Brackin, Asa Pardue	
Brackun, A. J.	28476	Fannin		
Bradberry, J. E.	01658	Gregg		
Bradberry, John	Rej	Coryell		
Bradberry, Nancy Jane	25068	Panola	Bradberry, Joseph Wingo	
Bradburn, C. C.	Rej	Van Zandt		
Bradbury, Andrew Jackson	14471	Waller		
Bradbury, Ann	11692	Waller	Bradbury, Alfred	
Bradbury, Henry Clay	25791	Caldwell		
Bradbury, M. A. Mrs.	42234	Caldwell	Bradbury, Henry Clay	25791
Bradbury, Mary E.	17661	Fisher	Bradbury, Aaron G.	
Braddock, A. M. Mrs.	RejM	Travis		
Braddock, Callie Dorria	51672	Young	Braddock, Elbert Marion	
Braddock, J. S.	02437	Lamar		
Braddock, Joseph D. (John)	10222	Travis		
Braddock, K. H. Mrs.	34857	Brown	Braddock, Perry Greenfield	
Braddy, Ben J.	28189	Wilson		
Braddy, Eliza Ann	38051	Bosque	Braddy, James L.	27886
Braddy, James B.	03226	Palo Pinto		
Braddy, James J.	17361	Bowie		
Braddy, James L.	27886	Bosque		
Braddy, M. J. Mrs.	18569	Wood	Braddy, William J.	
Braden, Andreas Mrs.	46971	Colorado	Braden, Andreas	
Braden, Edward	07833B	Bexar		
Braden, Felix Grundy	29953	Hopkins		
Braden, M. A. Mrs.	46034	Bexar	Braden, John Corson	
Braden, M. J. Mrs.	50386	Hopkins	Braden, Felix Grundy	29953
Braden, Mathilda	43341	Matagorda	Braden, Adam Braden	
Braden, N. J. Mrs.	17877	Hopkins	Braden, Absalom D.	
Braden, Rachel P.	04649	Knox	Braden, Gabriel A.	
Braden, T. M.	26464	Hopkins		
Bradfield, J. O.	Home	Travis		
Bradfield, James O.	Rej	Harrison		
Bradfield, John A.	33132	Dallas		
Bradfield, John Randolph	20059	Upshur		
Bradfield, John Rufus	25183	Eastland		
Bradfield, Nettie	32920	Terry	Bradfield, John Rufus	25183
Bradford, Amanda Jane	10230	Waller	Bradford, Joseph Woods	
Bradford, Eliza	32721	Bastrop	Bradford, William Thomas	08177
Bradford, Emma	49139	Bell	Bradford, James Madison	31668
Bradford, Francis Caroline	06317	Henderson	Bradford, Frank	
Bradford, H. E.	14507	Bell		
Bradford, James Madison	31668	Limestone		
Bradford, Martha Virginia	29055	Wilbarger	Bradford, Samuel G.	27414

Index to Confederate Pension Applications

Name	No.	County	Veteran	No.
Bradford, Mary E.	Rej	Smith	Bradford, William A.	—
Bradford, Nancy H.	29579	Palo Pinto	Bradford, James Randolph	—
Bradford, Nathaniel C.	39165	Fannin	—	—
Bradford, Powell Luke	37430	Anderson	—	—
Bradford, Samuel G.	27414	Wilbarger	—	—
Bradford, Scottie Rebecca	39947	Anderson	Bradford, Powell Luke	37430
Bradford, William Thomas	08177	Austin	—	—
Bradley, A. V. Mrs.	34651	Hood	Bradley, George Alexander	21463
Bradley, Bettie Lee	49727	Tarrant	Bradley, John Mosby	16636
Bradley, Charity	46667	Ellis	Bradley, Joseph Fouler	—
Bradley, Crayton	01501	Franklin	—	—
Bradley, Dan	09403	Lavaca	—	—
Bradley, David Richardson	12118	Rusk	—	—
Bradley, E. J. Mrs.	20440	Rusk	Bradley, David Richardson	12118
Bradley, F. A.	23353	Callahan	—	—
Bradley, George	26407	Cooke	—	—
Bradley, George Alexander	21463	Erath	—	—
Bradley, George Ann	23138	Henderson	Bradley, William Frederick	—
Bradley, H. E. Mrs.	19040	Houston	Bradley, Madison Monroe	—
Bradley, H. E. Mrs.	43438	Limestone	Bradley, Samuel Alexander	24859
Bradley, Helen Sarah Chipman	30778	Dallas	Bradley, Joseph William	—
Bradley, Henry	Rej	Freestone	—	—
Bradley, Henry F.	Rej	Hamilton	—	—
Bradley, I. N.	02816	McLennan	—	—
Bradley, J. C.	25345	Hopkins	—	—
Bradley, J. J.	02427	Kimble	—	—
Bradley, J. M.	23321	Camp	—	—
Bradley, J. S.	11081	Parker	—	—
Bradley, James Warren	18200	Navarro	—	—
Bradley, John Bunyan, Sr. Mrs.	49801	Johnson	John Bunyan, Sr.	—
Bradley, John Firvin	31900	Grimes	—	—
Bradley, John Flem T.	17215	Van Zandt	—	—
Bradley, John Mosby	16636	Tarrant	—	—
Bradley, John R.	24915	Rusk	—	—
Bradley, John Williams	23308	McLennan	—	—
Bradley, Linnie	32986	Grimes	Bradley, John Firvin	31900
Bradley, Louisa	14234	Galveston	Bradley, Francis V.	—
Bradley, Martha	15166	Franklin	Bradley, Jasper Perry	—
Bradley, Mary E.	33034	Cooke	Bradley, George	26407
Bradley, Mary Ellen	19549	Van Zandt	Bradley, John Flem	17215
Bradley, Mary Lee	45058	Camp	Bradley, Crayton	01501
Bradley, N. H.	05400	Hill	—	—
Bradley, Nancy P.	00997	Coryell	Bradley, W. H.	—
Bradley, R. S.	07693	Collin	—	—
Bradley, Rebecca	45296	Rusk	Bradley, John R.	24915
Bradley, S. B.	11310	Erath	—	—
Bradley, Samuel Alexander	24859	Limestone	—	—
Bradley, Samuel J.	04030	Upshur	—	—
Bradley, Sarah D.	Rej	Lavaca	Bradley, Daw	—
Bradley, Silas	23916	Knox	—	—
Bradley, T. F.	05358	Grayson	—	—
Bradley, William	30103	Jefferson	—	—
Bradshaw, Cyrus Franklin	08593	Tarrant	—	—
Bradshaw, Faney	08558	Limestone	—	—
Bradshaw, H. F. Mrs.	39594	Parker	Bradshaw, William Franklin	33399
Bradshaw, John	02684	Limestone	—	—
Bradshaw, Josiah Allen	15927	Liberty	—	—
Bradshaw, Lanora Ann	30855	Bastrop	Bradshaw, Samuel Kendrick	00187
Bradshaw, M. E. Mrs.	16616	Smith	Bradshaw, Paschal Green	—

Index to Confederate Pension Applications

Name	App#	County	Veteran	Vet App#
Bradshaw, Mary	Rej	Grayson	Bradshaw, J. T.	
Bradshaw, Mary E.	Rej	Smith	Bradshaw, P. G.	
Bradshaw, Nancy Jane	21148	Liberty	Bradshaw, Josiah Allen	15927
Bradshaw, R. D.	50500	Lee		
Bradshaw, Samuel Kendrick	00187	Bastrop		
Bradshaw, Sarah E.	47833	Fayette	Bradshaw, Amzi Thornton	
Bradshaw, W. C.	05408	Hill		
Bradshaw, William Franklin	33399	Stephens		
Bradstreet, Clara Amando Josephine	44065	Wilbarger	Br(o)adstreet, Jos. Rawls	11948
Bradwell, Ellen	36692	Kerr	Bradwell, Thomas Marion	02414
Bradwell, Thomas Marion	02414	Kerr		
Brady, Alexander	01995	Hopkins		
Brady, Alfred E.	Rej	Milam		
Brady, Asa	01996	Hopkins		
Brady, J. C.	22323	Panola		
Brady, John W.	29937	Titus		
Brady, Joseph P.	27327	Leon		
Brady, King	Rej	Hood		
Brady, M. C. Mrs.	43235	Limestone	Brady, James T.	
Brady, Mary L.	08936	Hill	Brady, George W.	
Brady, Mary V.	18366	Shelby	Brady, Charles Underwood	
Brady, Owen	19035	Houston		
Brady, Rutha	19031	Hopkins	Brady, Alexander	01995
Brady, S. E. Mrs.	39752	Dallas	Brady, Alfred Edmond	
Brady, Sallie	39950	Panola	Brady, J. C.	22323
Brady, Susan	46677	Hood	Brady, King McDonald	
Brady, Susan C.	Rej	Denton	Brady, Phillip Gross	
Brady, W. J.	17848	Hopkins		
Brady, William W.	41123	Leon		
Brady, William Wilkins	39012	Leon		
Bragg, Emily Waters	49228	Jim Wells	Bragg, Thomas Miles	
Bragg, J. J.	35087	Haskell		
Bragg, Melissa P.	19666	Terry	Bragg, George Bruton	
Bragg, T. P.	23416	Tarrant		
Braim, Parthena Ann	02608	Leon	Braim, William	
Braley, Erastus Asberry	07275	Kimble		
Braley, Lena	Rej	Kimble	Braley, Erastus Asberry	07275
Braley, Mandy	Rej	Polk	Braley, James S.	
Braley, Martha	10468	Shelby	Braley, James	
Braley, Milledge B.	12354	Fannin		
Braley, V. A. Mrs.	27865	Bowie	Braley, Joseph Warren	
Bralley, Catherine B.	RejM	Fannin		
Bralley, Catherine L.	Rej	Cooke	Bralley, John	
Bralley, Sarah Ann	36987	Fannin	Bralley, James Dennie	
Braly, Frances E.	36806	Montague	Braly, Millege Britan	
Bramblitt, Elkana Columbus	43044	Dallas		
Brame, Richard Samuel	30335	Lamar		
Brame, Sallie	33691	Lamar	Brame, Richard Samuel	30335
Bramham, J. H.	06182	Dewitt		
Bramlet, S. G.	43154	Travis		
Bramlett, Amanda	21659	McLennan	Bramlett, James Thomas	21433
Bramlett, Francis J.	17934	Johnson	Bramlett, John Lenorah	
Bramlett, James Thomas	21433	McLennan		
Brammin, Samuel D.	23239	Dallas		
Bran, Emma D.	46363	Harris	Bran, Samuel Edwards	
Branan, Emma	Rej	Upshur	Branan, Jessie Turison	
Branan, I. J. Mrs.	Rej	Hopkins	Branan, Luther B.	
Branan, Ida	49509	Hopkins	Branan, Luther Birrens	
Branch, Anthony Martin Mrs.	29053	McLennan	Branch, Anthony Martin	

Index to Confederate Pension Applications

Branch, Bama G.	37526	Walker	Branch, James Law	—
Branch, Dollie	Rej	Delta	Branch, Tom	—
Branch, Henry	Rej	Cherokee	—	—
Branch, J. W.	02231	Irion	—	—
Branch, L. A. Gilchriest Mrs.	49105	Jasper	Gilchriest, S. A.	15759
Branch, Laru Clemantine	26914	Rusk	Branch, James Burt	—
Branch, Lucinda E.	30516	Collin	Branch, John Thomas	—
Branch, Martha Susan	30871	McLennan	Branch, William	20732
Branch, Mary	Rej	Collin	Branch, Thomas Andrew	—
Branch, Mary E.	20128	Frio	Branch, La Fayette	—
Branch, Nancy Jane	43701	Cooke	Branch, James Evert	—
Branch, Sallie	35579	Hunt	Branch, Sam	28888
Branch, Sam	28888	Hunt	—	—
Branch, William	20732	Stephens	—	—
Brand, Alexander	13090	Travis	—	—
Brand, D. P. M.	Rej	Somervell	—	—
Brand, Malisa Jane	51143	Johnson	Brand, Robert Matthias Cleveland	22551
Brand, Margaret S.	40118	Lamar	Brand, William Henry	—
Brand, Robert Matthias Cleveland	22551	Johnson	—	—
Brandenburg, Sarah Josephene	47393	Dallas	Brandenburg, Benjamin Franklin	—
Brandenburg, Theresa Montgomery	03785	Tarrant	Brandenburg, Solomon I.	—
Brandes, F. W.	40336	Austin	—	—
Brandon, Artimecia	29647	Young	Brandon, Rufus Lafayette	24346
Brandon, J. Dewitt Mrs.	39957	Van Zandt	Brandon, J. Dewitt	—
Brandon, J. W.	23277	Johnson	—	—
Brandon, Mary S.	37568	Hamilton	Brandon, William	—
Brandon, N. G.	26853	Nacogdoches	—	—
Brandon, Rufus Lafayette	24346	Young	—	—
Brandon, William Jordan	Rej	Delta	—	—
Brandstatter, Alexander	01467	Fayette	—	—
Brandstatter, Alexander Mrs.	18808	Fayette	Brandstatter, Alexander	01467
Brandt, H. A.	Rej	Fayette	—	—
Brandt, Nancy	51722	Washington	Brandt, Henry Christian	—
Branham, John T.	23230	Walker	—	—
Brannan, George W.	09714	Irion	—	—
Brannan, James C.	21555	Taylor	—	—
Brannan, Nancy	06234	Coleman	Brannan, W. W.	—
Brannan, W. L.	12665	Van Zandt	—	—
Brannen, Ann Foster	37299	Erath	Brannen, John Adams William	25668
Brannen, John Adams Williams	25668	Erath	—	—
Brannon, Beverly Bazel	15431	Henderson	—	—
Brannon, Ellen	23302	Ellis	Brannon, Ishmael	—
Brannon, G. B.	Rej	Titus	—	—
Brannon, M. A. Mrs.	RejM	Hill	—	—
Brannon, Martha Ann	31698	Henderson	Brannon, Beverly Bazel	15431
Branom, A.	47917	Hopkins	—	—
Branom, William Jefferson	47365	Hopkins	—	—
Branom, William Jefferson Mrs.	Rej	Hopkins	Branom, William Jefferson	47365
Branon, James D.	38666	Lavaca	—	—
Bransom, J. B. Mrs.	51210	Van Zandt	Bransom, James B.	31230
Bransom, James B.	31230	Van Zandt	—	—
Bransom, James William	42167	Johnson	—	—
Bransom, Martha E.	Rej	Anderson	Bransom, Stephen Allen	—
Bransom, Nancy J.	42398	Johnson	Bransom, James William	42167
Branson, A. J.	33679	Ellis	—	—
Branson, Araminta	43933	McLennan	Friend, Nathaniel	—
Branson, G. W.	02295	Johnson	—	—
Branson, James Sanford	06004	Morris	—	—
Branson, Mattie Elizabeth	50965	Anderson	Branson, Stephen Allen	—

Index to Confederate Pension Applications

Brant, A. G.	24960	Jack		
Brant, Harriet Jane	33066	Jack	Brant, A. G.	24960
Brantley, Anna W.	21438	Burleson	Brantley, Robert Augustus	
Brantley, Eben	01538	Glasscock		
Brantley, H. T. Mrs.	Rej	Collin	Brantley, Henry Taylor	40226
Brantley, Henry Taylor	40226	Collin		
Brantley, J. D.	02769	Mason		
Brantley, John	49353	Titus		
Brantley, M. P. Mrs.	09599	Glasscock	Brantley, E.	
Brantley, Mineriva M.	31881	Brown	Brantley, John Hightower	
Brantley, S. A. Mrs.	29204	Red River	Brantley, John Henry	
Brantley, Thomas	05978	Fisher		
Branton, Adeline L.	46814	Grimes	Branton, Henry Hamilton	
Branton, William E.	09018	Galveston		
Branum, James M.	00186	Bastrop		
Branum, Sarah F.	32994	Wharton	Branum, James M.	00186
Branum, Thomas P.	Rej	Franklin		
Brasell, Bettie	36447	Erath	Brasell, Roland Franklin	15090
Brasell, Roland Franklin	15090	Erath		
Braselton, J. R.	38832	Parker		
Braser, Rachel	18236	Panola	Braser, Richard Stewart	
Brashear, B. A.	RejM	Lever		
Brashear, B. C.	17952	Jefferson		
Brashear, C. P. Mrs.	Rej	Leon	Brashear, John Brazil	
Brashear, L. T.	13526	Tarrant		
Brashear, M. R. Mrs.	02661	Liberty	Brashear, Neville D.	
Brashear, Martha	36158	Bosque	Brashear, Morgan Walter	24610
Brashear, Minnie	51942	Harris	Brashear, William Claude	35001
Brashear, Morgan Walter	24610	Bosque		
Brashear, Permelia	05357	Grayson	Brashear, Levi	
Brashear, Rhodes R.	43938	Comanche		
Brashear, Stephen B.	00732	Chambers		
Brashear, William Claude	35001	Harris		
Brashears, Elizabeth	00026	Angelina	Brashears, Jesse W.	
Brashears, Frances S.	04716	Freestone		
Brashears, L. A. Mrs.	50072	Eastland	Brashears, William Colonel Runnels	
Brashears, W. C.	Rej	Parker		
Brasher, C. E. Mrs.	32481	Coryell	Brasher, Samuel	
Brasher, E. T., Rev.	15586	Houston		
Brasher, Julia Catherine	35363	Hamilton	Brasher, T. H.	06704
Brasher, M. E. Mrs.	18570	Wood	Brasher, George Thomas	
Brasher, T. H.	06704	Bosque		
Brashier, James Thomas	12036	Lynn		
Brashier, Sallie E.	34848	Tarrant	Brashier, James Thomas	12036
Brassell, James M.	43279	Panola		
Brassell, Mary Francis	51944	Panola	Brassell, James M.	43279
Brassell, W. T.	41369	Navarro		
Brassell, W. T. Mrs.	50477	Navarro	Brassell, W. T.	41369
Braswell, B. A.	Rej	Lee		
Braswell, George Washington	33163	Nolan		
Braswell, M. E. Mrs.	29910	Falls	Braswell, William Nicholas	
Braswell, S. N.	13282	Dallas		
Bratcher, Amanda	49940	Tarrant	Bratcher, William Paxton	
Bratton, David L.	07289	McCulloch		
Bratton, Eliza	16088	Morris	Bratton, Y. Earvan	06005
Bratton, Laura R. Fulks	52019	Kerr	Fulks, Edmund Newton	
Bratton, Lavinia N.	Rej	Tarrant	Bratton, Thomas	
Bratton, Mary J.	18417	Tarrant	Bratton, James Alexander	
Bratton, W. H.	03901	Travis		

Index to Confederate Pension Applications

Bratton, Y. Earvan	06005	Morris	—	
Braun, Fredericka	19898	Victoria	Braun, August Fernand	—
Braun, Pauline	36695	Harris	Braun, Henry Carl	—
Braun, Theresa	19058	Jefferson	Braun, Louis Mannon	—
Brawley, John Addison	37039	Hill	—	
Brawley, John Addison Mrs.	37301	Hill	Brawley, John Addison	37039
Brawner, M. M. Mrs.	23980	Erath	Brawner, John Floyd	—
Bray, Isaac Manley	34120	Van Zandt	—	
Bray, James	30314	Hardeman	—	
Bray, James H.	32762	Bexar	—	
Bray, James L.	Rej	Wise	—	
Bray, Jesse N.	14147	Cass	—	
Bray, John Stanford	29142	Fannin	—	
Bray, M. A. Mrs.	24557	Harrison	Bray, Lewis Ranson	—
Brazeal, E. P. Mrs.	34437	Limestone	Brazeal, John Thomas	—
Brazeale, Ellen Jane	31697	Burnet	Brazeale, Jeff	—
Brazee, S. F. Mrs.	04412	Williamson	Brazee, W. C.	—
Brazel, Missouri Ann	49124	Tarrant	Brazel, Elijah Valentine	—
Brazele, Kate	51277	Hale	Brazele, William Clarke	—
Brazell, I. P.	47369	Shackelford	—	
Brazell, L. C. Mrs.	05816	Cass	Brazell, James C.	—
Brazell, Martha R.	27775	Kaufman	Brazell, Oliver Hazard	—
Brazelton, Hannah Margaret	34037	Brazoria	Brazelton, Richard Oliver	26701
Brazelton, Richard Oliver	26701	Brazoria	—	
Brazelton, Sue A.	34944	Runnels	Brazelton, John Cadmus	—
Braziel, A. C.	41919	Smith	—	
Braziel, Ann C.	23275	Hardeman	Braziel, Alonzo Derastus	—
Braziel, Elizabeth	18268	Rains	Braziel, Thomas Butler	—
Brazier, F. H.	22747	Ellis	—	
Brazier, Laura	45054	Denton	Brazier, William Edwin	—
Brazier, Mary Ida	40554	Cherokee	Brazier, William Henry Harrison	39239
Brazier, William Henry Harrison	39239	Cherokee	—	
Brazil, M. A. Mrs.	29839	Angelina	Brazil, Andrew Jackson	—
Brazil, Mary Ann	23185	Wise	Brazil, William Harding	—
Brazil, Moses B.	35682	Clay	—	
Brazille, A.	02879	Llano	—	
Brazzel, Fannie E.	41854	Tarrant	John H., Sr.	22586
Brazzel, John H., Sr.	22586	Tarrant	—	
Brazzil, G. A. Mrs.	36992	Harrison	Brazzil, John Wesley	—
Brazzil, J. W.	Rej	Coryell	—	
Brazzil, Mary A.	00985	Coryell	Brazzil, Riggou	—
Brazzil, William Nicholas	43714	Wharton	—	
Brazzil, Winnie E.	51164	Victoria	Brazzil, William Nichols	43714
Breazeale, Ann	18577	Angelina	Breazeale, John	—
Breazeale, Clinton	15934	Llano	—	
Breazeale, David Jenkins	17178	Angelina	—	
Breazeale, Dolly	28025	Harrison	Breazeale, Francis Marion	—
Breazeale, Harrison	36191	Burnet	—	
Breazeale, Manda A.	33724	Angelina	Breazeale, Marshall E.	—
Breazeale, Mary E.	45314	Burnet	Breazeale, Harrison	36191
Breazeale, Victoria	41983	Angelina	Breazeale, David Jenkins	17178
Breazeale, William Bruce	46932	Dallas	—	
Brecheen, James M.	06837	Wise	—	
Breckeen, Elizabeth A.	01121	Delta	Breckeen, William T.	—
Breckeen, James Edward	43957	Lamar	—	
Breckeen, Mary	51974	Lamar	Breckeen, James Edward	43957
Bredel, Anton	00128	Austin	—	
Breecheen, Sophia	Rej	Wise	Breecheen, James M.	—
Breed, G. A. Mrs.	14754	Brown	Breed, William Nathan	—

Index to Confederate Pension Applications

Name	App #	County	Veteran	Vet App #
Breed, James C., Sr.	39443	Hays	—	—
Breeding, Columbus Patton	45475	Uvalde	—	—
Breeding, D. S.	02416	Kerr	—	—
Breeding, Mollie E.	49539	Uvalde	Breeding, Columbus Patton	45475
Breeding, Nancy Jane	Rej	Callahan	Breeding, Francie Marion	—
Breeding, Susan	30508	McLennan	Breeding, James Able	—
Breedlove, Henry C.	20662	Wise	—	—
Breedlove, Mary A.	27348	El Paso	Breedlove, William Alexander	—
Breedlove, Thomas A.	15416	Hays	—	—
Breedlove, W. A.	Rej	Brewster	—	—
Brees, Jennie Shannon	45901	Johnson	Shannon, Fines Marion	—
Breeze, James	15592	Houston	—	—
Breeze, S. A. Mrs.	18797	Houston	Breeze, James	15592
Breitling, Alfred Jacob	35907	Smith	—	—
Breitling, S. A. Mrs.	42848	Smith	Breitling, Alfred Jacob	35907
Breland, F. A. Mrs.	07606	Grimes	Breland, R. A.	—
Bremer, Henry	Rej	Fayette	—	—
Bremner, John Leslie	09195	Dallas	—	—
Bremner, Mollie	31699	Navarro	Bremner, John Leslie	09195
Brendle, M. E.	06220	Red River	—	—
Brennan, Mary	36619	Harris	Brennan, Isaac J.	—
Brenshihan, J. D.	38527	Travis	—	—
Brent, James A., Sr.	38529	Houston	—	—
Brent, Lucy Jane	27476	Grayson	Brent, Harrison	—
Brett, Josephine Millican	38486	Milam	Brett, John	—
Bretton, W. S.	29586	McLennan	—	—
Brewer, A. R.	10772	Van Zandt	—	—
Brewer, Andrew Jackson	29145	Cherokee	—	—
Brewer, Ann T.	13910	Johnson	Brewer, Holland	—
Brewer, C. C.	14159	Cherokee	—	—
Brewer, E. R.	02294	Johnson	—	—
Brewer, Edward L.	19626	Dallam	—	—
Brewer, F. A. Mrs.	10121	Johnson	Brewer, E. R.	02294
Brewer, G. W.	11431	Erath	—	—
Brewer, George W.	22767	Cherokee	—	—
Brewer, Hardy	Rej	Wood	—	—
Brewer, Isabella	30000	Harris	Brewer, Silas Samuel W.	—
Brewer, J. H.	01289	Ellis	—	—
Brewer, J. H.	20566	Williamson	—	—
Brewer, J. J.	07832	Hood	—	—
Brewer, Jacob	09697	Fayette	—	—
Brewer, James Shadrick	41581A	Henderson	—	—
Brewer, James W.	20867	Brazos	—	—
Brewer, Jennie Virginia	41844	Henderson	Brewer, James Shadrick	41581A
Brewer, John A. N.	28454	Delta	—	—
Brewer, John Henry	46477	Hidalgo	—	—
Brewer, John R.	05723	Collin	—	—
Brewer, John Willis	40701	Brown	—	—
Brewer, Kinion Kendrick	13762	Concho	—	—
Brewer, Lewis Gorden	22884	Ellis	—	—
Brewer, Lizzie	31043	Ellis	Brewer, Lewis Gorden	22884
Brewer, Lou Ann	38827	Kaufman	Brewer, Henry Dallas	—
Brewer, M. V.	50221	Eastland	—	—
Brewer, Martha Ann	Rej	Bowie	Brewer, Linson	—
Brewer, Martha Jane	42981	Brown	Brewer, John Willis	40701
Brewer, Mary	03202	Orange	Brewer, John D.	—
Brewer, N. Mrs.	34438	Hood	Brewer, James Jasper	—
Brewer, Pennince	26973	Cooke	Brewer, Hardy	—
Brewer, Peyton G.	04158	Van Zandt	—	—

Index to Confederate Pension Applications

Brewer, Rebecca A.	28882	Dewitt	Brewer, Samuel Bolling	—
Brewer, S.	08354M	Hood	—	—
Brewer, Sallie A.	34197	Falls	Brewer, Edward L.	19626
Brewer, Sarah F.	26583	Angelina	Brewer, James Augustus	—
Brewer, Silas	11360	Burleson	—	—
Brewer, Victoria Adaline	46032	Comanche	Brewer, Kinneen (Kinion) Kendrick	13762
Brewer, Virginia	45101	Bandera	Brewer, Greene Washington	—
Brewer, W. J.	Rej	Navarro	—	—
Brewer, William Jordon	23295	Delta	—	—
Brewier, N. A.	Rej	Nacogdoches	—	—
Brewster, Blake	00284	Bell	—	—
Brewster, E. A. Mrs.	17138	Navarro	Brewster, John	—
Brewster, E. M.	22744	Williamson	—	—
Brewster, J. F.	23305	Tarrant	—	—
Brewster, N. J.	47984	Shackelford	—	—
Brewton, Eva S.	20364	Bexar	Brewton, Isaac Harris	18830
Brewton, Isaac Harris	18830	Bexar	—	—
Brewton, M. C. Mrs.	18953	Fort Bend	Brewton, William Harrison	—
Brewton, Samuel	04368	Wharton	—	—
Brewton, Susan Jane	05190	Houston	Brewton, John David	—
Brian, A. A.	20836	Knox	—	—
Brians, Eliza W.	17651	Fannin	Brians, Henly Chapman	—
Brice, Bettie	34786	Bastrop	Brice, James Wilson	31865
Brice, Bettie	34971	Real	Brice, John Nuton (Newton)	11339
Brice, David Jasper	09202	Edwards	—	—
Brice, J. J.	19143	Montgomery	—	—
Brice, J. W.	Rej	Nueces	—	—
Brice, James Wilson	31865	Bastrop	—	—
Brice, John Newton (Nuton)	11339	Bandera	—	—
Brice, John W.	37051	Atascosa	—	—
Brice, Mary A.	36567	Bell	Brice, Charles L.	—
Brickhouse, Joseph Abraham	02567	Lee	—	—
Brickhouse, Mary D.	37376	Jefferson	Brickhouse, Joseph Alexander	02567
Brickley, Hanah M.	28553	Dallas	Brickley, James Monroe	—
Bridewell, Clara F.	42236	Dallas	Bridewell, John Thomas	—
Bridge, Jean P. Routh	51135	Guadalupe	Bridge, Robert Berry	—
Bridgeman, Rebecca	03299	Parker	Bridgeman, A. J.	—
Bridgers, Maggie	35680	Lampasas	Bridgers, Leonodas Moon	—
Bridges, A. J.	22134	Navarro	—	—
Bridges, Aaron Lafayette	19207	Robertson	—	—
Bridges, Albert	20547	Dallas	—	—
Bridges, Altonia	43674	Dallas	Bridges, Albert	20547
Bridges, Asbury F.	00580	Burnet	—	—
Bridges, Benjamin Franklin	42412	Shelby	—	—
Bridges, Brancie	39328	Cherokee	Bridges, Neri	—
Bridges, C. C. Mrs.	19925	Shelby	Bridges, James Thomas	—
Bridges, E. F.	06374	Anderson	—	—
Bridges, Eliza	08471M	Smith	—	—
Bridges, Estaline	Rej	Tarrant	Bridges, Adam Henry	—
Bridges, F. E. Mrs.	27903	Navarro	Bridges, Francis Marion	—
Bridges, J. H.	10535	Clay	—	—
Bridges, J. H.	22816	McCulloch	—	—
Bridges, James Elonzo	31658	Cooke	—	—
Bridges, James Elonzo Mrs.	43406	Dallas	Bridges, James Elonzo	31658
Bridges, Jane E.	37898	Cass	Bridges, William Edward	12047
Bridges, Jasper	39226	Camp	—	—
Bridges, John James	10279	Limestone	—	—
Bridges, M. C. Mrs.	28334	Limestone	Bridges, John James	10279
Bridges, M. E. Mrs.	27299	Hopkins	Bridges, Russell Jeremiah	—

Index to Confederate Pension Applications

Name	No.	County	Related	No.
Bridges, Martha A.	35902	Jefferson	Bridges, William L.	—
Bridges, Mary Ellen	40611	Williamson	Bridges, Alfred Theodore	—
Bridges, Mary Louise	51272	Shelby	Bridges, Benjamin Franklin	42412
Bridges, Minnie Armfield	50781	Grimes	Bridges, Edward Langford	—
Bridges, Mollie	28493	Robertson	Bridges, Aaron Lafayette	19207
Bridges, Penelope Ake	00311	Bell	Bridges, B. F.	—
Bridges, S. A. Mrs.	16984	Wise	Bridges, James Allen	—
Bridges, Sallie Elizabeth	35846	Hopkins	Bridges, Pleasant Clingmen	—
Bridges, Susan E. M.	30808	Clay	Bridges, J. H.	10535
Bridges, Thomas H.	29448	Bell		
Bridges, William Edward	12047	Marion		
Bridwell, A. A. Mrs.	38893	Rusk	Bridwell, Joseph N.	37236
Bridwell, Joseph N.	37236	Rusk		
Brieger, Daniel T.	31971	Jim Wells		
Brieger, Maria	32301	Mason	Brieger, Daniel T.	31971
Brietz, Georgia S.	35090	Bowie	Brietz, Alexander Charles	—
Brigam, William C.	09685	Dallas		
Brigance, Elias	03198	Nueces		
Briggs, Alice	50268	Grayson	Briggs, Charlie Cain	—
Briggs, B. J. Mrs.	29029	Hopkins	Briggs, Benjamin Franklin	—
Briggs, Daniel	06810	Panola		
Briggs, Francis Marion	15567	Hopkins		
Briggs, James	13395	Kaufman		
Briggs, John Clinton	22579	Ellis		
Briggs, John Jackson	19184	Panola		
Briggs, John W.	15396	Harrison		
Briggs, Leroy Marshall	27531	Falls		
Briggs, M. A. Mrs.	36721	Hopkins	Briggs, Francis Marion	15567
Briggs, Martha	22506	Harrison	Briggs, John W.	15396
Briggs, Mary Ann	32561	Falls	Briggs, Leroy Marshall	27531
Briggs, Mattie Virginia	Rej	Tarrant	Briggs, John Clinton	22579
Briggs, W. W.	29569	Ellis		
Briggs, Washington	Rej	Hall		
Brigham, Benjamin	32599	Travis		
Brigham, Henry	28160	Hunt		
Bright, Alice	39576	Sabine	Bright, J. S. D.	33266
Bright, E. E. Mrs.	20213	Dallas	Bright, William Harrison	—
Bright, E. G. Mrs.	17572	Dallas	Bright, John Henry	—
Bright, Eleanor Annie	34972	Medina	Bright, George Washington	07624
Bright, Elizabeth J.	04522	Wood	Bright, Marmaduke	—
Bright, Ella E.	17547	Dallas	Bright, William Harrison	—
Bright, George Washington	07624	Medina		
Bright, Helen	50045	Navarro	Bright, William Roy	—
Bright, J. S. D.	33266	Nacogdoches		
Bright, John	07494	Hopkins		
Brightman, H. C. Mrs.	34858	Comanche	Brightman, Lyman	—
Brightman, Lyman	00922	Comanche		
Brightwell, Amanda E.	00184	Bastrop	Brightwell, Andrew J.	—
Brightwell, Margaret C.	41659	Rusk	Brightwell, Charles	—
Briley, B. C.	21660	Smith		
Briley, Felix G.	25484	Nacogdoches		
Briley, John Alexander	14221	Fannin		
Briley, Nancy	30378	Grayson	Briley, William W.	26902
Briley, S. R.	04828	Nacogdoches		
Briley, Sue M.	34859	Palo Pinto	Briley, John Alexander	14221
Briley, William W.	26902	Grayson		
Brill, Emma Anna	47630	Ellis	Brill, Henry Johnson	—
Brim, John D.	10557	Angelina		
Brim, L. R.	11064	Navarro		

Index to Confederate Pension Applications

Name	App. No.	County	Veteran	Vet. No.
Brimberry, George Anderson	15587	Houston	—	—
Brimberry, George Anderson Mrs.	38755	Houston	Brimberry, George Anderson	15587
Brimberry, L. A. Mrs.	Rej	Houston	Brimberry, Peter	—
Brimberry, M. E. Mrs.	Rej	Houston	Brimberry, Elbert	—
Brimer, N. A. Mrs.	Rej	Nacogdoches	Brimer, Harrison	—
Brimer, N. A. Mrs.	18188	Nacogdoches	Brimer, William Henry	—
Brimlee, George R.	14935	Collin	—	—
Bringhurst, Minnie Abercrombie	51190	Harris	Bringhurst, John Henry	—
Brink, J.	10151	Milam	—	—
Brinker, Jennie	46893	Cass	Brinker, Henry Washington	—
Brinkley, John William	10290	Colorado	—	—
Brinkley, M. J. Mrs.	45186	Madison	Brinkley, John William	10290
Brinkley, Martha	28181	Baylor	Brinkley, James Anderson	—
Brinkley, Peter	00885	Colorado	—	—
Brinkman, Mary Wilkening	41667	Washington	Wilkening, Henry William	—
Brinlee, Hiram Carroll	22338	Grayson	—	—
Brinlee, Sarah Ann	30157	Baylor	Brinlee, David Francis	—
Brinlee, Susan Elizabeth	41103	Collin	Brinlee, Hiram Carroll	22338
Brinley, M. J. Mrs.	33487	Donley	Brinley, William Ryan	04640
Brinley, William Ryan	04640	Donley	—	—
Brinson, James P.	05536	Harris	—	—
Brinson, Jason Burrel	25376	Mills	—	—
Brinson, John	40078	Shelby	—	—
Brinson, Phillip Mercer	18582	Cass	—	—
Brinson, S. A. Mrs.	33404	Cass	Brinson, Phillip Mercer	18582
Brinson, Sarah Ann	23347	Cherokee	Brinson, John Preston	—
Brisco, Nancy Fannie	50224	Jack	Brisco, William	—
Briscoe, Henry	05349	Grayson	—	—
Briscoe, I. N.	12451	Hunt	—	—
Briscoe, John B.	33754	Reeves	—	—
Briscoe, Margaret A.	36892	Cooke	Briscoe, William Henry	21661
Briscoe, Margarett	17518	Cooke	Briscoe, Henry	05349
Briscoe, Nancie Adeline	19660	Upshur	Briscoe, William P.	—
Briscoe, William Henry	21661	Cooke	—	—
Brisendine, John Thomas	06315	Henderson	—	—
Brisenham, Kate	10924	Falls	Brisenham, William	—
Brison, G. R. A.	17213	Upshur	—	—
Brison, M. E. Mrs.	16830	Upshur	Brison, Robert T.	—
Brison, M. J. Mrs.	14805	Camp	Brison, John A.	—
Brister, Ellen V.	24012	Navarro	Brister, Francis Marion	13473
Brister, Francis Marion	13473	Navarro	—	—
Brister, Frankey Mrs.	41616	Wilson	Brister, Wiley Franklin	—
Brister, George W.	21549	Coleman	—	—
Brister, Margaret	36329	Bee	Brister, Daniel Jasper	—
Brister, Mat Cordelia	46277	Atascosa	Brister, Yancey Goodall	—
Brister, W. J. (Jack)	06728	Mason	—	—
Bristley, Mathias	02664	Liberty	—	—
Bristol, William Henry	49964	Galveston	—	—
Briston, Annie E.	29836	Henderson	Briston, Abner L.	—
Bristow, C. S.	06690	Henderson	—	—
Bristow, J. A.	Rej	Henderson	—	—
Bristow, Mary C.	11766	Henderson	Bristow, C. S.	06690
Britain, Benjamin Meady Mrs.	47556	Baylor	Britain, Benjamin Meady	—
Britain, James M.	34241	Dallas	—	—
Brite, Thomas Benton	26966	Wise	—	—
Britt, B. F.	29757	Hunt	—	—
Britt, E. A. Mrs.	45607	Hood	Britt, Ruben	—
Britt, George W.	27739	Tarrant	—	—
Britt, Jonathan	03945	Travis	—	—

Index to Confederate Pension Applications

Name	App #	County	Veteran	Vet App #
Britt, Josie	Rej	Milam	Britt, John	
Britt, M. M. Mrs.	12644	Travis	Britt, Jonathan	03945
Britt, Martha	22415	Bosque	Britt, Patrick Miles	
Brittain, Annie E.	50348	San Augustine	Brittain, Thomas Tolan	
Brittain, D. A. Mrs.	16543	Shelby	Brittain, William David	06258
Brittain, Eliza Texana	36803	Llano	Brittain, George Hamilton	
Brittain, Ella Sarah	42609	Jefferson	Brittain, Onsolo Euclid	
Brittain, Henry B.	23482	Kaufman		
Brittain, J. B.	07131	Anderson		
Brittain, T. F.	20499	Shelby		
Brittain, W. F.	13064	Shelby		
Brittain, William David	06258	Shelby		
Britton, Carrie	29851	Wharton	Britton, James Alfred	
Britton, Cornelius Columbus	11365	Caldwell		
Britton, George L.	Rej	Denton		
Britton, James Madison	01347	Erath		
Britton, John Hampton	05073	McLennan		
Britton, John Robert	33596	Houston		
Britton, M. A. Mrs.	40687	Wood	Britton, Marcellus Louis	
Britton, M. L. Mrs.	49455	Erath	Britton, James Madison	01347
Britton, Margaret Ann	42921	Tarrant	Britton, Samuel Thomas	
Britton, Mary C.	39346	Houston	Britton, John Robert	33596
Britton, S. C. Mrs.	09513	Taylor	Britton, John Hampton	05073
Britton, W. M.	Rej	Panola		
Broadaway, M. A. Mrs.	38019	Hill	Broadaway, William Marshall	
Broaddus, Charles A.	19923	Burleson		
Broaddus, Henry Clay	10599	Burleson		
Broaddus, Henry Clay Mrs.	45298	Johnson	Broaddus, Henry Clay	10599
Broaddus, Leland W.	00566	Burleson		
Broaddus, Rueben Garland	10007	Burleson		
Broaderd, Jasper	30539	Dallas		
Broadhurst, James W.	33346	Dallas		
Broadhurst, Martha Frances	51387	Zavala	Broadhurst, William Edmond	
Broadstreet, Joseph Rawls	11948	Henderson		
Broadstreet, S. E. Mrs.	22669	Titus	Broadstreet, Parris Columbus	
Broadstreet, Sarah A.	03297	Parker	Broadstreet, James	
Broadwater, Thomas Jefferson	03624	Shelby		
Brock, B. C.	08607	Dallas		
Brock, Bertha	46345	Tarrant	Brock, John Augustus Ted Donavan	
Brock, Eli	25805	Bell		
Brock, F. M.	Home	Travis		
Brock, F. M.	Rej	Tarrant		
Brock, Granville B.	09874	Cooke		
Brock, Henry	25687	Erath		
Brock, J. B.	20367	Eastland		
Brock, J. F.	Rej	Archer		
Brock, J. J.	03356	Polk		
Brock, John E.	31262	Tarrant		
Brock, Laura A.	05375	Grayson	Brock, John T.	
Brock, Leatha	40322	Tarrant	Brock, John E.	31262
Brock, M. E. Mrs.	18060	Limestone	Brock, William Henry	
Brock, M. E. Mrs.	39347	Wilbarger	Brock, Lewis	
Brock, M. M.	23346	Scurry		
Brock, Martha	40507	Bell	Brock, Eli	25805
Brock, Mary E.	28035	McCulloch	Brock, David Oliver	
Brock, Mary Jane	36774	McLennan	Brock, Thomas Samuel	
Brock, Phebe	38391	Dallas	Brock, Young Allen	
Brock, Philpena	28019	Irion	Brock, Emanuel	
Brock, Polly S.	22348	Parker	Brock, John Henry	

Index to Confederate Pension Applications

Brock, S. P.	37200	Hamilton		
Brock, Sarah	Rej	Dallas	Brock, Marion	
Brock, Thursey B. Mrs.	14848	Cass		
Brock, W. A.	24902	Eastland		
Brock, Zebodee T.	29118	Collin		
Brockenbrough, S. F. Mrs.	21586	Brazoria	Brockenbrough, Marias Carter	
Brocker, Joe	46338	Lavaca		
Brocker, Mollie	51901	Lavaca	Brocker, Joe	46338
Brodie, C. A. Mrs.	Rej	Johnson	Brodie, J. B.	
Brodie, Charles E.	11648	Tarrant		
Brodie, E. P. Mrs.	34629	Lamar	Brodie, John Ligon	33712
Brodie, John Ligon	33712	Lamar		
Brodnax, Oran W.	08637	Callahan		
Brodnax, Thomas James	42942	Burleson		
Broers, Fannie	Rej	Bexar	Broers, Peter	
Broesche, W. C.	39753	Washington		
Brogden, Darthula	41902	Upshur	Brogden, Hubbard	
Brogden, L. C. Mrs.	38268	Parker	Brogden, Alexander Buggy	
Brogdon, H. G. Mrs.	31700	Brazos	Brogdon, George Washington	
Brogdon, Laura H.	39828	Brazos	Brogdon, William Joseph	
Brogdon, M. A. Mrs.	39662	Wood	Brogdon, Noah Richmond	
Broiles, John M.	25333	McLennan		
Bromley, J. J.	20924	Rusk		
Bromley, M. A. Mrs.	26967	Hopkins	Bromley, J. Smith	
Bronnum, Catherine	32580	Galveston	Bronnum, John S.	
Broocke, Lydia Ann	49457	Brown	Broocke, Rufus King Anderson	
Brooke, Martha Francis	36958	Wood	Brooke, William Wallace	27248
Brooke, William Wallace	27248	Wood		
Brookenbrough, John F.	23253A	Mills		
Brooker, Emma F.	35922	Harris	Brooker, William Henry	
Brookman, John	07686	Webb		
Brooks, A. J.	08622	Bexar		
Brooks, Abner R.	31268	Burnet		
Brooks, Allen Turner	06343	Hays		
Brooks, Amelia	25567	Hale	Brooks, Robert Write	
Brooks, Andrew Jackson	21189	Callahan		
Brooks, Annie E.	05863	Falls	Brooks, William	
Brooks, Augusta C.	33565	Harris	Brooks, Jesse Sylvester	12880
Brooks, Belle	Rej	Madison	Brooks, Madison Decalv	
Brooks, C. C. Mrs.	47381	Hidalgo	Brooks, Jacob Warren	31528
Brooks, Carroll Nathaniel	25617	Ellis		
Brooks, Carroll Nathaniel Mrs.	39079	Henderson	Brooks, Carroll Nathaniel	25617
Brooks, Charley W.	15122	Falls		
Brooks, David	Rej	Hood		
Brooks, Dewitt C.	50244	Collingsworth		
Brooks, Dora	50764	Hill	Brooks, Tom	
Brooks, E. Mrs.	10373	Fort Bend	Brooks, Josephus D.	
Brooks, Emma	51997	Howard	Brooks, William Corsey	44067
Brooks, Evant	31231	Hamilton		
Brooks, Fannie	33858	Navarro	Brooks, Charley W.	15122
Brooks, George Washington	31834	Eastland		
Brooks, H. I.	21214	Tarrant		
Brooks, H. P. Mrs.	08237	Burleson	Brooks, T. J.	
Brooks, Helena	25737	Hays	Brooks, Allen Turner	06343
Brooks, Henderson	30906	Brown		
Brooks, J. A.	10480	Tarrant		
Brooks, J. B.	Rej	Cherokee		
Brooks, J. F.	28417	Panola		
Brooks, J. H.	Rej	Limestone		

Index to Confederate Pension Applications

Name	App. No.	County	Veteran	Vet. App. No.
Brooks, J. J.	40148	Houston		
Brooks, J. R. K.	28926	Rusk		
Brooks, J. T.	47591	Ellis		
Brooks, Jacob Warren	31528	Eastland		
Brooks, James M., Sr.	11859	Colorado		
Brooks, James S.	02113	Hunt		
Brooks, Jennie B.	23986	Wheeler	Brooks, James Franklin	
Brooks, Jesse Sylvester	12880	Harris		
Brooks, Jesse W.	28707	Rusk		
Brooks, Jim	Rej	Gonzales		
Brooks, John	07216	Guadalupe		
Brooks, John D.	25642	Mitchell		
Brooks, John F.	18109	McLennan		
Brooks, John R.	05685	Denton		
Brooks, John Richard	16225	Panola		
Brooks, John W.	Rej	Guadalupe		
Brooks, Julia Helen	32852	Freestone	Brooks, William Haley	13812
Brooks, Julia Virginia	49660	Grimes	Brooks, Thomas Jefferson	
Brooks, Letitia	33465	Bastrop	Brooks, Calvin Herlock	
Brooks, Louis Pinkney	47447	Young		
Brooks, Louis Pinkney Mrs.	50445	Young	Brooks, Louis Pinkney	47447
Brooks, Louise F.	46066	Wood	Brooks, Stephen H.	
Brooks, M. S.	09728	Madison		
Brooks, Malcom Buie	16828	Upshur		
Brooks, Martha F.	47773	McLennan	Brooks, Dewitt Clint	
Brooks, Mary	36092	Brown	Brooks, Henderson	30906
Brooks, Mary E.	46383	Limestone	Brooks, James Hampton	
Brooks, Mary Veracruse	Rej	Walker	Brooks, Robert Logan	16913
Brooks, Mollie	45691	Rusk	Brooks, Jessie Watson	
Brooks, N. A. Mrs.	20314	Upshur	Brooks, Malcom Buie	16828
Brooks, N. I. Mrs.	31274	Runnels	Brooks, Pleasant Hampton	
Brooks, Nancy J.	37451	Parker	Brooks, John D.	25642
Brooks, Nancy White	17610	El Paso	Brooks, Belvidere	
Brooks, Phoebe	09168	Cherokee		
Brooks, R. L.	Rej	Schleicher		
Brooks, R. L.	11013	Kinney		
Brooks, Rachel	42463	Wichita	Brooks, William Calvin	
Brooks, Rebecca E.	Rej	Bowie	Brooks, Napoleon B.	
Brooks, Reding L.	Rej	Walker		
Brooks, Robert L. Mrs.	45571	Walker	Brooks, Robert L.	16913
Brooks, Robert Logan	16913	Robertson		
Brooks, Robert Manuel	30682	Grayson		
Brooks, S. H.	02609	Leon		
Brooks, S. H.	13640	Wood		
Brooks, Sallie O.	38149	Grimes	Brooks, Richard Preston	
Brooks, Sarah Ann	Rej	Lavaca	Brooks, John C.	
Brooks, Sarah Ann	45788	Limestone	Brooks, T. W.	34332
Brooks, Sarah P.	00348	Bexar	Brooks, D. J.	
Brooks, Sue	39822	Grayson	Brooks, Robert Manuel	30682
Brooks, T. A. Mrs.	36564	Eastland	Brooks, George Washington	31834
Brooks, T. W.	34332	Limestone		
Brooks, Victoria	29070	Wood	Brooks, Thomas Wheeler	
Brooks, W. G.	20559	Shelby		
Brooks, W. W.	08518M	Williamson		
Brooks, W. W.	14774	Burnet		
Brooks, Walter Green	26552	Cherokee		
Brooks, Weldon	Rej	Hill		
Brooks, William Corsey	44067	Howard		
Brooks, William Haley	13812	Freestone		

Index to Confederate Pension Applications

Name	No.	County	Veteran	Vet. No.
Brooks, William Henry Mrs.	43189	Tom Green	Brooks, William Henry	—
Brooks, William Lunsford	Rej	Wilbarger	—	—
Brooks, William S.	Rej	Kaufman	—	—
Brooks, William T.	Rej	Henderson	—	—
Brooksher, Harriet V.	49651	Tarrant	Brooksher, George M. D.	—
Brookshire, J. W.	00058	Angelina	—	—
Brookshire, Margaret Ann	10813	Angelina	Brookshire, J. W.	00058
Brookshire, Martha Jane	44026	Hill	Brookshire, William Leonard	—
Broom, J. P.	38504	Rusk	—	—
Broom, Madison	13731	Brown	—	—
Broom, Martin H.	29991	Comanche	—	—
Broom, Nancy C.	16893	Victoria	Broom, William Alexander	05918
Broom, William Alexander	05918	Victoria	—	—
Broome, Hannah M.	22472	Grayson	Broome, James Franklin	—
Brosius, M. A. Mrs.	12519	Lamar	Brosius, G. W.	—
Bross, S. A.	28785	Mills	—	—
Brothers, Elizabeth F.	46205	Gonzales	Brothers, Robert Jetton	—
Brothers, George	05265	Upshur	—	—
Brotton, Elizer Mrs.	Rej	Morris	Brotton, Y. E.	—
Brougher, D. M.	19468	Milam	—	—
Broughton, Eliza	29013	Anderson	Broughton, William David	—
Broughton, M. E. Mrs.	30878	Smith	Broughton, Edward Thomas	—
Broughton, Sarah	28786	Eastland	Broughton, Edward Thomas	—
Broun, Thomas Rogers	38956	Wise	—	—
Broun, Thomas Rogers Mrs.	42717	Wise	Broun, Thomas Rogers	38956
Broussard, Marguerite	47077	Jefferson	Broussard, Theodore	—
Browder, Cynthia L.	49639	Lee	Browder, Francis Marion	—
Browder, Mary H.	47760	Limestone	Browder, William Hosa	—
Browder, W. B.	35383	Austin	—	—
Brown, A. A.	06631	Madison	—	—
Brown, A. E. Mrs.	Rej	Brown	Brown, William Lunceford	—
Brown, A. E. Mrs.	38117	Henderson	Brown, Ausiluin Washington	12411
Brown, A. L.	Rej	Henderson	—	—
Brown, Abram James	42178	McCulloch	—	—
Brown, Albert Galerton	01018	Crockett	—	—
Brown, Alcy Mrs.	13445	Mills	Brown, Thaddeus Paten	03020
Brown, Alfred E.	21056	Brown	—	—
Brown, Alice	Rej	Tarrant	Brown, Francis Marion	—
Brown, Alice	47535	Hale	Brown, James Oliver	—
Brown, Allen Charles	41863	Smith	—	—
Brown, Allura	51451	Medina	Brown, John F.	37199
Brown, Amanda	50730	Dallas	Brown, Valentine O.	—
Brown, Amanda Ann	51580	Dallas	Brown, Francis Marion	—
Brown, Amanda J.	30844	Navarro	Brown, David	—
Brown, Amelia	07663	Smith	Brown, A. G.	—
Brown, Anderson	05508	Hopkins	—	—
Brown, Andrew J.	Rej	Parker	—	—
Brown, Andrew J.	10710	Shelby	—	—
Brown, Andrew J.	21346	Wise	—	—
Brown, Andrew J. Mrs.	30390	Wise	Brown, Andrew J.	21346
Brown, Andrew Jackson	01217	Ellis	—	—
Brown, Andrew Jackson	03679	Smith	—	—
Brown, Andrew Jackson	04159	Van Zandt	—	—
Brown, Andrew Jackson	28136	Navarro	—	—
Brown, Andrew Jackson Mrs.	Rej	Shelby	Brown, Andrew Jackson	—
Brown, Ann	36977	Grayson	Brown, William	—
Brown, Anna Regina Burch	45204	El Paso	Burch, Pulaski Thomas Hinds	—
Brown, Annie	20394	Tom Green	Brown, William Lunsford	—
Brown, Annie L.	41147	Collin	Brown, Addison Nathaniel	—

Index to Confederate Pension Applications

Name	App #	County	Veteran	Vet App #
Brown, Arthur	46916	Falls	—	—
Brown, Artie C.	28962	Wood	Brown, John S.	—
Brown, Aurora R.	48018	Fisher	Brown, Isaac Neely	—
Brown, Ausiluin Washington	12411	Henderson	—	—
Brown, Benjamin	38340	Jackson	—	—
Brown, Benjamin F.	14755	Brown	—	—
Brown, Benjamin F.	28349	Stephens	—	—
Brown, Benjamin Franklin	Rej	Bell	—	—
Brown, Bernard L.	08929	Lavaca	—	—
Brown, Bryant	10388	Hardin	—	—
Brown, C. C. Mrs.	26122	Hopkins	Brown, William Marion	—
Brown, C. D.	12434	Hopkins	—	—
Brown, C. T.	Rej	Shelby	—	—
Brown, Caroline Emily	47647	Freestone	Brown, Hary	—
Brown, Carrie E.	29189	Harris	Brown, Samuel Hancock	19003
Brown, Charles Sanford	36355	Coryell	—	—
Brown, Cora L.	35810	Burleson	Brown, Thomas	17533
Brown, Cynthia Caroline	17289	Angelina	Brown, William H.	—
Brown, D. J.	Rej	Hamilton	—	—
Brown, Daniel P.	06731	Newton	—	—
Brown, Daniel Richard	06480	Johnson	—	—
Brown, David Tollet	31987	Menard	—	—
Brown, Donna	51912	Harris	Brown, James David	—
Brown, E. B.	Rej	Llano	—	—
Brown, E. R.	30570	Freestone	—	—
Brown, Ed M.	Rej	Navarro	—	—
Brown, Elbridge	23345	Milam	—	—
Brown, Elbridge Mrs.	38130	Lee	Brown, Elbridge	23345
Brown, Elijah C.	07516	McLennan	—	—
Brown, Eliza T.	29977	Navarro	Brown, Jackson	—
Brown, Elizabeth	26857	Smith	Brown, James	25086
Brown, Elizabeth Panline	42000	Hays	Brown, Ossiam Tigers	—
Brown, Emily	30591	Callahan	Brown, James Allen	02954
Brown, Emma G.	33478	Travis	Brown, John Mathews	21265
Brown, Esther E.	42594	Denton	Brown, William	40999
Brown, Evan	06832	Wise	—	—
Brown, Ezekiel Meriman Mrs.	42011	Tom Green	Brown, Ezekiel Meriman	—
Brown, Ezeladah Mrs.	09707	Hardin	Brown, Frank	—
Brown, F. M.	30231	Montague	—	—
Brown, Fannie	42147	Comanche	Brown, Thomas	—
Brown, Fannie A.	46206	Navarro	Brown, Henry Clay	—
Brown, Fannie E.	36555	Titus	Brown, James Madison	23340
Brown, Florence S.	36000	Cooke	Brown, Napoleon B.	—
Brown, Francis Marion	04264	Walker	—	—
Brown, Franklin Columbus	03782	Tarrant	—	—
Brown, G. H.	Rej	Clay	—	—
Brown, G. S.	26702	McLennan	—	—
Brown, G. T.	08616	Bell	—	—
Brown, George B.	39302	Dallas	—	—
Brown, George D.	23324	Coryell	—	—
Brown, George Robinson	13096	Trinity	—	—
Brown, George T.	18046	Limestone	—	—
Brown, George W.	10108	Hill	—	—
Brown, Georgia	Rej	Smith	Brown, Allen Charles	41863
Brown, Georgia A.	42957	Cooke	Brown, Robert Jefferson	28301
Brown, Gordon	35452	Burnet	—	—
Brown, Gordon Mrs.	Rej	Burnet	Brown, Gordon	35452
Brown, Grace Vedder	42657	Bexar	Brown, Milton	—
Brown, Gustus B.	36984	Travis	—	—

Index to Confederate Pension Applications

Brown, H. D.	00309	Bell		
Brown, Harriett	42776	Johnson	Brown, John	
Brown, Hassie S.	41519	Navarro	Brown, Hiram S.	22395
Brown, Hattie G.	47273	McLennan	Brown, John Brunyan	
Brown, Helen	34151	McLennan	Brown, Erasmus A.	
Brown, Helen	51331	Bosque	Brown, Martin Andrew	32191
Brown, Henry	00889	Colorado		
Brown, Henry Etta	43481	Titus	Brown, John Oliver	
Brown, Henry Jackson	40169	Anderson		
Brown, Henry Justus Mrs.	43384	Harris	Brown, Henry Justus	
Brown, Henry Moses	38475	Houston		
Brown, Heppie	Rej	Nolan	Brown, Samuel Sheilds	
Brown, Hiram S.	22395	Navarro		
Brown, I. L.	37629	Gregg		
Brown, I. L. Mrs.	40401	Gregg	Brown, I. L.	37629
Brown, I. N.	23234	Jefferson		
Brown, Ida	Rej	Kaufman	Brown, Thomas Jefferson	32034
Brown, Imogenia	08724	Hill	Brown, Thomas	
Brown, Ira B.	40074	Comanche		
Brown, Isaac M.	01038	Dallas		
Brown, Isaiah	07610	Harrison		
Brown, J. A.	09258	Johnson		
Brown, J. A.	18410	Tarrant		
Brown, J. A. Mrs.	08641	Coke	Brown, J. W.	
Brown, J. D.	Rej	Titus		
Brown, J. F.	03780	Tarrant		
Brown, J. H.	05525	Grimes		
Brown, J. M.	Rej	Harris		
Brown, J. M.	05219	Lamar		
Brown, J. P.	Rej	Eastland		
Brown, J. P.	Rej	Lavaca		
Brown, J. P.	21577	McCulloch		
Brown, J. P. S.	06585	Tarrant		
Brown, J. S.	05977	Fisher		
Brown, J. S.	32438	Houston		
Brown, J. W.	Rej	Van Zandt		
Brown, James	25086	Smith		
Brown, James A.	05834	Cooke		
Brown, James Allen	02954	Milam		
Brown, James C.	16327	Robertson		
Brown, James Franklin	23472	Cottle		
Brown, James G.	10597	Brazoria		
Brown, James Jefferson	11256	Milam		
Brown, James Jefferson Mrs.	33262	Tarrant	Brown, James Jefferson	11256
Brown, James L.	47735	Eastland		
Brown, James Leonidas	14604	Atascosa		
Brown, James M.	20614	Fannin		
Brown, James Madison	23340	Titus		
Brown, James P.	13110	Walker		
Brown, James R. Mrs.	38936	Parker	Brown, James R.	
Brown, James V.	12216	Wood		
Brown, Jennie Elizabeth	15352	Harris	Brown, Hiram Walter	
Brown, Jeptha	28762	Scurry		
Brown, Jesse	17543	Dallas		
Brown, Jesse C.	23609	Pecos		
Brown, Jessie C. Mrs.	42315	Tom Green	Brown, Jessie C.	23609
Brown, Joanna Alexander	47001	Travis	Alexander, Thomas Hope	
Brown, Joe H.	08265	Coryell		
Brown, John	Rej	Jefferson		

Index to Confederate Pension Applications

Name	App#	County	Veteran	Vet#
Brown, John	21663	Houston		
Brown, John	35882	Bexar		
Brown, John (Jack) William	09608	Leon		
Brown, John F.	09132	Angelina		
Brown, John F.	37199	Medina		
Brown, John H.	41305	Bell		
Brown, John Houston	25947	Dallas		
Brown, John Mathews	21265	Travis		
Brown, John R.	27321	Burnet		
Brown, John S.	17923	Johnson		
Brown, John W.	31269	Anderson		
Brown, John William	29150	Karnes		
Brown, John William Mrs.	39976	Atascosa	Brown, John William	29150
Brown, Jonathan	25857	Bosque		
Brown, Joseph	02436	Lamar		
Brown, Joseph M.	36932	Tarrant		
Brown, Joseph Marshall	18047	Limestone		
Brown, Joseph Palestine	39320	Lavaca		
Brown, Joseph Palestine Mrs.	51671	Dewitt	Brown, Joseph Palestine	39320
Brown, Josie	45397	Burnet	Brown, Gordon	03545
Brown, Julia	01777	Harris	Brown, Gorham T.	
Brown, Julia A.	37264	Collin	Brown, James Malone	
Brown, Kate	50712	Coryell	Brown, Charles Sanford	36355
Brown, L. E. Mrs.	17571	Dallas	Brown, John William	
Brown, Lillie	28144	Tarrant	Brown, Mark A.	22354
Brown, Lizzie Virginia	41181	Limestone	Brown, Joseph Marshall	18047
Brown, Lottie	27023	Falls	Brown, David Ely	
Brown, Lou	24864	Smith	Brown, Joseph Warren	
Brown, Lou	35038	Hopkins	Brown, Anderson	05508
Brown, Lou Addie	42189	Bastrop	Brown, Alfred Ferman	
Brown, Louisa	06798	Galveston	Brown, John D.	
Brown, Lucinda	09194	Dallas	Brown, Isaac M.	01038
Brown, Lucinda Brown	Rej	Bexar	Brown, John	
Brown, Lucinda E.	Rej	Coryell	Brown, James R.	
Brown, Luticia A.	Rej	Rusk	Brown, George W.	
Brown, Luvenia	Rej	Panola	Brown, Andrew Jackson	
Brown, Luvina Ann	43761	Lavaca	Brown, James	
Brown, M. A. Mrs.	10709	Nacogdoches	Brown, John O.	
Brown, M. A. Mrs.	41666	Bell	Brown, John H.	41305
Brown, M. E.	20389	Montague	Brown, Lewis Alexander	
Brown, M. E. Mrs.	14871	Chambers	Brown, George Hardeman	
Brown, M. E. Mrs.	23235	Wise	Brown, Jake	
Brown, M. E. Mrs.	40723	Montague	Brown, F. M.	30231
Brown, M. J. Mrs.	07451	Coleman	Brown, George F.	
Brown, M. M. Mrs.	21664	Williamson	Brown, Simeon Keene	
Brown, M. O. Mrs.	27419	Red River	Brown, George Washington	
Brown, M. S. Mrs.	32689	Johnson	Brown, Daniel Richard	06480
Brown, Malinda	08259	Comanche	Brown, Thomas S.	
Brown, Mandy	49163	Collin	Brown, William Dave	
Brown, Margaret	35329	Bexar	Brown, Oliver	33559
Brown, Margaret Farr	52092	Johnson	Brown, Earl Young	
Brown, Marinda A.	48061	McCulloch	Brown, Abram James	42178
Brown, Mark A.	22354	Tarrant		
Brown, Martha	Rej	Hill	Brown, Frank M.	
Brown, Martha	00439	Blanco	Brown, Willis T.	
Brown, Martha	40984	Tarrant	Brown, Samuel Harrison	16635
Brown, Martha	42402	Brazos	Brown, Thomas Henry	
Brown, Martha A.	Rej	Nacogdoches	Brown, John O.	
Brown, Martha A.	32898	Shelby	Brown, Daniel	

Index to Confederate Pension Applications

Name	App#	County	Veteran	Vet#
Brown, Martha Ann	Rej	Nacogdoches	Brown, Gilford Green	
Brown, Martha Delilah	05317	Montague	Brown, W. V.	
Brown, Martha J.	10357	Dallas	Brown, Thomas	
Brown, Martha J.	40702	Hamilton	Brown, Thomas H.	
Brown, Martin Andrew	32191	Bosque		
Brown, Martin Francis	46353	Denton		
Brown, Mary	Rej	Shelby	Brown, Andrew Jackson	
Brown, Mary	RejM	Travis		
Brown, Mary	17909	Hunt	Brown, Andrew Jackson	03679
Brown, Mary	38608	Shelby	Brown, Andrew Jackson	28136
Brown, Mary	45366	Grayson	Brown, John Samuel	
Brown, Mary A.	12106	Rains	Brown, William S.	
Brown, Mary A.	18892	Colorado	Brown, Henry	
Brown, Mary A.	50110	Tarrant	Brown, Joseph M.	36932
Brown, Mary A. Kennedy	45029	Cherokee	Kennedy, William Henry	
Brown, Mary C.	49589	Dallas	Brown, Henry Clay	
Brown, Mary E.	Rej	Montague	Brown, Lewis A.	
Brown, Mary E.	19831	Robertson	Brown, James C.	16327
Brown, Mary Ellen	42310	Harris	Brown, George Robinson	13096
Brown, Mary Jane	40295	McCulloch	Brown, David Tollet	31987
Brown, Mary Julia	51479	Atascosa	Brown, James Leonidas	14604
Brown, Mary L.	38072	Houston	Brown, John	21663
Brown, Mary Lea	36668	Travis	Brown, William Morton	
Brown, Mary M.	18432	Titus	Brown, John Henry Davis	
Brown, Mary S.	Rej	Dallas	Brown, G. W.	
Brown, Mary S.	43870	Blanco	Brown, Robert A.	
Brown, Matilda	14254	Harris	Brown, William	07389
Brown, Mattie	50512	McLennan	Brown, Stephen Cowart	
Brown, Mattie A.	34358	Grayson	Brown, Richmond Nolley	
Brown, Mattie L.	Rej	Freestone	Brown, Phillip Clark	
Brown, Mildred	Rej	Concho	Brown, James Thomas	
Brown, Millie A.	12253	Angelina	Brown, John F.	09132
Brown, Milvina Ann	06070	Harris	Brown, Joseph D.	
Brown, Minerva Idella	40481	Johnson	Brown, W. J.	35800
Brown, Minnie Reaville	46599	Harris	Brown, Joseph Alvine	
Brown, Mollie A.	33923	Scurry	Brown, Jeptha	28762
Brown, Mollie S.	45583	Hunt	Brown, George	
Brown, Mountsie	49053	Brazos	Brown, Calvin Andrew Jackson	
Brown, N. E. Mrs.	05674	Coleman		
Brown, Nancy C.	27670	Titus	Brown, Albert Galiton	
Brown, Nancy E.	36135	San Jacinto	Brown, Robert Pinkney	16469
Brown, Nancy Elizabeth	35545	Ellis	Brown, Andrew Jackson	01217
Brown, Nannie E.	17528	Coryell	Brown, Robert Valentine	
Brown, Narsissa	39207	Rusk	Brown, J. W.	
Brown, Octavia	51926	Dallas	Brown, Stephen Decatur	
Brown, Oliver	33559	Atascosa		
Brown, Ophelia Alice	49256	Tarrant	Brown, Francis Marion	
Brown, P. M.	19319	Walker		
Brown, P. T.	Rej	Hill		
Brown, Parris	36187	Titus		
Brown, Peter	41122	Gonzales		
Brown, Peter R.	Rej	Fisher		
Brown, Phoebe Lue	14688	Bell		
Brown, Polly Ann	51637	Travis	Brown, Henry Moses	38475
Brown, R. F.	11349	Bell		
Brown, R. G. Mrs.	14341	Mitchell	Brown, H. D.	00309
Brown, R. N.	Rej	Grayson		
Brown, R. U.	27597	Atascosa		
Brown, Rachel Rebecca	Rej	Hill	Brown, Perry Oliver	

Index to Confederate Pension Applications

Name	App. No.	County	Veteran	Vet. App. No.
Brown, Reason	21665	McLennan	—	—
Brown, Rebecca	18957	Franklin	Brown, James Sylvester	—
Brown, Rebecca	20518	Walker	Brown, Francis Marion	04264
Brown, Robert D.	03021	Mills	—	—
Brown, Robert H.	27578	Fannin	—	—
Brown, Robert Jefferson	28301	Cooke	—	—
Brown, Robert M., Jr.	22600	Wharton	—	—
Brown, Robert Pinkney	16469	San Jacinto	—	—
Brown, Robert T.	19918	Navarro	—	—
Brown, Roney	44034	Coryell	Brown, Louis Henry	—
Brown, Ruben Robinson	30789	Hardeman	—	—
Brown, Ruth Ann	41204	Dawson	Brown, James McCloud	—
Brown, S. A. Mrs.	22151	Eastland	Brown, Ezeikel	—
Brown, S. A. Mrs.	33772	Bosque	Brown, Jonathan	25857
Brown, S. J. Mrs.	45916	Hunt	Brown, John R.	—
Brown, Sam A.	37676	Williamson	—	—
Brown, Sam J.	Rej	Potter	—	—
Brown, Samuel Hancock	19003	Harris	—	—
Brown, Samuel Harrison	16635	Tarrant	—	—
Brown, Sarah	Rej	Hall	Brown, Charles Lewis	—
Brown, Sarah	29209	Parker	Brown, James Richard	—
Brown, Sarah Angelina	Rej	Tarrant	Brown, Hyram	—
Brown, Sarah Ann	43713	Cooke	Brown, William George	41917
Brown, Sarah C.	35684	McLennan	Brown, John	—
Brown, Sarah E.	30788	Burnet	Brown, John R.	27321
Brown, Sarah Jane	12575	Parker	Brown, Thomas Murphy	—
Brown, Sarah P.	47876	Hill	Brown, Robert Bolan	—
Brown, Silas	21138	Bandera	—	—
Brown, Sophrona	24998	Lampasas	Brown, Robert Henry	—
Brown, Starling	27271	Jones	—	—
Brown, Susana	41282	Nacogdoches	Brown, James Benjamin	—
Brown, T. A.	Rej	Collin	—	—
Brown, T. S.	43627	Houston	—	—
Brown, Thaddeus Paten	03020	Mills	—	—
Brown, Thomas	17533	Crockett	—	—
Brown, Thomas A.	38210	Collin	—	—
Brown, Thomas Jefferson	32034	Kaufman	—	—
Brown, Thomas M. Mrs.	38400	Dallam	Brown, Thomas M.	—
Brown, Truelock	43040	Harrison	Brown, Andrew Jackson	—
Brown, Tyre Harris Mrs.	32100	Caldwell	Brown, Tyre Harris	—
Brown, Vernon Mrs.	35302	Limestone	Brown, George T.	18046
Brown, Victoria C.	15915	Leon	Brown, John (Jack) William	09608
Brown, Virgil S.	Rej	Freestone	—	—
Brown, W. A.	49371	Parker	—	—
Brown, W. B.	Rej	Denton	—	—
Brown, W. H.	09305	Panola	—	—
Brown, W. H.	09689	Ellis	—	—
Brown, W. H. C.	39912	Haskell	—	—
Brown, W. J.	35800	Johnson	—	—
Brown, W. L.	Rej	Mills	—	—
Brown, W. M.	27028	Tarrant	—	—
Brown, W. P.	Rej	Wise	—	—
Brown, W. P.	15731	Jack	—	—
Brown, W. W.	Rej	McLennan	—	—
Brown, William	Rej	Henderson	—	—
Brown, William	02075	Houston	—	—
Brown, William	07389	Wilson	—	—
Brown, William	35830	Johnson	—	—
Brown, William	40999	Denton	—	—

Index to Confederate Pension Applications

Brown, William A.	Rej	Parker	—	—
Brown, William Allen	47664	Cherokee	—	—
Brown, William C.	Rej	McMullen	—	—
Brown, William C.	46935	Cooke	—	—
Brown, William Carysle	30244	Denton	—	—
Brown, William Carysle Mrs.	34324	Denton	Brown, William Carysle	30244
Brown, William Columbus	11792	Bee	—	—
Brown, William George	41917	Cooke	—	—
Brown, William H.	Rej	Wise	—	—
Brown, William H.	19093	Limestone	—	—
Brown, William Harrison	Rej	Wise	—	—
Brown, William M.	35724	Parker	—	—
Brown, William Marion	17101	Hill	—	—
Brown, William Marion Mrs.	37211	Dawson	Brown, William Marion	17101
Brown, William Mattox	25726	Clay	—	—
Brown, William P.	26397	Knox	—	—
Brown, William Richard Mrs.	Rej	Dallas	Brown, William Richard	—
Brown, William Seal	28966	Aransas	—	—
Brown, Willis Moseley	25000	Cherokee	—	—
Brown, Willis Moseley Mrs.	45292	Cherokee	Brown, Willis Moseley	25000
Brown, Zachariah	21662	Houston	—	—
Brown, Zany M. Mrs.	07918	Montague	Brown, Louis N.	—
Browne, John T.	Rej	Harris	—	—
Browne, Mary Elizabeth	51042	Mitchell	Browne, Needham Pearson Polk	—
Browner, John Wilson	34352	Smith	—	—
Browner, John Wilson Mrs.	36897	Van Zandt	Browner, John Wilson	34352
Brownfield, Charles E.	07736	Wise	—	—
Brownfield, W. A.	Rej	Scurry	—	—
Browning, A. P.	06347	Kimble	—	—
Browning, Aaron	23424	Hood	—	—
Browning, B. C. Mrs.	17010	Wood	Browning, Thomas	—
Browning, B. N.	18405	Tarrant	—	—
Browning, Emma	30402	Callahan	Browning, Frank Marion	—
Browning, Eugene T.	41668	Navarro	—	—
Browning, Francis Jackson	15426	Henderson	—	—
Browning, Ida	Rej	Camp	Browning, Pleasant West	14803
Browning, J. E. Mrs.	46015	Collin	Browning, James Wellington	—
Browning, J. R.	39707	Parker	—	—
Browning, J. V.	Rej	Milam	—	—
Browning, John G.	08281	Dallas	—	—
Browning, John I.	Rej	Wood	—	—
Browning, John Wesley	25175	Franklin	—	—
Browning, M. A. Mrs.	05601	Hunt	Browning, F. H.	—
Browning, Maggie	32706	Franklin	Browning, John Wesley	25175
Browning, Martha Elizabeth	00343	Bexar	Browning, Nathan P.	—
Browning, Maryetta S.	10341	Camp	Browning, Benjamin W.	—
Browning, Perry	28150	Sabine	—	—
Browning, Peyton Graves	Rej	Lavaca	—	—
Browning, Pleasant West	14803	Camp	—	—
Browning, S. A. E. Mrs.	19751	Cass	Browning, James Andrew Daniel	—
Browning, Sallie	20629	Henderson	Browning, Francis Jackson	15426
Browning, Sarah Jane	42199	Mason	Browning, Alfred Parks	—
Browning, Virginia C.	29528	Smith	Browning, Monterville B.	—
Browning, William	27215	Sabine	—	—
Browning, Woodson Heard	47157	Lampasas	—	—
Browning, Woodson Heard Mrs.	51929	Reeves	Browning, Woodson Heard	47157
Brownlee, C. A.	05574	Kaufman	—	—
Brownlee, Celia E.	42905	Madison	John Middleton, Sr.	18507
Brownlee, J. W.	24983	Comanche	—	—

Index to Confederate Pension Applications

Brownlee, John Middleton, Sr.	18507	Madison		
Brownlee, S. C. Mrs.	11517	Lamar	Brownlee, C. C.	
Brownlee, Sallie C.	16485	Shackelford	Brownlee, Benjamin Franklin	
Brownlow, Martha Ann	37493	Denton	Brownlow, James Columbus	
Brownlow, W. J.	25532	Ellis		
Brownson, Bernice Lynch	31329	Dewitt	Brownson, Thadeus Jesse	
Broyles, G. M.	18639	Smith		
Broyles, Georgia A.	50505	San Saba	Broyles, Thomas Jefferson	
Broyles, James R.	13393	Jones		
Broyles, Mary Jane	31347	Hill	Broyles, Benjamin Alexander	
Broyles, Sallie	42424	Anderson	Broyles, Robert Washington	
Bruce, Arthur Cleveland	19922	Matagorda		
Bruce, G. W.	Rej	Gonzales		
Bruce, Holland H. Mrs.	13469	Nacogdoches	Bruce, Jasper A. (T.)	04865
Bruce, J. C.	17419	Cass		
Bruce, J. L.	00627	Caldwell		
Bruce, Jasper T.	04865	Nacogdoches		
Bruce, John C.	08260	Comanche		
Bruce, M. Ellen Mrs.	Rej	Trinity	Bruce, John B.	
Bruce, Malinda E.	27636	Red River	Bruce, Francis Bruton	
Bruce, Martha	07665	Stephens	Bruce, Phillip A.	
Bruce, Mary	37788	Matagorda	Bruce, Arthur Cleveland	19922
Brumback, Silas Alexander	01261	Ellis		
Brumbelow, I. M. Mrs.	17664	Fort Bend	Brumbelow, Isaac Lafayette	
Brumblow, M. V.	12088	Navarro		
Brumfield, D. C.	13681	Anderson		
Brumfield, Elvira H.	13434	McLennan	Brumfield, George W.	12492
Brumfield, George W.	12492	McLennan		
Brumley, A. J.	00533	Brown		
Brumley, B.	07200	Eastland		
Brumley, Luke L.	34376	Coke		
Brumley, Thomas B.	23227	Crockett		
Brummett, M. J. Mrs.	04517	Wood	Brummett, S. J.	
Brummett, Nancy	36101	Bastrop	Brummett, John	
Brummett, Robert Cherry	32538	Tarrant		
Brundage, Helen	49824	Ellis	Brundage, William Andrew	
Brundidge, W. E.	41019	Johnson		
Brundrett, Florilla E.	50881	Aransas	Brundrett, George Albert	
Brundrett, J. M.	38995	Aransas		
Brundrett, Lula Ida	50872	Aransas	Brundrett, J. M.	38995
Brune, Fannie	23683	Austin	Brune, Henry	06895
Brune, Henry	06895	Colorado		
Bruner, Fannie	12211	Wise	Bruner, J. K. P.	
Bruner, G. H.	03098	Navarro		
Bruner, J. H.	00498	Brazoria		
Bruner, J. J.	17207	Navarro		
Bruner, Major J.	11841	Cass		
Bruner, Mary E.	13257	Cass	Bruner, Major J.	11841
Brunk, John Hendrix	46779	Montague		
Brunk, Sarah R.	51107	Montague	Brunk, John Hendrix	46779
Bruns, Agnes	40700	Goliad	Bruns, Gerhardt Henry	17693
Bruns, Gerhardt Henry	17693	Gonzales		
Bruns, Lisette	Rej	Fayette	Bruns, John Alberto	
Brunson, Newton J.	11150	Travis		
Brunson, Sarah	14901	Cherokee	Brunson, E. C.	
Brunson, Thomas J.	26091	Collin		
Brunson, William Henry	23348	Harris		
Bruton, Arthur S.	14316	Llano		
Bruton, Carrie Pheobeline	50535	Red River	Bruton, Alonzo Douglas	

Index to Confederate Pension Applications

Bruton, George Asbury	46696	Comanche	—	
Bruton, George Asbury Mrs.	51517	Comanche	Bruton, George Asbury	46696
Bruton, Nancy E.	Rej	Bandera	Bruton, James R.	—
Bruton, W. R.	23460	Callahan	—	
Bryan, A. B.	23714	Shelby	—	
Bryan, Alice V.	39538	Dallas	Bryan, Henry Monroe	—
Bryan, Allen B.	31959	Wood	—	
Bryan, Allis Caroline	38925	Shelby	Bryan, Owen Jefferson	36817
Bryan, Dorothy Ophelia	51480	Johnson	Bryan, John Albert	—
Bryan, E. R.	36137	McLennan	—	
Bryan, Elizabeth	51438	Erath	Bryan, Nicholas	33509
Bryan, Emily	28156	Runnels	Bryan, John David	—
Bryan, F. D.	23223	Dallas	—	
Bryan, Frances	29141	Bastrop	Bryan, Samuel Wesley	—
Bryan, Henrietta A.	43598	Bosque	Bryan, Henry Martin	23782
Bryan, Henry M.	01069	Dallas	—	
Bryan, Henry Martin	23782	Bosque	—	
Bryan, J. A.	17491	Colorado	—	
Bryan, J. T.	Rej	Lamar	—	
Bryan, Jacob Apples	23313	Archer	—	
Bryan, Joe K.	10087	Freestone	—	
Bryan, John A.	15858	Lamar	—	
Bryan, Josephine Hart	43309	Montague	Bryan, Moses Austin	—
Bryan, Kittie Cate	Rej	Floyd	Cate, Jacob	—
Bryan, Mahaly	33475	Anderson	Bryan, James W.	—
Bryan, Martha	29140	Tom Green	Bryan, John Samuel Phelps	—
Bryan, Mary	Rej	San Augustine	Bryan, Seburn J.	—
Bryan, Mary D.	42343	Shelby	Bryan, William Jack	—
Bryan, Mary Eliza	33701	Milam	Bryan, Daniel Fox	—
Bryan, Nancy J.	24871	Hale	Bryan, James Harvey	—
Bryan, Nicholas	33509	Erath	—	
Bryan, Owen Jefferson	36817	Shelby	—	
Bryan, Polycarp L.	23184	Brazoria	—	
Bryan, Rena	22367	Anderson	Bryan, John Walker Knight	—
Bryan, S. A. Mrs.	39632	Archer	Bryan, Jacob Apples	23313
Bryan, S. E. Mrs.	42034	Hamilton	Bryan, F. W.	—
Bryan, Sallie M.	31439	Bowie	Bryan, James Parks	—
Bryan, Sarah A.	31046	Shelby	Bryan, Edward Fox	—
Bryan, Sarah Jane	46508	Clay	Bryan, John Neely	—
Bryan, Sue E.	49186	Dallas	Bryan, James Bracken	—
Bryan, Terrell	05638	Erath	—	
Bryant, A.	03355	Polk	—	
Bryant, A. G.	26618	Red River	—	
Bryant, Bell	49522	Bexar	Bryant, Benjamin Brittan	—
Bryant, Belle	Rej	Dallas	Bryant, Ben Newton	—
Bryant, Benjamin Franklin	07382	Van Zandt	—	
Bryant, Berry Benson	13657	Cooke	—	
Bryant, Eleanor C.	09126	Wood	Bryant, Howard	—
Bryant, Eliza	10938	Floyd	Bryant, Jesse	08303
Bryant, Elizabeth M.	01251	Ellis	Bryant, William T.	—
Bryant, Ella	34973	Coleman	Bryant, Berry Benson	13657
Bryant, Frances Codelia	Rej	Hopkins	Bryant, Lucius Rhods	—
Bryant, Frank	Rej	Limestone	—	
Bryant, George Newton Mrs.	43012	Wood	Bryant, George Newton	—
Bryant, George T.	33675	Milam	—	
Bryant, Hardy B.	25749	Smith	—	
Bryant, Henrietta	39154	Van Zandt	Bryant, Benjamin Franklin	07382
Bryant, Isaac	26649	Falls	—	
Bryant, J. M.	08422M	Navarro	—	

Index to Confederate Pension Applications

Name	App #	County	Veteran	Vet #
Bryant, James Franklin	01997	Hopkins		
Bryant, James Wesly	21666	Henderson		
Bryant, Jesse	08303	Floyd		
Bryant, Joe	46496	Terry		
Bryant, Joe Eleck	Rej	Terry		
Bryant, Joseph Calvin	29044	Montague		
Bryant, Joseph Robert	12332	Denton		
Bryant, Josephine	42553	Milam	Bryant, Roman	37041
Bryant, Josephine	47207	Montague	Bryant, Joseph Calvin	29044
Bryant, Laura E.	25792	Collin	Bryant, Robert Sylvanus	
Bryant, Lewis Henry	30035	Jack		
Bryant, Louisa	31537	Shelby	Bryant, Milton Rogers	25699
Bryant, M. M. Mrs.	Rej	Grimes	Bryant, Thomas Needham	
Bryant, Martha	01110	Delta	Bryant, William	
Bryant, Mary	27108	McLennan	Bryant, William Andrew	
Bryant, Mary	34336	Smith	Bryant, Hardy B.	25749
Bryant, Mary A.	40537	Navarro	Bryant, William Pursley	
Bryant, Mary D.	23245	Hardin	Bryant, William Owen	00727
Bryant, Mary E.	36470	Henderson	Bryant, James Wesley	21666
Bryant, Milian Mirandy	Rej	Leon	Bryant, David Washington	
Bryant, Milton Rogers	25699	Travis		
Bryant, N. J. Mrs.	24973	Wilbarger	Bryant, George J. Nitcheltree	
Bryant, Nancy Ann	26285	Collin	Bryant, Joseph Roberts	12332
Bryant, Nettie	20907	Navarro	Bryant, John	
Bryant, P. H.	02434	Lamar		
Bryant, R.	49848	Erath		
Bryant, R. J.	30821	Limestone		
Bryant, Roman	37041	Milam		
Bryant, Sallie C.	40349	Jack	Bryant, Lewis Henry	30035
Bryant, Samuel Alexander Mrs.	Rej	San Saba	Bryant, Samuel Alexander	
Bryant, Sarah Alice	47254	Cass	Bryant, John Patrick	
Bryant, Sarah Ann	20023	Hopkins	Bryant, James Franklin	01997
Bryant, Sarah Elizabeth	05022	Nueces	Bryant, Martin V.	
Bryant, Sterling	29926	Fannin		
Bryant, T. L.	40876	Johnson		
Bryant, T. N.	Rej	Grimes		
Bryant, T. Y.	19596	Montague		
Bryant, Thomas L.	42406	Franklin		
Bryant, Thomas R.	Rej	Fannin		
Bryant, William H.	08029	Dallas		
Bryant, William Owen	00727	Chambers		
Bryce, D. W.	22444	Williamson		
Bryce, John A.	06917	Rusk		
Bryce, Millie	09620	Rusk	Bryce, John A.	06917
Bryce, Peter (Perry)	18347	Shelby		
Bryce, Rebecca Eveline Poole	31163	Upshur	Poole, Thomas Masten	24449
Brymer, Amanda Catherine	35305	Tarrant	Brymer, John Tucker	
Brymer, John T.	Rej	Tarrant		
Brymer, Mary	44025	Williamson	Brymer, Amos Posey	
Brymer, N. P. Mrs.	33179	Burleson	Brymer, James	
Bryson, A. C.	05722	Collin		
Bryson, E. S. Mrs.	33146	Burnet	Bryson, Joseph Goodson	
Bryson, George Washington Mrs.	45504	Cooke	Bryson, George Washington	
Bryson, J. D.	06171	Nolan		
Bryson, J. H.	04833	Red River		
Bryson, John Franklin Mrs.	43370	Ellis	Bryson, John Franklin	
Bryson, Josephine	36513	Williamson	Bryson, Thomas Noble	
Bryson, Margreate Henrietta	Rej	McLennan	Bryson, William Wiley	
Bryson, S. M. Mrs.	36757	Mitchell	Bryson, J. D.	06171

Index to Confederate Pension Applications

Bryson, Samuel	07952	Rusk	—	
Bryson, Teresa	01689	Grimes	Bryson, William	
Buchan, L. A. P. Mrs.	01201	Eastland	Buchan, James E.	
Buchan, William Hector, Sr.	29619	Upshur	—	
Buchanan, Armandia	04810	Nacogdoches	—	
Buchanan, Eula Jane	46404	Hunt	Buchanan, Marcus Theophulus	—
Buchanan, Fannie	Rej	Goliad	Buchanan, Samuel Beaty	
Buchanan, Frances	42282	Real	Buchanan, William Andrews	37735
Buchanan, G. W.	08443M	Parker	—	
Buchanan, George A.	15826	Kaufman	—	
Buchanan, George A.	18550	Wise	—	
Buchanan, George Craig	28590	Scurry	—	
Buchanan, Henry Clay	43505	Hunt	—	
Buchanan, J. C.	16686	Titus	—	
Buchanan, J. T.	38760	Collin	—	
Buchanan, James Wesley	23541	Upshur	—	
Buchanan, Jane	08834	Palo Pinto	Buchanan, G. W.	08443M
Buchanan, John Neullin	12086	Navarro	—	
Buchanan, Josephine D.	45802	Hill	Buchanan, Samuel Edwin	08729
Buchanan, L. J. Mrs.	39172	Upshur	Buchanan, James Mesley	23541
Buchanan, Marinda A.	Rej	Bastrop	Buchanan, William Alexander	12259
Buchanan, Mary Ann	31880	Comanche	Buchanan, William B.	17501
Buchanan, Mary Clark	Rej	Hunt	Buchanan, Henry Clay	43505
Buchanan, Molly S.	42798	Wichita	Buchanan, John C.	
Buchanan, Nancy Ann	04988	Williamson	Buchanan, F. M.	
Buchanan, Ola	52050	Henderson	Buchanan, John Neullin	12086
Buchanan, R. J.	25836	Travis	—	
Buchanan, R. W.	08748	Lampasas	—	
Buchanan, S. L. Mrs.	41931	Cooke	Buchanan, Oliver Perry	
Buchanan, S. L. Z. Mrs.	35314	Lamar	Buchanan, William Philander	24987
Buchanan, S. P. Mrs.	39393	Van Zandt	Buchanan, Seborn Pruitt	25467
Buchanan, Sallie	49576	Dallas	Buchanan, John B.	
Buchanan, Samuel Edwin	08729	Hill	—	
Buchanan, Sarah C.	51287	Scurry	Buchanan, George Craig	28590
Buchanan, Seborn Pruitt	25467	Van Zandt	—	
Buchanan, Susan T.	20548	Wise	Buchanan, George A.	18550
Buchanan, T. A.	01534	Gillespie	—	
Buchanan, W. L.	23352	Burnet	—	
Buchanan, William Alexander	12259	Bastrop	—	
Buchanan, William Andrews	37735	Real	—	
Buchanan, William B.	17501	Comanche	—	
Buchanan, William Philander	24987	Lamar	—	
Buck, Georgia T.	44045	Erath	Buck, Silas Calmes	
Buck, J. G. H.	Rej	Anderson	—	
Buck, Sarah Matilda	31701	Montague	Buck, Pleasant	
Buckalew, Fanny L.	43245	Henderson	Buckalew, John Christopher	
Buckingham, C. S. Mann Mrs.	Rej	Denton	Mann, Brice William	
Buckles, L. A. Mrs.	27771	Callahan	Buckles, Edward Robinson Antillius	—
Buckley, Lou H.	32722	Denton	Buckley, Cornelius	
Buckley, Mamie A.	47823	Dallas	Buckley, Ruben E.	
Buckley, Sarah J.	28271	Harris	Buckley, John Cornelius	
Buckner, Edmonia	24885	Navarro	Buckner, Eli Franklin	
Buckner, Emily	07295	McLennan	Buckner, George Washington	
Buckner, F. (Jennie) V.	17622	Erath	Buckner, William Ayleth	07071
Buckner, James Washington	38844	Bastrop	—	
Buckner, M. L. Mrs.	43522	Bastrop	Buckner, James Washington	38844
Buckner, Missouri Elizabeth Moore	38060	Polk	Moore, Thomas C.	
Buckner, Myrtis Euphrazier	16390	Rusk	Buckner, Artur Washington	—
Buckner, Susan Isabella	35766	Nacogdoches	Buckner, Isaac Newton	

Index to Confederate Pension Applications

Buckner, William Ayleth	07071	Limestone	—	
Buckow, Joe	Rej	Harris	—	
Budde, Louis	39007	Dewitt	—	
Budde, Theresa	40216	Dewitt	Budde, Louis	39007
Buechmann, Minna	43552	Austin	Buechmann, John	
Buff, Lem	35424	Grimes	—	
Buffington, Ada	42464	Houston	Buffington, Samuel Edward	
Buford, Amanda	50403	Van Zandt	Buford, Edward L.	
Buford, D. S. Mrs.	23251	Gonzales	Buford, William Henry	
Buford, Edward	Rej	Van Zandt	—	
Buford, Emma J.	35006	Guadalupe	Buford, James Wilburn	14789
Buford, James Edward	07160	Burnet	—	
Buford, James Wilburn	14749	Brown	—	
Buford, M. C. Mrs.	19640	Coke	Buford, James Edward	07160
Buford, M. J. Mrs.	20572	Scurry	Buford, Alexander Jasper	
Buford, Serena	19789	Harris	Buford, James William	
Bugg, J. P.	26509	McLennan	—	
Bugg, Malinda	06416	Cooke	Bugg, John S.	
Buice, J. B.	00911	Comanche	—	
Buie, Amanda C.	29452	Van Zandt	Buie, John Archin	
Buie, Malcom	23462	Smith	—	
Buie, R. D.	12003	Kaufman	—	
Bulger, Phillip	13087	Travis	—	
Bulger, William Jefferson	29745	Tom Green	—	
Bulger, William Jefferson Mrs.	42737	Tom Green	Bulger, William Jefferson	29745
Bull, C. V. Mrs.	Rej	Coleman	Bull, John Campbell	
Bull, George W.	07916	Mills	—	
Bull, Isabell A.	28041	Hamilton	Bull, James Convey	
Bull, Jessie M.	05309	Montague	—	
Bull, John C.	13756	Coleman	—	
Bull, M. E. Mrs.	30447	Hunt	Bull, William Hamilton	
Bull, Mahala E.	43100	Montague	Bull, Robert Campbell	
Bull, Millie E.	20598	Coleman	Bull, John C.	13756
Bull, Robert C.	07566	Coleman	—	
Bull, T. D.	Rej	Eastland	—	
Bullard, Amanda M.	01752	Hamilton	Bullard, Stephen A.	
Bullard, Asa	31570	Johnson	—	
Bullard, B. F.	Rej	Tarrant	—	
Bullard, Benjamin	Rej	Shelby	—	
Bullard, Charley Lee	22734	Upshur	—	
Bullard, Henry S.	05568	Kaufman	—	
Bullard, Isaac H.	37456	Reeves	—	
Bullard, J. B.	28076	Gonzales	—	
Bullard, J. E.	31845	Tarrant	—	
Bullard, Jap	03383	Rains	—	
Bullard, Lorenzo Dow Mrs.	41203	Dallam	Bullard, Lorenzo Dow	
Bullard, M.	RejM	Smith	—	
Bullard, M. E. Mrs.	40512	Upshur	Bullard, Charley Lee	22734
Bullard, Mary A.	00974	Cooke	Bullard, Ephraim I.	
Bullard, Mary A.	34945	Mitchell	Bullard, James Francis	
Bullard, Mary Ann	Rej	Real	Bullard, Christopher Columbus	
Bullard, N. A. H.	Rej	Wood	—	
Bullard, Rebecca Elizabeth	45375	Upshur	Bullard, William Thomas	23341
Bullard, Sally E.	Rej	Collin	Bullard, William	
Bullard, Savilla Matilda	41035	Johnson	Bullard, Asa	31570
Bullard, Susan C.	32102	Smith	Bullard, Wiley Mackalister	
Bullard, Wiley M.	Rej	Smith	—	
Bullard, William Thomas	23341	Upshur	—	
Buller, N. C.	30071	Polk	—	

Index to Confederate Pension Applications

Name	App #	County	Veteran	Vet App #
Bullington, Elizabeth	28015	Fannin	Bullington, Joseph	—
Bullington, James Newton	27208	Williamson	—	—
Bullington, John R.	22454	Parker	—	—
Bullington, Mary D.	09063	Lamar	Bullington, John D.	—
Bullington, Mary Isabell	40319	Williamson	Bullington, James Newton	27208
Bullion, C. A. Mrs.	Rej	Mitchell	Bullion, George Wilson	—
Bulloch, D. L.	13059	Shelby	—	—
Bulloch, Emiline	19366	Shelby	Bulloch, David	—
Bullock, A. E. Mrs.	40690	Upshur	Ransom Lamar, Sr.	23518
Bullock, E. J. Mrs.	35538	Dallas	Bullock, William Lowery	—
Bullock, Jane	24911	Hopkins	Bullock, Cornelius	—
Bullock, John M. V.	34639	Stonewall	—	—
Bullock, Laura C.	10954	Grayson	Bullock, William H.	08701
Bullock, Mary E.	46230	Nueces	Bullock, Joseph	—
Bullock, Mary Jane	10815	Austin	Bullock, Alfred	—
Bullock, Napoleon B.	12328	Dallas	—	—
Bullock, Ransom Lamar, Sr.	23518	Upshur	—	—
Bullock, S. N.	05533	Harris	—	—
Bullock, Sarah R.	03563	San Augustine	Bullock, Thad W.	—
Bullock, Thomas Franklin	24641	Tom Green	—	—
Bullock, William H.	08701	Grayson	—	—
Bullock, William Lowery Mrs.	Rej	Dallas	Bullock, William Lowery	—
Bulls, C. H. Mrs.	21564	Hunt	Bulls, James Henry	20749
Bulls, James Henry	20749	Hunt	—	—
Bumguardner, M. J. Mrs.	20801	McCulloch	Bumguardner, Sylvester S.	06565
Bumguardner, Sylvester S.	06565	McCulloch	—	—
Bumpas, H. E. Mrs.	01039	Dallas	Bumpas, William Madison	—
Bunch, Ava J.	36700	Caldwell	Bunch, Henry Holcombe	25568
Bunch, Flavia H.	50758	Dallas	Bunch, Eugene Franklin	—
Bunch, Henry Holcombe	25568	Caldwell	—	—
Bundick, Ellen	45776	Gonzales	Bundick, Milton Pruett	—
Bundick, Laura P.	18099	McCulloch	Bundick, Martin W.	—
Bundick, Martin W.	Rej	Guadalupe	—	—
Bundrant, Mary S.	45593	Coryell	Bundrant, Daniel Gillie	—
Bundren, John W.	Rej	Bexar	—	—
Bundy, Martha	Rej	Williamson	Bundy, Zachery Taylor	—
Bundy, Mary Y.	30025	Smith	Bundy, David Thomas	—
Bunge, William W. Mrs.	49214	Colorado	Bunge, William W.	—
Bunker, John W.	06712	Comanche	—	—
Bunker, Mary C.	21667	Dewitt	Bunker, Thaddeus	08669
Bunker, N. I. Mrs.	14952	Comanche	Bunker, John W.	06712
Bunker, Thaddeus	08669	Dewitt	—	—
Bunn, John G.	09932	Limestone	—	—
Bunn, Mary A.	11659	Tom Green	Bunn, W. M.	—
Bunn, Wiley	Rej	Dallas	—	—
Bunn, William	00292	Bell	—	—
Bunt, Delana	23395	Gregg	—	—
Bunt, Mary Arminda	38955	Gregg	Bunt, Delana	23395
Buntin, Alice A.	30351	Erath	Buntin, John Adams	23344
Buntin, John Adams	23344	Erath	—	—
Buntin, Sarah L.	41462	Parker	Buntin, William Edward Harrison	—
Bunting, Alonzo Sidney	38865	Palo Pinto	—	—
Bunting, Alonzo Sidney Mrs.	47320	Palo Pinto	Bunting, Alonzo Sidney	38865
Bunton, Elizabeth	35039	Bastrop	Bunton, Joseph Loyd	23550
Bunton, Jane	06143	Gillespie	Bunton, Robert	—
Bunton, John W.	Rej	Sutton	—	—
Bunton, Joseph Loyd	23550	Bastrop	—	—
Bunton, Thomas H.	32601	Real	—	—
Burcalow, Jesse	04032	Upshur	—	—

Index to Confederate Pension Applications

Name	No.	County	Related	No.
Burcalow, Sarah E.	17170	Upshur	Burcalow, Jesse	04032
Burch, Burman Dotty	28621	Cooke	—	—
Burch, J. C.	09033	Hale	—	—
Burch, Martha J.	34359	Cooke	Burch, Burman Dotty	28621
Burch, Mary	08262	Cooke	Burch, Joseph R.	—
Burch, Thomas	19920	Polk	—	—
Burcham, Joe R.	23293	Jones	—	—
Burchfield, G. W.	07391	Wood	—	—
Burchfield, George Washington	35034	Kaufman	—	—
Burden, A. J.	05878	Fannin	—	—
Burden, Carroll	04408	Williamson	—	—
Burden, Matilda	20055	Montgomery	Burden, John G.	—
Burden, Rebecca	37409	Grimes	Burden, George L.	—
Burden, W. T.	08277	Dallas	—	—
Burdett, Abner G.	17825	Hill	—	—
Burdett, Augusta A.	03902	Travis	—	—
Burdett, Benjamin Apling	05966	Bosque	—	—
Burdette, Isabella F.	35964	Hill	Burdette, Abner G.	17825
Burdette, M. E. Mrs.	37588	Bosque	Burdette, Benjamin Apling	05966
Burdick, Alf L.	01990	Hopkins	—	—
Burditt, A. B. Mrs.	Rej	Atascosa	Burditt, Jessie F.	—
Burditt, J. S.	37194	Fort Bend	—	—
Burford, A. W.	21641	Tarrant	—	—
Burgamy, S. C. Mrs.	15693	Henderson	Burgamy, John Collinsworth	—
Burge, J. W.	09540	Collin	—	—
Burge, Jerry N.	03418	Red River	—	—
Burge, Julia Ann	09679	Collin	Burge, J. W.	09540
Burge, K. F.	08451M	Red River	—	—
Burge, L. T.	02438	Lamar	—	—
Burge, Mary E.	03681	Smith	Burge, B. W.	—
Burge, Rowan A.	07613	Hill	—	—
Burge, T. F.	Rej	Denton	—	—
Burge, Tom W.	50450	Cameron	—	—
Burger, Bertha	25261	Bell	Burger, Feodar	21384
Burger, Feodor	21384	Bell	—	—
Burger, Louisa	49140	Medina	Burger, Hubert	—
Burger, Mary R.	RejM	Cherokee	—	—
Burger, W. M.	06346	Kaufman	—	—
Burges, Gray	49242	Guadalupe	Burges, Richard Joseph	—
Burges, Mary Lou Jefferson	42684	Bexar	Burges, William Henry	—
Burgess, A. S.	Rej	Henderson	—	—
Burgess, David Francis	25172	Polk	—	—
Burgess, Elizabeth	10426	Milam	Burgess, Robert	02955
Burgess, F. C. Mrs.	04384	Wichita	Burgess, W. H.	—
Burgess, F. J. Mrs.	Rej	Rains	Burgess, J. T.	—
Burgess, F. J. Mrs.	31508	Rains	Burgess, Ellis Green	—
Burgess, John J.	Home	Travis	—	—
Burgess, Laura	01998	Hopkins	Burgess, John M.	—
Burgess, Lemuel C.	50037	Tarrant	—	—
Burgess, Matilda E.	01908	Hill	Burgess, Lewis Wesley	—
Burgess, Mattie	36758	Navarro	Burgess, Charley H.	—
Burgess, N. A. Mrs.	32104	Tarrant	Burgess, William Franklin	28432
Burgess, Nettie	33665	Polk	Burgess, David Francis	25172
Burgess, Penelope Clark	51073	Tarrant	Burgess, Lemuel C.	50037
Burgess, Robert	02955	Milam	—	—
Burgess, Sallie	19701	San Saba	Burgess, William M.	07899
Burgess, T. B.	Rej	Shelby	—	—
Burgess, Thomas Madison Jasper	51732	Crosby	—	—
Burgess, W. B.	31348	Dallas	—	—

Index to Confederate Pension Applications

Name	No.	County	Veteran	No.
Burgess, William Franklin	28432	Tarrant	—	
Burgess, William M.	04553	Burleson	—	
Burgess, William M.	07899	Milam	—	
Burget, S. J. Mrs.	23183	Tarrant	Burget, Andrew Jackson	
Burgoon, Mary V.	42881	Tarrant	Burgoon, Henry	
Burk, C. B.	09468	Gonzales	—	
Burk, Elizabeth	Rej	Rusk	Burk, R. T.	
Burk, John Alonzo	07794	Denton	—	
Burk, John Henry	26673	Harris	—	
Burk, M. C. Mrs.	50786	Hamilton	Burk, Richard	
Burke, A. C. Mrs.	Rej	San Saba	Burke, James Polk	
Burke, Annie R.	49621	Cherokee	Burke, Francis William	
Burke, Ben	21669	Trinity	—	
Burke, Bettie	17723	Gregg	Burke, Archibald Turk	
Burke, C. G.	08323	Grayson	—	
Burke, Daniel	Rej	Harris	—	
Burke, Daniel Marion	20777	Harris	—	
Burke, David	RejM	Harris	—	
Burke, Elizabeth Ann	23557	Milam	Burke, John Franklin	
Burke, Emma L.	34550	Angelina	Burke, James Dowen	29611
Burke, Etta K.	41465	Tarrant	Burke, Francis Marion	38747
Burke, Fannie A.	41718	Denton	Burke, Robert Lafayette	15042
Burke, Francis A.	Rej	Guadalupe	—	
Burke, Francis M.	Rej	Upshur	—	
Burke, Francis Marion	38747	Tarrant	—	
Burke, G. F.	RejM	Polk	—	
Burke, G. W.	23549	Fannin	—	
Burke, George P.	10223	Travis	—	
Burke, I. R.	16967	Williamson	—	
Burke, James	05730	Dallas	—	
Burke, James Dowen	29611	Angelina	—	
Burke, James Oliver	27763	Trinity	—	
Burke, Joseph Calvin Mrs.	42200	Grayson	Burke, Joseph Calvin	
Burke, Kate Elizabeth Thomas	46471	Harris	James, Jr.	
Burke, M. E. Mrs.	30879	Hunt	Burke, Samuel Duncan	
Burke, Martha	35351	Trinity	Burke, Ben	
Burke, Nancy	51169	Harris	Burke, Daniel Marion	20777
Burke, Petronia Josephine	40531	Madison	Burke, Preston Pinckney	26372
Burke, Preston Pinckney	26372	Madison	—	
Burke, Rebecca Jane	14560	Angelina	Burke, James Monroe	
Burke, Robert Lafayette	15042	Denton	—	
Burke, Samuel D.	40297	Lubbock	—	
Burke, Sarah	32974	Trinity	Burke, James Oliver	27763
Burke, Thomas P.	40075	Denton	—	
Burke, Tobias	Rej	Travis	—	
Burke, William	31846	Fayette	—	
Burkehalter, Frances	Rej	Sabine	Burkehalter, James D.	
Burket, Fred	05193	Delta	—	
Burkett, Charles M.	18382	Smith	—	
Burkett, Frank A.	15277	Grayson	—	
Burkett, J. C.	40988	Grayson	—	
Burkett, Jabez Lafayette	28282	Fannin	—	
Burkett, Martha F.	08643	Collin	Burkett, James Monroe	
Burkett, N.	12944	Karnes	—	
Burkett, Ollie	43853	Collin	Burkett, Josiah	
Burkett, Sarah	00392	Bexar	Burkett, Alexander	
Burkett, Sarah A.	20140	Lamar	Burket(t), Fred	05193
Burkett, Sarah P.	40203	Fannin	Burkett, Jabez Lafayette	28282
Burkhalter, A.	13583	Cass	—	

Index to Confederate Pension Applications

Name	Number	County	Related	Related #
Burkhalter, Ebenezer M.	06893	Bowie		
Burkhalter, Elender Adline	34562	Shelby	Burkhalter, William	
Burkhalter, G. G.	12183	Van Zandt		
Burkhalter, H. M.	30099	Kaufman		
Burkhalter, Sarah R.	08226	Bowie	Burkhalter, Ebben M.	
Burkham, E. B.	09709	Hopkins		
Burkham, Fannie	50726	Childress	Burkham, Charles	
Burkham, Mary A.	31275	Uvalde	Burkham, Thomas Jefferson	26370
Burkham, Thomas Jefferson	26370	Uvalde		
Burkhart, Della	46479	Williamson	Burkhart, John Harvey	42204
Burkhart, Emma A.	33702	Matagorda	Burkhart, Alexander Christian	
Burkhart, Granville Martin	33628	Milam		
Burkhart, J. C.	05664	Collin		
Burkhart, James McDonnal	Rej	McLennan		
Burkhart, John Harvey	42204	Williamson		
Burkhart, Mary A.	17953	Jefferson	Burkhart, William H.	
Burkhart, Mary Ann	50511	Milam	Burkhart, Granville Martin	33628
Burkhart, Nancy White	Rej	Hopkins	Burkhart, Stephen Houston	
Burkhead, Solon E.	38765	Harris		
Burks, Andrew J.	18985	Grimes		
Burks, Benjamin F.	Rej	Polk		
Burks, Caroline	33570	Polk	Burks, Hardy D.	12101
Burks, Ellen D.	51852	Dallas	Burks, Nathan	
Burks, Exah M. Mrs.	21395	Comanche	Burks, Thomas J.	17500
Burks, Hardy D.	12101	Polk		
Burks, Harriet	19497	Smith	Burks, James Armstrong	
Burks, J. F.	47160	Ellis		
Burks, J. L.	06709	Cherokee		
Burks, J. W.	06391	Ellis		
Burks, James K. Polk	13760	Comanche		
Burks, Josephine	Rej	Polk	Burks, Benjamin Franklin	
Burks, Joshua	Rej	Bastrop		
Burks, M. C. Mrs.	23323	McLennan	Burks, James Washington	
Burks, M. J. Mrs.	Rej	Van Zandt	Burks, Maston Milton	
Burks, Mary E.	38430	Grayson	Burks, John William	
Burks, Mary Jane	41656	Taylor	Burks, Berry Maximilian	
Burks, Nancy	12078	Nacogdoches	Burks, William	
Burks, Nancy C.	07476	Gonzales	Burks, O. H. K.	
Burks, Sudie A.	34689	Comanche	Burks, James K. Polk	13760
Burks, Thomas J.	17500	Comanche		
Burks, William	10763	Travis		
Burleson, A. T.	07599	Grayson		
Burleson, Aaron James	22559	Limestone		
Burleson, D. W.	08261	Comanche		
Burleson, E. E. Mrs.	00436	Blanco	Burleson, Joseph Rogers	
Burleson, Fannie	47392	Travis	Burleson, Jefferson Warren	
Burleson, J. A.	Rej	Fannin		
Burleson, James R.	10569	Freestone		
Burleson, John F.	Rej	Bastrop		
Burleson, John Garvan	10366	Edwards		
Burleson, John J.	29504	Eastland		
Burleson, Josephine Elizabeth	Rej	Mills	Burleson, William Harrison	
Burleson, Josie	50165	Limestone	Burleson, Aaron James	22559
Burleson, M. A. Mrs.	42289	Freestone	Burleson, Augustus Lawhorn	
Burleson, Martha J.	19965	Bastrop	Burleson, John Baptin	
Burleson, Martha Jane	32979	Dawson	Burleson, Joseph Pride	
Burleson, Mary	Rej	Travis	Burleson, Jacob	
Burleson, S. J. Mrs.	49320	Johnson	Burleson, William Curtis	
Burleson, Sarah Ann	05098	Comanche	Burleson, Wiley	

Index to Confederate Pension Applications

Name	No.	County	Veteran	No.
Burleson, Thomas J.	09960	Erath	—	
Burleson, Viola	21293	San Augustine	Burleson, John	—
Burnam, J. H.	27341	Ellis	—	
Burnes, Henry	46730	Bexar	—	
Burnes, James W.	19764	Palo Pinto	—	
Burnes, Sarah Ann	Rej	Leon	Burnes, William Alexander	—
Burnett, Alexander Hamiilton	22895	Grayson	—	
Burnett, Columbus Price	15091	Erath	—	
Burnett, Eliza A.	03562	San Augustine	Burnett, J. R.	—
Burnett, Francis M.	26942	Terry	—	
Burnett, Henry Clay	11913	Galveston	—	
Burnett, J. M.	10932	Fannin	—	
Burnett, James H.	15092	Erath	—	
Burnett, Jennie	Rej	Grayson	Burnett, Alexander Hamilton	22895
Burnett, John F.	17328	Bexar	—	
Burnett, Julia E.	14191	Dallas	Burnett, S. C.	—
Burnett, M. A. Mrs.	Rej	Borden	Burnett, Isaac	—
Burnett, M. E. Mrs.	39943	Swisher	Burnett, Lafayette	—
Burnett, M. V. Mrs.	43199	Jack	Burnett, Lorenzy Dow	—
Burnett, Mattie R.	33839	Harrison	Burnett, Samuel	—
Burnett, N. P. Mrs.	Rej	Williamson	Burnett, J. L.	—
Burnett, N. P. Mrs.	08360M	Hopkins	—	
Burnett, Nissie	Rej	Washington	Burnett, William S.	—
Burnett, P. C.	Rej	Van Zandt	—	
Burnett, R. J. Mrs.	02248	Jasper	Burnett, T. G.	—
Burnett, S. F. Mrs.	20171	Erath	Burnett, Columbus Price	15091
Burnett, Sarah Margaret	Rej	Montague	Burnett, Robert Middleton	—
Burnett, Thomas Raynes Mrs.	33528	Dallas	Burnett, Thomas Raynes	—
Burnett, William	02768	Mason	—	
Burney, Belinda McNair	46120	Uvalde	Burney, Madison Weir	—
Burney, James Sylvanus	12979	Limestone	—	
Burney, John H.	10649	Harris	—	
Burney, M. E. Mrs.	32101	Limestone	Burney, James Sylvanus	12979
Burney, Martha Tatum	50254	Kerr	Burney, William Dewitt Clinton	—
Burney, Mary	18629	Limestone	Burney, Tom S.	11037
Burney, N. M. Mrs.	17772	Harris	Burney, James Lawrence	—
Burney, S. A. Mrs.	38396	Erath	Burney, William R.	15093
Burney, Tom S.	11037	Limestone	—	
Burney, William R.	15093	Erath	—	
Burnham, John H.	00952	Cooke	—	
Burnham, Marion Legran	27623	Newton	—	
Burnham, Marion Legran Mrs.	39188	Newton	Burnham, Marion Legran	27623
Burnham, William T.	14561	Angelina	—	
Burns, A. U. Mrs.	40717	Taylor	Burns, John Strauther	38339
Burns, Addie	Rej	Cass	Burns, John H.	23464
Burns, Alabama Victoria	34246	Brown	Burns, Joseph Shrock	—
Burns, Andrew S.	00048	Angelina	—	
Burns, B. F.	RejM	Bexar	—	
Burns, B. F.	00243	Bell	—	
Burns, B. F.	10927	Falls	—	
Burns, C. C.	Rej	Caldwell	—	
Burns, Charles George Mrs.	21670	Deaf Smith	Burns, Charles George	—
Burns, Charles W.	46175	Fayette	—	
Burns, Christopher Columbus, Sr.	26687	Dimmit	—	
Burns, D. S.	RejM	Grayson	—	
Burns, D. T.	Rej	Franklin	—	
Burns, Dovey S.	28414	Navarro	Burns, Alford Eli	—
Burns, E. A.	45945	Lee	—	
Burns, E. E. Mrs.	06280	Hopkins	Burns, S. J.	—

Index to Confederate Pension Applications

Name	App. No.	County	Veteran	Vet. No.
Burns, E. H. Mrs.	00117	Austin	Burns, Thomas H.	—
Burns, Elizabeth	09789	Taylor	Burns, John M.	—
Burns, Elizabeth	43852	Cooke	Burns, John W.	—
Burns, Elvira	03620	Shelby	Burns, John M.	—
Burns, Eunice	45862	Parker	Burns, John Wesley	40523
Burns, Fannie	31045	Bowie	Burns, William	—
Burns, Felix H.	33656	Austin	—	—
Burns, G. D. Mrs.	50366	Uvalde	Burns, Henry Luther	—
Burns, Georgiana	35784	Dimmit	Christopher Columbus, Sr.	26687
Burns, Isham L.	Rej	Grayson	—	—
Burns, J. H.	27319	Bexar	—	—
Burns, J. W.	15716	Hopkins	—	—
Burns, John	03836	Titus	—	—
Burns, John	09965	Limestone	—	—
Burns, John	17327	Bexar	—	—
Burns, John	39269	Austin	—	—
Burns, John H.	23464	Cass	—	—
Burns, John R.	37797	Navarro	—	—
Burns, John Strauther	38339	Taylor	—	—
Burns, John W.	07153	Brown	—	—
Burns, John Wesley	40523	Parker	—	—
Burns, John, Sr.	Rej	Karnes	—	—
Burns, L.	21668	Montgomery	—	—
Burns, Lizzie	03784	Tarrant	Burns, W. O.	—
Burns, Lizzie	49590	Milam	Burns, Simeon Maxwell	—
Burns, Louisa	RejM	Collin	—	—
Burns, Lydia	05598	Hunt	Burns, James J.	—
Burns, Martha Ellen	36595	Hardeman	Burns, Thomas Hue	01768
Burns, Mary A.	09134	Angelina	Burns, Andrew S.	00048
Burns, Mary E.	17657	Fayette	Burns, James Thomas	—
Burns, N. A. Mrs.	06674	Collin	Burns, W. W.	—
Burns, Nancy H.	Rej	Shelby	Burns, William Reece	—
Burns, O. W.	01323	Erath	—	—
Burns, Peter	26083	Bowie	—	—
Burns, R. L. Mrs.	16860	Van Zandt	Burns, Martin Vanburen	—
Burns, R. M.	01636	Grayson	—	—
Burns, Robert Mrs.	17771	Harris	Burns, Robert	—
Burns, Rose G. L.	51376	Austin	Burns, John	39269
Burns, S. W. Mrs.	Rej	Grimes	Burns, Reason Robert	—
Burns, Sallie	09527	Williamson	Burns, John R.	—
Burns, Samanthy Millirons	45991	Navarro	Burns, John Lawrence	—
Burns, Thomas Hue	01768	Hardeman	—	—
Burns, W. M.	05604	Hunt	—	—
Burns, William Denis	15152	Fayette	—	—
Burns, William Penn Mrs.	40549	Shelby	Burns, William Penn	—
Burnsed, N. A. Mrs.	23233	Gonzales	Burnsed, James Hutson	—
Burnsed, S. J. Mrs.	28671	Dallas	Burnsed, Jordon Huliet	—
Burnside, Anna L.	21363	Bexar	Burnside, James Augustus	—
Burnside, Fannie E.	24766	Rains	Burnside, S. N.	03384
Burnside, S. N.	03384	Rains	—	—
Burr, Mary Elizabeth	38550	Madison	Burr, Timothy Waldron	—
Burrage, John E., Sr.	45601	Collin	—	—
Burrage, Mattie J.	50383	Collin	John E., Sr.	45601
Burrage, Thomas Allen Mrs.	49311	Karnes	Burrage, Thomas Allen	—
Burrage, William Henry	50485	Bexar	—	—
Burran, N. J. Mrs.	46090	Houston	Burran, John Milton	—
Burran, W. A.	37625	Hansford	—	—
Burrell, Eliza J.	26286	Parker	Burrell, William Graham	—
Burrell, Frederick Walter	02246	Jasper	—	—

Index to Confederate Pension Applications

Name	No.	County	Veteran	Vet. No.
Burrell, Martha	45696	Jefferson	Burrell, Robert David	
Burrell, Rachel	15754	Jasper	Burrell, Frederick Walter	
Burrell, W. G.	Rej	Parker		
Burrer, John Gottilieb	15243	Gillespie		
Burrer, Katherina	32961	Gillespie	Burrer, John Gottilieb	15243
Burris, A. J.	02367	Karnes		
Burris, B. F.	Rej	Bexar		
Burris, J. W.	27252	Erath		
Burris, Jane E.	31409	Bexar	Burris, Benjamin Franklin	
Burris, John H.	17395	Caldwell		
Burris, Ruth E.	37783	Karnes	Burris, Lemuel Wells	
Burris, Samuel J.	33190	Grayson		
Burriss, J. J.	08693	Goliad		
Burrough, W. E.	Rej	Tarrant		
Burroughs, Cassie Jane	52069	Wood	Burroughs, William Alexander	
Burroughs, James Howard	06137	Upshur		
Burroughs, M. A. Mrs.	06656	Taylor	Burroughs, William J.	
Burroughs, M. J. Mrs.	32723	Harris	Burroughs, William Thomas	
Burroughs, S. E. Mrs.	37479	Upshur	Burroughs, James Howard	06137
Burroughs, Tom	Rej	Shelby		
Burroughs, W. S.	18256	Polk		
Burrow, B. C.	Rej	Lampasas		
Burrow, Catherine A.	Rej	Panola	Burrow, John Alexander	
Burrow, Claudia	31855	Jones	Burrow, Wiley Thompson	
Burrow, Henry A.	13017	Navarro		
Burrow, J. I.	10171	Navarro		
Burrow, Mildred P.	07789	Dallas	Burrow, Elias W.	
Burrow, Nancy Sue	46448	Grayson	Burrow, Charles H.	
Burrows, A. P.	29960	Madison		
Burrows, Ameta	19914	Bastrop	Burrows, Jacob Thompson	
Burrows, George Madison	26257	Madison		
Burrows, Henrietta	28046	Runnels	Burrows, Lewis Francis	
Burrows, John, Sr.	31424	Nacogdoches		
Burrows, Josiah	03518	Rusk		
Burrows, M. J. Mrs.	04665	Gonzales	Burrows, William A.	
Burrows, Martha Jane	45154	Mills	Burrows, Thomas	33741
Burrows, Nancy J.	40691	Parker	Burrows, W. E.	23454
Burrows, Rebekiah Ann	17724	Gregg	Burrows, Thomas Easton	07941
Burrows, Thomas	33741	Mills		
Burrows, Thomas Easton	07941	Parker		
Burrows, Thomas Jefferson	19119	McLennan		
Burrows, V. L. Mrs.	42301	Runnels	Burrows, George Madison	26257
Burrows, W. E.	23454	Parker		
Burrus, Mary A.	43977	Collin	Burrus, William Carroll	
Burrus, Nancy Louisa	45322	Collin	Burrus, William Campbell	40980
Burrus, William Campbell	40980	Collin		
Burruss, Flora J.	51421	Cameron	Burruss, Joe Frank	
Bursey, N. R. Mrs.	35119	Erath	Bursey, James Henry	
Burson, John Mack	23320	Erath		
Burson, Mary Jane	10983	Houston	Burson, Jonathan Dennis	
Burson, Mary Jane	29139	Smith	Burson, John Milton	
Burson, S. E. Mrs.	46333	Erath	Burson, John Mack	23320
Burt, Elizabeth J.	49810	Tarrant	Burt, John Thomas	
Burt, Emma Garrett	Rej	Bell	Burt, Henry McGuire	
Burt, Fannie Lou	50213	Bexar	Burt, John Pittman	
Burt, Goode W.	27722	Palo Pinto		
Burt, Henry M.	Rej	Bell		
Burt, J. B.	23879	Haskell		
Burt, James H.	05280	Dallas		

Index to Confederate Pension Applications

Name	App#	County	Veteran	Vet#
Burt, P. M.	01247	Ellis	—	—
Burt, R. E.	18884M	Collin	—	—
Burt, Weltha	17382	Brazos	Burt, William Jefferson	08020
Burt, William Jefferson	08020	Jasper	—	—
Burton, Adaline Eliza	04574	Panola	Burton, Thomas A.	—
Burton, Bertrand S.	42179	Fannin	—	—
Burton, Catherine L.	07368	Shelby	Burton, George W.	—
Burton, Charles Clark	47475	Wise	—	—
Burton, Charles Clark Mrs.	50802	Wise	Burton, Charles Clark	47475
Burton, Cynthia Ann	51041	Llano	Burton, Wiley Wood	21217
Burton, D. F.	14408	Smith	—	—
Burton, Fannie	30880	Dallas	Burton, Jobe	22467
Burton, Fannie	50770	Hill	Burton, William	—
Burton, Frederick Abbey	36185	Orange	—	—
Burton, George W.	38986	Rusk	—	—
Burton, Helen	Rej	Ellis	Burton, Zenas Leland Boggs	—
Burton, James C.	10939	Fort Bend	—	—
Burton, Jobe	22467	Dallas	—	—
Burton, John G.	03201	Orange	—	—
Burton, John I.	02076	Houston	—	—
Burton, Julia	46439	Kaufman	Burton, David Elijah	—
Burton, Julia H.	32360	Washington	Burton, Travis Jefferson	30984
Burton, L. E. Mrs.	Rej	Armstrong	Burton, William Franklin	—
Burton, Lewis	33677	Liberty	—	—
Burton, M. A.	05231	Lamar	—	—
Burton, M. A. F. Mrs.	Rej	Shackelford	Burton, William Thomas Jarrell	—
Burton, M. C. Mrs.	06648	Smith	Burton, S. J.	—
Burton, M. D. L.	07965	Somervell	—	—
Burton, Mattie	45004	Fannin	Burton, Bertrand S.	42179
Burton, N. B.	22968	Somervell	—	—
Burton, Owen W., Sr.	35636	Orange	—	—
Burton, Sarah Elizabeth	Rej	Harrison	Burton, Nathaniel	—
Burton, Susan Pamala Persons	51505	Briscoe	Persons, William Amos	—
Burton, Thomas J.	50275	Tarrant	—	—
Burton, Travis Jefferson	30984	Washington	—	—
Burton, W. H. P.	05915	Taylor	—	—
Burton, Wiley Wood	21217	Burnet	—	—
Burton, William F.	30399	Wise	—	—
Burts, Nancy	46542	Robertson	Burts, William	06635
Burts, William	06635	Madison	—	—
Burtt, Mary Cornick	51825	Bee	Burtt, William Thomas	—
Busby, A. J.	08566	Dallas	—	—
Busby, Cornelius Vandervort	10943	Frio	—	—
Busby, Daniel	00991	Coryell	—	—
Busby, Frances	43074	Tarrant	Busby, John Stephen	23844
Busby, G. J.	11393	Comanche	—	—
Busby, Georgia Ann	49602	Harris	Busby, Isaiah Sellers	—
Busby, H. P.	06651	Parker	—	—
Busby, John R.	22956	Karnes	—	—
Busby, John Stephen	23844	Tarrant	—	—
Busby, John W.	20624	Harrison	—	—
Busby, W. A.	Rej	Upshur	—	—
Busby, William Henry Harrison	Rej	Sabine	—	—
Bush, Albin C.	39637	Llano	—	—
Bush, Alvina	16163	Navarro	Bush, Johnson Delaware	—
Bush, Arminda	07042	Robertson	Bush, Thomas	—
Bush, Daniel Henry	46931	Atascosa	—	—
Bush, E. C. Mrs.	21481	Newton	Bush, Hope Hull Christian	16187
Bush, Ellie	Rej	Clay	Bush, William Rhodes	—

Index to Confederate Pension Applications

Name	No.	County	Spouse/Related	No.
Bush, Emma C.	17063	Young	Bush, Louis B.	
Bush, George W.	31516	Collin		
Bush, Hope Hull Christian	16187	Newton		
Bush, Isaac	01618	Grayson		
Bush, James Calvin	42521	Taylor		
Bush, James Calvin Mrs.	45358	Taylor	Bush, James Calvin	42521
Bush, Lorenzo Dow	21026	Shelby		
Bush, Louisa M.	08324	Grayson	Bush, Isaac	01618
Bush, Martha Frances	30371	Shelby	Bush, Lorenzo Dow	21026
Bush, Mary E.	32014	Harris	Bush, Robert Thomas	19007
Bush, Mary Jane	43732	Harris	Bush, Charles Thomas	
Bush, Mollie C.	47440	Hunt	Bush, Thomas J.	
Bush, Nora V.	21409	Harris	Bush, Winfield Scott	01778
Bush, R. F. Mrs.	30048	McLennan	Bush, Edmond Artton	
Bush, Richard Rhodes Mrs.	49317	Taylor	Bush, Richard Rhodes	
Bush, Robert Thomas	19007	Harris		
Bush, Sarah F.	49690	Bosque	Bush, Thomas P.	
Bush, Winfield Scott	01778	Harris		
Bushart, Sallie	30207	Cass	Bushart, John Cornelius	
Bushwall, Frank	41857	Austin		
Busick, N. M. Mrs.	06273	Grimes	Busick, D. B.	
Bussell, Amanda M.	28239	Hopkins	Bussell, Henry	
Bussey, Annie L.	Rej	Dallas	Bussey, Charles Henry	
Bussey, Delaney Elizabeth	45781	Jefferson	Bussey, Edward Moody	
Bussey, J. C.	01999	Hopkins		
Bussey, John B., Dr.	42481	Shelby		
Bussey, John Frazier Mrs.	19538	Wichita	Bussey, John Frazier	
Bussey, John Lion	15293	Gregg		
Bussey, Laura	49985	Tarrant	Bussey, William	
Bussy, Hezekiah	28474	Shelby		
Buster, Usuly Ann	19367	Falls	Buster, William Preston	12961
Buster, William Preston	12691	Falls		
Butchee, H. M. Mrs.	09238	Hill	Butchee, Abraham	
Butler, Albert Brown	42193	Bee		
Butler, Albert Brown Mrs.	42718	Bee	Butler, Albert Brown	42193
Butler, Alphonzo Carlos	10988	Hunt		
Butler, Amanda M.	37380	Panola	Butler, Samuel Thomas	
Butler, Andrew Jackson	09884	Houston		
Butler, Benjamin Franklin	33133	Fannin		
Butler, C. E.	10441	Navarro		
Butler, Catherine	32613	Jones	Butler, William Thomas	12941
Butler, Clara	46359	Live Oak	Butler, James Ira Bird	
Butler, Clarisa A.	28174	Lamar	Butler, William T.	
Butler, Della	39815	Palo Pinto	Butler, Henry Clinton	21062
Butler, Donnie E. Mrs.	29559	Mills	Butler, William Madison	
Butler, E. C. Mrs.	35712	Haskell	Butler, Lilburn Mercer	32465
Butler, Elmira	19376	Houston	Butler, Andrew Jackson	09884
Butler, Ester	49695	Tarrant	Butler, William Buford	
Butler, Francis A.	18863	Callahan		
Butler, Francis Y.	33517	Trinity	Butler, Tom	33373
Butler, Henrietta L.	26800	Montgomery	Butler, John Beech	
Butler, Henry Clay	47336	Guadalupe		
Butler, Henry Clinton	21062	Palo Pinto		
Butler, Henry J.	37319	Comanche		
Butler, J. B.	Rej	Red River		
Butler, J. K.	37528	Angelina		
Butler, J. P.	46064	Wood		
Butler, J. S.	20687	Hunt		
Butler, Jack Richard	23459	Hunt		

Index to Confederate Pension Applications

Name	App. No.	County	Veteran	Vet. App. No.
Butler, James	Rej	Mitchell		
Butler, James Kibble	10447	Palo Pinto		
Butler, James W.	31799	Clay		
Butler, James William	14707	Bowie		
Butler, John	11542	Limestone		
Butler, John B.	21591	Red River		
Butler, John Kirkly	18234	Panola		
Butler, John Thomas	05658	Bowie		
Butler, Judith	12708	Titus		
Butler, L.	29958	Gonzales	Butler, George Ball	
Butler, Laura	31986	Houston	Butler, Stephen	10862
Butler, Lilburn Mercer	32465	Haskell		
Butler, Lizzie T.	Rej	Henderson	Butler, Marshal Neigh	12409
Butler, Louisa	10177	Parker	Butler, A. J.	
Butler, M. C. Mrs.	19916	Caldwell	Butler, William G.	
Butler, M. E. Mrs.	Rej	Morris	Butler, Solomon Anderson	
Butler, M. Mrs.	00760	Cherokee	Butler, J. W.	
Butler, M. R. Mrs.	10389	Hays	Butler, David B.	
Butler, Manerva W.	10640	Grimes		
Butler, Margaret	41615	Bowie	Butler, James William	14707
Butler, Marshal Neigh	12409	Henderson		
Butler, Martha E.	27231	Comanche	Butler, John R.	
Butler, Mary Ann	10790	Young	Butler, Benjamin F.	
Butler, Mary H.	50878	Llano	Butler, William Thomas	
Butler, Mary L.	25002	Childress	Butler, Elliott Lafayett	
Butler, Milton	10617	Coryell		
Butler, N. M. Mrs.	19300	Trinity	Butler, Benjamin Franklin	
Butler, Nancy Ann	06485	Kaufman	Butler, John	
Butler, Nancy C.	18628	Jones	Butler, Alphonzo Carlos	10988
Butler, Nancy C.	38678	Hunt	Butler, Thomas Newton	15724
Butler, Polly	32236	Fannin	Butler, John Thomas	05658
Butler, Preston Irvin	31754	Freestone		
Butler, Preston Irvin Mrs.	38887	Freestone	Butler, Preston Irvin	31754
Butler, R. N.	07327	Montgomery		
Butler, S. E. Mrs.	40877	Panola	Butler, John Kirkly	18234
Butler, Sallie	49868	Fannin	Butler, Benjamin Franklin	33133
Butler, Sarah J.	42255	Bell	Butler, Thomas Steward	
Butler, Sarah Wilson	45017	Harris	Butler, James Cox	
Butler, Stephen	10862	Cherokee		
Butler, T. A.	08746	Karnes		
Butler, Talitha M.	37487	Bexar	Butler, James K. Polk	
Butler, Thomas Newton	15724	Hunt		
Butler, Tom	33373	Trinity		
Butler, Virginia	Rej	Dallas	Butler, Joe W.	
Butler, W. F.	26776	Milam		
Butler, William	02956	Milam		
Butler, William	35906	Red River		
Butler, William Thomas	12941	Jones		
Butner, Lorenzia Dow Mrs.	41074	Stonewall	Butner, Lorenzia Dow	
Butt, Josephine E.	47271	Tarrant	Butt, Frances Augustus	
Butt, M. A. Mrs.	06689	Henderson	Butt, J. M.	
Butt, Mondicai R.	23322	Fannin		
Butt, Rosia	51512	Fannin	Butt, Mondicai R.	23322
Butterfield, William H.	Rej	Cass		
Butterworth, Fannie C.	25422	Panola	Butterworth, Josiah Washington	
Buttfield, J. B.	Rej	Jefferson		
Butts, Ida M.	45722	Gregg	Butts, Charles Mongomery	
Butts, J. T.	43613	Gregg		
Butts, Priscilla S. R. A.	01376	Falls	Butts, Thomas J.	

Index to Confederate Pension Applications

Buxton, William Martin	32332	Cherokee	—	—
Buzbee, J. E.	06240	Eastland	—	—
Buzbee, Levi Simuel	19082	Lamar	—	—
Buzbee, Martha Elizabeth	27035	Lamar	Buzbee, Levi Simeul	19082
Byars, Charles Terrell	38374	Bastrop	—	—
Byars, D. W.	20892	Hunt	—	—
Byars, Euphrie S.	Rej	Bastrop	Byars, Charles Terrell	38374
Byars, G. A. M. Mrs.	35094	Hays	Byars, Joseph Jeremiah	—
Byars, James	39497	Colorado	—	—
Byars, James Marion	07573	Dewitt	—	—
Byars, L. A. Mrs.	38239	Parker	Byars, Baylor Triant	—
Byars, Martha Ophelia	10685	Lavaca	Byars, W. H.	09889
Byars, Sarah C.	15979	McCulloch	Byars, John Ferdinand	—
Byars, Sophonia C.	15053	Dewitt	Byars, Joseph	—
Byars, T. J.	03296	Parker	—	—
Byars, W. H.	09889	Lavaca	—	—
Bybee, Mollie D.	43059	Montgomery	Bybee, Clinton	—
Byerley, Lavina	17954	Jefferson	Byerley, John	—
Byerley, Margret F.	15772	Jefferson	Byerley, Steven John	—
Byerly, Frank	16188	Newton	—	—
Byerly, James Robert	15755	Jasper	—	—
Byerly, L. M. Mrs.	20156	Jasper	Byerly, James Robert	15755
Byerly, Micajah	14154	Chambers	—	—
Byerly, Stephen John	Rej	Fayette	—	—
Byerly, William	25596	Jasper	—	—
Byers, Edward Leonidas	18081	Madison	—	—
Byers, Ella Belle	51874	Harris	Byers, William Riley	16894
Byers, Hannah R.	41856	Hunt	Byers, William M.	—
Byers, J. A.	28599	Madison	—	—
Byers, Jennie	47376	Tarrant	Byers, Thomas Jefferson	—
Byers, Katherine	30288	Madison	Byers, Edward Leonidas	18081
Byers, Sarah Elizabeth	17761	Harris	Byers, Robert Hamilton	—
Byers, W. W.	17232	Coleman	—	—
Byers, William Riley	16894	Victoria	—	—
Byler, Cirene	10990	Irion	Byler, E. R.	—
Byne, Joseph H.	05447	Bowie	—	—
Bynum, Arminta	16688	Titus	Bynum, James Wesley	13155
Bynum, D. W.	16687	Titus	—	—
Bynum, Daniel B. A.	08461M	Scurry	—	—
Bynum, Eliza	Rej	Ellis	Bynum, Asa	—
Bynum, I. L.	Rej	Titus	—	—
Bynum, James Wesley	13155	Titus	—	—
Bynum, M. B.	Rej	Lampasas	—	—
Bynum, Martha	29373	Smith	Bynum, Elijah Gray	—
Bynum, Nancy Catherine Wilson	Rej	Taylor	Wilson, Matt Frederick	—
Bynum, R. E. Mrs.	07784	Coryell	Bynum, Benjamin	—
Bynum, R. L. Mrs.	Rej	Comanche	Bynum, Jesse Ellis	—
Bynum, S. L. Mrs.	36940	Titus	Bynum, D. W.	16687
Bynum, W. L.	10071	Falls	—	—
Bynum, William R.	00671	Camp	—	—
Byram, John A.	Rej	Clay	—	—
Byram, Sallie	Rej	Red River	Byram, Samuel M.	—
Byrd, A. C.	15715	Hopkins	—	—
Byrd, A. W.	12075	Nacogdoches	—	—
Byrd, Allice	19964	Hopkins	Byrd, Wiley A.	—
Byrd, Andrew Jackson	23297	Panola	—	—
Byrd, Elizabeth A.	10725	Parker	Byrd, P. A.	—
Byrd, Elizabeth A.	22095A	Navarro	Byrd, George P.	03099
Byrd, Elizabeth Ellen	35774	Nacogdoches	Byrd, Andrew Jackson	23297

Index to Confederate Pension Applications

Name	App#	County	Related	Related#
Byrd, Ellen Tyler	51193	Dickens	Byrd, Vallentine Ausburn	—
Byrd, Emma	51329	Titus	Byrd, William Washington	50908
Byrd, Evie Mae	Rej	Robertson	Byrd, Isaac Wilburn (bird)	49935
Byrd, F. C. Mrs.	Rej	Baylor	Byrd, Thomas S.	—
Byrd, George P.	03099	Navarro	—	—
Byrd, J. W.	Rej	Eastland	—	—
Byrd, James D.	12085	Navarro	—	—
Byrd, Joe H.	08542	Wood	—	—
Byrd, John E.	00162	Bastrop	—	—
Byrd, L. P. Mrs.	Rej	Smith	Byrd, Monroe Washington	31319
Byrd, M. A. Mrs.	Rej	Erath	Byrd, A. J.	—
Byrd, Margarett	27706	Milam	Byrd, William Leander	—
Byrd, Martha E.	32810	Hopkins	Byrd, Judson Peter	—
Byrd, Mary Jane	06736	Bastrop	Byrd, Richard	—
Byrd, Monroe Washington	31319	Smith	—	—
Byrd, Rachel M.	31983	Wise	Byrd, Pleasant Wisley	—
Byrd, William	05088	Dewitt	—	—
Byrd, William Washington	50908	Morris	—	—
Byrne, James A.	46111	Galveston	—	—
Byrne, Marie Louise	32326	Harris	Byrne, Charles Hubert	—
Byrne, Martha E. Walker	Rej	Falls	Walker, William E.	—
Byrne, Mary E.	21247	Goliad	Byrne, Thomas King	—
Byrnes, John Patrick	15679	Harris	—	—
Byrnes, John Patrick Mrs.	20167	Harris	Byrnes, John Patrick	15679
Byrns, James P.	22332	Jefferson	—	—
Byrom, J. A.	13958	Montague	—	—
Byron, L. V. Mrs.	39266	Parker	Byron, William Henry	—
Byrum, H. B.	03676	Smith	—	—
Byrum, James C.	00185	Bastrop	—	—
Byrum, Mary A.	Rej	Coleman	Byrum, E. W.	—
Byrun, T. C.	RejM	Titus	—	—
Byus, Mary Elizabeth	21671	McLennan	Byus, John Franklin	—
Bywaters, Laura	49128	Bexar	Bywaters, Branson	—

C

Name	App#	County	Related	Related#
Cabaniss, Columbia A.	33891	Bell	Cabaniss, Napoleon B.	20838
Cabaniss, Mary E.	37221	Caldwell	Cabaniss, Jesse Miltiades	—
Cabaniss, Napoleon B.	20838	Bell	—	—
Cabell, William H.	35384	Hamilton	—	—
Cabitt, John W.	RejM	Upshur	—	—
Cable, J. H.	Rej	Collin	—	—
Cable, John Franklin	01666	Gregg	—	—
Cable, Sarah Elizabeth	18983	Gregg	Cable, John Franklin	01666
Cabler, Gaston Davidson	Rej	Baylor	—	—
Cabler, Laura D.	38814	Swisher	Cabler, Charles D.	—
Cabler, Sophronia	41867	Baylor	Cabler, John Quincy	—
Cabler, Susan	49354	Baylor	Cabler, Gaston Davidson	Rej
Cabron, Frank	21672	Milam	—	—
Caddell, A. O. Mrs.	46018	Grayson	Caddell, William T.	—
Caddell, J. B.	Rej	McLennan	—	—
Cade, Annie C. Holloway	46061	Collin	Holloway, Napoleon Bonaparte	—
Cade, D. H.	04165	Van Zandt	—	—
Cade, Frank M.	16868	Van Zandt	—	—
Cade, H. C.	15688	Henderson	—	—
Cade, Harriet Ellen	25529	Newton	Cade, Robert	—
Cade, James C.	02711	Live Oak	—	—
Cade, James Landrich	19980	Tom Green	—	—
Cade, M. C. Mrs.	11776	Van Zandt	Cade, D. H.	04165

Index to Confederate Pension Applications

Name	App #	County	Veteran	Vet App #
Cade, Robert R.	21673	Van Zandt	—	
Cade, Sarah	27420	Tom Green	Cade, James Landrich	19980
Cade, Susan A.	19164	Nacogdoches	Cade, William Bedford	13627
Cade, Thomas	16154	Nacogdoches	—	
Cade, Thomas Mrs.	32092	Nacogdoches	Cade, Thomas	16154
Cade, William Bedford	13627	Nacogdoches	—	
Cadenhead, Dora	45783	McLennan	Cadenhead, Francis Marion	
Cadenhead, Ephraim Sanders	13568	Walker	—	
Cadenhead, Homer T.	03252	Panola	—	
Cadenhead, James M.	Rej	Camp	—	
Cadenhead, M. V. Mrs.	32724	Panola	Cadenhead, Thomas Alexander	
Cadenhead, Mary S.	23861	Van Zandt	Cadenhead, William Henry	
Cadenhead, Powell	28731	Van Zandt	—	
Cadenhead, S. A. Mrs.	10353	Comanche	Cadenhead, T. S.	00474
Cadenhead, Sallie	32336	Montgomery	Cadenhead, Ephraim Sanders	13568
Cadenhead, T. S.	00474	Bosque	—	
Cadey, A. H.	Rej	Harris	—	
Cadle, Lucinda	11236	Lamar	Cadle, James Preston	
Cadwell, M. E. Mrs.	15149	Fayette	Cadwell, James Alexander	
Caffall, Thomas	Rej	Karnes	—	
Caffey, Francis Elmira	Rej	Brown	Caffey, Abraham	
Caffey, Rebecca	39999	Milam	Caffey, Elijah Charles	
Cage, Clara P.	38407	Wood	Cage, John William	
Cage, James House Mrs.	47387	Erath	Cage, James House	
Cagle, A. J.	23115	Smith	—	
Cagle, Charles	01046	Dallas	—	
Cagle, N. S. Mrs.	39066	Lamar	Cagle, John Hampton	
Cagle, Virginia Frances	Rej	Navarro	Cagle, James Pinkney	
Cahill, E. A.	37743	Red River	—	
Cain, A. J.	Rej	Upshur	—	
Cain, A. J.	13577	Wood	—	
Cain, A. P.	08427M	Newton	—	
Cain, C. C.	18343	Shelby	—	
Cain, E. D.	06726	Lamar	—	
Cain, Frank D.	32763	Lavaca	—	
Cain, Issac E.	12814	Denton	—	
Cain, J. P.	28951	Wood	—	
Cain, James A.	Rej	Limestone	—	
Cain, John	50552	Collin	—	
Cain, Lizzie	51033	Bexar	Cain, Whitfield H.	46526
Cain, Lucy A.	12516	Montague	Cain, John	
Cain, M. E. Mrs.	50561	Lee	Cain, Robert Leonidas	
Cain, Martha	Rej	Henderson	Cain, Ferdinand C.	
Cain, Martha	08345	Henderson	—	
Cain, Mary A.	06617	Hunt	Cain, Dempsey G.	
Cain, Mary J.	27892	Briscoe	Cain, William Thomas	
Cain, Nancy J.	32811	Childress	Cain, Joseph Harland	
Cain, Nannie P.	41872	Cooke	Cain, Jedidah Callaway	
Cain, Richard A.	11045	McLennan	—	
Cain, Sarah A.	Rej	Freestone	Cain, William	
Cain, Susanna	46648	Lee	Cain, Isaac Cosby	
Cain, Whitfield H.	46526	Robertson	—	
Cain, William	Rej	Freestone	—	
Caison, T. M. Mrs.	40536	Denton	Caison, W. J.	23159
Caison, W. J.	23159	Cooke	—	
Calahan, Pricilla	51940	Throckmorton	Calahan, William Franklin	
Calahan, Vibella C.	43715	Blanco	Calahan, William	
Calaway, Dollie	50355	Montague	Calaway, William	47312
Calaway, James Daniel	27684	Mills	—	

Index to Confederate Pension Applications

Name	No.	County	Related	No.
Calaway, William	47312	Montague		
Calder, Margania	27310	Bell	Calder, William Washington	16046
Calder, William Washington	16046	Mills		
Caldwell, Annie R.	38331	Palo Pinto	Caldwell, Hopkins Ethelton	19975
Caldwell, Augustus K.	02000	Hopkins		
Caldwell, C. A.	02960	Milam		
Caldwell, C. H.	29812	Shelby		
Caldwell, Casper Wister	35352	Bell		
Caldwell, Daniel R.	21219	Smith		
Caldwell, Delia Mary	14619	Bastrop	Caldwell, Perry N.	
Caldwell, E. B. Mrs.	25526	Callahan	Caldwell, Wiley Thomas	
Caldwell, Eliza A.	22573	Nacogdoches	Caldwell, Joseph Thadeus	
Caldwell, Elizabeth W.	18755	Lamar	Caldwell, Orville Howard	15848
Caldwell, Emily	52058	Fort Bend	Caldwell, Wylie Harrison	21675
Caldwell, Endora C.	39382	McLennan	Caldwell, Samuel Thomas	35245
Caldwell, Fannie	35645	Bell	Caldwell, Casper Wister	35352
Caldwell, H. W.	09997	Bosque		
Caldwell, Harriet A.	13975A	Sabine	Caldwell, Hugh Lawson	13975
Caldwell, Hopkins Ethelton	19975	Grayson		
Caldwell, Hugh Lawson	13975	Sabine		
Caldwell, Ida Waggoner	39156	Van Zandt	Waggoner, Lisby	
Caldwell, J. T.	02115	Hunt		
Caldwell, James William	32926	Galveston		
Caldwell, John W.	25497	Dallas		
Caldwell, L. M. Mrs.	09963	Hunt	Caldwell, J. T.	02115
Caldwell, Leonidas Beecher	23474	Fannin		
Caldwell, Lura	46947	Dallas	Caldwell, Thomas Joseph	
Caldwell, Martha R.	23476	Ellis	Caldwell, Hugh Lawson White	
Caldwell, Mary C.	34691	Dallas	Caldwell, John W.	25497
Caldwell, Mary Etta	33776	Coryell	Caldwell, R. N.	
Caldwell, Mary H.	34801	Kaufman	Caldwell, Whitfield Sledge	22481
Caldwell, N. D.	22528	Van Zandt		
Caldwell, Nancy	06950	Limestone	Caldwell, George Washington	
Caldwell, Nettie	31056	Bell	Caldwell, Matthew Moss	
Caldwell, O. B.	Rej	Travis		
Caldwell, Orville Howard	15848	Lamar		
Caldwell, R. N. Mrs.	31614	Red River	Caldwell, Benjamin Phineas	
Caldwell, S. H.	37635	Bee		
Caldwell, Sallie	35558	Galveston	Caldwell, James William	32926
Caldwell, Samuel Thomas	35245	McLennan		
Caldwell, Selena	Rej	Dallas	Caldwell, William	
Caldwell, W. Emily	Rej	Van Zandt	Caldwell, Wylie Harrison	21675
Caldwell, W. H.	05170	Bell		
Caldwell, Whitfield Sledge	22481	Kaufman		
Caldwell, William Henry H. Mrs.	47976	Dallas	Caldwell, William Henry Harrison	
Caldwell, William M.	20214	Smith		
Caldwell, Wylie Harrison	21675	Van Zandt		
Cale, Joseph H.	18539	Wilson		
Caler, George N.	49188	Randall		
Caler, S. J. Mrs.	49989	Randall	Caler, George N.	49188
Calfee, Alpha P.	47812	Hill	Calfee, Calvin J.	
Calfee, J. F. Mrs.	31552	Red River	Calfee, William Judson	29776
Calfee, William Judson	29776	Lamar		
Calhoun, A. C. Mrs.	22203	Van Zandt	Calhoun, Thomas Nathan	09947
Calhoun, Annie Deliah	29289	Dewitt	Calhoun, John Richard	26151
Calhoun, Augusta	31791	Houston	Calhoun, George M.	23524
Calhoun, Bettie	42818	Calhoun	Calhoun, Frank (Francis) Henry	32927
Calhoun, Elizabeth	21002	Smith	Calhoun, Albert Jefferson	
Calhoun, Ellen Gilmer	43727	Jefferson	Calhoun, John Caldwell	

Index to Confederate Pension Applications

Calhoun, Francis Henry	32927	Calhoun	—	
Calhoun, George M.	23524	Houston	—	
Calhoun, J. M.	Rej	Coryell	—	
Calhoun, John	05736	Jack	—	
Calhoun, John A.	15691	Henderson	—	
Calhoun, John C.	19725	Grayson	—	
Calhoun, John Richard	26151	Dewitt	—	
Calhoun, Lela G.	Rej	Jefferson	Calhoun, Benjamin Franklin	—
Calhoun, Lou J.	40062	Grayson	Calhoun, John C.	19725
Calhoun, Mary A.	06926	Galveston	Calhoun, John C.	—
Calhoun, Mary Ann	08004	Van Zandt	Calhoun, Robert R.	04171
Calhoun, N. A. Mrs.	16806	Upshur	Calhoun, Elias Washington	—
Calhoun, N. E.	18404	Tarrant		
Calhoun, Nancy E.	36281	Dewitt	Calhoun, Samuel Daniel	27261
Calhoun, R. P. H.	04960	Bexar		
Calhoun, Robert R.	04171	Van Zandt		
Calhoun, Samuel Daniel	27261	Dewitt		
Calhoun, Theodore	42211	Jefferson		
Calhoun, Thomas Nathan	09947	Van Zandt		
Calhoun, W. L.	16803	Upshur		
Calhound, Martha E.	Rej	Travis	Calhound, William Henry	—
Call, William H.	41944	Delta		
Callaghan, Rita S.	30657	Bexar	Callaghan, Juan	—
Callaham, Benjamin G.	Rej	Bosque		
Callahan, Annie D.	12805	Dallas	Callahan, Wesley S.	—
Callahan, James C.	14060	Van Zandt		
Callahan, James T.	13328	Gregg		
Callahan, John A.	43068	Floyd		
Callahan, Matthew William	01621	Grayson		
Callahan, N.	11461	Gonzales		
Callahan, Nancy E.	26519	Grayson	Callahan, Matthew William	01621
Callahan, S. J. Mrs.	33773	Johnson	Callahan, James Adison	—
Callan, Alice	31633	Mitchell	Callan, Marian Maxamillian	—
Callan, J. J.	10700	Menard		
Callan, M. M.	27350	Mitchell		
Callan, Margaret M.	34652	Menard	Callan, J. J.	10700
Callan, Mary	27658	Travis	Callan, George Joseph	—
Callaway, C. P. Mrs.	37288	Harrison	Callaway, James Madison	—
Callaway, Enoch Job	21674	McLennan		
Callaway, Enoch Jobe	25030	Jones		
Callaway, G. C.	01047	Dallas		
Callaway, J. D.	23053	Upshur		
Callaway, J. I.	Rej	Limestone		
Callaway, Joe	23432	Morris		
Callaway, Joe Anna	Rej	Houston	Callaway, Elijah Holcomb	—
Callaway, John A.	17169	Tyler		
Callaway, Josephine R.	40179	Matagorda	Callaway, William Hillery	34121
Callaway, Leona	Rej	Red River	Callaway, James A.	—
Callaway, Letha	33067	Jones	Callaway, Enoch Job	25030
Callaway, Mary V.	44004	Smith	Callaway, Alonzo Newell	—
Callaway, Melvina Elizabeth	46086	Wichita	Callaway, Erastus Jasper	—
Callaway, Samuel B.	21075	Bee		
Callaway, V. R.	17615	Erath		
Callaway, William Hillery	34121	Matagorda		
Callaway, William J.	Rej	Brown		
Callaway, William Jonathan	19324	Waller		
Callaway, William McWhorter	13908	Johnson		
Callaway, William S.	00473	Bosque		
Callen, M.	42529	Collingsworth		

Index to Confederate Pension Applications

Name	No.	County	Related	Related No.
Callens, George Monroe	41807	Van Zandt		
Callens, Mary	43544	Van Zandt	Callens, George Monroe	41807
Calley, J. M.	Rej	Comanche		
Callicoate, M. J., Ashley Mrs.	39434	Lamar	Ashley, John Willis	—
Callicoatte, Lucy A.	23365	Camp	Callicoatte, Harrison C.	—
Callihan, Annie	39951	Brazoria	Callihan, William Clark	00497
Callihan, James M.	03357	Polk		
Callihan, Margaret	14780	Caldwell	Callihan, Thomas Jefferson Lafayette	
	19293			
Callihan, William Clark	00497	Brazoria		
Callison, Alex	Rej	Colorado		
Callison, J. C.	13546	Val Verde		
Calloway, John A.	34539	Wood		
Calloway, Joshua Sanford Mrs.	33204	Potter	Calloway, Joshua Sanford	—
Calloway, Nora	47933	Bailey	Calloway, James Madison	—
Calloway, Steve	04672	Rockwall		
Calson, A. V. Mrs.	15328	Grimes	Calson, William Loraine	—
Calvert, Adeline Jane	32508	Jack	Calvert, Jesse A.	08184
Calvert, C. M. Mrs.	15080	Ellis	Calvert, William Carroll	—
Calvert, David	25463	McLennan		
Calvert, Indiana	38930	McLennan	Calvert, David	25463
Calvert, J. N.	16805	Upshur		
Calvert, Jesse A.	08184	Jack		
Calvert, S. J. Mrs.	19286	Tarrant	Calvert, John Calvin	—
Calvery, John H.	00069	Angelina		
Calvery, William Johnson	Rej	Hill		
Calvin, Mollie	36731	Kerr	Calvin, George Washington	—
Cameron, Annie E.	36323	Travis	Cameron, Zachary Taylor	—
Cameron, Archie Smith	47846	Titus		
Cameron, Benjamin Thomas	23075	Cherokee		
Cameron, Bettie	19441	Lampasas	Cameron, William Jasper	—
Cameron, Camilla Mildred	37763	Cherokee	Cameron, Benjamin Thomas	23075
Cameron, Daniel Littleton	25021	Lavaca		
Cameron, Daniel Littleton Mrs.	42089	Leon	Cameron, Daniel Littleton	25021
Cameron, Eleanor Amanda	18012	Lee	Cameron, Daniel Munn	—
Cameron, Elizabeth	43153	Cherokee	Cameron, James Samuel	11847
Cameron, J. A.	13349	Harris		
Cameron, James M.	14842	Cass		
Cameron, James M. Mrs.	43626	Cass	Cameron, James M.	14842
Cameron, James Madison	02232	Irion		
Cameron, James Samuel	11847	Cherokee		
Cameron, Margaret	43632	Medina	Cameron, Hugh	—
Cameron, Martha M.	21677	Johnson	Cameronte, Allen Willis	—
Cameron, Mary J.	50747	Titus	Cameron, Archie Smith	47846
Cameron, Mattie Bird	47705	Bexar	Cameron, Benjamin Franklin	—
Cameron, Mollie	Rej	Bowie	Cameron, William Cannon	—
Cameron, Robert S.	15105	Erath		
Cameron, S. E. Mrs.	21611	Travis	Cameron, James Madison	02232
Cameron, William Lochiel	30529	Galveston		
Camfield, John Freeman	03232	Palo Pinto		
Camfield, Maggie	19657	Palo Pinto	Camfield, John Freeman	03232
Cammack, H. E. Mrs.	40151	Shelby	Cammack, Eugene Alonzo	—
Cammack, James Madison	27474	Shelby		
Cammack, Mary	12039	Madison	Cammack, John Lewis	—
Cammack, Mary E.	45712	Shelby	Cammack, James Madison	27474
Cammack, Sallie F.	23087	Harris	Cammack, Addison Irvin	—
Cammack, Thomas Jefferson	14405	Shelby		
Cammack, V. E. Mrs.	26752	Tyler	Cammack, John Richard	—
Camp, Asbury M.	49929	Milam		

Index to Confederate Pension Applications

Name	No.	County	Veteran	No.
Camp, B. M.	47167	Hopkins	—	
Camp, Burwell Washington	42637	Anderson	—	
Camp, J. C.	09222	Grayson	—	
Camp, J. M.	29218	Trinity	—	
Camp, John Clark	23363	Cass	—	
Camp, John L.	47795	Grayson	—	
Camp, Laura	42052	Upshur	Camp, James Daniel	
Camp, Logan T.	41303	Denton	—	
Camp, Loucinda	36499	Bexar	Camp, John Franklin	
Camp, Louisa	44031	Anderson	Camp, Burwell Washington	42637
Camp, Lula Belle	49510	Cherokee	Camp, George Washington	
Camp, M. J. Mrs.	14059	Upshur	Camp, W. S.	
Camp, Mary A.	13171	Madison	Camp, T. J.	
Camp, Mary E.	Rej	Hunt	Camp, William Lafayette	22722
Camp, Mary E.	36715	Atascosa	Camp, Samuel S.	
Camp, Seborn Lewis	45687	Hopkins	—	
Camp, William J.	37604	Jones	—	
Camp, William Lafayette	22722	Kaufman	—	
Camp, Zach Taylor	29360	Lamar	—	
Campbell, A. C. Mrs.	Rej	Knox	Campbell, John Alexander	
Campbell, A. E. Mrs.	36754	Dickens	Campbell, Joshua Madison	10764
Campbell, A. J. Mrs.	Rej	Harris	Campbell, Ephraim McLain	
Campbell, A. W.	05199	Houston	—	
Campbell, Alexander	10819	Bastrop	—	
Campbell, Annie Lou	50566	McLennan	Campbell, John Ira	43466
Campbell, Bettie M.	25385	Irion	Campbell, Alvin Upshaw	
Campbell, Charles	Rej	Walker	—	
Campbell, Cooper Clarency	30779	Travis	—	
Campbell, D. W.	32469	Houston	—	
Campbell, E. D.	06460	Johnson	—	
Campbell, E. H. Mrs.	38381	Tarrant	Campbell, William Smith	
Campbell, E. J. Mrs.	49765	Hamilton	Campbell, William L.	
Campbell, Ella R.	50931	Wichita	Campbell, Elias Hardin	
Campbell, Emily	31263	Upshur	Campbell, Green	
Campbell, F. J. Mrs.	08577AM	Wise	—	
Campbell, Fannie E.	30779A	Travis	Campbell, Cooper Clarency	30779
Campbell, Francis M.	12972	Limestone	—	
Campbell, G. Jefferson	32402	Cottle	—	
Campbell, G. W.	04634	Nolan	—	
Campbell, George W.	02610	Leon	—	
Campbell, Granison M. Mrs.	39683	Bosque	Campbell, Granison M.	
Campbell, Harriet Alice	21678	Colorado	Campbell, James Martin	13388
Campbell, Harriett E.	21561	Caldwell	Campbell, John	06425
Campbell, Henry	10907	Denton	—	
Campbell, Isaac Anderson Mrs.	47307	Bastrop	Campbell, Isaac Anderson	
Campbell, Isabella	17279	Anderson	Campbell, William Henry	
Campbell, J. H.	33406	Nacogdoches	—	
Campbell, J. I.	Rej	Williamson	—	
Campbell, J. M.	03100	Navarro	—	
Campbell, J. M.	11058	Motley	—	
Campbell, J. W.	07564	Cass	—	
Campbell, James	19066	Jones	—	
Campbell, James L.	23326	Wise	—	
Campbell, James Martin	11388	Colorado	—	
Campbell, John	06425	Wilson	—	
Campbell, John C.	02077	Houston	—	
Campbell, John Holmes	05657	Bowie	—	
Campbell, John Ira	43466	McLennan	—	
Campbell, John J.	26164	Tarrant	—	

Index to Confederate Pension Applications

Name	App. No.	County	Veteran	Vet. App. No.
Campbell, John M.	10315	Atascosa	—	
Campbell, John Wesley	12954	Knox	—	
Campbell, John Wilson Mrs.	46397	Comanche	Campbell, John Wilson	
Campbell, Joseph Clemmons	24903	Nacogdoches	—	
Campbell, Joseph Clemmons Mrs.	38427	Nacogdoches	Campbell, Joseph Clemmons	24903
Campbell, Joshua Madison	10764	Travis	—	
Campbell, L. B. Mrs.	45141	Motley	Campbell, Henry Harrison	
Campbell, L. M.	00686	Cass	—	
Campbell, Laura	40129	Nolan	Campbell, Joe Castillo	
Campbell, Louisa T.	36134	Navarro	Campbell, Samuel L.	
Campbell, Louise	44062	Navarro	Campbell, Joseph Patterson	
Campbell, M. E. Mrs.	39899	Hunt	Campbell, Robert David	20448
Campbell, M. F. Mrs.	40254	Cherokee	Campbell, John W.	
Campbell, M. L. Mrs.	32899	Angelina	Campbell, Walter D.	
Campbell, Maggie Pearson	35073	Lamar	Campbell, George Washington	
Campbell, Marcus Lafayette	39784	Cass	—	
Campbell, Martha	01744	Guadalupe	Campbell, James	
Campbell, Martha C.	42183	Wood	Campbell, Henry Newton	
Campbell, Martha J.	21016	Lubbock	Campbell, John William	
Campbell, Mary	31306	Harrison	Campbell, Elias L.	
Campbell, Mary	49864	Atascosa	Campbell, John	
Campbell, Mary Elizabeth	51829	Titus	Campbell, John Newton	
Campbell, Mary Elizabeth Dennis	42806	Burnet	Campbell, Marcus Lafayette	39784
Campbell, Mary F.	Rej	Mills	Campbell, Thomas Jefferson	
Campbell, Matilda Tabatha	05555	Kaufman	Campbell, Enos Mitcheal	
Campbell, Mattie	28044	Bowie	Campbell, John Holmes	05657
Campbell, N. E. Mrs.	28613	Coryell	Campbell, Alexander James	
Campbell, Nancy Ann	43973	Mills	Campbell, James Harvey	
Campbell, Pauline M.	14752	Brown	Campbell, James Mifflen	
Campbell, R. S.	16777	Tyler	—	
Campbell, Robert David	20448	Hunt	—	
Campbell, Rosella P.	30130	Bexar	Campbell, Edwin Francis	
Campbell, S. E. Mrs.	27042	Coryell	Campbell, Daniel Archable	
Campbell, Sarah A.	04730	Bandera	Campbell, J. D.	
Campbell, Singleton	22578	Tarrant	—	
Campbell, Susan L.	46735	Navarro	Campbell, Robert Bedford	
Campbell, Tennie B.	25616	Lampasas	Campbell, William Lewis	
Campbell, Thomas Jefferson	14012	Travis	—	
Campbell, Thomas P.	27044	Lamar	—	
Campbell, W. H.	Rej	Houston	—	
Campbell, W. M.	22147	Houston	—	
Campbell, Warren	10256	Galveston	—	
Campbell, William Blanton	16870	Van Zandt	—	
Campbell, William Blanton Mrs.	41849	Foard	Campbell, William Blanton	16870
Campbell, William Henry	40487	Brazos	—	
Camper, James Munroe	13617	Ellis	—	
Camper, Sarah Elizabeth	36644	Ellis	Camper, James Munroe	13617
Campion, Mary J.	33600	Lavaca	Campion, Joseph Andrew	
Campion, Mary Mc Tiernan	Rej	Nueces	Campion, William S.	
Campos, Eulogio	09122	Webb	—	
Camron, Martha	32577	Freestone	Camron, Robert Newton	
Camster, G. H.	12580	Red River	—	
Canady, Archulius Byrd	32905	Johnson	—	
Canady, Archulius Byrd Mrs.	36429	Johnson	Canady, Archulius Byrd	32905
Canady, H.	06316	Henderson	—	
Canady, Lucy L.	40631	Falls	Canady, Thomas Jefferson	
Canady, Richard Edward	26904	Grayson	—	
Canady, Snowie	35663	Grayson	Canady, Richard Edward	26904
Canafax, E. J.	05351	Grayson	—	

Index to Confederate Pension Applications

Name	App #	County	Veteran	Vet #
Canant, T. C.	25821	Van Zandt	—	
Canard, Robert	Rej	Hopkins	—	
Canavara, Lucretia D.	13200	Aransas	Canavara, Antonio	
Canble, Nannie Mae	RejM	Hill	—	
Candle, William T.	18292	Runnels	—	
Candler, M. L. Mrs.	26666	Jack	Candler, Joseph Halt	
Canfield, N. J. Mrs.	19372	Jefferson	Canfield, Augustin Royall	
Canion, George Washington	45309	Gonzales	—	
Canion, Roxie	47843	Gonzales	Canion, George Washington	45309
Cannaday, Mary E.	45819	Burnet	Cannaday, John Frances	
Cannaday, Mollie S.	45658	Wood	Cannaday, Stephen Jasper	
Cannan, E. B.	49152	Brazoria	—	
Cannon, A. V. Mrs.	03104	Navarro	Cannon, W. T.	
Cannon, Alfred	39043	Childress	—	
Cannon, Benjamin Bartlett	34300	Parker	—	
Cannon, Charles	29742	Cherokee	—	
Cannon, D.	03303	Parker	—	
Cannon, David	07901	Milam	—	
Cannon, David Etherly	21679	Sterling	—	
Cannon, Della	Rej	Trinity	Cannon, David Crockett	
Cannon, Fannie	41249	Cherokee	Cannon, Charles	29742
Cannon, Harriett	38943	Hunt	Cannon, John Nichols	
Cannon, James D.	17741	Hamilton	—	
Cannon, James Harrison	24980	Cherokee	—	
Cannon, James William	Rej	Hunt	—	
Cannon, John C.	03195	Nueces	—	
Cannon, John L.	Rej	Hopkins	—	
Cannon, John W.	22782	Hunt	—	
Cannon, Kate	18689	Cass	Cannon, Jesse Denson	
Cannon, L. C.	26276	Houston	—	
Cannon, L. F. Mrs.	38005	Dallas	Cannon, Emberry	
Cannon, Leander Mrs.	35055	Galveston	Cannon, Leander	
Cannon, Maggie A.	40005	El Paso	Cannon, Benjamin Bartlett	34300
Cannon, Mary	17621	Erath	Cannon, Robert C.	
Cannon, N. C. Mrs.	32384	Sterling	Cannon, David Etherly	21679
Cannon, R. F.	06257	Shelby	—	
Cannon, Rebecca	15705	Hopkins	Cannon, Thomas	
Cannon, Robert Tunnel	14694	Bexar	—	
Cannon, Saphronia	37088	Tarrant	Cannon, William Green	
Cannon, T. J.	02078	Houston	—	
Cannon, V. F. Mrs.	09561	Shelby	Cannon, R. F.	06257
Cannon, Warren P.	37729	Smith	—	
Cannon, Warren P. Mrs.	42213	Smith	Cannon, Warren P.	37729
Canon, Amanda L.	03358	Polk	Canon, Robert T.	
Canon, E. F.	20739	Polk	—	
Canon, John W.	07133	Aransas	—	
Cansler, G. P.	41089	Newton	—	
Cansler, Lizzie	49388	Hill	Cansler, Thomas Green	
Cansler, N. E. Mrs.	19140	Montague	Cansler, Robert Abraham	
Canter, James Christopher	23085	Liberty	—	
Canter, Julia Ann	35478	Liberty	Canter, James Christopher	23085
Cantrell, Alexander C.	Rej	Coryell	—	
Cantrell, Alice	51648	Tarrant	Cantrell, Henry C.	
Cantrell, B. A. Mrs.	45697	Henderson	Cantrell, Shade	18703
Cantrell, B. F.	Rej	Van Zandt	—	
Cantrell, Banister	24128	Dallas	—	
Cantrell, David Martin Mrs.	35958	Anderson	Cantrell, David Martin	
Cantrell, Eliza J.	49072	Van Zandt	Cantrell, Ben Franklin	
Cantrell, Emma	33182	Bell	Cantrell, James Marshall	

Index to Confederate Pension Applications

Cantrell, J. C.	Rej	Henderson		
Cantrell, J. R.	19505	Henderson		
Cantrell, Jim	47357	Young		
Cantrell, Lora	38032	Dallas	Cantrell, Banister	24128
Cantrell, Maggie E.	08608	Angelina	Cantrell, James R.	
Cantrell, Miles	Rej	Travis		
Cantrell, S. S. Mrs.	50741	Young	Cantrell, Jim	47357
Cantrell, Sarah F.	Rej	Coryell	Cantrell, Alexander C.	Rej
Cantrell, Shade	18703	Henderson		
Cantrell, Shadrach	Rej	Anderson		
Cantu, Donaciano	10244	Bexar		
Cantwell, M. B.	02412	Kerr		
Cantwell, Suzanne E.	41644	Grayson	Cantwell, William Thomas	
Canuteson, Christian	27386	Bosque		
Canuteson, Kestie	30268	Bosque	Canuteson, Neal	28640
Canuteson, Neal	28640	Bosque		
Canuteson, O. A.	30798	Bosque		
Cape, Myra M.	42801	Concho	Cape, William David	
Capehart, Mary Ann	01037	Dallas	Capehart, James E.	
Capel, M. J. Mrs.	30098	Cass	Capel, James Jackson	
Capell, C. F.	38861	Dallas		
Capers, Caleb Leonidas	32369	San Jacinto		
Capers, Caleb Leonidas Mrs.	39098	San Jacinto	Capers, Caleb Leonidas	32369
Caperton, Andy W.	30683	Karnes		
Caperton, Belle	41995	Travis	Caperton, Reuben Scrivener	00103
Caperton, John M.	32216	Jim Wells		
Caperton, Louise E.	07010	Hill	Caperton, W. W.	
Caperton, M. M. Mrs.	17263	Runnels	Caperton, Alfred H.	
Caperton, Reuben Scrivener	00103	Archer		
Caplen, Louisiana	15676	Harris	Caplen, Charles Selim	
Caples, Nancy Ann	46095	Angelina	Caples, Thomas Richard	
Capon, Mary E.	45790	Bee	Capon, George Walcot	
Cappleman, C. C. Mrs.	20075	Grayson	Cappleman, David Boozer	15276
Cappleman, D. R.	15314	Grimes		
Cappleman, David Boozer	15276	Grayson		
Cappleman, H. S.	06718	Fannin		
Cappleman, Sarah Taylor	49451	Fannin	Taylor, Whitfield Rogers	
Capps, Elvira Ann Ligett	Rej	Dallas	Ligett, James	
Capps, H. H.	37344	Grimes		
Capps, J. Q. A.	00007	Anderson		
Capps, J. W.	17203	Montague		
Capps, James A.	01370	Falls		
Capps, James Marion	14985	Crockett		
Capps, Levina	32038	Anderson	Capps, William M.	
Capps, M. C. Mrs.	00675	Camp	Capps, A. J.	
Capps, Margaret E.	31588	Smith	Capps, George Walter	
Capps, Mary A.	05302	Grimes	Capps, John R.	
Capps, Mary E.	45363	Matagorda	Capps, Robert James	33519
Capps, Matt C. (Mathew)	04023	Upshur		
Capps, Ransom	18091	Mason		
Capps, Robert James	33519	Matagorda		
Capps, S. A. Mrs.	16804	Upshur	Capps, Mathew C.	04023
Capshaw, J. J. Mrs.	34360	Williamson	Capshaw, Caswell Carver	
Caradine, Ailsey J. Mrs.	06353	Wood		
Caradine, John Elliot	06510	Kaufman		
Caradine, M. C. Mrs.	34899	Childress	Caradine, Robert	
Caradine, R.	Rej	Childress		
Caradine, U. C. Mrs.	21351	Jasper	Caradine, John Elliott	06510
Caraway, Adam	43551	Nacogdoches		

Index to Confederate Pension Applications

Name	No.	County	Spouse/Related	Ref.
Caraway, Albert S.	42632	Hunt	—	
Caraway, Amanda	42838	Gonzales	Caraway, George Washington	—
Caraway, C. M.	RejM	Comanche	—	
Caraway, Henry	13139	Gonzales		
Caraway, Maria Jane	47269	Gonzales	Caraway, Martin Van Buren	—
Caraway, Martha L.	40004	Comanche	Caraway, Calvin Marshall	—
Caraway, Mary A.	08061	Sabine	Caraway, N. J.	
Caraway, Mollie P.	42181	Grayson	Caraway, William Garner	
Caraway, Sarah Ann Elizabeth	28872	Grimes	Caraway, Archie Ezekial	
Caraway, W. T.	32803	Coke	—	
Cardell, A. L.	29035	Anderson	—	
Cardenas, Amelia	10784	Wilson	Cardenas, Pablo	
Cardenas, Nicanor	10338	Caldwell	—	
Carder, Alice	51657	Potter	Carder, James Frank	45009
Carder, James Frank	45009	Potter	—	
Cardin, P.	32643	Delta	—	
Cardwell, A. F.	Rej	Childress	—	
Cardwell, Aaron D.	05588	Hunt	—	
Cardwell, Henry C.	15785	Johnson	—	
Cardwell, Mattie	50677	Caldwell	Cardwell, John Madison	
Cardwell, T. W.	24382	Haskell	—	
Cardwell, William Mankin	22641	McLennan	—	
Cardwell, William Mankin Mrs.	38615	Brazoria	Cardwell, William Mankin	22641
Carey, A. L. Mrs.	00467	Bosque	Carey, Joel Gordon	—
Carey, Dan J.	11552	McLennan	—	
Carey, James C.	13831	Hardin	—	
Carey, John James	02818	McLennan	—	
Carey, M. A. Mrs.	10417	McLennan	Carey, John James	02818
Cargal, William Calvin (Cargle)	07694	Collin	—	
Cargill, Alfred	01294	Erath	—	
Cargill, J. P.	28963	Tarrant	—	
Cargill, Mary G.	36565	Robertson	Cargill, Andrew Jackson	—
Cargill, Sarah C.	42327	Tarrant	Cargill, John Wesley	—
Cargill, T. D.	Rej	Kinney	—	
Cargle, Jennie	34407	Fannin	Cargle, William Calvin (Cargal)	07694
Carico, Charles	15850	Lamar	—	
Carico, M. L. Mrs.	36172	Lamar	Carico, Charles	15850
Cariker, Percival M.	37705	Cherokee	—	
Cariker, W. W.	05860	Falls	—	
Carillo, Carmen Jaimes De	00326	Bexar	Carillo, Jose Nestor	—
Carithers, Georgia A.	20331	Ellis	Carithers, Hugh McGowan	01252
Carithers, Hugh McGowan	01252	Ellis	—	
Carl, Mary Elizabeth	39168	Bexar	Carl, John Hammock	—
Carleton, M. A. Mrs.	18355	Shelby	Carleton, George Washington	—
Carleton, S. D. Mrs.	22514	Ellis	Carleton, William Monroe	01220
Carleton, William Monroe	01220	Ellis	—	
Carleton, Willie	45337	Milam	Carleton, James Monroe	—
Carley, Rebecca E.	04712	Freestone	Carley, William T.	—
Carley, S. A. Mrs.	06809	Mitchell	Carley, J. W.	—
Carlile, H. J.	01709	Grimes	—	
Carlile, J. D.	49512	Williamson	—	
Carlile, J. S.	07304	Montague	—	
Carlile, James	00750	Cherokee	—	
Carlile, James Wesley	16472	San Jacinto	—	
Carlile, Mollie	45511	San Jacinto	Carlile, James Wesley	16472
Carlile, Robert H.	09127	Wood	—	
Carlile, T. J.	25536	Upshur	—	
Carlisle, Alexander Emmett Mrs.	49762	Dallas	Carlisle, Alexander Emmett	—
Carlisle, Annie B.	33932	Gregg	Carlisle, William Beach	—

Index to Confederate Pension Applications

Name	App #	County	Veteran	Vet App #
Carlisle, Annie E.	19711	Bexar	Carlisle, John Hutsell	—
Carlisle, Billie	43388	Mills		
Carlisle, Billie Mrs.	51570	Mills	Carlisle, Billie	43388
Carlisle, E. M. Mrs.	18688	Cass	Carlisle, James W.	—
Carlisle, F. M.	04934	Brown		
Carlisle, G. A.	24981	Jack		
Carlisle, John	Rej	Callahan		
Carlisle, John	43982	Kaufman		
Carlisle, Lawrence	Rej	Bee		
Carlisle, Martha	51027	Dickens	Carlisle, Jonas	—
Carlisle, Mary D.	47123	Travis	Carlisle, James Newton	—
Carlisle, Natalie Taylor	51998	Harris	Carlisle, John King	—
Carlisle, T. P.	06291	Kaufman		
Carlock, James Jackson	29269	Bell		
Carlock, William Voules Culton	19623	Mills		
Carlow, Samuel Joseph	13585	Cass		
Carlow, Sarah C.	14148	Cass	Carlow, Samuel Joseph	13585
Carlton, Elizabeth Jane	03992	Trinity	Carlton, John S.	—
Carlton, G. W.	32843	Young		
Carlton, Hennie	29722	McLennan	Carlton, William Henry	—
Carlton, Henry Harrison	16412	Sabine		
Carlton, J. T. Mrs.	33774	Robertson	Carlton, John Thomas	—
Carlton, Laura Elizabeth	20903	Sabine	Carlton, Henry Harrison	16412
Carlton, Lucy V.	49392	Hays	Carlton, John Peter	—
Carlton, Margaret	08495M	Trinity		
Carlton, Missouri Ann	27123	Cass	Carlton, William Haston	—
Carlton, N. A. Mrs.	Rej	Gregg	Carlton, Coleman Columbus	—
Carmack, David R.	41705	Terry		
Carmack, Emma	45641	Tarrant	Carmack, George Lilburn	—
Carmichael, Crockett N.	50461	Wilson		
Carmichael, Etta	46968	Gonzales	Carmichael, Hugh McCall	—
Carmichael, Flem	Rej	Orange		
Carmichael, George Washington	15933	Llano		
Carmichael, L. J. Mrs.	26126	Llano	Carmichael, George Washington	15933
Carmichael, R. R.	16869	Van Zandt		
Carmichael, S. E.	29669	Clay		
Carmichael, Sarah A.	03251	Panola	Carmichael, G. W.	—
Carnahan, Andrew Jackson Mrs.	21680	Tarrant	Carnahan, Andrew Jackson	—
Carnathan, Mary Ann	41099	Camp	Carnathan, James Monroe	—
Carnathan, Mattie J.	45536	Dallas	Carnathan, Wylie J.	—
Carner, James A.	Rej	Dimmit		
Carnes, Alice Greenwood	47884	Jefferson	Carnes, Joseph Malcolm	—
Carnes, Andrew Jackson	11866	Comanche		
Carnes, Dave	22140	Tarrant		
Carnes, James, Jr.	18897	Comanche		
Carnes, John	10878	Comanche		
Carnes, John Daniel	12011	Lamar		
Carnes, Joseph M.	35453	Wilson		
Carnes, Kate	23558	Brown	Carnes, John	10878
Carnes, Mary E.	22806	Comanche	Carnes, Andrew Jackson	11866
Carnes, N. C. Mrs.	26441	Montgomery	Carnes, James Marshal	—
Carnes, S. E. Mrs.	04887	Nacogdoches	Carnes, J. N.	—
Carnes, Sarah	31330	Lamar	Carnes, John Daniel	12011
Carnes, Sarah Elizabeth	47814	Tarrant	Carnes, William Davis Gowen	—
Carnes, W. F.	33134	Nacogdoches		
Carnes, William	10877	Comanche		
Carney, Rebecca	Rej	Wise	Carney, George W.	—
Carnochan, Kate	45610	Travis	Carnochan, Nicholas	22906
Carnochan, Nicholas	22906	Montgomery		

Index to Confederate Pension Applications

Carnohan, Annie E.	38628	Tarrant	Carnohan, Joseph Battle	29703
Carnohan, Joseph Battle	29703	Dallas	—	—
Carnoline, William	Rej	Angelina	—	—
Caro, J. M.	Rej	Starr	—	—
Carother, J. A. Mrs.	09990	Bell	Carother, S. D.	—
Carothers, A. M.	Rej	Travis	—	—
Carothers, Ada Ledbetter	51555	Bexar	Carothers, Robert Simian	02926M
Carothers, Henry O.	23979	Collin	—	—
Carothers, Ophelia M.	18373	Scurry	Carothers, James Howell	—
Carothers, R. J.	00258	Bell	—	—
Carothers, Robert Simian	02926M	—	—	—
Carothers, Samuel Moore	26455	Mills	—	—
Carothers, Stephen E.	22973	McLennan	—	—
Carpenter, Allen R.	Rej	Limestone	—	—
Carpenter, Amelia F.	28215	McCulloch	Carpenter, George W.	—
Carpenter, B. F.	26845	Cooke	—	—
Carpenter, Benjamin F.	42032	Ellis	—	—
Carpenter, Benjamin Franklin	06252	Van Zandt	—	—
Carpenter, Conrad H.	01438	Fannin	—	—
Carpenter, Edmund Lilly	09197	Dallas	—	—
Carpenter, Edmund Lilly Mrs.	20388	Dallas	Carpenter, Edmund Lilly	09197
Carpenter, Elizabeth	26809	Foard	Carpenter, Benjamin Artemas	—
Carpenter, Elizabeth C.	17841	Hood	Carpenter, William Sanford	01977
Carpenter, F. W.	28696	Hopkins	—	—
Carpenter, Harriet F.	12351	Fannin	Carpenter, Conrad H.	01438
Carpenter, Hattie	Rej	Dallas	Carpenter, John Robert	—
Carpenter, Henry	10326	Bexar	—	—
Carpenter, James Madison	46923	Bell	—	—
Carpenter, Jennie L.	35605	Bowie	Carpenter, Uriah	31382
Carpenter, John J.	17330	Bexar	—	—
Carpenter, L. C.	03946	Travis	—	—
Carpenter, Lawrence T.	00347	Bexar	—	—
Carpenter, M. J. Mrs.	32271	Van Zandt	Carpenter, Benjamin Franklin	06252
Carpenter, Margaret	10326A	Bexar	Carpenter, Henry	10326
Carpenter, Margaret A.	40435	Hopkins	Carpenter, Richard	33837
Carpenter, Mariah	26844	Bexar	Carpenter, John J.	17330
Carpenter, Mary	Rej	Bexar	Carpenter, Frank	—
Carpenter, Mary	41894	Bell	Carpenter, Thomas F.	—
Carpenter, Mary	49414	Titus	Carpenter, William Green	—
Carpenter, Mary A.	09958	Travis	Carpenter, L. C.	—
Carpenter, Mary A.	19913	Tom Green	Carpenter, Andrew Jackson	—
Carpenter, Matilda Ireland	34106	Harris	Carpenter, Evan Shelby	—
Carpenter, N. J. Mrs.	Rej	Hunt	Carpenter, Owen Lovel	—
Carpenter, P. Banks Mrs.	50832	Navarro	Banks, Thomas Calhoun	—
Carpenter, Richard	33837	Hopkins	—	—
Carpenter, Tom C.	50806	King	—	—
Carpenter, Uriah	31382	Bowie	—	—
Carpenter, William Sanford	01977	Hood	—	—
Carper, John Henry Mrs.	50986	Johnson	Carper, John Henry	—
Carr, A. M. Mrs.	27752	Robertson	Carr, David Milton	—
Carr, Annie	45162	Tarrant	Carr, Harry Benjamin	25883
Carr, Dabney W.	05405	Hill	—	—
Carr, Eliza Ann	47380	Dallas	Carr, Henry Stephen	—
Carr, F. W.	06620	Hunt	—	—
Carr, H. C. Mrs.	10305	Hunt	Carr, F. W.	06620
Carr, Harry Benjamin	25883	Franklin	—	—
Carr, Hugh	10421	Medina	—	—
Carr, J. C.	00335	Bexar	—	—
Carr, J. C.	05707	Erath	—	—

Index to Confederate Pension Applications

Name	No.	County	Soldier	No.
Carr, James C.	19352	Shelby	—	—
Carr, James F.	12877	Harris	—	—
Carr, James W.	37195	Randall	—	—
Carr, Jennie	19670	Burleson	Carr, William	00385
Carr, Joel Stanley	00493	Bowie	—	—
Carr, Laura Jane	21373	Bowie	Carr, Joel Stanley	00493
Carr, Martha Jane Shell	39348	Robertson	Shell, John Ezekiel	—
Carr, Mary C.	17091	Gonzales	Carr, Emanuel	—
Carr, Mary S.	23059	Delta	Carr, John	—
Carr, Polly	21681	San Patricio	Carr, Hugh	10421
Carr, R. S.	24112	Travis	—	—
Carr, Robert A.	25725	Eastland	—	—
Carr, Sarah	40618	Cottle	Carr, Thomas M.	21603
Carr, Susan	11713	Bexar	Carr, J. C.	—
Carr, Susan	46129	Dallas	Carr, Madison Hawkins	—
Carr, Thomas M.	21603	Cottle	—	—
Carr, William	00385	Bexar	—	—
Carr, William L.	08565	Dallas	—	—
Carr, Z. T.	45368	Hunt	—	—
Carraway, David O.	45942	Bexar	—	—
Carraway, J. E., Capt.	39327	Fannin	—	—
Carrell, James Joseph	09402	Delta	—	—
Carrell, L. V. Mrs.	43689	Van Zandt	Carrell, Summey	—
Carrell, Melissa J.	30990	Grayson	Carrell, William M.	—
Carrell, Pacia Ann	36288	Delta	Carrell, James Joseph	09402
Carrell, R.	43473	Wood	—	—
Carrell, Thomas I.	14562	Angelina	—	—
Carrell, Thomas I. Mrs.	42534	Angelina	Carrell, Thomas I.	14562
Carrico, H. H.	12465	Johnson	—	—
Carrier, Mary	Rej	Nacogdoches	Carrier, J. E.	—
Carrier, Thomas S.	34936	Tarrant	—	—
Carrigan, Obediance Mrs.	01912	Hill	Carrigan, Allen	—
Carriker, Elizabeth Jordan	40882	Shelby	Carriker, Henry James	—
Carriker, Mary A.	24761	Wheeler	Carriker, Adam Pinkney	—
Carriker, Rachel Catherine	42767	Palo Pinto	Carriker, Samuel Manualis	—
Carrington, Daniel	18485	Upshur	—	—
Carrington, Ida S.	19011	Harris	Carrington, Edward J.	—
Carrington, Lucius Marion	28579	Bexar	—	—
Carrington, M. E. Mrs.	36018	Travis	Carrington, Robert Emmett	—
Carrington, Margaret G.	19690	Freestone	Carrington, Duncan Cameron	—
Carrington, Margaret L.	31910	Dallas	Carrington, Lucius Marion	28579
Carrol, Narcisus B.	36589	Limestone	Carrol, John William	—
Carroll, Abe, Sr.	27691	Ellis	—	—
Carroll, Ada	29297	Montgomery	Carroll, David A.	—
Carroll, Amanda C.	30346	Polk	Carroll, James Monroe	20806
Carroll, Ami Bass Mrs.	Rej	Harris	Carroll, Ami Bass	—
Carroll, B. A. Mrs.	Rej	Shelby	Carroll, John Jesse	—
Carroll, C. E. Thompson Mrs.	45020	Upshur	Thompson, Augustus L.	—
Carroll, C. G.	35760	Wharton	—	—
Carroll, David Vinson	10085	Freestone	—	—
Carroll, E. J. Mrs.	14518	Anderson	Carroll, Abner M.	—
Carroll, E. M.	RejM	Jackson	—	—
Carroll, Emma B.	Rej	Freestone	Carroll, David Vinson	10085
Carroll, F. E. Mrs.	51092	Navarro	Carroll, Nathaniel Henderson	10714
Carroll, G. A. Mrs.	46945	Navarro	Carroll, Benjamin Franklin	—
Carroll, Hattie Meek	40748	Dallas	Abe, Sr.	27691
Carroll, J. C.	20129	Delta	—	—
Carroll, James Caswell	20469	Anderson	—	—
Carroll, James Monroe	20806	Polk	—	—

Index to Confederate Pension Applications

Name	App#	County	Veteran	Vet#
Carroll, James R.	27788	Jasper		
Carroll, Jennie	17512	Comanche	Carroll, Steadman D.	
Carroll, John Jesse Mrs.	24135	Shelby	Carroll, John Jesse	
Carroll, John William	05775	Dallas		
Carroll, John William (Pete)	17614	Erath		
Carroll, Joseph Milton	11051	Milam		
Carroll, Josephine	Rej	McLennan	Carroll, John Giles	
Carroll, L.	46625	Hopkins		
Carroll, L. E. Mrs.	Rej	Rusk	Carroll, J. C.	
Carroll, Lucinda	24654	Bastrop	Carroll, Patrick	
Carroll, M. S. Mrs.	25392	Harris	Carroll, John Newton	
Carroll, M. Z. Mrs.	37591	Van Zandt	Carroll, Thomas Jefferson	12712
Carroll, Margaret	38577	Smith	Carroll, Robert N.	
Carroll, Margret	16259	Parker	Carroll, Nicholas	07937
Carroll, Mary E.	18827	Bell	Carroll, Thomas Henderson	
Carroll, Mary E.	38087	Anderson	Carroll, James Caswell	20469
Carroll, Mary Elizabeth	42845	Navarro	Carroll, John W.	
Carroll, Mary Ennis	03102	Navarro	Carroll, John W.	
Carroll, Mary J.	18918	Dallas	Carroll, John William	05775
Carroll, Mary N.	49292	Hopkins	Carroll, L.	46625
Carroll, Nancy Emiline	24127	Tarrant	Carroll, John Marion	
Carroll, Nathaniel Henderson	10714	Navarro		
Carroll, Nicholas	07937	Parker		
Carroll, P. P.	39158	Brazos		
Carroll, R. M.	10977	Hill		
Carroll, Rebecca E.	36914	Wichita	Carroll, William George	09227
Carroll, Sallie	35227	Shelby	Carroll, Thomas	17228
Carroll, Samantha A.	37798	Brown	Carroll, Wilbur Pipkin	
Carroll, Sarah Jane	49869	San Saba	Carroll, John Bunyan	
Carroll, Smith F.	02940	Midland		
Carroll, Susan C.	04022	Upshur	Carroll, Stephen G.	
Carroll, Thomas	17228	Shelby		
Carroll, Thomas Benton	23080	Hopkins		
Carroll, Thomas Benton Mrs.	40377	Hopkins	Carroll, Thomas Benton	23080
Carroll, Thomas Jefferson	12712	Van Zandt		
Carroll, Thomas Madison	39103	Henderson		
Carroll, Thomas Madison Mrs.	39630	Anderson	Carroll, Thomas Madison	39103
Carroll, W. H.	Rej	McLennan		
Carroll, William George	09227	Hill		
Carroll, Wilson R.	11686	Walker		
Carruth, Charles Robert	49931	Comanche		
Carruth, John T.	23097	Eastland		
Carruth, Mary Jane	51899	Comanche	Carruth, Charles Robert	49931
Carruthers, Permelia Adaline	39001	Kaufman	Carruthers, George Madison	
Carslile, T. R.	14863	Cass		
Carson, Bransonia	46997	Gonzales	Carson, John William	
Carson, Elizabeth	51374	Dewitt	Carson, John F.	
Carson, Elizabeth C.	18657	Montgomery	Carson, Elihu Lemuel	
Carson, Emma J.	22916	Coleman	Carson, Robert Pattner	
Carson, Henry S.	32787	Hill		
Carson, James	02296	Johnson		
Carson, John Charles	05480	Henderson		
Carson, John Pinkney	46382	Bell		
Carson, Julia A.	29228	Harris	Carson, George William	
Carson, M. O. Mrs.	41183	Harris	Carson, James Sanders	
Carson, Marguritte Annie	46292	Mason	Carson, Hazel Albert	
Carson, Martha Ann	41888	Coryell	Carson, Thomas William	
Carson, Mary A.	Rej	Madison	Carson, T. H.	
Carson, Mary S.	19206	Red River	Carson, Samuel	

Index to Confederate Pension Applications

Carson, Nancy Jane	50332	Cooke	Carson, Wilie	
Carson, Nancy L.	34188	Leon	Carson, Thomas Henderson	
Carson, S. F. Mrs.	47066	Cherokee	Carson, Robert Pinkney	
Carson, Saleta A.	26049	Lamar	Carson, Owen R.	
Carson, Sallie M.	11382	Collin	Carson, William Stewart	
Carson, Sarah M.	Rej	Collin	Carson, William Stewart	
Carson, Seburn F.	Rej	Hemphill		
Carson, Thomas G.	26041	Johnson		
Carson, Thomas Jefferson	08823	Edwards		
Carson, V. A. Mrs.	21682	Johnson	Carson, James	02296
Carstens, L. V. Mrs.	27026	Harris	Carstens, Christian H.	
Carswell, Lydia	27463	Mills	Carswell, William Texas	
Carswell, Oliver Perry	44066	Panola		
Carter, A. E. Mrs.	27846	Jones	Carter, Thomas Randolph	
Carter, A. H.	43128	Colorado		
Carter, Alfred	05148	Brazoria		
Carter, Alfred H.	Rej	Freestone		
Carter, Amanda C.	06358	Grimes	Carter, Hampston Wesley	
Carter, Anna	20790	Waller	Carter, Daniel Jamison	
Carter, Ben Alice	50185	Hartley	Carter, Edward Franklin	
Carter, Benjamin F.	00964	Cooke		
Carter, Bernetie Hanah	Rej	Brown	Carter, Alexander Aulkie	
Carter, C. W.	39301	Baylor		
Carter, Charlie P.	22818	Collin		
Carter, Dan M.	36369	Tyler		
Carter, Darrinda	23067	Wood	Carter, John Elvis	
Carter, David Edmond (Edwin)	17808	Henderson		
Carter, Davidson L.	01910	Hill		
Carter, E. F. Mrs.	14519	Anderson	Carter, Nicholas	
Carter, E. L. Mrs.	32150	Dallas	Carter, George Fitzhugh	
Carter, E. S. Mrs.	32385	Tarrant	Carter, Samuel	19279
Carter, Eda	35804	Harris	Carter, Harry Pearson	26734
Carter, Edward F.	36435	Dallam		
Carter, Elizabeth	Rej	Parker	Carter, Joseph Wilson	
Carter, Elizabeth Franklin	04613	Panola	Carter, Perry	
Carter, Eula	45478	Hood	Carter, Charley Powell	
Carter, F. E. Mrs.	42333	Bailey	Carter, William James	
Carter, F. M.	Rej	Angelina		
Carter, F. M.	37461	Hamilton		
Carter, Fannie	19438	Kaufman	Carter, John L.	
Carter, Granberry W.	26438	Ellis		
Carter, Hannibal	01555	Galveston		
Carter, Hannibal Mrs.	11477	Hays	Carter, Hannibal	01555
Carter, Harriett Ann	39476	Bell	Carter, William Haywood	
Carter, Harry Pearson	26734	Harris		
Carter, Henrietta	40383	Ellis	Carter, John James	29090
Carter, Hugh	15690	Henderson		
Carter, J. M.	Rej	Erath		
Carter, J. M.	40488	Bowie		
Carter, J. O.	10380	Grayson		
Carter, James Houston	23553	Henderson		
Carter, James Thomas	29534	Nacogdoches		
Carter, Jane	02440	Lamar	Carter, B. P.	
Carter, Jane Ann Newland	07201	Fisher	Carter, Samuel H.	
Carter, Jane C.	49615	Cooke	Carter, Robert William	41455
Carter, Jennie	45798	Stephens	Carter, Clark Britton	
Carter, Joe C.	00293	Bell		
Carter, John C.	01407	Fannin		
Carter, John H.	33869	Harrison		

Index to Confederate Pension Applications

Carter, John Henry Mrs.	Rej	Eastland	Carter, John Henry	
Carter, John James	29090	Johnson	—	
Carter, John T.	28379	Dallas	—	
Carter, John Temple	11616	Runnels	—	
Carter, Julia Bell	25122	Lamar	Carter, Andrew Jackson	
Carter, L. B.	14621	Bastrop	—	
Carter, Lewis Allen	05875	Fannin	—	
Carter, Lou F. Mrs.	04838	Red River	Carter, Virgil J.	
Carter, Lou T. Mrs.	21683	Hays	Carter, Haley McCalister	
Carter, Luella G.	45381	Tarrant	Carter, James Houston	23553
Carter, M. A. Mrs.	28692	McCulloch	Carter, James Uriah	
Carter, M. E. Mrs.	50968	Callahan	Carter, William Thomas	25929
Carter, M. M. Moseley Mrs.	48079	Limestone	Moseley, William P.	
Carter, Madison James	18694	Hamilton	—	
Carter, Marcia R.	36104	Colorado	Carter, John A.	
Carter, Margaret	13111	Walker	Carter, Thomas J.	12673
Carter, Margaret	37446	Henderson	Carter, David Edwin (Edmond)	17808
Carter, Martha F.	21477	Grayson	Carter, Thomas Wister	
Carter, Mary	20939	Wilbarger	Carter, Charles Wasten	
Carter, Mary A.	39740	Rains	Carter, Blake Anderson	
Carter, Mary Emly	17244	Henderson	Carter, Hugh	15690
Carter, Mary L.	42663	Freestone	Carter, Alfred Henry	
Carter, Mary P.	36759	Panola	Carter, William Fincher	
Carter, Mattie E.	45553	Panola	Carter, Alexander	
Carter, Mildred Ann Roper	00632	Caldwell	Carter, John Q. A.	
Carter, Minerva Shelfer	49384	Angelina	Carter, Mike C.	
Carter, N. C. Mrs.	03450	Robertson	Carter, J. H.	
Carter, Nancy A.	25661	Collin	Carter, John C.	01407
Carter, Nancy Catherine	25555	Wichita	Carter, Louis McKendill	
Carter, Nancy E.	12507	Milam	Carter, Benjamin A.	
Carter, Nancy J.	15706	Hopkins	Carter, Robert Augustus	
Carter, Nancy M.	13287	Denton	Carter, Joseph C.	
Carter, Nancy Maro	52075	Smith	Carter, Thomas Abraham	27447
Carter, Oliver	18048	Limestone	—	
Carter, Perlina Ellen	23388	Bell	Carter, James Beaver	
Carter, R. E.	23123	Navarro	—	
Carter, R. E. Mrs.	45170	Lamar	Carter, R. E.	23123
Carter, R. J.	10973	Hays	—	
Carter, Rachel Henrietta	45757	Tarrant	Carter, George Thomas	
Carter, Robert Augustus	05295	Gregg	—	
Carter, Robert William	41455	Cooke	—	
Carter, S. H. Mrs.	05220	Lamar	Carter, John Milton	
Carter, S. M.	38364	Eastland	—	
Carter, Samuel	19279	Tarrant	—	
Carter, Sefronia E.	33933	Ellis	Carter, Granberry W.	26438
Carter, St. Clair Blake	13438	Milam	—	
Carter, Susan M.	Rej	Shelby	Carter, Hubbard	
Carter, Tennie	34946	Milam	Carter, St. Clair Blake	13438
Carter, Thomas	35439	Comanche	—	
Carter, Thomas Abraham	27447	Smith	—	
Carter, Thomas Alexander	24688	Johnson	—	
Carter, Thomas Alexander Mrs.	37032	Johnson	Carter, Thomas Alexander	24688
Carter, Thomas C.	29381	Brazos	—	
Carter, Thomas J.	Rej	Delta	—	
Carter, Thomas J.	12673	Walker	—	
Carter, Thomas Jefferson	23096	Fannin	—	
Carter, Virginia F.	21318	Wilbarger	Carter, Lewis (Louis) Allen	05875
Carter, W. G.	32859	Van Zandt	—	
Carter, W. N.	15689	Henderson	—	

Index to Confederate Pension Applications

Name	No.	County	Veteran	Ref
Carter, Wade H.	Rej	Panola	—	—
Carter, Wade H.	19183	Panola	—	—
Carter, William Fincher	14364	Panola	—	—
Carter, William H.	33046	Harrison	—	—
Carter, William L.	09235	Hill	—	—
Carter, William Mrs.	Rej	Kinney	Carter, William	—
Carter, William Thomas	25929	Brown	—	—
Cartwright, C. W.	Rej	Bastrop	—	—
Cartwright, David J.	10817	Bandera	—	—
Cartwright, George W.	21325	Bandera	—	—
Cartwright, J. L.	Rej	Johnson	—	—
Cartwright, J. T.	26825	Denton	—	—
Cartwright, James McGowen	09397	Nacogdoches	—	—
Cartwright, Joanna	16066	Montgomery	Cartwright, Pleasant L.	—
Cartwright, L. M.	09927	Hill	—	—
Cartwright, Madison P.	11805	Bexar	—	—
Cartwright, Martha L.	16155	Nacogdoches	Cartwright, James McGowen	09397
Cartwright, Osa	Rej	Shelby	—	—
Cartwright, Susan	19681	Jefferson	Cartwright, Madison P.	—
Cartwright, Susan Caroline	04319	Webb	Cartwright, James S.	—
Cartwright, William W.	Rej	Nacogdoches	—	—
Caruth, M. E. Mrs.	13797	Fannin	Caruth, Thomas C.	—
Caruth, M. L. Mrs.	45868	Collin	Caruth, George Michael	—
Caruthers, Elizabeth	Rej	Wise	Caruthers, Benjamin Newton	—
Caruthers, Permelia	RejM	Kaufman	—	—
Caruthers, Rachel	10387	Hardin	Caruthers, Euclid	—
Caruthers, Richard Walter Mrs.	42358	Johnson	Caruthers, Richard Walter	—
Carvajal, Vincente F.	Rej	Wilson	—	—
Carver, C.	06473	Johnson	—	—
Carver, D. Lucinda	06019	San Jacinto	Carver, Levi	—
Carver, J. C.	10307	Henderson	—	—
Carver, James Anderson	13213	Bell	—	—
Carver, John S.	15692	Henderson	—	—
Carver, Mary	04729	Bandera	Carver, James	—
Carver, Mary	18541	Wilson	Carver, Isaac	—
Carver, Missouri	41225	Bell	Carver, James Anderson	13213
Carwile, Elizabeth	08477	Tarrant	—	—
Carwile, M. J. Mrs.	25694	Cass	Carwile, John Schuyler	—
Carwile, Milton S.	07996	Tarrant	—	—
Casanova, Juan	00401	Bexar	—	—
Casas, Joaquin	00381	Bexar	—	—
Casbeer, Amy	39493	Williamson	Casbeer, William Madison	39258
Casbeer, Joseph Lamar	02491	Lampasas	—	—
Casbeer, Kate	41451	Crockett	Casbeer, Joseph Lamar	02491
Casbeer, William Madison	39258	Williamson	—	—
Casber, Millie E.	RejM	Shelby	—	—
Case, Mary E.	40627	Cooke	Case, W.	14962
Case, N. A. Mrs.	39391	Erath	Case, William Marion	—
Case, Susan C.	04805	Nacogdoches	Case, Pinkney	—
Case, W.	14962	Cooke	—	—
Casey, A. A.	Rej	Hood	—	—
Casey, A. T.	Rej	Wise	—	—
Casey, Azlee D. Mrs.	14620	Bastrop	Casey, James Wilkins	08529M
Casey, D. M. Mrs.	32386	Newton	Casey, Henry James	20611
Casey, Elva A.	50155	Fisher	Casey, David Newton	—
Casey, George Washington	13183	Donley	—	—
Casey, Henrietta	33500	Wise	Casey, Abner Tipton	—
Casey, Henry James	20611	Newton	—	—
Casey, Hugh	20937	Williamson	—	—

Index to Confederate Pension Applications

Casey, Izora Joan Gentry	50300	Mills	Gentry, Jesse A.	
Casey, J. Isabel	04415	Williamson	Casey, Willis	
Casey, James Wilkins	08529M	Caldwell	—	
Casey, Martha B.	01490	Franklin	Casey, William H.	
Casey, Mary Francis	23271	Bastrop	Casey, Alfred	
Casey, Nancy	33035	Falls	Casey, Rufus Martin	27534
Casey, P. Houston	27498	Titus	—	
Casey, Preston	01735	Guadalupe	—	
Casey, Rufus Martin	27534	Falls	—	
Casey, Texana	27020	Falls	Casey, Thomas Calvin	
Casey, William J.	31597	Coleman	—	
Casey, William Thomas	33560	Cherokee	—	
Cash, B. J.	29928	Leon	—	
Cash, Benjamin R.	Rej	Wood	—	
Cash, Joel Franklin	16537	Shelby	—	
Cash, T. J.	08180	Brown	—	
Cashell, A. L.	28359	Kinney	—	
Cashion, Charlotte J.	15786	Johnson	Cashion, John W.	
Cashion, Jones Elija Mrs.	41024	Grimes	Cashion, Jones Elija	
Cashion, Mary A.	25405	Ellis	Cashion, Andrew Jackson	
Casillas, Casimiro, Sr.	06208	Bexar	—	
Caskey, Almanza A.	28755	Collin	Caskey, James A.	
Caskey, Cordelia A.	36675	Williamson	Caskey, George Decolb	32906
Caskey, George Decolb	32906	Williamson	—	
Caskey, L. M. Mrs.	14520	Anderson	Caskey, William Madison	
Casner, Emma L.	37176	McCulloch	Casner, Hiram	
Cason, Belle Mrs.	15206	Freestone	Cason, William Henry	
Cason, Benjamin L.	20568	Navarro	—	
Cason, F. A. Mrs.	30128	Fannin	Cason, Isaac Marina	
Cason, Jane L.	03230	Palo Pinto	Cason, P. E.	
Cason, O. S. Mrs.	05593	Hunt	Cason, Elihu	
Casper, Columbus H.	Rej	Lampasas	—	
Casper, Dora	20729	Coke	Casper, Hampton Harmon	07177
Casper, Frank Samuel Mrs.	33244	Travis	Casper, Frank Samuel	
Casper, Hampton Harmon	07177	Coke	—	
Cass, Bettie	50240	Haskell	Cass, James Madison	45181
Cass, James Madison	45181	Haskell	—	
Cass, S. J. Mrs.	07278	Lamar	Cass, J. M.	
Cassady, Elizabeth Jane	Rej	Leon	Cassady, Francis Marion	12034
Cassady, Francis Marion	12034	Llano	—	
Cassell, Henry Thomas	17516	Cooke	—	
Cassell, Henry Thomas Mrs.	44023	Cooke	Cassell, Henry Thomas	17516
Cassells, George Henry	13695	Bastrop	—	
Cassidy, Julia	41979	Gonzales	Cassidy, Michael	
Castanon, Rumalda	Rej	Atascosa	Castanon, Luis	
Castellaw, Almeda	23120	Lamar	Castellaw, Andrew Jackson	10402
Castellaw, Andrew Jackson	10402	Lavaca	—	
Castello, Vincenta V.	21096	Bexar	Castello, Alcario	
Castillo, Juanita	34189	Bexar	Castillo, Sevariano	
Castle, Calvin Columbus	26357	Anderson	—	
Castle, George W.	41179	Fannin	—	
Castle, Laura T.	25448	Smith	Castle, John Martin	
Castle, Mollie	50529	Titus	Castle(s), James W.	22499
Castle, R. L.	08251	Clay	—	
Castle, Rachel	30033	Anderson	Castle, Calvin Columbus	26357
Castle, William T.	37710	Montague	—	
Castleberry, Ida Mae	Rej	Wilbarger	Castleberry, Archibald H.	
Castleberry, Ira	09347	Travis	—	
Castleberry, James	Rej	Gregg	—	

Index to Confederate Pension Applications

Castleberry, James	11767	Henderson		
Castleberry, L. A. Mrs.	23121	Van Zandt	Castleberry, Edward	
Castleberry, Margaret J.	20641	Tarrant	Castleberry, Samuel Elbert	16655
Castleberry, Martha	36036	Travis	Castleberry, Ira	09347
Castleberry, Mollie	40599	Harrison	Castleberry, Richard W.	22485
Castleberry, Reuben V.	14348	Nacogdoches		
Castleberry, Richard W.	22485	Gregg		
Castleberry, S. Mrs.	34900	Nacogdoches	Castleberry, Simeon	13878
Castleberry, Simeon	13878	Nacogdoches		
Castlebery, Samuel Elbert	16655	Tarrant		
Castlebury, E. C. Mrs.	02439	Lamar	Castlebury, Joshua G.	
Castleman, J. M.	05900	Palo Pinto		
Castles, Arelia	39121	Leon	Castles, Samuel Alexander	34401
Castles, B. T.	07757	Bell		
Castles, James Alexander	33400	Wise		
Castles, James W.	22499	Franklin		
Castles, Samuel Alexander	34401	Leon		
Castles, Susan Ann	36392	Wise	Castles, James Alexander	33400
Castner, S. S. Mrs.	09710	Hopkins	Castner, W. H.	
Castro, Mary	39615	Nacogdoches	Castro, Narcese	
Castro, Ursula W.	04964	Bexar	Castro, Jesus Torres	
Caswell, Fannie M.	17603	Ellis	Caswell, James Russell	
Caswell, J. M.	27653	Jefferson		
Cate, Ann E.	41739	Denton	Cate, David H.	20734
Cate, David H.	20734	Denton		
Cate, Eliza Jane	35951	Mason	Cate, James Abner	06727
Cate, James Abner	06727	Mason		
Cate, James J.	06464	Johnson		
Cate, John Thomas	11247	Mason		
Cate, Mary Jane	19215	Runnels	Cate, Robert	
Cate, Matilda Ann	03772	Tarrant	Cate, William	
Cater, Belle	50436	Bexar	Cater, D. J.	45618
Cater, D. J.	45618	Bexar		
Cates, Anna Elizabeth	21045	Cass	Cates, James Littleton	
Cates, David Berry	40031	Cass		
Cates, Elizabeth	20178	Hopkins	Cates, Phillip	15704
Cates, Elvira	23161	McCulloch	Cates, Robert C.	
Cates, Fidelia	20613	Knox	Cates, William J.	
Cates, I. H. Mrs.	01265	Ellis	Cates, Thomas P.	
Cates, Jane	14781	Caldwell	Cates, William Houston	
Cates, Joshua	13249	Caldwell		
Cates, Lucynda	50390	Floyd	Cates, Hiram	
Cates, Marshall M.	13390	Johnson		
Cates, Mary Catherine	41078	Cass	Cates, David B.	40031
Cates, Nancy	06891	Wichita	Cates, R. B.	
Cates, Phillip	15704	Hopkins		
Cates, Rebecca	39424	Van Zandt	Cates, Thomas Jefferson	35935
Cates, Rowena Hale	Rej	Wise	Cates, Charles Donahue	
Cates, Thomas Jefferson	35935	Van Zandt		
Cathcart, J. F.	Rej	San Saba		
Cathcart, Joseph H.	22795	McLennan		
Cathcart, Sarah E.	43915	Tarrant	Cathcart, Joseph H.	22795
Cathey, Alice E. Matthews	41980	Travis	Matthews, Thomas Riley	
Cathey, Eliza Elizabeth	35570	Wood	Cathey, Benjamin F.	
Cathey, Elizabeth	42775	Hunt	Cathey, James A.	
Cathey, Fannie Mae	35537	Dallas	Cathey, Jethro Brown	26920
Cathey, Jethro Brown	26920	Dallas		
Cathey, Martha	01911	Hill	Cathey, M. R.	
Cathey, Mary Emily	50608	Houston	Cathey, Wilson Harrison	

Index to Confederate Pension Applications

Name	App #	County	Veteran	Vet App #
Cathey, Mary Hannah	40677	Coleman	Cathey, Griffith Rutherford	
Cathey, N. C. Mrs.	14633	Borden	Cathey, William Jackson	
Catlett, Benjamin L.	16802	Upshur		
Catlett, J. D.	23068	Upshur		
Catlett, Virginia Elizabeth	47877	Donley	Catlett, Henry Buin	
Cato, A. P. Mrs.	19145	Montgomery	Cato, Phillip Hamilton	
Cato, C. J. Mrs.	25643	Travis	Cato, William Alexander	
Cato, G. S.	27875	Johnson		
Cato, Z. T.	10308	Lamar		
Caton, Rebecca Tommas	45678	Hopkins	Caton, Charles Henry	
Caton, S. M. Mrs.	32230	Montague	Caton, William Alexander	
Caton, Sallie M.	46432	Red River	Caton, James H.	
Catterton, Benjamin Nicholson	33332	Gregg		
Catterton, Sarah S.	33340	Gregg	Catterton, Benjamin Nicholson	33332
Catvery, W. J.	RejM	Hill		
Cauble, D. B.	01909	Hill		
Cauble, James K. Polk Mrs.	45183	Johnson	Cauble, James K. Polk	
Cauble, James L.	36045	Hill		
Cauble, Nannie Mae	51850	Hill	Cauble, James L.	36045
Cauble, Thomas F.	50671	Hill		
Caudle, G. L. Mrs.	10062	Erath	Caudle, C. B.	
Caudle, J. H.	08358M	Hopkins		
Caudle, J. H.	23091	Comanche		
Caudle, Mary Francis	47206	Hardeman	Caudle, John Hiram	
Caughron, John William	48068	Collin		
Cauldwell, Catherine	21676	Cooke	Cauldwell, Thomas	
Cauley, W. C.	05341	Grayson		
Causey, John T.	27565	Robertson		
Causey, John W.	27370	Franklin		
Causey, Josephine	32310	Bexar	Causey, William Joseph	
Causey, Nannie Miller	51452	Franklin	Causey, John W.	27370
Causey, Nathaniel Green	11653	Titus		
Causey, W. R.	29162	Gregg		
Causey, W. S.	22170	Bandera		
Causseaux, Nannie	47755	Taylor	Causseaux, Peter Ballard	
Cauthen, John G.	Rej	Callahan		
Cauthen, L. C. Mrs.	25955	Taylor	Cauthen, John Thomas	
Cauthon, N. E. Mrs.	09521	Walker	Cauth(r)on, William James	06351
Cauthron, William James	06351	Walker		
Cave, A. J. Mrs.	49835	Fisher	Cave, Hiram David	
Cave, Sarah	38700	Nolan	Cave, Clark	
Cavender, George Washington	27725	El Paso		
Cavender, Helen	Rej	Parker	Cavender, John Calvin	
Cavender, Mary Jane	35228	Uvalde	Cavender, George Washington	27725
Cavender, S. J. Mrs.	41853	Frio	Cavender, Thomas Jefferson	
Cavener, Thomas D.	05839	Cooke		
Caveness, William A.	14892	Cherokee		
Caver, Annie	37018	Cherokee	Caver, William Thomas	
Caver, Nancy Q.	38751	Nacogdoches	Caver, Samuel Thompson	21441
Caver, S. L. Mrs.	25671	Erath	Caver, Robert Pinkney	
Caver, Samuel Thompson	21441	Nacogdoches		
Caver, W. T.	43475	Nolan		
Cavett, William Beatty	13821	Gonzales		
Cavin, Edmond Washington	05718	Bowie		
Cavin, Mary E.	38847	Bowie	Cavin, Edmond Washington	05718
Cavines, N. J. Mrs.	15851	Lamar	Cavines, William Lewis	
Caviness, Lucy	07324	Montague	Caviness, David	
Caviness, T. C.	15939	Dewitt		
Cavitt, John W.	Rej	Upshur		

Index to Confederate Pension Applications

Name	App #	County	Veteran	Vet App #
Cavitt, William A.	10627	El Paso	—	
Cavnar, Martha A. C.	29370	Lamar	Cavnar, William B.	
Cavness, Robert	02771	Mason	—	
Cawthon, Fannie M.	Rej	McLennan	Cawthon, Nathan	
Cawthon, James Christopher	32488	Cherokee	—	
Cawthon, Mary E.	35293	Cherokee	Cawthon, James Christopher	32488
Cawthon, Susan L.	23487	Cherokee	Cawthon, John Oliver	
Cawthon, Thomas J.	11846	Cherokee	—	
Cawthron, Thomas H.	01715	Grimes	—	
Cayce, G. L.	13298	Ellis	—	
Cayce, George B.	14771	Burnet	—	
Cayce, Henry Petty	14213	Erath	—	
Cayce, James Martin Mrs.	24119	Robertson	Cayce, James Martin	
Caylor, Addie L.	37063	Grayson	Caylor, Robert A.	
Caylor, F. M.	05444	Palo Pinto	—	
Caylor, Jennie	46738	Fannin	Caylor, Jacob Laban	
Caylor, John Henry	31757	Mason	—	
Cayton, Emeline	06936	Limestone	Cayton, James Calvin	
Ceballos, Rosa F. De	04317	Webb	Ceballos, Pedro	
Cecil, Frances A.	39550	Fannin	Cecil, William Wallace	33755
Cecil, William Wallace	33755	Fannin	—	
Cellum, E. J.	17452	Cherokee	—	
Cellum, L. I. Mrs.	28364	Delta	Cellum, Erastus Webb	
Cellum, Mary E.	20489	San Patricio	Cellum, Robert Washington	
Cellum, Thomas J.	21684	Harrison	—	
Cely, Maggie Jane	45032	Anderson	Cely, John Frank	
Center, Fleming W.	12436	Hopkins	—	
Cervantes, Francisco	08969	Bexar	—	
Cervantes, Manuel	08965	Bexar	—	
Cervantes, Senovia	33576	Bexar	Cervantes, Manuel	08965
Cessna, Borena	46106	Leon	Cessna, Daniel Adkins	
Cessna, Green K.	Rej	Fort Bend	—	
Chaddick, M. A. Mrs.	40421	Morris	Chaddick, George Martin	
Chaddick, R. C.	18686	Brown	—	
Chaddick, Ruth	46996	Collin	Chaddick, William Huett	
Chadick, S. R.	06047	Upshur	—	
Chadwell, James K. Mrs.	40776	Cooke	Chadwell, James K.	
Chadwell, John Richard	37757	Coleman	—	
Chadwell, John Richard Mrs.	51227	Coleman	Chadwell, John Richard	37757
Chadwick, A. H.	10283	Panola	—	
Chadwick, Mary Beatrice Fite	38438	Panola	Fite, Abraham Monroe	
Chadwick, William J.	45008	Panola	—	
Chaffin, Christopher Columbus	26050	Anderson	—	
Chaffin, Green	15719	Hunt	—	
Chaffin, J. H.	05340	Grayson	—	
Chaffin, Mariah E.	38837	Anderson	Chaffin, Christopher Columbus	26050
Chaffin, W. M.	41637	Grayson	—	
Chaffin, W. R.	44007	Hill	—	
Chaffin, W. T.	42450	Bosque	—	
Chalk, Robert L.	23367	Bexar	—	
Chalker, Emily Amanda	30281	Stephens	Chalker, John Marshal	
Chalker, Mary	36614	Bowie	Chalker, Charles Amos	
Chamberlain, Bettie	13860	Houston	Chamberlain, Benj. F.	
Chamberlain, Carmen	50997	Bexar	Chamberlain, William Chapman	
Chamberlain, David Bird	22427	Parker	—	
Chamberlain, Elva Lee	42146	Brown	Chamberlain, Wiley Jackson	
Chamberlain, George	10798	Bandera	—	
Chamberlain, J. A.	14606	Bandera	—	
Chamberlain, M. F. Mrs.	32934	Bandera	Chamberlain, J. A.	14606

Index to Confederate Pension Applications

Chamberlain, Martha Jane	42601	Burnet	Chamberlain, John Tate	
Chamberlain, Mary E.	41883	Parker	Chamberlain, David Bird	22427
Chamberlain, William C.	33460	Bexar		
Chamberlin, D. C.	22768	Dallas		
Chambers, Benjamin Franklin	20810	Anderson		
Chambers, Bettie	52039	Anderson	Chambers, Benjamin Franklin	20810
Chambers, Clara B.	35380	Comanche	Chambers, William Chambers	00925
Chambers, Edwin Glover	15996	McLennan		
Chambers, Ella	Rej	Denton	Chambers, Joseph Taylor	
Chambers, Francis	Rej	Milam	Chambers, William	
Chambers, J. A.	49006	Comanche		
Chambers, J. T.	Rej	Denton		
Chambers, James R.	39137	Denton		
Chambers, Jesse F.	19635	Comanche		
Chambers, John G.	00836	Coleman		
Chambers, John S.	23118	Jones		
Chambers, Josephine	51492	Harris	Chambers, James A.	
Chambers, Julia H.	50137	Collin	Chambers, Zachariah Taylor	
Chambers, Landon Clay	09654	Liberty		
Chambers, Laura Ann	Rej	Taylor	Chambers, Henry Freeman	
Chambers, Maranda	Rej	Coryell	Chambers, S. A.	08268
Chambers, Mary A.	18660	Milam	Chambers, Henry Columbus	
Chambers, Mary Ellen	18262	Presidio	Chambers, James Henry	
Chambers, Mattie E.	50807	Coleman	Chambers, Limuel	
Chambers, N. F.	05640	Erath		
Chambers, Nancy	31952	Comanche	Chambers, Jesse F.	19635
Chambers, Oliver Perry	12544	Liberty		
Chambers, R. J. Gage Mrs.	45704	Harris	Gage, Thomas Clarke	
Chambers, R. N.	17665	Franklin		
Chambers, S. A.	08268	Coryell		
Chambers, Sallie P.	29825	Morris	Chambers, George Caperton	
Chambers, Sarah Elizabeth	38624	McLennan	Chambers, Edwin Glover	15996
Chambers, Sarah Jane	38685	Walker	Chambers, Oliver Perry	12544
Chambers, Silas	15936	Lynn		
Chambers, Susan Francis	45072	Gray	Chambers, Joseph Henry	
Chambers, T. D.	03480	Rockwall		
Chambers, Taylor	Rej	Denton		
Chambers, Thomas J.	27861	Liberty		
Chambers, William	00925	Comanche		
Chamblee, Isham B.	17089	Freestone		
Chamblee, Laura Francis	19486	Karnes	Chamblee, Henry Freeman	
Chamblee, Louise	18701	Victoria	Chamblee, Andrew Jackson	
Chamblee, M. H. Mrs.	23114	Cass	Chamblee, John	
Chamblee, R. I.	09259	Johnson		
Chambles, H. F.	Rej	Karnes		
Chambles, Louise	Rej	Victoria	Chambles, Jackson	
Chambless, Eliza Amanda	Rej	Harris	Chambless, James Madison	
Chambless, Ephraim	Rej	Tyler		
Chambless, Ephraim	25400	Tyler		
Chambless, Hellen A.	Rej	Leon		
Chambless, J. A., Dr.	Rej	Red River		
Chambless, John Levi	21685	Taylor		
Chambless, William Perryman Mrs.	36247	Tarrant	Chambless, William Perryman	
Chambliss, Adelaide Almira	12257	Bastrop	Chambliss, Henry Fulton	
Chambliss, Delphia	20671	Limestone	Chambliss, Henry Gilmore	18052
Chambliss, Francis Marion	18079	Madison		
Chambliss, Henry Gilmore	18052	Limestone		
Chambliss, Littleton Marion	12616	Shelby		
Chambliss, Susan Ann	Rej	Lee	Chambliss, Joseph	

Index to Confederate Pension Applications

Name	No.	County	Veteran	Vet. No.
Chamness, Benjamin C., Sr.	16240	Panola	—	
Chamness, Mattie	Rej	Panola	Chamness, Ben C.	
Chamness, S. M.	20291	Shelby	—	
Champion, John	04392	Williamson	—	
Champion, L. E. Mrs.	41381	Tarrant	Champion, William Wiley	26733
Champion, Louisa	02686	Limestone	Champion, William H.	
Champion, M. F. Mrs.	Rej	Brown	Champion, George Wesley	
Champion, Mary E. Clark	42145	Freestone	Clark, Lawrence	
Champion, Richard Marion	30061	Shelby	—	
Champion, Richard Marion Mrs.	38012	Shelby	Champion, Richard Marion	30061
Champion, William Wiley	26733	Tarrant	—	
Chance, Benajah	30266	Bowie	—	
Chance, D. H.	Rej	Hardin	—	
Chance, Elenora	05121	Hardin	Chance, E. M.	
Chance, Mary J.	18880	Clay	Chance, Joseph Choffin	
Chance, Nancy E.	00667	Camp	Chance, Stephen	
Chance, Stephen	03626	Shelby	—	
Chancellor, A. L. A. Mrs.	25959	Stephens	Chancellor, Wesley Houston	
Chancellor, Daniel Jackson	08686	Freestone	—	
Chancellor, George Washington	18145	Montague	—	
Chancellor, J. M.	04876	Nacogdoches	—	
Chancellor, Jacob W.	15066	Eastland	—	
Chancellor, John Henly	00948	Cooke	—	
Chancellor, M. S. Mrs.	16122	Nacogdoches	John Asa Whetstone, Dr.	
Chancellor, Sarah Jane	38966	Montague	Chancellor, George Washington	18145
Chancellor, Sarah M.	37482	Cooke	Chancellor, John Henly	00948
Chancellor, W. H.	16872	Van Zandt	—	
Chancellor, Wade Hampton	00918	Comanche	—	
Chancy, Catherine	04652	Angelina	Chancy, John C.	
Chancy, Randolph	20027	Angelina	—	
Chancy, S. J. Mrs.	22656	Tarrant	Chancy, David	
Chandler, Adams M.	15682	Haskell	—	
Chandler, Angelina	30745	Fannin	Chandler, Jabas Ezra	
Chandler, Ann V.	Rej	Sabine	Chandler, John	
Chandler, Bettie	14373	Polk	Chandler, Rufus F.	
Chandler, Clara	49059	Wilbarger	Chandler, H. G.	23360
Chandler, D. N.	00993	Coryell	—	
Chandler, Earl Harrison Mrs.	49553	Erath	Chandler, Earl Harrison	
Chandler, Elizabeth A.	04835	Nacogdoches	Chandler, C. L.	
Chandler, Ella Josephine Johnston	47278	Travis	Johnston, Cary Moore	
Chandler, Elvira	20590	Childress	Chandler, William Jones	
Chandler, Emma E.	39261	Leon	Chandler, Robert Francis	38119
Chandler, Emma J.	39055	Upshur	Chandler, Thomas Henry	04026
Chandler, Emma Lee	47400	Hunt	Chandler, Marshall Marion	
Chandler, Enoch	08765	Milam	—	
Chandler, Essie Maldra	51115	Red River	Chandler, Joseph Marion	
Chandler, Euphamia A.	39451	Reeves	Chandler, William Washington	
Chandler, George W.	Rej	Montgomery	—	
Chandler, Georgia	Rej	McLennan	Chandler, Joseph Alvin	
Chandler, H. G.	23360	Wilbarger	—	
Chandler, H. M. Mrs.	Rej	Young	Chandler, John Lemuel	
Chandler, Hallan J.	Rej	Limestone	—	
Chandler, Isaac	Rej	Cass	—	
Chandler, J. M.	37334	Orange	—	
Chandler, J. N.	Rej	Hood	—	
Chandler, James W.	15903	Leon	—	
Chandler, Jane	18798	Polk	Chandler, Ransom D.	10183
Chandler, Joseph M.	16479	San Saba	—	
Chandler, M. A. Mrs.	15717	Houston	Chandler, E. H.	

Index to Confederate Pension Applications

Chandler, M. S. Mrs.	15828	Kaufman	Chandler, J. C.	
Chandler, Martin Alford	14618	Bastrop		
Chandler, Nancy J.	35903	Limestone	Chandler, Holland (Hollow) Jessie	
Chandler, P. H.	23559	Brazoria		
Chandler, R. A. Mrs.	16871	Van Zandt	Chandler, John Crawford	
Chandler, Ransom D.	10183	Polk		
Chandler, Robert Francis	38119	Freestone		
Chandler, S. A. Mrs.	03105	Navarro	Chandler, F. M.	
Chandler, Sallie	29067	Wharton	Chandler, William A. J.	
Chandler, Samuel T.	14436	Tarrant		
Chandler, Sanders	37685	Houston		
Chandler, Sarah A.	13742	Cass	Chandler, Isaac	
Chandler, Sarrah Ellen	15007	Dallas	Chandler, Edward	
Chandler, Stephen H.	36242	McLennan		
Chandler, Susan Elizabeth	32725	Bee	Chandler, Thomas Alonzo	18823
Chandler, T. H.	50996	Navarro		
Chandler, T. J.	24855	Montague		
Chandler, Thomas	Rej	Live Oak		
Chandler, Thomas Alonzo	18823	Bee		
Chandler, Thomas Henry	04026	Upshur		
Chandler, Washington W.	Rej	Reeves		
Chaney, Elizabeth	28845	Erath	Chaney, Hiram Jackson	
Chaney, M. M.	16843	Uvalde		
Chaney, Mary Catherine	47106	Lamar	Chaney, Walter Overton Tazelton	
Chaney, Nannie	21573	Val Verde	Chaney, W. T.	
Chaney, Sarah P.	45579	Fannin	Chaney, Cephas Joe Anderson	
Chaney, Thomas	17283	Angelina		
Chaney, W. J.	06514	Parker		
Channell, H. J.	Rej	Cass		
Chapa, Bernardo	10320	Bexar		
Chapman, A. E.	50379	Henderson		
Chapman, A. E. Mrs.	22412	Erath	Chapman, William P.	10061
Chapman, Adeline	38370	Van Zandt	Chapman, Arch Thomas	32372
Chapman, Al J.	Rej	Collin		
Chapman, Arch Thomas	32372	Van Zandt		
Chapman, Caroline C.	05472	Henderson	Chapman, Morgan	
Chapman, Celenda	08754	Llano	Chapman, James	00141
Chapman, Daniel	23081	Ellis		
Chapman, Dora	35040	Tyler	Chapman, William Payne	
Chapman, E. C. Mrs.	41688	Waller	Chapman, William Gardiner	
Chapman, Edward Algenown	41168	Navarro		
Chapman, Erasmus S.	26503	Mills		
Chapman, F. M.	28558	Hunt		
Chapman, F. T.	Rej	Uvalde		
Chapman, Frank J.	16807	Upshur		
Chapman, Frank T.	39236	Val Verde		
Chapman, G. W.	20427	Hood		
Chapman, George Washington	10303	Kaufman		
Chapman, Gillford Ratliff	10147	Menard		
Chapman, Gillford Ratliff Mrs.	41261	Menard	Chapman, Gillford Ratliff	10147
Chapman, H. E.	26771	Runnels		
Chapman, H. R. Mrs.	18794	Hopkins	Chapman, Willis Wilshire	17854
Chapman, H. S. Mrs.	Rej	Harris	Chapman, Enoch Ordillo	
Chapman, Henry M.	01380	Falls		
Chapman, Husie T.	Rej	Colorado	Chapman, David Madison	
Chapman, Isaac S.	07770	Burnet		
Chapman, J. M. Mrs.	15008	Dallas	Chapman, James Marion	05782
Chapman, J. N.	14173	Collin		
Chapman, James	00141	Bandera		

Index to Confederate Pension Applications

Chapman, James C.	14404	Shelby	—	
Chapman, James Calvin	47165	Collin	—	
Chapman, James Marion	05782	Dallas	—	
Chapman, Jane J.	31611	Cherokee	Chapman, Jasper Newton	
Chapman, Lavina Ann	Rej	Williamson	Chapman, William	
Chapman, Lorenzo Dow Mrs.	40621	Johnson	Chapman, Lorenzo Dow	
Chapman, M. A. Mrs.	17980	Kaufman	Chapman, George Washington	10303
Chapman, M. A. Mrs.	37399	Hays	Chapman, William Thomas	
Chapman, Maggie Griffith	47897	Denton	Chapman, James S.	
Chapman, Malinda	12911	Hopkins	Chapman, E. R.	
Chapman, Martha J.	47073	Williamson	Chapman, Thomas Allen	
Chapman, Mary E.	13494	Robertson	Chapman, William C.	07979
Chapman, Mary Jane	06622	Jones	Chapman, Jacob Hudson	
Chapman, Mary Jane	27119	Cass	Chapman, Samuel Newton	
Chapman, Mollie D.	49086	Collin	Chapman, James Calvin	47165
Chapman, N. E. Mrs.	26962	Upshur	Chapman, John Wesley	
Chapman, Nancy M.	02116	Hunt	Chapman, T. A.	
Chapman, R. C.	33210	Ellis	—	
Chapman, Robert D.	14192	Dallas	—	
Chapman, Rosanna A.	19757	Menard	Chapman, Benjamin Laurence	
Chapman, Sallie B.	Rej	Kaufman	Chapman, William Benjamin	
Chapman, Sam H.	31059	Tarrant	—	
Chapman, Sara	43740	Ellis	Chapman, Edward Algenown	41168
Chapman, Solomon D. Mrs.	30881	Lee	Chapman, Solomon D.	
Chapman, T. J.	23538	Smith	—	
Chapman, Thomas Benton Mrs.	47225	Collin	Chapman, Thomas Benton	
Chapman, W. A.	23054	Fisher	—	
Chapman, W. M.	25908	Rusk	—	
Chapman, William C.	07979	Trinity	—	
Chapman, William G.	10687	Lavaca	—	
Chapman, William H.	11159	Van Zandt	—	
Chapman, William M.	25759	San Saba	—	
Chapman, William P.	10061	Erath	—	
Chapman, Willis Wilshire	17854	Hopkins	—	
Chappelear, Benjamin Franklin	14841	Cass	—	
Chappelear, C. A. Mrs.	17437	Cass	Chappelear, Benjamin Franklin	14841
Chappell, Carrie F.	25649	Wilson	Chappell, George Washington	
Chappell, J. D.	23398	Brown	—	
Chappell, Jane	04173	Van Zandt	Chappell, Mastin	
Chappell, M. E. Johnson Mrs.	Rej	Harris	Johnson, Henry Clay	
Chappell, R. M.	25289	Anderson	—	
Chappell, W. J.	15208	Freestone	—	
Charles, Joel (Joseph) Barksdale	16174	Navarro	—	
Charles, Mattie	Rej	Dallas	Charles, Joseph (joel) Barksdale	16174
Charo, Refugio	14041	Webb	—	
Charpiot, J. C. J.	19773	Jefferson	—	
Charske, M.	39159	Dallas	—	
Charters, Carrie Amanda	38235	Brown	Charters, Samuel	
Charters, Robert Edward	51410	Brown	—	
Charwane, Mary H.	43376	Harris	Charwane, William James	
Chase, Laura S.	27198	Denton	Chase, George Nelson	
Chase, Martha	50522	Bosque	Chase, William Riley	
Chastain, Ezriah Mrs.	20130	Stephens	Chastain, Raney Franklin	
Chastang, William Henry Mrs.	49623	Harris	Chastang, William Henry	
Chasteen, Jerusha Emma	30444	Milam	Chasteen, William Wiley	12064
Chasteen, William Wiley	12064	Milam	—	
Chasten, Joseph Milton	17950	Jefferson	—	
Chasten, Mary Elizabeth	41053	Jefferson	Chasten, Joseph Milton	17950
Chastian, Edward Harold	10386	Hardeman	—	

Index to Confederate Pension Applications

Chastian, O. J. Mrs.	35442	Throckmorton	Chastian, Edward Harold	10386
Chastine, Sallie A.	25143	Bowie	Chastine, Henry Smith	—
Chatham, A. S.	18153	Montgomery	—	—
Chatham, Emergene	18162	Montgomery	Chatham, Thomas Jefferson	—
Chatham, Fannie E.	47726	Brazos	Chatham, Roland Kinchen	—
Chatham, Jane S.	00262	Bell	Chatham, M. H.	—
Chatham, Martha Jane	Rej	Montgomery	Chatham, Andrew Singleton	—
Chatten, William Wade	23125	Dallas	—	—
Chatwell, Lucy	21686	Parker	Chatwell, Thomas Sanders	—
Chaucy, Mary M.	20680	Van Zandt	Chaucy, Thomas Washington	—
Chaudion, Annie	13149	Milam	Chaudion, W. L. (Chaudoin)	02957
Chaudoin, P. W.	30432	Atascosa	—	—
Chaudoin, W. L.	02957	Milam	—	—
Chaves, Mariano	04975	Bexar	—	—
Chavez, Bernardino	04316	Webb	—	—
Cheairs, A. J.	01754	Hamilton	—	—
Cheairs, J. J.	24084	Red River	—	—
Cheatham, James W.	01575	Gonzales	—	—
Cheatham, Lewis Robertson	03103	Navarro	—	—
Cheatham, Mary E.	12996	McLennan	Cheatham, Lewis Robertson	03103
Cheatwood, Samuel M.	12612	Shelby	—	—
Chebret, Salina	31800	Liberty	Chebret, Soustan	—
Cheek, C. S. Mrs.	Rej	Comanche	Cheek, Thomas Jackson	—
Cheek, J. W.	Rej	Foard	—	—
Cheek, Jane	45987	Dallas	Cheek, John C.	—
Cheek, John Burroughs	04524	Wood	—	—
Cheek, John W.	19910	Foard	—	—
Cheek, Julia Octavia Wicker	45679	Ellis	Cheek, John Eldridge	—
Cheek, Martha	17041	Wood	Cheek, John Burroughs	04524
Cheek, R. M.	21015	Parker	—	—
Cheesman, C. F.	19055	Jefferson	—	—
Cheesman, Mary E.	38637	Harris	Cheesman, Robert George	—
Chenault, J. B.	14079	Kimble	—	—
Chenault, James Monroe	22542	Ellis	—	—
Chenault, Julia	12935	Jefferson	Chenault, Alanson T.	—
Chenault, Kate	35982	Dallas	Chenault, John	—
Chenault, M. E. Mrs.	Rej	Ellis	Chenault, James Monroe	22542
Chenault, Ruth Ann	Rej	Dallas	Chenault, William	—
Chenault, Sophie Ann	32205	Gonzales	Chenault, James Reed	—
Chenault, Stephen	14374	Potter	—	—
Cheney, W. C.	Rej	Comanche	—	—
Chennault, Thomas Henderson	25802	Lamar	—	—
Chenoweth, Joseph	05780	Dallas	—	—
Chenoweth, Rebecca Ann	36386	Dallas	Chenoweth, Joseph	05780
Chenoweth, T. J.	Rej	Grayson	—	—
Chenowith, Elizabeth	41802	Grayson	Chenowith, Thomas James	—
Chenowith, Hannah	07737	Wise	Chenowith, T. L.	—
Chenowith, Thomas L.	06847	Wise	—	—
Cherry, Cordelia	15338	Guadalupe	Cherry, Robert Pinckney	—
Cherry, Ella O.	40258	Tarrant	Cherry, Fielding Wilhoite	34734
Cherry, Emma	21687	Titus	Cherry, Hancell Lilly	—
Cherry, Fielding Wilhoite	34734	Tarrant	—	—
Cherry, George Buchanan Mrs.	38047	Red River	Cherry, George Buchanan	—
Cherry, Geory A.	16478	San Saba	Cherry, Robert Washington	02568
Cherry, J. E.	Rej	Milam	—	—
Cherry, James A.	37784	Erath	—	—
Cherry, James O.	05255	Lavaca	—	—
Cherry, Jesu W.	08447	Rains	—	—
Cherry, John Randolph	Rej	Hood	—	—

Index to Confederate Pension Applications

Name	App #	County	Related	Related #
Cherry, Joseph Franklin	06952	Limestone	—	—
Cherry, Mary R.	31594	Grayson	Cherry, David	—
Cherry, Mattie A.	36548	Harrison	Cherry, Henry Dixon	—
Cherry, Robert Washington	02568	Lee	—	—
Cherry, Sallie	Rej	Panola	Cherry, Joshua W.	—
Cheshire, G. P.	Rej	Nolan	—	—
Cheshire, G. P.	21688	Madison	—	—
Cheshire, H. Lee	27330	Cooke	—	—
Chesney, Leah Jane	25185	Fannin	Chesney, William Alexander	—
Chesnut, Sarah E.	39412	Delta	Chesnut, William Henry	21689
Chesnut, William Henry	21689	Delta	—	—
Chesnutt, Sarah	23056	Bee	Chesnutt, Isaac	—
Chesser, Christopher Columbus	10158	Mills	—	—
Chesser, Mendocia	12514	Mills	Chesser, Christopher Columbus	10158
Chesser, S. A. Mrs.	26653	Cass	Chesser, William Andrew Jackson	14838
Chesser, William Andrew Jackson	14838	Cass	—	—
Chessher, J. A.	18469	Trinity	—	—
Chessher, Melvina George	47397	Cherokee	George, David N.	—
Chester, B. Louisa	17868	Hopkins	Chester, John C.	—
Chester, J. C.	Rej	Hopkins	—	—
Chester, Martha M.	17870	Hopkins	Chester, William Gilbert	02001
Chester, Sidney J.	31060	Nacogdoches	—	—
Chester, W. Y.	23055	Johnson	—	—
Chester, William Gilbert	02001	Hopkins	—	—
Chevalier, Margarita C. De	40137	Webb	Chevalier, Archibald Stuart	—
Cheves, W. B.	49750	Young	—	—
Chew, Annie T.	32039	Fort Bend	Chew, Vernon T.	—
Chick, George Washington	33944	Comanche	—	—
Chick, Martha A.	38542	Erath	Chick, George Washington	33944
Chiddix, L. A. S.	18141	Montague	—	—
Chilcoat, Dorcas Mrs.	05241	Navarro	Chilcoat, W. P.	—
Chilcoat, G. E.	12470	Kaufman	—	—
Chilcoat, James Ephraim Mrs.	22123	Tarrant	Chilcoat, James Ephraim	—
Childers, Addie	22644	Hill	Childers, John Henry	—
Childers, Bettie	21690	Navarro	Childers, Joseph Terrell	—
Childers, Candace	03204	Orange	Childers, J. P.	—
Childers, J. P.	20470	Harris	—	—
Childers, James A.	23124	Rains	—	—
Childers, James Mrs.	47781	Ellis	Childers, James	—
Childers, Jennie Alabama	46734	Dallam	Childers, Absalom Fortenberry	—
Childers, John H.	08580	Hill	—	—
Childers, Mary Emily	31244	Rains	Childers, James Anderson	—
Childers, Nancy Susan	50836	Nueces	Childers, Wiley Thomas	—
Childers, William Fletcher	26386	Comanche	—	—
Childers, William Fletcher Mrs.	39903	Haskell	Childers, William Fletcher	26386
Childre, Fannie	38756	Harris	Childre, Oran Ivy	17726
Childre, Oran Ivy	17726	Grimes	—	—
Childress, A. J.	11821	Bosque	—	—
Childress, Abe	32201	Anderson	—	—
Childress, Delilah	01377	Falls	Childress, Thomas A. J.	—
Childress, F. M.	Rej	Red River	—	—
Childress, F. M.	49254	Red River	—	—
Childress, H. C.	03837	Taylor	—	—
Childress, J.	06625	Jones	—	—
Childress, James	Rej	Ellis	—	—
Childress, John Hale	02118	Hunt	—	—
Childress, John W.	19523	Travis	—	—
Childress, John W. Mrs.	39689	Travis	Childress, John W.	19523
Childress, Joseph	13586	Cass	—	—

Index to Confederate Pension Applications

Childress, Louis	50071	Limestone		
Childress, Louis Mrs.	51807	Limestone	Childress, Louis	50071
Childress, M. D. Mrs.	33183	Erath	Childress, William Preston	07581
Childress, M. J. W. Mrs.	26109	Rusk	Childress, Guilford Bush	
Childress, Mary	16536	Shelby	Childress, William Russell	
Childress, Mary F.	50755	Atascosa	Childress, Samuel Hardy Nelms	
Childress, Minerva	03107	Navarro	Childress, J. W.	
Childress, Nellie Kennard	51635	Bexar	Childress, Thomas Beverly	50866
Childress, Peyton Franklin Mrs.	Rej	Clay	Childress, Peyton Franklin	
Childress, R. G.	06170	Nolan		
Childress, Rufus E.	29290	Tarrant		
Childress, Rufus E. Mrs.	41654	Wichita	Childress, Rufus E.	29290
Childress, S. E. Mrs.	20472	Hunt	Childress, John Hale	02118
Childress, Samuel	10895	Dallas		
Childress, Thomas Beverly	50866	Bexar		
Childress, William Preston	07581	Erath		
Childry, June	01913	Hill	Childry, James	
Childs, C. S. Mrs.	27624	Cass	Childs, James Clark	
Childs, Edward Washington	04715	Freestone		
Childs, H. C. Mrs.	18721	Freestone	Childs, Henry Joyce	
Childs, James Lafayette	51882	Freestone		
Childs, James Matthew	28396	McLennan		
Childs, Sarah	50606	Lamar	Childs, John L.	
Childs, Susan	29240	Coryell	Childs, William Thomas	
Chiles, John L.	19462	Travis		
Chiles, Maggie	Rej	Bowie	Chiles, Archibald Henry	
Chipman, Joseph A.	42351	Taylor		
Chipman, Thomas J.	15905	Leon		
Chisholm, John A.	18143	Montague		
Chisholm, M. E. Mrs.	34718	Montague	Chisholm, John A.	18143
Chism, Fannie	30448	Uvalde	Chism, Daniel Washington	
Chism, Lydia C.	47616	Burnet	Chism, Alexander Valentine	
Chism, Mary A.	03613	Shackelford	Chism, Jacob	
Chism, Sarah E. Quirl	49386	Brown	Quirl, Joseph	
Chism, W. E.	07365	Shelby		
Chisum, A. J.	18179	Nacogdoches		
Chisum, J. M.	40649	Grayson		
Chisum, James A.	45995	Runnels		
Chivers, J. M.	19054	Jackson		
Choat, H. N. Mrs.	17644	Fannin	Choat, John C.	06722
Choat, Jasper	09274	Llano		
Choat, John C.	06722	Fannin		
Choat, Julia	46145	Erath	Choat, James Allen	
Choat, S. C.	18348	Shelby		
Choate, Amanda	07687	Travis	Choate, Pryor	
Choate, Christopher C.	13811	Franklin		
Choate, D. B.	05383	Hill		
Choate, David McKenzie	19783	Shelby		
Choate, Elizabeth	22794	Shelby	Choate, David McKenzie	19783
Choate, Frank G.	13284	Delta		
Choate, J. M.	13913	Karnes		
Choate, Nicholas H.	02819	McLennan		
Choate, Olley	19439	Tarrant		
Choate, Richard	14186	Coryell		
Choate, Zelda	14474	Wharton	Choate, J. M.	
Choates, Mary J.	Rej	Kaufman	Choates, James Rufus	
Chowning, A. J.	17580	Denton		
Chowning, Malinda C.	25270	Denton	Chowning, Uriah Johnson	
Chrane, Sarah F.	09420	Taylor	Chrane, William E.	

Index to Confederate Pension Applications

Name	App. No.	County	Veteran	Vet. App. No.
Chreitzberg, Mary M.	29137	Wood	Chreitzberg, Elzy Franklin	—
Chrestman, Francis Lavisa	Rej	Terry	Chrestman, Thomas Jarrot	—
Chrestman, J. M.	17297	Archer	—	—
Chrestman, L. M.	37709	Van Zandt	—	—
Chriesman, O. W. Mrs.	09158	Burleson	Chriesman, O. W.	—
Chrietzberg, Belle P.	29351	Williamson	Chrietzberg, Bond English	—
Chrisman, Albert Sanford	15695	Hill	—	—
Chrisman, Albert Sanford Mrs.	39549	Johnson	Chrisman, Albert Sanford	15695
Chrisman, Henry Clay	29160	Hill	—	—
Chrisman, Henry Clay Mrs.	39551	Johnson	Chrisman, Henry Clay	29160
Chrisman, James Riley	13827	Gregg	—	—
Chrisman, John Henry	10528	Bell	—	—
Chrisman, Julia T.	42859	Johnson	Chrisman, Thomas J.	—
Chrisman, M. L. Mrs.	Rej	Dallas	Chrisman, Wallace Alexander	—
Chrisman, Mary P.	34901	Gregg	Chrisman, James Riley	13827
Chrisman, Wallace A.	03773	Tarrant	—	—
Christal, Sallie	51159	Dallas	Christal, Rolland	—
Christian, Adam	Rej	Morris	—	—
Christian, Ann E.	38981	Milam	Christian, Charles Samuel	23065
Christian, Charles Samuel	23065	Milam	—	—
Christian, Elizabeth Victoria	46969	Gonzales	Christian, Obie Mast	—
Christian, Frederick Abdy (Abeda)	28395	McLennan	—	—
Christian, Frederick Abeda Mrs.	31491	McLennan	Christian, Frederick Abeda (Abdy)	28395
Christian, George W.	17532	Cottle	—	—
Christian, Gid	08179	Taylor	—	—
Christian, Harriett	41986	San Saba	Christian, James Thomas	40135
Christian, J. C.	31529	Dallas	—	—
Christian, J. R.	29088	Upshur	—	—
Christian, James H.	13510	Smith	—	—
Christian, James Thomas	40135	San Saba	—	—
Christian, Jennie H.	42264	Parker	Christian, Lewis	—
Christian, John	46763	Collin	—	—
Christian, John E.	16123	Nacogdoches	—	—
Christian, John E. Mrs.	38091	Nacogdoches	Christian, John E.	16123
Christian, John Samuel	26938	Tarrant	—	—
Christian, L. H. Mrs.	11120	Shelby	Christian, Stephen Chappel	—
Christian, M. M. Mrs.	13308	Franklin	Christian, E. Louis	—
Christian, Mary J.	Rej	Montgomery	Christian, James K.	—
Christian, Nancy E.	13934	Leon	Christian, Constantine C.	—
Christian, Nathan Jeptha	35180	Gonzales	—	—
Christian, P. W.	18342	Shelby	—	—
Christian, Peruvia	Rej	Hunt	Christian, James D.	—
Christian, R. T.	Rej	Newton	—	—
Christian, R. T.	Rej	Jasper	—	—
Christian, Sarah Ann	48008	Hill	Christian, James Cumberland	—
Christian, Sarah Elizabeth	38983	Gonzales	Christian, Nathan Jeptha	35180
Christian, Susan	42931	Tarrant	Christian, John Samuel	26938
Christian, T. H. P.	16365	Rusk	—	—
Christian, W. A.	Rej	Milam	—	—
Christian, W. L.	06899	Dallas	—	—
Christie, B. A.	50938	San Saba	—	—
Christie, Dora	26402	Galveston	Christie, George A.	—
Christie, Ellen	22765	Angelina	Christie, John C.	—
Christie, J. W.	25290	Navarro	—	—
Christmas, Benjamin S.	18333	San Saba	—	—
Christmas, E. J.	06095	Travis	—	—
Christmas, J. K.	18152	Montgomery	—	—
Christmas, W. S.	29401	Eastland	—	—
Christoff, Joseph F.	18513	Waller	—	—

Index to Confederate Pension Applications

Name	App #	County	Veteran	Vet #
Christopher, A. C.	09364	Waller		
Christopher, E. A. Mrs.	16158	Nacogdoches	Christopher, John Daniel	
Christopher, Ella Cargill	36436	Harris	Christopher, George	
Christopher, Joseph H.	25632	Taylor		
Christopher, Mary Lou	31234	Freestone	Christopher, James Dubose	
Christopher, W. L.	Rej	Nacogdoches		
Christy, John	Rej	Angelina		
Chrosby, Jesse	23284	Tyler		
Chumley, Aria	40212	San Augustine	Chumley, Thomas Monroe	16457
Chumley, John I.	00778	Cherokee		
Chumley, Thomas Monroe	16457	San Augustine		
Chumney, Sarah Virginia	51058	Hamilton	Chumney, George Washington	
Church, Mary E.	13781	Eastland	Church, B. F.	
Church, Mastin	04483	Wise		
Church, Nancy A.	14499	Wise	Church, Mastin	
Church, Serene H.	Rej	Comal	Church, Caleb I.	
Churchill, Delfenia M.	43735	Live Oak	Churchill, William W.	30797
Churchill, William W.	30797	Zavala		
Churchman, James P.	14317	Llano		
Churchman, John R.	23551	Johnson		
Churchman, Sallie A.	27801	Johnson	Churchman, John R.	23551
Churchwell, George W.	06422	Parker		
Churchwell, John M.	Rej	San Saba		
Ciprian, Cecilio	Rej	Webb		
Ciprian, R. S. De Mrs.	06255	Webb	Ciprian, Pablo	
Cissell, Vincent	Rej	Taylor		
Clabaugh, John Anion	18104	McLennan		
Clabaugh, Sophia D.	37013	McLennan	Clabaugh, John Anion	18104
Clack, M. R.	Rej	Rockwall		
Clack, Sallie	Rej	Wheeler	Clack, James Thomas	
Claiborne, Ella Holbrook	46743	Dallas	Claiborne, John Marshall	
Claiborne, Ethel	Rej	Grayson	Claiborne, John Harrison	15855
Claiborne, Holbert T.	Rej	Bastrop		
Claiborne, John Harrison	15855	Lamar		
Clamon, Emily	32299	Henderson	Clamon, John	
Clamp, William Jacob	18303	Rusk		
Clamp, William Jacob Mrs.	27307	Rusk	Clamp, William Jacob	18303
Clampitt, Elisha Galveston	12709	Titus		
Clampitt, George Washington Mrs.	41577	Wharton	Clampitt, George Washington	
Clampitt, Nancy J.	20313	Upshur	Clampitt, Elisha Galveston	12709
Clampitt, R. D. Mrs.	45857	Smith	Clampitt, Sterling Nehemiah	40375
Clampitt, Sterling Nehemiah	40375	Smith		
Clanahan, Martha Ann	19641	Dallas	Clanahan, James	
Clanahan, Mollie Elizabeth	36155	Henderson	Clanahan, William Ross	15687
Clanahan, William Ross	15687	Henderson		
Clancy, Alfred J.	12547	Limestone		
Clancy, Pinkney D.	29512	Smith		
Clanton, E. J. Gilreath	36004	Williamson	Gilreath, Nathan David	
Clanton, George Washington	27877	Baylor		
Clanton, J. G.	33713	Aransas		
Clanton, Mollie	35353	Wood	Clanton, Wyley Richard	20335
Clanton, N. C. Mrs.	42595	Haskell	Clanton, George Washington	27877
Clanton, Wyley Richard	20335	Wood		
Clapp, Carrie V.	16958	Wharton	Clapp, Alfred Henderson	
Clapp, E. D.	10352	Colorado		
Clapp, John F.	26534	Robertson		
Clapp, Peter L.	Rej	Waller		
Clapp, Sarah Ann	34096	Colorado	Clapp, Eli Dawson	
Clapp, Suffield	04372	Wharton		

Index to Confederate Pension Applications

Name	No.	County	Veteran	No.
Clapp, Suffield Mrs.	42321	Wharton	Clapp, Suffield	04372
Clapp, William	43250	Hood		
Clardy, A. D.	40422	Van Zandt		
Clardy, I. A. Mrs.	19263	Shelby	Clardy, James Harvey	
Clardy, Jesse Washington	34616	Wise		
Clardy, Mary R.	40516	Mills	Clardy, William Franklin	22930
Clardy, William Franklin	22930	Mills		
Clare, Martha	15891	Lee	Clare, James Daniels	
Clarie, E. F. Mrs.	RejM	Harris		
Clark, A. E. Mrs.	06767	Nacogdoches	Clark, M. V.	
Clark, A. J.	Rej	Dallas		
Clark, A. J. Mrs.	15190	Freestone	Clark, Stephen F. Austin	
Clark, Adolphus J.	37654	Dallas		
Clark, Amanda	38691	San Patricio	Clark, Newton Jasper	32300
Clark, Annie	50972	Navarro	Clark, William Thomas	
Clark, Annie M.	Rej	Limestone		
Clark, Antonette Elizabeth	Rej	Caldwell	Clark, John	
Clark, B. B.	Rej	Taylor		
Clark, B. C. Mrs.	07233	Harris	Clark, B. C.	
Clark, B. M. C.	00288	Bell		
Clark, Bettie	37628	Van Zandt	Clark, George Washington	10123
Clark, Birdie	52030	Gonzales	Clark, William Luke	
Clark, Burgess	11496	Hunt		
Clark, Caroline Isabel	49766	Jefferson	Clark, William Martin	
Clark, Charity A.	39982	Armstrong	Clark, Silas Jefferson	
Clark, Charles D.	51267	Travis		
Clark, Charles H.	43321	Limestone		
Clark, Daniel James Edwin	23421	Young		
Clark, Dutton M.	14282	Hopkins		
Clark, E. B.	19537	Red River	Clark, James Madison	
Clark, E. F. Mrs.	30882	Gonzales	Clark, John Allen	
Clark, E. F. Mrs.	46134	Harris	Clark, Edmund	
Clark, E. H.	Rej	Bowie		
Clark, Edward Levi	13850	Henderson		
Clark, Elenor C.	20261	San Jacinto	Clark, Charles Canty	
Clark, Elizabeth	09330	Sabine	Clark, Paschal	03552
Clark, Elizabeth	47007	Calhoun	Clark, Thomas	
Clark, Elizabeth Jane	Rej	Newton	Clark, Oliver Comistock	
Clark, Ellen Mandie	50766	Van Zandt	Clark, Joseph	37525
Clark, Emily Silicy	21103	Wichita	Clark, Michael J.	14241
Clark, F. N.	Rej	Dallas		
Clark, Fannie	35666	Burnet	Clark, William Taylor	18856
Clark, Fannie Lee	51808	Dallas	Clark, Adolphus J.	37654
Clark, G. K.	27902	Nacogdoches		
Clark, G. W.	Rej	Dallas		
Clark, George B.	41822	Hunt		
Clark, George Edward	16793	Upshur		
Clark, George Lafayette	20633	Tarrant		
Clark, George Washington	10123	Kaufman		
Clark, Georgia	32495	Trinity	Clark, William Wallace	08425M
Clark, H. T.	50410	Glasscock		
Clark, H. V. Mrs.	34902	Rusk	Clark, Wade H.	26199
Clark, Harriet Caroline	06942	Limestone	Clark, John McCoy	
Clark, Hattie	01006	Coryell	Clark, E. W.	
Clark, Isaac Wesley Mrs.	49485	Grayson	Clark, Isaac Wesley	
Clark, J. A.	11649	Tarrant		
Clark, J. A.	41589	Hunt		
Clark, J. C.	25486	Kaufman		
Clark, J. G.	21691	Erath		

Index to Confederate Pension Applications

Name	No.	County	Veteran	No.
Clark, J. H.	21132	Lubbock		
Clark, J. H.	36150	Lampasas		
Clark, J. K.	RejM	Williamson		
Clark, J. L.	Rej	Cooke		
Clark, J. O. A.	41383	Erath		
Clark, J. P.	03106	Navarro		
Clark, J. R.	20697	Williamson		
Clark, J. T.	15096	Erath		
Clark, James A.	09661	Scurry		
Clark, James H.	Rej	Lubbock		
Clark, James Jackson	12402	Harrison		
Clark, James W.	13372	Hunt		
Clark, Jamima S.	40214	Bell	Collier, Willis B.	09912
Clark, Jerry	Rej	Bowie		
Clark, Jim H.	20746	Harrison		
Clark, John	03686	Smith		
Clark, John	32316	Tarrant		
Clark, John A.	10381	Grayson		
Clark, John Ann Mrs.	23071	Ellis	Clark, Thomas David	
Clark, John D.	11065	Navarro		
Clark, John D.	22896	Hamilton		
Clark, John Lewis	27407	Fisher		
Clark, John Matthew	41337	Brown		
Clark, John Mrs.	17552	Dallas	Clark, John	03686
Clark, John Stewart	25044	Runnels		
Clark, John William	19086	Leon		
Clark, Joseph	37525	Van Zandt		
Clark, Joseph John	06920	Rusk		
Clark, Joseph Wright Mrs.	51345	Grayson	Clark, Joseph Wright	
Clark, L. F. Mrs.	09400	Rusk	Clark, Joseph John	06920
Clark, L. J. Mrs.	34589	Bexar	Clark, Charles	
Clark, Laura	28618	Hopkins	Clark, William Wesley	
Clark, Laura Ann	20089	Upshur	Clark, George Edward	16793
Clark, Laura Josephine	29211	El Paso	Clark, William Breckenridge	
Clark, Lavina R.	49339	Jones	Clark, Oliver Harrison	
Clark, Lester	04294	Washington		
Clark, Lewis	12750	Brown		
Clark, Lizzie M.	52084	Collin	Clark, Richard C.	45043
Clark, Lou English	50967	Travis	Clark, Pat Benjamin	
Clark, M. C. Mrs.	15532	Hopkins	Clark, James Perry	
Clark, M. E. Mrs.	07653	Parker	Clark, Jeptha	
Clark, M. J. Mrs.	29753	Sabine	Clark, Elias	
Clark, M. L.	04592A	Brown		
Clark, M. O. Mrs.	17148	Rockwall	Clark, Micajah Rogers	
Clark, Margaret J.	51572	Montgomery	Clark, William C.	
Clark, Marjorie Victoria	51663	Harris	Clark, Isaac Benton	
Clark, Marrie E.	17794	Haskell	Clark, Thomas B.	
Clark, Martha Ann	Rej	Hill	Clark, David Garrison	
Clark, Martha Manning	51710	Harris	Clark, John James	
Clark, Martha P.	26929	Smith	Clark, Hiram Ballard	
Clark, Martin Van Buren	09885	Houston		
Clark, Mary	28798	Travis	Clark, Lewis	12750
Clark, Mary Ann	11299	Bell	Clark, B. M. C.	00288
Clark, Mary B.	50705	Bexar	Clark, James	
Clark, Mary Catherine	42585	Harris	Clark, John Wesley	
Clark, Mary E.	28433	Shelby	Clark, William Henry	11637
Clark, Mary Ellen	36739	Delta	Clark, William Jasper	32542
Clark, Mary F.	Rej	Tarrant	Clark, Ephriam Elisha	
Clark, Mary J.	36490	Tarrant	Clark, George L.	20633

Index to Confederate Pension Applications

Clark, Mary Jane	47996	Williamson	Clark, John Alexander White	—
Clark, Mary Jane Letney	13869	Hunt	Clark, Burgess	11496
Clark, Mary L.	40746	Hall	Clark, Daniel James Edwin	23421
Clark, Mary Lou	45421	Palo Pinto	Clark, Edward Levi	13850
Clark, Mary Susan	33692	Brooks	Clark, John Dastin	—
Clark, Mattie Orr	47718	Milam	Clark, James Asbury	—
Clark, Michael J.	14241	Grayson	—	—
Clark, Minerva J.	40459	Mitchell	Clark, John J.	—
Clark, Mollie	39136	Robertson	Clark, John William	19086
Clark, Myra Elizabeth	46394	Navarro	Crow, Beverly	—
Clark, N. E. Mrs.	23060	Parker	Clark, Kneely Paschal	—
Clark, N. J. Mrs.	35161	Hopkins	Clark, Thomas Law	—
Clark, Nancy H.	23516	Fannin	Clark, Morris Burn	—
Clark, Newton Jasper	32300	Bexar	—	—
Clark, P. C.	Rej	Houston	—	—
Clark, Paschal	03552	Sabine	—	—
Clark, Phronie	46009	Camp	Clark, James	—
Clark, Randolph	43998	Erath	—	—
Clark, Rebecca Elizabeth	37776	Wilson	Clark, William Charles	21692
Clark, Richard C.	45043	Collin	—	—
Clark, Richard J., Sr.	50197	Lavaca	—	—
Clark, Robert Harrison	29339	Jasper	—	—
Clark, Robert Harrison Mrs.	45087	Angelina	Clark, Robert Harrison	29339
Clark, Rosa H.	08031	Hill	Clark, Franklin P.	—
Clark, S. A. Mrs.	19440	Denton	Clark, Lemuel Newton	—
Clark, S. C. Mrs.	15069	Ellis	Clark, Horatio Perry	—
Clark, Sallie	42029	Eastland	Clark, Lewis Marion	—
Clark, Sarah	33747	Brown	Clark, John Stewart	25044
Clark, Sarah E.	37583	Caldwell	Clark, Hugh Ervin	—
Clark, Sarah E.	45390	Trinity	Clark, Martin Van Buren	09885
Clark, Sarah Elizabeth	51335	Haskell	Clark, Robert A.	—
Clark, Sarah J.	26200	Bowie	Clark, William	—
Clark, Sarah Jane	28797	Harrison	Clark, James Jackson	12402
Clark, Sela Ann	Rej	Delta	Clark, Wellington	—
Clark, Susan Ann	Rej	Houston	Clark, John Anderson	—
Clark, T. C. Mrs.	21261	Cass	Clark, William Thomas	18856
Clark, T. F.	46055	Caldwell	—	—
Clark, Tabitha	38915	Tom Green	Clark, William Asa	32870
Clark, Thomas	02525	Lavaca	—	—
Clark, Thomas J.	25885	Bell	—	—
Clark, Virgil A.	07553	Angelina	—	—
Clark, Virginia L. Moore	51930	Hill	Clark, James Rabb	—
Clark, W. A. Mrs.	Rej	Tom Green	Clark, W. A.	—
Clark, W. D.	03775	Tarrant	—	—
Clark, W. F. Mrs.	47669	Fannin	Clark, William Fletcher	20030
Clark, W. J.	08785	San Jacinto	—	—
Clark, W. M.	39499	Comanche	—	—
Clark, Wade H.	26199	Rusk	—	—
Clark, William Asa	32870	Coleman	—	—
Clark, William Boland	15191	Freestone	—	—
Clark, William Boland Mrs.	41137	Freestone	Clark, William Boland	15191
Clark, William Charles	21692	Gonzales	—	—
Clark, William Fletcher	20030	Dallas	—	—
Clark, William Hainey Mrs.	17553	Dallas	Clark, William Hainey	—
Clark, William Henry	11637	Shelby	—	—
Clark, William Jasper	32542	Delta	—	—
Clark, William M.	42414	Hockley	—	—
Clark, William M. Mrs.	16622	Smith	Clark, William M.	—
Clark, William R.	29426	Bastrop	—	—

Index to Confederate Pension Applications

Name	No.	County	Veteran	No.
Clark, William T. Mrs.	Rej	Navarro	Clark, William T.	
Clark, William Thomas	00704	Cass		
Clark, William Thomas	18856	Burnet		
Clark, William Wallace	08425M	Navarro		
Clarke, I. V.	Rej	Harrison		
Clarke, Pickens Rutledge	25510	Montgomery		
Clarke, Sarah Lou	40114	Montgomery	Clarke, Pickens Rutledge	25510
Clarke, W. J.	00525	Brazos		
Clary, Benjamin Franklin	31755	Collin		
Clary, E. B.	11899	Erath		
Clary, E. J. Mrs.	08548M	Erath		
Clary, Edwin P.	03903	Travis		
Clary, M. E. Mrs.	19679	Travis	Clary, Edwin P.	03903
Clary, Maggie J. Mrs.	38412	Collin	Clary, Benjamin Franklin	31755
Clary, S. R.	16207	Henderson		
Clary, Susan J.	16037	Milam	Clary, John Postow	
Clary, W. T. Mrs.	51503	Wise	Clary, Thomas Chester	
Claterbaugh, W. E.	08297	Fannin		
Claud, M. E. Mrs.	15758	Jasper	Claud, James Washington	
Claude, Emil	10684	Lavaca		
Claunch, E. E. Mrs.	35269	Kaufman	Claunch, Thomas Jefferson	14466
Claunch, J. P.	47043	Ellis		
Claunch, Sarah A.	33783	Dallas	Claunch, William Truehart	
Claunch, Thomas Jefferson	14466	Van Zandt		
Clausel, T. N.	08361M	Hopkins		
Clausell, N. E. Mrs.	22785	Hopkins	Clausell, Thomas N.	
Clave, Ann Eliza	02526	Lavaca	Clave, Thomas B.	
Clawson, Jacob Brown	13001	Milam		
Clawson, Mary Jane	31623	Falls	Clawson, William Martin	23126
Clawson, William Martin	23126	Falls		
Clay, Alice	20215	Smith	Clay, William	
Clay, Alice Mary	34525	Taylor	Clay, Robert Phelix	
Clay, Charles B. D.	11125	Shelby		
Clay, Cyntha	47769	Limestone	Clay, James Tolbert	
Clay, E. B.	06509	Kaufman		
Clay, Elizabeth	51824	Grayson	Clay, John Harrison	50674
Clay, Esse Jane	20653	McLennan	Clay, William Coon	
Clay, Francis Marion	06300	Bell		
Clay, Francis Marion Mrs.	16704	Tom Green	Clay, Francis Marion	06300
Clay, Godfrey B.	06611	Falls		
Clay, J. C.	26615	Titus		
Clay, J. F.	08636	Calhoun		
Clay, Jane	Rej	Wheeler	Clay, E. B.	
Clay, John Harrison	50674	Hunt		
Clay, Kate P.	51123	Washington	Clay, Atreus McClery	
Clay, L. E. Mrs.	49972	Wilbarger	Clay, James Monroe	
Clay, Lizzie	43842	Jefferson	Clay, Henry Calvin	
Clay, Margaret	28835	Somervell		
Clay, Mary	50521	Dallas	Parr, Thomas	05437
Clay, Mary Vernell	51587	Scurry	Clay, Thomas Jefferson	11377
Clay, Melissa	40699	Shelby	Clay, Charles B. D.	11125
Clay, R. N.	23400	Hill		
Clay, Sarah Franice	46654	Jack	Clay, William	
Clay, Thomas Jefferson	11377	Cherokee		
Clayton, A. A. Mrs.	08452	Rusk		
Clayton, G. A. Mrs.	29056	Cass	Clayton, Thomas Jefferson	
Clayton, John (Jessie) Franklin	02117	Hunt		
Clayton, John H.	Rej	Gonzales		
Clayton, Kittie	36690	Hunt	Clayton, Jessie (John) Franklin	02117

Index to Confederate Pension Applications

Name	App #	County	Veteran	Vet #
Clayton, Laura E.	00197	Bastrop	Clayton, Henry Webster	
Clayton, Mary A.	06856	Wise	Clayton, Norman B.	
Clayton, Mary Ann	00029	Angelina	Clayton, William A.	
Clayton, Nettie	17790	Harrison	Clayton, William Riley	
Clayton, P. L.	07678	Wilson		
Clayton, Rebecca	26824	Hopkins	Clayton, William Benton	19981
Clayton, Rosa	Rej	Hardin	Clayton, Josephus	
Clayton, William Benton	19981	Hopkins		
Claytor, Nancy Amanda	51101	Denton	Claytor, William Arthur	
Cleaves, Mary J.	40514	Parker	Cleaves, Alonzo Baron	
Cleere, A. M.	02297	Johnson		
Cleere, Frances Caroline	31276	Freestone	Cleere, Cornelius E.	
Cleere, M. E. Mrs.	17676	Freestone	Cleere, George Robert	
Clegg, J. H.	33882	San Augustine		
Clegg, S. A. E. Mrs.	Rej	Trinity	Clegg, William Owen	
Cleghorn, J. B.	08210	Atascosa		
Cleland, Bluford T.	23084	Titus		
Clem, Charlotte	47431	Dallas	Clem, John	
Clement, Francis (Frank)	25066	Milam		
Clement, Joseph, Sr.	31578	Brazoria		
Clement, Louisa G.	40493	Calhoun	Clement, Thomas Houlton	
Clements, A. N.	04947	Bexar		
Clements, Adam Quincy	17318	Bell		
Clements, E. L. Mrs.	28652	Ellis	Clements, William Allen	
Clements, Ella	51017	Parker	Clements, Maning Thomas	
Clements, Fannie	07834	Bexar	Clements, Alexander N.	
Clements, Irvin Walter	02958	Milam		
Clements, J. R.	07172	Coke		
Clements, Jesse	Rej	Cass		
Clements, Jesse Mrs.	42773	Cass	Clements, Jesse	
Clements, John W.	33380	Taylor		
Clements, M. A. Mrs.	16644	Tarrant	Clements, Manning	
Clements, M. E. Mrs.	28438	Erath	Clements, Irvin Walter	02958
Clements, Mary Ellen	11851	Coke	Clements, J. R.	07172
Clements, Mildred Amanda	Rej	Smith	Clements, Jephthah S.	
Clements, Nancy A.	29077	Callahan	Clements, James C.	
Clements, S. J. Mrs.	Rej	Burleson	Clements, A. E.	
Clements, Sarah H.	35974	Kerr	Clements, Adam Quincy	17318
Clements, T. M.	01264	Ellis		
Clements, W. D.	24905	Van Zandt		
Clementson, Iona Coffin	52076	San Patricio	Clementson, William	
Clemmer, Leander Roberts	42570	Callahan		
Clemmer, Leander Roberts Mrs.	45911	Callahan	Clemmer, Leander Roberts	42570
Clemmer, Mary Ann	23051	Hamilton	Clemmer, William Henry	
Clemmons, Benjamin T.	24192	Bowie		
Clemons, Alice	Rej	Taylor	Clemons, David Godfrey	
Clemons, Lucy Jane	49031	Navarro	Clemons, James	
Clendening, Elizabeth C.	22120	McLennan	Clendening, Wm. Thomas Benton	
Clendening, T. B.	25147	Parker		
Clendennen, J.M.	00001	Anderson		
Clendennen, James E.	14072	Haskell		
Clepper, Joseph C.	11188	Burleson		
Clepper, Penelope	18764	Burleson	Clepper, Joseph C.	11188
Clepper, Sarah Ann	Rej	Waller	Clepper, Lorenzo D.	
Cleveland, C. H.	11807	Bexar		
Cleveland, C. L.	20164	Johnson		
Cleveland, D. L.	16464	San Jacinto		
Cleveland, David D.	23287	Hays		
Cleveland, F. J.	15456	Henderson		

Index to Confederate Pension Applications

Name	App. No.	County	Veteran	Vet. App. No.
Cleveland, J. W.	15268	Gonzales	—	
Cleveland, L. J. Mrs.	41742	McLennan	Cleveland, Eli John	
Cleveland, Leander	07058	Galveston	—	
Cleveland, Lucile Neal	12721	Anderson	Cleveland, William	
Cleveland, Sarah P.	14600	Archer	Cleveland, John Franklin	
Cleveland, Wiley B.	24107	Clay	—	
Cleveland, William M.	39182	Bosque	—	
Clevenger, Margaret M.	Rej	Angelina	Clevenger, William	
Clevenger, Margarett M.	20102	Angelina	Clevenger, William	
Clevenger, Mary Jane	37210	Franklin	Clevenger, William Joseph	
Clevenger, Sam	05773	Dallas	—	
Clevenger, William H.	13864	Hunt	—	
Clewis, J. C.	01577	Gonzales	—	
Clews, Mary	08314	Gonzales	Clews, J. A.	
Cliburn, Thomas C.	16761	Tyler	—	
Click, H.	29929	Hopkins	—	
Click, Henry Tolliver	14878	Cherokee	—	
Click, J. M.	04694	Bandera	—	
Click, John	Rej	Johnson	—	
Click, John	49112	Johnson	—	
Click, Joseph H.	07956	Sabine	—	
Click, Lucy A.	01106	Delta	Click, Eldridge E.	
Click, M. L. Mrs.	34015	Shackelford	Click, Henry Tolliver	14878
Click, Rufus	Rej	Medina	—	
Click, W. E.	00739	Cherokee	—	
Cliett, James Roberto	18517	Waller	—	
Cliett, Joseph M.	18518	Waller	—	
Cliett, Margaret C.	37662	Waller	Cliett, James Roberto	18517
Clift, Lenora A.	34212	Dallas	Clift, Stephen Alexander	
Clifton, Annie	16982	Wise	Clifton, Merit	14049
Clifton, D. M.	15530	Hopkins	—	
Clifton, Eliza A.	47274	Tarrant	Clifton, James Martin	11144
Clifton, Eliza Ann	21181	Hopkins	Clifton, James Daniel Cornelius	15529
Clifton, F. L.	12431	Hopkins	—	
Clifton, James Daniel Cornelius	15529	Hopkins	—	
Clifton, James Martin	11144	Tarrant	—	
Clifton, Jane	21360	Hopkins	Clifton, John David Cornelius	15529
Clifton, M. A. Johnson Mrs.	49084	Lamar	Johnson, Benjamin Franklin	
Clifton, M. A. Mrs.	35566	Hopkins	Clifton, Thomas Nathan	15531
Clifton, Merit	14049	Wise	—	
Clifton, Rhoda Elizabeth	11279	Travis	Clifton, Felix H.	
Clifton, Sarah O'boyle	51717	Bexar	Clifton, Job	
Clifton, Thomas Nathan	15531	Hopkins	—	
Clifton, William	11564	Menard	—	
Climer, Willie T.	42520	Hill	Climer, John Trimble	
Clindining, A. F.	26541	Hunt	—	
Cline, Elizabeth M.	18785	Bell	Cline, Sylvester	12686
Cline, H. C. Mrs.	32962	Erath	Cline, James Knox Polk	29526
Cline, James Knox Polk	29526	Erath	—	
Cline, Margaret N.	45867	Tarrant	Cline, Perry Robert	
Cline, Marion P.	11423	Erath	—	
Cline, Martha	22954	Morris	Cline, Wade Franklin	
Cline, Sylvester	12686	Bell	—	
Clines, Emily C.	01048	Dallas	Clines, L. W.	
Clinglesmith, H. E. Mrs.	15136	Fannin	Clinglesmith, Henry W.	11435
Clinglesmith, Henry W.	11435	Fannin	—	
Clingman, Julia A.	31053	Brown	Clingman, Alexander Michael	
Clinkscales, Abner Lewis	29439	Dallas	—	
Clinkscales, B. T.	12678	Williamson	—	

Index to Confederate Pension Applications

Name	No.	County	Soldier	No.
Clinkscales, James Thomas	36009	Bexar		
Clinton, D. M.	Rej	Smith		
Clinton, F. C. Mrs.	27230	Taylor	Clinton, Thomas Jefferson	
Clinton, John Sterling	31934	Fannin		
Clinton, Mary Ann	16621	Smith	Clinton, Derias M.	
Clinton, T. M.	27810	Martin		
Cloar, John	23470	Matagorda		
Cloer, F. E. Mrs.	35838	Montague	Cloer, William J.	15730
Cloer, William J.	15730	Jack		
Cloninger, Amos B.	14824	Cass		
Cloninger, J. R.	36205	Tarrant		
Cloninger, M. L.	22652	Cass		
Cloninger, Nancy L.	Rej	Cass	Cloninger, Amos B.	14824
Cloninger, W. B.	50459	Cass		
Clopton, Henry Harrison	33341	Wilbarger		
Clopton, Hoggatt	10491	Travis		
Clopton, M. S. Mrs.	19593	Hays		
Clopton, Martha Ann	33307	Bastrop	Clopton, Hoggatt	10491
Clopton, Mattie	45468	Wilbarger	Clopton, Henry Harrison	33341
Clopton, Mortiman L.	20576	Harrison		
Clopton, Reuben M.	11571	Montgomery		
Clopton, Texanna T.	19168	Navarro	Clopton, Benjamin Micheu	
Clopton, Willie E.	35945	Montgomery	Clopton, Reuben M.	11571
Close, R. E. Mrs.	41202	Coleman	Close, William Lindsey	36705
Close, Sarah	18116	McLennan	Close, John Smith	
Close, William Lindsey	36705	Coleman		
Closs, Sarah Margaret	28087	Brazos	Closs, Junious Theodore	
Clothier, Mary Campell	34653	Jeff Davis	Clothier, George English	
Cloud, Adam Erastus	16068	Montgomery		
Cloud, James W.	37678	Brazos		
Cloud, Jane E.	00118	Austin	Cloud, Alexander	
Cloud, John Jefferson	Rej	Concho		
Cloud, Lydia	36264	Travis	Cloud, William Laswell	
Cloud, Mary	RejM	Van Zandt		
Cloud, W. J.	05712	Kimble		
Clough, Luella	49664	Navarro	Clough, Medicus E.	12559
Clough, Mary	Rej	Van Zandt	Clough, George W.	
Clough, Medicus E.	12559	Navarro		
Clough, S. A. Mrs.	29227	Tyler	Clough, Joseph Philip	
Clover, Elizabeth	26220	Navarro	Clover, Thomas Coke	
Clower, A. T. Mrs.	40210	Franklin	Clower, Augustus Marion	33047
Clower, Augustus Marion	33047	Franklin		
Clower, John H. D.	18243	Parker		
Clower, John Thomas	22583	Harris		
Clower, Johnathan S.	33251	Cottle		
Clower, Maggie J.	35921	Harris	Clower, John Thomas	22583
Clower, Mary H.	49889	Cottle	Clower, Johnathan S.	33251
Clower, Pemelia Jane	38609	Coryell	Clower, James Madison	
Clowers, Davis Harrison Mrs.	47374	Falls	Clowers, Davis Harrison	
Clowers, S. J. Mrs.	18499	Van Zandt	Clowers, George Ashley	
Cloyd, B. F.	08610	Angelina		
Cloyd, Emaline	43207	Dallas	Cloyd, William David	
Cloyd, Mary L.	47347	Collin	Cloyd, Thomas James	
Cloyd, William C.	31609	Travis		
Clubb, W. R.	02270	Jefferson		
Cluck, Barbara E.	29362	Williamson	Cluck, Joseph Jackson	
Cluck, R. J.	04413	Williamson		
Clutts, G. B.	07375	Trinity		
Clyburn, M. H.	28841	Jones		

Index to Confederate Pension Applications

Name	No.	County	Veteran	No.
Clymer, C. M. Mrs.	49099	Llano	Clymer, John	
Clynch, Alexander Knox	49113	Wichita		
Coalson, C.	02772	Mason		
Coalson, J. K.	04735	Waller		
Coalson, Julia Ann	43110	Brown	Coalson, McDonald C.	25140
Coalson, Mary E.	42751	Parker	Coalson, John M.	
Coalson, McDonald C.	25140	Brown		
Coates, Addie	40688	Dallas	Coates, Washington Ford	
Coats, Destie	28604	Rusk	Coats, John Wesley	27055
Coats, Ellen	16393	Rusk	Coats, Martin V.	
Coats, Fannie	33543	Wood	Coats, Moses Butler	
Coats, H. A.	04884	Nacogdoches		
Coats, Harriet P.	10437	Nacogdoches	Coats, J. H.	
Coats, Harriett Virginia	19982	Dallas	Coats, M. A.	06904
Coats, John Wesley	27055	Rusk		
Coats, M. A.	06904	Dallas		
Coats, N. E. Mrs.	28024	Cass	Coats, Cornelius Butcher	
Coats, O. P.	14877	Cherokee		
Coats, S. C. Mrs.	09733	Nacogdoches	Coats, Henry	
Coats, S. F. Mrs.	02444	Lamar	Coats, A. J.	
Coats, W. B.	18265	Rains		
Coats, William Thomas	36718	Collingsworth		
Cobb, A. B.	19962	McCulloch		
Cobb, Albert G.	36762	Robertson		
Cobb, Alexander	Rej	Titus		
Cobb, Alice Ann	51915	Matagorda	Cobb, James Harper	17692
Cobb, Alice Burnett	32812	Tarrant	Cobb, William Jesse	
Cobb, Amanda I.	43340	Fannin	Cobb, Charles Robert	38162
Cobb, Arabella F.	40532	Dallas	Cobb, Charles Albert	
Cobb, Burwell Edward	06838	Wise		
Cobb, Calvin L.	RejM	Fannin		
Cobb, Charles Robert	38162	Fannin		
Cobb, D. J.	23072	Wood		
Cobb, Dillard E.	36410	Rusk		
Cobb, Elizabeth	43581	Grayson	Cobb, Joseph Benton	36374
Cobb, Frances Ann	27918	Gonzales	Cobb, William Benjamin	15264
Cobb, George	04481	Wise		
Cobb, Harriet E.	17602	Ellis	Cobb, John Edwards	
Cobb, Henry Platt	12291	Burleson		
Cobb, J. E.	01272	Ellis		
Cobb, J. H. W.	33407	Fort Bend		
Cobb, J. L.	21693	Jefferson		
Cobb, J. W.	07022	Marion		
Cobb, J. W.	14340	Mitchell		
Cobb, J. W.	31425	Wood		
Cobb, Jacob Hilman	26685	Shelby		
Cobb, James E.	28369	Childress		
Cobb, James Harper	17692	Gonzales		
Cobb, James Warren	15323	Grimes		
Cobb, John D.	16550	Shelby		
Cobb, Joseph Benton	36374	Grayson		
Cobb, Julia E.	29405	Nolan	Cobb, Richard Howard	
Cobb, Lizzie (Elizabeth)	43670	Collingsworth	Cobb, Thomas Wheeler	
Cobb, Lydia A.	16435	Sabine	Cobb, Lafayette	
Cobb, M. S. Mrs.	41781	Grayson	Cobb, John Tatum	
Cobb, Mary	Rej	San Augustine	Cobb, Elcona C.	
Cobb, Mary E.	30845	Brown	Cobb, John Clark	
Cobb, Mary E.	42879	Navarro	Cobb, Carie	
Cobb, Mary Jane Lewis	Rej	Jefferson	Lewis, Alexander	

Index to Confederate Pension Applications

Applicant	Number	County	Veteran	Number
Cobb, Mary L.	33835	Wood	Cobb, D. J.	23072
Cobb, N. A. Mrs.	38253	Rusk	Cobb, Dillard E.	36410
Cobb, Ralla Maxey	28895	Dallas	Cobb, James Warren	15323
Cobb, Robert	22204	Wichita	—	—
Cobb, Sallie A.	19189	Panola	Cobb, Joseph Elija	—
Cobb, Sarah	15265	Gonzales	Cobb, William Andrew	—
Cobb, Sarah Elizabeth	24982	Harris	Cobb, Malachia Austin	—
Cobb, Sarah J. Mrs.	07331	Montgomery	Cobb, J. G.	—
Cobb, Steve	10930	Fannin	—	—
Cobb, Susan Jane	40424	Falls	Cobb, Jacob Hilman	26685
Cobb, Vina	35007	Cooke	Cobb, Steve	10930
Cobb, Virginia	28581	Wichita	Cobb, Robert	22204
Cobb, William Benjamin	04382	Wharton	—	—
Cobb, William Benjamin	15264	Gonzales	—	—
Cobb, William Hamilton	20157	Fannin	—	—
Cobble, Sallie E.	42400	Cherokee	Cobble, Thomas Henderson	—
Coble, A. E. Mrs.	33958	McCulloch	Coble, George Washington	29604
Coble, Calvin Luther	Rej	Fannin	—	—
Coble, George Washington	29604	McCulloch	—	—
Coble, J. R.	39215	Terry	—	—
Coble, Mary Elizabeth	49245	Tarrant	Coble, Alfred Madison	—
Cobler, G. W.	Rej	Grayson	—	—
Coburn, Emily J.	33725	Madison	Coburn, William Canna	—
Coburn, Martha A.	23066	Parker	Coburn, John	—
Cochran, Abraham Marshall	28245	Callahan	—	—
Cochran, Alice	38611	Harrison	Cochran, Pleasant Vanburon	—
Cochran, Amanda	35946	Rains	Cochran, John Edmond	05109
Cochran, Amanda M.	47079	Dallas	Cochran, William Porter	—
Cochran, Blanche	41341	Cooke	Cochran, Stephen Tyler	—
Cochran, Callie	49731	Bosque	Cochran, Benjamin Franklin	—
Cochran, E. M. Mrs.	42090	Hill	Cochran, William Benton	—
Cochran, Emma A.	Rej	Young	Cochran, David Jackson	—
Cochran, Emma Campbell	45092	Young	Campbell, Louis	—
Cochran, Enoch Elijah	45874	San Saba	—	—
Cochran, Enoch Elijah Mrs.	46848	San Saba	Cochran, Enoch Elijah	45874
Cochran, Etna	35068	Callahan	Cochran, Abraham Marshall	28245
Cochran, Fannie	Rej	Henderson	Cochran, David James	—
Cochran, Florence	32182	Cherokee	Cochran, Nehemiah	—
Cochran, J. R.	28051	Cooke	—	—
Cochran, John A.	30158	Panola	—	—
Cochran, John Edmond	05109	Rains	—	—
Cochran, John L.	03888	Tom Green	—	—
Cochran, John W.	26107	Lamar	—	—
Cochran, Joseph M.	36671	Gonzales	—	—
Cochran, L. D.	01659	Gregg	—	—
Cochran, L. N.	17834	Hood	—	—
Cochran, L. T.	17593	Dickens	—	—
Cochran, Lazirus Andrews	18425	Titus	—	—
Cochran, Lucinda C.	03205	Orange	Cochran, Jacob	—
Cochran, M. A.	08137M	Newton	—	—
Cochran, M. A. Mrs.	13873	Hunt	Cochran, L. D.	01659
Cochran, M. F. Mrs.	24968	San Jacinto	Cochran, William James Brown	17155
Cochran, Margarette A.	22803	Newton	Cochran, John Lewis	—
Cochran, Martin B.	04634A	Hays	—	—
Cochran, Maryetta	49507	Montgomery	Cochran, Richard Fulton	—
Cochran, Minerva Elizabeth	38036	Jasper	Cochran, William Green	—
Cochran, Missouri Ann	05026	Jasper	Cochran, Alfred James	—
Cochran, P. M. Mrs.	Rej	Williamson	Cochran, James	—
Cochran, Sam Houston	26118	San Jacinto	—	—

Index to Confederate Pension Applications

Name	App #	County	Veteran	Vet App #
Cochran, Sam Houston Mrs.	40747	San Jacinto	Cochran, Sam Houston	26118
Cochran, Susan D.	18801	Titus	Cochran, Lazirus Andrews	18425
Cochran, Travis Spraggin Mrs.	29333	Polk	Cochran, Travis Spraggin	—
Cochran, W. A.	30430	Milam	—	
Cochran, William J.	25236	Harrison	—	
Cochran, William James Brown	17155	San Jacinto	—	
Cockburn, James P.	Rej	Red River	—	
Cockburn, Nancy O.	28149	Parker	Cockburn, Clark Terrel	—
Cocke, Araminta Jane	41464	Burnet	Cocke, Bowman William	—
Cocke, H. D.	04148	Uvalde	—	
Cocke, Joseph J.	41022	Cameron	—	
Cocke, Lizzie Y.	43884	Williamson	Cocke, Thomas Foster	11273
Cocke, Martha C.	45599	Cherokee	Cocke, Thomas Augustin	—
Cocke, Mattie J.	49738	Washington	Cocke, James Norfolk	—
Cocke, Thomas Foster	11273	Tom Green	—	
Cocke, William G.	21541	Bexar	—	
Cockerell, W. H.	51214	Navarro	—	
Cockerham, John David	Rej	Tarrant	—	
Cockerham, Nancy M.	25193	Fannin	Cockerham, Pleasant Leroy	—
Cockrell, James William	18107	McLennan	—	
Cockrell, John A.	22453	Baylor	—	
Cockrell, John A. Mrs.	41827	Baylor	Cockrell, John A.	22453
Cockrell, Mary Virginia	50795	Bexar	Cockrell, Quintus Jupitus	—
Cockrell, Sallie A.	46485	Hill	Cockrell, Mark Samuel	—
Cockrell, Sarah	29815	Caldwell	Cockrell, Edward Harrison	—
Cockrell, Sarah	35247	McLennan	Cockrell, James William	18107
Cockrell, Willis M.	11956	Hill	—	
Cody, J. A. Mrs.	42678	Hunt	Cody, Robert D.	—
Cody, William S.	08887	Red River	—	
Coe, John	13309	Franklin	—	
Coe, M. K. Mrs.	30532	Franklin	Coe, John	13309
Cofer, Malinda Jane	35607	Henderson	Cofer, William Madison	34697
Cofer, William Madison	34697	Henderson	—	
Coffee, F. E. Mrs.	30619	Brown	Coffee, William Madison	—
Coffee, Francis V. Haddox	42707	Comanche	Haddox, Timothy Rasbern	—
Coffee, Lou V.	47131	Randall	Coffee, Thomas Dean	—
Coffelt, Henry	19091	Limestone	—	
Coffelt, Nancy Margaret	31538	Limestone	Coffelt, Henry	19091
Coffey, Almeda	37490	Travis	Coffey, Charles Lineus	13534
Coffey, Benjamin Franklin	15973	Mason	—	
Coffey, Charles Lineus	13534	Travis	—	
Coffey, Cleora Ann	32658	Dallas	Coffey, Thomas Jessup	11405
Coffey, Emer Maria	46080	Brown	Coffey, John Nathan	—
Coffey, Fannie	32921	San Saba	Coffey, Hiram Van	—
Coffey, Hooper Van	00204	Bastrop	—	
Coffey, L. E. Mrs.	42276	Llano	Coffey, Benjamin Franklin	15973
Coffey, M. Smith	42191	Bandera	—	
Coffey, Mary Elizabeth	49092	Mason	Coffey, John Henderson	—
Coffey, Matthew Slaughter	46089	Grayson	—	
Coffey, Mattie	27929	Bastrop	Coffey, Hooper Van	00204
Coffey, Milton Sinclair	11772	Morris	—	
Coffey, Thomas Jessup	11405	Dallas	—	
Coffey, Virginia	46249	Grayson	Coffey, Matthew Slaughter	46089
Coffield, Mary B.	46746	Milam	Coffield, Charles Hunter	—
Coffield, S. T.	11697	Wichita	—	
Coffin, E. Mrs.	17563	Dallas	Coffin, Arthur	—
Coffin, Helen W.	49003	Hill	Coffin, Charles Ignatius	—
Coffin, John Randolph	32304	Hill	—	
Coffin, Mary E.	35812	Hill	Coffin, John Randolph	32304

Index to Confederate Pension Applications

Name	No.	County	Spouse/Related	Related No.
Coffman, Elizabeth A.	23781	Collin	Coffman, Leroy Wilson	
Coffman, Frank	25498	Hopkins		
Coffman, James M.	31562	Callahan		
Coffman, John Green	27010	Red River		
Coffman, M. J. Mrs.	38255	Red River	Coffman, John Green	27010
Cofield, Maggie J.	25871	Hardeman	Cofield, George Thomas	
Cofield, W. M.	29934	Red River		
Cogburn, E. B.	19219	Rusk		
Cogburn, James Macom	13085	Travis		
Cogdell, Carrie	47628	Hill	Cogdell, Alfred Banfill	
Cogdell, Nancy Jane	21694	Foard	Cogdell, William Henry	
Cogdell, William	30039	Bastrop		
Cogdill, John R.	25506	Delta		
Cogdill, Zachary T.	22691	Collin		
Coggin, Andrew J.	21695	Taylor		
Coggin, Andrew Jackson	14717	Bowie		
Coggin, J. R.	10080	Fisher		
Coggins, William Ivy	11207	Ellis		
Cogswell, L. M.	09562	Shelby		
Cogswell, Sallie	11735	Shelby	Cogswell, L. M.	09562
Cohea, Nancy C.	04663	Gonzales	Cohea, A. T.	
Cohen, Clara	39948	Bexar	Cohen, Isaac	10828
Cohen, Hyan, Dr.	21696	Hill		
Cohen, Issac	10828	Bexar		
Cohen, Lawrence L.	27033	Harris		
Cohen, Mary	45636	Dallas	Cohen, Simon	34402
Cohen, Mattie	46232	McLennan	Hyan, Dr.	21696
Cohen, Simon	34402	Dallas		
Cohran, Eliza J.	51990	Throckmorton	Cohra(or o)n, Felix Gilbert	27168
Cohron, Felix Gilbert (Cohran)	27168	Throckmorton		
Coile, Mary M.	19364	Lamar	Coile, Nicholas Warren	14305
Coile, Nicholas Warren	14305	Lamar		
Coke, Martha Curtis	35056	Nolan	Coke, Robert Payne	21598
Coke, Robert Payne	21598	Cass		
Coker, A. P.	20464	Polk		
Coker, Caroline	45321	Bexar	Coker, Leonard Tarrant	34583
Coker, Fannie J.	21698	Comanche	Coker, Payton L.	14953
Coker, Hiram Green	26512	Erath		
Coker, James T.	21697	Henderson		
Coker, Jose Ann	18709	Bandera	Coker, James Harrison	
Coker, Josephine	31232	Tarrant	Coker, James Alexander	
Coker, Leonard Tarrant	34583	Bexar		
Coker, Lillie L.	34841	Atascosa	Coker, Hiram Green	26512
Coker, M. F. Mrs.	15454	Henderson	Coker, William	
Coker, Martha	32651	Smith	Coker, Robert	16625
Coker, Mollie A.	22327	Comanche	Coker, Leonard Thomas	
Coker, Nancy Elizabeth	35331	Rains	Coker, Squire John	03387
Coker, P. E. Mrs.	09385	Lamar	Coker, H. D.	
Coker, Payton L.	14953	Comanche		
Coker, R. S.	25610	Tarrant		
Coker, Robert	16625	Smith		
Coker, Robert Griffin	10826	Bell		
Coker, Robert W.	12412	Henderson		
Coker, Sarah E.	02713	Live Oak	Coker, Alexander	
Coker, Squire John	03387	Rains		
Coker, Virginia	26154	Polk	Coker, Robert Griffin	10826
Coker, W. J.	03101	Navarro		
Coker, William Smith	12895	Henderson		
Coker, William Thomas	25512	Fisher		

Index to Confederate Pension Applications

Colbath, Winthrop Sinclear	09221	Frio		
Colbath, Winthrop Sinclear Mrs.	21440	Frio	Colbath, Winthrop Sinclear	09221
Colbert, B. F.	02079	Houston		
Colbert, George Washington	27844	Bell		
Colburn, A. H.	04373	Wharton		
Colburn, C. C.	23078	San Saba		
Colburn, George Henry	18295	Runnels		
Colburn, John Henry	14133	Bosque		
Colburn, Mary	51820	Eastland	Colburn, George Henry	18295
Colding, Sue E.	04953	Bexar	Colding, Joseph Dell	
Coldwell, P. C.	26650	Van Zandt		
Cole, Annie R.	35529	Parker	Cole, George Washington	
Cole, C.	49459	Navarro		
Cole, E. A. Mrs.	Rej	Hunt	Cole, John	
Cole, Eliza	19254	Scurry	Cole, Jacob	
Cole, Elizabeth	50464	Cass	Cole, Jacob Scott	35888
Cole, Elizabeth A.	36469	Fayette	Cole, George Washington	
Cole, Ellen	20458	Nacogdoches	Cole, James Manton	
Cole, Frances A.	40790	Hamilton	Cole, William J.	
Cole, Frances P.	07270	Kaufman	Cole, J. L.	
Cole, Francis Asbury	19255	Shackelford		
Cole, Francis Asbury Mrs.	23393	McLennan	Cole, Francis Asbury	19255
Cole, George Washington	23440	Bell		
Cole, I. F.	25589	Morris		
Cole, J. A.	40564	Jefferson		
Cole, J. C.	Rej	Tarrant		
Cole, J. C.	28622	Dallas		
Cole, J. E. Mrs.	26861	Dallas	Cole, Lafayette Newton	
Cole, J. G.	Rej	Van Zandt		
Cole, J. H.	02354	Jones		
Cole, J. H.	04685	Gonzales		
Cole, J. H., Sr.	Rej	Van Zandt		
Cole, J. M.	00537	Brown		
Cole, J. M.	06274	Shelby		
Cole, J. W.	16795	Upshur		
Cole, Jacob Scott	35888	Cass		
Cole, Jasper Newton Mrs.	49722	Brazos	Cole, Jasper Newton	
Cole, Jennie	42589	Washington	Cole, George Washington	
Cole, John Bishop	35197	Caldwell		
Cole, John M.	26860	Ellis		
Cole, John R.	06655	Parker		
Cole, John Randolph	41207	Bosque		
Cole, Joseph Larkin	47155	Dallas		
Cole, Julia	30215	Tarrant	Cole, Green Alexander	
Cole, Julia A.	04260	Victoria	Cole, Gabriel	
Cole, Julia A.	30162	Brazos	Cole, Flournoy Jefferson	
Cole, Julia A.	32106	Tarrant	Cole, Greene Alexander	
Cole, Julie A.	25775	Van Zandt	Cole, Nickolson David	16859
Cole, Larkin Granville	Rej	Terry		
Cole, M. C. Mrs.	13206	Bell	Cole, J. D.	
Cole, M. E. Mrs.	51460	Erath	Cole, John Randolph	41207
Cole, M. S.	Rej	Cherokee		
Cole, Mahala Elizabeth	43180	Caldwell	Cole, John Bishop	35197
Cole, Margaret L.	07933	Parker	Cole, John R.	06655
Cole, Martha A.	31504	Rains	Cole, Acy Thomas	
Cole, Martha H.	38614	Cherokee	Cole, Aaron Shannon	
Cole, Mary E.	17955	Jefferson	Cole, Robert William	
Cole, Mary Elizabeth	23157	Oldham	Cole, Daniel Franklin	
Cole, Mary Elizabeth	37044	Dallas	Cole, Samuel Love	

Index to Confederate Pension Applications

Name	Number	County	Related	Related No.
Cole, Mattie	45227	Collin	Cole, Thomas Jefferson	—
Cole, Nickolson David	16859	Van Zandt	—	—
Cole, Phalisa J. Stanley	36908	Robertson	Stanley, Lysander Edward	—
Cole, Providence William	26435	Sabine	—	—
Cole, Providence William Mrs.	40109	Sabine	Cole, Providence William	26435
Cole, Rebecca Jane	32548	Caldwell	Richard, Sr.	11368
Cole, Richard, Sr.	11368	Caldwell	—	—
Cole, Robert M.	49155	Robertson	—	—
Cole, Rosana	28285	Floyd	Cole, James McDonald	—
Cole, S. B.	23112	Red River	—	—
Cole, S. B. Mrs.	35401	Bosque	Cole, William Turner	—
Cole, Sarah A.	15680	Harrison	Cole, William Bright	—
Cole, Sarah Francis	35773	Nacogdoches	Cole, Thomas Pinckney	19153
Cole, Susan	34094	Austin	Cole, Austin Bryan	—
Cole, Susan Elizabeth	40820	Bell	Cole, George Washington	23440
Cole, Thomas Pinkney	19153	Nacogdoches	—	—
Cole, Victoria A.	29486	Wheeler	Cole, James Lilburn	—
Cole, W. G.	01226	Ellis	—	—
Cole, W. R.	06873	Donley	—	—
Cole, W. T.	16858	Van Zandt	—	—
Cole, William Samuel	39498	Smith	—	—
Coleman, A. E. Mrs.	34611	Morris	Coleman, William Harrison	23158
Coleman, A. S.	05762	Dallas	—	—
Coleman, Albert	Rej	Harrison	—	—
Coleman, Anna Elizabeth	43693	Leon	Coleman, Ben A.	43453
Coleman, Ary A. Mrs.	26947	Uvalde	Coleman, John Enos	—
Coleman, Ben A.	43453	Leon	—	—
Coleman, Ben F.	33539	Wood	—	—
Coleman, Caroline	15192	Freestone	Coleman, William Wallace	—
Coleman, Cornelia S.	25862	Walker	Coleman, William Gooden	—
Coleman, David Swain	29680	Henderson	—	—
Coleman, Elijah Lynch	27797	Anderson	—	—
Coleman, Elijah Lynch Mrs.	35606	Anderson	Coleman, Elijah Lynch	27797
Coleman, Eliza	29135	Henderson	Coleman, Joseph W.	—
Coleman, Ellen	38857	Wilbarger	Coleman, William Henry	09524
Coleman, Eloise	35273	Henderson	Coleman, David Swain	29680
Coleman, George T.	50478	Bandera	—	—
Coleman, George Washington	38283	Coryell	—	—
Coleman, Henry B.	38045	Johnson	—	—
Coleman, I. H.	19775	Liberty	—	—
Coleman, J. C.	Rej	Denton	—	—
Coleman, J. W.	Rej	Henderson	—	—
Coleman, James	21410	Coryell	—	—
Coleman, James H.	Rej	Bosque	—	—
Coleman, James Mrs.	25717	Coryell	Coleman, James	21410
Coleman, John H.	50363	Trinity	—	—
Coleman, John W.	35502	McLennan	—	—
Coleman, John Wesley Mrs.	49148	Runnels	Coleman, John Wesley	—
Coleman, L. E. Mrs.	19730	San Augustine	Coleman, Manning C.	—
Coleman, Lewis	01779	Harris	—	—
Coleman, Louisa	00751	Cherokee	Coleman, James H.	—
Coleman, M. A. Mrs.	19636	Borden	Coleman, Jesse H.	—
Coleman, M. C.	18320	San Augustine	—	—
Coleman, M. J. Mrs.	46281	Hood	Coleman, Thomas Bluett	—
Coleman, M. V. Mrs.	39125	Coryell	Coleman, George Washington	38283
Coleman, Martha M.	19790	Harrison	Coleman, Albert	Rej
Coleman, Mary A.	16304	Red River	Coleman, William Stephens	—
Coleman, Mary A.	31058	Titus	Coleman, Mathew W.	03851
Coleman, Mary Eliza Livingston	51497	Erath	Coleman, James Burr Head	—

Index to Confederate Pension Applications

Name	No.	County	Veteran	No.
Coleman, Mary J.	33607	Clay	Coleman, Thomas Smith	28912
Coleman, Mary McGregor	38633	Matagorda	Coleman, William Hayden Leavel	—
Coleman, Mathew W.	03851	Titus	—	
Coleman, Michel Henry	12971	Limestone	—	
Coleman, Michel Henry Mrs.	18059	Limestone	Coleman, Michel Henry	12971
Coleman, Millie	08325	Grayson	Coleman, Anderson	—
Coleman, Mittie A.	Rej	Dewitt	Coleman, Edward Perry	—
Coleman, N. E. Mrs.	45642	Burleson	Coleman, Robert William	—
Coleman, R. B.	12366	Frio	—	
Coleman, Robert Foster Mrs.	34287	Jefferson	Coleman, Robert Foster	—
Coleman, Rufus	29509	Travis	—	
Coleman, Sarah J.	50856	Wood	Coleman, Ben F.	33539
Coleman, Sarah Jane	51454	Trinity	Coleman, John H.	50363
Coleman, Susan E.	14141	Burleson	Coleman, William J.	—
Coleman, Thomas Smith	28912	Clay	—	
Coleman, Virginia E.	28119	Harrison	Coleman, John H.	—
Coleman, W. C.	Rej	Tarrant	—	
Coleman, W. H.	08628	Bowie	—	
Coleman, W. W.	21699	Montague	—	
Coleman, W. W.	23107	Hays	—	
Coleman, William Harrison	23158	Morris	—	
Coleman, William Henry	09524	Wilbarger	—	
Coleman, Wyley D.	20288	El Paso	—	
Coleman, Youngs O.	29720	Webb	—	
Coleman, Youngs O. Mrs.	36056	Webb	Coleman, Youngs O.	29720
Coleson, Joe	36363	Jasper	Coleson, James Marion	—
Coley, J. C.	13009	Montgomery	—	
Coley, Louisa M.	22631	Titus	Coley, Charley Capers	—
Colgan, James	11337	Archer	—	
Colgin, Annie E.	39524	Freestone	Colgin, Richard Ewing	—
Colkin, Richard C.	37679	Houston	—	
Colkin, Richard C. Mrs.	40659	Houston	Colkin, Richard C.	37679
Collard, Elizabeth Louise	45382	Harris	Collard, William E.	—
Collard, Mary Jane	Rej	Brazos	Collard, Joe Larrison	—
Collard, Tennie Randall	45452	Wichita	Felix Robert, Sr.	—
Collett, Martha Ellen	49959	Brown	Collett, Abraham Hoss	—
Colley, A. W.	05266	Coryell	—	
Colley, Amanda	47110	Travis	Colley, James F.	10301
Colley, D. N.	15094	Erath	—	
Colley, Edmund C.	43399	Gonzales	—	
Colley, Henry C.	35108	McLennan	—	
Colley, James F.	10301	Hunt	—	
Colley, John Turner	15866	Lampasas	—	
Colley, Julia Virginia	50920	Milam	Colley, John	—
Colley, Mattie A.	18004	Lampasas	Colley, John Turner	15866
Collie, Lue	32675	Hays	Collie, Albert Weich	—
Collier, A. J.	Rej	Jack	—	
Collier, Amanda Jane	37151	Hays	Collier, Smith	12228
Collier, Arrimenta J.	33784	Hunt	Collier, Thaddeus Bridges	—
Collier, B. W.	33381	Limestone	—	
Collier, Elizabeth	05228	Tyler	Collier, J. G.	—
Collier, Elizabeth	16067	Montgomery	Collier, A. B.	—
Collier, Francis Marion	30907	Bosque	—	
Collier, Francis Marion Mrs.	50000	Bosque	Collier, Francis Marion	30907
Collier, H. L. W.	11043	McCulloch	—	
Collier, Henry M.	15675	Hardin	—	
Collier, Isham	07907	Montague	—	
Collier, J. Dallas	21448	Tyler	—	
Collier, J. F.	22713	Haskell	—	

Index to Confederate Pension Applications

Name	App #	County	Veteran	Vet App #
Collier, J. M.	28461	Dallas	—	—
Collier, J. W.	Rej	Tyler	—	—
Collier, James B.	12335	Denton	—	—
Collier, Jesse	22606	Callahan	—	—
Collier, John	22193	Jefferson	—	—
Collier, John J.	RejM	Cherokee	—	—
Collier, John T.	11281	Upshur	—	—
Collier, Joseph John	23069	Wilson	—	—
Collier, Lou Mrs.	02820	McLennan	Collier, Rufus	—
Collier, Malinda	45543	Grayson	Collier, William Jasper	19961
Collier, Mary Alma	Rej	Bexar	Collier, John Joseph	—
Collier, Mary C.	00740	Cherokee	Collier, John	—
Collier, Mary Elizabeth	Rej	Montague	Collier, Johnathan	—
Collier, N. C. Mrs.	07046	Robertson	Collier, William C.	—
Collier, Nicodemus	00859	Collin	—	—
Collier, R. A. Mrs.	35869	Tyler	Collier, William Granberry	16762
Collier, S. Z.	30460	Tyler	—	—
Collier, Smith	12228	Kerr	—	—
Collier, W. B.	Rej	Kimble	—	—
Collier, W. M.	00099	Archer	—	—
Collier, William Austin	32170	Anderson	—	—
Collier, William Granberry	16762	Tyler	—	—
Collier, William Jasper	19961	Grayson	—	—
Collier, Willis B.	09912	Williamson	—	—
Collins, Albert Gonzales	32602	Irion	—	—
Collins, Alexander	38921	Denton	—	—
Collins, Alzena	Rej	Fannin	Collins, J. S.	—
Collins, Andrew Jackson	05956	Bandera	—	—
Collins, Anna P.	34787	Gonzales	Collins, Albert Horn	—
Collins, Asberry Sebastian	10156	Mills	—	—
Collins, Barbara Peyton	45249	Bandera	Collins, James Charleton	41907
Collins, Bettie	14757	Burleson	Collins, Samuel S.	—
Collins, C. C.	Rej	Harrison	—	—
Collins, Caroline	35274	Cherokee	Collins, John Bonaparte	32217
Collins, Charles C.	07629	McLennan	—	—
Collins, Delaney Mrs.	07484	Henderson	Collins, W. L.	—
Collins, Della	Rej	Hidalgo	Collins, James Rice	—
Collins, Dora	52043	Irion	Collins, Albert Gonzales	32602
Collins, Eli L.	09753	Mason	—	—
Collins, Eliza Blackshear	Home	Travis	Collins, Charles C.	07629
Collins, Elizabeth	10864	Cherokee	Collins, John V.	—
Collins, Elizabeth	34974	Frio	Collins, Lee George	33975
Collins, Elizabeth	46097	Garza	Collins, Eli L.	09753
Collins, Elizabeth Ford	51794	Galveston	Collins, Jonas Ephrodis	—
Collins, Elizabeth Mary Ann	28410	Throckmorton	Collins, Wyatt	—
Collins, Emily Josephine	16204	Nolan	Collins, William Green	10099
Collins, George W.	24106	Tarrant	—	—
Collins, Hannah J.	38233	Tarrant	Collins, Thomas Benton	28564
Collins, Henrietta	45602	Hood	Collins, Andrew Jackson	—
Collins, Henry Dock	10847	Bowie	—	—
Collins, Ida	Rej	Shelby	Collins, Arthur	—
Collins, J. L.	11891	Eastland	—	—
Collins, J. O.	Rej	Shelby	—	—
Collins, J. Q. A.	01232	Ellis	—	—
Collins, James Charleton	41907	Bandera	—	—
Collins, James H.	30404	Grayson	—	—
Collins, James Henry	09920	Eastland	—	—
Collins, Jane	41638	Milam	Collins, Johnson	—
Collins, Japhet	Rej	—	—	—

Index to Confederate Pension Applications

Name	App#	County	Soldier	Soldier App#
Collins, Jesse M.	15729	Jack		
Collins, Jessie O.	Rej	Foard	Collins, Thomas Luman	19578
Collins, John Bonaparte	32217	Cherokee		
Collins, John Franklin	12728	Bell		
Collins, John Jackson	09591	Cherokee		
Collins, John O.	22293	Shelby		
Collins, Joseph William	50070	Bell		
Collins, Josephine B.	26234	Dallas	Collins, John White	
Collins, Josiah M. Mrs.	Rej	Grayson	Collins, Josiah M.	
Collins, Lavanda Tinnie	36846	Wise	Collins, Willis Green	26748
Collins, Lee D.	28839	Grayson	Collins, William Maton	
Collins, Lee George	33975	Atascosa		
Collins, Levi F.	Rej	Taylor		
Collins, Lizzie	43547	Tarrant	Collins, Marshall Reed	
Collins, Lorena	22490	Coleman	Collins, Henry Wilburn	
Collins, Lucy Etta	27575	Wichita	Collins, William Gregory	04709
Collins, Lusendy Jane	42235	Polk	Collins, M. C.	41265
Collins, M. A. Mrs.	03060	Montgomery	Collins, J. L.	
Collins, M. A. Mrs.	25921	Parmer	Collins, William Brame	02770
Collins, M. A. Mrs.	47730	Coleman	Collins, Nathan D.	
Collins, M. C.	41265	Polk		
Collins, M. C. Mrs.	23070	Harris	Collins, Van Buren	
Collins, M. V. Mrs.	47390	Hopkins	Collins, Redden	
Collins, Margaret A.	27277	Wise	Collins, Robert Marion	
Collins, Martha	45198	Bowie	Collins, Henry Dock	10847
Collins, Mary	46415	Polk	Collins, James Madison	
Collins, Mary A.	22834	McLennan	Collins, James Henry	09920
Collins, Mary A.	47649	Harris	Collins, John	
Collins, Mary Ann	20256	McLennan	Collins, William Thomas	20153
Collins, Mary C.	09982	Bell	Collins, William	
Collins, Mary Elizabeth	42761	Matagorda	Collins, Pleasanton Bohanan	09058
Collins, Mary F.	29041	Dallas	Collins, Thomas Palmer	20965
Collins, Mattie	34903	San Saba	Collins, Thomas Jefferson	08917
Collins, Mattie Kee Ellison	51597	Bosque	Collins, Columbus Franklin	
Collins, Mollie	30149	Travis	Collins, Robert Crittenden	
Collins, N. E. Mrs.	39617	Erath	Collins, James	
Collins, Nancy	33129	Mitchell	Collins, Levi Feaster	
Collins, Nannie M.	36256	Austin	Collins, Japhet	Rej
Collins, Olivia	51799	Bell	Collins, Joseph William	50070
Collins, Olivia Russell	47256	Tom Green	Collins, John Ford	
Collins, Pleasanton Bohanan	09058	Karnes		
Collins, R. C.	47792	Ellis		
Collins, Romulus Madison Mrs.	Rej	Tom Green	Collins, Romulus Madison	
Collins, S. K.	11695	Wilbarger		
Collins, Sarah P.	31340	Polk	Collins, Thomas Jefferson	
Collins, T. H. Mrs.	39967	Bexar	Collins, James W.	
Collins, Thomas Benton	28564	Tarrant		
Collins, Thomas Jefferson	08917	Limestone		
Collins, Thomas Luman	19578	Foard		
Collins, Thomas P.	Rej	Grayson		
Collins, Thomas Palmer	20965	Grayson		
Collins, Thomas R.	11804	Bexar		
Collins, V. V. Mrs.	11311	Harrison	Collins, Christopher C.	
Collins, W. J.	09424	Anderson		
Collins, William	04844	Nacogdoches		
Collins, William Brame	02770	Mason		
Collins, William Green	10099	Haskell		
Collins, William Gregory	04709	Freestone		
Collins, William L. Sr.	00049	Angelina		

Index to Confederate Pension Applications

Collins, William Thomas	20153	McLennan		
Collins, Willis Green	26748	Wise		
Collinsworth, E. J. Mrs.	32066	Dallas	Collinsworth, James Gideon	
Collinsworth, J. M.	00590	Caldwell		
Collinsworth, Joel	04843	Nacogdoches		
Collinsworth, Laura Marildia	19960	Bastrop	Collinsworth, Willis Bonner	
Collinsworth, Sarah A.	08632	Caldwell	Collinsworth, J. M.	00590
Collom, Amanda	21091	Stonewall	Collom, Josiah Wilson	
Collom, Jesse Lemuel	17074	Bowie		
Collom, Lee	51866	McLennan	Collom, George	
Collom, Nancy Jane	41429	Bowie	Collom, Spencer Rice	
Collum, Rebecca	48078	Bowie	Collum, Charles Collin	
Colson, A. S.	23089	Bosque		
Colson, William L.	01682	Grimes		
Coltharp, A. B.	Rej	Henderson		
Coltharp, H. M. Mrs.	15455	Henderson	Coltharp, William Henry	
Coltharp, Maryetta	Rej	Henderson	Coltharp, Abel Bruce	
Coltharp, Oscar John Robert	18140	Montague		
Coltharp, Z. L. Mrs.	19141	Montague	Coltharp, Oscar John Robert	18140
Columbus, Sarah L.	43850	Hamilton	Columbus, Louis Samuel	
Colville, Mary D.	Rej	San Patricio	Colville, William Thomas	
Colvin, F. B.	22128	Coleman		
Colvin, J. E.	20909	Erath		
Colvin, W. D.	03771	Tarrant		
Colwell, P. H. Loftin Mrs.	46645	Nolan	Loftin, Thomas Benton	
Colwell, W. N.	07803	Ellis		
Combow, Thomas L.	45780	Dallas		
Combs, Daniel W.	Rej	Burleson		
Combs, Fannie A.	47219	Hays	Combs, James Henry	
Combs, Mary C.	34266	Dallas	Combs, Robert Martin	
Combs, S. E. Mrs.	45417	Franklin	Combs, Thomas Jackson	26504
Combs, Sarah	Rej	Carson	Combs, Zur David	
Combs, Thomas Jackson	26504	Hopkins		
Comegys, Susan Harris	33844	Cooke	Comegys, Edward Freeman	
Comer, Calvin Hampton	22418	Tarrant		
Comer, Calvin Hampton Mrs.	Rej	Tarrant	Comer, Calvin Hampton	22418
Comer, Don	Rej	Harris		
Comer, Martha Isabel	28016	Fannin	Comer, Charles Allen	
Comer, Thomas J.	02119	Hunt		
Comer, William Henry	38474	Johnson		
Comer, William Henry Mrs.	46322	Johnson	Comer, William Henry	38474
Commander, E. L. Mrs.	08497M	Tyler		
Commander, Emeline	31054	Tarrant	Commander, Madison	
Como, Angie Sophia	42934	Harris	Como, Desire	
Compton, Braston William	01308	Erath		
Compton, Edilda Victoria	36052	Throckmorton	Compton, Aaron	
Compton, G. W.	11376	Cherokee		
Compton, Henry Thomas	30908	Wharton		
Compton, J. A. Mrs.	23090	Freestone	Compton, William Francis	
Compton, John Perkins	27297	Harris		
Compton, L. L. Mrs.	22776	Dallas	Compton, Bishop	
Compton, Martha	14395	Rusk	Compton, William C.	
Compton, Mary Elizabeth	15926	Liberty	Compton, John Lewis	
Compton, Mary Elizabeth	47275	Wilbarger	Compton, Smith Nathan	
Compton, Mary Louise	49419	Fannin	Compton, John Wesley	
Compton, Melvina W. Mrs.	18058	Limestone	Compton, George Washington	
Compton, Sarah	29508	Milam	Compton, William Washington	
Compton, Sarah L.	01978	Hood	Compton, Yelverton O.	
Compton, Sarah M.	23407	Knox	Compton, Braston William	01308

Index to Confederate Pension Applications

Applicant	App. No.	County	Veteran	Vet. No.
Compton, T. P. Mrs.	Rej	Harris	Compton, John Perkins	27297
Conaway, Helen C.	39695	Bexar	Conaway, Jesse Lafayette	—
Conaway, M. J. Mrs.	49688	Travis	Conaway, William B.	—
Conaway, Sarah A.	22520	Smith	Conaway, John Basel	—
Conder, Sarah E.	07502	Hunt	Conder, Berry B.	—
Condict, V. G. Mrs.	31801	Camp	Condict, Louis Vernon	—
Condra, L. B.	28254	Williamson	—	—
Condra, L. T. Mrs.	38737	Runnels	Condra, L. T. (Condrey)	17474
Condrey, L. T. (Condra)	17474	Coleman	—	—
Condrey, N. J. Mrs.	04917	Bastrop	Condrey, Elijah	—
Condron, Melissa	49252	Donley	Condron, W. H.	—
Condron, Riley Nelson Mrs.	47801	Throckmorton	Condron, Riley Nelson	—
Condron, Thomas M.	22205	Comanche	—	—
Cone, Edna Ann	41112	Van Zandt	Cone, William Oliver	25641
Cone, Elmira	04169	Van Zandt	Cone, T. C.	—
Cone, Eva	47434	Montague	Cone, Samuel Overton	—
Cone, George Washington	15324	Grimes	—	—
Cone, J. T.	29410	Limestone	—	—
Cone, James Thomas	14942	Colorado	—	—
Cone, Laura Emmaline	47525	El Paso	Cone, George Washington	—
Cone, M. E. Mrs.	02080	Houston	Cone, Isham	—
Cone, Maggie	Rej	Grimes	Cone, Henry Shrock	—
Cone, Mary F.	Rej	Hunt	Cone, W. C.	—
Cone, Mattie A.	39567	Grimes	Cone, George Washington	15324
Cone, R. R. Mrs.	37064	Grayson	Cone, Fletcher Asberry	—
Cone, T. J.	27440	Harris	—	—
Cone, William Oliver	25641	Van Zandt	—	—
Conerly, Myra Jane	40727	Harrison	Conerly, Buxton Reeves	—
Congalton, John Alexander	Rej	Hill	—	—
Congalton, Mattie	22614	Hill	Congalton, John Alexander	Rej
Conger, Martha Francis	26795	Nolan	Conger, Samuel Weir	—
Conger, Sarah Elizabeth	31802	Hunt	Conger, Thomas Eli	—
Conine, James Britain	43509	Tarrant	—	—
Conkle, Catherine	06677	Collin	Conkle, John	—
Conklin, T. B.	08479M	Tarrant	—	—
Conley, Olivia E.	45306	Dallas	Conley, Samuel Osburne (Oswell)	44064
Conley, Samuel Oswell (Osburne)	44064	Dallas	—	—
Conly, N. V. Mrs.	05887	Franklin	Conly, George B.	—
Conn, J. G.	Rej	Madison	—	—
Conn, J. M.	Rej	Parker	—	—
Conn, M. E. Mrs.	28794	Tarrant	Conn, Jefferson Suddeth	—
Conn, Mary Ann	33821	Bexar	Conn, John William	—
Conn, Ruth C.	14063	Clay	Conn, William F.	09442
Conn, William F.	09442	Clay	—	—
Connally, Charles	36391	Somervell	—	—
Connally, Charles P.	Rej	Garza	—	—
Connally, Mary Alice	46602	Somervell	Connally, Charles	36391
Connally, Mary C.	31233	Hopkins	Connally, Drury	—
Connally, S. E. Mrs.	30766	Hopkins	Connally, James Polk	—
Connally, Sarah C.	40364	Stephens	Connally, George Birdwell	—
Connally, William L.	15168	Franklin	—	—
Connally, Winfield Scott	50738	McLennan	—	—
Connaway, Octavia C.	18927	Edwards	Connaway, Wiley Thomas	—
Connell, John Posey	39623	Nueces	—	—
Connell, Kate	51703	Nueces	Connell, John Posey	39623
Connelly, John	02355	Jones	—	—
Connelly, John Larkin Mrs.	30307	Hays	Connelly, John Larkin	—
Conner, Amanda E.	50014	Hopkins	Conner, Festus Osbourne	—
Conner, Ellen	Rej	Washington	Conner, James Monroe	13007

Index to Confederate Pension Applications

Name	No.	County	Related	Related No.
Conner, Frances E.	25146	Parker	Conner, John Daniel	
Conner, J. F., Sr.	00822	Coke		
Conner, James C.	00199	Bastrop		
Conner, James Monroe	13007	Montgomery		
Conner, James P.	Rej	Bailey		
Conner, Julius Augustus	46684	Briscoe		
Conner, Kittie	39895	Hopkins	Conner, Presley Arnold	15533
Conner, M. A. Mrs.	20532	Tarrant	Conner, Jessee Russell	
Conner, M. E. Mrs.	17460	Cherokee	Conner, Jesse Jackson	
Conner, Morning Mrs.	16763	Tyler	Conner, Lewis Henry Jackson	
Conner, N. J.	28064	Hopkins		
Conner, N. Mrs.	17975	Kaufman	Conner, Joseph Hart	
Conner, Presley Arnold	15533	Hopkins		
Conner, Sarah Jane	20934	Kaufman	Conner, Shadrick James	16173
Conner, Shadrick James	16173	Navarro		
Conner, Susan A.	34325	McCulloch	Conner, William Dunn	12984
Conner, T.	26735	Van Zandt		
Conners, John	Rej	Hill		
Connolly, S. J. Mrs.	Rej	Ellis	Connolly, Owen	
Connon, James William	RejM	Hunt		
Connor, Ed Tom	25395	Harris		
Connor, M. J. Mrs.	06901	Dallas	Connor, Robert J.	
Connor, William Dunn	12984	McCulloch		
Conoley, Alexander H.	42861	Milam		
Conoly, Alice	21700	Bexar	Conoly, Clay C.	
Conor, Elmira	37495	Panola	Conor, Mickael	
Conor, Mattie E.	31460	Madison	Conor, Francis Marion	
Conrad, Emma	10327	Bexar	Conrad, John Baptiste	00340
Conrad, John Baptiste	00340	Bexar		
Consford, J. T.	Rej	San Augustine		
Conway, Charles	12466	Johnson		
Conway, J. D.	00509	Brazos		
Conway, L. H.	12613	Shelby		
Conway, Nannie	42774	Caldwell	Conway, Silas Perry	
Conway, Thomas	09091	Panola		
Conwill, John Ciseroe	15054	Dewitt		
Conwill, John Ciseroe Mrs.	41050	Dewitt	Conwill, John Ciseroe	15054
Cook, A. M.	Rej	Callahan		
Cook, Abraham James	28038	Smith		
Cook, Alice	Rej	Atascosa	Cook, Caswell Washington	12729
Cook, Allen T.	40955	Wichita		
Cook, Almira	42453	Terry	Cook, James Maderson	28686
Cook, Alpheus	11500	Johnson		
Cook, Anderson	00811	Clay		
Cook, Austin Young	11327	Anderson		
Cook, Austin Young Mrs.	46459	Smith	Cook, Austin Young	11327
Cook, Belle	43851	Gonzales	Cook, Louis Dawson	
Cook, Camelia Lou	38313	Hood	Cook, Alpheus	11500
Cook, Caswell Washington	12729	Bee		
Cook, Cynthia M.	Rej	Bexar	Cook, William Montgomery	
Cook, D. J.	Rej	Madison		
Cook, D. L.	07948	Red River		
Cook, E. E. Mrs.	Rej	Titus	Cook, Jasper	
Cook, E. J. Mrs.	10059	Ellis	Cook, George W.	
Cook, E. W.	32827	Fayette		
Cook, Elias Wilburn	35057	Fayette		
Cook, Eliza	01891	Hays	Cook, Gustave	
Cook, Eliza	22475	Titus	Cook, Jasper	
Cook, Eliza	32206	Harris	Cook, Robert Slaughter	

Index to Confederate Pension Applications

Cook, Elizabeth	Rej	Upshur	Cook, David	
Cook, Elizabeth	06235	Coleman	Cook, Francis M.	
Cook, Elizabeth	18638	Lee	Cook, William Sanford	
Cook, Elizabeth	20321	Houston	Cook, William Houston	15570
Cook, Elizabeth Frances	50974	Brewster	Cook, John Enoch	
Cook, Ella	51938	McLennan	Cook, James D.	47852
Cook, Emily	37008	Burnet	Cook, James Gwin	36267
Cook, Emily Jane	Rej	Henderson	Cook, George W.	
Cook, Emma	50607	Callahan	Cook, J. T.	50005
Cook, Ermine	39132	Brown	Cook, Nathan Fairchild	
Cook, F. A. Mrs.	41454	Red River	Cook, William Walter	
Cook, Fannie	28986	Hill	Cook, Henry Clay	
Cook, Francis Marion	00592	Caldwell		
Cook, George A.	17822	Hill		
Cook, George A. Mrs.	32343	Lampasas	Cook, George A.	17822
Cook, George Washington	27387	Grimes		
Cook, H. A. Mrs.	Rej	Travis	Cook, Eli	
Cook, Harmon	26516	Tarrant		
Cook, Henry H.	06889	Wichita		
Cook, Hulda	02941	Midland	Cook, John Andrew	
Cook, J. D.	28957	Angelina		
Cook, J. J.	13543	Titus		
Cook, J. J.	27159	Bell		
Cook, J. R.	38541	Upshur		
Cook, J. T.	50005	Callahan		
Cook, Jackie Ann	47228	Limestone	Cook, John Patillo	
Cook, James D.	47852	McLennan		
Cook, James Gwin	36267	Burnet		
Cook, James Hollis	05631	Erath		
Cook, James Maderson	28686	Coryell		
Cook, James Madison, Sr.	19546	Anderson		
Cook, James R.	25008	Hill		
Cook, James R.	51256	Atascosa		
Cook, James W. Mrs.	Rej	Harris	Cook, James W.	
Cook, Jasper Newton	47663	Red River		
Cook, John	34748	Sabine		
Cook, John Henry Mrs.	Rej	Fannin	Cook, John Henry	
Cook, John P.	12849	Gillespie		
Cook, John P.	26080	Comanche		
Cook, John Thomas Calvin	08000	Van Zandt		
Cook, John Walter Mrs.	51316	Houston	Cook, John Walter	
Cook, Joseph T.	23684	Collin		
Cook, Josiah M.	16034	Milam		
Cook, Julia Ann	41990	Fayette	Cook, Elias Wilburn	35057
Cook, L. J. Mrs.	17863	Hopkins	Cook, William Russell	
Cook, Laban M.	25192	Kent		
Cook, Laura Lavina	47282	Comanche	Cook, John P.	26080
Cook, Lizzie	29652	Dewitt	Cook, John David	
Cook, Lucinda	49335	Denton	Cook, Joseph William	
Cook, Lydia A.	31432	Kent	Cook, Laban M.	25192
Cook, M. A. Mrs.	32151	Jasper	Cook, John Bootie	
Cook, M. C. Mrs.	36856	Grimes	Cook, George Washington	27387
Cook, M. Mrs.	Rej	Erath	Cook, James Edward	
Cook, Maggie	Rej	Bexar	Cook, James Franklin	
Cook, Mahala	Rej	Travis	Cook, James Edward	
Cook, Malinda	01780	Harris	Cook, Vol. R.	
Cook, Martha Ann	07814	Fayette	Cook, John C.	
Cook, Martha E. T.	10503	Wilbarger	Cook, Henry H.	06889
Cook, Mary	25006	Morris	Cook, James Jasper	

Index to Confederate Pension Applications

Name	No.	County	Related	No.
Cook, Mary A.	15940	Eastland	Cook, James Hollis	05631
Cook, Mary Ann	06684	Henderson	Cook, Benjamin Parker	—
Cook, Mary E.	47754	Tarrant	Cook, Samuel Walter	42048
Cook, Mary F.	22442	Tarrant	Cook, Richard Shelton	—
Cook, Mary Frances	39578	Montague	Cook, James D.	—
Cook, Mary L.	Rej	Hamilton	Cook, William Washington	—
Cook, Mary L.	38237	Cherokee	Cook, Green Berry	—
Cook, Matilda A.	33456	Clay	Cook, Harmon	26516
Cook, Mattie A.	40854	Hemphill	Cook, Addison Forbs	—
Cook, N. E. Mrs.	23539	Henderson	Cook, John Riley	—
Cook, N. J. Mrs.	31702	Montague	Cook, Solomon	—
Cook, Nancy	41213	Cass	Cook, Thomas Mayberry	37224
Cook, Nancy D.	28927	Shelby	Cook, Newton Franklin	—
Cook, Nancy Jane	46507	Harris	Cook, Thomas Annisy	—
Cook, O.	01737	Guadalupe	—	
Cook, Parthenia	39366	Cass	Cook, James W.	—
Cook, Penelope R.	34755	Falls	Cook, John	—
Cook, R. S.	09901	Parker	—	
Cook, Rebecca	03684	Smith	Cook, David	—
Cook, Richard F.	Rej	Lavaca	—	
Cook, S. A. Mrs.	17109	Jack	Cook, William C.	—
Cook, S. A. Mrs.	43808	Van Zandt	Cook, John Thomas Calvin	08000
Cook, S. D.	25164	Young	—	
Cook, Samantha L.	41328	Travis	Cook, William Austin	16717
Cook, Samuel	00861	Collin	—	
Cook, Samuel D.	21500	Parker	—	
Cook, Samuel Walter	42048	Tarrant	—	
Cook, Sarah A.	21703	Anderson	James Madison, Sr.	19546
Cook, Sarah E.	20691	Collin	Cook, Samuel	00861
Cook, Susan Ann	23457	Caldwell	Cook, Francis Marion	00592
Cook, Susan C.	33968	Henderson	Cook, Francis Marion	—
Cook, Tempie J.	41496	Hill	Cook, John Bunyan	—
Cook, Thomas	19915	Montague	—	
Cook, Thomas J.	14280	Hood	—	
Cook, Thomas Jefferson	15571	Houston	—	
Cook, Thomas Jefferson Mrs.	51384	Houston	Cook, Thomas Jefferson	15571
Cook, Thomas Mayberry	37224	Cass	—	
Cook, Viney Ragan	Rej	Houston	Ragan, Alfred Asa	13143
Cook, W. H.	Rej	Houston	—	
Cook, W. H.	Rej	Knox	—	
Cook, W. H.	Rej	Mitchell	—	
Cook, W. H.	12280	Bosque	—	
Cook, W. J.	00462	Bosque	—	
Cook, W. L.	05027	Jasper	—	
Cook, W. W.	Rej	Camp	—	
Cook, William Andrew	26212	Tom Green	—	
Cook, William Artus	32998	Erath	—	
Cook, William Austin	16717	Travis	—	
Cook, William E.	12109	Red River	—	
Cook, William Francis	28717	Clay	—	
Cook, William Francis Mrs.	38873	Clay	Cook, William Francis	28717
Cook, William Henderson	39751	Nacogdoches	—	
Cook, William Henderson Mrs.	50743	Nacogdoches	Cook, William Henderson	39751
Cook, William Houston	15570	Houston	—	
Cook, William J.	23445	Mitchell	—	
Cook, William Jasper	10035	Collin	—	
Cook, William Reuben Mrs.	42643	Erath	Cook, William Reuben	—
Cook, William S.	12112	Robertson	—	
Cook, Zipporah Adeline	34770	Tarrant	Cook, Richard Royston	—

Index to Confederate Pension Applications

Name	App. No.	County	Veteran	Vet. App. No.
Cooke, Annie E.	37703	Waller	Cooke, Hugh	
Cooke, Elizabeth Ann	38463	Bandera	Cooke, William G.	17303
Cooke, George Martin Mrs.	Rej	Johnson	Cooke, George Martin	
Cooke, Hattie Grimes	34225	Harrison	Cooke, Samuel Alonza	
Cooke, Henry Clay	39237	Dallas		
Cooke, Jasper Newton	10427	Milam		
Cooke, Mary Elizabeth	21020	Milam	Cooke, Jasper Newton	10427
Cooke, William G.	17303	Bandera		
Cooksey, Catherine	26873	Mitchell	Cooksey, Samuel	
Cooksey, E. M.	28346	Bell		
Cooksey, Elizabeth H.	35188	Gonzales	Cooksey, Andrew Jackson	
Cooksey, James W.	00306	Bell		
Cooksey, Sam	Rej	Mitchell		
Cooksey, Sarah Ann	38825	Denton	Cooksey, Joseph Hill	
Cooksey, William M. Mrs.	42608	Knox	Cooksey, William M.	
Cooley, C. H. Mrs.	40006	Titus	Cooley, John Franklin	36485
Cooley, Ellen B.	00394	Bexar	Cooley, Simeon W.	
Cooley, John Franklin	36485	Titus		
Cooley, Katherine Milligan	49799	Limestone	Milligan, Henry Johnson	
Coombs, Daniel	31756	Harris		
Coon, David Calvin	23117	Delta		
Coon, Emily	26818	Delta	Coon, David Calvin	23117
Coon, Leander W.	Rej	Burnet		
Coon, M. A. Mrs.	41441	Hunt	Coon, William Paily	25004
Coon, Martha A.	51283	Kaufman	Coon, Robert Anderson	32133
Coon, N. A. Mrs.	31052	Burnet	Coon, John Marian	
Coon, Robert Anderson	32133	Kaufman		
Coon, Virginia	17393	Burnet	Coon, Leander Wilson	
Coon, William Paily	25004	Hunt		
Cooner, Mary Jane	12793	Comanche	Cooner, William M.	
Cooner, S. E.	15967	Marion	Cooner, Franklin Noah	
Cooney, Sarah	49713	Wilbarger	Cooney, Patrick	
Coonrad, T. J.	15278	Grayson		
Coonrod, John	09923	Fannin		
Coonrod, John Mrs.	37177	Fannin	Coonrod, John	09923
Coonrod, Susan E.	12449	Hunt	Coonrod, John L.	
Cooper, Albert James	21701	Fisher		
Cooper, Amelia	42744	Sabine	Cooper, James Amberson	33200
Cooper, Barshaba	25853	McLennan	Cooper, William J.	
Cooper, Burwell Zacariah	16050	Mitchell		
Cooper, Cain	03385	Rains		
Cooper, Charles Carter	18139	Montague		
Cooper, Charles S.	00464	Bosque		
Cooper, Christopher Columbus	14772	Burnet		
Cooper, Columbus	09933	Matagorda		
Cooper, Cynthia	28311	Henderson	Cooper, James Henry	22206
Cooper, Eliza	33113	Travis	Cooper, Albert Newton	
Cooper, Elizabeth Monroe	04555	Hall	Cooper, William M.	
Cooper, Elizabeth Ricks	41669	Bexar	Cooper, George W.	39942
Cooper, Emily L.	49709	Haskell	Cooper, Thomas Jefferson	
Cooper, F. P. Mrs.	Rej	Bosque	Cooper, Benjamin Franklin	
Cooper, Florence C.	Rej	Floyd	Cooper, Samuel Thomas	49052
Cooper, Frank M.	10174	Orange		
Cooper, Frank M. Mrs.	45787	Orange	Cooper, Frank M.	10174
Cooper, George A.	Rej	Nolan		
Cooper, George W.	Rej	Menard		
Cooper, George W.	39942	Bexar		
Cooper, Harriet	05093	Dewitt	Cooper, Sylvester	
Cooper, Henry	Rej	Burleson		

Index to Confederate Pension Applications

Name	No.	County	Soldier	No.
Cooper, Henry	08594	Tarrant	—	
Cooper, Henry	34574	Johnson	—	
Cooper, Henry Mrs.	20304	Tarrant	Cooper, Henry	08594
Cooper, Henry Payton	Rej	Bosque	—	
Cooper, Henry Wilkerson	15924	Liberty	—	
Cooper, J. B.	22148	Hunt	—	
Cooper, J. C.	Rej	Colorado	—	
Cooper, J. H.	09411	Eastland	—	
Cooper, J. M.	10056	Eastland	—	
Cooper, J. M.	23113	Dallas	—	
Cooper, J. P.	18906	Dallas	—	
Cooper, James	38056	Johnson	—	
Cooper, James Amberson	33200	Sabine	—	
Cooper, James Franklin	21357	Shelby	—	
Cooper, James Green	18418	Taylor	—	
Cooper, James Henry	22206	Henderson	—	
Cooper, James Monroe	12989	McLennan	—	
Cooper, James Thomas	14127	Bexar	—	
Cooper, James Thomas Mrs.	34439	Bexar	Cooper, James Thomas	14127
Cooper, James W.	Rej	Fannin	—	
Cooper, Janie	51849	Johnson	Cooper, Henry	34574
Cooper, John	01630	Grayson	—	
Cooper, John Alexander	44042	Coleman	—	
Cooper, John F.	15925	Liberty	—	
Cooper, John M.	07062	Dallas	—	
Cooper, John Thomas	07192	Ellis	—	
Cooper, Johnathan Carter	36251	Colorado	—	
Cooper, Joseph Smith	09810	Hamilton	—	
Cooper, L. P. Mrs.	42546	Waller	Cooper, William	
Cooper, Laura Sophronia	37103	Mitchell	Cooper, Burwell Zacariah	16050
Cooper, Lecie	20960	Fannin	Cooper, Calvin	—
Cooper, Lem	16391	Rusk	—	
Cooper, M. E. Mrs.	21613	Ellis	Cooper, John Thomas	07192
Cooper, M. E. Mrs.	29235	Liberty	Cooper, Henry Wilkerson	15924
Cooper, M. E. Mrs.	35567	Fisher	Cooper, Albert James	21701
Cooper, Maggie M.	42485	El Paso	Cooper, Joseph Smith	09801
Cooper, Malinda Jane	50454	Hill	Cooper, William F.	46117
Cooper, Margaret	21702	Grayson	Cooper, John	01630
Cooper, Mary	04170	Van Zandt	Cooper, J. M.	
Cooper, Mary	35294	Montague	Cooper, Charles Carter	18139
Cooper, Mary	42538	Jefferson	Cooper, H. Thomas	—
Cooper, Mary	48039	Tarrant	Cooper, James D.	—
Cooper, Mary Ann	11826	Bowie	Cooper, Matthew	—
Cooper, Mary D.	Rej	Dallas	Cooper, John Maoy	—
Cooper, Mary Elizabeth	25650	Burnet	Cooper, Christopher Columbus	14772
Cooper, Mary Elizabeth	40741	Colorado	Cooper, Johnathan Carter	36251
Cooper, Mary Elizabeth	41135	Smith	Cooper, William Lewis	—
Cooper, Mary Ella	51449	Harris	Cooper, Isaac	—
Cooper, Mary Lee	21125	Dallas	Cooper, John M.	07062
Cooper, Mary M.	03947	Travis	Cooper, Sam C.	—
Cooper, Mary M.	19519	Coleman	Cooper, Quintas Leonidas	—
Cooper, Mary Susan	35835	Erath	Cooper, James Monroe	12989
Cooper, Mattie	Rej	Dallas	Cooper, William	—
Cooper, Milla E.	40883	Shelby	Cooper, James Franklin	21357
Cooper, Molly	49523	Johnson	Cooper, James	38056
Cooper, Newton Lee Mrs.	17839	Hood	Cooper, Newton Lee	—
Cooper, Peter	14753	Brown	—	
Cooper, R. A. Mrs.	35414	Rains	Cooper, Cain	03385
Cooper, R. E. Mrs.	36308	Franklin	Cooper, Thomas Marial	17188

Index to Confederate Pension Applications

Name	No.	County	Veteran	No.
Cooper, Rebecca Catherine	06549	Falls	Cooper, Benjamin F.	
Cooper, Richmond C.	25922	Knox		
Cooper, Robert Lee	07015	Hill		
Cooper, Rufus K.	19614	Nueces		
Cooper, S. A. Mrs.	05321	Montague	Cooper, R. J.	
Cooper, S. A. Mrs.	32274	Taylor	Cooper, James Green	18418
Cooper, S. C.	22287	Ellis		
Cooper, S. C. Mrs.	08041	Erath	Cooper, J. H.	
Cooper, S. H.	16392	Rusk		
Cooper, Samuel Thomas	49052	Floyd		
Cooper, Sarah A. E.	06275	Shelby	Cooper, W. H.	
Cooper, Sarah E.	25986	San Augustine	Cooper, Robert Lee	07015
Cooper, T. A.	28470	Shelby		
Cooper, Thaddeus S.	02120	Hunt		
Cooper, Thomas Jefferson	19182	Panola		
Cooper, Thomas Marial	17188	Franklin		
Cooper, W. A.	06834	Wise		
Cooper, W. H.	31440	Sabine		
Cooper, W. L.	30358	Leon		
Cooper, William	Rej	Collin		
Cooper, William	12598	Rusk		
Cooper, William F.	46117	Hill		
Cooper, William Joseph	37497	Bell		
Coopwood, Martha	Rej	Bastrop	Coopwood, John	
Cootes, Harriet	15025	Dallas	Cootes, George W.	
Coots, Caroline	Rej	Bexar	Coots, George W.	
Cope, C. W.	Rej	Limestone		
Cope, Francis R.	27587	Camp	Cope, John W.	20158
Cope, J. M.	07438	Bell		
Cope, John W.	20158	Camp		
Cope, Mason L.	15043	Denton		
Cope, William Henry Harrison	27158	Camp		
Cope, Z. V. Mrs.	37869	Camp	Cope, William Henry Harrison	27158
Copeland, Benjryman Lewis	36015	Parker		
Copeland, Benjryman Lewis Mrs.	40293	Parker	Copeland, Benjryman Lewis	36015
Copeland, C. J. Mrs.	16272	Polk	Copeland, John J.	
Copeland, C. M.	17275	Anderson		
Copeland, C. M. Mrs.	35248	Anderson	Copeland, C. M.	17275
Copeland, Callie	45877	Childress	Copeland, William M.	18697
Copeland, Daniel	02959	Milam		
Copeland, F. C.	10263	Henderson		
Copeland, Fannie M.	16003	McLennan	Copeland, John B.	
Copeland, Frances	41497	Titus	Copeland, James Lafayette	
Copeland, Georgia A.	26993	Montague	Copeland, Charles Calvin	
Copeland, Henry	24086	Leon		
Copeland, J. A.	11105	Robertson		
Copeland, J. B. Mrs.	38948	Hill	Copeland, James Baley	15697
Copeland, J. E. Mrs.	19811	Jones	Copeland, James M.	06035
Copeland, J. K. P.	26161	Ellis		
Copeland, James Alexander	17924	Johnson		
Copeland, James Baley	15697	Hill		
Copeland, James M.	06035	Smith		
Copeland, James Marion	14822	Cass		
Copeland, Jonathan Craig	13946	McCulloch		
Copeland, Josias S.	42185	Eastland		
Copeland, Kissiah Mrs.	09832	Coryell	Copeland, J. B.	
Copeland, L. C. Mrs.	18386	Smith	Copeland, Alexander K.	
Copeland, Laura	44047	Collin	Copeland, Hilliard Andrew	
Copeland, Laura C.	50833	Dallas	Copeland, Joab	

Index to Confederate Pension Applications

Copeland, M. A. Mrs.	17775	Cass	Copeland, Richard McNutty	—
Copeland, M. A. Mrs.	26424	Erath	Copeland, Jonathan Craig	13946
Copeland, M. J. Mrs.	18765	Johnson	Copeland, James Alexander	17924
Copeland, Martha C.	13418	Leon	Copeland, J. P.	—
Copeland, Mary	30966	Cass	Copeland, Daniel	02959
Copeland, Mary E.	46276	Parmer	Copeland, Ruben C.	36585
Copeland, Mary Susan	45466	Harris	Copeland, Henry Clay	—
Copeland, R. G.	11939	Harrison	—	—
Copeland, R. M.	09413	Galveston	—	—
Copeland, Richard Marion	Rej	Bell	—	—
Copeland, Ruben C.	36585	Cherokee	—	—
Copeland, S. F.	28981	Eastland	—	—
Copeland, S. M. Mrs.	46213	Cass	Copeland, James Marion	14822
Copeland, W. L.	25844	Wise	—	—
Copeland, William M.	18697	Motley	—	—
Copelin, M. E. Mrs.	03853	Titus	Copelin, T. B.	—
Copley, John McLemore Mrs.	19753	Dallas	Copley, John McLemore	—
Coppedge, May	Rej	Hunt	Coppedge, James J.	—
Coppedge, Serena A.	26244	Hopkins	Coppedge, Charles Clark	—
Copperell, Charles S. (Copprell)	10264	Henderson	—	—
Copprell, Sarah Jane	11946	Henderson	Copprell, Charles S. (Copperell)	10264
Corbell, Felix Houston	09010	Erath	—	—
Corbell, Maloney E.	32614	Wilbarger	Corbell, Felix Houston	09010
Corbett, Carrie	38489	Travis	Corbett, Meredith	—
Corbin, Addie	29906	Jefferson	Corbin, William	—
Corbin, Drury H.	11802	Bell	—	—
Corbin, Matilda C. Perrigo	51822	Dallas	Perrigo, Greenberry Jordan	—
Corbin, Nancy	38883	Johnson	Corbin, William Henry	22352
Corbin, S. A. Mrs.	17869	Hopkins	Corbin, Granville	—
Corbin, William Henry	22352	Johnson	—	—
Corbitt, James Madison Mrs.	26675	Hill	Corbitt, James Madison	—
Corbitt, M. A.	22844	Shelby	—	—
Cordaway, Manuel	06626	Karnes	—	—
Corder, Assenieth E.	22330	Taylor	Corder, Jacob Elias	—
Corder, Elba Ann	27825	Wilson	Corder, Sheppard Bayles	—
Corder, Etna G.	Rej	Wichita	Corder, Joel Gillum	—
Corder, M. C. Mrs.	13930	Lee	Corder, M. C.	—
Corder, S. M. P.	13575	Wharton	—	—
Corder, Susan V.	18525	Wharton	Corder, S. M. P.	13575
Cordray, Isabell Elizabeth	27383	Caldwell	Cordray, Charles Sidney	—
Cordray, Martha	31279	Sabine	Cordray, Daniel C.	—
Cordway, Angela M.	Rej	Hidalgo	Cordway, J. C.	02368
Cordway, J. C.	02368	Karnes	—	—
Cork, B. B.	00105	Dallas	—	—
Cork, K. S.	25876	Bowie	—	—
Corker, E. A. Mrs.	07764	Smith	Corker, J. A.	—
Corker, Elizabeth	12389	Harris	Corker, Robert Henry	—
Corley, A.	27560	Nacogdoches	—	—
Corley, A. B.	19257	Shelby	—	—
Corley, A. E. Mrs.	07947	Red River	Corley, John A.	—
Corley, Andrew Boswell	01836	Harrison	—	—
Corley, B. L.	30159	Tarrant	—	—
Corley, Carrie M.	13040	Red River	Corley, A. P.	—
Corley, David P.	12868	Grimes	—	—
Corley, Gabriel Rudolphus Wash.	17158	Shelby	—	—
Corley, H. K.	08650	Comanche	—	—
Corley, James	50035	Hopkins	—	—
Corley, John R.	43431	Bowie	—	—
Corley, Josephine	33892	Bell	Corley, Thomas Haynes	17317

Index to Confederate Pension Applications

Name	App#	County	Soldier	Soldier App#
Corley, P. L. Mrs.	12239	Freestone	Corley, Sam M.	—
Corley, Ruth	Rej	Henderson	Corley, L. A.	—
Corley, S. J. Mrs.	17106	Harrison	Corley, Andrew Boswell	01836
Corley, Sam M.	09879	Freestone	—	
Corley, Sare Elizabeth	32944	Shelby	Corley, Gabriel Rudolphus Wash.	17158
Corley, Sophia E.	45156	Tarrant	Corley, B. L.	30159
Corley, Tabitha Bedford	38582	Hill	Corley, Catlick Petty	—
Corley, Thomas Haynes	17317	Bell	—	
Cormany, M. E. Mrs.	51741	McLennan	Cormany, Martin Luther	51040
Cormany, Martin Luther	51040	McLennan	—	
Corn, Kate Roff	36478	Brazoria	Roff, Nighram Burnett	—
Cornelison, J. E. Mrs.	26901	Clay	Cornelison, William Franklin	—
Cornelison, Jesse Porter	11286	Wilson	—	
Cornelius, A. F. Mrs.	15294	Gregg	Cornelius, Preston Owen	07664
Cornelius, Cynthia	43886	Dallas	Cornelius, Miles Anderson	41352
Cornelius, E. C. Mrs.	23101	Hunt	Cornelius, Francis Daniel	—
Cornelius, Emma	Rej	Parker	Cornelius, Warren Woodson	—
Cornelius, Miles Anderson	41352	Hill	—	
Cornelius, Pheba K.	12461	Jack	—	
Cornelius, Preston Owen	07664	Smith	—	
Corner, James A.	RejM	Dimmit	—	
Cornett, Augustus Americus	14433	Tarrant	—	
Cornett, J. T.	26070	Motley	—	
Cornett, James K.	32547	Johnson	—	
Cornett, Lucy J.	36906	Bexar	Cornett, Augustus Americus	14433
Cornett, M. M. Mrs.	21381	Uvalde	Cornett, William	—
Cornitius, Louise	20933	Harris	Cornitius, Walter Albert Bernard	19006
Cornituis, Walter Albert Bernard	19006	Harris	—	
Cornley, M. A. Mrs.	04866	Nacogdoches	Cornley, William	—
Cornutt, Susan F.	06581	San Saba	Cornutt, Reuben	—
Cornwall, Elizabeth P.	46201	Dallas	Walker, Edward Lea	19769
Cornwall, Richard Owens	42892	Dallas	—	
Cornwell, G. A.	19404	Anderson	—	
Cornwell, Jerome N.	01127	Delta	—	
Cornwell, Josie	Rej	Eastland	Cornwell, George Washington	—
Cornwell, M. A. Mrs.	00020	Anderson	Cornwell, William	—
Corona, Antonia G. De	04315	Webb	—	
Corona, Pas	Rej	Webb	—	
Corona, Ylario	04318	Webb	—	
Correll, Edward Monroe	23052	Jackson	—	
Corrigan, Thomas	Rej	Brazoria	—	
Corry, George Crimes	21606	Van Zandt	—	
Corry, Mary Francis	33934	Van Zandt	Corry, George Crimes	21606
Corsbie, James Blakemore	01730	Guadalupe	—	
Corsbie, S. F. Mrs.	19357	Caldwell	Corsbie, James Blakemore	01730
Corzine, S. A. Mrs.	14478	Wilbarger	Corzine, G. J.	—
Corzine, Sallie	12835	Fannin	Corzine, William R.	—
Cosby, J. W.	Rej	Milam	—	
Cosby, M. E. Mrs.	41238	Dawson	Cosby, Lemuel Pryor	—
Cosby, Mollie	36903	Robertson	Cosby, William Wallace	—
Cosgrove, John E.	06406	Ellis	—	
Coskrey, J. C.	22207	Coryell	—	
Cosper, Columbus H.	09930	Lampasas	—	
Cosper, Elizabeth	51496A	Travis	Cosper, Hampton Monroe	45800
Cosper, Hampton Monroe	45800	Gaines	—	
Cosper, Lue Braddock	48065	Uvalde	Braddock, John D. (Joseph)	10222
Cosper, Martha Elizabeth	21225	Fisher	Cosper, Proccer Charles Clements	11020
Cosper, Proccer Charles Clements	11020	Lampasas	—	
Cosper, Rebecca A.	13128	Lampasas	Cosper, Columbus H.	09930

Index to Confederate Pension Applications

Name	App. No.	County	Veteran	Vet. No.
Costellom, J. B.	02527	Lavaca	—	—
Costen, E. P.	Rej	Jack	—	—
Coston, Amanda L.	51986	Dallas	Coston, Owen Franklin	—
Coston, Ann Eliza	31553	Titus	Coston, James Francis	—
Coston, Doyle O'hanlon	10693	Matagorda	—	—
Coston, Hannah A.	38669	Matagorda	Coston, Doyle O'hanlon	10693
Coston, Isom Alexander Mrs.	50064	Delta	Coston, Isom Alexander	—
Coston, J. F.	07374	Titus	—	—
Cotharn, Joseph D.	35206	Milam	—	—
Cotharn, Rosa	38100	Milam	Cotharn, Joseph D.	35206
Cothran, J. C.	Rej	Lamar	—	—
Cothran, Martha Ezell L.	45682	Freestone	Cothran, Thomas Jefferson	—
Cothran, Thursey Mrs.	05006	Denton	Cothran, John	—
Cothran, Wiley Monroe	Rej	Leon	—	—
Cotney, Harriet	31803	Harris	Cotney, James Alexander	—
Cotrell, J. W.	06036	Smith	—	—
Cotten, Joab Harris	06750	Comanche	—	—
Cotten, L. Elizabeth	22491	Hamilton	Cotten, Joab Harris	06750
Cotten, N. L. Mrs.	Rej	Henderson	Cotten, William Thomas	50312
Cotten, Peter Clay	13687	Anderson	—	—
Cotten, Virginia W.	28071	Anderson	Cotten, Peter Clay	13687
Cotten, William Thomas	50312	Henderson	—	—
Cotter, J. J.	Rej	Kimble	—	—
Cotter, John Thomas	23366	Camp	—	—
Cotter, Joseph Benjamin	33764	Cass	—	—
Cotter, Joseph Benjamin Mrs.	42248	Cass	Cotter, Joseph Benjamin	33764
Cottingham, Frances E.	06087	Travis	—	—
Cottingham, Mary	07044	Robertson	Cottingham, D. P.	—
Cottingham, Sophronia	Rej	Bexar	Cottingham, John Rowe	—
Cotton, A. B. Teague Mrs.	39856	Llano	Teague, Colonel Boggs	—
Cotton, Alexander Black	14969	Coryell	—	—
Cotton, Andrew E.	00366	Bexar	—	—
Cotton, Eula	22153	McLennan	Cotton, James Melbon	—
Cotton, Fannie	29769	Bexar	Cotton, William Lindsey	10602
Cotton, I. A. Mrs.	36701	Coryell	Cotton, Alexander Black	14969
Cotton, J. J.	09704	Harris	—	—
Cotton, J. K. P.	14320	Marion	—	—
Cotton, Joseph, Sr.	10732	Polk	—	—
Cotton, L. J. Mrs.	00294	Bell	Cotton, Robert B.	—
Cotton, Louisa Elizabeth	20735	Hardin	Cotton, Jefferson Napoleon	—
Cotton, M. A. Mrs.	Rej	Hunt	Cotton, Allen	—
Cotton, Napoleon B.	00576	Burnet	—	—
Cotton, Richard Calhoun	19514	Taylor	—	—
Cotton, Shedrick M.	13422	Limestone	—	—
Cotton, Shedrick M. Mrs.	Rej	Travis	Cotton, Shedrick M.	13422
Cotton, Thomas Wiley Mrs.	33608	Tarrant	Cotton, Thomas Wiley	—
Cotton, William	16902	Walker	—	—
Cotton, William Lindsey	10602	Caldwell	—	—
Couch, Aaron Thomas	23077	Bell	—	—
Couch, Doctor Franklin	34543	Karnes	—	—
Couch, Elisha Peter	19045	Hunt	—	—
Couch, Fannie	37419	Cherokee	Couch, Henry Andrew	17453
Couch, Henry Andrew	17453	Cherokee	—	—
Couch, J. Calvin	Rej	Hamilton	—	—
Couch, James Thomas	10126	Lamar	—	—
Couch, Jesse Pinkney	08762	McLennan	—	—
Couch, Jimmie Mrs.	49707	Kaufman	Couch, William J.	19074
Couch, L. C. Mrs.	19911	Hunt	Couch, Elisha Peter	19045
Couch, M. J. Mrs.	05562	Kaufman	Couch, J. M.	—

Index to Confederate Pension Applications

Name	No.	County	Related	No.
Couch, Mahalia J.	32873	Lamar	Couch, James Thomas	10126
Couch, Martha Ann	32726	Bell	Couch, Aaron Thomas	23077
Couch, Mary	Rej	Howard	Couch, Josiah Calvin	—
Couch, Mary	03687	Smith	Couch, Drew	—
Couch, N. E. Mrs.	37859	Karnes	Couch, Doctor Franklin	34543
Couch, Nancy	29805	McLennan	Couch, Laufton Kinslow	—
Couch, Robert Newton Mrs.	46906	Ellis	Couch, Robert Newton	—
Couch, William J.	19074	Kaufman	—	—
Couey, Ella	51209	McLennan	Couey, Isham Houze	30700
Couey, Isham Houze	30700	McLennan	—	—
Coughanour, Lucinda A.	33224	Dallas	Coughanour, Richard David	—
Coughlin, John P.	14402	San Saba	—	—
Coughtry, Hattie	45281	Dallas	Coughtry, Joseph R.	—
Couling, H.	Rej	Duval	—	—
Coulon, Ida Collins	34016	Shelby	Coulon, Arthur Ad	—
Coulter, J. J.	22696	Caldwell	—	—
Council, Belle	32093	Johnson	Council, Benjamin Franklin	31009
Council, Benjamin Franklin	31009	Johnson	—	—
Council, Martha M.	23408	Nacogdoches	Council, Joseph Carson	—
Countryman, Martha	40809	Grimes	Countryman, John Marion	—
Counts, Henrieta Virginia	43657	Collin	Counts, Hasten Alexander	—
Counts, Julia Francis	41142	Shelby	Counts, Simeon	—
Counts, Mary E.	Rej	Tarrant	Counts, William	—
Counts, N. E. Mrs.	32727	Fannin	Counts, Thomas Bradford	25757
Counts, Thomas Bradford	25757	Fannin	—	—
Counts, W. M. Mrs.	50495	Ellis	Counts, William	—
Coupland, Andrew Adams	32648	Kaufman	—	—
Coupland, Sallie Battle	36473	Kaufman	Coupland, Andrew Adams	32648
Courrage, Mary	06807	Galveston	Courrage, Hilare	—
Coursey, Amanda	32294	Donley	Coursey, Virgil	20868
Coursey, J. A.	17270	Anderson	—	—
Coursey, Virgil	20868	Donley	—	—
Coursey, W. L.	11168	Wheeler	—	—
Courson, John Holcomb	02002	Hopkins	—	—
Courson, Nina	34975	Hopkins	Courson, John Holcomb	02002
Court, James M.	02271	Jefferson	—	—
Court, Julia Ann	11498	Jefferson	Court, James M.	02271
Court, Louise Mohl	Rej	Harris	Court, Charles	—
Court, Paul P.	23848	Aransas	—	—
Court, S. E. Mrs.	31804	Comanche	Court, Thomas Jefferson	—
Court, Sarah Chapman	45928	Aransas	Court, Paul P.	23848
Courtney, Carrie	38641	Robertson	Courtney, Jesse Myer	23058
Courtney, Frank	07033	Robertson	—	—
Courtney, G. A. Mrs.	36458	Angelina	Courtney, Reuben William	14565
Courtney, Jacob	03386	Rains	—	—
Courtney, Jesse Myer	23058	Robertson	—	—
Courtney, Mary Elizabeth	10589	Bell	Courtney, Frank	—
Courtney, Ollie Matilda	Rej	Kerr	Courtney, Thomas Jefferson	—
Courtney, Reuben William	14565	Angelina	—	—
Courtney, Sarah E.	04867	Nacogdoches	Courtney, Amos	—
Courtney, Sol J.	16740	Trinity	—	—
Courtney, Solomon	05417	Hill	—	—
Courtney, Vinson M.	14564	Angelina	—	—
Couser, M. E. Mrs.	Rej	Collin	Couser, Marvin Alexander	—
Cousins, Celia Jane	50681	Somervell	Cousins, John Richards	—
Cousins, Mary H.	07520	McLennan	Cousins, Richard H.	—
Cousins, Sallie A.	22146	Colorado	Cousins, William M.	11860
Cousins, William M.	11860	Colorado	—	—
Coussins, Julia G.	27759	Sabine	Coussins, William Thomas	—

Index to Confederate Pension Applications

Name	App #	County	Veteran	Vet App #
Covey, G. C. Mrs.	40884	Rains	Covey, George C.	13964
Covey, George C.	13964	Rains	—	—
Covey, Jacob	01602	Grayson	—	—
Covey, Jennetta	03852	Taylor	Covey, William V.	—
Covey, Laura	21348	Erath	Covey, William Harrison	—
Covey, Maria M.	Rej	Val Verde	Covey, Joseph	—
Covey, S. W. Mrs.	31838	Rockwall	Covey, Enoch	—
Covey, Thomas Jefferson Mrs.	Rej	Upshur	Covey, Thomas Jefferson	—
Covin, J. W.	02390	Kaufman	—	—
Covin, Jim L., Sr.	26208	Harrison	—	—
Covin, Martha Jane	15825	Kaufman	Covin, J. W.	—
Covington, Emma McJimsey	35312	Gregg	Covington, William Jasper	—
Covington, H. H.	14377	Red River	—	—
Covington, Joe Sorrelo	26606	Wise	—	—
Covington, John Calvin	20597	Nacogdoches	—	—
Covington, Julia	34976	Tarrant	Covington, Joe Sorrelo	26606
Covington, Larkin Anderson	06612	Falls	—	—
Covington, M. B. Mrs.	15119	Falls	Covington, Larkin Anderson	06612
Covington, M. Leodicea	35697	Nacogdoches	Covington, John Calvin	20597
Covington, Queen Elizabeth	43961	Mills	Covington, Leonard	—
Covington, S. A. Mrs.	38382	Hopkins	Covington, William M.	21704
Covington, Sarah J.	32431	Red River	Covington, Maston Crawford	—
Covington, W. E.	13263	Cherokee	—	—
Covington, William M.	21704	Hunt	—	—
Cowan, C. Mrs.	15419	Hays	Cowan, Samuel Franklin	—
Cowan, Eliza	Rej	Foard	Cowan, William Wallace	—
Cowan, J. H.	00765	Cherokee	—	—
Cowan, James Washington Mrs.	Rej	Bell	Cowan, James Washington	—
Cowan, John Abraham	25593	Lampasas	—	—
Cowan, Margaret Elizabeth	23362	Hill	Cowan, William Marion	—
Cowan, Margrette Ann	43935	Kaufman	Cowan, Montgomery	—
Cowan, Maria Alice	20736	Tarrant	Cowan, Benjamin Franklin	—
Cowan, Mary	Rej	Grayson	Cowan, Maron C.	—
Cowan, Mary	RejM	Collin	—	—
Cowan, Nathan V.	22724	Coryell	—	—
Cowan, Sam	39104	Shelby	—	—
Cowan, Sarah Ann	06142	Carson	Cowan, A. P.	—
Cowan, Sebron Montgomery	02687	Limestone	—	—
Cowan, Stephen D.	34640	Young	—	—
Cowan, Susan E.	39150	Lampasas	Cowan, John Abraham	25593
Cowan, William H.	19536	Navarro	—	—
Coward, Ara	51834	Lamar	Coward, Lawrence Brock	47449
Coward, John N.	17284	Angelina	—	—
Coward, Lawrence Brock	47449	Lamar	—	—
Coward, Miranda	14495	Harris	—	—
Coward, W. Elizabeth	32279	Harris	Coward, Miranda	14495
Coward, Willis B.	Rej	Harris	—	—
Cowart, A. C. Mrs.	Rej	Wood	Cowart, Andrew Jackson	17024
Cowart, Andrew Jackson	17024	Wood	—	—
Cowart, Bessie	43634	San Jacinto	Cowart, Benjamin Franklin	—
Cowart, J. C.	15193	Freestone	—	—
Cowart, John William	20616	Randall	—	—
Cowart, John William Mrs.	31558	Randall	Cowart, John William	20616
Cowart, Julia A.	07958	San Saba	Cowart, Stephen B.	—
Cowart, L. E.	12560	Navarro	—	—
Cowart, Lawrence Pictman	28061	Tyler	—	—
Cowart, Mary	36366	Tarrant	Cowart, Seaborn	07269
Cowart, Nancy	39595	Tyler	Cowart, Lawrence Pictman	28061
Cowart, Sarah J.	34904	Palo Pinto	Cowart, Thomas Jones	22819

Index to Confederate Pension Applications

Cowart, Seaborn	07269	Kaufman	—	—
Cowart, Stephen B.	03601	San Saba	—	—
Cowart, Thomas Jones	22819	Palo Pinto	—	—
Cowden, James Monroe	06418	Lamar	—	—
Cowell, Winnie M.	48069	Red River	Cowell, J. Riley	—
Cowen, Joseph B.	13397	Kaufman	—	—
Cowen, Zilphia Gayosa	17551	Dallas	Gayosa, Ferdinand	—
Cowey, Hester Ann	29148	Guadalupe	Cowey, Charles William	—
Cowley, Andrew Jackson	40321	Dallas	—	—
Cowley, Josephine	49063	Dallas	Cowley, Andrew Jackson	40321
Cowling, Sidneyham W. Mrs.	23419	Wise	Cowling, Sidneyham W.	—
Cowsar, Elizabeth	46478	Knox	Cowsar, John Samuel	—
Cowser, Mandy A.	15978	McCulloch	Cowser, William F.	—
Cox, A. A. Mrs.	Rej	Wilson	Cox, Frank Marion	—
Cox, A. J.	26775	Limestone	—	—
Cox, Allen R.	22208	Robertson	—	—
Cox, Anna B.	18510	Walker	Cox, Lewis Alexander	—
Cox, Annie	12345	Erath	Cox, J. G.	05689
Cox, Arch	30046	Kinney	—	—
Cox, Asberry Garrison	20705	Upshur	—	—
Cox, Ausborn P.	04024	Upshur	—	—
Cox, Belle C. Muller	46011	Wilbarger	Muller, Christopher	—
Cox, C. B. Mrs.	Rej	Falls	Cox, John Marshal	—
Cox, C. C.	25139	Eastland	—	—
Cox, C. E. Mrs.	32456	Tarrant	Cox, Stephen M.	—
Cox, Callie	48005	Lamar	Cox, Robert Bowen	—
Cox, Carolina B.	50528	Falls	Cox, J. M.	—
Cox, Charles W.	19857	Maverick	—	—
Cox, Clarinda Sutton	51783	Jefferson	Cox, Samuel William	—
Cox, Clemmie	50579	Hunt	Cox, Joe P.	49360
Cox, Curd	29832	Burnet	—	—
Cox, Cynthia Jane	46159	Grayson	Cox, William M.	—
Cox, D. B.	10041	Dallas	—	—
Cox, D. J. Mrs.	17369	Bowie	Cox, J. J.	—
Cox, E. C. Mrs.	16645	Tarrant	Cox, James	09103
Cox, E. E. Mrs.	16684	Titus	Cox, Edward	—
Cox, E. T. Mrs.	25781	Uvalde	Cox, William David	—
Cox, Edwin Ruby	13520	Tarrant	—	—
Cox, Elias	01781	Harris	—	—
Cox, Eliza	28482	Limestone	Cox, Obediah	21706
Cox, Eliza B.	Rej	Walker	Cox, James Rambean	—
Cox, Elizabeth	09755	Stephens	Cox, Ephraim	07170
Cox, Elizabeth Louvicia	Rej	Tarrant	Cox, George	—
Cox, Ellen B.	09138	Bastrop	Cox, Ruben W.	04919
Cox, Elmira M.	21404	Taylor	Cox, Jeremiah Elexas	—
Cox, Emily Jane	21705	Taylor	—	—
Cox, Emma V.	49439	Hill	Cox, John Pinckney	—
Cox, Emma W.	38413	Cherokee	Cox, James Lafayette	17445
Cox, Ephraim	07170	Carson	—	—
Cox, Fannie	41690	Kinney	Cox, Arch	30046
Cox, Fannie Elizabeth	49622	Dawson	Cox, William Harrison	—
Cox, George W.	15910	Leon	—	—
Cox, H. P.	17175	Wood	—	—
Cox, Harvey Harrison	11988	Jackson	—	—
Cox, Henry White	35985	Harris	—	—
Cox, Huldah Ann	50641	Comanche	Cox, Carmelion Jackson	—
Cox, Ike	30116	Kinney	—	—
Cox, Irene	45564	Palo Pinto	Cox, James Cary	—
Cox, Issac Harvey	12964	Leon	—	—

Index to Confederate Pension Applications

Cox, J. B.	17487	Collin	—	—
Cox, J. D.	02441	Lamar	—	—
Cox, J. G.	05689	Erath	—	—
Cox, J. L.	23232	Panola	—	—
Cox, J. P.	23057	Hunt	—	—
Cox, J. T.	27207	Lampasas	—	—
Cox, James	Rej	Dallas	—	—
Cox, James	09103	Tarrant	—	—
Cox, James Edwin	21193	Shelby	—	—
Cox, James Henry	20975	Wood	—	—
Cox, James Lafayette	17445	Cherokee	—	—
Cox, James Nelson	16305	Red River	—	—
Cox, James W.	31991	Bexar	—	—
Cox, Jim S.	50501	Titus	—	—
Cox, Joe P.	49360	Hunt	—	—
Cox, John	08747	Kimble	—	—
Cox, John	10636	Gonzales	—	—
Cox, John C.	16624	Smith	—	—
Cox, John H.	22539	Erath	—	—
Cox, John Henry	00815	Childress	—	—
Cox, John R.	35246	Harris	—	—
Cox, John W.	13242	Brazoria	—	—
Cox, John Wesley	Rej	Lampasas	—	—
Cox, John Wesley Mrs.	42489	Coryell	Cox, John Wesley	—
Cox, Joseph B.	23160	Eastland	—	—
Cox, Joseph H.	14253	Harris	—	—
Cox, Joseph P.	36855	Cass	—	—
Cox, Joshua	30117	Kinney	—	—
Cox, Josiah Green	04773	Eastland	—	—
Cox, Julia	47782	Ellis	Cox, William Alexander	—
Cox, Julius M.	14296	Houston	—	—
Cox, L. H. Mrs.	RejM	Hunt	—	—
Cox, Lawrence Scarbrough	12755	Caldwell	—	—
Cox, Lou A.	42257	Hunt	Cox, Newton H.	—
Cox, Louis Ibzan	49901	Eastland	—	—
Cox, Louiza U.	23119	Hill	Cox, Charley Gates	—
Cox, M. A. Mrs.	35120	Dallas	Cox, Jerry Melvin	—
Cox, M. B.	47637	Limestone	—	—
Cox, M. F. Mrs.	46847	Erath	Cox, John Henry	—
Cox, M. I. Mrs.	05178	Bell	Cox, James	—
Cox, M. J. Mrs.	02881	Llano	Cox, William B.	—
Cox, M. J. Mrs.	49391	Taylor	Cox, Allen R.	22208
Cox, M. L. Mrs.	40098	Red River	Cox, James Nelson	16305
Cox, Maggie A.	23074	Grayson	Cox, William Allison	—
Cox, Margaret E.	18112	McLennan	Cox, George Simpson	—
Cox, Marietta	10367	Ellis	Cox, Robert B.	01244
Cox, Martha A.	11890	Eastland	Cox, Thomas H.	10914
Cox, Martha E.	31051	Shelby	Cox, Wright P.	—
Cox, Martha Elizabeth	17166	Tarrant	Cox, John Henry	00815
Cox, Mary	Rej	Wood	Cox, C. W.	—
Cox, Mary H.	16794	Upshur	Cox, Samuel Alexander	—
Cox, Mary J.	17920	Jackson	Cox, Harvey Harrison	11988
Cox, Mary Jane Riddles	50163	Nolan	Riddles, Hiram Franklin	—
Cox, Mattie Cox	46104	Hidalgo	Cox, Aaron Washington	—
Cox, Mattie Ellen	50989	Eastland	Cox, Louis Ibzan	49901
Cox, Melvina Jane	10423	Midland	Cox, W. B.	—
Cox, Metella J.	17023	Wood	Cox, William W.	12683
Cox, Mollie	33125	Kinney	Cox, Ike	30116
Cox, Mollie H.	29549	Tarrant	Cox, James Fred	—

Index to Confederate Pension Applications

Name	No.	County	Veteran	No.
Cox, N. C. Mrs.	20409	Caldwell	Cox, Lawrence Scarbrough	12755
Cox, N. J. Mrs.	03449	Robertson	Cox, S. W.	—
Cox, Nancy Ann	05177	Bell	Cox, James W.	—
Cox, Nancy Jane	37014	Nacogdoches	Cox, John William	—
Cox, Obediah	21706	Limestone	—	—
Cox, Polk	30618	Coke	—	—
Cox, Rebecca	50810	Cass	Cox, Robert Tedanals	—
Cox, Robert B.	01244	Ellis	—	—
Cox, Robert M.	08574	Grimes	—	—
Cox, Ruben W.	04919	Bastrop	—	—
Cox, S. E. Mrs.	27146	Dallas	Cox, Andrew Jackson	—
Cox, S. E. Mrs.	45019	Shelby	Cox, James Edwin	21193
Cox, S. J. Mrs.	36845	Upshur	Cox, Asberry Garrison	20705
Cox, Sallie F.	36421	Collin	Cox, J. B.	17487
Cox, Sallie J.	33684	Wood	Cox, James Henry	20975
Cox, Samuel Jefferson	22555	Kaufman	—	—
Cox, Samuel Jefferson Mrs.	50335	Kaufman	Cox, Samuel Jefferson	22555
Cox, Samuel Lee	21707	Wichita	—	—
Cox, Sarah	34947	Guadalupe	Cox, John	10636
Cox, Sarah Ann	06010	Morris	Cox, Thomas Jefferson	—
Cox, Sarah Ann	33969	Mitchell	Cox, Polk	30618
Cox, Sarah E.	15911	Leon	Cox, Issac Harvey	12964
Cox, Sarah P.	19347	Wood	Cox, John Alexander	—
Cox, Sarah S.	30883	Grimes	Cox, Arthur Beard	—
Cox, Susan	39953	Ellis	Cox, William	27118
Cox, Susan A.	21420	Eastland	Cox, Josiah Green	04773
Cox, T. H.	09629	Erath	—	—
Cox, Thomas	00871	Collin	—	—
Cox, Thomas H.	10914	Eastland	—	—
Cox, Tina	32107	Parker	Cox, Edwin Hansford	—
Cox, V. C. Mrs.	25052	Angelina	Cox, Elias	01781
Cox, W. E.	11680	Van Zandt	—	—
Cox, W. H.	05363	Grayson	—	—
Cox, W. J., Sr.	32764	Leon	—	—
Cox, W. M.	16547	Shelby	—	—
Cox, W. T.	Rej	Grayson	—	—
Cox, William	27118	Comanche	—	—
Cox, William A.	39390	Wood	—	—
Cox, William H.	11205	Eastland	—	—
Cox, William H.	43900	Cooke	—	—
Cox, William Pinkney	18825	Bell	—	—
Cox, William Thomas	13794	Falls	—	—
Cox, William W.	12683	Wood	—	—
Coy, Candelaria C. Mrs.	00397	Bexar	Coy, Antonio S.	—
Coyle, Alexander Irvin	34068	Falls	—	—
Coyle, George Worthy	Rej	Ward	—	—
Coyle, James	07716	Galveston	—	—
Coyle, M. J. Mrs.	37205	Falls	Coyle, Alexander Irvin	34068
Coyle, Mary E.	50616	Hopkins	Coyle, James Acklen	—
Coyle, Nancy Jane	23094	Dallas	Coyle, Walker Jones	—
Cozart, Urunta Helen	18356	Shelby	Cozart, Matthew Henderson	—
Cozart, Walter A., Sr.	25019	Taylor	—	—
Cozby, F. M. Mrs.	Rej	Cooke	Cozby, John Chatten Calhoun	11731
Cozby, J. A.	29617	Hamilton	—	—
Cozby, J. A. Mrs.	37454	Hamilton	Cozby, J. A.	29617
Cozby, John Chatten Calhoun	11731	San Jacinto	—	—
Cozby, Margarette Anna	17744	Hamilton	Cozby, Roswell Greene	—
Cozby, Robert M.	13371	Hunt	—	—
Crabb, Columbus Warren	15954	Madison	—	—

Index to Confederate Pension Applications

Crabb, G. K., Sr.	23116	Lavaca	—	—
Crabb, Hulda Eugene	34223	Madison	Crabb, Columbus Warren	15954
Crabb, J. D.	Rej	Wise	—	—
Crabb, J. L.	00923	Comanche	—	—
Crabb, Lizzie	33018	Fannin	Crabb, Robert Logan	25581
Crabb, Malissa	36941	Wise	Crabb, William Burton	19339
Crabb, Permelia J.	08258	Comanche	—	—
Crabb, Robert Logan	25581	Fannin	—	—
Crabb, T. J.	04166	Van Zandt	—	—
Crabb, William Burton	19339	Wise	—	—
Crable, J. M.	10733	Rains	—	—
Crabtree, Eliza	26707	Delta	Crabtree, James McCuller	—
Crabtree, Joe Mrs.	50259	Van Zandt	Crabtree, John William	30153
Crabtree, John William	30153	Van Zandt	—	—
Crabtree, Martha	29959	Grayson	Crabtree, Rhesa (Reece)	—
Crabtree, Martha Adeline	22452	Hopkins	Crabtree, John Whittier	—
Crabtree, W. B.	34889	Hardin	—	—
Cracker, George	13815	Galveston	—	—
Craddock, M. J. Mrs.	09837	Grayson	Craddock, W. W.	—
Craddock, Sarah Ellen	47831	Erath	Craddock, John David	—
Craddock, Sarah J.	17026	Wood	Craddock, William James	—
Craddock, Thomas H.	46437	Dallas	—	—
Craft, Charity P.	06842	Wise	Craft, Joshua B.	—
Craft, J. S.	19083	Lampasas	—	—
Craft, James Wiley	19080	Kimble	—	—
Craft, Mary A.	41484	Bastrop	Craft, William Samuel	—
Craft, Thomas J.	25858	Denton	—	—
Crafton, R. W.	24118	McLennan	—	—
Crager, Martin	00059M	Angelina	—	—
Crager, Mary J.	35492	Angelina	Crager, Francis A.	—
Craig, A. M.	31541	Tarrant	—	—
Craig, Alice	43514	Johnson	Craig, James Patterson	—
Craig, Archibald Neblo Mrs.	27090	Tarrant	Craig, Archibald Neblo	—
Craig, Archie Mason	05197	Houston	—	—
Craig, Belle	12373	Glasscock	Craig, J. M.	03887
Craig, Blanche	50113	Victoria	Craig, William Johnson	—
Craig, C. J. Mrs.	14087	Nacogdoches	Craig, William	—
Craig, C. L.	40962	Dallas	—	—
Craig, E. R. Mrs.	22784	Tarrant	Craig, Robert Lysander	—
Craig, Emma	48094	Ellis	Craig, Edward Everett	—
Craig, J. F.	20882	Ellis	—	—
Craig, J. M.	03887	Tom Green	—	—
Craig, J. P.	14459	Upshur	—	—
Craig, Joel	26425	Sabine	—	—
Craig, Kate	46805	Navarro	Craig, William Henry	—
Craig, Margaret B.	37023	Nueces	Craig, Milton Philip	—
Craig, Margaret M.	18882	Coleman	Craig, Robert G.	—
Craig, Mary C.	49734	Delta	Craig, Thomas Jefferson	—
Craig, Missouri Elizabeth	29456	Houston	Craig, Archie Mason	05197
Craig, P. B.	20703	Rusk	—	—
Craig, Pheby	33852	Liberty	Craig, Thomas W.	28987
Craig, Ruth L.	02003	Hopkins	Craig, A. F.	—
Craig, Susan	Rej	Freestone	Craig, Samuel R.	—
Craig, Thomas W.	28987	Liberty	—	—
Craig, W. J.	03302	Parker	—	—
Craig, William P.	23463	Collin	—	—
Craigen, Edward	17948	Jefferson	—	—
Craigen, Ellen	18616	Jefferson	Craigen, Edward	17948
Craighead, Bytha E.	Rej	Dallas	Craighead, William E.	30909

Index to Confederate Pension Applications

Name	App#	County	Veteran	Vet#
Craighead, John S.	41376	Wilson	—	—
Craighead, Mattie Elliott	34656	McLennan	Elliott, William Monroe	26053
Craighead, William Alexander Mrs.	47441	Stephens	Craighead, William Alexander	—
Craighead, William E.	30909	Dallas	—	—
Craigo, Emma	37082	Red River	Craigo, James Thomas	—
Crain, Anna Corinne	26180	Harris	Crain, Ephrim Jesse	—
Crain, Annie Elizabeth	18760	Bowie	Crain, Thomas Freeman	—
Crain, Billy	Rej	Fannin	—	—
Crain, Elizabeth S.	17962	Karnes	Crain, George W.	02369
Crain, George W.	02369	Karnes	—	—
Crain, J. D.	Rej	Matagorda	—	—
Crain, James M.	14236	Galveston	—	—
Crain, M. J. Mrs.	02442	Lamar	Crain, W. T.	—
Crain, Mary A.	07316	Montague	Crain, Giles B.	—
Crain, Mattie P.	11925	Gregg	John R., Dr.	—
Crain, Mollie	33068	Tarrant	Crain, John L.	—
Crain, Stephen	31805	Nolan	—	—
Crain, W. B. Mrs.	45734	Williamson	Crain, Uriah Yorke	—
Crain, W. W.	Rej	Fannin	—	—
Craine, Harrison	17428	Cass	—	—
Crainer, Frank	17682	Galveston	—	—
Cramer, Edward Christopher	10948	Galveston	—	—
Cramer, Henrietta	17212	Travis	Cramer, (Ferdinand) Theo. Emil	03904
Cramer, Mary E.	20044	Galveston	Cramer, Edward Christopher	10948
Cramer, S. A. Mrs.	46701	Morris	Cramer, Samuel Joseph	—
Cramer, Sarah J.	40823	Harris	Cramer, Joseph	—
Cramer, Theodore Emil (Ferdinand)	03904	Travis	—	—
Crane, A. J.	Rej	Erath	—	—
Crane, Andrew Jackson	26859	Childress	—	—
Crane, E. C. Mrs.	28783	Bexar	Crane, Eugene Colton	13217
Crane, Elizabeth	31792	Angelina	Crane, Jerry C.	00051
Crane, Eugene	Rej	Bexar	—	—
Crane, Eugene Colton	13217	Bexar	—	—
Crane, James Madison	33202	Gregg	—	—
Crane, Jerry C.	00051	Angelina	—	—
Crane, Leonard V.	21708	Ellis	—	—
Crane, Lola A.	36766	Childress	Crane, Andrew Jackson	26859
Crane, M. A. Mrs.	33371	Gregg	Crane, James Madison	33202
Crane, M. J. Mrs.	29575	Uvalde	Crane, William Ambrose	—
Crane, M. M.	24152	Bowie	—	—
Crane, Nick	14563	Angelina	—	—
Crane, William H.	19028	Hopkins	—	—
Cranford, Angie B.	22521	Franklin	Cranford, John White	—
Cranford, Elias R.	36755	Ellis	—	—
Cranford, J. W.	Rej	Franklin	—	—
Cranford, J. W.	32928	Navarro	—	—
Cranford, L. A. Mrs.	36293	Panola	Cranford, Virgil Dennis	—
Cranford, Leobian Shelton	35150	Harris	—	—
Cranford, Leobian Shelton Mrs.	37463	Harris	Cranford, Leobian Shelton	35150
Cranford, Thomas	08369M	Hunt	—	—
Crass, Mark L.	20782	Lampasas	—	—
Craton, William G.	22836	Upshur	—	—
Craven, Lottie E.	01629	Grayson	Craven, Newton S.	—
Craven, Mary A.	22978	Burnet	Craven, Richard Walker	03948
Craven, Mary M.	01626	Grayson	Craven, Elijah J.	—
Craven, Richard Walker	03948	Travis	—	—
Craver, Abigail	01837	Harrison	Craver, Henry	—
Craver, Elizabeth	37545	Harrison	Craver, James Philip	—
Craver, Fannie E.	22667	Hall	Craver, David Hilliard	—

Index to Confederate Pension Applications

Craver, Joseph	12885	Harrison		
Craver, K. F. Mrs.	05823	Cass	Craver, Mike	
Craver, Mollie	28196	Wood	Craver, Samuel M.	17025
Craver, S. M. Mrs.	42753	Collin	Craver, S. M.	
Craver, Samuel M.	17025	Wood		
Cravey, Andrew Jackson	03625	Shelby		
Cravey, Elizabeth	21035	Shelby	Cravey, Andrew Jackson	03625
Cravey, Henry C.	42852	Kent		
Cravey, J. H.	01782	Harris		
Cravey, James M.	08808	Upshur		
Cravey, Mary Elizabeth	45311	Kent	Cravey, Henry C.	42852
Cravey, William R.	15376	Harris		
Crawford, Amanda M.	18224	Palo Pinto	Crawford, James Morrow	05644
Crawford, Annie	50861	Henderson	Crawford, William Anderson	
Crawford, Annie E.	50698	Nacogdoches	Crawford, Oliver Henry Perry	
Crawford, Callie C.	51047	Wise	Crawford, Henry P.	32603
Crawford, Charles Hume	13595	Jefferson		
Crawford, Daniel Steele	01283	Ellis		
Crawford, David O.	34527	Brown		
Crawford, E. J. Mrs.	49023	Dallas	Crawford, Merriwether Lewis	
Crawford, Eliza	Rej	Montgomery	Crawford, Francis Marion	
Crawford, Eliza A.	04274	Waller	Crawford, Robert W.	
Crawford, Elizabeth	50745	Dallas	Crawford, Joseph Alexander	
Crawford, Elizabeth Ann	18814	Anderson	Crawford, William Benjamin	
Crawford, Felix G.	39163	Live Oak		
Crawford, Felix G. Mrs.	50792	Live Oak	Crawford, Felix G.	39163
Crawford, Francis A.	14823	Cass		
Crawford, G. W.	12079	Nacogdoches		
Crawford, George Andrew	44032	Coryell		
Crawford, George Andrew Mrs.	Rej	Coryell	Crawford, George Andrew	44032
Crawford, George Marion	37760	Medina		
Crawford, George W.	04637	Angelina		
Crawford, Henry P.	32603	Wise		
Crawford, J. B.	Rej	Ellis		
Crawford, J. L.	03108	Navarro		
Crawford, J. M.	Rej	Johnson		
Crawford, James H.	03600	San Saba		
Crawford, James Morrow	05644	Erath		
Crawford, James P.	14776	Anderson		
Crawford, James Thomas	16152	Nacogdoches		
Crawford, James Warren	45756	Upshur		
Crawford, John	09678	Collin		
Crawford, John E.	13853	Houston		
Crawford, John T., Sr.	25208	Gray		
Crawford, Josiah	06992	Erath		
Crawford, L. S. Mrs.	19187	Panola	Crawford, A. J.	
Crawford, Luella	17267	Harris	Crawford, Lytle	15375
Crawford, Lytle	15375	Harris		
Crawford, M. E. Mrs.	45329	Nacogdoches	Crawford, James Thomas	16152
Crawford, M. E. Mrs.	47318	Lamar	Crawford, Ellsworth Robert	
Crawford, Mary E.	27437	McLennan	Crawford, Joel Hayden	
Crawford, Mattie	26069	Ellis	Crawford, Daniel Steele	01283
Crawford, Mattie	45878	Dallas	Crawford, James Allen	
Crawford, Mildred	33217	Coleman	Crawford, Charles Sinclair	
Crawford, O. H. P.	Rej	Nacogdoches		
Crawford, P. A. Mrs.	42597	Medina	Crawford, George Marion	37760
Crawford, R. H.	Rej	Brewster		
Crawford, S. L.	Rej	Comanche		
Crawford, Sallie Josephine	35008	Brazos	Crawford, Charles Lewis	

Index to Confederate Pension Applications

Name	App #	County	Veteran	Vet App #
Crawford, Samuel H. Mrs.	47519	Denton	Crawford, Samuel H.	—
Crawford, Susan Caroline	43803	Panola	Crawford, Edmund Turner	—
Crawford, T. J.	19241	San Augustine	—	
Crawford, Thomas S.	23073	Wood	—	
Crawford, W. H. Mrs.	12082	Nacogdoches	Crawford, W. H.	—
Crawford, W. Y.	11578	Nacogdoches	—	
Crawford, William	15793	Johnson	—	
Crawford, William C.	19912	Hale	—	
Crawford, William Hamilton	Rej	Bowie	—	
Crawley, Harrington M.	09919	Cooke	—	
Crawley, Robert Ransom	27957	Fannin	—	
Crawley, Sarah B.	41550	Fannin	Crawley, Robert Ransom	27957
Crawson, Jennie	RejM	Fannin	—	
Crayton, Adline	02611	Leon	Crayton, J. P.	—
Crayton, Margaret Louise	45925	Wichita	Crayton, Thomas Jefferson	31806
Crayton, Rebecca H.	42721	Harris	Crayton, Walter Looney	—
Crayton, Thomas Jefferson	31806	Dimmit	—	
Creager, Larkin Ferrol	28422	Erath	—	
Creager, Larkin Ferrol Mrs.	35058	Erath	Creager, Larkin Ferrol	28422
Creager, Martha	39314	Grayson	Creager, Thomas H.	—
Creagle, Sallie	06251	Van Zandt	Creagle, Henry	—
Creamer, Garison C.	06747	Comanche	—	
Creamer, John C.	19071	Kaufman	—	
Creasey, Mary E.	15594	Houston	Creasey, William Harrison	—
Creasy, M. C. Mrs.	Rej	Clay	Creasy, John Burton	—
Creath, J. H.	11356	Brazos	—	
Crebbs, Mattie	27404	Colorado	Crebbs, William Conrad	21011
Crebbs, William Conrad	21011	Colorado	—	
Creech, Aaron C.	19258	Shelby	—	
Creecy, Susie	30684	Franklin	Creecy, George Taylor	—
Creecy, T. Asberry	05679	Denton	—	
Creed, Joseph M.	17377	Brazos	—	
Creed, Joseph M. Mrs.	43224	Brazos	Creed, Joseph M.	17377
Creekmore, A. J.	11088	Parker	—	
Creekmore, Elizabeth Francis	21439	Bowie	Creekmore, Henry Clay	13720
Creekmore, Henry Clay	13720	Bowie	—	
Creekmore, Mary A.	07169	Cass	Creekmore, J. C.	—
Creekmore, R. F.	03304	Parker	—	
Creel, Eusilia Shaw	49980	Dallas	Shaw, Josiah	—
Creel, Harris	18249	Polk	—	
Creel, Isaiah	33638	Cherokee	—	
Creel, James Tyler	16273	Polk	—	
Creel, James Tyler Mrs.	41831	Polk	Creel, James Tyler	16273
Creel, Martha	39397	Cherokee	Creel, Isaiah	33638
Creel, Neelie M.	42525	Jackson	Creel, Felix Thomas	—
Creel, S. A. Mrs.	30027	Nacogdoches	Creel, Elijah	—
Creighton, T. N.	02443	Lamar	—	
Crelia, S. C.	18408	Tarrant	—	
Crenshaw, Edward Hodge	49789	Hill	—	
Crenshaw, Eula	Rej	McLennan	Crenshaw, John Benjamin	39484
Crenshaw, John Benjamin	39484	McLennan	—	
Crenshaw, Lewis Doison	18547	Wise	—	
Crenshaw, M. E. Mrs.	10474	Tarrant	Crenshaw, M. L.	01608
Crenshaw, M. L.	01608	Grayson	—	
Crenshaw, M. V.	03905	Travis	—	
Crenshaw, M. W. Mrs.	22620	Wise	Crenshaw, Lewis Doison	18547
Crenshaw, Mary E.	45996	McLennan	Crenshaw, Drewery Micajah	—
Crenshaw, Nettie	34132	Howard	—	
Crenshaw, Nicholas A.	11598	Palo Pinto	—	

Index to Confederate Pension Applications

Name	App. #	County	Veteran	Vet. App. #
Crenshaw, Sallie E.	Rej	Brazos	Crenshaw, Samuel Perry	—
Crenshaw, Thomas C.	50138	Harris	—	—
Cresswell, A. N. Mrs.	47774	Johnson	Cresswell, Roford Wert	—
Cresswell, William	09340	Tarrant	—	—
Creswell, Jane Vaginni	33814	Hill	Creswell, Lennard Collins	11955
Creswell, Lennard Collins	11955	Hill	—	—
Creswell, Lytle B.	03774	Tarrant	—	—
Creswell, Pheoba Ann	06995	Erath	Creswell, William Anderson	—
Creswell, R. L.	23099	Erath	—	—
Cretsinger, Mary Hardman	51535	Palo Pinto	Hardman, Squire Christopher	—
Cretsinger, S. J.	11092	Parker	—	—
Crew, S. M.	20604	Johnson	—	—
Crewes, Rebecca	10850	Brazos	Crew(e)s, James	08528M
Crews, Cora	17984	Kendall	Crews, Thomas C.	—
Crews, H. E. Mrs.	50105	Hamilton	Crews, Fleming J.	—
Crews, Henry Harrison Mrs.	50693	Kaufman	Crews, Henry Harrison	—
Crews, James	08528M	Brazos	—	—
Crews, James Alvan	36117	Coleman	—	—
Crews, James M.	13174	Rusk	—	—
Crews, John Jefferson	25490	Tyler	—	—
Crews, Lora D.	36538	Eastland	Crews, James Alvan	36117
Crews, Nancy	48051	Red River	Crews, Beverly Jones	—
Crews, S. J. Mrs.	Rej	Tyler	Crews, John Jefferson	25490
Crews, Simeon Jasper	34301	Cherokee	—	—
Crews, Simeon Jasper Mrs.	35979	Cherokee	Crews, Simeon Jasper	34301
Crews, T. A.	07884	Kendall	—	—
Cribbs, P. A.	03094	Motley	—	—
Crick, Cornelia W.	Rej	Wichita	Crick, Charles Newton	—
Crider, James Henry	30620	Limestone	—	—
Crider, Mattie J.	37815	Limestone	Crider, James Henry	30620
Crider, Sarah A.	38337	Travis	Crider, Martin Calvin	—
Crim, Lucinda	18312	Rusk	Crim, Zacariah H.	—
Crimm, M. L. Mrs.	20142	Van Zandt	Crimm, Thomas Newton	04167
Crimm, Thomas Newton	04167	Van Zandt	—	—
Criner, Mary L.	34977	Johnson	Criner, Sam Green	30164
Criner, Sam Green	30164	Johnson	—	—
Crisman, James Morris	27077	Tarrant	—	—
Crisman, James Morris Mrs.	41015	Tarrant	Crisman, James Morris	27077
Crisp, Elizabeth	19030	Hopkins	Crisp, Carroll	—
Crisp, John Henry	26808	Anderson	—	—
Crisp, P. W.	04852	Nacogdoches	—	—
Crisp, Wealth Jane	04168	Van Zandt	Crisp, William Riley	—
Crisswell, William (Criswell)	08885	Parker	—	—
Crist, F.	28103	Taylor	—	—
Crist, George L.	29540	Jasper	—	—
Crist, W. H.	09086	Navarro	—	—
Criswell, David Peace	18241	Parker	—	—
Criswell, Franklin G.	10721	Palo Pinto	—	—
Criswell, J. H.	Rej	Colorado	—	—
Criswell, M. J. Mrs.	20854	Haskell	Criswell, David Peace	18241
Criswell, Martha C.	49921	Van Zandt	Criswell, William C.	—
Criswell, Sarah	31016	Parker	Cris(s)well, William	08885
Crittenden, Bettie	05559	Kaufman	Crittenden, John	—
Crittenden, Gilbert Lafayette	11721	Fannin	—	—
Crittenden, Martha Elizabeth	39890	Fannin	Crittenden, Gilbert Lafayette	11721
Critz, Ella R.	51343	Coleman	Critz, George Edward	22209
Critz, George Edward	22209	Concho	—	—
Crocker, Arzena	38595	San Augustine	Crocker, George Washington	27863
Crocker, George Washington	27863	San Augustine	—	—

Index to Confederate Pension Applications

Name	App. No.	County	Veteran	App. No.
Crocker, Jane	36956	Titus	Crocker, T. J.	33574
Crocker, Jennie M.	38709	Wise	Crocker, Peter Harry	12682
Crocker, Peter Harry	12682	Wise	—	—
Crocker, T. J.	33574	Navarro	—	—
Crockett, A. E. Mrs.	39533	Fort Bend	Crockett, William Henry Harrison	36610
Crockett, Agnes Mercer	33859	Travis	Crockett, Edward Richardson	10594
Crockett, Callie	03683	Smith	Crockett, John C.	—
Crockett, Edward Richardson	10594	Bell	—	—
Crockett, John Richardson	09692	Fayette	—	—
Crockett, Lizzie Scholl	20701	Kerr	Crockett, Andrew Monroe	—
Crockett, Mary Francis	42938	Taylor	Crockett, Walter Preston	27291
Crockett, S. J. Mrs.	25163	Comanche	Crockett, Anthony C.	—
Crockett, Walter Preston	27291	Scurry	—	—
Crockett, William Henry Harrison	36610	Fort Bend	—	—
Crofford, M. A. Mrs.	17356	Bosque	Crofford, Simeon Lafayette	—
Croft, E. D.	09962	Hunt	—	—
Croft, M. E. Mrs.	12224	Harrison	George W., Sr.	—
Croft, M. J. Mrs.	36035	Limestone	Croft, Richard T.	—
Croft, W. C.	14259	Harrison	—	—
Crofton, Cora Love	43123	Taylor	Crofton, Marcus Lenox	—
Cromeans, Andrew Jackson	11895	Edwards	—	—
Cromeans, Francis Marion	43654	Burnet	—	—
Cromeans, Thomas	15068	Edwards	—	—
Cromeens, J. W.	05984	Leon	—	—
Cromer, E. A. Mrs.	18492	Upshur	Cromer, John G.	—
Cromer, Jarrett	04414	Williamson	—	—
Cromer, John C.	14821	Cass	—	—
Cromer, S. H.	Rej	Wood	—	—
Cromer, Thomas L.	12302	Cass	—	—
Cromwell, A. G.	03993	Trinity	—	—
Cromwell, Sina Ann	08782	Panola	Cromwell, Washington Laf.05020	13298
Cromwell, Washington Lafayette	05020	Panola	—	—
Cronan, Fannie	33205	Harris	Cronan, Thomas Winfor	—
Crone, Franklin M.	30699	Wood	—	—
Crook, Georgia S.	Rej	McLennan	Crook, Samuel Joshua	—
Crook, Joseph L.	29973	Morris	—	—
Crook, M. A. Mrs.	03519	Rusk	Crook, Lafayette	—
Crook, M. Violet	23088	Houston	Crook, Alfred Barry	—
Crook, Susan	Rej	Smith	Crook, Ruben Franklin	—
Crook, Ulta	33586	Lamar	Crook, George McKenzie	—
Crooks, Anna Elizabeth	27580	Titus	Crooks, Louis M.	—
Crooks, Thomas J.	10541	Grayson	—	—
Crooks, William A.	12579	Red River	—	—
Croom, John Wesley	10054	Eastland	—	—
Cropper, J. S.	Rej	Hamilton	—	—
Crosby, E. Victoria	20179	Falls	Crosby, Thomas Eli	—
Crosby, Elizabeth	34821	Hardin	Crosby, William	30759
Crosby, J. F.	05304	Montague	—	—
Crosby, Ophelia Dexter	09822	Blanco	Crosby, Charles Adolphus	—
Crosby, W. R.	07317	Montague	—	—
Crosby, William	06411	Ellis	—	—
Crosby, William	30759	Hardin	—	—
Crosley, J. A. Mrs.	21458	Bosque	Crosley, Valentine Vanhuse	20993
Crosley, Valentine Vanhuse	20993	Bosque	—	—
Cross, Elizabeth Jane	47721	Lamar	Cross, William Calvin	—
Cross, Emma Rebecca	28328	Fannin	Cross, James Harvel	—
Cross, Francis Marion	06598	Brown	—	—
Cross, H. C.	07809	Fannin	—	—
Cross, Homer C.	23122	Bosque	—	—

Index to Confederate Pension Applications

Name	App#	County	Veteran	Vet App#
Cross, J. F.	Rej	Van Zandt	—	
Cross, J. J.	00108	Atascosa	—	
Cross, J. T.	07452	Coleman	—	
Cross, James Daniel	13936	Limestone	—	
Cross, James Franklin	16857	Van Zandt	—	
Cross, James R.	02004	Hopkins	—	
Cross, Josie E.	38098	Travis	Cross, Thomas Jefferson	21560
Cross, Judy C.	00975	Cooke	Cross, Albert M.	—
Cross, Julia	36276	Liberty	Cross, James Daniel	13936
Cross, L. L.	Rej	Lamar	—	
Cross, Martha Sebella	03682	Smith	Cross, Joel	—
Cross, Mary M.	26998	Montague	Cross, Elcona C.	—
Cross, Mary P.	Rej	Hill	Cross, William J.	—
Cross, Ruda	03231	Palo Pinto	—	
Cross, Ryla J.	04482	Wise	—	
Cross, Sallie M.	40166	Falls	Cross, Micaja Morgan	—
Cross, Sarah W.	30232	Hunt	Cross, James Franklin	16857
Cross, Susan Jane	06024	Smith	Cross, William W.	—
Cross, Thomas E.	16673	Tarrant	—	
Cross, Thomas Jefferson	21560	Taylor	—	
Cross, Virgil A. S.	11345	Bell	—	
Crossland, A. M.	09734	Navarro	—	
Crossland, Lucinda	19068	Jones	Crossland, Henry Strong	—
Crossland, Mary Elizabeth	43767	Nacogdoches	Crossland, William John	21531
Crossland, William John	21531	Nacogdoches	—	
Crossley, Bilpah L.	14508	Eastland	—	
Crossley, P. G.	09005	Eastland	—	
Crosslin, Caroline	15854M	Lamar	—	
Crosson, James Murray	16764	Tyler	—	
Crouch, Albert Gallatin	04877	Nacogdoches	—	
Crouch, Charles Louis	48072	Hays	—	
Crouch, Jane	51853	Hays	Crouch, Charles Louis	48072
Crouch, Jane C.	Rej	Rusk	Crouch, Joseph C.	—
Crouch, John A.	35282	Harrison	—	
Crouch, Martha Ann	40656	Johnson	Crouch, John Andrew	—
Crouch, Mary E.	42469	Coryell	Crouch, William Pleasant	23133
Crouch, Sarah Jane	05649	Harrison	Crouch, Isaac	—
Crouch, Susan T.	22210	Nacogdoches	Crouch, Albert Gallatin	04877
Crouch, W. F.	30961	Brazoria	—	
Crouch, William Pleasant	23133	Camp	—	
Crout, Mary Jane	50599	Denton	Crout, Walter Wm. Henry Wash.	—
Crow, Anna H.	47740	Taylor	Crow, William Pickens	—
Crow, Bettie	24976	Parker	Crow, Solomon McCall	—
Crow, Coleman C.	15792	Johnson	—	
Crow, David Franklin	18484	Upshur	—	
Crow, David Ile	29194	Lee	—	
Crow, Dollie R.	23197	Johnson	Crow, Coleman C.	15792
Crow, Florence	45817	Fisher	Crow, David Ile	29194
Crow, Isaac	26568	Comanche	—	
Crow, J. A.	27994	Hardin	—	
Crow, J. A., Sr.	08988	Cass	—	
Crow, J. V.	09835	Grayson	—	
Crow, James William	02961	Milam	—	
Crow, Jane	42225	Bell	Crow, Jesse Jackson	—
Crow, John C.	25460	Red River	—	
Crow, M. I.	Rej	Houston	—	
Crow, Mansel Smith	18475	Tyler	—	
Crow, Mary Ann	27705	Tom Green	Crow, Thomas English	17607
Crow, Moses M.	21110	Rusk	—	

Index to Confederate Pension Applications

Name	App. No.	County	Veteran	Vet. No.
Crow, Phebe A.	05378	Grayson	Crow, William H.	—
Crow, Rachel Anna	35430	Jasper	Crow, Mansel Smith	18475
Crow, Robert	10463	Rusk	—	—
Crow, Ruth M.	51044	Scurry	Crow, William M.	47044
Crow, S. C. Mrs.	24137	Tarrant	Crow, Andrew Jackson	—
Crow, Sarah Jane	12511	Milam	Crow, James William	02961
Crow, Solomon	Rej	Parker	—	—
Crow, Susan A.	05779	Dallas	Crow, C. C.	—
Crow, Thomas English	17607	El Paso	—	—
Crow, Thomas T.	37366	Haskell	—	—
Crow, W. W.	06333	Henderson	—	—
Crow, William M.	47044	Scurry	—	—
Crowder, G. W., Sr.	Rej	Harris	—	—
Crowder, Hulda	39750	Dallas	Crowder, Robert Scott	—
Crowder, S. M. Wood Mrs.	Rej	Hunt	Wood, Henry Clay	15548
Crowder, Susan	43997	Tarrant	Crowder, William Garrett	27685
Crowder, W. M.	26279	Parker	—	—
Crowder, William Garrett	27685	Erath	—	—
Crowe, Josiah A.	Rej	Hardin	—	—
Crowell, Amanda	51175	Menard	Crowell, Perry	44050
Crowell, Elizabeth A.	02005	Hopkins	Crowell, William G.	—
Crowell, G. M.	21185	Caldwell	—	—
Crowell, Hannah Jane	20272	Austin	Crowell, David Isaac	—
Crowell, Henry	25672	Sabine	—	—
Crowell, Laura	50299	Sabine	Crowell, Henry	25672
Crowell, Perry	44050	Dawson	—	—
Crowley, Dan	31485	Smith	—	—
Crowley, Daniel	23418	Coryell	—	—
Crowley, M. W. Mrs.	23108	Ellis	Crowley, Edwin	—
Crowley, T. U. Mrs.	30431	Dallas	Crowley, Robert Alexander	—
Crown, N. T. Mrs.	35330	Hardeman	Crown, Nimrod Hunter	—
Crownover, E. J. Mrs.	25167	Callahan	Crownover, Marion Rutes	—
Crownover, Rachel Susie	Rej	Tarrant	Crownover, James Melton	—
Crowson, Amanda	02081	Houston	Crowson, Richard	—
Crowson, David	28406	Jackson	—	—
Crowson, Jennie	41039	Fannin	Crowson, Asa Billingsley	—
Crowson, John	27194	McLennan	—	—
Crowson, L. E. Mrs.	43190	Houston	Crowson, (William) Lafayette	13098
Crowson, Lafayette	13098	Trinity	—	—
Crowson, O. L.	05185	Houston	—	—
Crowson, William L.	Rej	Hill	—	—
Crowson, William M.	15628	Hunt	—	—
Crowther, Minerva Ann	00344	Bexar	Crowther, Benjamin	—
Crozier, A. E. Mrs.	37019	Clay	Crozier, Andrew	—
Crozier, Anolia	41149	Caldwell	Crozier, James Henry	—
Crozier, E. M. Mrs.	24997	Washington	Crozier, Olander	—
Crozier, M. E. Mrs.	48053	Angelina	Crozier, Thomas Boston	—
Crozier, N. L. Mrs.	47377	Collin	Crozier, John Rufus	—
Cruce, S. A.	16303	Red River	—	—
Cruise, R. M.	09508	Red River	—	—
Crum, Adaline	15494	Hood	Crum, George	—
Crum, Bettie Virginia	46136A	Burnet	Crum, Earnest	41219
Crum, Earnest	41219	Burnet	—	—
Crum, George	01979	Hood	—	—
Crum, George Washington	16765	Tyler	—	—
Crum, George Washington Mrs.	41416	Tyler	Crum, George Washington	16765
Crum, Lucy	29576	Fayette	Crum, Winfield Scott	—
Crum, Mary A.	03688	Smith	Crum, David D.	—
Crumb, Leonard	06468	Johnson	—	—

Index to Confederate Pension Applications

Crumbley, J. A.	02801	McCulloch		
Crumbley, Martha	45550	Navarro	Crumbley, Henry Washington	
Crumley, L. T. Mrs.	30846	Lampasas	Crumley, Benjamin T.	
Crumley, Mary S.	41728	Hays	Crumley, Chapple Columbus	
Crummey, E. W.	21710	Bowie		
Crummey, Nancy Elizabeth	45675	Wichita	Crummey, William Ransom L.	30592
Crummey, William Ransom L.	30592	Cass		
Crump, Anna E.	51721	Wheeler	Crump, Robert Wilkerson	
Crump, Anna P.	39160	Hunt	Crump, John Ratekin	
Crump, Cornelia Elizabeth	Rej	Shelby	Crump, William James	16548
Crump, Cynthia Caroline	08985	Camp	Crump, Richard Phillip	
Crump, George Patrick	13927	Lavaca		
Crump, James Marion	40770	Menard		
Crump, John A.	22414	Dallas		
Crump, Madora	50950	Dallam	Crump, Thomas Edmon	
Crump, Mary Eliza	49812	McLennan	Crump, Madison	
Crump, Pollie	44015	Menard	Crump, James Marion	40770
Crump, Prudence T.	45625	Cooke	Crump, William Benton	
Crump, Q. V.	21161	McCulloch		
Crump, R. O.	25133	Hopkins		
Crump, Robert Monroe, Sr.	16549	Shelby		
Crump, Sallie	Rej	Morris	Crump, Winfield Scott	
Crump, Sarah	36353	Shelby	Robert Monroe, Sr.	16549
Crump, T. C. Mrs.	32690	Tarrant	Crump, William Donald	
Crump, T. J. Mrs.	35189	McCulloch	Crump, George Patrick	
Crump, William Dorsey	47837	Lubbock		
Crump, William James	16548	Shelby		
Crumpler, Cynthia V.	21709	Smith	Crumpler, Sam Houston	
Crumpler, James Wesley	04523	Wood		
Crumpler, John G.	18381	Smith		
Crumpler, Mary E.	50564	Wood	Crumpler, John Asa	
Crumps, America	37173	Austin	Crumps, James Waddie	
Crumpton, Luke Washington Mrs.	43261	Bowie	Crumpton, Luke Washington	
Crundwell, Joseph Mathias	30154	Brown		
Crundwell, Ruth M.	31055	Brown	Crundwell, Joseph Mathias	30154
Crunip, Florence E.	49582	Montague	Crunip, John Gray	
Crunk, Sarah Obedience	50230	Concho	Crunk, Ira Caswell	
Crunk, Susan M.	Rej	Concho	Crunk, Jos W.	
Cruse, Anderson P.	21336	Bosque		
Cruse, N. H. Mrs.	Rej	Lamar	Cruse, William Richard	
Cruse, S. J. F.	29712	Tyler		
Cruse, William F.	37144	Bastrop		
Crutcher, A. H. Mrs.	31985	Tarrant	Crutcher, Richard	07790
Crutcher, Dudley S. L.	18876	Clay		
Crutcher, Lelia M.	43878	Dallas	Crutcher, William Lee	
Crutcher, Mattie Della	46940	Nolan	Crutcher, Samuel W.	38584
Crutcher, Richard	07790	Dallas		
Crutcher, Samuel W.	38584	Nolan		
Crutchfield, Joanna	19618	Medina	Crutchfield, John	
Crutchfield, John D.	27157	Jones		
Crutchfield, Lucy	39273	Jones	Crutchfield, John D.	27157
Crutchfield, Mamie	51024	Grayson	Crutchfield, James Oscar	
Cruthirds, John Wesley	34069	Baylor		
Cruthirds, Tennessee	37071	Baylor	Cruthirds, John Wesley	
Cruz, Jenaro	00332	Bexar		
Cruze, Mary Kate	41601	Bexar	Cruze, Joseph S.	
Cryar, Nancy	21711	Tyler	Cryar, William Hanry	
Cubine, N. L. Mrs.	41625	Montague	Cubine, W. H.	
Cubit, Gilbert	Rej	Gonzales		

Index to Confederate Pension Applications

Name	No.	County	Related	Related No.
Cubley, J. G.	22839	Navarro		
Cubstead, Henry E.	26341	Walker		
Cudd, Sarah	49829	Dewitt	Cudd, A. R.	
Cude, Delia	40593	Gonzales	Cude, Richard D.	
Cude, G. A. Mrs.	19461	Grimes	Cude, William Johnson	01684
Cude, George Travis	13562	Upshur		
Cude, George W.	Rej	Comanche		
Cude, J. H.	06958	Robertson		
Cude, John	08994	Cooke		
Cude, Kate	Rej	Bexar		
Cude, Kate	41077	Medina	Cude, Nathian Wiley	29030
Cude, Kiziah (Kate) Allbright	37465	Bexar	Allbright, Benjamin R.	
Cude, Nathian Wiley	29030	Frio		
Cude, Tim J.	14657	Bee		
Cude, W. F. Mrs.	51023	Bexar	Cude, William F.	15223
Cude, William F.	15223	Frio		
Cude, William Johnson	01684	Grimes		
Culberson, Ovie	41809	Upshur	Culberson, James Isaac	
Culberson, William A.	35777	Hill		
Culbertson, Ellick Steward	10045	Dallas		
Culbertson, J. G.	13735	Burnet		
Culbertson, J. S.	32955	Comanche		
Culbertson, Mary M.	33703	Fannin	Culbertson, Israel Mariah	
Culbertson, Mildred H.	Rej	McLennan	James, Dr.	
Culbertson, R. W.	Rej	Shelby		
Culbertson, Ransom H.	32403	Shelby		
Culbertson, Samuel Green	06686	Henderson		
Culbertson, Sarah A.	18758	Dallas	Culbertson, Ellick Steward	10045
Culbertson, Susan D.	37119	Comanche	Culbertson, J. S.	32955
Culbertson, W. W.	26645	Shelby		
Culbesson, Elizabeth Ann	Rej	Hunt	Culbesson, Columbus Young	
Culbreth, Mary	17126	Madison	Culbreth, Warren	06636
Culbreth, Mary Jane	47422	Bell	Culbreth, Thomas Love	
Culbreth, Warren	06636	Madison		
Culbreth, William Henderson	40195	Navarro		
Culbreth, William Henderson Mrs.	41333	Navarro	Culbreth, William Henderson	40195
Cullefer, T. W.	12763	Callahan		
Cullen, Edwin Chipman	16716	Travis		
Cullin, Hortense A.	20762	Travis	Cullin, Edwin Chipman	16716
Cullom, Peter William	30461	Dallas		
Cullpepper, Sophie	47788	Fannin	Cullpepper, William Curtis	
Cullum, Elisha Garland	23361	Ellis		
Cullum, Elizabeth	41241	Ellis	Cullum, Elisha Garland	23361
Culp, A. F.	13437	McLennan		
Culp, B. D.	12324	Coryell		
Culp, C. A. Mrs.	Rej	Comanche	Culp, Amos Franklin	
Culp, Jerusha	26385	Mills	Culp, George Adam	
Culp, Martha Josephine	39523	Coleman	Culp, William Crawford	
Culp, Martha R.	14637	Bosque	Culp, Daniel	
Culp, Permelia	14636	Bosque	Culp, Greenville Casville	
Culp, Rebecca	06993	Erath	Culp, John F.	
Culpepper, Amos A.	21713	Caldwell		
Culpepper, Benjamin Franklin	23050	Upshur		
Culpepper, Elizabeth	39020	Bastrop	Culpepper, Amos A.	21713
Culpepper, I. F. Mrs.	34107	Upshur	Culpepper, Benjamin Franklin	23050
Culpepper, J. F.	02298	Johnson		
Culpepper, J. M.	23076	Hopkins		
Culpepper, Joel Tyler	16685	Titus		
Culpepper, John Alexander, Sr.	16623	Smith		

Index to Confederate Pension Applications

Culpepper, L. H. Mrs.	20491	Cass	Culpepper, Elijah Clark	—
Culpepper, M. C. Mrs.	21712	Harrison	Culpepper, James Pickens	—
Culpepper, M. C. Mrs.	26460	Titus	Culpepper, Joel Tyler	16685
Culpepper, M. C. Mrs.	41124	Wilson	Culpepper, John Thomas Jefferson	—
Culpepper, Martha	23405	Upshur	Culpepper, Thomas Jefferson	—
Culpepper, P. E. Mrs.	36494	Smith	John Alexander, Sr.	16623
Culpepper, Sophronia Jane	30182	Hardeman	Culpepper, John Asberry	—
Culpepper, Tempa	39769	Bexar	Culpepper, Shadrach Dixon	—
Culver, I. T.	08875	Gregg	—	—
Culver, Izora Henderson	51561	Grayson	Culver, John Michael	32171
Culver, John M.	03040	Montague	—	—
Culver, John Michael	32171	Grayson	—	—
Culver, Joseph	33229	Wilbarger	—	—
Culverhouse, T. J.	30701	Wood	—	—
Culwell, E. L. Mrs.	15095	Erath	Culwell, Thomas Berry	—
Culwell, M. M. Mrs.	35468	Tarrant	Culwell, Johnathan Jones	—
Culwell, Mary Ellen	42323	Parker	Culwell, William Thompson	—
Culwell, Sarah Belle	Rej	Parker	Culwell, Hezekiah	—
Cumba, Paul	07991	Henderson	—	—
Cumbie, Frances A.	20681	Cooke	Cumbie, Hiram Jackson	01625
Cumbie, Hiram Jackson	01625	Grayson	—	—
Cumbie, Sarah	13646	Freestone	Cumbie, Hansford	—
Cumbie, Sarah E.	04025	Upshur	Cumbie, Wiley B.	—
Cumbie, W. A.	26665	Wood	—	—
Cumby, Samantha C.	00257	Bell	Cumby, John W.	—
Cummings, Amanda Earl	34551	Cottle	Cummings, Thomas Phylander	—
Cummings, Bridget	Rej	Anderson	Cummings, Thomas	—
Cummings, C. C.	29187	Tarrant	—	—
Cummings, Caroline	43766	Bosque	Cummings, Jessie Edington	—
Cummings, Charles C.	00575	Burnet	—	—
Cummings, Clara	37677	Jackson	Cummings, Granville Newton	—
Cummings, David Martin	17754	Harris	—	—
Cummings, Granbury Mrs.	36208	Coryell	Cummings, Granbury	—
Cummings, Henry	03359	Polk	—	—
Cummings, J. F.	12513	Milam	—	—
Cummings, Jennie	49592	Harris	Cummings, David Martin	17754
Cummings, John Fletcher	19647	Knox	—	—
Cummings, John Fletcher Mrs.	46396	Knox	Cummings, John Fletcher	19647
Cummings, Pamelia J.	31057	Jones	Cummings, Wilson Hill	—
Cummings, William	01783	Harris	—	—
Cummins, Henry	28011	Hunt	—	—
Cummins, James M.	17312	Baylor	—	—
Cummins, Josephine B.	15024	Dallas	Cummins, John M.	—
Cummins, Mary E.	46384	Montague	Cummins, James A.	—
Cummins, Minnie C.	Rej	El Paso	Cummins, William Fletcher	—
Cummins, Nancy J.	40017	Hunt	Cummins, Henry	28011
Cummins, T. E. Mrs.	20683	Denton	Cummins, Robert Franklin	—
Cummons, Mary	50673	Dallas	Cummons, Rufus George	42868
Cummons, Rufus George	42868	Dallas	—	—
Cundieff, Sarah F.	18067	Limestone	Cundieff, William Keith	—
Cundiff, John William	38725	Leon	—	—
Cundiff, Maggie Robbins	43530	Leon	Cundiff, John William	38725
Cuney, Philip M.	30910	Waller	—	—
Cuniff, John	Rej	Jefferson	—	—
Cunliffe, Henry C.	10499	Upshur	—	—
Cunniff, John	10571	Jefferson	—	—
Cunningham, A. W.	05308	Montague	—	—
Cunningham, Angie	25009	Upshur	Cunningham, William Columbus	—
Cunningham, Aramittie Caroline	46962	Runnels	Cunningham, Mose	—

Index to Confederate Pension Applications

Cunningham, Arthur	26155	Bexar		
Cunningham, Clara	35162	Bexar	Cunningham, Arthur	26155
Cunningham, Daniel Mrs.	Rej	Childress	Cunningham, Daniel	
Cunningham, David	Rej	Lamar		
Cunningham, F. J. Mrs.	25847	Hunt	Cunningham, Jim Moore	
Cunningham, Fannie C.	46731	Ellis	Cunningham, Vincient A.	
Cunningham, Felix C.	10297	Erath		
Cunningham, Harriet Bryan	30770	Brooks	Cunningham, John Leander	19689
Cunningham, J. W.	Rej	Bee		
Cunningham, James Baker	15595	Houston		
Cunningham, James Baker Mrs.	33312	Houston	Cunningham, James Baker	15595
Cunningham, Jesse James	01125	Delta		
Cunningham, John Leander	17689	Goliad		
Cunningham, John V.	34377	Wise		
Cunningham, M. L.	12872	Hardin		
Cunningham, Mary Josephine	45720	Henderson	Cunningham, James Davidson	
Cunningham, Mary Melissie	43308	Brown	Cunningham, John Evans	
Cunningham, Matthew G.	11141	Tarrant		
Cunningham, N. C. Mrs.	09199	Eastland	Cunningham, John	
Cunningham, Richard T.	42677	Comanche		
Cunningham, Sarah J.	09141	Bexar	Cunningham, William H.	
Cunningham, Sarah Jane	43102	Collin	Cunningham, Pinkney Anderon	
Cunningham, Susan P. H.	18261	Potter	Cunningham, John	
Cunningham, T. A. Mrs.	10737	Roberts	Cunningham, J. W.	
Cunningham, Thomas Mabry Mrs.	Rej	Polk	Cunningham, Thomas Mabry	
Cupp, Elizabeth	31050	Milam	Cupp, Jim M.	09077
Cupp, Elizabeth C.	50190	Hill	Cupp, Sam Mede	46623
Cupp, James Monroe	24193	Hill		
Cupp, Jeannette	35074	Hill	Cupp, James Monroe	24193
Cupp, Jim M.	09077	Milam		
Cupp, Sam Mede	46623	Hill		
Curbella, Soloman	Rej	Bexar		
Curbo, S. A. Mrs.	Rej	Rusk	Curbo, Thomas Benton	
Curd, R. L.	39798	Childress		
Cureton, Robert M.	13423	Llano		
Cureton, T. K.	16151	Nacogdoches		
Curington, Margie Ann	20904	Tom Green	Curington, William Thomas	
Curington, W. H.	06014	Somervell		
Curl, James W.	19152	Nacogdoches		
Curl, O. C.	29394	Sabine		
Curlee, Emaline	51634	McLennan	Curlee, Archibald	
Curlee, Martha S.	46339	Milam	Moore, George Washington	
Curley, Louise	22604	Harris	Curley, John	
Curlin, Jackson Valentine Mrs.	46280	Ellis	Curlin, Jackson Valentine	
Curmett, Hiram R.	29641	Rusk		
Curnutt, Lilly Forest	45900	Smith	Curnutt, Hiram Richardson	
Curren, James Thomas	23109	Collin		
Curren, Tyrenia	32922	Collin	Curren, James Thomas	23109
Current, Levi M.	07709	Parker		
Currey, N. C. Mrs.	29627	Morris	Currey, Charles Dawsey	
Currie, A.	09905	San Jacinto		
Currie, Ann E.	12023	Limestone	Currie, William Ezekiel	08753
Currie, Archibald David	06048	Van Zandt		
Currie, David Blunt	38305	Concho		
Currie, Edward	11961	Hill		
Currie, Helen	43233	Johnson	Currie, Abram Whitaker	
Currie, Hester A.	36560	Houston	Currie, James Thomas	17880
Currie, James Thomas	17880	Houston		
Currie, John A. , Sr.	00148	Bandera		

Index to Confederate Pension Applications

Name	App#	County	Soldier	Soldier App#
Currie, Mary E.	42354	Concho	Currie, David Blunt	38305
Currie, Mary Mack	43460	San Jacinto	Currie, A.	09905
Currie, N. A. Mrs.	40428	Smith	Currie, Archibald David	06048
Currie, Naomi J.	19098	Llano	Currie, Cyrus C.	—
Currie, William Ezekiel	08753	Limestone	—	—
Currier, S. H. Mrs.	50412	Comanche	Currier, John Wesley	—
Currin, Addie Maroney	Rej	Hunt	Maroney, James	—
Currin, E. B. Mrs.	19380	Grayson	Currin, Sidney Thomas	—
Currin, Susan Alice	45250	Hunt	Currin, Stephen Beasley	—
Currington, Joseph Green	32907	Wilson	—	—
Currington, Lillie F.	Rej	Wilson	Currington, Joseph Green	32907
Curry, A. A. Mrs.	07645	Navarro	Curry, J. T.	—
Curry, Alexander	00551	Brown	—	—
Curry, Amry Marshall	40885	Eastland	—	—
Curry, Amy	08453M	Robertson	—	—
Curry, Ann	40774	McLennan	Curry, Daniel Bankston	—
Curry, Augusta Alexander Mrs.	32207	Milam	Curry, Augusta Alexander	—
Curry, B. F.	06990	Brown	—	—
Curry, Bettie	50417	Limestone	Curry, Thomas Levy	—
Curry, David Webster	Rej	Brown	—	—
Curry, Emarius Mrs.	19245	San Augustine	Curry, James Thomas	—
Curry, F. A.	03059	Montgomery	—	—
Curry, Frances	34170	Rockwall	Curry, Thomas M.	30694
Curry, G. B.	01242	Ellis	—	—
Curry, G. H.	26426	Hamilton	—	—
Curry, Israel I.	08761	McLennan	—	—
Curry, J. A.	23127	Milam	—	—
Curry, J. P.	17859	Hopkins	—	—
Curry, James Van	08959	Bastrop	—	—
Curry, John D.	35214	Gonzales	—	—
Curry, John Pickney Mrs.	Rej	Hopkins	Curry, John Pickney	—
Curry, Joseph E.	36656	Nueces	—	—
Curry, Joseph E. Mrs.	41825	Nueces	Curry, Joseph E.	36656
Curry, M. V. Mrs.	27069	Haskell	Curry, Hugh Franklin	—
Curry, Margret	Rej	Jones	Curry, John Wiseman	—
Curry, Mary	14610	Bastrop	Curry, James Van	08959
Curry, N. J. Mrs.	47493	Live Oak	Curry, John Thomas	—
Curry, Nancy	37658	Madison	Curry, William Joshua	—
Curry, Nancy Jane Willcoxon	49986	Montgomery	Willcoxon, Robert English	11057
Curry, Rebecca S.	Rej	Burnet	Curry, David Phillips	—
Curry, S. L. Mrs.	Rej	Brown	Curry, Benjamin Franklin	—
Curry, S. Mrs.	01270	Ellis	Curry, William P.	—
Curry, T. N.	04172	Van Zandt	—	—
Curry, Thomas Jefferson	42904	Limestone	—	—
Curry, Thomas Jefferson Mrs.	Rej	Limestone	Curry, Thomas Jefferson	42904
Curry, Thomas M.	30694	Rockwall	—	—
Curry, W. W.	50721	Travis	—	—
Curry, William	RejM	Unknown	—	—
Curry, William	21455	Jasper	—	—
Curry, William Wesley	25446	Bell	—	—
Curtis, A. J. Mrs.	26373	Newton	Curtis, Taylor	—
Curtis, Charles Phillip	13474	Navarro	—	—
Curtis, Clara	36387	Dallas	Curtis, Porter	30175
Curtis, Ella W.	19610	Navarro	Curtis, Charles Phillip	13474
Curtis, Gertrude	51002	Camp	Curtis, James Monroe	47454
Curtis, James Abner	22282	Van Zandt	—	—
Curtis, James Monroe	47454	Camp	—	—
Curtis, L. G.	32804	Cooke	—	—
Curtis, Luallen	05665	Collin	—	—

Index to Confederate Pension Applications

Curtis, Mary Jane	29017	Dallas	Curtis, James Claiborn	
Curtis, Mattie L.	42009	Van Zandt	Curtis, James Abner	22282
Curtis, Permelia	17573	Dallas	Curtis, Joshua Hering	
Curtis, Porter	30175	Dallas		
Curtis, W. H.	23086	Bosque		
Curtner, John Henry Mrs.	22783	Wise	Curtner, John Henry	
Curtright, C. R.	21134	Cass		
Custard, Mary M.	35313	Limestone	Custard, William	33945
Custard, William	33945	Limestone		
Custer, J. C.	02370	Karnes		
Custer, John	02712	Live Oak		
Custer, Rachel Elizabeth	Rej	Mason	Custer, Michael	
Cutbirth, Alvin	25719	Callahan		
Cutbirth, Lucy Ann	37206	Brown	Cutbirth, Sam	34242
Cutbirth, Sam	34242	Reagan		
Cutts, Elizabeth	02006	Hopkins	Cutts, Micajah	
Cypert, Harriet J.	45600	San Patricio	Cypert, Thomas F.	

D

Dabbs, Mary A. E.	29379	Williamson	Dabbs, Jesse Franklin	
Dabney, Clara Wamick	26477	Fannin	Dabney, James Watson	
Dabney, Fannie J.	19436	Galveston	Dabney, James Anderson	09017
Dabney, J. B.	26030	Wise		
Dabney, James Anderson	09017	Galveston		
Dabney, James Richard Mrs.	46520	San Jacinto	Dabney, James Richard	
Dabney, Joseph W.	14279	Hood		
Dabney, M. V. Mrs.	50336	Fannin	Dabney, Benjamin	
Dabney, Ruth J.	22211	Dallas	Dabney, John Haywood	
Dacus, M. K. Mrs.	51388	Knox	Dacus, Thomas D.	
Dacus, Maud	42770	Montgomery	Dacus, Judson (Judge) Berry	
Dade, Eugene	19014	Harrison		
Daeckel, William	19291	Travis		
Daffern, Henry	05669	Coleman		
Daffron, John M.	22851	Gray		
Dafft, A. A. Mrs.	33263	Houston	Dafft, James Nicholas	21719
Dafft, James Nicholas	21719	Houston		
Daggs, L. C. Mrs.	12226	Hill	Daggs, Hezekiah	
Dagnell, F. M.	03285	Panola		
Dahl, Emma	06808	Galveston	Dahl, John	
Dahl, Wilhamena	48002	Bee	Dahl, Henry Christopher	
Dail, Charles A.	06805	Galveston		
Dail, Delia	08691	Galveston	Dail, Charles A.	06805
Dailey, Christopher Pierce Mrs.	46818	Karnes	Dailey, Christopher Pierce	
Dailey, David Watson Mrs.	43136	Hays	Dailey, David Watson	
Dailey, Henry	Rej	Guadalupe		
Dailey, L. J.	46930	Hays		
Dailey, Samuel George Mrs.	43595	Karnes	Dailey, Samuel George	
Daily, James Westly	09435	Borden		
Daily, Jasper Newton	25695	Camp		
Daily, Jasper Newton Mrs.	40237	Camp	Daily, Jasper Newton	25695
Daimwood, Susan	08931	Sabine	Daimwood, Henry	
Dakan, Mary E.	19704	Montague	Dakan, Blake	
Dakin, Caroline M.	28344	Grimes	Dakin, Joseph	21720
Dakin, Joseph	21720	Grimes		
Dalby, Bettie	16963	Wilbarger	Dalby, Benjamin Bullock	
Dalby, Hayden	06496	Shelby		
Dalby, John Ward	28940	Cherokee		
Dalby, Mollie Adeline	21721	Bowie	Dalby, Fountain Moffitt	

Index to Confederate Pension Applications

Name	No.	County	Veteran	No.
Dalby, Robert Warren	12281	Bowie		
Dalby, Turza Q. Mrs.	00479	Bowie	Dalby, G. D.	
Dale, Charles C.	08899	Robertson		
Dale, Clarinda	02300	Johnson	Dale, G. W.	
Dale, Elizabeth	Rej	Mitchell	Dale, Edward	
Dale, Susan Ella	45746	Collin	Dale, Lewis	
Dale, T. F. Mrs.	10058	Ellis	Dale, Charles C.	08899
Dale, William M.	34617	Nacogdoches		
Dallar, J. W.	RejM	Collingsworth		
Dalrymple, Alice Josephine	21722	Llano	Dalrymple, William Tate	
Dalrymple, Charles M.	10508	Young		
Dalton, Charles Fox Mrs.	Rej	McLennan	Dalton, Charles Fox	
Dalton, E. S. Mrs.	Rej	Denton	Dalton, Jeremiah	
Dalton, Frank	52013	Travis		
Dalton, J. J.	40265	Dallas		
Dalton, Margaret Caroline	43011	Palo Pinto	Dalton, Levi Corlenius	
Dalton, Oscar Valentine Mrs.	15015	Dallas	Dalton, Oscar Valentine	
Dalton, T. B.	37524	Camp		
Daly, Michael	19992	Jefferson		
Daly, William Jones	43234	Limestone		
Dame, Valentine	Rej	Victoria		
Dameron, Mary E.	33271	Coleman	Dameron, James Calvin	
Dameron, Mattie Ann	02821	McLennan	Dameron, Jessie R.	
Damewood, Tilton H.	42762	Hunt		
Damon, Fannie P.	19840	Bastrop	Damon, Sam	11791
Damon, Jane	04374	Wharton	Damon, Warren	
Damon, Maggie Rogers	52067	Travis	Damon, Henry Gordon	
Damon, Sam	11791	Bastrop		
Dampier, Elihu A.	33793	Montgomery		
Damron, America	27803	Bell	Damron, Henry Clay	19766
Damron, Henry Clay	19766	Bell		
Damron, Nancy A.	34978	Brown	Damron, John Henry	
Damuth, Elizabeth	06065	Harris	Damuth, Julius	
Dancer, James Henry	03189	Nolan		
Dancer, Mary J. Gage	09174	Coke	Dancer, James Henry	03189
Dandridge, E. B. Mrs.	Rej	Hill	Dandridge, Joseph Robert	12417
Dandridge, Joseph Robert	12417	Hill		
Danford, Alex	15326	Grimes		
Danford, T. J.	15325	Grimes		
Danford, Winnie Mrs.	04276	Waller	Danford, John M.	
Daniel, A. C.	01579	Gonzales		
Daniel, A. W.	29808	Jones		
Daniel, Amanda	17829	Hill	Daniel, Littleton	
Daniel, Annie	42416	Williamson	Daniel, William Madison	
Daniel, Annie Elizabeth	33476	Dallas	Daniel, Walter Raleigh	26816
Daniel, B. H. Mrs.	32691	Morris	Daniel(s), Thomas E.	06002
Daniel, C. A.	03788	Tarrant		
Daniel, C. J. Mrs.	10916	Ector	Daniel, J. F.	
Daniel, Calvin B.	04040	Upshur		
Daniel, Celia Ann	10775	Van Zandt	Daniel, W. A.	
Daniel, Darthula	46514	Cass	Daniel, Samuel Isaac	
Daniel, E.	RejM	Liberty		
Daniel, Ellison A.	14193	Dallas		
Daniel, F. R.	12227	Johnson		
Daniel, Francis A. Mrs.	Rej	Johnson	Daniel, James Monroe	
Daniel, George Mayfield	29842	Smith		
Daniel, George Mayfield Mrs.	35295	Smith	Daniel, George Mayfield	29842
Daniel, George T.	36515	Cass		
Daniel, H. H.	03690	Smith		

Index to Confederate Pension Applications

Name	Number	County	Related	Rel. Number
Daniel, Henry Madison	00852	Collin		
Daniel, J. F.	Rej	Potter		
Daniel, J. M.	45027	Comanche		
Daniel, J. T.	06219	Lavaca		
Daniel, J. W.	Rej	Matagorda		
Daniel, James B.	17302	Bandera		
Daniel, James Jordan	02299	Johnson		
Daniel, Jane Ann	43243	Denton	Daniel, William Mack	
Daniel, John B.	Rej	Palo Pinto		
Daniel, John G.	11953	Hill		
Daniel, John R.	14697	Bexar		
Daniel, John S.	35355	Wood		
Daniel, Joseph Anderson	11863	Comanche		
Daniel, Josephine	17476	Collin	Daniel, Henry Madison	00852
Daniel, L. C. Mrs.	26708	Van Zandt	Daniel, William Jasper	16865
Daniel, Laura F.	22405	Kaufman	Daniel, Tilman N.	05558
Daniel, Laurah Winnifred	51586	Runnels	Daniel, Henry	
Daniel, Levina C.	16217	Palo Pinto	Daniel, Enoch E.	
Daniel, Louisa	27720	Wichita	Daniel, Wyatt Bibb	
Daniel, M. J. Mrs.	21061	Johnson	Daniel, James Jordan	02299
Daniel, Marion I.	12059	McLennan		
Daniel, Martha Minerva	15836	King	Daniel, James	
Daniel, Mary	28972	Liberty	Daniel, William Edward	
Daniel, Mary A.	10205	Tarrant	Daniel, C. A.	03778
Daniel, Mary Ann	Rej	Uvalde	Daniel, J. W.	
Daniel, Mary E.	50330	Dallas	Daniel, William Edgar	
Daniel, Mary Jane	37536	Navarro	Daniel, William Wells	04174
Daniel, Mary L.	37514	Wichita	Daniel, Joseph Anderson	11863
Daniel, Moses C.j	10885	Dallas		
Daniel, N. E. Mrs.	39429	Bell	Daniel, George Harris	
Daniel, Nancy	41256	Calhoun	Daniel, James Bennett	
Daniel, Nancy A.	08295	Erath	Daniel, Wiley E.	
Daniel, Robert Lafayette (Daniels)	26738	Frio		
Daniel, S. A.	20865	Nacogdoches		
Daniel, Samuel	10747	Tarrant		
Daniel, Samuel Isaac	29440	Cass		
Daniel, Sarah F.	22312	Bowie	Daniel, Jesse H.	
Daniel, T. B.	05764	Dallas		
Daniel, Thomas M.	Rej	Anderson		
Daniel, Tilman M.	05558	Kaufman		
Daniel, Virginia C.	19909	Harris	Daniel, William Lafayette	
Daniel, W. T.	22975	Callahan		
Daniel, Walter Raleigh	26816	Harris		
Daniel, William	Rej	Wise		
Daniel, William B.	06740	Colorado		
Daniel, William Brown	Rej	Camp		
Daniel, William E.	Rej	Liberty		
Daniel, William G.	00950	Cooke		
Daniel, William Jasper	16865	Van Zandt		
Daniel, William Wells	04174	Van Zandt		
Daniell, Elizabeth S.	07151	Brown	Daniell, Isaac D.	
Daniell, J. M.	Rej	Jones		
Daniell, L.	Rej	Bell		
Daniell, Martha J.	32305	Guadalupe	Daniell, William Issac	04662
Daniell, S. O. Mrs.	31784	Tarrant	Daniell, Aaron Compton	
Daniell, Susan	42170	Brown	Daniell, Jefferson Collie	
Daniell, William Isaac	04662	Gonzales		
Daniels, A. P.	47636	Tarrant		
Daniels, Eliza Lackey	47883	Tarrant	Daniels, A. P.	47636

Index to Confederate Pension Applications

Name	No.	County	Veteran	No.
Daniels, Henrietta	34044	Upshur	Daniel(s), Robert Lafayette	26738
Daniels, J. A.	26085	Cass	—	—
Daniels, James W.	03627	Shelby	—	—
Daniels, John W.	09770	Wharton	—	—
Daniels, Johnathon Macon	10084	Franklin	—	—
Daniels, M. T.	16238	Panola	—	—
Daniels, Martha A.	11259	Nacogdoches	Daniels, James M.	—
Daniels, Mary G.	46132	Angelina	Daniels, Hope Hull	—
Daniels, Nannie	31272	Panola	Daniels, Theophlis Bostwick	—
Daniels, Reania	Rej	Cherokee	Daniels, John Mark	—
Daniels, Thomas E. (Daniel)	06002	Morris	—	—
Daniels, W. H.	42384	Cass	—	—
Daniels, Williamson	07473	Fayette	—	—
Danley, Altha	42869	Bell	Danley, Charles Wesley	—
Danley, Charles W.	Rej	Bell	—	—
Danley, Eliza Jane	03630	Shelby	Danley, Alex	—
Danley, H. K.	34540	Erath	—	—
Danley, I.	39350	Erath	—	—
Danley, Martha C.	15037	Delta	Danley, John	—
Dann, Jacob G.	Rej	Cherokee	—	—
Dannelley, Fletcher Pinkney	21198	Caldwell	—	—
Dannelley, Green Franklin	27427	Caldwell	—	—
Dannelley, Madison Perry	11719	Edwards	—	—
Dannelley, Mary Isabella	38229	Caldwell	Dannelley, Fletcher Pinkney	21198
Dannelley, Sarah E.	33069	Caldwell	Dannelley, Green Franklin	27427
Danner, Dorthea	07840	Harris	Danner, Phillip	—
Dannheim, Clara	45240	Gillespie	Dannheim, William	—
Dansbee, W. W.	43980	Hamilton	—	—
Dansby, Amanda	43103	Erath	Dansby, Edward	—
Dansby, Caroline Eliza	46513	Brazos	Dansby, Durant Motier	—
Dansby, S. A. Mrs.	Rej	Bosque	Dansby, Jonathan	—
Dantzler, E. V. Mrs.	41029	Matagorda	Dantzler, Groves Howard	—
Danvers, Lydia Frances	49420	Bowie	Danvers, Charles Lionell	—
Darby, A. E. Mrs.	05761	Camp	Darby, B. F.	—
Darby, Benjamin C.	10857	Camp	—	—
Darby, James Wesley	01695	Grimes	—	—
Darby, John C.	14414	Smith	—	—
Darby, John Leeright	Rej	Hunt	—	—
Darby, M. E. Mrs.	40434	Cherokee	Darby, William R.	—
Darby, Mary Charity	Rej	Tarrant	Darby, Thomas Jefferson	26258
Darby, Mary Susan	41228	Grimes	Darby, James Wesley	01695
Darby, Riley G.	05028	Madison	—	—
Darby, Sallie J.	07725	Madison	Darby, Riley G.	05028
Darby, Sarah	09341	Tarrant	Darby, A. A.	—
Darby, Thomas A.	29538	Grayson	—	—
Darby, Thomas Jefferson	26258	Grimes	—	—
Darby, V. M.	17440	Cherokee	—	—
Darcy, S. A. Mrs.	Rej	Brazoria	Darcy, Jos	—
Darden, Alfred Britton Mrs.	Rej	McLennan	Darden, Alfred Britton	—
Darden, E. J.	07743	Llano	—	—
Darden, Elizabeth	10770	Upshur	Darden, Robert Seaborn	—
Darden, Ellen	49077	Bosque	Darden, William Henry	—
Darden, H. C.	12552	Nacogdoches	—	—
Darden, J. J.	11706	Wood	—	—
Darden, J. P.	35660	Taylor	—	—
Darden, James M.	32554	Wood	—	—
Darden, Lucy	22145	Bowie	Darden, Theopolus Stephens	—
Darden, M. E. Mrs.	04043	Upshur	Darden, T. G.	—
Darden, S. E. Mrs.	26374	Tarrant	Darden, Jesse T.	—

Index to Confederate Pension Applications

Name	No.	County	Soldier	Soldier No.
Darden, William	21723	Hunt	—	
Darden, William Jefferson	23444	Cherokee	—	
Dare, George J.	12967	Leon	—	
Dare, Maggie L.	19460	Leon	Dare, George J.	12967
Dargan, Kemp Strother Mrs.	51924	Dallas	Dargan, Kemp Strother	—
Dark, David L.	06649	Smith	—	
Dark, Emma	40721	Smith	Dark, William Green	16607
Dark, Sallie A.	50345	Liberty	Dark, Joseph Neal	—
Dark, William Green	16607	Smith	—	
Darley, James A.	47372	Menard	—	
Darley, James A. Mrs.	51129	Menard	Darley, James A.	47372
Darling, Andrew J.	40529	Fannin	—	
Darling, Delilah	Rej	Titus	Darling, Milas Madison	—
Darling, Frances	41559	Brewster	Darling, James	—
Darling, Leonidas	Rej	Fannin	—	
Darnall, Adeline	41016	Fannin	Darnall, Alfred Harris	—
Darnell, A. A.	02962	Milam	—	
Darnell, A. B. Mrs.	Rej	Morris	Darnell, Ugene Preston	—
Darnell, D. E.	30952	Van Zandt	—	
Darnell, L. C.	15966	Marion	—	
Darnell, Martha Jane Brown	Rej	Travis	Brown, Henry Jackson	40169
Darnell, Thomas M.	22484	Van Zandt	—	
Darnell, U. P.	13488	Polk	—	
Darow, F. W.	34234	Bandera	—	
Darr, H. L.	38969	Rockwall	—	
Darr, Levi	08784	Rockwall	—	
Darracott, John F.	07464M	Concho	—	
Darracott, Sallie E.	33490	Dallas	Darracott, William Herbert	—
Darrow, Christopher C.	28018	Dallas	—	
Darrow, Maria J.	46458	Dallas	Darrow, Christopher C.	28018
Darsey, Edward Hill	47424	Houston	—	
Darsey, Rezin M.	25327	Erath	—	
Darsey, Ruth	16000	McLennan	Darsey, Benjamin Wade	—
Dart, Nathalie Beatrice	47863	Kendall	Dart, Christopher	—
Darwin, Elizabeth	51111	Grayson	Darwin, Lon H.	47448
Darwin, Ella	45416	Bell	Darwin, Ritson Wildman	16033
Darwin, Ellen	36325	Brazos	Darwin, Thomas Howard	25864
Darwin, Etta	45464	Hunt	Darwin, James Polk	41153
Darwin, James Polk	41153	Hunt	—	
Darwin, Lewis Charles	23270	Cooke	—	
Darwin, Lon H.	47448	Grayson	—	
Darwin, Ritson Wylman	16033	Milam	—	
Darwin, Thomas Howard	25864	Brazos	—	
Dashiell, Marianna J.	38665	Kaufman	Dashiell, Wickliffe Bond	—
Dashner, G. H.	35796	Dallas	—	
Dashner, Harriet C.	34011	Hunt	Dashner, William Jackson	33583
Dashner, William Jackson	33583	Hunt	—	
Datson, M. A. Mrs.	19209	Robertson	Datson, James Louis	—
Dattner, August	15150	Fayette	—	
Dattner, Elise	19391	Harris	Dattner, August	15150
Dauchey, Adelbert R.	32661	Caldwell	—	
Dauchy, Annie E.	Rej	Bexar	Dauchy, Carey Cephus	—
Daughdrill, James Harolel	42671	Harris	—	
Daughdrill, James Harolel Mrs.	48086	Harris	Daughdrill, James Harolel	42671
Daugherty, Boone	38695	Denton	—	
Daugherty, E. R.	46100	Bexar	—	
Daugherty, J. K.	30462	Burnet	—	
Daugherty, James (Doddy)	12607	San Saba	—	
Daugherty, K. D.	11563	McMullen	—	

Index to Confederate Pension Applications

Name	No.	County	Related	Related No.
Daugherty, Laura V.	45717	Lubbock	Daugherty, Ferdinand Hamilton	—
Daugherty, M. A.	09598	Falls	—	—
Daugherty, M. E. Mrs.	43783	Bell	Daugherty, William	24958
Daugherty, Martha A.	32581	Harrison	Daugherty, Andrew P.	—
Daugherty, Martha Hanna	33014	Burnet	Daugherty, J. K.	30462
Daugherty, Mary A.	41291	Midland	Daugherty, William A.	—
Daugherty, Matt	03838	Taylor	—	—
Daugherty, R. F.	08478M	Tarrant	—	—
Daugherty, Sarah	06213	Bexar	Daugherty, John Q.	—
Daugherty, Sarah Ann	10104	Henderson	Daugherty, W. A.	—
Daugherty, Sarah C.	14425	Tarrant	Daugherty, William E.	—
Daugherty, Thomas Jefferson	11548	McCulloch	—	—
Daugherty, Thomas Jefferson Mrs.	42017	Dallas	Daugherty, Thomas Jefferson	11548
Daugherty, W. C.	41351	Culberson	—	—
Daugherty, William	24958	Bell	—	—
Daughety, Z.	07708	Marion	—	—
Daughtery, Cashan	13338	Hardeman	—	—
Daughtery, G. W., Jr.	Rej	Scurry	—	—
Daughtery, L. H.	Rej	Kaufman	—	—
Daughtrey, Josiah	30911	Brown	—	—
Dausby, A. S. Mrs.	31067	Brazos	Dausby, Daniel Muroe	—
Davanay, John James	28418	Hopkins	—	—
Davanay, S. J. Mrs.	29715	Hopkins	Davanay, John James	28418
Davault, Anthony J.	07179	Cooke	—	—
Davenport, Candis A.	34045	Falls	Davenport, George Hewlett	23044
Davenport, Charles J.	37328	Van Zandt	—	—
Davenport, E. A. Mrs.	23488	Eastland	Davenport, Overton Fletcher	—
Davenport, George Hewlett	23044	Milam	—	—
Davenport, Irene M.	19469	Walker	Davenport, William	—
Davenport, Isaac Shelby	46918	Frio	—	—
Davenport, J. H.	35637	Comanche	—	—
Davenport, J. L.	30449	Grimes	—	—
Davenport, J. M.	25356	Smith	—	—
Davenport, John A.	08864	Eastland	—	—
Davenport, Lou	40827	Gillespie	Davenport, Sam Houston	13620
Davenport, Lucinda	13258	Cass	Davenport, Sidney L.	—
Davenport, M. A. Mrs.	29778	Van Zandt	Davenport, Phillip P. Lafayette	—
Davenport, M. S. Mrs.	00316	Bell	Davenport, J. H.	—
Davenport, Marion Celesta	38735	Dallas	Davenport, William Harrison	23210
Davenport, Martha E.	Rej	Bowie	Davenport, William J.	—
Davenport, Mary Jane	47693	Frio	Davenport, Isaac Shelby	46918
Davenport, Nancy Elzabeth	14815	Cass	Davenport, John Emory	—
Davenport, R. H.	05822	Cass	—	—
Davenport, Rosa	32194	Cass	Davenport, William Lawson	14814
Davenport, Sam Houston	13620	Gillespie	—	—
Davenport, Sinkley R.	24614	Rusk	—	—
Davenport, Thomas Wesley	19340	Wise	—	—
Davenport, William Harrison	23210	Bexar	—	—
Davenport, William Lawson	14814	Cass	—	—
Daves, William P.	09399	Somervell	—	—
Davey, Nancy Ann	05470	Henderson	Davey, Thomas P.	—
David, F. E. Mrs.	36147	Polk	David, Joshua Augusta	—
David, James Clark	24656	Freestone	—	—
David, L. A. Mrs.	33524	Freestone	David, James Clark	24656
Davidson, Alfred Morris	27219	Fisher	—	—
Davidson, Alice	31277	Fannin	Davidson, John Daniel	—
Davidson, Anna M.	51308	Montague	Davidson, John Henry	—
Davidson, Della	46444	Panola	Davidson, Issac Newton	—
Davidson, Francis Marion	23048	Palo Pinto	—	—

Index to Confederate Pension Applications

Name	No.	County	Soldier	No.
Davidson, H. A.	Rej	Harris		
Davidson, Henry Clay	13548	Van Zandt		
Davidson, Henry Washington	05278	Fayette		
Davidson, J. M.	23042	Coryell		
Davidson, J. O.	25774	Sabine		
Davidson, James T.	27214	Sabine		
Davidson, Jane L.	09427	Austin	Davidson, George L.	
Davidson, Jane R.	01461	Fayette	Davidson, Wiliiam M.	
Davidson, John A.	14931	Collin		
Davidson, John Martin	18202	Navarro		
Davidson, John Martin Mrs.	37715	Navarro	Davidson, John Martin	18202
Davidson, John P.	46925	Nacogdoches		
Davidson, John Ransom	40425	Harrison		
Davidson, L. A. Mrs.	09745	Rains	Davidson, W. L.	
Davidson, L. C. Mrs.	37484	Kaufman	Davidson, Henry Clay	13548
Davidson, Littliton	39519	Van Zandt		
Davidson, Lucinda Levina	14875	Cherokee	Davidson, George W.	
Davidson, M. E. Mrs.	33670	Fisher	Davidson, Alfred Morris	27219
Davidson, Margaret Elizabeth	49181	Atascosa	Davidson, William Wesley	
Davidson, Margaret S.	32975	Palo Pinto	Davidson, Francis Marion	23048
Davidson, Mary J.	52024	Zavala	Davidson, Walter Young	
Davidson, Mary P.	22137	Bowie	Davidson, Thomas Jefferson	
Davidson, Mattie M.	35370	Jack	Davidson, Robert Alexander	
Davidson, Nalium Putney	10633	Gonzales		
Davidson, Ottawa Anna	38246	Hays	Davidson, Nalium Putney	10633
Davidson, Pedras Philips Mrs.	36776	Sabine	Davidson, Pedras Philips	
Davidson, S. J. Mrs.	41818	Harrison	Davidson, John Ransom	40425
Davidson, Sarah A.	12238	Van Zandt	Davidson, John K.	
Davidson, Sarah Josephine	43382	Sabine	Davidson, William Richard	16431
Davidson, T. L.	20265	Trinity		
Davidson, Thomas B.	06812	Sabine		
Davidson, Thomas D.	00617	Caldwell		
Davidson, W. L.	03388	Rains		
Davidson, William C.	30065	Comanche		
Davidson, William Richard	16431	Sabine		
Davie, Henrietta C.	37689	Travis	Davie, William Richardson	36971
Davie, Marshall Elias Mrs.	33423	Johnson	Davie, Marshall Elias	
Davie, N. J. Mrs.	46433	Lubbock	Davie, Daniel	
Davie, William Richardson	36971	Travis		
Davies, Susan A.	Rej	Travis	Davies, Anderson Dickson	
Davis, A. B.	27018	Hopkins		
Davis, A. C. Mrs.	30760	Camp	Davis, W. A. P.	28108
Davis, A. E. Austin	29364	Lamar	Davis, Joseph W.	
Davis, A. J.	09781	Marion		
Davis, A. J.	17894	Hunt		
Davis, A. M.	30602	Van Zandt		
Davis, Aaron Grigsby	16320	Robertson		
Davis, Abbie	31062	Lee	Davis, Regnald C.	
Davis, Addie	41128	Brazoria	Davis, Cornelius	
Davis, Adolphus	Rej	Tarrant		
Davis, Alfred W.	33602	Comanche		
Davis, Alice Ophelia	42763	McLennan	Davis, William Thomas	41474
Davis, Allen Wilson	16001	McLennan		
Davis, Allen Wilson Mrs.	32728	McLennan	Davis, Allen Wilson	16001
Davis, Almire S. Mrs.	05443	Palo Pinto		
Davis, Alonzo L.	31071	Navarro		
Davis, Amanda E.	47270	Cooke	Davis, Martin Joshua	
Davis, Amanda J.	25910	Ellis	Davis, William Ausburn	
Davis, Angelina Eliza	49631	Bexar	Davis, James O.	08349

Index to Confederate Pension Applications

Applicant	No.	County	Veteran	No.
Davis, Anna L.	51962	Cooke	Davis, William Owen	47173
Davis, Anne L.	35827	Denton	Davis, Samuel Lewis	28682
Davis, Annie Lou	46137	Travis	Davis, Andrew Jackson	—
Davis, Anthony W.	45218	Atascosa	—	—
Davis, Artie	36624	Wichita	Davis, Hilliard S.	—
Davis, Asa	06276	Shelby	—	—
Davis, Asariah	Rej	Hunt	—	—
Davis, B. F.	42696	Scurry	—	—
Davis, B. G., Sr.	25265	Rusk	—	—
Davis, B. W.	13015	Morris	—	—
Davis, Benjamin	Rej	Cooke	—	—
Davis, Bettie	21725	Wood	Davis, Francis Henry	11117
Davis, Betty	26640	Shelby	Davis, Asa	06276
Davis, Brazoria E.	19563	Washington	Davis, Easley Puloski	—
Davis, Burdine	03995	Trinity	—	—
Davis, C. B. Mrs.	30049	Upshur	Davis, Jesse Augustus Lane	04038
Davis, C. E. Mrs.	11839	Callahan	Davis, W. G.	—
Davis, C. W.	Rej	Johnson	—	—
Davis, C. W.	Rej	Collin	—	—
Davis, Caroline M.	06380	Hunt	Davis, C. G.	—
Davis, Caroline Malissie	34905	Red River	Davis, James Carson	28057
Davis, Cassy	22391	McLennan	Davis, William M.	12053
Davis, Celia Elizabeth	Rej	Erath	Davis, Wallace Parks	—
Davis, Charles	24624	Cass	—	—
Davis, Charles Andrew	50032	Upshur	—	—
Davis, Clara L.	42304	Dallas	Davis, John Lugar	—
Davis, Clarenda F.	38467	Bastrop	Davis, Marshall Thomas	22212
Davis, Clemmie	36221	Robertson	Davis, James Henry	—
Davis, Columbus Wilson	23019	Galveston	—	—
Davis, Cordelia	37619	Cherokee	Davis, Edwin King	13266
Davis, D. J.	05168	Bell	—	—
Davis, D. R.	30047	Fisher	—	—
Davis, D. Tom	Rej	Tarrant	—	—
Davis, Daniel A.	17086	Dallas	—	—
Davis, David Bright	23461	Clay	—	—
Davis, David Crockett Mrs.	Rej	Dallas	Davis, David Crockett	—
Davis, Dona	06231	Bexar	Davis, George W.	—
Davis, Donian Campbell	25371	Red River	—	—
Davis, E.	49900	Milam	—	—
Davis, E. D.	06769	Nacogdoches	—	—
Davis, E. F. Mrs.	19348	Wood	Davis, Hillary Foster	—
Davis, E. Mrs.	28822	Wise	Davis, Lunsford Green	—
Davis, E. Mrs.	51136	Falls	Davis, E.	49900
Davis, E. N.	09355	Upshur	—	—
Davis, E. T. Mrs.	24706	Dallas	Davis, Hezekiah Thomas	—
Davis, Edwin King	13266	Cherokee	—	—
Davis, Elisha Ann	13460	Nacogdoches	Davis, E. D.	06769
Davis, Eliza Little	49802	Titus	Davis, Thomas Sidney	30077
Davis, Elizabeth	04014	Tyler	Davis, Calvin	—
Davis, Elizabeth E.	03452	Robertson	Davis, Lewis C.	—
Davis, Ella F.	26895	Shelby	Davis, Robert Lee	—
Davis, Elleanor Ann	21070	Taylor	Davis, Thomas M.	—
Davis, Ellen	31461	Fannin	Davis, Henry Harrison	—
Davis, Ellen	38319	Trinity	Davis, Wilbur (William) Vist	18301
Davis, Ellen M.	51532	Matagorda	Davis, John L.	—
Davis, Ellen R.	16140	Nacogdoches	Davis, William Lytle	—
Davis, Elmina	39666	Navarro	Davis, Alonzo L.	31071
Davis, Emaline	01495	Franklin	Davis, Bluford	—
Davis, Emaline A.	36414	Henderson	Davis, Nathan	17811

Index to Confederate Pension Applications

Davis, Emily Francis	26671	Potter	Davis, Thomas Holland	
Davis, Emma D.	38967	Travis	Davis, John Springs	37402
Davis, Emma Rachel	20154	Gregg	Davis, Samuel Houston	
Davis, F. C.	16070	Montgomery		
Davis, F. E.	28955	Angelina		
Davis, F. M.	17029	Wood		
Davis, Fannie C.	09080	Mills	Davis, William C.	
Davis, Fannie M.	23035	Dallas	Davis, Joseph M.	
Davis, Fidelia	27092	Cooke	Davis, Thomas Jefferson	22642
Davis, Francis Elizabeth Robison	46873	Lee	Robison, James Ross	
Davis, Francis Henry	11117	Shelby		
Davis, Francis P.	26394	Wood	Davis, J. T.	
Davis, Francisco C.	11172	Wilson		
Davis, G. A.	Rej	Hunt		
Davis, G. C.	21726	Galveston		
Davis, G. D.	03306	Parker		
Davis, George	Rej	Kaufman		
Davis, George Martin Columbus	33918	Nueces		
Davis, George W.	22589	Coleman		
Davis, George W.	47189	Navarro		
Davis, George Washington	07658	Shelby		
Davis, George Washington	23678	Wichita		
Davis, George Washington	50285	Stephens		
Davis, George Washington Mrs.	50707	Stephens	Davis, George Washington	50285
Davis, H.	25465	Panola		
Davis, H. N. C.	Rej	Ellis		
Davis, Harriet	04417	Williamson	Davis, John P.	
Davis, Harrison	46669	Bandera		
Davis, Henry	36340	Anderson		
Davis, Henry Heslip	42690	Henderson		
Davis, Hezekiah B.	39827	Parker		
Davis, Ida M.	28791	Shelby	Davis, Richard Ferdinand	
Davis, Isaac	00823	Coke		
Davis, Isaac W.	Rej	Cooke		
Davis, Isham J.	03628	Shelby		
Davis, Issac P.	13079	Tarrant		
Davis, J. A.	Rej	Navarro		
Davis, J. A.	08583	Montague		
Davis, J. B.	Rej	Foard		
Davis, J. B.	Rej	Parker		
Davis, J. B.	31758	Jackson		
Davis, J. B.	35385	Morris		
Davis, J. C.	RejM	Freestone		
Davis, J. C.	39389	Camp		
Davis, J. C.	49938	Grimes		
Davis, J. C.	51200	Parker		
Davis, J. C. Bullock Mrs.	49579	Harris	Bullock, Thomas Jennings	
Davis, J. F.	40385	Grayson		
Davis, J. H.	Rej	Upton		
Davis, J. H.	04575	Harris		
Davis, J. I.	Rej	Leon		
Davis, J. P.	RejM	Robertson		
Davis, J. R.	20876	Jasper		
Davis, J. R.	33535	Hale		
Davis, J. S.	RejM	Leon		
Davis, J. W.	RejM	Navarro		
Davis, J. W.	00640	Callahan		
Davis, J. W.	08948	Anderson		
Davis, J. W.	11392	Comanche		

Index to Confederate Pension Applications

Davis, J. W.	27195	Lampasas	—	
Davis, James Anderson Monroe	13050	Runnels	—	
Davis, James B.	Rej	Dallas	—	
Davis, James Bradford	41834	McLennan	—	
Davis, James Carson	28057	Red River	—	
Davis, James Collins	14734	Brazos	—	
Davis, James H.	12192	Walker	—	
Davis, James I.	11912	Freestone	—	
Davis, James J.	Rej	Erath	—	
Davis, James Jefferson Mrs.	27311	Erath	Davis, James Jefferson	
Davis, James M.	03022	Mills	—	
Davis, James M.	03041	Montague	—	
Davis, James O.	08349	Hill	—	
Davis, James T.	16498	Shelby	—	
Davis, James Tillman	26214	Williamson	—	
Davis, James W.	Rej	Henderson	—	
Davis, James W.	03797	Tarrant	—	
Davis, Jane	05648	Harrison	Davis, Jasper N.	
Davis, Jane	24664	Collingsworth	Davis, William Wesley	
Davis, Jane	36240	Dallas	Davis, John Wesley	
Davis, Jasper Marion	50751	Wichita	—	
Davis, Jennie	21129	Brown	Davis, John Wesley	18685
Davis, Jennie	43080	Jones	Davis, Joseph Beckton	
Davis, Jesse Augustus Lane	04038	Upshur	—	
Davis, John Arnold	38994	Bastrop	—	
Davis, John E.	20626	Williamson	—	
Davis, John Easly	03286	Panola	—	
Davis, John Fletcher	27221	McLennan	—	
Davis, John H.	11707	Wood	—	
Davis, John H.	31486	Kaufman	—	
Davis, John L.	29259	Stephens	—	
Davis, John L.	47041	Williamson	—	
Davis, John Mack	Rej	Wichita	—	
Davis, John McMillen Mrs.	34837	Tarrant	Davis, John McMillen	
Davis, John Robert	12237	Trinity	—	
Davis, John S.	Rej	Travis	—	
Davis, John Springs	37402	Hays	—	
Davis, John W.	32908	Bexar	—	
Davis, John W.	49263	Grimes	—	
Davis, John Wesley	18685	Brown	—	
Davis, Joseph A.	16744	Trinity	—	
Davis, Julia A.	23397	Hill	Davis, Reps Alexander	
Davis, Julia A.	40294	Liberty	Davis, Leon	15923
Davis, Julia Caroline	51245	Wichita	Davis, Raleigh	
Davis, Julia Hill	47305	Milam	Davis, Daniel Grovener	
Davis, Kate	51994	Rains	Davis, Edward Benton	
Davis, Katie	51529	Coryell	Davis, Joseph Miller	
Davis, L. B. Mrs.	37447	Henderson	Davis, Thomas Richard	11224
Davis, L. H.	09043	Hopkins	—	
Davis, L. H. Mrs.	32707	Red River	Davis, Donian Campbell	25371
Davis, L. J.	02371	Karnes	—	
Davis, Lafayette	12509	Milam	—	
Davis, Laura A.	13621	Grimes	Davis, Charnick T.	
Davis, Laura L.	40259	Dallas	Davis, Washington	
Davis, Leon	15923	Liberty	—	
Davis, Leroy Ellington	13492	Robertson	—	
Davis, Levi Harvey	46242	Zavala	—	
Davis, Lila Lillian	42857	Limestone	Davis, Richard E.	
Davis, Lorenzo M.	11492	Houston	—	

Index to Confederate Pension Applications

Name	App #	County	Veteran	Vet #
Davis, Louie T. Mrs.	45114	Denton	Davis, Louie T.	—
Davis, Louisa	11872	Dallas	Davis, Jeter B.	—
Davis, Louisa	18491	Upshur	Davis, James M.	—
Davis, Louise E.	41430	Burleson	Davis, Sidney Smith	—
Davis, Lucy	42219	Clay	Davis, David Bright	23461
Davis, Lucy Ann	41691	Fannin	Davis, Richard Willis	—
Davis, Lucy J.	50404	Henderson	Davis, Henry Heslip	42690
Davis, Lucy Prudence	Rej	Terry	Davis, James Monroe	—
Davis, Lula R.	16257	Parker	Davis, Hugh Watkins	—
Davis, Lydia Minter	45023	Tarrant	Davis, Charles Mundin	—
Davis, M. A. Mrs.	Rej	Parker	Davis, Chancer Hine	—
Davis, M. A. Mrs.	10419	McLennan	Davis, William Riley	—
Davis, M. E. Mrs.	35527	Johnson	Davis, Thomas Young	27556
Davis, M. H.	39349	Coke	—	—
Davis, M. I.	Rej	Caldwell	—	—
Davis, M. J. Mrs.	Rej	Bell	Davis, William	—
Davis, M. J. Mrs.	34198	Johnson	Davis, John Thomas	—
Davis, M. J. Mrs.	38503	Taylor	Davis, James Anderson Monroe	13050
Davis, M. M.	19202	Red River	—	—
Davis, M. V.	13717	Blanco	—	—
Davis, Macon F. Mrs.	09577	Wilbarger	Davis, John P.	—
Davis, Manurvie	07326	Montague	—	—
Davis, Margaret Ann	50143	Brown	Davis, Pinkney	—
Davis, Margaret Caroline	13343	Harris	Davis, Francis Marion	—
Davis, Margaret Jenet	Rej	Upshur	Davis, William Allen	—
Davis, Margaret L.	46160	Cameron	Davis, William Perry	—
Davis, Margarett	17108	Hunt	Davis, Asariah	Rej
Davis, Mariah	46489	Dallas	Davis, David Crockett	—
Davis, Maroma	37005	Kent	Davis, Thomas Jefferson	—
Davis, Marshall Thomas	22212	Bastrop	—	—
Davis, Martha	25134	Ellis	Davis, Allen Walter	—
Davis, Martha A.	19541	McLennan	Davis, James Maliclu	—
Davis, Martha Ann	34326	Lamar	Davis, William Rasbury	02445
Davis, Martha Augustine	34095	Lamar	Davis, Samuel	—
Davis, Martha E.	08821	Coryell	Davis, William	—
Davis, Martha Eliza	08030	Limestone	Davis, George Tipton	—
Davis, Martha Ella	35095	Travis	Davis, William Granville	—
Davis, Martha J.	20618	Nacogdoches	Davis, Daniel Henderson	—
Davis, Martha Rebecca	41364	Comanche	Davis, J. W.	11392
Davis, Mary	23023	Dallas	Davis, John Copher	—
Davis, Mary	27466	Dallas	Davis, Tandy Walker	—
Davis, Mary	39332	Denton	Davis, Gerrad Preston	—
Davis, Mary Adeline	34108	Bexar	Davis, John Smith	—
Davis, Mary E.	18136	Milam	Davis, Lafayette	12509
Davis, Mary E.	49945	Cooke	Davis, James Wesley	—
Davis, Mary E.	50008	Scurry	Davis, B. F.	42696
Davis, Mary Ellen	Rej	Navarro	Davis, Andrew Jackson	—
Davis, Mary Francis	21497	Wichita	Davis, Franklin B.	—
Davis, Mary Francis	51566	Hansford	Davis, Thomas Richard	—
Davis, Mary H.	02082	Houston	Davis, J. J.	—
Davis, Mary J.	Rej	Jack	Davis, Nathan W.	—
Davis, Mary J.	47799	Collin	Davis, James Elnathan	—
Davis, Mary Jane	19959	Collin	Davis, Henry Sibly	—
Davis, Mary Jane	28710	Navarro	Davis, Benjamin Franklin	—
Davis, Mary Lou	46143	Harris	Davis, William Leonard	—
Davis, Mary Lucinda	35415	Marion	Davis, Mead L.	—
Davis, Mary M.	51697	Zavala	Davis, Levi Harvey	46242
Davis, Mary P.	Rej	Presidio	Davis, James Joshua	—
Davis, Mattie D.	46758	Brown	Davis, Newton Blackborn	—

Index to Confederate Pension Applications

Name	App. No.	County	Veteran	Vet. No.
Davis, Mattie E. Sinclair	36887	Panola	Sinclair, John Thomas	—
Davis, Maude V. Woods	47404	Kaufman	Woods, James Stanton	—
Davis, Mervyn B. Mrs.	23364	McLennan	Davis, Mervyn B.	—
Davis, Moses A.	01366	Falls	—	—
Davis, Moses C.	18907	Denton	—	—
Davis, N. J. Mrs.	15418	Hays	Davis, Andrew Lawson	—
Davis, N. S. A. Mrs.	18480	Tyler	Davis, Benjamin Haygood	—
Davis, N. V. Mrs.	03548	Sabine	Davis, Robert H.	—
Davis, Nancy	Rej	Van Zandt	Davis, Lafayette	—
Davis, Nancy	05530	Harris	Davis, James H.	—
Davis, Nancy C.	27356	Henderson	Davis, Saul Cicero	—
Davis, Nancy C.	32656	Brazos	Davis, James Collins	14734
Davis, Nancy C.	45003	Camp	Davis, Samuel Webster Daniel	—
Davis, Nannie L.	41286	Dallas	Davis, William Plummer	—
Davis, Nat. F.	11012	Kerr	—	—
Davis, Nathan	17811	Henderson	—	—
Davis, Nathan	22366	Wilson	—	—
Davis, Nesbit C.	Rej	Grayson	—	—
Davis, O. C. Mrs.	Rej	Jones	Davis, W. R.	—
Davis, Ophelia	51632	Upshur	Davis, Charles Andrew	50032
Davis, P. J. Mrs.	29065	Red River	Davis, John Wesley	—
Davis, Parilee	Rej	Parker	Davis, Adolphus	—
Davis, Patsey	14521	Anderson	Davis, Doctor Tinbrook	—
Davis, Pattie Kinnard	49195	Tarrant	Davis, George Franklin	—
Davis, Philip Martin	47579	Lampasas	—	—
Davis, Philip Martin Mrs.	51800	Lampasas	Davis, Philip Martin	47579
Davis, Phineas James	27999	Bexar	—	—
Davis, Plaina Ruth	49638	Wood	Davis, William B.	—
Davis, Prudiance Jane	31020	Red River	Davis, John Wesley	—
Davis, R. A. Mrs.	Rej	Cass	Davis, John Jones	—
Davis, R. B. Mrs.	18191	Nacogdoches	Davis, George Washington	07658
Davis, R. L.	Rej	Shelby	—	—
Davis, R. W.	11136	Sutton	—	—
Davis, Rachel Plumer	34341	Panola	Davis, Austin Lacy	—
Davis, Rebecca	35597	Trinity	Davis, John Robert	12237
Davis, Rebecca A.	25158	Harrison	Davis, John Jones	—
Davis, Richard W.	Rej	Bastrop	—	—
Davis, Robert H.	31070	Somervell	—	—
Davis, Robert J.	23379	Van Zandt	—	—
Davis, Robert Montgomery Mrs.	41846	Rockwall	Davis, Robert Mongomery	—
Davis, Roberta M.	04275	Waller	Davis, Mathias	—
Davis, Rosa A.	01223	Ellis	Davis, J. W.	—
Davis, Ruby	Rej	Jones	Davis, William	—
Davis, S. A. Mrs.	Home	Travis	Davis, Green Hunter	—
Davis, S. A. Mrs.	23530	Wilson	Davis, Nathan	22366
Davis, S. A. Mrs.	42551	Erath	Davis, Henry Fletcher	—
Davis, S. D.	27792	Sterling	—	—
Davis, S. E. Mrs.	05882	Fannin	Davis, A. C.	—
Davis, S. E. Mrs.	40557	Tarrant	Davis, Aaron Grigsby	16320
Davis, S. F.	13352	Harris	—	—
Davis, S. J. Mrs.	02963	Milam	Davis, James	—
Davis, S. J. Mrs.	08725	Hill	Davis, B. C.	—
Davis, S. T.	31237	Irion	—	—
Davis, Sallie A.	39563	Robertson	Davis, Leroy Ellington	13492
Davis, Sallie E.	36196	Morris	Davis, Alford Kingston	—
Davis, Sallie V.	31064	Eastland	Davis, James Madison	—
Davis, Sallie W.	30761	Anderson	Davis, William Henry	—
Davis, Sally Selman	42734	Dallas	Selman, William Harrison	—
Davis, Sam A.	50354	Limestone	—	—

Index to Confederate Pension Applications

Name	App. No.	County	Veteran	Vet. No.
Davis, Sampson I.	04036	Upshur	—	
Davis, Samuel Lewis	28682	Denton	—	
Davis, Sarah Ann Savannah	51594	Bandera	Davis, Harrison	46669
Davis, Sarah F.	20550	Bell	Davis, David J.	—
Davis, Sarah J.	09170	Cherokee	Davis, W. D. Y.	—
Davis, Sarah J.	14940	Collingsworth	Davis, William Alexander	—
Davis, Sarah J.	24183	Llano	Davis, Caleb A.	—
Davis, Sislie Francis	40515	Burnet	Davis, James Tillman	26214
Davis, Stafford	11398	Coryell	—	
Davis, Susan	06466	Johnson	Davis, Pleasant J.	—
Davis, Susan H.	00067	Angelina	Davis, Harrison	—
Davis, Susan S.	37034	Cass	Davis, Warren Pinkney	—
Davis, T. A.	Rej	Kendall	—	
Davis, T. H.	26765	Ellis	—	
Davis, T. J.	Rej	Kent	—	
Davis, T. M., Sr.	04416	Williamson	—	
Davis, Theophilus W.	34022	Colorado	—	
Davis, Thomas Jefferson	13407	Lamar	—	
Davis, Thomas Jefferson	22642	Cooke	—	
Davis, Thomas Murphy Mrs.	Rej	Medina	Davis, Thomas Murphy	—
Davis, Thomas Richard	11224	Henderson	—	
Davis, Thomas Sidney	30077	Red River	—	
Davis, Thomas Sparton	27233	Bell	—	
Davis, Thomas Young	27556	Harris	—	
Davis, W. A. P.	28108	Camp	—	
Davis, W. D. Y.	00781	Cherokee	—	
Davis, W. F.	27109	Morris	—	
Davis, W. L.	16141	Nacogdoches	—	
Davis, W. L. Mrs.	37443	Galveston	Davis, Columbus Wilson	23019
Davis, W. M.	Rej	McLennan	—	
Davis, W. M.	10020	Cass	—	
Davis, W. P. Mrs.	Rej	Rusk	Davis, W. P.	—
Davis, W. S.	04991	Williamson	—	
Davis, W. S.	06007	Morris	—	
Davis, Waddy T.	17852	Hopkins	—	
Davis, Warren	13500	San Augustine	—	
Davis, Wesley	13694	Atascosa	—	
Davis, Will A.	14092	Palo Pinto	—	
Davis, William	Rej	Gonzales	—	
Davis, William	51539	Upshur	—	
Davis, William (Wilbur) Vist	18301	Rusk	—	
Davis, William Anderson Mrs.	41471	Travis	Davis, William Anderson	—
Davis, William B.	37786	Anderson	—	
Davis, William Evan	28001	Bexar	—	
Davis, William H.	07340	Montgomery	—	
Davis, William H.	25777	Comanche	—	
Davis, William Jasper	13207	Bee	—	
Davis, William M.	12053	McLennan	—	
Davis, William Owen	47173	Cooke	—	
Davis, William P.	17150	Rusk	—	
Davis, William Rasbury	02445	Lamar	—	
Davis, William Riley Mrs.	30405	Lubbock	Davis, William Riley	—
Davis, William Thomas	41474	McLennan	—	
Davison, Bruce Cisero	20250	Shelby	—	
Davison, Mattie	40616	Dallas	Davison, George Washington	—
Davison, Sarah Elizabeth	51790	Harris	Davison, John James	—
Daviss, William Rogers	15200	Freestone	—	
Davlin, A. J.	08377M	Kaufman	—	
Davlin, Emma	26366	Robertson	Davlin, John T.	08900

Index to Confederate Pension Applications

Name	App. No.	County	Veteran	Vet. No.
Davlin, F. P. I.	13306	Fannin	—	—
Davlin, H.	Rej	Van Zandt	—	—
Davlin, J. P.	Rej	Robertson	—	—
Davlin, John T.	08900	Robertson	—	—
Davlin, Mahala J.	40817	Fannin	Davlin, F. P. I.	13306
Davlin, Martha	23033	Kaufman	Davlin, Hugh	—
Daw, Nancy S.	03629	Shelby	Daw, Thomas S.	—
Dawdy, R. Mrs.	43925	Medina	Dawdy, William Alfred	—
Dawdy, William A.	Rej	Medina	—	—
Dawes, Sophia Ellen	45836	Lamar	Dawes, John	—
Dawkins, H. S.	25162	Hill	—	—
Dawkins, Levi	10886	Dallas	—	—
Dawson, A. M.	Rej	Red River	—	—
Dawson, Amanda J.	22771	Coke	Dawson, Enoch	—
Dawson, Annie	Rej	Marion	Dawson, G. W. L.	—
Dawson, Arizona	Rej	Harris	Dawson, Benjamin Thomas	—
Dawson, B. B. Mrs.	47258	McCulloch	Dawson, James	—
Dawson, B. F.	09688	Ellis	—	—
Dawson, Charles Wesley Mrs.	Rej	Dallas	Dawson, Charles Wesley	—
Dawson, D. E. Mrs.	35523	Burnet	Dawson, Hiram Kerkindall	20895
Dawson, David Duncan	01880M	Brazos	—	—
Dawson, David Duncan Mrs.	21728	Brazos	Dawson, David Duncan	01880M
Dawson, Elbert	46136	Ellis	—	—
Dawson, Ella	38742	Van Zandt	Dawson, Franklin A.	—
Dawson, Ephrim A.	17515	Cooke	—	—
Dawson, Fannie	39771A	Milam	Dawson, William Cash	—
Dawson, G. D.	36303	Johnson	—	—
Dawson, G. W.	29740	Hopkins	—	—
Dawson, Henry Jefferson	11364	Burnet	—	—
Dawson, Hiram Kerkindall	20895	Burnet	—	—
Dawson, Isaac H.	30780	Bosque	—	—
Dawson, James Harrison	26055	Goliad	—	—
Dawson, Jimmie Edmiston	45284	Van Zandt	Dawson, William McQuiston	32701
Dawson, Katherine	07905	Wise	Dawson, P.	—
Dawson, Lucinda	41792	Cooke	Dawson, Ephrim A.	17515
Dawson, M. M. Mrs.	13778	Denton	Dawson, H. H.	—
Dawson, Mary	05315	Montague	Dawson, Nicholas H.	—
Dawson, Mary F.	21524	Trinity	Dawson, William Wyatt	—
Dawson, Mary J.	17391	Burnet	Dawson, Henry Jefferson	11364
Dawson, Mary Jane	46840	Ellis	Dawson, Elbert	46136
Dawson, Mary L.	15853	Lamar	Dawson, Isaac Newton	—
Dawson, Mattie A.	26317	Rockwall	Dawson, James O.	—
Dawson, N. A. Mrs.	28768	Nacogdoches	Dawson, James Monroe	—
Dawson, P. T. Mrs.	28559	Van Zandt	Dawson, William	—
Dawson, Peter Thomas	Rej	Freestone	—	—
Dawson, S. S. Mrs.	07660	Smith	Dawson, C. L.	—
Dawson, Sudie	50683	Delta	Dawson, Thomas Benton	—
Dawson, Susan	Rej	Parker	Dawson, Henry Frank	—
Dawson, Thomas M.	01097	Delta	—	—
Dawson, Thomas P.	27101	Burnet	—	—
Dawson, Wiley J.	28079	Bastrop	—	—
Dawson, William McQuiston	32701	Van Zandt	—	—
Day, Lizzie Beth	21279	Eastland	Day, William Hart	01185
Day, Ann	05141	Leon	Day, Thomas Warren	—
Day, B. F.	Rej	Comanche	—	—
Day, C. F. Mrs.	15536	Hopkins	Day, Joseph N.	—
Day, C. I.	14721	Bowie	—	—
Day, Christina H.	Rej	Wood	Day, Joseph Richard	—
Day, E. Mrs.	17776	Harris	Day, Ballard Newton	—

Index to Confederate Pension Applications

Name	No.	County	Veteran	No.
Day, Elbert Elaxander Mrs.	31912	Madison	Day, Elbert Elaxander	26628
Day, Elbert Elexander	26628	Madison	—	—
Day, Elizabeth Julia	17891	Houston	Day, James Madison	14295
Day, Ethelbert Morgan Mrs.	Rej	Henderson	Day, Ethelbert Morgan	—
Day, Frank Preston	18407	Tarrant	—	—
Day, G. J.	Rej	Shelby	—	—
Day, George C.	08310	Galveston	—	—
Day, George Washington	23544	Young	—	—
Day, George Washington Mrs.	39089	Coleman	Day, George Washington	23544
Day, Georgia	21729	Montague	Day, Martin V.	—
Day, Georgia Ann	50395	Jones	Day, Dempsey Wilburn	—
Day, H. C.	Rej	Dallas	—	—
Day, H. J. Mrs.	35096	Freestone	Day, Andrew Jackson	—
Day, Helen A.	16608	Smith	Day, William Chesterfield	03689
Day, Henry Taylor	37355	Scurry	—	—
Day, Ida V.	32584	Tarrant	Day, Frank Preston	18407
Day, J. A.	40524	Nacogdoches	—	—
Day, J. N.	Rej	Wood	—	—
Day, James D.	Rej	Wichita	—	—
Day, James Madison	14295	Houston	—	—
Day, James W.	04278	Waller	—	—
Day, Jefferson Allen	07795	Denton	—	—
Day, Jefferson Allen Mrs.	46516	Denton	Day, Jefferson Allen	07795
Day, John Wesley	37832	Hopkins	—	—
Day, L. M. Mrs.	28409	Comanche	Day, Franklin	—
Day, M. L. Mrs.	41746	Tarrant	Day, Henry Taylor	37355
Day, Maggie	42764	Hopkins	Day, John Wesley	37832
Day, Margaret M.	28582	Freestone	Day, William Jackson	—
Day, Martha A.	00630	Caldwell	Day, John T.	—
Day, Mary Joanna Wood	49416	Fannin	Wood, Wallace Wilson	—
Day, N. C. Mrs.	Rej	Collin	Day, James Marshall	—
Day, Nancy D.	28527	Cooke	Day, James Marion	—
Day, Rausel N.	04042	Upshur	—	—
Day, Robert M.	Rej	Stephens	—	—
Day, S. F. M.	25318	Red River	—	—
Day, Stephen M.	25266	Tyler	—	—
Day, Susan R.	17292	Angelina	Day, Eli A.	—
Day, Thomas	08671	Dimmit	—	—
Day, Thomas O.	Rej	Taylor	—	—
Day, W. Z.	30822	Anderson	—	—
Day, William Chesterfield	03689	Smith	—	—
Day, William Hart	01185	Eastland	—	—
Dayton, H.	06572	Navarro	—	—
Dayton, Nicholas	28485	Williamson	—	—
De Arman, J. N.	18944	Fannin	—	—
De Blanc, Oscar	07077	Liberty	—	—
De Bord, James	02952	Milam	—	—
De Grafenreid, Bell	11025	Leon	—	—
De Graffenreid, T. R.	02614	Leon	—	—
De Groott, Henry	02915	Medina	—	—
De Hay, Zachariah A.	09387	Limestone	—	—
De Leon, Guadalupe	16981	Wilson	De Leon, Antonio	—
De Mendiola, Paula Gonzales	24587	Webb	De Mendiola, Santiago	—
De Moss, Elizabeth	01784	Harris	De Moss, G. W.	—
De Moss, James	11257	Mitchell	—	—
De Moss, James Mrs.	12069	Mitchell	De Moss, James	11257
De Steiguer, Julia W.	47539	Hays	De Steiguer, Edward	—
De Vaughan, Elijah Allen	22152	Ellis	—	—
Deal, C. Mrs.	28609	Angelina	Deal, James Franklin	—

Index to Confederate Pension Applications

Name	Number	County	Related Name	Related Number
Deal, William E.	14237	Galveston	—	
Dean, Alva W.	02121	Hunt	—	
Dean, Anna	31703	Shelby	Dean, Simeon	
Dean, Annie J.	Rej	Tyler	Dean, Jesse B.	12170
Dean, Charles K.	22577	Cass	—	
Dean, D. C.	30393	Henderson	—	
Dean, Daniel Franklin	12410	Henderson	—	
Dean, Dosia	41114	Anderson	Dean, Daniel Franklin	12410
Dean, E. A. Mrs.	47932	Jones	Dean, Charlie Samuel	
Dean, Eliza J.	35865	Cass	Dean, Charles K.	22577
Dean, Fannie	45981	Wise	Dean, Wayman Attison	
Dean, Frances E.	43630	Houston	Dean, William Herreld	
Dean, Francis Jane	25842	Fisher	Dean, Wiley	
Dean, Georgeanne Luranie	37255	Leon	Dean, William Jackson	
Dean, Georgiana	50602	Hill	Dea(or e)n, Thomas Jefferson	28399
Dean, J. A.	Rej	Harrison	—	
Dean, James D.	11114	San Jacinto	—	
Dean, James Laban Mrs.	Rej	Shelby	Dean, James Laban	
Dean, James M.	30847	Panola	—	
Dean, Jesse B.	12170	Tyler	—	
Dean, Jessie Jackson	50031	Collin	—	
Dean, Jessie Jackson Mrs.	51288	Collin	Dean, Jessie Jackson	50031
Dean, John Calhoun Mrs.	46595	Dallas	Dean, John Calhoun	
Dean, John W.	31487	Comanche	—	
Dean, John Wesley	13552	Van Zandt	—	
Dean, John Wesley Mrs.	36613	Van Zandt	Dean, John Wesley	13552
Dean, Joseph Eli	31418	Kerr	—	
Dean, Martha J.	36277	Madison	Dean, William Julius	26537
Dean, Mary A.	10160	Montague	Dean, Joshua	
Dean, Mary Hammack	43576	Grayson	Dean, William Ridley	
Dean, Mary J.	08535M	Ellis	—	
Dean, Mattie A.	50050	Kaufman	Dean, John	
Dean, N.	RejM	Limestone	—	
Dean, Nancy P.	37771	Panola	Dean, William Underwood	16239
Dean, Perry	11972	Hunt	—	
Dean, Rachel (Sarah)	Rej	Grimes	Dean, Thomas Zacheria	
Dean, Rachel Susan	36042	Grayson	Dean, Henry Clay Lewis	
Dean, Sarah E.	05753	Montague	Dean, John	
Dean, Sarah E.	14139	Bowie	Dean, Joshua Warren	
Dean, Sarah M.	46290	Parker	Dean, Shearr Christopher	03307
Dean, Shearr Christopher	03307	Parker	—	
Dean, Sophia	34152	Bowie	Dean, William Henry	31358
Dean, T. Z.	RejM	Grimes	—	
Dean, William Henry	31358	Bowie	—	
Dean, William Julius	26537	Madison	—	
Dean, William Underwood	16239	Panola	—	
Deane, Charles Ludwig	34070	Aransas	—	
Deane, James Henry	08766	Milam	—	
Deane, John Darnell	03889	Tom Green	—	
Deane, Laura A.	15108	Erath	Deane, John Darnell	03889
Deane, M. E. Mrs.	27981	Hill	Deane, Jobus Washington	
Deans, E. L. Mrs.	30379	Limestone	Deans, Neverson	
Dearcy, L. A. Mrs.	RejM	Brazoria	—	
Dearing, M. E. Mrs.	08797	Tarrant	Dearing, B. F.	
Dearman, Kate	42827	Tarrant	Dearman, Wellington Brooks	26862
Dearman, Rhoda L.	Rej	Goliad	Dearman, John	
Dearman, Rice W.	11424	Erath	—	
Dearman, Sidney	41750	Burleson	—	
Dearman, Wellington Brooks	26862	Wise	—	

Index to Confederate Pension Applications

Name	App#	County	Veteran	Vet App#
Dearmore, G. W.	37327	Navarro	—	—
Deason, Annie	47439	Johnson	Deason, Elbert Robinson	—
Deason, Daniel M.	47462	Potter	—	—
Deason, J. S.	01313	Erath	—	—
Deason, John	32063	McLennan	—	—
Deason, Marina Harriet	51502	Potter	Deason, Daniel M.	47462
Deason, Martha	16384	Rusk	Deason, James Henry	—
Deason, Rebecca	37594	Brazos	Deason, William Knox	—
Deatherage, Emery D.	07890	Lavaca	—	—
Deatherage, Louise	18837	Bexar	Deatherage, Emery D.	07890
Deatley, Anna	42047	Lamar	Deatley, Henry	—
Deaton, A. E. Mrs.	49417	Brown	Deaton, Greenberry	—
Deaton, Annie M.	Rej	Eastland	Deaton, Frank Carl	23040
Deaton, Frank Carl	23040	Eastland	—	—
Deaton, J. C.	Rej	Palo Pinto	—	—
Deaton, J. C.	20713	Smith	—	—
Deaton, J. T., Sr.	Rej	Trinity	—	—
Deaton, John C.	39155	Smith	—	—
Deaton, Nancy Ann	29414	Cherokee	Deaton, Cornelius Dowd	—
Deaton, Rachel	Rej	Trinity	Deaton, James Turner	—
Deaton, Sarah Elizabeth	46499	Stephens	Deaton, Isaac Morrison	—
Deats, Mary	39105	Llano	Deats, Louis Matthew	—
Deaver, Cornelia	38644	Harris	Deaver, Thomas Melton	—
Deaver, Mary M.	10384	Grayson	Deaver, Elijah Nelson	—
Deaver, T. M. Mrs.	RejM	Houston	—	—
Debardeleben, Mary C.	45799	Williamson	Debardeleben, John Frederick	—
Deberry, J. W.	Rej	Leon	—	—
Deberry, W. S.	40998	Travis	—	—
Deblanc, Charlotte	Rej	Liberty	Deblanc, Louis	—
Deblanc, Hanah	28429	Jefferson	Deblanc, Martin (le Blanc)	20119
Deblance, Eva	31441	Liberty	Deblance, Simeon	—
Debo, Fannie W.	46869	Runnels	Debo, Thomas B.	25171
Debo, Mary R.	47497	Burnet	Debo, Cornelius Payton	—
Debo, Thomas B.	25171	Bell	—	—
Deborah, J. L. P.	Rej	Lavaca	—	—
Debord, Ica	50742	Lavaca	Debord, George Washington	—
Debord, John H.	Rej	Lavaca	—	—
Debord, Martha J.	14674	Bell	Debord, James	—
Debusk, Sarah Catherine	49122	Brown	Debusk, Elijah	—
Decaussey, Emma	34171	Freestone	Decaussey, Marion	—
Decherd, Harriet F.	14675	Bell	Decherd, Benjamin Spikes	—
Decherd, Mattie Susan	12260	Bastrop	Decherd, Alfred Henderson	—
Decherd, Sallie Frances	42277	Robertson	Decherd, Johnathan	—
Dechman, Henrietta Belle	42190	Dallas	Dechman, Alexander McRae	—
Decker, Amzy Calvin	27974	Mills	—	—
Decker, J. I. Mrs.	45803	Comanche	Decker, Amzy Calvin	27974
Decker, Permila	24944	Hardeman	Decker, John Thomas	—
Deel, John Washington	00101	Archer	—	—
Deel, Mary Alice	16056	Montague	Deel, John Washington	00101
Deel, R. C.	06721	Fannin	—	—
Deen, Martha Jane	03906	Travis	Deen, Burditt Walter	—
Deen, T. C. Mrs.	22406	Leon	Deen, Thomas Jefferson	11024
Deen, Thomas Jefferson	11024	Leon	—	—
Deen, Thomas Jefferson (Dean)	28399	Hill	—	—
Deer, Christian Mildred	40176	Falls	Deer, Joseph S.	—
Dees, A. B.	22602	Gonzales	—	—
Dees, Berry	45323	Limestone	—	—
Dees, Elmira Jane	41997	Wichita	Dees, Aaron Sam	—
Dees, Fannie	49387	Limestone	Dees, Berry	45323

Index to Confederate Pension Applications

Name	App #	County	Veteran	Vet App #
Dees, John C.	25159	Sabine	—	—
Dees, John Peyton	29855	Cherokee	—	—
Dees, John W.	23915	Angelina	—	—
Dees, Mary	30355	Angelina	Dees, John W.	23915
Dees, Nancy	00066	Angelina	Dees, Andrew J.	—
Dees, Willoughby Gadi Mrs.	41435	Reeves	Dees, Willoughby Gadi	—
Defee, Ella	45310	Hunt	Defee, Harmon Pratt	—
Defee, J. J.	02730	Madison	—	—
Defee, Margaret A.	19712	Bowie	Defee, Green P.	—
Defee, Naomi E.	19784	Shelby	Defee, William P.	14403
Defee, R. A. Mrs.	38177	Polk	Defee, William Henry	14292
Defee, Richard King	34567	Madison	—	—
Defee, S. F. Mrs.	41633	Madison	Defee, Richard King	34567
Defee, V. A. Mrs.	31976	Tarrant	Defee, John McLemore	—
Defee, William Henry	14292	Houston	—	—
Defee, William P.	14403	Shelby	—	—
Defoor, J. R.	Rej	Palo Pinto	—	—
Defoor, Mary	08943	Madison	Defoor, E. B. R.	—
Deford, Emma	39761	Morris	Deford, Nolan Richford	33657
Deford, Nolan Richford	33657	Palo Pinto	—	—
Defriend, J. B. Mrs.	Rej	Shelby	Defriend, Phillip Henry	—
Defur, Andrew Jackson	07246	Henderson	—	—
Defur, S. A. Mrs.	15437	Henderson	Defur, Andrew Jackson	07246
Degan, Lucy A.	10909	Denton	Degan, James H.	—
Degen, Jacob	12209	Wilson	—	—
Degen, Phillip	14622	Bastrop	—	—
Deggs, E. C. Mrs.	27688	Polk	Deggs, Benjamin Berry	—
Dehart, A. H.	02249	Jasper	—	—
Dehart, B. D.	13728	Brazos	—	—
Dehart, James Monroe	23046	Uvalde	—	—
Dehart, Mary Elizabeth	52051	Hill	Dehart, Thomas Alexander	13229
Dehart, P. N. Rhodes Mrs.	46849	Angelina	Rhodes, Barney R.	—
Dehart, Roberta Adelia	39641	Wilson	Dehart, James Monroe	23046
Dehart, Thomas Alexander	13229	Bosque	—	—
Deisher, Nancy Susan	49347	Erath	Deisher, William Mike	—
Deishler, Ann	27422	Mason	Deishler, Christopher Benjamin	05985
Deishler, Christopher Benjamin	05985	Liberty	—	—
Dejarnatte, Margaret K.	29480	Fannin	Dejarnatte, John De	—
Dejarnett, W. T.	41723	Johnson	—	—
Dejarnette, Archibald McBryde	15014	Dallas	—	—
Dejarnette, Evelyn Lewis	17548	Dallas	Dejarnette, Archibald McBryde	15014
Dejean, Homer L. Mrs.	49994	Jefferson	Dejean, Homer L.	—
Delafield, James Crockett	16300	Red River	—	—
Delafield, James Crockett Mrs.	19205	Red River	Delafield, James Crockett	16300
Delane, Freeman Wilson Mrs.	47507	Throckmorton	Delane, Freeman Wilson	—
Delaney, John W.	33334	Jefferson	—	—
Delaney, Mary	49246	Brazoria	Delaney, Edward	—
Delaney, Sam H.	17750	Harris	—	—
Delano, Mary Hellon	16957	Wharton	Delano, Oliver	—
Delano, Oliver J.	16269	Polk	—	—
Delap, Anna E.	33846	Cooke	Delap, Joseph Franklin	24613
Delap, Joseph Franklin	24613	Cooke	—	—
Delashaw, M. E. Mrs.	46804	Grayson	Delashaw, George Washington	—
Delay, Burgess	05724	Collin	—	—
Delay, J. N.	33413	Fannin	—	—
Delbrel, Frank	30185	Dallas	—	—
Delbrel, Josie	36372	Dallas	Delbrel, Frank	30185
Delesdernier, Eliza Granger	Rej	Harris	Delesdernier, Louis Frederick	—
Deleza, Andrea F.	04320	Webb	Deleza, Clemente	—

Index to Confederate Pension Applications

Delgado, Clemente	42614	Dallas	—	—
Delgao, Servera	08533M	Victoria	—	—
Delhis, M. Z. Mrs.	RejM	Kaufman	—	—
Delhom, Jean Marie	Rej	Bexar	—	—
Delk, Fletcher Lafayette	40889	Dallas	—	—
Delk, M. Elizabeth	51008	Dallas	Delk, Fletcher Lafayette	40889
Dell, Georgia Virgina	21730	Cass	Dell, Jasper Newton	—
Delleney, Margaret M.	17475	Coleman	Delleney, Martin P.	—
Dellinger, A. M.	Rej	Marion	Dellinger, Mike	—
Dellinger, Noah D.	32885	Bell	—	—
Dellinger, Sophia	Rej	Bowie	Dellinger, Cepha Crooks	—
Dellis, Mary E.	45986	Limestone	Dellis, Samuel Ferguson	—
Dellis, Mary Z.	37821	Kaufman	Dellis, William Pleasant	32588
Dellis, William Pleasant	32588	Kaufman	—	—
Delno, M. H. Mrs.	Rej	Wharton	Delno, O. H.	—
Deloach, Fannie E.	46830	Bowie	Deloach, Alfred Burton	—
Deloney, Lewis H.	Rej	Dewitt	—	—
Dement, Hannah R.	18298	Runnels	Dement, Charles William Gil(l)bert	22801
Dement, J. C.	12405	Hays	—	—
Dement, Joel D.	05991	Milam	—	—
Dement, Lurell T.	13247	Caldwell	—	—
Dement, Nancy	04046	Upshur	Dement, James	—
Demere, Lena	49498	Nolan	Demere, Paul Raymond	—
Demoss, Elias	41558	Grayson	—	—
Demoss, Lewis	16301	Red River	—	—
Demoss, William M.	17214	Upshur	—	—
Demoss, William M. Mrs.	40320	Upshur	Demoss, William M.	17214
Demoville, Emma	37191	Runnels	Demoville, J. A.	33100
Demoville, J. A.	33100	Runnels	—	—
Denbow, James A.	13885	Navarro	—	—
Denby, John Henry	25263	Sabine	—	—
Denby, John Henry Mrs.	Rej	Sabine	Denby, John Henry	25263
Denby, Samuel P.	13065	Shelby	—	—
Dendy, Fannie	44084	Lamar	Dendy, Lawrence Edgefield	34735
Dendy, L. A. Mrs.	29128	Bowie	Dendy, James Hogan	—
Dendy, Lawrence Edgefield	34735	Lamar	—	—
Denham, James D.	09467	Gonzales	—	—
Denham, Marcellus Andrew	19107	Mason	—	—
Denison, George Henry	23452	Mills	—	—
Denman, America Victoria	27607	Harris	Denman, Moses Richard	—
Denman, Izola F.	39966	Bell	Denman, William Marion	—
Denman, James A.	49930	Comanche	—	—
Denman, Joshua Word	19504	Hill	—	—
Denman, Mary Catherine	51396	Comanche	Denman, James A.	49930
Denman, Mary Ellen	33681	Titus	Denman, Joshua Word	19504
Denman, Moses Harvey	09242	Houston	—	—
Denman, Ruth Ella	17890	Houston	Denman, Moses Harvey	09242
Denman, Sophronia A.	36558	Mills	Denman, William Absolam	31434
Denman, T. J. Mrs.	49654	Angelina	Denman, Felix Gilbert	—
Denman, William Absolam	31434	Brazos	—	—
Denman, William S.	30339	Nacogdoches	—	—
Denman, William S. Mrs.	33582	Nacogdoches	Denman, William S.	30339
Denmark, Emily S.	45033	Gonzales	Denmark, Alexander J.	—
Denmark, J. W.	Rej	Newton	—	—
Dennard, Fannie	37271	Panola	Dennard, Littleberry Kennedy	—
Denney, Alice Sands Pannell	Rej	Tarrant	Pannell, Charles C.	—
Denning, Evline	04688	Wilson	Denning, John W.	—
Dennis, A. E. Mrs.	10069	Erath	Dennis, G. W.	—
Dennis, Caleb B.	Rej	Fannin	—	—

Index to Confederate Pension Applications

Name	No.	County	Veteran	No.
Dennis, Dora	47003	Dallas	Dennis, James Thomas	—
Dennis, Elcana B.	13131	Bexar	—	—
Dennis, Fannie	35584	Milam	Dennis, William Rue	17135
Dennis, George W.	23039	Caldwell	—	—
Dennis, Henry	39869	Cass	—	—
Dennis, Jane	42539	Hood	Dennis, William	—
Dennis, John Q.	13970	Runnels	—	—
Dennis, Lucy	41748	Bexar	Dennis, Elcana B.	13131
Dennis, M. E. Mrs.	41116	Hopkins	Dennis, William T.	27075
Dennis, Martha	33031	Comanche	Dennis, John Q.	13970
Dennis, Mary A.	08433M	Nolan	—	—
Dennis, Mollie	50629	Brown	Dennis, William Thomas	39731
Dennis, Noah	20155	Wise	—	—
Dennis, O.	04633A	Nolan	—	—
Dennis, S. E. Gregory Mrs.	Rej	Mills	Gregory, Riley Burvine	—
Dennis, Sophina T.	40684	Harris	Dennis, Phillip Henderson	—
Dennis, W. N. Mrs.	35190	Jim Wells	Dennis, William Neel	—
Dennis, William Rue	17135	Milam	—	—
Dennis, William T.	27075	Hopkins	—	—
Dennis, William Thomas	39731	Brown	—	—
Dennison, E. D.	14328	McLennan	—	—
Dennison, Henry	04485	Wise	—	—
Denny, Eliza C.	26183	Motley	Denny, William Hays	—
Denny, J. D.	11090	Parker	—	—
Denson, (Lizzie) M. E.	49834	Lamar	Denson, James Isaac	—
Denson, A. C. Mrs.	35216	Williamson	Denson, James Madison	—
Denson, A. D.	Rej	Bell	—	—
Denson, G. W.	00666	Camp	—	—
Denson, J. C.	45623	Bosque	—	—
Denson, James Harvey Mrs.	46874	Williamson	Denson, James Harvey	—
Denson, James M.	02422	Kimble	—	—
Denson, Joseph	13157	Wilson	—	—
Denson, Laura E.	28714	Hunt	Denson, George Washington	—
Denson, Lavenia Adaline	46518	Atascosa	Denson, Shadrach Thomas	—
Denson, M. E. Mrs.	40046	Upshur	Denson, William Byron	—
Denson, M. J. Mrs.	13714	Bexar	Denson, James M.	02422
Denson, Madison Monroe	23269	Upshur	—	—
Denson, Mariah V.	32349	Upshur	Denson, Madison Monroe	23269
Denson, Mary F.	19698	Williamson	Denson, William Henry	—
Denson, Mary H.	20326	Bee	Denson, Joseph	13157
Denson, Nelson	Rej	Falls	—	—
Denson, R. K.	09268	Lampasas	—	—
Denson, T. H.	27131	Fannin	—	—
Denson, Whitfield Watson	Rej	San Jacinto	—	—
Dent, Anna M.	45365	Sabine	Dent, John Turner	27305
Dent, Delia	15771	Jefferson	Dent, James Cade	—
Dent, John Turner	27305	Sabine	—	—
Denton, (Catherine) Elnora	46853	Johnson	Denton, John Edward	—
Denton, A. Mrs.	14160	Cherokee	Denton, John	—
Denton, Abraham Lincoln	07650	Palo Pinto	—	—
Denton, Alice	51478	Taylor	Denton, John Carl William	—
Denton, Amanda	13151	Parker	Denton, Jonathan F.	03308
Denton, Benjamin Franklin	18524	Wharton	—	—
Denton, Benjamin Franklin Mrs.	35543	Wharton	Denton, Benjamin Franklin	18524
Denton, J. L.	38849	Crosby	—	—
Denton, J. W.	RejM	Newton	—	—
Denton, James C.	20052	Madison	—	—
Denton, Jane	28849	Jones	Denton, Francis Marion	—
Denton, John Burnard	08250	Clay	—	—

Index to Confederate Pension Applications

Name	No.	County	Related	No.
Denton, Jonathon F.	03308	Parker	—	—
Denton, Lucy Eveline	49529	Hill	Denton, Joseph E.	—
Denton, Mattie E.	27740	Comanche	Denton, Thomas S.	14951
Denton, N. A. Mrs.	10055	Eastland	Denton, W. B.	—
Denton, Thomas S.	14951	Comanche	—	—
Denton, W. B.	07704	Coke	—	—
Denton, William	05251	Wilson	—	—
Denton, William H.	24633	Dallam	—	—
Denys, Johanna	02528	Lavaca	Denys, John H.	—
Denzer, Carl	11390	Comal	—	—
Depew, Nancy	11014	Orange	Depew, J. N.	—
Depp, Edwin	03907	Travis	—	—
Depp, Mary A.	09280	McLennan	Depp, Edwin	03907
Derden, R. W.	15436	Henderson	—	—
Derden, Sue	15438	Henderson	Derden, James Kimble	—
Derden, Texanna	36334	Hill	Derden, David	—
Derieux, George Lewis	Rej	Childress	—	—
Derieux, George Lewis Mrs.	49290	Childress	Derieux, George Lewis	Rej
Derozier, Alexander	09106	Tarrant	—	—
Derr, Henrietta	08824	Ellis	Derr, James F.	01034
Derr, James F.	01034	Dallas	—	—
Derrick, Clara E.	46470	Zavala	Derrick, George Washington	—
Derrick, H. C. Mrs.	50377	Jack	Derrick, William Vinson	—
Derrick, Mary A.	28906	Upshur	Derrick, Joseph	—
Derrick, Mary C.	47993	Galveston	Derrick, John William	—
Derrick, Mary J.	06281	Hopkins	Derrick, G. C.	—
Derrick, Thomas Jefferson	17704	Grayson	—	—
Derrough, John Harvey Mrs.	23041	Tarrant	Derrough, John Harvey	—
Derrough, W. G.	00766	Cherokee	—	—
Derryberry, Chris W.	Rej	Cooke	—	—
Derryberry, Christopher W. Mrs.	45852	Cooke	Derryberry, Christopher William	—
Derryberry, Henry A.	06859	Wise	—	—
Derryberry, Mary A.	15295	Gregg	Derryberry, Samuel Whitfield	01661
Derryberry, Samuel Whitfield	01661	Gregg	—	—
Derryberry, Sarah	08570	Wise	Derryberry, Henry A.	06859
Derryberry, William Taylor	06322	Henderson	—	—
Deshane, P. E. Mrs.	42639	Jack	Deshane, Orsenath Madison	—
Deshang, N. P.	17991	Lamar	—	—
Deshazo, Andrew Emmett	12840	Franklin	—	—
Deshazo, Elizabeth	11479	Hill	Deshazo, Elbert Henderson	—
Deshazo, Jimmie Mrs.	22522	Franklin	Deshazo, Andrew Emmett	12840
Deshazo, L. C. Mrs.	42028	Terry	Deshazo, Thomas	26968
Deshazo, N. E. Mrs.	01502	Franklin	Deshazo, J. L. T.	—
Deshazo, Thomas	26968	Terry	—	—
Deskin, America	15266	Gonzales	—	—
Deskin, M. E. Sublett Mrs.	38440	Bexar	Sublett, Daniel Ward	—
Desnoyer, F. M.	27326	Montague	—	—
Despain, C. A. Mrs.	10574	Montague	Despain, David M.	05629
Despain, David M.	05629	Montague	—	—
Despain, Henry Clay	18979	Grayson	—	—
Despain, James Wilson	08382	Kimble	—	—
Despain, Joseph M.	Rej	Hopkins	—	—
Despain, Laura M.	30166	Uvalde	Despain, James Wilson	08382
Despain, Sarah Emma	45661	Grayson	Despain, Henry Clay	18979
Despain, William M.	29912	Hall	—	—
Detterly, Annie M.	40466	Dallas	Detterly, Jacob Henry	—
Dettmer, Christian	01084	Dallas	—	—
Dettmer, Dorothea	10889	Dallas	Dettmer, Christian	01084
Deupree, Annie	45903	Fannin	Deupree, Joseph E.	38721

Index to Confederate Pension Applications

Name	No.	County	Veteran	No.
Deupree, Joseph E.	38721	Fannin	—	—
Devall, E. M.	07236	Hardeman	—	—
Devenport, A. B. Mrs.	30838	Erath	Devenport, Richard	06994
Devenport, Henry	06754	El Paso	—	—
Devenport, L. J. Mrs.	43010	Hardeman	Devenport, William Jasper	—
Devenport, M. S. Mrs.	22802	Hunt	Devenport, James Willis	—
Devenport, Richard	06994	Erath	—	—
Dever, H. H.	31585	Liberty	—	—
Devereaux, J. M.	09557	Palo Pinto	—	—
Devine, Mary Jane	27485	Freestone	Devine, Miles Marion	—
Deviney, Elizabeth	45950	Guadalupe	Deviney, T. A.	—
Devore, Emma	Rej	Liberty	Devore, Warren	—
Dew, Alice	30969	Fort Bend	Dew, Thomas Tristram	—
Dew, Ellen M.	27572	Jackson	Dew, Lee Marion	—
Dew, M. J. Mrs.	30812	Taylor	Dew, John Hiniard	—
Dewalt, Mary R.	35783	Johnson	Dewalt, William Boyce	32023
Dewalt, William Boyce	32023	Clay	—	—
Dewberry, E. C. Mrs.	17813	Henderson	Dewberry, James Marion	—
Dewberry, H. C. Mrs.	22798	Falls	Dewberry, James Franklin	11433
Dewberry, James Franklin	11433	Falls	—	—
Dewberry, Mollie	31068	Henderson	Dewberry, Thomas Messer	—
Dewberry, T. M.	Rej	Henderson	—	—
Dewberry, William H.	06162	Fannin	—	—
Dewees, Annie	43698	Wilson	Dewees, John Oatman	—
Dewees, Bettie I.	50842	Bexar	Dewees, Thomas	—
Dewees, Daniel J.	33414	Jefferson	—	—
Dewees, J. W.	35989	Wise	—	—
Dewees, James M.	12150	Tarrant	—	—
Dewees, Nellie	32837	Bexar	Dewees, William Preston	—
Deweese, Joe Wright	34071	Lamar	—	—
Deweese, Lewis Wright	33742	Lamar	—	—
Deweese, Lewis Wright Mrs.	43635	Lamar	Deweese, Lewis Wright	33742
Deweese, M. M. Mrs.	21714	Hunt	Deweese, Goodman	—
Dewey, Ellen E.	39949	El Paso	Dewey, William Spencer	31677
Dewey, William Spencer	31677	Calhoun	—	—
Dewitt, Charles Asbury	34568	Shackelford	—	—
Dewitt, Francis L.	Rej	Hill	Dewitt, Dewitt Clinton	—
Dewitt, John E.	Rej	Erath	—	—
Dewitt, John E.	01335	Erath	—	—
Dewitt, L. L.	23031	Navarro	—	—
Dewitt, M. J. Mrs.	27577	Galveston	Dewitt, Wallace M.	—
Dewitt, W. A. Mrs.	49562	Navarro	Dewitt, L. L.	23031
Dexter, John F.	30975	Montague	—	—
Dezell, Ira A.	41380	Leon	—	—
Dezell, John T.	Rej	Leon	—	—
Dial, Elizabeth	45432	Cherokee	Dial, John Jackson	34749
Dial, Garlington C.	26578	Jones	—	—
Dial, James L.	18540	Wilson	—	—
Dial, John Jackson	34749	Cherokee	—	—
Dial, Joseph	02007	Hopkins	—	—
Dial, L. V. Mrs.	20180	Falls	Dial, Napoleon	—
Dial, Louisa	28430	McLennan	Dial, Sam Napoleon	—
Dial, M. M. Mrs.	34906	Wilson	Dial, James L.	18540
Dial, Mary Jane	33726	Jones	Dial, Garlington C.	26578
Dial, R. C.	17030	Wood	—	—
Dial, Thomas C.	37681	Wichita	—	—
Dial, William Allen	41868	Rockwall	—	—
Dial, William Allen Mrs.	45488	Rockwall	Dial, William Allen	41868
Diamond, George W.	Rej	Grayson	—	—

Index to Confederate Pension Applications

Applicant	App. No.	County	Veteran	Vet. No.
Diamond, Paralee Cook	18574	Wood	Diamond, Green Berry	
Diaz, Victoriana Mrs.	18832	Bexar	Diaz, Victoriana	
Dibrell, Jeptha W.	34220	Bexar		
Dick, A. P.	Rej	Red River		
Dick, Amanda	28473	Galveston	Dick, John	
Dick, C. H.	RejM	Austin		
Dick, G. A. Mrs.	23402	Lampasas	Dick, Charles Madison	
Dick, Jacob J.	11314	Colorado		
Dick, John	Rej	Galveston		
Dick, John P., Sr.	46926	Red River		
Dick, Sallie E.	39944	Red River	Dick, Archie Prentis	
Dick, Susan A.	11384	Colorado	Dick, Jacob J.	
Dickard, M. A.	Rej	Harrison		
Dickens, Harriet	31704	Dimmit	Dickens, Thomas Ewing	06547
Dickens, Mollie Brown	47218	Coleman	Dickens, James Robert	
Dickens, Thomas Ewing	06547	Dimmit		
Dickerman, Nancy J.	00973	Cooke	Dickerman, Charles L.	
Dickerson, Catherine V.	40614	Coryell	Dickerson, William Jackson	35151
Dickerson, E. Mrs.	07822	Grayson	Dickerson, J. F.	
Dickerson, Edward Elisha	40340	San Augustine		
Dickerson, Edward Elisha Mrs.	51104	San Augustine	Dickerson, Edward Elisha	40340
Dickerson, G. W.	43027	Goliad		
Dickerson, J. R.	29178	Tyler		
Dickerson, James C.	18307	Rusk		
Dickerson, John	43694	Grayson		
Dickerson, John Cullen	08930	Sabine		
Dickerson, John Marshall	25907	San Augustine		
Dickerson, Laura L.	28372	Limestone	Dickerson, Rufus Crayton	25504
Dickerson, Lizzie	Rej	San Augustine	Dickerson, John Marshall	25907
Dickerson, M. I.	32084	Kaufman		
Dickerson, Martha	25868	Hill	Dickerson, George Scott	
Dickerson, Mary L.	33935	Kleberg	Dickerson, John Funston	
Dickerson, Mollie	29419	Mills	Dickerson, Cornelius Brown	
Dickerson, Nehemiah G.	12016	Lampasas		
Dickerson, P. M. Mrs.	34502	Palo Pinto	Dickerson, William Tyler	08670
Dickerson, Rufus Crayton	25504	Limestone		
Dickerson, Sarah D.	21716	Rusk	Dickerson, William J.	
Dickerson, Susan	02714	Live Oak	Dickerson, John S.	
Dickerson, T. A. Mrs.	49162	Fannin	Dickerson, John Calvin	
Dickerson, William Jackson	35151	Coryell		
Dickerson, William Tyler	08670	Dewitt		
Dickey, A. J.	Rej	Tarrant		
Dickey, Alice	39877	Atascosa	Dickey, James Wilson	
Dickey, Anna Green	43487	Brown	Dickey, Thomas Marion	42280
Dickey, Barkley Martin	21718	Fisher		
Dickey, D. H.	18435	Tom Green		
Dickey, Eliza Ann	32574	Cherokee	Dickey, Robert	
Dickey, H. M.	34957	Tarrant		
Dickey, J. D.	00003	Anderson		
Dickey, James Harvey Mrs.	49050	Throckmorton	Dickey, James Harvey	
Dickey, James Lewis	46474	Collingsworth		
Dickey, John S.	17189	Grayson		
Dickey, John Wheeler	49153	Lamar		
Dickey, Jonathan D.	07123	Anderson		
Dickey, Lemuel Milton	25744	Cherokee		
Dickey, Leonidas C.	21717	Johnson		
Dickey, M. A. Mrs.	Rej	Hunt	Dickey, J. J.	
Dickey, M. H.	08912	Leon		
Dickey, Martha A.	14294	Houston	Dickey, Jonathan D.	07123

Index to Confederate Pension Applications

Name	App. No.	County	Veteran	Vet. No.
Dickey, Mary	Rej	Knox	Dickey, Robert Andrew	—
Dickey, Mattie E.	15908	Leon	Dickey, John Reeves	—
Dickey, Robert	28276	Grayson	—	
Dickey, Robert Calvin Mrs.	41622	Tarrant	Dickey, Robert Calvin	—
Dickey, Rufus James	Rej	San Patricio	—	
Dickey, S. J. Mrs.	38324	Fisher	Dickey, Barkley Martin	21718
Dickey, Samantha Josephine	39898	Cherokee	Dickey, Lemuel Milton	25744
Dickey, Sarah Ann	51725	Collingsworth	Dickey, James Lewis	46474
Dickey, Thomas Franklin	34683	Dallas		
Dickey, Thomas Marion	42280	Brown		
Dickey, W. A.	02615	Leon		
Dickey, W. H.	08537M	Houston		
Dickey, W. N.	Rej	Jackson		
Dickie, J. L.	27338	Jackson		
Dickinson, Alonzo	11186	Bosque		
Dickinson, F. N.	08530M	Callahan		
Dickinson, George F.	49838	Dewitt		
Dickinson, J. I.	43129	Tarrant		
Dickinson, Mary C.	16430	Sabine	Dickinson, James Lenard	—
Dickinson, Mary Ellen	33785	Dallas	Dickinson, Alonzo	11186
Dickinson, Neomi Kats	47064	Gonzales	Dickinson, Edward	—
Dickinson, S. T.	05757	Burleson		
Dickinson, W. A.	22777	Gray		
Dickson, A. W.	19374	Panola		
Dickson, Addie	29992	Cooke	Dickson, James Marion	05835
Dickson, Agnes	46812	Hill	Dickson, William Henry	—
Dickson, Anna Mae	28314	Johnson	Dickson, Isaac Jefferson	21592
Dickson, Bud	Rej	Harrison		
Dickson, Crayton	03481	Rockwall		
Dickson, E. J. Mrs.	47286	San Saba	Dickson, John Martin	—
Dickson, Elizabeth	38806	Houston	Dickson, John Newton	—
Dickson, Ellar Ringold	24934	Hopkins		
Dickson, Green B.	29346	Titus		
Dickson, Henrietta F.	19851	Baylor	Dickson, Robert Temple	—
Dickson, Isaac Jefferson	21592	Johnson		
Dickson, James Benton	Rej	Shelby		
Dickson, James M.	46794	Donley		
Dickson, James Marion	05835	Cooke		
Dickson, James R. Mrs.	45146	Erath	Dickson, James Robert	21063
Dickson, James Robert	21063	Bosque		
Dickson, John Brantley	Rej	Shelby		
Dickson, John R.	20792	Travis		
Dickson, K. G. Mrs.	39186	Rusk	Dickson, B. C.	—
Dickson, M. J. Mrs.	42222	Ellis	Dickson, William Crawford	—
Dickson, M. M. Mrs.	46435	Wise	Dickson, John Nixon	—
Dickson, Martha	37640	Red River	Dickson, George Henry	—
Dickson, Mary P.	29195	Tarrant	Dickson, John William	—
Dickson, Mary Rosanah	45112	Hopkins	Dickson, Ellar Ringold	24934
Dickson, Mattie L.	36481	Falls	Dickson, Horace Mortimer	—
Dickson, R. H.	37094	Harris	—	
Dickson, Senira Jane	40765	Palo Pinto	Dickson, Noah Thomas	—
Dickson, V. C. Mrs.	15537	Hopkins	Dickson, Thomas C.	—
Dickson, W. C.	01603	Grayson	—	
Dickson, W. H.	Rej	Red River	—	
Dickson, William Henry Mrs.	46040	Lamar	Dickson, William Henry	—
Dicus, Martin	26897	Milam		
Dicus, Mary	39485	Milam	Dicus, Martin	26897
Die, Elias	19195	Polk	—	
Diedrich, Auguste Mrs.	Rej	Colorado	Diedrich, Henry W.	—

Index to Confederate Pension Applications

Name	App No.	County	Veteran	Vet App No.
Dielman, F.	Rej	Marion		
Dielmann, Katherine	13427	Marion	Dielmann, Frederick	
Diemer, S. L.	31530	Waller		
Dierlam, Christopher	08038	Calhoun		
Dierlam, John, Sr.	11837	Calhoun		
Dierlem, Elmira	Rej	Calhoun	Dierlem, Christian	08038
Dierlem, John, Sr.	Rej	Calhoun		
Diesing, William	Rej	Lampasas		
Dietrich, Jack	Rej	Matagorda		
Dietrich, Sebastian	05955	Aransas		
Dietz, Sophie	15244	Gillespie	Dietz, Heinrich	
Diffey, James Peter	36960	Dallas		
Diffey, Mary V.	40732	Dallas	Diffey, James Peter	36960
Diffey, N. M. Mrs.	19630	Camp	Diffey, William	
Digby, Elmira Tennessee	38171	Bell	Digby, Martin Van Buren	
Diggs, B. H.	Rej	Childress		
Diggs, Benjamin H.	26035	Lamar		
Diggs, Dora	43570	Bexar	Diggs, David Edward	
Dike, W. F.	28274	Van Zandt		
Dikeman, Nancy	21732	Montgomery	Dikeman, William Kellog	16069
Dikeman, William Kellog	16069	Montgomery		
Dikes, G. G.	09465	Gonzales		
Dildy, E. Robert	35889	Coryell		
Dildy, E. Robert Mrs.	Rej	Coryell	Dildy, E. Robert	35889
Dildy, Mattie Marlin	43807	Coryell	Marlin, Ben Waller	
Dill, A. J.	Home	Travis		
Dill, Isaac Newton	23032	Nacogdoches		
Dill, Lou Murray	Rej	Bexar	Dill, Charles R.	
Dill, Sallie (Sarah Frances)	40886	Nacogdoches	Dill, Isaac Newton	23032
Dillahay, J. G.	10486	Travis		
Dillann, E. Mrs.	RejM	Bowie		
Dillard, Allan B.	Rej	Uvalde		
Dillard, Bettie	37671	El Paso	Dillard, George	36282
Dillard, Edward L.	31759	Jack		
Dillard, Emma	39054	Cooke	Dillard, Robert	
Dillard, George	36282	Bexar		
Dillard, H. A. Mrs.	10708	Nacogdoches	Dillard, John B.	
Dillard, H. B. Mrs.	Rej	Limestone	Dillard, Edward M.	
Dillard, Jane	43690	San Jacinto	Dillard, William Tiring	18327
Dillard, Jane C.	10590	Bell	Dillard, R. R.	08392
Dillard, K. H. Mrs.	29978	Lavaca	Dillard, William M.	
Dillard, M. A. Mrs.	42270	Van Zandt	Dillard, William Nuchels	22436
Dillard, M. H. Mrs.	26722	Johnson	Dillard, Joel Lewis	
Dillard, M. J. Mrs.	05156	Bell	Dillard, Thomas M.	
Dillard, Mahala	03789	Tarrant	Dillard, Joshua B.	
Dillard, Margaret Wooley	Rej	Falls	Wooley, R. C.	
Dillard, Martha S.	00754	Cherokee	Dillard, Thomas J.	
Dillard, Miram Virginia	18940	Falls	Dillard, William Scurrock	
Dillard, Peter R.	27025	Denton		
Dillard, R. R.	08392M	Lee		
Dillard, Rosa	27785	Wichita	Dillard, James Eldredge	
Dillard, S. A. Mrs.	Rej	Parker	Dillard, John Lovett	
Dillard, W. A.	38141	Tarrant		
Dillard, William Nuchels	22436	Van Zandt		
Dillard, William Tiring	18327	San Jacinto		
Dillard, William W.	42283	Harrison		
Dillard, Z.	06564	Hunt		
Dillashaw, L. T.	01033	Dallas		
Dillehay, James Alexander Mrs.	46813	Hunt	Dillehay, James Alexander	

Index to Confederate Pension Applications

Name	App. No.	County	Veteran	Vet. App. No.
Dilleshaw, E. M.	04779	Brazos		
Dilleshaw, S. J. Mrs.	47853	Harris	Dilleshaw, Marion Godfrey	
Dilleshaw, Sarah J.	21324	Harris	Dilleshaw, Marion Godfrey	
Dilliard, Allen B.	11676	Uvalde		
Dillinder, Andrew Jackson	33062	Palo Pinto		
Dillinder, Clarinda	36775	Palo Pinto	Dillinder, Andrew Jackson	33062
Dillingham, R. V.	22612	Parker		
Dillion, Ancil G. Mrs.	04967	Bexar	Dillion, Ancil G.	
Dillman, F.	RejM	Marion		
Dillman, John	RejM	Calhoun		
Dillon, J. J.	20463	Polk		
Dillon, J. L.	13962	Morris		
Dillon, M. A. Mrs.	27365	Rusk	Dillon, Andrew Richard	
Dillon, M. E. Mrs.	18061	Limestone	Dillon, James William	
Dillon, Mary Elizabeth	39618	Dallas	Dillon, Andrew Roane	
Dills, M. C. Mrs.	31929	Cooke	Dills, Henry Casper	
Dilworth, M. A. Hysaw Mrs.	49271	Madison	Hysaw, Nathaniel A.	
Dimmitt, Alamo A.	Rej	Guadalupe		
Dimmitt, Texas P.	40695	Bexar		
Dingler, Beni F.	17835	Hood		
Dingler, J. P.	Rej	Comanche		
Dingler, Larissa	43930	Henderson	Dingler, B.	17835
Dinkins, James M.	04277	Waller		
Dinn, James	42336	Jim Wells		
Dinquid, Edwin S.	10626	Ellis		
Dinter, Pauline	06184	Dewitt	Dinter, Anton	
Dirr, Alice	32980	Hemphill	Dirr, Louis W.	18239
Dirr, Louis W.	18239	Parmer		
Dirr, S. A. Mrs.	43898	Coryell	Dirr, Charles M.	
Disheroon, Andrew Jackson	25679	Hall		
Disheroon, M. J. Mrs.	31063	Hall	Disheroon, Andrew Jackson	25679
Dishman, Bettie	27856	Taylor	Dishman, Jeremiah	
Dishman, C. H.	02197	Jack		
Dishough, M. C. Mrs.	21456	Harris	Dishough, Jacob Stadler	
Dismuke, M. A. Mrs.	Rej	Henderson	Dismuke, Robert Mosley	
Dismuke, T. J.	17444	Cherokee		
Dismukes, A. B.	05500	Hill		
Dismukes, Cora	Rej	McLennan	Dismukes, Marcus Lavett	
Dismukes, F. Alice	46091	Lee	Dismukes, John Bell	
Dismukes, M. L.	23043	McLennan		
Ditmore, Henry	34221	Tom Green		
Dittess, Jacob	35181	Freestone		
Dittmar, Emilie Johanna	42162	Travis	Dittmar, George	
Dittmar, Emmy	51883	Bexar	Dittmar, H. C. W. Albert	
Dittmor, August	Rej	Austin		
Ditto, J. S.	Rej	Tarrant		
Ditto, John	16032	Milam		
Ditto, Josiah	16031	Milam		
Ditto, Mattie	49106	Tarrant	Ditto, John Washington	
Ditto, Nannie	39758	Montague	Ditto, Thomas Benton	29994
Ditto, Sarah Jane Owens	Rej	Sterling	Owens, Joe	
Ditto, Thomas Benton	29994	Montague		
Dix, John J.	14696	Bexar		
Dixon, A. L. Mrs.	32532	Hood	Dixon, Thomas Burton	29591
Dixon, Alice M.	33026	Dimmit	Dixon, Shadrach (Shady) F.	11454
Dixon, Elender C.	33365	Lampasas	Dixon, William Henry	
Dixon, Elizabeth	14967	Coryell	Dixon, Jessie	
Dixon, Eugenia Josephine	Rej	Van Zandt	Dixon, James Tillman	
Dixon, George B.	15372	Harris		

Index to Confederate Pension Applications

Name	Number	County	Veteran	Number
Dixon, George Franklin	00040	Angelina		
Dixon, J. S.	13798	Fannin		
Dixon, James H.	13825	Grayson		
Dixon, John W.	38694	Dallas		
Dixon, Joseph H.	46914	Mills		
Dixon, Joseph H. Mrs.	51678	Mills	Dixon, Joseph H.	46914
Dixon, Judge Legrand	00371	Bexar		
Dixon, Julia A.	39111	Lubbock	Dixon, William Henry Harrison	
Dixon, L. A. Mrs.	19323	Waller	Dixon, Green Berry	
Dixon, M. V.	29688	Ellis		
Dixon, Margaret J.	33126	Dallas	Dixon, James Polk	
Dixon, Martha	46424	Parker	Dixon, Samuel Franklin	
Dixon, Martha V.	25051	Angelina	Dixon, George Franklin	00040
Dixon, Mary	33727	Cherokee	Dixon, Robert	
Dixon, Mary A.	31898	Coryell	Dixon, William M.	
Dixon, Mary E.	40374	Dallas	Dixon, Samuel Gilliand	
Dixon, Mary H.	Rej	Parker	Dixon, Thomas	
Dixon, Mary M. Sumner	46723	Falls	Sumner, William J.	
Dixon, Mary P.	Rej	Panola	Dixon, John W.	
Dixon, Prudie E.	10724	Panola		
Dixon, Rosa A.	38332	Hunt	Dixon, Shradic (Shady) E.	15839
Dixon, Sarah E.	30534	Potter	Dixon, John Koger	
Dixon, Sarah Elizabeth	08623	Bexar	Dixon, Judge Legrand	00371
Dixon, Shadrach F.	11454	Frio		
Dixon, Shady (Shradic) E.	15839	Knox		
Dixon, Thomas Burton	29591	Kaufman		
Dixon, Thomas J.	20174	Anderson		
Dixon, Wynona Ann	50520	Dallas	Dixon, John W.	38694
Dixson, Luvisa	31705	Parker	Dixson, William	
Dizard, Germain	06555	Hays		
Dizard, Mary	14792	Callahan	Dizard, Germain	06555
Doak, M. E. Mrs.	35041	Scurry	Doak, William R.	31807
Doak, Mary A.	Rej	Hill	Doak, James B.	
Doak, Robert S.	07016	Hill		
Doak, William R.	31807	Scurry		
Doan, Alexander M.	08835	Palo Pinto		
Doan, Maggie	33552	Palo Pinto	Doan, Alexander M.	08835
Dobbins, Jenkins T.	46712	Dallas		
Dobbins, Minnie Clyde	43452	Hays	Dobbins, William German	
Dobbins, Thomas M.	01656	Gregg		
Dobbs, A. B.	25763	Camp		
Dobbs, Jabez N.	15134	Fannin		
Dobbs, Margaret	50439	Bexar	Dobbs, John Henry	
Dobbs, Margaret Adaline	43672	Hood	Dobbs, Johnathan	
Dobbs, N. E. Mrs.	32945	Comanche	Dobbs, William T.	
Dobkins, William Calloway Mrs.	Rej	Tarrant	Dobkins, William Calloway	
Dobson, Callie	45535	Childress	Dobson, William S.	
Dobson, E. M. Mrs.	32240	Eastland	Dobson, William J.	07574
Dobson, Mary Lou	Rej	Brown	Dobson, Marshall Melton	
Dobson, Sol	12788	Collin		
Dobson, William	31610	Grayson		
Dobson, William J.	07574	Eastland		
Doby, Emma	28002	Potter	Doby, John	
Docharty, L. O.	Rej	Tarrant		
Dockens, Silas Shadrick	17222	Shelby		
Dockers, Isabell	33531	Shelby	Dockers, Silas Shadrick	17222
Dockery, L. Y. Mrs.	48031	Lamar	Dockery, William Jasper	
Dockery, Louis K.	13919	Kent		
Dockery, Louis Kilbum Mrs.	30805	Tarrant	Dockery, Louis Kilbum	

Index to Confederate Pension Applications

Name	Number	County	Related	Number
Dockray, M. E. Mrs.	14122	Bell	Dockray, Samuel R.	05159
Dockray, S. J. Mrs.	07886	Lamar	Dockray, B. S.	—
Dockray, Samuel R.	05159	Bell	—	
Dockrey, J. M.	42263	Hunt	—	
Docus, Maud	RejM	Montgomery	—	
Dodd, Ann	45128	Matagorda	Dodd, Thomas Curtis	—
Dodd, Arrena Winfred	33218	Cherokee	Dodd, Francis Elbert	—
Dodd, Cornelia Augusta	51225	Hunt	Dodd, John Newton	36722
Dodd, E. J. Mrs.	26848	Wise	Dodd, William Short	—
Dodd, J. B.	Rej	Travis	—	
Dodd, John Newton	36722	Hunt	—	
Dodd, Joseph Andrew	07865	Lavaca	—	
Dodd, Joseph Washington	Rej	Fannin	—	
Dodd, Mahala	40534	Milam	Dodd, James Riley	—
Dodd, N. J. Mrs.	29288	Dewitt	Dodd, Joseph Andrews	07865
Dodd, T. C.	Rej	Matagorda	—	
Dodd, W. E.	05703	Erath	—	
Dodds, Joseph	02967	Milam	—	
Dodds, William	02965	Milam	—	
Doddy, Linnie	18712	San Saba	Doddy, James (Daugherty)	12607
Dodge, Fannie	33114	McLennan	Dodge, John Washington	31551
Dodge, John Washington	31551	McLennan	—	
Dodgen, Dora	Rej	Dallam	Dodgen, James Harris	29949
Dodgen, James Harris	29949	Harris	—	
Dodgen, John Lewis	24740	Coleman	—	
Dodgen, John Lewis Mrs.	42251	Coleman	Dodgen, John Lewis	24740
Dodgen, Miranda	25977	Waller	Dodgen, Eli Washington	—
Dodson, Adela	14733	Brazos	Dodson, L. G.	—
Dodson, Alf	Rej	Ellis	—	
Dodson, Amanda	34778	Harris	Dodson, Charles Columbus	—
Dodson, Ben F.	39514	Wood	—	
Dodson, Bessie E.	29224	McLennan	Dodson, Wesley Clarke	20591
Dodson, C. J. Mrs.	45524	Lamar	Dodson, James Brown	—
Dodson, Eliza J.	21715	Wood	Dodson, Swep (S. G.)	—
Dodson, Elizabeth	07072	Navarro	Dodson, John R.	—
Dodson, Elizabeth J.	Rej	Rains	Dodson, George Hampton	—
Dodson, Franklin Clark	23272	Johnson	—	
Dodson, George W.	27561	Burnet	—	
Dodson, J. L.	20617	Coleman	—	
Dodson, J. M.	18498	Van Zandt	—	
Dodson, L. A. Mrs.	43137	Grayson	Dodson, Francis Marion	—
Dodson, L. J. Mrs.	05043	Collingsworth	—	
Dodson, Louisa Frances	46199	Johnson	Dodson, Franklin Clark	23272
Dodson, M. A. Mrs.	47661	Hunt	Dodson, Cicere	—
Dodson, Margaret Jane	23466	Lee	Dodson, Marcus	—
Dodson, Martha Emeline	29996	Anderson	Dodson, Marion Leonadis	—
Dodson, Milton M.	47444	San Patricio	—	
Dodson, Newton J.	13723	Bowie	—	
Dodson, Noami S.	33197	Travis	Dodson, George W.	27561
Dodson, Sarah Adaline	Rej	Comanche	Dodson, William Stephens	—
Dodson, Thomas	03494	Runnels	—	
Dodson, Wesley Clarke	20591	McLennan	—	
Doe, E. S.	Home	Travis	—	
Doggett, Augustus Smith	13984	Shelby	—	
Doggett, E. M.	03023	Mills	—	
Doggett, Isabel	36022	Parker	Doggett, Thomas Jefferson	31542
Doggett, Sallie J.	20560	Shelby	Doggett, Augustus Smith	13984
Doggett, Sarah E.	13592	Hamilton	Doggett, William H.	01763
Doggett, Sarah Elizabeth	36800	Hunt	Doggett, John Wesley	—

Index to Confederate Pension Applications

Name	App. No.	County	Veteran	Vet. No.
Doggett, Thomas Jefferson	31542	Parker		
Doggett, William H.	01763	Hamilton		
Doggette, Amanda	42448	Smith	Hanson, Thomas Silas	
Doherty, Sarah Elizabeth	Rej	Bexar	Doherty, George Patrick	
Dohmann, Anna	51784	Goliad	Dohmann, Werner	
Doigg, Mattie	40047	Dallas	Doigg, Mathew	
Doke, Fielding Yeager Mrs.	43443	Hunt	Doke, Fielding Yeager	
Dolan, Cecila	37849	Live Oak	Dolan, Mike	
Dolan, Mary H.	30407	Bee	Dolan, Patrick	
Dollahite, Hillery Bongerant	20733	Atascosa		
Dollahite, James C.	07835	Bexar		
Dollahite, John Wiley	24590	Harrison		
Dollahite, Louise E.	27418	Atascosa	Dollahite, Hillery Bongerant	20733
Dollahite, M. A. E. Mrs.	42503	Harrison	Dollahite, John Wiley	24590
Dollahite, Mollie	41614	Blanco	Dollahite, James C.	07835
Dollahite, Tennessee	29371	Harrison	Dollahite, William Adkerson	
Dollahite, Z. R. Mrs.	28953	Erath	Dollahite, Charles Wesley	
Dollar, J. M., Dr.	37345	Milam		
Dollar, J. W.	Rej	Collingsworth		
Dollins, Romulus Culver	42076	Bexar		
Dollins, Susie	42604	Travis	Dollins, Romulus Culver	42076
Dolman, Mary A.	15852	Lamar	Dolman, Abram Hickman	
Dom, Wilhelmina Minnie	15236	Galveston		
Dominy, Benjamin M.	15572	Houston		
Dominy, C. E. Mrs.	15573	Houston	Dominy, Daniel Jasper	
Dominy, Caroline G.	31554	Trinity	Dominy, Seaborn	18462
Dominy, Georgia A.	37723	Houston	Dominy, Benjamin M.	15572
Dominy, Seaborn	18462	Trinity		
Donaho, B. B.	30354	Navarro		
Donaho, Hattie	27142	Wilson	Donaho, William	04456
Donaho, Lurinda Elizabeth	12274	Bexar	Donaho, Wilson	
Donaho, William	04456	Wilson		
Donaho, Wilson	04956	Bexar		
Donahoe, D. M.	26564	Leon		
Donald, Fannie Elizabeth	46986	Montague	Donald, John Franklin	26535
Donald, John Franklin	26535	Montague		
Donald, Mattie C.	42511	Wise	Donald, Robert Steven	41754
Donald, Mildred Ann	21429	Taylor	Donald, Theophilus Theodore	19437
Donald, R. Q.	RejM	Wise		
Donald, Robert Steven	41754	Wise		
Donald, Theophilus Theodore	19437	Taylor		
Donaldson, John Richard	32046	Jones		
Donaldson, M. C. Mrs.	06152	Grayson	Donaldson, R. S.	
Donaldson, Maria	38533	Childress	Donaldson, John Richard	32046
Donaldson, Martha	04484	Wise	Donaldson, Calvin	
Donaldson, N. M. Mrs.	02966	Milam	Donaldson, J. S.	
Donaldson, Olive Elizabeth	38443	Coryell	Donaldson, John Lucky	
Donaldson, Rebecca	14331	Milam	Donaldson, Thomas J.	
Donaldson, Sarah Elizabeth	16258	Parker	Donaldson, James C.	
Donaldson, W. J. W.	03389	Rains		
Donalson, E. A. Mrs.	38613	Wichita	Donalson, Dan Webster	
Donathan, Francis Jane	49190	Terry	Donathan, John Baptist	
Donathan, M. E. Mrs.	30794	Hood	Donathan, James Westly	
Donegan, Hattie	49169	Guadalupe	Donegan, John	
Donegan, M. Mrs.	19161	Nacogdoches	Donegan, Marion	
Donelson, Charles	RejM	Galveston		
Doney, Emma N.	15374	Harris	Doney, Alonzo G. Van Voltenbery	19885
Donham, James Polk	38189	Hill		
Donham, W. J.	36483	Hill		

Index to Confederate Pension Applications

Name	No.	County	Veteran	Vet. No.
Donhoo, Calvin C.	Rej	Johnson		
Donly, John Mrs.	50262	Dallas	Donly, John	
Donnan, Jennie	51157	Travis	Donnan, John Knox	49839
Donnan, John Knox	49839	Travis		
Donnel, W. J. W.	25029	Bosque		
Donnelan, Jessamine	37680	Harris	Donnelan, Thuston John	
Donnell, Bettie	18415	Tarrant	Donnell, Alfred Portervino	
Donnell, D. B.	42793	Donley		
Donnell, Dan (Don)	28620	Henderson		
Donnell, Eliza Anne	49863	Baylor	Donnell, Lemuel Amzi	
Donnell, F. A. Mrs.	37297	Henderson	Donnell, Don (Dan)	28620
Donnell, H. W.	19282	Tarrant		
Donnell, Martha Ann	06989	Brown	Donnell, Stephen H.	
Donnell, Mary E.	49483	Tarrant	Donnell, Stephen Mitchell	
Donnell, Mattie P.	47842	McLennan	Donnell, Robert	
Donnell, Stephen H.	00535A	Brown		
Donnelson, Artimisa Elizabeth	Rej	Leon	Donnelson, James Henry	
Donnelson, Pauline	25878	Galveston	Donnelson, Charles	
Donnerberg, Bernhard	Rej	Comal		
Donoho, G. W.	37801	Tarrant		
Donohoo, Henry	15409	Haskell		
Donohue, Charles	Rej	Palo Pinto		
Donoldson, Buck W.	40076	Wise		
Donovan, Camille	51847	Dallas	Donovan, Patrick Henry	
Donovan, Elmina	35020	Gregg	Donovan, William A.	04039
Donovan, James	01699	Grimes		
Donovan, William A.	04039	Upshur		
Doolen, Bettie	31278	Dallas	Doolen, James Madison	
Dooley, George Travis	08509M	Victoria		
Dooley, James Luther	Rej	Williamson		
Dooley, John Bell	02492	Lampasas		
Dooley, Lewis	49319	Hale		
Dooley, M. J. Mrs.	41255	Comanche	Dooley, James Littleton	
Dooley, Mary B.	30499	Lampasas	Dooley, John Bell	02492
Dooling, Mary J.	Rej	Upshur	Dooling, Pat	16798
Dooling, Pat	16798	Upshur		
Doolittle, Alice	18542	Wilson	Doolittle, Abram Marshal	
Doors, John B.	07285	Liberty		
Doran, L. E. Mrs.	50892	San Saba	Doran, William Russell	
Doran, Rebecca A.	22281	Milam	Doran, John	
Dorety, Elizabeth A.	10358	Dallas	Dorety, W. B.	01080
Dorety, W. B.	01080	Dallas		
Dorgon, Margaret	Rej	Marion	Dorgon, M. V.	
Dorman, Catherine Talbert	41329	El Paso	Dorman, Henry Fletcher	
Dorman, Elizabeth J.	03631	Shelby	Dorman, John B.	
Dorn, Sarah S.	28661	McLennan	Dorn, Robert Marshall	
Dorough, E. A. Mrs.	Rej	Van Zandt	Dorough, James Willis	
Dorough, Mary Elizabeth	35215	Dallas	Dorough, Robert Toombs	
Dorries, D. J. (Dorris)	11618	Rusk		
Dorris, Annie	22825	Hill	Dorri(e)s, David Jackson	11618
Dorris, B. P. Mrs.	17618	Erath	Dorris, James Elvis	
Dorris, Elias	05706	Erath		
Dorris, Elizabeth C.	09633	Hunt	Dorris, Elias	05706
Dorris, Emma	39109	Erath	Dorris, Erastus Bennett	15109
Dorris, Erastus Bennett	15109	Erath		
Dorris, J. A. Mrs.	11470	Hamilton	Dorris, W. R.	
Dorris, M. C. Mrs.	32692	Bastrop	Dorris, George Harrington	
Dorris, Mary Jane	03908	Travis	Dorris, Elias	
Dorroh, Mattie E.	43410	Williamson	Dorroh, David L.	

Index to Confederate Pension Applications

Dorroh, Sarah P.	29121	Upshur	Dorroh, James Madison	—
Dorrough, John Thomas	22213	Robertson	—	
Dorrough, Martha M. E.	36890	Robertson	Dorrough, John Thomas	22213
Dorsett, Eliza L.	05049	Anderson	Dorsett, E. L.	—
Dorsett, Elizabeth Jennie	12202	Williamson	Dorsett, Theodore James	—
Dorsett, Frances Arkadelphia	43978	Falls	Dorsett, Charles	—
Dorsett, M. V. Mrs.	43283	Galveston	Dorsett, Monroe Theodore	18967
Dorsett, Monroe Theodore	18967	Galveston	—	
Dorsett, W. A.	02569	Lee	—	
Dorsey, Aggie	20552	Kaufman	Dorsey, William James	02391
Dorsey, Thomas A.	29921	Collin	—	
Dorsey, William James	02391	Kaufman	—	
Dortch, William Edward	07670	Taylor	—	
Dortic, Mary Ellen	34654	Harris	Dortic, Charles Adolphus	—
Doshier, Johnathan	32368	Montague	—	
Doshier, S. E. Mrs.	40888	Montague	Doshier, Johnathan	32368
Dosier, John R.	Rej	Hardin	—	
Doss, A. S.	18552	Wise	—	
Doss, Augusta	39818	Milam	George Anton, Sr.	39115
Doss, Bertha A.	32466	McLennan	Doss, Richard Antonio	—
Doss, Bettie	38053	Waller	Doss, William Holman	18519
Doss, Fannie	12247	Anderson	Doss, Seaborn P.	—
Doss, George Anton, Sr.	39115	Milam	—	
Doss, Harmon (Hiram) Wilson	20567	Bell	—	
Doss, J. F.	Rej	Parker	—	
Doss, J. L.	Rej	Mitchell	—	
Doss, J. V.	27130	Wood	—	
Doss, John P.	Rej	Hill	—	
Doss, M. A. Mrs.	30950	Burleson	Doss, Marcus Lafayette	—
Doss, M. L.	Rej	Burleson	—	
Doss, Mary J.	02392	Kaufman	Doss, David T.	—
Doss, Mary Virginia	27432	Montgomery	Doss, Washington Alvin	04557
Doss, S. J. Mrs.	32615	Cass	Doss, William Newton	17426
Doss, Sallie E.	36320	Bell	Doss, Hiram (Harmon) Wilson	20567
Doss, Washington Alvin	04557	Brown	—	
Doss, William Holman	18519	Waller	—	
Doss, William Newton	17426	Cass	—	
Dossett, A. L. Mrs.	32963	Cherokee	Dossett, John	10498
Dossett, John	10498	Upshur	—	
Dossett, Larry	Rej	Comanche	—	
Dossey, Elizabeth	43992	Coryell	Dossey, Thomas Franklin	—
Dossey, James Thomas	38740	Brown	—	
Dotson, Annie S.	42606	Harris	Dotson, Elisha Milton	34488
Dotson, Campbell	23417	Taylor	—	
Dotson, Elisha Milton	34488	McLennan	—	
Dotson, J. N.	30064	Fannin	—	
Dotson, Jerry	02083	Houston	—	
Dotson, L. V. Mrs.	02749	Marion	Dotson, J. B.	—
Dotson, Leonidus Constantin	13122	Wise	—	
Dotson, M. E. Mrs.	22898	Wise	Dotson, Leonidus Constantin	13122
Dotson, Mary	00200	Bastrop	Dotson, James	—
Dotson, Miranda G.	20529	Harris	Dotson, James Jackson	—
Dotson, Mollie	30353	Nolan	Dotson, James Monroe	—
Dotson, Mollie F.	39872	Runnels	Dotson, William T.	—
Dotson, Sallie	20726	Robertson	Dotson, William Burtsfield	03451
Dotson, Susan	27972	Houston	Dotson, Jerry	—
Dotson, Virginia	40635	Taylor	Dotson, Campbell	23417
Dotson, William Burtsfield	03451	Robertson	—	
Doty, C. E. Mrs.	43572	Bowie	Doty, John Wesly	—

Index to Confederate Pension Applications

Doud, Sarah Abbigill	51016	Brown	Doud, William Charles	—
Dougherty, Annie	40780	Brazoria	Dougherty, Clandin	—
Dougherty, Eliza	18913	Dallas	Dougherty, Robert Henry	—
Dougherty, J. N.	05885	Franklin	—	
Dougherty, Nannie Kyle	41968	Dallas	Dougherty, William Fulton	23082
Dougherty, Thomas Wisdom Mrs.	39732	Taylor	Dougherty, Thomas Wisdom	—
Dougherty, Urania	21724	Eastland	Dougherty, Francis Bascom	—
Dougherty, William Fulton	23082	Dallas	—	
Doughorty, Clarisy Jane	07647	Newton	Doughorty, Marshall Joseph	—
Doughtie, John Simpson	28824	Nacogdoches	—	
Doughtie, Mary S.	18512	Walker	Doughtie, Jacob Franklin	—
Doughty, J. M.	01609	Grayson	—	
Doughty, L. S. Mrs.	29334	Polk	Doughty, James Rogers	—
Douglas, Alexander Mrs.	42063	Tarrant	Douglas, Alexander	—
Douglas, Burtice Ferrell	21044	Fannin	—	
Douglas, Della Lee	51970	Limestone	Douglas, Napoleon Bonaparte	50422
Douglas, Dora	Rej	Anderson	Douglas, William Lipscomb	05264
Douglas, Elizabeth	44082	Collingsworth	Douglas, John Stanley	—
Douglas, Eugene Murphy Mrs.	43941	Cherokee	Douglas, Eugene Murphy	—
Douglas, James Knox Polk	40758	Cooke	—	
Douglas, James Postell Mrs.	50906	Smith	Douglas, James Postell	—
Douglas, Linnie M.	Rej	Fannin	Douglas, John	—
Douglas, Lucy Catherine	44024	Randall	Douglas, Robert Emmett	—
Douglas, Mary	30202	Collin	Douglas, Alfred Mason	—
Douglas, N. A. Mrs.	23369	Hunt	Douglas, Hamilton	—
Douglas, Nancy Stewart	47610	Hamilton	Douglas, Jesse	—
Douglas, Napoleon Bonaparte	50422	Limestone	—	
Douglas, Sarah	50824	Cooke	Douglas, James Knox Polk	40758
Douglas, William Lipscomb	05264	Houston	—	
Douglass, A. J.	25863	Taylor	—	
Douglass, Albert B.	21542	Tarrant	—	
Douglass, Amanda	21734	Franklin	Douglass, William Alnomac	19849
Douglass, Berta J.	33511	Kaufman	Douglass, Robert Parrish	—
Douglass, Edward E.	35749	Kaufman	—	
Douglass, Elisha F.	Rej	Tarrant	—	
Douglass, Emily	01545	Goliad	Douglass, W. S.	—
Douglass, F. M.	Rej	Milam	—	
Douglass, Francis Marion	40224	Milam	—	
Douglass, J. C.	Rej	Karnes	—	
Douglass, J. C.	33919	Williamson	—	
Douglass, James W.	Rej	McLennan	—	
Douglass, John Joel Mrs.	47785	Tarrant	Douglass, John Joel	—
Douglass, Lee Mosby	29147	Llano	Douglass, Camillus	—
Douglass, M. J. Mrs.	Rej	Grayson	Douglass, Elbridge Garey	—
Douglass, Mary	01086	Dallas	Douglass, W.r.	—
Douglass, Mary	41605	Milam	Douglass, Francis Marion	40224
Douglass, Mary Jane	14208	Ellis	Douglass, Alsey Monroe	—
Douglass, Perry Oliver Mrs.	38033	McLennan	Douglass, Perry Oliver	—
Douglass, Robert George	19305	Upshur	—	
Douglass, Robert George Mrs.	45402	Upshur	Douglass, Robert George	19305
Douglass, Sudie	50568	Kaufman	Douglass, William George	35705
Douglass, William Alnomac	19849	Franklin	—	
Douglass, William Cantrell	28306	Henderson	—	
Douglass, William George	35705	Kaufman	—	
Dougless, Sarah	31065	Franklin	Dougless, James T.	—
Douphrate, Kate	Rej	Upshur	Douphrate, J. W.	—
Douthit, Dora B.	13443	Milam	J. Emory, Dr.	—
Douthit, Evan Vandevander	30235	Anderson	—	
Douthit, Isabelle	35303	Anderson	Douthit, Evan Vandevander	30235

Index to Confederate Pension Applications

Douthit, James Eden Mrs.	36662	Tom Green	Douthit, James Eden	
Dove, Ernestine	38497	San Saba	Dove, Henry Clay	38000
Dove, Henry Clay	38000	San Saba		
Dove, Hugh Godfrey	46029	Falls		
Dover, Alfred Lafayette	32047	Cherokee		
Dowd, Lou	33848	Dallas	Dowd, W. D.	20696
Dowd, W. D.	20696	Denton		
Dowda, Celia Ann	21330	Kerr	Dowda, James Monroe	17986
Dowda, James Monroe	17986	Kerr		
Dowdle, A. O.	26616	Palo Pinto		
Dowdle, E. J. Mrs.	27317	Van Zandt	Dowdle, Robert Price	
Dowdle, M. A. Mrs.	00755	Cherokee	Dowdle, D. M.	
Dowdy, James	51578	Dallas		
Dowdy, Jesse Lafayette	33916	Bexar		
Dowdy, Julia A.	39078	Travis	Dowdy, Jesse Lafayette	33916
Dowdy, Nancy Jane	39140	Brown	Dowdy, John Samuel	
Dowell, Louisa A.	09744	Polk	Dowell, John R.	
Dowell, M. I. Mrs.	30518	Madison	Dowell, James	
Dowell, Mary	17014	Wood	Dowell, John Franklin	
Dowis, E. J. Mrs.	23062	Smith	Dowis, Tyra Jackson	
Dowlen, Martha A.	51172	Wichita	Dowlen, John W.	
Dowling, Mary K. Hodge	43500	Kaufman	Hodge, Warren	
Dowling, W. J.	09924	Grayson		
Dowling, W. W.	10866	Cherokee		
Downer, W. A.	Rej	Wheeler		
Downey, H. J. Mrs.	42660	Montague	Downey, John Curtis	23045
Downey, J. Ann	21727	Navarro	Downey, John Anderson	
Downey, James	09099	Somervell		
Downey, John Curtis	23045	Montague		
Downing, Asa Marshall	03287	Panola		
Downing, Emma	45616	Camp	Downing, William B.	38115
Downing, Mary	26846	Bosque	Downing, Carter Tarrant	
Downing, S. E. Mrs.	09337	Smith	Downing, Henry	
Downing, William B.	38115	Camp		
Downman, Lillie C.	30972	Waller	Downman, Henry Pontus	
Downs, Amelda	04551	Zavala	Downs, J. M.	
Downs, Charles Mitchell	12713	Van Zandt		
Downs, D. N.	Rej	Harrison		
Downs, Edwin L.	39640	Uvalde		
Downs, Elizabeth	Rej	Coryell	Downs, W. A.	
Downs, Erastus Roberts	12664	Van Zandt		
Downs, Erastus Roberts Mrs.	33671	Van Zandt	Downs, Erastus Roberts	12664
Downs, Francis	50199	McLennan	Downs, John Wesley	Rej
Downs, J. A.	Rej	Harrison		
Downs, John Wesley	Rej	McLennan		
Downs, Mary Ellen	45699	Potter	Downs, William	
Downs, Matilda	Rej	Van Zandt	Downs, Charles Mitchell	12713
Downs, Sophie Caroline	03909	Travis	Downs, Thomas Jones	
Downs, Susan T.	29834	Harrison	Downs, Daniel Norwood	
Downs, W. A.	Rej	Harris		
Downs, W. A.	01000	Coryell		
Dowty, Jennie	35283	Brown	Dowty, Samuel James	
Doyel, Lugenia Franklin	38267	Lamar	Doyel, Henry Clay	
Doyle, A. E. Mrs.	RejM	Lee		
Doyle, Bettie	43725	Bastrop	Doyle, Felix Houston	
Doyle, C. E. Mrs.	06707	Bosque	Doyle, Daniel T.	
Doyle, Elizabeth R.	07713	Eastland	Doyle, David P.	
Doyle, F. M. Mrs.	25195	Erath	Doyle, Eli Jackson	
Doyle, James Hogan	43983	Hood		

Index to Confederate Pension Applications

Name	No.	County	Related	No.
Doyle, James J.	14874	Cherokee	—	
Doyle, Kate	51294	Hood	Doyle, James Hogan	43983
Doyle, M. C. Mrs.	46267	Lampasas	Doyle, John	
Doyle, M. S. Mrs.	Rej	Eastland	Doyle, Albert B.	
Doyle, Mary A.	Rej	Travis	Doyle, Michael J.	
Doyle, Mary Ann	19435	Bexar	Doyle, Thomas L.	00409
Doyle, Mary J.	Rej	Callahan	Doyle, Francis W. A.	
Doyle, Miles J.	31965	Johnson		
Doyle, Mirabeau Monroe	30301	Stephens		
Doyle, R. E. Mrs.	Rej	Lee	Doyle, F. H.	
Doyle, R. J.	07940	Parker		
Doyle, S. P. Mrs.	04995	Williamson	Doyle, W. G.	
Doyle, Susie	31808	Tarrant	Doyle, James Madison	
Doyle, Thomas L.	00409	Bexar		
Doyle, William C.	08298	Fayette		
Doyle, William E.	50305	Freestone		
Dozier, Argive	38941	Waller	Dozier, William Smith	
Dozier, Dora F.	52029	Tom Green	Dozier, Benjamin Wesley	
Dozier, E. M. A. Mrs.	04743	Waller	Dozier, James M.	
Dozier, James Absolam	36937	Franklin		
Dozier, John L.	39307	Smith		
Dozier, Marshall Elias Mrs.	50559	Williamson	Dozier, Marshall Elias	
Dozier, Sarah	45998	Brown	Dozier, James Absolam	36937
Dragoo, Benjamin Crawford	29172	Tom Green		
Dragoo, J. M.	09490	Kimble		
Drake, Aaron	Rej	Madison		
Drake, Aaron	20795	Jefferson		
Drake, Amanda	12648	Tyler	Drake, F. M.	05224
Drake, Belle	24736	Kaufman	Drake, James	
Drake, Ezekiel Nicolas	05792	Hardin		
Drake, F. M.	05224	Tyler		
Drake, Fannie	30408	Jefferson	Drake, Aaron	20795
Drake, J. D.	28050	Haskell		
Drake, James M.	02822	McLennan		
Drake, James Riley	23047	Tarrant		
Drake, James Riley Mrs.	49249	Tarrant	Drake, James Riley	23047
Drake, John A.	Rej	Trinity		
Drake, John Wyatt	12008	Lamar		
Drake, Julius Nichols	11473	Hardin		
Drake, Katie A.	29412	Smith	Drake, Pressley Newly	
Drake, Louisa J.	17594	Eastland	Drake, James Gilbert	
Drake, M. A. Mrs.	38977	Brewster	Drake, Francis Marion	
Drake, Mary E.	30702	Galveston	Drake, Sidney Albert	
Drake, Mary Jane	37618	Hardin	Drake, Ezekial Nicolas	05792
Drake, P. N.	01215	Smith		
Drake, Sarah A.	18799	Red River	Drake, John Wyatt	12008
Drake, Sarah E.	26252	Erath	Drake, Sidney Ciscero	
Drake, T. J.	01208	Eastland		
Drane, Elizabeth	42836	Robertson	Drane, Wesley	
Drape, Laura	36942	Brown	Drape, Holden Ivens	
Draper, C. Mrs.	47656	San Saba	Draper, George Washington	
Draper, Ellen Elizabeth	49547	Upshur	Draper, Joseph Leonard	
Draper, Hattie	36500	Burleson	Draper, Richard Edward	14761
Draper, Hollie	51039	Cass	Draper, J. S.	25941
Draper, J. M.	22214	Williamson		
Draper, J. M.	28946	Rusk		
Draper, J. S.	25941	Cass		
Draper, J. S.	37523	Cass		
Draper, Martha E.	33609	Bexar	Draper, James Patrick	

Index to Confederate Pension Applications

Name	App #	County	Veteran	Vet App #
Draper, Richard Edward	14761	Burleson	—	
Draper, Thomas J.	28528	Dallas	—	
Draper, W. M.	04684	Clay	—	
Drefflich, Ella	50437	Bexar	Drefflich, August Frederick	
Dreher, Benjamin F.	03400	Rains	—	
Drehr, Sallie Neely	35811	Harris	Drehr, Joseph	
Drennan, Bettie	35356	Sabine	Drennan, Jim Moses	25571
Drennan, Isaac Alexander	23489	Wood	—	
Drennan, J. A. Mrs.	41056	Johnson	Drennan, J. A.	
Drennan, Jim Moses	25571	Sabine	—	
Drennan, M. E. Mrs.	18873	Cherokee	Drennan, Joseph Charles	
Drennan, Mary Francis	35354	Wood	Drennan, Isaac Alexander	23489
Drennen, William C.	Rej	Wise	—	
Drennon, S. A.	29115	Rusk	—	
Drennon, Susan Hamm	27434	Grayson	Drennon, John H.	
Drew, Bettie	35809	Brown	Drew, Samuel Joseph	13244
Drew, John H.	39986	Camp	—	
Drew, Rosa	45200	Camp	Drew, John H.	39986
Drew, Samuel Joseph	13244	Brown	—	
Dreyer, Josephine	Rej	Dewitt	Dreyer, Gideon	
Driggers, James	21733	Shelby	—	
Driggers, James L.	Rej	Henderson	—	
Driggers, Nancy D.	04045	Upshur	Driggers, John	
Drinkard, Arimatha	49355	Limestone	Drinkard, Allen M.	
Drinkard, Callie Dony Crow	42118	Travis	Crow, David Franklin	18484
Drinkard, John S.	13678	Trinity	—	
Drinkard, Mary Ann	41258	Brown	Drinkard, Evans Itham	
Driscoll, Cornelius	01563	Galveston	—	
Driscoll, Mary	51917	Galveston	Driscoll, Cornelius	01563
Driskell, Columbus Washington	25603	Lamar	—	
Driskell, Joseph Littleton	42368	Houston	—	
Driskell, Lucretia Jane	51955	Houston	Driskell, William Lafayette	38215
Driskell, Mary Elizabeth	46549	Houston	Driskell, Joseph Littleton	42368
Driskell, W. F.	15401	Harrison	—	
Driskell, William Lafayette	38215	Houston	—	
Driskill, W. H.	01326	Erath	—	
Driver, Andrew Jackson	26622	Nueces	—	
Driver, E. E. Mrs.	10299	Hunt	Driver, J. M.	
Driver, E. L.	26791	Taylor	—	
Driver, Ichabod	00056	Angelina	—	
Driver, J. W.	05244	Navarro	—	
Driver, M. J. Mrs.	27335	Fisher	Driver, Joel Yantis	
Driver, M. J. Mrs.	35929	Johnson	Driver, William James	
Driver, Martha	51761	Williamson	Driver, Andrew Jackson	26622
Driver, Rachel	37780	Harris	Driver, James	
Driver, Sarah Emily	11582	Navarro	Driver, John Wesley	
Driver, William	03233	Palo Pinto	—	
Dromgoole, A. F. Mrs.	00540	Brown	Dromgoole, P. G.	
Dromgoole, Leroy	31467	Bexar	—	
Dromgoole, Minerva	01731	Guadalupe	Dromgoole, John G.	
Dromgoole, William A.	01157	Dewitt	—	
Drouet, Mary	41340	Bexar	Drouet, Adolph	
Drum, Gilla Elizabeth	31307	Parker	Drum, Hiram Duncan	21128
Drum, Hiram Duncan	21128	Parker	—	
Drummond, Charles O.	Rej	Duval	—	
Drury, James H.	Rej	Hall	—	
Dry, Hattie	34337	Sabine	Dry, William Rufus	09211
Dry, Henry	26156	Panola	—	
Dry, Jane Alice	29348	Panola	Dry, Henry	26156

Index to Confederate Pension Applications

Name	No.	County	Related	No.
Dry, Lucindy Caroline	26979	Shelby	Dry, Lawson Alexander	—
Dry, William Rufus	09211	Falls	—	—
Dryman, Jasper Newton	27816	Robertson	—	—
Dryman, Louisa C.	38959	Robertson	Dryman, Jasper Newton	27816
D'spain, Alonzo L.	18773	Comanche	—	—
D'spain, J. A. Mrs.	27961	Gray	D'spain, Thomas Carlin	—
D'spain, J. R.	16008	Menard	—	—
D'spain, Mary E.	38517	Hays	D'spain, Alonzo L.	18773
Dubberly, Henry Clay	22820	McLennan	—	—
Dubberly, Louis Allen	00857	Collin	—	—
Dublin, A. C.	14873	Cherokee	—	—
Dublin, A. C. Mrs.	42648	Cherokee	Dublin, A. C.	14873
Dublin, Charity C.	13750	Cherokee	Dublin, W. C.	—
Dubois, Justin M.	13043	Refugio	—	—
Dubois, Lucas, Jr.	06780	Refugio	—	—
Dubois, Sarah Williams	45040	Leon	Williams, Zachariah	—
Dubose, Carline Olivia	51716	Harris	Dubose, May Banks	—
Dubose, David Stanton	31236	Shelby	—	—
Dubose, Fannie R.	42433	Panola	Dubose, David Stanton	31236
Dubose, Frances Elizabeth	40055	Navarro	Dubose, Jules Augustus	09737
Dubose, Frank B.	25087	Titus	—	—
Dubose, Friendly H. Mrs.	30450	Bee	Dubose, Friendly H.	—
Dubose, G. W.	26948	Navarro	—	—
Dubose, J. A.	03582	San Patricio	—	—
Dubose, Jules Augustus	09737	Navarro	—	—
Dubose, Margaret	45671	Navarro	Dubose, Wildo Peter	—
Dubose, Tabitha	09089	Newton	Dubose, A.	—
Dubose, Wade (William) H. Mrs.	Rej	Titus	Dubose, Wade (william) Hampton	16691
Dubose, William (Wade) Hampton	16691	Titus	—	—
Dubose, William Storton	26743	Medina	—	—
Duce, Mark Gallespy	Rej	Bastrop	—	—
Duck, Nancy Adaline	31066	Harris	Duck, Manning Langly	—
Duckett, E. J.	36514	Williamson	—	—
Duckett, Mary E.	05293	Gregg	Duckett, W. J.	—
Duckworth, George W.	33090	Delta	—	—
Duckworth, J. N.	12357	Fannin	—	—
Duckworth, Jane	47768	Fannin	Duckworth, James	—
Duckworth, T. T.	23401	Panola	—	—
Duclos, Josephine	15373	Harris	Duclos, Louis	—
Ducos, Jean	Rej	Bexar	—	—
Dudley, A.	09272	Lavaca	—	—
Dudley, Ann	11298	Gregg	Dudley, W. C.	03305
Dudley, Barbara D.	39997	Archer	Dudley, Benjamin Franklin	—
Dudley, Benjamin F.	Rej	Cooke	—	—
Dudley, Frances Marion	25407	Taylor	—	—
Dudley, Franklin Whitaker	22543	Crockett	—	—
Dudley, John Edwin Quinton	31847	Trinity	—	—
Dudley, Lula	26452	Polk	Dudley, William Hardy	—
Dudley, M. J. Mrs.	40602	Taylor	Dudley, Frances Marion	25407
Dudley, Margaret	43940	Cherokee	Dudley, George Washington	—
Dudley, Martha Porter	37127	Trinity	Dudley, John Edwin Quinton	31847
Dudley, Mary	20026	Angelina	Dudley, Elijah Nelson	—
Dudley, Mary Lou	Rej	Bexar	Dudley, William Agusta F.	—
Dudley, Peggie Ann	12456	Hunt	Dudley, John H.	—
Dudley, Sarah Francis	35374	Harris	Dudley, Franklin Whitaker	22543
Dudley, W. C.	03305	Parker	—	—
Dudley, William	01302	Erath	—	—
Dudley, William R.	Rej	Lamar	—	—
Dudley, William Riley Mrs.	43649	Lamar	Dudley, William Riley	—

Index to Confederate Pension Applications

Name	App. No.	County	Veteran/Spouse	Ref. No.
Dudley, William Wallace	39013	McLennan	—	
Duease, Katie Lavene	Rej	Hill	Duease, George Buchanan	
Duelberg, Hueda Seekamp	51557	Dewitt	Seekamp, Albert Nicholas	
Duey, Amelia W.	20979	Williamson	Duey, James	03602
Duey, G. W.	38206	Lee	—	
Duey, James	03602	San Saba	—	
Duff, A. H., Sr.	05407	Hill	—	
Duff, Altha G.	17960	Jefferson	Duff, Fred Paul	
Duff, C. D. Mrs.	05215	Lamar	Duff, William	
Duff, D. A.	09060	Kaufman	—	
Duff, J. B.	10240	Wise	—	
Duff, John Carson	08756	Llano	—	
Duff, Joseph	32218	Dallas	—	
Duff, Katharine	17697	Gonzales	Duff, Marion Jasper	
Duff, Mattie Ann	34760	Llano	Duff, John Carson	08756
Duff, S. J.	37212	Harris	—	
Duff, Sarah A.	50421	Montague	Duff, Wilson Alexander	
Duff, Sarah J.	01227	Ellis	Duff, A. M.	
Duffel, Isiah	05151	San Saba	—	
Duffell, Mahaley D.	28602	Titus	Duffell, Francis Marion	
Duffey, Callie	43285	Trinity	Duffey, Willis Braxton	
Duffey, S. E. Mrs.	16799	Upshur	Duffey, George Washing	
Duffie, Rebecca A.	14968	Coryell	Duffie, S. F.	
Duffy, August Mrs.	39181	Matagorda	Duffy, August	
Dufner, Annie Elizabeth	33362	Lavaca	Dufner, Hilary	
Dufnik, Annie	25283	Karnes	Dufnik, Joseph	
Dugan, James Polk	45859	Tom Green	—	
Dugan, James Polk Mrs.	51477	Tom Green	Dugan, James Polk	45859
Dugan, Thomas	18242	Parker	—	
Dugas, Elmina	27186	Jefferson	Dugas, Joseph Gontrond	
Dugat, C. Mrs.	41287	Brewster	Dugat, James Taylor	
Dugat, Ellen	Rej	Bee	Dugat, W. S.	
Dugat, Emma C.	31615	San Patricio	Dugat, Wilber Meredith	
Dugat, John	14866	Chambers	—	
Dugat, Joseph A.	Rej	Uvalde	—	
Dugat, Louise	02272	Jefferson	Dugat, Giles	
Duggan, Medie	42668	Dallas	Duggan, Alston	
Duggan, Susan Elizabeth	Rej	Eastland	Duggan, Benjamin Frederick	
Dugi, Martin	47794	Karnes	—	
Dugi, Martin Mrs.	51897	Wilson	Dugi, Martin	47794
Duhig, Frances	15013	Dallas	Duhig, Jack	05788
Duhig, Jack	05788	Dallas	—	
Duhon, Cellise	25919	Orange	Duhon, Joseph F.	
Duhon, J. F.	18218	Orange	—	
Duke, A.	09310	Parker	—	
Duke, B. A. Mrs.	37269	Tarrant	Duke, Joseph Jennings	
Duke, B. S.	17409	Camp	—	
Duke, Bell	36075	Shackelford	Duke, Nick	
Duke, Carrie M.	51577	Hall	Duke, James Kelly	
Duke, E. J. Mrs.	37125	McCulloch	Duke, John Marshall	10137
Duke, E. K.	Rej	Anderson	—	
Duke, Edmond King	18812	Anderson	—	
Duke, Emily Jane	29522	Collin	Duke, Perry W.	
Duke, Francis M.	10824	Bell	—	
Duke, Frank Mrs.	23079	Parker	Duke, John Coleman	
Duke, George Washington	41964	Dallas	—	
Duke, Henry	08907	Van Zandt	—	
Duke, Henry Jasper	16606	Smith	—	
Duke, Hiram Lonzo	29913	Bell	—	

Index to Confederate Pension Applications

Name	Number	County	Related	Related #
Duke, Hubbard	06739	Colorado		
Duke, Isaac Jefferson	28007	Grayson		
Duke, Isaac Jefferson Mrs.	51367	Grayson	Duke, Isaac Jefferson	28007
Duke, J. D.	34023	Jefferson		
Duke, J. F.	Rej	Denton		
Duke, Jack Brinson	13897	Panola		
Duke, Jimmie Cleason	26731	Rusk		
Duke, John F.	10362	Dallas		
Duke, John Marshall	10137	McCulloch		
Duke, John W.	10514	Erath		
Duke, Joseph Benton	28976	Hays		
Duke, Lafayette Washington	26898	Smith		
Duke, Lafayette Washington Mrs.	45342	McLennan	Duke, Lafayette Washington	26898
Duke, Laura J.	21736	Anderson	Duke, Edmond King	18812
Duke, Leonidas	17242	Van Zandt		
Duke, Lucindy	41743	Panola	Duke, Jack Brinson	13897
Duke, M. J. Mrs.	38718	Shelby	Duke, Walter Newton	16497
Duke, Margret	45871	Rusk	Duke, Jimmie Cleason	26731
Duke, Martha Caroline	34979	Bell	Duke, Hiram Lonzo	29913
Duke, Mary Ann	30031	Comanche	Duke, William C.	
Duke, Mary Jane	32482	Fannin	Duke, Owens H. Kinion	22788
Duke, Millie	45005	Kaufman	Duke, James Worth	
Duke, Mollie	35873	Brazoria	Duke, Monroe Jackson	25574
Duke, Monroe Jackson	25574	Colorado		
Duke, Nancy Elizabeth	29938	Panola	Duke, George Lewis	
Duke, Owens H. Kinion	22788	Fannin		
Duke, Phebe E.	07580	Erath		
Duke, S. A. Mrs.	15495	Hood	Duke, W. A.	
Duke, S. Irwin	23020	Bell		
Duke, Sarah Alice	43013	McCulloch	Duke, Stephen Austin	
Duke, Sarah Ann	32197	Parker	Duke, Adolphus	
Duke, Sarah E.	13843	Haskell	Duke, Thomas H.	
Duke, Sarah J.	00888	Colorado	Duke, Joseph M.	
Duke, Susan Ann	03253	Panola	Duke, Ransom	
Duke, T. A.	29038	Limestone		
Duke, Walter Newton	16497	Shelby		
Duke, William H.	25433	Bell		
Duke, William J. Mrs.	46077	Bell	Duke, William J.	
Duke, Z. P.	04037	Upshur		
Dukel, A.	02964	Milam		
Dukeminier, Richard Pruitt	23394	Navarro		
Dukeminier, Richard Pruitt Mrs.	32564	Navarro	Dukeminier, Richard Pruitt	23394
Dukes, Clarinda	08287	Delta	Dukes, Henry	
Dukes, Gennie	45148	Rusk	Dukes, John James	16387
Dukes, Henry	07466	Delta		
Dukes, John James	16387	Rusk		
Dula, D. F.	Rej	Brown		
Dulaney, Harvey T.	41419	Knox		
Dulaney, Lucy A.	25177	Hardeman	Dulaney, William Henry	
Dulaney, Lucy Ann	46985	Collin	Dulaney, Joseph Elkaney	
Dulaney, Olive	45246	Knox	Dulaney, Harvey T.	41419
Dulaney, Rachel Jane	22626	Dallas	Dulaney, James Madison	
Dulaney, Theodore Freeling	02008	Hopkins		
Dulaney, William Henry	Rej	Hardeman		
Dulany, Margaret S.	30206	Hunt	Dulany, Theodore Freeling	02008
Dulany, Matilda R.	52006	Montgomery	Dulany, Henry Preston Cook	
Dumas, Henry C.	23977	McLennan		
Dumis, R. W.	26216	Parker		
Dunagan, Alfred M.	Rej	Freestone		

Index to Confederate Pension Applications

Name	Number	County	Related	Related #
Dunagan, Alfred M.	17083	Dallas	—	
Dunagan, M. E. Mrs.	34563	Hood	Dunagan, George Washington	—
Dunagin, Millie	30621	Robertson	Dunagin, Riley	—
Dunavant, James Urban	43669	Bell	—	
Dunaway, Alice	38054	Grayson	Dunaway, Henry Turner	15279
Dunaway, Elvin	19297	Trinity	—	
Dunaway, Henry Turner	15279	Grayson	—	
Dunaway, Ida	Rej	Trinity	Dunaway, Elvin	19297
Dunaway, J. M.	26769	Ellis	—	
Dunaway, Rebecca Clara	Rej	Wichita	Dunaway, James Cicero	—
Dunbar, Olive R.	04558	Aransas	Dunbar, Adam	—
Dunbar, Thomas G.	28838	Montague	—	
Dunbar, William	32252	Matagorda	—	
Duncan, Abijah Elam	05140	San Saba	—	
Duncan, Alex V.	26473	Hays	—	
Duncan, Ann Elizar	06121	Gonzales	Duncan, R. M.	—
Duncan, Caroline	39854	Grayson	Duncan, Jesse Asberry	—
Duncan, Charles J.	21557	Travis	—	
Duncan, Daniel B.	38157	Dallas	—	
Duncan, David	33988	Cooke	—	
Duncan, Dora	05416	Hill	Duncan, W. W.	—
Duncan, Edmon	24637	Eastland	—	
Duncan, Fannie A.	25814	Jack	Duncan, William Garner	—
Duncan, Francis	45974	Parker	Duncan, Edmon	24637
Duncan, G. W.	42330	Titus	—	
Duncan, George W.	20255	Rusk	—	
Duncan, George W.	26227	Tom Green	—	
Duncan, Hugh L.	06160	Fannin	—	
Duncan, Idella	Rej	Ellis	Duncan, William Tucker (dunkin)	19024
Duncan, James Allen	28327	Fannin	—	
Duncan, James Franklin	11785	Anderson	—	
Duncan, James Samuel	49784	Smith	—	
Duncan, Jennie	Rej	Reagan	Duncan, William Moses (dick)	—
Duncan, Jessie L.	47569	Victoria	Duncan, Thomas Green	—
Duncan, Joab M.	31069	Hall	—	
Duncan, John A.	22650	Cass	—	
Duncan, John F.	35861	San Saba	—	
Duncan, John Green	31239	Hill	—	
Duncan, John McCurry	25184	Smith	—	
Duncan, John William	21413	Tom Green	—	
Duncan, Joseph W. Mrs.	46002	Coleman	Duncan, Joseph W.	—
Duncan, Julia Ann	20754	Caldwell	Duncan, Hewell L.	—
Duncan, Lovina A.	50456	San Saba	Duncan, Robert Jenkins	—
Duncan, M. A. Mrs.	Rej	Eastland	Duncan, W. B.	—
Duncan, M. M. Mrs.	36517	San Saba	Duncan, Abijah Elam	05140
Duncan, Margaret T.	35866	Cass	Duncan, John A.	22650
Duncan, Margia Ann	20688	Fannin	Duncan, John Wiley	—
Duncan, Mary A.	02773	Mason	Duncan, James	—
Duncan, Mary Walter	19506	Anderson	Duncan, James Franklin	11785
Duncan, Mattie B.	41508	Fannin	Duncan, James Allen	28327
Duncan, Mollie L.	43856	Rusk	Duncan, A. M.	—
Duncan, N. R. Mrs.	36060	Hill	Duncan, John Green	31239
Duncan, Nora A.	26732	Smith	Duncan, John McCurry	25184
Duncan, R. Mrs.	34609	Llano	Duncan, Charles J.	21557
Duncan, Rhodes	33568	Eastland	—	
Duncan, Rhodes Mrs.	43780	Eastland	Duncan, Rhodes	33568
Duncan, S. S., Sr.	03520	Rusk	—	
Duncan, Sarah	Rej	Gonzales	Duncan, Ashley Summerfield	—
Duncan, T. W.	34192	Angelina	—	

Index to Confederate Pension Applications

Name	App#	County	Related	Rel#
Duncan, Wade Alexander	30127	Navarro	—	—
Duncan, Wade Alexander Mrs.	37855	Navarro	Duncan, Wade Alexander	30127
Dunford, Donnie	19023	Hill	Dunford, James Thomas	02343
Dunford, James Thomas	02343	Johnson	—	—
Dungan, Mollie	51192	Burleson	Dunga(or e)n, Joe Frank	49374
Dungan, Moses H.	Rej	Collin	—	—
Dungen, Joe Frank (Dungan)	49374	Burleson	—	—
Dunham, John Henry Mrs.	33544	Denton	Dunham, John Henry	—
Dunham, M. A. C. Mrs.	42898	Lamar	Dunham, James Hawkins	—
Dunham, Nancy Anne Bowdoin	Rej	Guadalupe	Bowdoin, Simeon Travis	—
Dunivan, M. E. Mrs.	30080	Johnson	Dunivan, John	—
Dunk, John	34958	Lee	—	—
Dunken, J. A.	34072	Ellis	—	—
Dunkin, John T.	16386	Rusk	—	—
Dunkin, M. L. Mrs.	40460	Angelina	Dunkin, Robert Alexander	09969
Dunkin, Robert Alexander	09969	Angelina	—	—
Dunkin, William Tucker (Duncan)	19024	Hood	—	—
Dunkle, Susan L.	35163	Wheeler	Dunkle, John Joseph	—
Dunklin, J. H.	11619	Rusk	—	—
Dunks, John	33303	Harris	—	—
Dunlap, A. W. Mrs.	10228	Uvalde	Dunlap, M. M.	06589
Dunlap, David Crockett	Rej	Trinity	—	—
Dunlap, Davis Collins Bell	13888	Palo Pinto	—	—
Dunlap, F. L. Mrs.	28142	Brazos	Dunlap, William Henry	04783
Dunlap, Hiram C.	05747	Mills	—	—
Dunlap, J. T.	01914	Hill	—	—
Dunlap, John	25925	Bell	—	—
Dunlap, Josiah	29524	Erath	—	—
Dunlap, M. G.	16959	Wharton	—	—
Dunlap, M. M.	06589	Uvalde	—	—
Dunlap, Marion E.	12152	Throckmorton	—	—
Dunlap, Mary Josephine	36443	Palo Pinto	Dunlap, Davis Collins Bell	13888
Dunlap, Thomas L.	23034	Bosque	—	—
Dunlap, Vonie	Rej	Nolan	Dunlap, Robert M.	—
Dunlap, W. C.	Rej	Cass	—	—
Dunlap, William Henry	04783	Brazos	—	—
Dunlavy, Annie Victorie	43664	Lee	Dunlavy, John James	—
Dunlavy, James Harvey	40194	Tarrant	—	—
Dunlavy, Mary Isabell	40566	Tarrant	Dunlavy, James Harvey	40194
Dunlavy, W. D.	10030	Colorado	—	—
Dunlop, Clara	11246	Marion	Dunlop, Thomas	—
Dunman, Kate	Rej	Cameron	Dunman, Daniel	—
Dunman, Lucinda E.	47615	Coleman	Dunman, Robert Leander	—
Dunman, Rebecca	34288	San Patricio	Dunman, Robert	32238
Dunman, Robert	32238	San Patricio	—	—
Dunn, Aaron W.	12887	Haskell	—	—
Dunn, Amanda	20693	Dallas	Dunn, George W.	—
Dunn, Benjamin L.	37213	Cooke	—	—
Dunn, Cassie Ann Malinda	35207	Travis	Dunn, Andrew Jackson	—
Dunn, Celia	14106	Hood	Dunn, William Thomas	—
Dunn, Christina M.	00390	Bexar	Dunn, James	—
Dunn, Cora	20377	Montague	Dunn, Palinas Abiham	—
Dunn, Fannie	33245	Victoria	Dunn, Uriah H.	—
Dunn, G. W.	Rej	McLennan	—	—
Dunn, G. W. Mrs.	RejM	Unknown	—	—
Dunn, Harriett	19133	Milam	Dunn, Martin Emmett	—
Dunn, Henry Crittenden	34141	Sterling	—	—
Dunn, Ishmael P.	26198	Haskell	—	—
Dunn, John T.	02250	Jasper	—	—

Index to Confederate Pension Applications

Name	App#	County	Veteran	Vet#
Dunn, Joseph W.	09303	Nueces	—	
Dunn, Katy L.	40887	Sterling	Dunn, Henry Crittenden	34141
Dunn, Leah A.	Rej	Lampasas	Dunn, Joseph T.	
Dunn, Lemuel Elisha	31235	Jefferson	—	
Dunn, Levisa E.	45879	Dallas	Dunn, Thomas Franklin	
Dunn, Louise Jane	Rej	Dallas	Dunn, Luke William	
Dunn, M. A. Mrs.	50790	Navarro	Dunn, William	
Dunn, M. E. Mrs.	31238	Jim Wells	Dunn, Marlin Emmett	
Dunn, M. E. Mrs.	32900	Travis	Dunn, Myddleton Shann	
Dunn, M. E. Mrs.	36951	Coryell	Dunn, Aaron	
Dunn, Maggie Bishop	51121	Ector	Dunn, Aaron W.	12887
Dunn, Mary V.	43138	Jefferson	Dunn, Lemuel Elisha	31235
Dunn, Musa	45924	Ellis	Dunn, Isham L.	
Dunn, Nancy Ann	33822	Shackelford	Dunn, James	
Dunn, Nannie	41011	Williamson	Dunn, Thomas Newton	
Dunn, S. A.	06302	Bell	—	
Dunn, S. A. Mrs.	06308	Burleson	Dunn, C. J.	
Dunn, S. M.	42741	Comanche	—	
Dunn, S. M.	43893	Comanche	—	
Dunn, Samuel H.	04979	Williamson	—	
Dunn, Sarah A.	31509	Cooke	Dunn, Matthew Hale	
Dunn, Sarah O.	01785	Harris	Dunn, George	
Dunn, Selina	37781	Freestone	Dunn, Jacob F.	
Dunn, Talitha	11293	Harrison	Dunn, C. H.	
Dunn, Thomas P.	20262	McLennan	—	
Dunn, W. Henry	23037	Van Zandt	—	
Dunn, William M.	35638	Brown	—	
Dunn, William T.	01980	Hood	—	
Dunnam, Alzada M.	Rej	Trinity	Dunnam, Sidney H.	
Dunnam, Evander Jerome	18328	San Jacinto	—	
Dunnam, James Wesley	18406	Tarrant	—	
Dunnam, Letitia A.	11592	Nueces	Dunnam, Montalvon A.	03110
Dunnam, M. A.	03110	Navarro	—	
Dunnam, Sarah	45206	Trinity	Dunnam, John Joseph	
Dunnam, T. W.	09485	Houston	—	
Dunnam, Tillie	39206	Brown	Dunnam, Evander Jerome	18328
Dunnam, Viola J.	Rej	Tarrant	Dunnam, James Wesley	18406
Dunnam, Virginia Evans	21735	Bowie	Dunnam, Alexander James Chobine	—
Dunnaway, C. M.	31901	Grimes	—	
Dunnaway, Jackson R.	30060	Llano	—	
Dunnica, A. G.	00506	Brazos	—	
Dunning, J. E.	Rej	Wheeler	—	
Dunning, N. E. Mrs.	17257	Hays	Dunning, Samuel Washington	11277
Dunning, Roanzy	Rej	Gregg	—	
Dunning, Samuel Washington	11277	Travis	—	
Dunnington, Pattie Griggs	19587	Travis	Dunnington, John James	
Dunson, S. A. Mrs.	19162	Nacogdoches	Dunson, Hamilton Franklin	
Dunson, William Harrison	30406	Tom Green	—	
Dunson, William M.	47092	Travis	—	
Dunton, Mary	Rej	Henderson	Dunton, William Henry	
Dupree, Annie E.	32901	Eastland	Dupree, Franklin L.	04646
Dupree, Antonette	09459	Fannin	Dupree, Mitchell T.	07592
Dupree, Austin Morrow	26465	Harris	—	
Dupree, Charlie Calhoun	19005	Harris	—	
Dupree, Ella	42967	Bell	Dupree, Herod Gossaway	11710
Dupree, F. G.	21731	Montgomery	—	
Dupree, Franklin L.	04646	Eastland	—	
Dupree, Herod Gossaway	11710	Bell	—	
Dupree, J. E.	RejM	Fannin	—	

Index to Confederate Pension Applications

Name	No.	County	Related	No.
Dupree, J. R.	19001	Harris	—	—
Dupree, James M.	22880	Cass	—	—
Dupree, John Henry	19510	Hunt	—	—
Dupree, John L.	21039	Harris	—	—
Dupree, Laura Etta	39086	Harris	Dupree, Austin Morrow	26465
Dupree, Mitchell T.	07592	Fannin	—	—
Dupree, S. L.	15865	Lampasas	—	—
Dupree, Sallie	34289	Hunt	Dupree, John Henry	19510
Dupree, Susan	36021	Cass	Dupree, James M.	22880
Dupree, V. T. Mrs.	07578	Erath	—	—
Dupriest, John	08441	Panola	—	—
Dupuy, C. M. Mrs.	36027	Harris	Dupuy, James Alva	12882
Dupuy, Flora M.	05739	Jackson	Dupuy, Bartholomew	—
Dupuy, James Alva	12882	Harris	—	—
Dupuy, Katie Alexander	51052	Falls	Dupuy, Henry Guerrant	—
Dupuy, Marcus Cicero Mrs.	38175	Houston	Dupuy, Marcus Cicero	—
Duran, Antee D.	31061	Collin	Duran, Joseph E.	23475
Duran, James M., Sr.	00169	Bastrop	—	—
Duran, Joseph E.	23475	Collin	—	—
Duran, Josephine	50664	Rusk	Duran, John Reuben	—
Durant, D. R.	12428	Hood	—	—
Durant, George W.	11993	Jefferson	—	—
Duraud, Adelada	51239	Hays	Duraud, Nacleto	—
Durdin, A. F. Mrs.	27154	Jasper	Durdin, John Jephtha	—
Durdin, Alexas Maltermore Mrs.	39688	San Jacinto	Durdin, Alexas Maltermore	—
Duren, Calvin (Calvonestic) A.	35504	Wichita	—	—
Duren, Calvonestic A. Mrs.	36306	Wichita	Duren, Calvonestic (Calvin) A.	35504
Duren, John W.	19166	Navarro	—	—
Duren, Philip D.	21427	Mills	—	—
Duren, William H.	15574	Houston	—	—
Durfee, Nannie B.	36069	Travis	Durfee, Alvin A.	—
Durham, Alice	Rej	Young	Durham, Rufus Edward	—
Durham, Docia Mae	52052	Hamilton	Durham, John Jack	—
Durham, Eliza	05195	Houston	Durham, George G.	—
Durham, Eliza S.	Rej	Coryell	Durham, Wiley M.	—
Durham, Emma M.	23385	Llano	Durham, James Knox	—
Durham, Fannie E.	40457	Dallas	Durham, John Landrum	39002
Durham, Frances A.	16770	Tyler	Durham, William Starnes	—
Durham, Jennie	27770	Brazoria	Durham, John Lafayette	—
Durham, John	02493	Lampasas	—	—
Durham, John Landrum	39002	Coke	—	—
Durham, Lou	47757	Limestone	Durham, Charles Anderson	—
Durham, Louisa	08219	Bell	Durham, W. G.	00269
Durham, M. A. Mrs.	28952	Hunt	Durham, William Green	—
Durham, Mary B.	26910	Young	Durham, Francis Marion	—
Durham, Mary C.	39719	Wheeler	Durham, S. C. S.	36086
Durham, Mildred Adella	42860	Collin	Durham, Richard Waverly	28290
Durham, Milley	01728	Guadalupe	Durham, M. J.	—
Durham, Nancy Jane	36534	Victoria	Durham, Green Harvey	—
Durham, Paulina	Rej	Trinity	Durham, H. L. T.	—
Durham, Richard	42133	Cooke	—	—
Durham, Richard Waverly	28290	Collin	—	—
Durham, S. C. S.	36086	Wheeler	—	—
Durham, W. G.	00269	Bell	—	—
Durington, Malinda	02393	Kaufman	Durington, Thomas	—
Durkee, A. G.	01660	Gregg	—	—
Durkee, P. A. Mrs.	06310	Harrison	Durkee, J. A.	—
Durnett, Alexander Aaron	38791	Harris	—	—
Durnett, Alexander Aaron Mrs.	46240	Harris	Durnett, Alexander Aaron	38791

Index to Confederate Pension Applications

Name	No.	County	Veteran	Ref
Durning, Charlie Steward Mrs.	47105	Grayson	Durning, Charlie Steward	
Durrett, F. R.	10220	Travis	—	
Durrett, G. W.	04858	Nacogdoches	—	
Durrett, Hose	Rej	Cherokee	—	
Durrett, Lewis	23285	Cherokee	—	
Durrett, Mary J.	50831	Dallas	Durrett, Morpheus A.	
Durrett, Mary Jane	19160	Nacogdoches	Durrett, George Washington	
Durrett, Millie Adline	45220	Cherokee	Durrett, Louis (Lewis)	23285
Durrett, Robert W.	09765	Young	—	
Durrett, Sallie	46824	Ellis	Durrett, William Ivy	
Durrett, T. C.	05776	Dallas	—	
Durrett, T. H.	31320	Angelina	—	
Durrett, T. H. Mrs.	37830	Angelina	Durrett, T. H.	31320
Durrett, William J.	Rej	Cooke	—	
Durst, Horatio Mrs.	47530	Houston	Durst, Horatio	
Durst, Lilla Kittrell	43594	Kimble	Durst, John Sterling	
Durst, Mortimer Thorn Mrs.	49875	Bexar	Durst, Mortimer Thorn	
Durst, Sophie	40272	Mason	Durst, Jacob John	
Durst, Texana M.	25686	Leon	Durst, Bruno	
Durst, W. E.	07703	Hill	—	
Dutart, Charles John	28401	Jackson	—	
Dutart, Nellie	32474	Jackson	Dutart, Charles John	28401
Dutton, Amanda	41582	McCulloch	Dutton, Abraham	
Dutton, George W.	37569	Grayson	—	
Dutton, James Marion	10210	Travis	—	
Dutton, Josie	Rej	Coryell	Dutton, A. J. (drew)	
Duty, Mollie	50679	McLennan	Duty, Robert Barton	
Duval, A. D. Mrs.	40577	Clay	Duval, Edwin Lafayette	
Duval, D. S.	08945	Anderson	—	
Duval, Mary E.	07748	Anderson	Duval, T. J.	
Duval, Rufus	04041	Upshur	—	
Duvall, Martha	Rej	Johnson	Duvall, Joseph Dabney	
Dwight, F. M.	15727	Jack	—	
Dwight, L. J. Mrs.	36963	Jack	Dwight, F. M.	15727
Dwight, O. A. Mrs.	07823	Grayson	Dwight, R. B.	
Dwire, Sallie E.	29824	Trinity	Dwire, Thomas Jefferson	
Dwyer, Mike	35113	Harris	—	
Dycus, N. C. Mrs.	Rej	Williamson	Dycus, E. H.	
Dye, B. F.	12659	Uvalde	—	
Dye, James W., Sr.	02009	Hopkins	—	
Dye, Mary J.	20797	Titus	James W., Sr.	02009
Dyer, A. E. Mrs.	43210	Hunt	Dyer, F. F.	
Dyer, B. F.	03109	Navarro	—	
Dyer, B. P.	22845	Travis	—	
Dyer, Bettie J.	51260	Ward	Dyer, George W.	
Dyer, D. C.	Rej	Palo Pinto	—	
Dyer, E. L. Mrs.	19317	Van Zandt	Dyer, William Henderson	
Dyer, Edwin William Mrs.	38798	Hale	Dyer, Edwin William	
Dyer, Evalyn E.	43051	Fannin	Dyer, John Calhoun	
Dyer, Icie Nola	39287	Dallas	Dyer, Jerome	34476
Dyer, James C.	00810	Clay	—	
Dyer, James G.	19333	Wilbarger	—	
Dyer, Jerome	34476	Dallas	—	
Dyer, John	43390	Tarrant	—	
Dyer, John Mrs.	45626	Tarrant	Dyer, John	43390
Dyer, Martha A.	02446	Lamar	Dyer, John L.	
Dyer, Mary Samantha	51237	Montague	Dyer, Calib Williams	
Dyer, Orpha A.	26997	Dallas	Dyer, Joel Sylvester	
Dyer, S. A. E. Mrs.	26745	Hill	Dyer, Andrew Jackson	

Index to Confederate Pension Applications

Name	No.	County	Veteran	No.
Dyer, S. F.	33048	Grimes	—	—
Dyer, Sarah D.	11584	Navarro	Dyer, B. F.	03109
Dyer, T. F. Mrs.	05323	Montague	Dyer, Dwight	—
Dyer, W. A.	Rej	Comanche	—	—
Dyess, John George	23029	Hill	—	—
Dyess, John J.	05959	Bell	—	—
Dyess, Reuben Henry	23030	Tarrant	—	—
Dyess, Reuben Henry Mrs.	34765	Tarrant	Dyess, Reuben Henry	23030
Dykes, Ida	46585	Burnet	Dykes, Thomas Jefferson	11324
Dykes, M. V.	Rej	Bexar	—	—
Dykes, Martin Van Buren	Rej	Hays	—	—
Dykes, Thomas Jefferson	11324	Travis	—	—
Dysart, Sarah Jane	06156	Grayson	Dysart, Thomas Jefferson	—
Dyson, E.	19373	Polk	—	—
Dyson, Emily	11992	Jefferson	Dyson, William	—
Dzuik, Alexander Mrs.	47601	Karnes	Dzuik, Alexander	—

www.ingramcontent.com/pod-product-compliance
Lightning Source LLC
Chambersburg PA
CBHW080723300426
44114CB00019B/2478